William Shakespeare

HIS WORLD · HIS WORK
HIS INFLUENCE

New York Shakespeare Festival's 1984 production of *Henry V,*
presented at Central Park's Delacorte Theater.

WILLIAM SHAKESPEARE

His World · His Work

His Influence

VOLUME III

HIS INFLUENCE

John F. Andrews

EDITOR

CHARLES SCRIBNER'S SONS · NEW YORK

Through the kind permission of the publisher, portions of the article "Ethical and Theological Questions in Shakespeare's Dramatic Works" were adapted from " 'The Purpose of Playing': Catharsis in *Hamlet*" by John F. Andrews, which appeared in *Poetry and Drama in the English Renaissance:* In Honour of Professor Jiro Ozu (Tokyo: Kinokuniya, 1980).

Material from the article "Tradition, Style, and the Shakespearean Actor Today" was previously published as "Tradition, Style, and the Theatre Today" by Sir John Gielgud in *Shakespeare Survey* (New York: Cambridge University Press, 1951), and it is reprinted here with the permission of the publisher.

All credits for illustrations are included in this volume in the *List of Illustrations.*

Library of Congress Cataloging in Publication Data

Main entry under title:

William Shakespeare: his world, his work, his influence.

Includes bibliographies and index.
Contents: v. 1. His world—v. 2. His work—
v. 3. His influence.
1. Shakespeare, William, 1564–1616—Criticism and
interpretation.   2. Shakespeare, William, 1564–1616—
Contemporary England.   3. Shakespeare, William, 1564–1616
—Influence.   4. Great Britain—Civilization—16th
century.   5. Great Britain—Civilization—17th century.
I. Andrews, John, 1942–
PR2976.W5354   1985   822.3'3   85-8305
ISBN 0–684–17851–6 (Set)
ISBN 0–684–18773–6 (Volume 1)
ISBN 0–684–18774–4 (Volume 2)
ISBN 0–684–18775–2 (Volume 3)

90-0913

Contents

VOLUME I

hIS WORLD

v

CONTENTS

VOLUME II

hIS WORK

VOLUME III

HIS INFLUENCE

CONTENTS

ix

William Shakespeare

HIS WORLD · HIS WORK
HIS INFLUENCE

The Publishing and Editing of Shakespeare's Plays

GEORGE WALTON WILLIAMS

When we speak of *publishing,* we now think almost exclusively of the printed word. With Shakespeare it was not so; for him the term meant no more than "making public." Thus, King Lear proposes to "publish" his daughters' different dowries: he does so by announcing his decisions publicly to the court. Similarly, performance was the publication that Shakespeare sought for his plays, and with it he seems to have been entirely content.

For two poems, he had a different attitude. He published in print his *Venus and Adonis* (1593) and *The Rape of Lucrece* (1594) at the beginning of his career, when only six or seven of his plays had been published on stage. Because he wanted his poems to be well printed, he turned—it must have seemed the natural thing—to a fellow citizen of Stratford, Richard Field, like himself an expatriate in London, and almost certainly a personal acquaintance, if not a friend. (Their fathers were well known to one another back home.) The publication of these two poems raises the question of Shakespeare's purpose: Did the man who was already on the way to becoming a successful popular dramatist consider the possibility of seeking the kind of permanent fame available to poets? Probably not. The sophistication of the style and the congeries of themes and images seem to date the composition of the poems at the years of their publication (thus precluding their being juvenilia, brought up to London in Shakespeare's bags) and to make reasonably certain the hypothesis that while the theaters were closed

against the plague from midsummer 1592 to June 1594, Shakespeare turned to poetry as a means of earning some income.

Shakespeare's first publication in print, *Venus and Adonis,* is a cleanly printed work; its neatness suggests that Shakespeare was careful in the preparation of the manuscript he sent to the printer and that Field regarded the production of the poem seriously. Perhaps Shakespeare took the pains—unusual for his time—of personally seeing his manuscript through the press. The volume was very successful, requiring a second printing in the next year and, in all, eight more printings in Shakespeare's lifetime. Shakespeare called it "the first heire of my invention"; he must have been proud of it.

His second poem to be printed, *The Rape of Lucrece,* followed in 1594, an attempt, we may suppose, to exploit the success of the first and, like many sequels, less remarkable than its predecessor; it enjoyed five more printings in Shakespeare's lifetime. Other poems, "The Passionate Pilgrim" and "The Phoenix and Turtle," appeared in anthologies in 1599 and 1601, respectively. There is no indication whether these were authorized or not, but the next collection was almost certainly not authorized, *Shake-speares Sonnets,* published by Thomas Thorpe in 1609. This volume provides the text of 154 sonnets and, as a sort of appendix, "A Lover's Complaint."

The long attack of the plague during the years 1592 through 1594 forced the closing of the theaters. Times were hard for the players; they needed income. One source was the sale of plays. Many plays were printed in those black years, and four of Shakespeare's seem to have been sold to the printers by various companies of players. *Titus Andronicus* was entered in the Stationers' Register (of books being printed) on 6 February 1594; *The First Part of the Contention Betwixt the Two Famous Houses of York and Lancaster (Henry VI, Part 2)* was entered on 12 March 1594; *The Taming of a Shrew* (presumably a debased version of *The Taming of the Shrew*) was entered on 2 May 1594; and *The True Tragedy of Richard Duke of Yorke (Henry VI, Part 3)* was printed in 1595.

The appearance of these plays in print was further demonstration of the financial motives that produced the printings of the poems in the same years. But as there is every reason to suppose that Shakespeare initiated the printing of his poems and that it was not by accident that Field was the printer, so there is no reason to suppose that Shakespeare took the slightest interest in the printing of his plays. In fact, each of the plays just mentioned was printed in a text inferior to the complete text of the play as Shakespeare had written it. Though each of these plays had several reprintings during his lifetime, Shakespeare evidently made no efforts in those later printings to correct the inadequacies of these texts.

The poems of 1593 and 1594 were dedicated to Henry Wriothesley, earl of Southampton, a wealthy patron of letters and a favorite dedicatee of hopeful authors. The dedication of *Venus and Adonis* is formal and distant; it might have been written to a stranger. That of the *Rape* is written under the warrant "of acceptance," as if to a friend. The first promised "some graver labour" if *Venus and Adonis* "pleased" the earl; the *Rape* is the fulfilling of that promise. An old tradition holds that the earl's imagination was sufficiently caught by the dedications that he gave Shakespeare a substantial sum of money. The legend is not improbable: dedicatees were supposed to reward tangibly those who had honored them intangibly. Still more speculative is the hypothesis that Shakespeare used this patronage to buy a share in a company of players, just the sort of purchase that Hamlet proposed when his little play had succeeded in catching the conscience of the King.

The facts are that *The Rape of Lucrece* was entered in the Stationers' Register on 9 May 1594 and that in June 1594 Shakespeare was a member of an acting company with William Kempe and Richard Burbage, the nucleus of the group that was to become the Lord Chamberlain's Men and later the King's Men, the premier acting company of the period. If the response to the dedications of his poems bought Shakespeare a place in this company, we have much for which we may thank the earl of Southampton. At any rate, after 1594, Shakespeare published no more poems in print and concentrated his efforts on publishing his plays on stage. When Shakespeare had Hamlet say, "The play's the thing," he had in mind the performance, not the printed book. Others thought otherwise; actors, printers, booksellers, and publishers saw to it that the texts of the plays, already published on stage, should be published in print.

According to the Pelican standard chronology of his works, Shakespeare began writing in 1590 with *The Comedy of Errors* and concluded his career with either *Henry VIII* or *The Two Noble Kinsmen* in 1613. During the first half of this span of twenty-four years (1590–1601), Shakespeare wrote twenty-three of his plays, of which sixteen were printed, approximately 70 percent of the total. In the second half (1602–1613), he wrote fifteen of his plays, of which three were printed, 20 percent of the total. (Two more were printed after his death.) It is not easy to explain the disparity between these two ratios. Perhaps the King's Men became more jealous of their privileges as time went on, for though plays of the first period continued to be reprinted regularly throughout the second period (in popularity of varying degrees), few new plays came on the market. It does not appear that Shakespeare's lack of interest in the printing of his plays changed throughout his career, nor, as he neared the end of that career, did Shakespeare seem to develop an interest in reserving his plays for printing in a collected edition.

Before the appearance of that collected edition of 1623 (the First Folio), assembled by his fellow actors, twenty plays had appeared in print, nineteen during Shakespeare's lifetime and one after his death. Of seventeen comedies and romances, seven were printed: *The Taming of the Shrew* (1594), *Love's Labor's Lost* (1598), *A Midsummer Night's Dream, The Merchant of Venice, Much Ado About Nothing* (all in 1600), *The Merry Wives of Windsor* (1602), and *Pericles* (1609). Of ten histories, seven were printed: *Henry VI, Part 2* (1594), *Henry VI, Part 3* (1595), *Richard III* (1597), *Richard II* (1597), *Henry IV, Part 1* (1598), *Henry IV, Part 2*

(1600), *Henry V* (1600)—three plays of the first tetralogy and all of the second. Of eleven tragedies, six were printed: *Titus Andronicus* (1594), *Romeo and Juliet* (1597), *Hamlet* (1603), *King Lear* (1608), *Troilus and Cressida* (1609), *Othello* (1622). One romance, *The Two Noble Kinsmen,* attributed to Shakespeare in collaboration with John Fletcher, was printed in 1634. All of these plays were printed in separate volumes; all but one of them appeared in a format termed "quarto," a term which describes the way the sheet of paper is printed and folded, each printed leaf being one-fourth the size of the sheet of paper. The size of the average quarto of the period was 7.5 inches by 10.0 inches, though trimming at the bindery reduced the dimensions of most books.

These twenty-one quartos are classified by scholars into two groups: "bad" and "good." (Though the terms are not well chosen, they still have a currency and a use.) The bad quartos are characterized, in varying degrees of corruptness, by brevity and by faulty readings. Because scholars detect in some of these misreadings evidence of faulty memory, they have concluded that the group derives somehow from the actors and that each text has been assembled from the recitation or performance of the actors. Among the quartos cited above, those marked by such memorial reconstruction are *Henry VI, Part 2; The Taming of the Shrew; Henry VI, Part 3; Romeo and Juliet; Henry V; The Merry Wives of Windsor; Hamlet;* and *Pericles.* Some scholars would add to the list *Richard III* and *King Lear;* other scholars would argue that these quartos—or some of them—represent versions of Shakespeare's early drafts rather than actors' versions derived subsequently from the final texts. There was, presumably, also a bad quarto of *Love's Labor's Lost,* though no copy now survives, because the good quarto announces on its title page that it is superseding an earlier defective text. It would appear that Shakespeare's company made available to the printers correct texts of *Love's Labor's Lost, Romeo and Juliet,* and *Hamlet,* which were published in quartos of 1598, 1599, and 1604–1605, respectively, but it took no interest in replacing the other bad quartos.

The printers of these dramatic quartos were not remarkable men, neither the best nor the worst of Elizabethan and Jacobean printers—though perhaps their number included a few of each group. They approached the task of printing these priceless documents of the human mind with somewhat less zeal and care than they gave to run-of-the-mill sermons; but they were professional men, and they did the best they could with what were surely on many occasions messy manuscripts. As no manuscripts of Shakespeare survive, we must find in this miscellaneous collection of printing jobs the only surviving records of those men who actually knew what Shakespeare's manuscripts looked like before they went into print.

In 1619, William Jaggard, one of the leading printers of the early seventeenth century, joined his friend, Thomas Pavier, a bookseller, in a project to reprint the quartos of Shakespeare's plays. As the two men seem to have conceived of the venture as no more than a mere reprinting, they did not enlist the services of the King's Men, who apparently took offense, intervened, and halted the project. Jaggard and Pavier produced ten plays (the "Pavier quartos"), all attributed to Shakespeare, though two were the work of other hands: *The Whole Contention between the two Famous Houses, Lancaster and York . . . Divided into Two Parts (Henry VI, Part 2* and *Henry VI, Part 3); Pericles; A Yorkshire Tragedy* (probably by George Wilkins); *The Merchant of Venice; Sir John Falstaff (The Merry Wives of Windsor); King Lear; Henry V; Sir John Oldcastle, Part 1* (by Michael Drayton, Anthony Munday, and others); and *A Midsummer Night's Dream.*

The interruption of this ill-conceived and ill-informed project may have served a useful purpose, in that it may have effected the collaboration of the printers and the players that produced the first collected edition of Shakespeare's plays four years later. We may even hazard the guess that before he gave up the 1619 production, Jaggard agreed with the players to collaborate in a new venture. Having jealously guarded their stock in trade, the players may well have resented Jaggard's making that stock public on the grand scale. As they had never thought that plays should be published in print, it must have seemed strange to them when Ben Jonson, once a player, now a playwright, undertook in 1616 to publish his plays in print in a large and handsome volume, just as if they were literary works and as important as poems. Still, Jonson's collected edition of his plays provided a model for Shakespeare's fellow players, now turned compilers.

Of Shakespeare's close friends, the only ones surviving in the company from the old days were John Heminge and Henry Condell; they took upon themselves the task of identifying the canon and providing manuscript copies of the plays. Not literary men, and certainly not editors, Heminge and Condell in their letter "to the great Variety of Readers" prefacing their volume spoke of "their care, and paine" in collecting and publishing in print the texts of the plays that they had so joyously published on stage many times. To help them, they enlisted that literary man, Ben Jonson, who knew how to do this kind of thing; Jonson wrote a commendatory poem, "To the memory of my beloved, The Author, . . . And what he hath left us," and probably the letter and the dedication, both signed by the players. (It may be mentioned that though he was no doubt of great assistance to Heminge and Condell, Jonson did not assist them so much as to prepare a volume more handsome than his own.) This collected edition was printed in a format termed "folio," a term which describes the way the sheet of paper is printed and folded, each printed leaf being half the size of the sheet. The size of the average folio of the period is 10 inches by 15 inches. The folio of 1623 is called the "First Folio."

The care and pain of the compilers resulted in a volume of thirty-six plays, all of the plays that they could find that were certifiable as Shakespeare's. The compilers did not include *Pericles,* perhaps because they could not locate a complete text (none has yet been found); and they did not include *The Two Noble Kinsmen,* perhaps because they thought this collaboration more Fletcher's than Shakespeare's (though they did include *Henry VIII,* another such collaboration—more Shakespeare's than Fletcher's presumably). But they provided good texts of the bad quartos for which no good quartos had been printed: *Henry VI, Part 2* and *Part 3; The Taming of the Shrew; Henry V;* and *The Merry Wives of Windsor.* They reprinted the good quartos: *Love's Labor's Lost; Romeo and Juliet; Hamlet; Titus Andronicus* (with a scene, III. ii, not included in the quarto); *Richard III; Richard II; Henry IV, Part 1; A Midsummer Night's Dream; The Merchant of Venice; Much Ado About Nothing;* and *Troilus and Cressida.* Perhaps they provided fresh copy for *Henry IV, Part 2; King Lear;* and *Othello.* They provided manuscript copy for the plays not previously printed: *The Tempest; The Two Gentlemen of Verona; Measure for Measure; The Comedy of Errors; As You Like It; All's Well That Ends Well; Twelfth Night; The Winter's Tale; King John; Henry VI, Part 1; Henry VIII; Coriolanus; Timon of Athens; Julius Caesar; Macbeth; Antony and Cleopatra;* and *Cymbeline.* Many of the texts in the First Folio reprinted from quartos show signs of interpolations and changes that must have derived from changes in stage practice that occurred after their original composition; the text of *Macbeth,* printed from a theatrical prompt book, even gives indication of a fair amount of interpolated material written by another hand.

The First Folio was undertaken by William Jaggard in his print shop in the early months of 1622, and his son Isaac listed the volume in the *Mess-Katalog* of the Frankfurt Book Fair as to be published before October 1622, a date perhaps more hopeful than actually attainable. The printing of the volume was interrupted several times while Jaggard printed other books. The comedies and the first pages of the histories were printed before the end of 1622; the histories were finished by May 1623; the tragedies were printed from April through October. The volume was ready for publication by 8 November 1623.

The colophon of the First Folio, printed on the last page of text, probably in late October, declares that the volume was "Printed at the Charges of W. Jaggard, Ed. Blount, I. Smethweeke, and W. Aspley." These booksellers, or, as we now call them, publishers, bore the substantial charges of financing the manufacture of the volume. The title page, printed as usual after the body of the text had been finished and probably in early November, declares that the volume was "Printed by Isaac Iaggard and Ed. Blount. 1623." The prominence given to Edward Blount on the title page even though he was not the printer testifies to the fact that he was one of the two principal members of the syndicate, John Smethwicke (Smethweeke) and William Aspley being minor figures only. The other principal member was William Jaggard, in whose shop the entire volume was printed. His name does not appear on the title page, for William had died shortly before 4 November, his son Isaac taking over the operation of the shop and the position of first place on the title page of Shakespeare's works.

With the publication of the First Folio, Shakespeare's dramatic monument was complete, save for the addition of *Pericles* and *The Two Noble Kinsmen* many years later. Though Shakespeare's plays continued to be published on stage, they had moved from the theater into a new mode, the printed page.

The publication of Shakespeare's works in print in the seventeenth century discloses several trends. The most important is the series of reprintings of the plays in folio. The First Folio was followed by the Second in 1632, by the Third in 1664, and by the Fourth in 1685. It may be argued that perhaps with the exception of a few years during the Puritan interregnum, a collected edition of Shakespeare's plays was always in print throughout the century. To this series we shall return.

Less important but perhaps of more interest is the sequence of printings of the plays in quarto. Some plays were not reprinted, and others were reprinted frequently; but by 1660 the reprinting of the twenty-one plays originally printed in quarto had run its course and ceased (in the years indicated): 1600 *Henry IV, Part 2,* and *Much Ado About Nothing;* 1607 *Love's Labor's Lost;* 1609 *Troilus and Cressida;* 1611 *Titus Andronicus;* 1619 (Pavier) *Henry VI, Part 2* and *Part 3, Henry V,* and *A Midsummer Night's Dream;* 1634 *Richard III, Richard II,* and *The Two Noble Kinsmen* (collected thereafter into the Beaumont and Fletcher canon in the folio of 1647); 1635 *Pericles* (collected thereafter into the Shakespeare canon in the Third Folio of 1664); 1637 *Hamlet* and *Romeo and Juliet;* 1639 *Henry IV, Part 1;* 1652 *Merchant of Venice;* and 1655 *King Lear* and *Othello.* From the full texts in the First Folio—not from their bad quartos—were printed in single editions *The Merry Wives of Windsor* in 1630 and *The Taming of The Shrew* in 1631. One tradition of publishing individual plays was at an end.

The preparation, printing, and publishing of the plays in quarto and in folio up to this time had been entirely in the hands of the printers. When a new tradition of printing individual plays began in 1660, the initiating agents were the players. The quartos that follow are described as "players' quartos," a title that defines their distinctiveness from the "printers' quartos" that have been described, and points to the new prominence given to the theater by the reestablishment of the monarchy. They had the sponsorship of the theater rather than of the print shop, and they record post-Restoration productions—often quite specific ones.

Quartos of three plays demonstrate the shift that occurred in the last third of the century. The last of the printers' quartos was the *Othello* of 1655. Its title page advertised that "it hath beene divers times Acted at the Globe, and at the Black-Friers." The *Othello* series resumed with a fourth quarto in 1681, "acted at the Globe, and at the Black-Friers, and now at the Theater Royal." This quarto reprinted the second quarto (1630), perhaps because the third quarto (1655) had never found its way into the collection of the players while they suf-

fered under proscription. The series continued with quartos in 1687, 1695, and 1705, each printed from its predecessor. *Julius Caesar,* "as it is Now Acted at the Theatre Royal," appeared in 1684, "in response to renewed public interest in the play," following its revival in 1682 by Thomas Betterton. This quarto reprinted the text in the First Folio; four undated quartos followed, and a fifth, dated 1691, concluded the series. The text shows signs of some playhouse alterations. *K. Henry IV (Henry IV, Part 1)* appeared in 1700, subtitled "a Tragi-Comedy. . . . Revived, with Alterations. Written Originally by Mr. Shakespear." These alterations consist of acting cuts only, the remainder of the text deriving, like *Caesar,* from the Folio. The quarto texts of these three plays are the only quarto printings of Shakespeare's plays to have survived the interregnum intact. Though one is slightly altered and another is cut, they remain on the whole faithful to the original texts and to Shakespeare's conception.

Very different are the scores of players' quartos that flooded the market after the Restoration, the texts in some of them so thoroughly altered as to be scarcely Shakespeare's. The first such quarto— it is typical—is the 1661 edition of *A Midsummer Night's Dream,* reduced by Robert Cox to *The Merry Conceited Humors of Bottom, the Weaver.* Adaptations of Shakespeare became the norm on stage and, in consequence, the norm in the print shop. The most famous adapter was John Dryden, whose versions of *The Tempest, Antony and Cleopatra (All for Love),* and *Troilus and Cressida* (subtitled by him *Truth Found Too Late*) commanded the stage. Sir William Davenant adapted *Macbeth* and *Hamlet* and made *Much Ado About Nothing* and *Measure for Measure* coalesce in his *Law Against Lovers.* Nahum Tate adapted *Coriolanus* and *Richard II.* His version of *King Lear* in 1681 is the most important of all the adaptations, holding the stage for a century and a half. With unfeigned surprise and delight Tate describes his ingenuity in one rearrangement:

'Twas my good fortune to light on one Expedient to rectifie what was wanting in the Regularity and Probability of the Tale [in Shakespeare's version], which was to run through the whole A Love betwixt Edgar and Cordelia, that never chang'd word with each other in the Original. . . . This Method necessarily threw me on making the Tale conclude in a Success to the innocent distrest Persons: Otherwise I must have incumbred the Stage with dead Bodies.

To record the other variant texts of altered Shakespeare by Thomas Shadwell, Edward Ravenscroft, Thomas Otway, Thomas D'Urfey, Calley Cibber, John Dennis, and others would pass from the record of publishing to the history of dramatic literature and encumber the page with dead bodies. Suffice it to say that "Shakespeare adapted" was regularly reprinted in quarto through the seventeenth century and on into the eighteenth century, but in such texts as would have astonished their grand original. The texts of the authentic Shakespeare, however, marched stately on above the pack of yelping pups in the series of folio editions of 1632, 1664, and 1685.

The Second Folio was published by Thomas Cotes and Robert Allot, Cotes having acquired the Jaggard interest in the copyrights by purchase from Isaac Jaggard's widow (Isaac died in 1627), and Allot, the Blount interest. John Smethwicke and William Aspley maintained their shares, and Richard Hawkins and Richard Meighen joined the syndicate. Thomas Cotes printed the volume, a page-for-page reprint of the First Folio.

A collation of the two folios reveals that though the second is not so carefully printed as the first, it bears the marks of careful attention. For the first time in the history of the transmission of Shakespeare's text (and the only time in the seventeenth century), a person not of the printing house, trained in literary matters and in metrics and with a sense of English history, supervised the text of a volume. We should call this person an editor. This editor provided more than 1,600 emendations of the text, of which some six hundred are accepted in modern editions; he supplied words that had been inadvertently omitted by the printers; he adjusted passages in Latin, Italian, and French; he corrected inconsistencies and errors of fact by a thorough knowledge of each play and of history; most remarkably, he corrected rhyme and metrical errors with a keen ear for the rhythm and movement of Shakespeare's verse. Many of his corrections have been rejected by modern editors because they were made with an eye to the linguistic or grammatical patterns of 1632 and with no awareness of the desirability of recovering the patterns of an earlier generation, but his achievement was remarkable. Later adapters responded to the texts as theatrical documents; he responded to them as literature.

The Third Folio was published by Philip Chetwinde, who had acquired the copyrights belonging to Allot as he acquired other rights in marrying Allot's widow. He seems also to have acquired the rights of the other members of the syndicate, for no other publisher is mentioned in his volume. Nor is any printer, for Chetwinde distributed the work among three printers, presumably to speed the manufacture. Though their names do not appear, these have been identified as Roger Daniel, John Hayes or Thomas Ratcliffe, and Alice Warren. The volume is a page-for-page reprint of the Second Folio, and though it is more carefully printed than the Second Folio, it is less carefully edited. The editor was not, apparently, a literary man, and his emendations tend to be "unexciting": corrections of typographical errors, changes of words that had become obscure or obsolete, reduction of unusual or unorthodox expressions to clearer or more literal phrases, attempts to regularize the flexible metrics of Shakespeare's verse. The volume may possibly have been issued in 1663, but its date is usually set at 1664 because a "second" issue appeared in that year, containing a supplement of seven plays attributed to Shakespeare. *Pericles* is the first of this group and the only one to have been accepted as a genuine addition to the canon.

The Fourth Folio was published by a syndicate headed by Henry Herringman and including Edward Brewster, Richard Chiswell, and Richard Bentley. Herringman acquired the copyrights formerly held by Thomas Cotes and then by Cotes's widow from her estate. Like the Third, the Fourth Folio was also parceled out among three printers; of these, only Robert Roberts, printer of the preliminaries and the comedies, has been identified. The Fourth Folio had no editor, but in neatness and correctness of typography it profited from the attention of proofreaders in three shops. These proofreaders aimed at a handsome piece of typography, interesting themselves in neither literary nor dramatic questions. As a result, the Fourth is the cleanest and most readable of the folios. It looks as if the volume had benefited from the increased interest in style and sophistication usually associated with continental printing, and it sets a new standard of elegance anticipating the fine printing of the next century.

In one sense, the series of collected editions continued unabated into the eighteenth century: the Fourth Folio followed the Third Folio by twenty-one years; the next edition (1709) followed the Fourth Folio by twenty-four years. But in two matters the first eighteenth-century edition differed markedly from its predecessors: it was in a multivolume set in octavo, not in folio; and it was supervised by an editor, a dramatist of literary pretensions.

The first eighteenth-century edition of Shakespeare's works derives from the energy and promotion of the publisher, Jacob Tonson, who recognized the need for a fresh edition of Shakespeare. He conceived of the task in the same terms that earlier publishers had seen it: he reprinted the edition immediately preceding his own. But recognizing also that times and tastes had changed, he engaged the services of Nicholas Rowe to oversee the project. Rowe had been since 1700 an extremely popular dramatist (his *Tamerlane* was presented annually on 5 November until 1815); he was also a translator and an adapter of other men's works and had attempted a tragedy in the style of Shakespeare. A poet of some note, he was named poet laureate in 1715. He was a likely candidate for the post of editor of Shakespeare, and it is clear that he undertook the office seriously.

Three of Rowe's contributions to the format of an edition of Shakespeare's plays are with us still. First, he prepared a biography, "An Account of the Life and Writings of the Author," printed as an introduction to the edition. This, the first attempt at an authoritative biography of Shakespeare, became the standard biography of the century, appearing in all subsequent editions until 1803. Many of the details of Shakespeare's life recorded in Rowe's account may be apocryphal, though they derive from the traditions of the seventeenth-century stage transmitted through the actor Thomas Betterton. But without Rowe's record of them, they would not have been preserved at all. Second, Rowe provided a list of the dramatis personae for each play; only eight such lists had appeared in the folios. Though such lists do not affect the texts of the plays, they do provide a useful and conspicuous part of all modern editions. Third, Rowe provided act and scene divisions for all of the plays which had appeared in the folios inadequately or incorrectly divided or divided not at all. Rowe's divisions, modified now in many particulars, remain the standard for theatrical performance (where act-divisions are represented as intervals still) and for critical reference. Though producers and critics in the second half of the twentieth century tend to minimize the value of such divisions in production and in editing, Rowe's tradition is still very much with us.

Rowe's edition appeared in six octavo volumes,

in June 1709; an immediate success, it was followed by a second edition, dated and presumably printed the same year, so exact a reprint that not until the twentieth century did scholars realize that the two were not one. The fact that a second edition was required demonstrates convincingly that a new reading public of substantial dimensions had suddenly appeared, a phenomenon marked by two subsequent reactions.

Since Rowe, a man of the theater, had followed the Fourth Folio, "Rowe's Shakespeare" contained none of the poems. To remedy this omission, in 1710, the publisher Edmund Curll, a businessman not famed for his integrity, issued a volume of Shakespeare's poems, "with Critical Remarks on his Plays, [and] an Essay on the Art, Rise and Progress of the Stage in Greece, Rome and England." He entitled the volume *The Works of Mr. William Shakespeare, Volume the Seventh* and printed it in the same format as Rowe's six volumes. In consequence, the "standard" Rowe's Shakespeare became a seven-volume set, most purchasers probably not aware of the split nature of their acquisition. Thereafter, all editions of the complete works included the poems as a natural part of the canon.

The second response to the increase in the size of the audience manifested itself on the Continent. The first edition of Rowe's Shakespeare served as the copy text not only for the second edition in London but also for the first two volumes of *A Collection of the Best English Plays,* published in 1711–1712 by Thomas Johnson, an English bookseller living in The Hague. Johnson printed eight plays from Rowe in the Netherlands for sale in England. He introduced two new traditions in the printing of Shakespeare's plays. He advertised that his "Choice Collection of all the best English Plays [was] neatly and correctly printed in small Volumes fit for the pocket" and that as each volume contained four plays, the set made in all "10 handsom Volumes, when bound together: [but] They are also sold single." Johnson's *Collection* was reissued in 1720–1722 and again in 1750, printed still in The Hague for sale in the streets of London. Johnson's printing method, by which he could sell the same sheets singly or in a collection, was a marketing device of considerable acumen and was copied in England by many publishers throughout the century. His other trick was equally ingenious: he popularized the paperback pocket book.

Rowe's edition had appeared in large octavo measuring about 4.5 by 7.5 inches; Johnson's *Col-*

lection appeared in small octavo to emphasize its pocketability. That plays in a smaller size could be sold singly demonstrated that the reading public now included folk of more limited means than had hitherto constituted the market. Tonson responded by producing a third edition of Rowe in 1714, printed in eight volumes in duodecimo, measuring about 3.75 by 6.5 inches. Immediately Curll provided a ninth volume in the same format; Rowe's two formats, supplemented by Curll's volumes, seem to have served in particular a dual function: the large format reposed in gentlemen's libraries for display; the small rested in their pockets for reading or was intended for the use of their children. In consequence, many copies of the 1709 editions survive well preserved, but few copies of the 1714, which was read to pieces.

As Rowe had been primarily a dramatist, not an editor, so the next literary man to engage Shakespeare's works was primarily a poet, not an editor. Alexander Pope, having completed his translation of one classic, Homer's *Iliad,* consented to edit another. He labored with much industry but with little editorial acumen for four years until the publication of his edition of Shakespeare was finished in 1725. Repeating the lesson he had learned, Tonson published the 1725 edition in a sumptuous quarto format; his second edition, 1728, in duodecimo. The two markets having once been identified and distinguished, Tonson was quick to capitalize on them. A third market appeared: in 1726, George Grierson and George Ewing reprinted, probably without authority, Pope's first edition in Dublin. The Irish market had opened.

Pope's edition, attended with the highest of expectations, fell very short of fulfilling them. That Tonson should have chosen this poet to be an editor shows how little he understood the task of an editor; Pope's acceptance of the task displays the same deficiency. Dr. Johnson believed that Pope "understood but half his undertaking." One virtue his edition had: Pope rejected from the canon the seven plays that had been added in the Third Folio. Had he rejected only six of them, leaving *Pericles* in his volumes, he would have done that part of his job perfectly. The seven plays were again included in Pope's 1728 edition. And another advantage: Pope designated with precision the locations of the scenes.

In matters of prime importance, however, Pope was inadequate to the task of an editor and, therefore, because of his great prestige, often mislead-

ing. Pope said that he had collated the texts of the earliest quartos and folios; he did so only occasionally. He declared that he never admitted to his text his own private conjecture; he did so constantly and without any notice. He boasted that he had explained the obsolete words; he explained very few, often explained them incorrectly, and sometimes explained words differently in different places in the text. Passages that he disliked he omitted or placed out of context at the foot of the page in small type, because he assumed they could not have been written by Shakespeare. Passages he could not understand he omitted. Pope's consuming care was meter, and to bring Shakespeare's metrical practice into conformity with the regularity of his century, Pope labored long and hard—dropping or adding syllables and rearranging words so that each line should be precise.

In the tradition of the editing of Shakespeare's plays, Pope did more harm than good. The evils that he did as an editor lived too long after him. But correctives came into action immediately. In 1726 appeared Lewis Theobald's critique, *Shakespeare Restored: or, a Specimen of the Many Errors, as Well Committed, as Unamended by Mr. Pope in His Late Edition of This Poet.*

Theobald followed this attack on Pope's edition with an edition of his own in seven volumes (1733), "collated with the Oldest Copies, and Corrected." He placed on the title page this motto from Virgil: "I, Decus, i, nostrum: melioribus utere Fatis" ("Go, my handsome one; enjoy a better fate"). But before this edition was published, Theobald had already been made infamous. *Shakespeare Restored,* his critique of Pope's edition, would have demolished the work of any man less famous than Pope; but Theobald was demolished by it, being raised by Pope to the bad eminence of King of Dullness in *The Dunciad* in 1728. Pope's vilification of Theobald initiated a tradition of personal abuse that colored and disfigured the development of textual criticism throughout the century, one of the less attractive aspects of Shakespearean scholarship. Furthermore, the power of Pope's name was so considerable as the century progressed that it tended to raise Pope's textual work far beyond its worth and so to deprecate Theobald's.

The first particular successor to Pope was Sir Thomas Hanmer, who published at Oxford a handsome quarto edition of the *Works* in 1743–1744, expressly designed to be more elegant than Pope's. The edition was reprinted in London in 1745,

1747, 1748, 1751, 1760, in Edinburgh in 1761, and in Oxford in 1771. Pope's second successor was William Warburton, a clergyman who was to become bishop of Gloucester. Warburton became a friend of Pope's in the poet's later years, and it was presumably at Pope's suggestion that the critical work that Warburton had been preparing should appear as a new collaborative edition, though, in fact, all of the work of the edition was Warburton's. In 1747 appeared *The Works of Shakespeare in Eight Volumes. The Genuine Text (collated with all the former Editions, and then corrected and emended) is here settled: Being restored from the Blunders of the first Editors, and the Interpolations of the two Last . . . by Mr. Pope and Mr. Warburton.* The "two last" were, of course, Hanmer and Theobald, to whom the word "restored" glances, and the "first Editors" were the printers of the quartos and folios and Rowe; but the "Genuine Text" was far from being "settled" by this edition, for Warburton was more inventive than Pope had been and showed everywhere a more casual attitude toward the integrity of the text than had any previous editor.

A further sad commentary on the bitter rivalry of the eighteenth-century editors is the fact that they knew one another by correspondence, if not in person. Pope and Theobald corresponded, Theobald and Warburton corresponded, Warburton and Hanmer corresponded; each offered contributions to the text of his correspondent. What should have been a group of editors working together became a group at one another's throats.

The only editor in this series who had a genuine understanding of his task was Theobald, whose edition, in spite of the vilification he suffered, went on steadily in new printings of 1740, 1752, 1757, 1762, 1767, 1772, and 1773. Theobald brought to his task a serious interest in the dull work of an editor: he collated as many of the early quartos as he could find—though his standards were not so thorough as those of later editors—and he read extensively in the dramatic literature of the period. He vaunted the claim that he had read eight hundred plays in preparing his Shakespeare, a boast characteritic of Theobald's worst temper (not so many plays survived), but his library did include some two hundred original quartos. Dr. Johnson, overmuch influenced by the tradition of Pope, nevertheless admitted of Theobald that he was "zealous for minute accuracy, and not negligent in pursuing it. . . . What little he did was commonly right."

The second editor who has earned the respect of modern textual critics is Edward Capell. Capell understood clearly two precepts of modern scholarship: he rejected the eighteenth-century tradition (traced to Rowe) of reprinting the edition immediately preceding, and he founded his edition on the first substantive quarto or on the First Folio. His edition was published in 1767–1768, preceded by his *Prolusions* (1760) and followed by his *Notes and Various Readings* (1779–1783). Because Capell was not a member of what seems to have been a clique of Shakespeareans, Capell's Shakespeare had only one edition, but it was, as the modern critic G. B. Evans has said, "textually the most important of all eighteenth-century editions."

The great figure who sums up the editorial work of the first half of the eighteenth century and launches that of the nineteenth is Samuel Johnson. Like Capell, though less exactly, Johnson understood that the First Folio was superior to all the later folios and that "the reading of the ancient books is probably true. . . . As I practised conjecture more, I learned to trust it less." A scholar has said of his edition, "We may now abandon his text; . . . but, wherever a difficulty can be solved by common sense, we shall never find his notes antiquated. . . . In disputed passages he has an almost unerring instinct for the explanation which alone can be right." The edition was reprinted in the year of issue, 1765, and in 1768.

In 1766, George Steevens published *Twenty of the Plays of Shakespeare . . . printed in Quarto during his life-time.* On the strength of this publication Steevens joined forces with Johnson to publish a new edition of Shakespeare (1773). Steevens' preface to this edition disclaims any use of Capell's edition, but in fact Steevens incorporated without acknowledgment many of Capell's readings and notes. The title page announces that the plays are printed "with the Corrections and Illustrations of Various Commentators." One reworking of this edition appeared in 1778, depending still more heavily on Capell, and another in 1785, in which the name of a new editor was added, Isaac Reed. Reed was responsible also for the editions of 1793, 1803, and 1813; the series concludes with the edition of 1821, edited by James Boswell, son of the famous biographer. One of Boswell's friends and associates was Edmond Malone, another influential editor at the end of the eighteenth century. Malone's edition was published in 1790 and reprinted in 1794 in Dublin. As late as 1864, the names of

Steevens and Malone appeared on the title page of an edition of Shakespeare, so impressive was the influence of these two eighteenth-century scholars in the nineteenth century.

The publication of the first four editions of Shakespeare's collected works spanned eighty-five years (1623–1708); the publication of the second four editions spanned sixteen (1709–1725). That was only the beginning of a publication record extraordinary for its energy, diversity, and acrimony. In the score of years from 1709 to 1730, six editions of the collected works were published; from 1731 to 1750, ten; from 1751 to 1770, twelve; from 1771 to 1790, fifteen; from 1791 to 1810, twenty-two. The various printings in any score of years included simple reprints, revised editions, and new editions. Among them may be mentioned Hugh Blair's edition, published in Edinburgh (1753); Charles Wagner's edition, published in Brunswick, Germany (1797–1801); Samuel Ayscough's edition, published by Stockdale (1784), the first single-volume complete works since the Fourth Folio (printed in large octavo format with tiny print); and the first American edition, a reprint of Dr. Johnson's edition, published in Philadelphia (1795–1796).

The frequent issuing of complete editions continued into the nineteenth century, as it has done to this day. Only a few of the many can be mentioned, but among those should be the work of Thomas Bowdler, whose *Family Shakespeare* (twenty plays only), first published in 1807, ran through more than a score of editions in the century. The value of this edition lies not in its text, which was bowdlerized, but in the view that it offers of the omnipresence of Shakespeare's plays not merely in the libraries of the learned but in the homes of all sorts of people. Another popularizer was Charles Knight, who capitalized on new techniques of lithography to produce "Pictorial Editions." The first of Knight's many editions was published in 1838–1843, issued in fifty-five monthly parts and then collected into eight volumes. Gulian C. Verplanck followed suit in New York, his monthly parts appearing from 1844 to 1847, the whole collection in three volumes in 1847 as the "Illustrated Shakespeare." Scholarly editions continued to appear: by John Payne Collier (1842–1844), Henry N. Hudson (1851–1856), James O. Halliwell (1853–1865), Nicolaus Delius (Leipzig, 1854), Alexander Dyce (1857), Richard Grant White (1857–1866), and so on.

Notable in the century is the presence of editions published in English in Germany. Delius' work enjoyed five editions and was supplanted by an edition of Wilhelm Wagner and Ludwig Proescholdt published in Hamburg (1879–1891), and that in turn by an edition published in Darmstadt (1925). In the United States, Hudson and Grant White published many reprints and new editions of their work; the latter's second edition (Boston, 1883) was the "Riverside Edition," the first of a notable line. Another series, edited by William J. Rolfe, was reissued many times and revised at least three times officially; Rolfe's texts from 1870 to 1911 formed the standard text for many American classrooms. The latter third of the century was marked by the publication of constantly increasing numbers of school series for use in Great Britain; the most famous of these series, the "Temple Shakespeare," annotated by Israel Gollancz, was published by Dent in 1902.

Though the publication of Shakespeare's works flourished in Germany and the United States as well as in Great Britain, it did not do so in the capitals of the empire. British publishing houses followed the flag, establishing their branches around the globe so that the sun never set on the publishing of Shakespeare. But independent ventures did show their faces in Calcutta (1878, an incomplete edition), Madras (1898), and Bombay (1939). The first Canadian edition, a revised "Swan Shakespeare," appeared in Toronto in 1948. Foreign translations abounded: into German (1762, by Wieland), French (1776, by Le Tourneur), Italian (1797), Russian (1841, incomplete; 1865), and fifteen other languages. Shakespeare was not of one place but for all climes.

Two major events in the publishing of Shakespeare's works occurred at the end of the nineteenth century, one in England, one in America. The first was the publication of the works of Shakespeare by the University of Cambridge, edited by John Glover, William George Clark, and William Aldis Wright in nine volumes (1863–1866). One textual critic, Fredson Bowers, has said that this "first editorial recasting of the text since the Malone Variorum of the turn of the century . . . became the modern foundation, or source, text of Shakespeare. . . . The critical sense of these editors was broad, humane, and shrewd; and their excellent taste served in some part to repair the blunders of their occasionally faulty textual theories." The significance of this edition was more than scholarly, for its editors published a one-volume edition of their work for the popular market, the "Globe Shakespeare" (1864). The Globe text, with its act, scene, and line numbering, became the absolute standard for most readers of the English-speaking world and a reference for scholarship that could scarcely be assailed. For over a century, the Globe Shakespeare has dominated the market and the public mind. As recently as 1978 a commercial venture, *The Annotated Shakespeare,* simply reprinted the Globe text as the basis for its edition. The good work of Glover, Clark, and Wright continues—as if there had been no scholarly improvement made to the text of Shakespeare since then.

The other considerable event was American: the publication of the "New Variorum." This series was undertaken by Horace Howard Furness with the appearance of *Romeo and Juliet* in 1871. Furness, a Philadelphia lawyer, was personally responsible for the editing of fourteen plays from 1871 to 1907; he was succeeded by his son and namesake, who edited five plays from 1908 to 1928; and he in turn was succeeded in 1936 by the Modern Language Association, which continued the series. The New Variorum, like its predecessors, sought to collect in one volume the remarks of various commentators on the text and on the dramatic sense of the play; unlike its predecessors, it also included a systematic record of every textual variant in all the early editions and in the important later editions. The New Variorum was one of the first works of American scholarship to be accepted as a significant document by major British critics and scholars.

As we have noted, George Steevens issued the first reprints of original texts in 1766. Reprints of the quartos and of the folios became increasingly available as the nineteenth century progressed. At first these were type facsimiles, but as techniques improved, lithography and photography became the standard methods of reproduction. The first series of lithographic facsimiles of the quartos, published by E. W. Ashbee and edited by J. O. Halliwell-Phillipps, was issued in a limited edition—"for private circulation only"—from 1861 to 1871, in forty-eight volumes. The second series was the "Shakspere Quarto Facsimiles," in forty-three volumes, issued in photolithography under the direction of F. J. Furnivall by William Griggs and Charles Praetorius from 1880 to 1889. The third series, "Shakespeare Quartos in Collotype Facsimile," was undertaken by W. W. Greg at Ox-

ford in 1939 and continued after the war by Charlton Hinman; sixteen items have appeared in this series. In 1983, Kenneth Muir and Michael J. B. Allen produced in a single volume by fine-screen offset facsimiles of all the first quartos and the good second quartos.

The first reprint of a folio—the First Folio—was produced in type facsimile in 1807; a second followed in 1864, printed by Lionel Booth. A photographic facsimile appeared under the direction of Howard Staunton (1866), a second, by J. O. Halliwell-Phillipps, reduced in size, was published in 1876 (reissued in New York in 1887). Another reduced facsimile, "The Double Text Dallastype Shakespeare," presented the First Folio text by a process of "photographic engraving" on pages facing "the modern text as determined by the late Charles Knight," published in 1895. The best of all the early folio facsimiles was that prepared by Sidney Lee and published at Oxford in 1902. This was followed by the Methuen series of the four folios: the Fourth in 1904, the Third in 1905, the Second in 1909, and the First in 1910. A popular facsimile, inexpensively produced, was prepared at Yale University in 1954, published by photo-offset.

The most distinctive of all the facsimiles is that prepared by Charlton Hinman at the Folger Library. Published in 1968 by W. W. Norton, this facsimile is unique in reproducing not simply the best copy available but the best copy in the corrected state of each page; in all, thirty of the copies of the First Folio at the Folger were used in assembling the clearest pages for the facsimile. The technique used was fine-screen offset. Hinman took the occasion of the production of his facsimile to provide also a complete numbering system on a scheme originating in but not perfected in the "Bankside Shakespeare," edited by Appleton Morgan and published by the New York Shakespeare Society (1888–1906). In each play every line of print in the folio is given a number. This system of "through line numbering" offers a standard that will be invariable for all editions. (For example, Macbeth's great speech, "To-morrow, and to-morrow, and to-morrow," in the Globe numbering V. v. 19–28, is TLN 2340–2349.)

Scripture tells us that of the making of books there is no end; editions of Shakespeare constitute an important subset for that rule. The twentieth century has been dominated by several major editions or series amid a host of lesser ones. Perhaps the leader of the group is the "Arden Shakespeare," appearing under the general editorship of W. J. Craig and R. H. Case from 1899 to 1944, individual volumes being regularly revised. After the second World War, the series was reinstated as the "new Arden," under the editorship of, successively Una Ellis-Fermor, Harold Brooks, Harold Jenkins, and Brian Morris. Volumes of the new Arden appeared from 1951 until 1982. A fresh reworking is proposed now for some of the earlier volumes of the new Arden.

Another notable series has been that issuing from Cambridge, in succession to the magisterial edition of 1863–1866, itself revised by W. A. Wright in 1891–1893. The "Cambridge New Shakespeare" began publication in 1921, the editors expecting to finish the work in a decade; the last volume appeared in 1966. A list of scholarly monographs, *Shakespeare Problems,* was published as supplementary to the texts. The first editors were Arthur Quiller-Couch and John Dover Wilson, the latter succeeding to the sole editorship after the death of "Q" and being joined in the last volumes by younger scholars. Cambridge has undertaken another edition, its fourth, under the general editorship of Philip Brockbank, the first volumes appearing in 1984. Not quite in the class of scholarship of these series but very popular in the United States has been the "Yale Shakespeare," edited by Wilbur Cross and C. F. Tucker Brooke, from 1917 to 1928, and then in a revised edition, commencing in 1954, by Helge Kökeritz and C. T. Prouty.

Responding to the growing number of college undergraduates in the United States, editors provided collections of selected plays of Shakespeare for classroom use: Hardin Craig (1931), G. B. Harrison (1948), and O. J. Campbell (1949). Craig and Harrison issued the complete works in 1951 and in 1952, respectively; both of these editions reprinted the Globe text, "exactly," as said one, and in response to public demand, as said the other. The days when editors could seriously recommend the Globe text had long gone, but the tradition refused to die. In 1938, George Lyman Kittredge produced his complete one-volume edition (revised by Irving Ribner in 1966–1969), and in 1942, William A. Neilson and Charles J. Hill published a one-volume revision (the second Riverside Shakespeare) of a text prepared by Neilson in 1906. In Great Britain two editions, comparable in nature though without annotations aimed at undergraduates, were prepared by Peter Alexander (1951) and Charles J. Sisson (1954).

In the mid-twentieth century, four series of Shakespeare in paperback pocket books came on the market. The first issued from the imaginative publishers Penguin Books. The "Penguin Shakespeare," edited singly by G. B. Harrison, was published in England (1937–1959); it has been succeeded by the "New Penguin," edited successively by T. J. B. Spencer and Stanley Wells, with separate editors (usually British) for each play, beginning in 1967, a series superior in text and annotation to its predecessor. In the United States, following that model, Penguin Books issued the "Pelican Shakespeare" (1956–1967), with Alfred Harbage as general editor and separate editors (usually American) for each play. This edition contributed notably to the editorial tradition by reducing act and scene indications to a minimum (those that Rowe had inserted prominently) and by rejecting location indicators completely (those that Pope had invented) so as to reproduce to modern eyes reading the text the sense of continuously flowing action that Elizabethan eyes must have experienced seeing the original productions. Signet Books produced its "Signet Classic Shakespeare," with Sylvan Barnet as general editor and separate editors (1963–1968). The Folger Shakespeare Library gave its name to a series edited by Louis B. Wright and Virginia Lamar. The Pelican Shakespeare and the Signet Shakespeare were both collected into single volumes for undergraduate courses, in 1969 and 1972, respectively. Two other single-volume editions have also appeared: one is a revision of Hardin Craig's 1958 volume, prepared by David Bevington in 1973 (now itself revised entirely by Bevington, 1980); the other is the third Riverside Shakespeare, the text prepared by G. B. Evans with supporting annotations and commentary by many hands (1974). It seems impossible to glut the market for editions of Shakespeare's works.

Though it took the lead in 1740 in publishing Sir Thomas Hanmer's edition, the first sponsored by a university press, the University of Oxford yielded primacy to Cambridge in 1863 on the appearance of the Cambridge Shakespeare; in the same year that the Cambridge Shakespeare was undergoing its revision (1891), Oxford University Press published its second Oxford edition, the work of W. J. Craig. A reissue was published in 1911–1912, with an introduction by Algernon C. Swinburne. In 1982, the Oxford University Press published the first volumes of a new Oxford Shakespeare, under the general editorship of Stanley Wells and Gary

Taylor, with Samuel Schoenbaum the American advisory editor.

This edition will appear finally in three different formats, one of which will print the plays in the spellings of the Elizabethan and Jacobean period, thereby producing a text of Shakespeare as close to Shakespeare's actual spelling and Shakespeare's actual words as modern scholarship can create. At the other end of the scale is a series, "The Contemporary Shakespeare," prepared by A. L. Rowse, that aims at restoring Shakespeare to the average reader by "translating" into modern usage all the spellings of the early texts, all obsolete and archaic words, all words that have changed meaning, and all aberrant grammatical forms. The first volumes were released in 1984.

It would be difficult to imagine two approaches to the publishing and editing of Shakespeare's plays more opposite in philosophy or in practice. Yet the two series, appearing simultaneously, demonstrate the energy and vitality that still animate the tradition of Shakespearean textual study, the purposes of which have been and will be to identify with the most scrupulous care precisely the words that Shakespeare wrote and to communicate the full meaning of the plays to the largest number of readers and playgoers possible. The publication of these most recent editions would seem to suggest that editors and their publishers are seeking to fill both these needs now in new and different ways.

BIBLIOGRAPHY

M. J. B. Allen and K. Muir, *Shakespeare's Plays in Quarto* (1981). M. W. Black and M. A. Shaaber, *Shakespeare's Seventeenth-century Editors* (1937). Fredson Bowers, *On Editing Shakespeare* (1966). Folger Shakespeare Library, *Catalog of the Shakespeare Collection* (1972). H. L. Ford, *Shakespeare 1700–1740* (1935). W. W. Greg, *The Editorial Problem in Shakespeare* (1951) and *The Shakespeare First Folio* (1955).

Charlton Hinman, *The First Folio of Shakespeare,* The Norton Facsimile (1968) and *The Printing and Proofreading of the First Folio of Shakespeare* (1963). R. Hosley, R. Knowles, and R. McGugan, *Shakespeare Variorum Handbook* (1971). T. H. Howard-Hill, *Shakespearian Bibliography and Textual Criticism* (1971). A. W. Pollard and G. R. Redgrave, *A Short-Title Catalogue of Books Printed . . . 1475–1640* (1926; rev. ed., 1976). Samuel Schoenbaum, *William Shakespeare: A Documentary Life* (1975).

Shakespeare on the English Stage

STANLEY WELLS

The history of Shakespeare's plays in the theater is, in part, the history of their adaptation to the theatrical conditions and tastes of the age in which they were being performed; in very small part, it is the history of attempts to adapt theatrical conditions to imitate those of the period in which the plays were written; to a large extent, especially in more recent times, it is the history of attempts to realize the scripts as Shakespeare wrote them in terms acceptable to contemporary audiences. It is also the history of the actors, directors, designers, composers, theater managers, and everyone else concerned with the process of performance. Here one can hope only to sketch the major developments from Shakespeare's time to our own.

To 1672

During the years between Shakespeare's death in 1616 and the suppression of the theaters in 1642, there appears to have been little change in the conditions under which Shakespeare's plays had initially been performed. Certainly his own company, the King's Men, continued to act them, as we know principally from records of performances at court. Presumably the plays were given much as they had originally been, for the tradition was continuous. The King's Men were granted a new patent in 1619, confirming their right to play at the Globe and the Blackfriars; the patent was renewed on the accession of Charles I in 1625. Their personnel changed, of course: Richard Burbage, the leading actor in Shakespeare's time, died in 1619; but they remained the most important theater company right down to 1642.

In that year occurred one of the most decisive and disruptive events in the history of the English theater: a parliamentary edict forbade the performance of plays as "spectacles of pleasure too commonly expressing lascivious mirth and levity." The Globe theater was pulled down in 1644, and though public performances resumed in 1647, they were rapidly suppressed by Parliament, which made an order of imprisonment for actors caught performing. This was not uniformly obeyed. Among the pieces surreptitiously acted were a number of simplified adaptations ("drolls") of pre-Commonwealth plays given in, for instance, fairground theaters. A collection of twenty-six of these texts first published in 1662 as *The Wits* includes several based on Shakespeare; they are *The Merry Conceits of Bottom the Weaver* (based on *A Midsummer Night's Dream*), *The Bouncing Knight* (based on *Henry IV, Part 1*), and *The Grave-Makers* ("out of *Hamlet*"). The frontispiece to the collection is an interesting, though somewhat mysterious, document. It apparently depicts an improvised stage on which are represented characters from several plays; the figures include Shakespeare's Falstaff and Mistress Quickly, and are of interest as the first pictorial depictions of these characters.

The Commonwealth represents not an absolute hiatus in theater history but an immensely significant break in continuity. In the theater following the restoration of the monarchy in 1660, conditions were very different from those that had obtained less than twenty years before. Initially, some of the old buildings were used—the Cockpit, the Red Bull, and Salisbury Court. But in August 1660, Thomas Killigrew and Sir William Davenant were granted permission "to erect two companies of players, consisting respectively of such persons as they shall choose and appoint, and to purchase, build, and erect, or hire at their charge, as they shall think fit, two houses or theatres . . . for the representation of tragedies, comedies, plays, operas, and all other entertainments of that nature, in convenient places." This same grant suppressed all other companies of actors within the area of London and Westminster, giving to Killigrew and Davenant a virtual monopoly of theatrical activity in the capital. The resulting stranglehold had many regrettable consequences, but it does greatly simplify the history of the London stage during this period.

The two companies played initially in converted indoor tennis courts. The King's Company, under Killigrew, in performances at Gibbon's Tennis Court from November 1660, appears to have been closer to the prewar traditions, not using scenery; but the Duke's Company, under Davenant, opened Lisle's Tennis Court, near Lincoln's Inn Fields, in June 1661 with a version of *The Siege of Rhodes* employing "shutter scenes" (or "flat scenes"), in which a pair of painted shutters called flats placed about halfway up the depth of the stage could be slid across the stage, meeting in the middle. There were also "scenes of relief," using cut-out wings or side scenes set in succession before a backcloth. In 1663, Killigrew moved to an old riding school in Bridges Street, off Drury Lane, where he probably used scenery. Davenant, in rivalry, commissioned Christopher Wren to plan a new theater, and though Davenant himself died in 1668, his company transferred to this new Duke's House (Dorset Garden Theatre) in 1671. In the following year Killigrew's theater burned down, and he, too, commissioned from Wren a new building, which became the ancestor of all the succeeding Drury Lanes.

Though the break in theatrical tradition imposed by the Commonwealth was crucial, there were links between pre- and post-Restoration theater. Both Killigrew and Davenant had been active in the theater before 1642. Killigrew belonged to a literary circle centered on Queen Henrietta Maria during the 1630s and wrote two extant plays. He served the royal family as a messenger on the Continent during their period of exile; his theater patent was a reward for this service. Davenant was even more closely bound up with the theater and claimed to have had intimate links with Shakespeare. Indeed, according to John Aubrey, Davenant boasted that he was Shakespeare's natural son. It is ironical that a man who was to bastardize Shakespeare should have claimed to be Shakespeare's bastard. The first of Davenant's many plays dates from 1629. After Ben Jonson's death in 1637, Davenant became a semiofficial poet laureate, and he had a close association with the performance of masques at court. His *Salmacida Spolia* (1640) was the last masque written for Charles I. A fervent royalist, he was arrested on his way to America in 1650 and imprisoned in the Tower of London until 1654. After his release he presented a number of entertainments, evading the law by giving them privately and by disguising plays as musical performances. His association with the elaborate staging techniques of court masques influenced his later staging of plays and is partly responsible for the fact that the post-Restoration theater was closer in many ways to the tradition of pre-Commonwealth court entertainments than to the public theaters of that period.

The new theater buildings were enclosed, unlike the great public theaters of Shakespeare's time. Though the stage projected into the auditorium, it did so less prominently than that of its forebears, and the forestage was marked off from the rear-stage by an embellished proscenium arch such as Inigo Jones had employed for court masques. Entries could be made through doors at each side of the proscenium; a curtain could conceal the area behind the arch from the audience; representational scenery could be painted on wings and on pairs of flats. Staging was highly conventionalized. In general, the actors spoke on the forestage; the settings, which were illustrational rather than representational and which often did duty for many different plays, changed in view of the audience; it was unusual for the curtain to fall between acts. A green carpet signified that the play was a tragedy. (This custom continued to be observed until well into the nineteenth century.) Lighting was by means of chandeliers hanging above the performers in outdoor as well as indoor scenes. Efforts to keep spectators off the stage were generally unsuccessful.

One immensely important convention of the pre-

Commonwealth stage was abandoned—the portrayal of women by boys. The actors available to Killigrew and Davenant included some who had belonged to the King's Men before the Commonwealth. A prologue to *Othello* written by Thomas Jordan, probably for a performance very shortly after the Restoration and published in 1664, suggests that among them may have been former boy actors still playing women's parts:

> Our women are defective, and so siz'd
> You'd think they were some of the guard disguis'd;
> For to speak truth, men act that are between
> Forty and Fifty, wenches of fifteen;
> With bone so large and nerve so incompliant,
> When you call *Desdemona,* enter *Giant.*

But the prologue has news for the audience:

> I come, unknown to any of the rest
> To tell you news, I saw the lady drest;
> The Woman playes today, mistake me not,
> No man in gown, or page in petticoat.

He is aware that there may be something shocking about this, and offers a defense:

> Do you not twitter, gentlemen? I know
> You will be censuring, do't fairly though;
> 'Tis possible a vertuous woman may
> Abhor all sorts of looseness, and yet play;
> Play on the stage, where all eyes are upon her,
> Shall we count that a crime France counts an Honour?

It took only a short time for playgoers to accept the change. The age of the professional actress had arrived.

Like the staging methods, the Restoration audience, too, was closer to that of the earlier private theaters and of court performances than to that of the public theaters. Royal influence was strong; whereas earlier the theater had gone to the court, now the court attended the theater. The repertory included, along with new plays, many revivals of earlier ones; but tastes had changed, with the result that some older plays soon dropped out of the repertory and others were heavily adapted to make them more suitable both for the new theater conditions and for the tastes of the spectators. After seeing *Hamlet* in 1661, the diarist John Evelyn wrote, "The old play began to disgust this refined age." But Samuel Pepys saw the same play frequently and

admired it greatly, especially when Thomas Betterton, the greatest actor of the age, played the Prince. In 1661, for example, Pepys noted seeing the play "done with scenes very well, but above all Betterton did the prince's part beyond imagination." He saw it again twice that year. In 1668 he was "mightily pleased with it, but above all with Betterton, the best part, I believe, that ever man acted." Between 1660 and 1669, Pepys records some 350 visits to the theater, including forty-one performances of twelve plays by Shakespeare; he saw *Macbeth* nine times, *The Tempest* eight. As these statistics suggest, Shakespeare was not dominant in the repertoire. Among older dramatists, Jonson and Beaumont and Fletcher, appear to have been more popular. The right to perform Shakespeare's plays was divided between the two companies. Davenant was awarded *The Tempest, Measure for Measure, Much Ado About Nothing, Romeo and Juliet, Twelfth Night, Henry VIII, King Lear, Macbeth, Hamlet,* and *Pericles,* all of which he declared he would "reform and make fitt for the Company of Actors appointed under his direction and command."

This phrasing acknowledges that the plays had come to be viewed as old-fashioned. They might need to be "reformed" before being acceptable. Spectators with neoclassical leanings found Shakespeare barbarously free in his plotting. Those who went to the theater hoping for music, dancing, and spectacular stage effects were liable to find him dull. And all theatergoers had difficulty in understanding him. Nevertheless, some plays were given more or less as written. Killigrew mounted *Othello* and *Julius Caesar,* for instance, with little adaptation. Davenant was more radical in his treatment of the texts, though his *Hamlet* for Betterton (acted in 1661, published in 1676) was relatively unaltered apart from some stylistic changes and the omission of around 850 lines—significant enough, it may be thought, but comparable in quantity with the cuts in many modern productions, such as Peter Hall's 1965 staging. Davenant's next adaptation was more radical. *The Law Against Lovers* (1662) combines the main plot of *Measure for Measure* with the Benedick-Beatrice episodes of *Much Ado About Nothing,* along with many other alterations and additions. Essentially, this is a new play drawing heavily on Shakespeare. Pepys found it "a good play and well performed, especially the little girl's (whom I never saw act before) dancing and singing," but an anonymous satirist complained that Davenant

Was a far better Cooke then a Poet
And only he the Art of it had
Of two good Playes to make one bad.

The Law Against Lovers was not revived after the year of its first performance.

Far more successful and influential was Davenant's version of *Macbeth,* dating from 1663–1664. This is a thorough adaptation, reshaping the play according to the tenets of neoclassical criticism, refining its language ("The devil damn thee black, thou cream-faced loon!" becomes "Now Friend, what means thy change of Countenance?"), giving it a more explicit moral purpose with an emphasis on the folly of ambition. Malcolm calls for Macbeth's body to

Hang upon
A pinnacle in *Dunsinane,* to shew
To future Ages what to those is due,
Who others Right, by Lawless Power pursue.

On a more practical level, Davenant fattened the actresses' parts (arranging a meeting between Lady Macbeth and Lady Macduff, for example) and added to the spectacle, especially by elaborating the witch scenes with song, dance, and flying machines. Though Dryden satirized it and Thomas Duffett parodied it, Davenant's *Macbeth* was a success. John Downes, prompter to the Duke's Company, wrote of its "being drest in all it's Finery, as new Cloath's, new Scenes, Machines, as flyings for the Witches," and said that "with all the Singing and Dancing in it . . . it being all Excellently perform'd, being in the nature of an Opera, it Recompens'd double the Expense." Davenant's *Macbeth* totally supplanted Shakespeare's play on the stage until David Garrick's performance of 1744, and it was more than a century after that before the acting text was finally purged of his accretions.

Davenant enlisted the help of the young John Dryden for his adaptation of *The Tempest,* or *The Enchanted Island,* successfully performed in 1667. The plot is regularized by providing a sister for Miranda and a brother for Ferdinand. As Dryden put it in his preface, Davenant, "as he was a man of quick and piercing imagination, soon found that somewhat might be added to the Design of *Shakespear* . . . he design'd the Counter-part to *Shakespear's* Plot, namely, that of a Man who had never seen a Woman; that, by this means, those two characters of Innocence and Love might the more illustrate and commend each other." Scenes of po-

tentially lubricious comedy when the young people first become aware of the opposite sex have aroused disapproval (Odell calls this "the worst perversion of Shakespeare in the two-century history of such atrocities"), but the play has life of its own and is more easily acceptable for its inventiveness and originality than are mere debasements of Shakespeare. It was itself adapted in 1674 in a spectacularly operatic version ascribed (by Downes) to Thomas Shadwell. This had music by John Banister, Pelham Humfrey, and Matthew Locke; Henry Purcell composed a new score for performance in 1690. These adaptations kept Shakespeare's play off the stage until the late eighteenth century and went on influencing productions well into the nineteenth century. (The "operatic" version was revived at the Old Vic, London, in 1959 for the tercentenary of Purcell's birth.)

Other Shakespeare plays were performed during the early years of the Restoration. Killigrew presented John Lacy's *Sauny the Scot,* an adaptation of *The Taming of the Shrew,* in 1667; it had some success. Davenant's company gave *Twelfth Night* (from 1661); *Romeo and Juliet* (in a lost version, according to John Downes, adapted "into a Tragicomedy, by Mr *James Howard,* he preserving *Romeo* and *Juliet* alive; so that when the Tragedy was Reviv'd again, 'twas Play'd Alternately, Tragical one day and Tragicomical another; for several Days together"); *Henry VIII;* and *King Lear* (as written, according to Downes). But it is Davenant's *Macbeth,* his acting text of *Hamlet,* and his and Dryden's *Tempest* that are of continuing importance in the history of Shakespearean performance.

1672–1745

The Dorset Garden Theatre, built by Christopher Wren for the Duke's Company, opened successfully in 1671 and proved particularly suitable for spectacular shows—so much so that Thomas Shadwell, in his second epilogue for *The Tempest,* expressed doubts about the wisdom of overelaboration:

When you of Witt and sence were weary growne,
Romantic riming, fustian Playes were showne,
We then to flying Witches did advance,
And for your pleasure traffic'd into France.
From thence new arts to please you we have sought,
We have machines to some perfection brought.

The King's Company's new Drury Lane Theatre opened in 1674 and survived with few changes until 1791. But the company collapsed in 1682, and in that year Betterton and his colleagues moved into Drury Lane, forming a new United Company with former members of the King's Company. The Dorset Garden Theatre declined and was demolished in 1709. Even the United Company had problems, especially the financial machinations and tyrannical exploitation of the actors by Christopher Rich, who had bought the patent from Davenant's son; and in 1695, Betterton broke away from Drury Lane and formed a new company playing at Lincoln's Inn Fields. This company moved in 1705 to Sir John Vanbrugh's magnificent new theater, the Haymarket, but the enterprise failed, and within a few years the theater became an opera house. The patent companies came together again at Drury Lane, which from 1712 to about 1732 was successfully managed by the "Triumvirate" of Robert Wilks, Barton Booth (who had rapidly replaced Thomas Doggett), and Colley Cibber, whose *Apology for the Life of Mr. Colley Cibber, Comedian* (1740) is one of the most important and entertaining sources of knowledge about the theater of his time. In 1714 a rebuilt Lincoln's Inn Fields opened its doors and soon became a rival to Drury Lane. It closed in 1732, when Covent Garden, then a comparatively small theater, opened. This established a long-lasting pattern, with Covent Garden and Drury Lane as the two main theaters in London, occupied by the two patent companies. There were occasional attempts to break the monopoly, but essentially it remained in force until 1843.

The London theater of the period, now remembered mainly for the comedies of Wycherley, Congreve, Farquhar, and Vanbrugh, attracted audiences in its own day with the plays of Dryden, Shadwell, Nathaniel Lee, and others, but it also fed on the past. Shakespeare was only one of many pre-Commonwealth authors whose plays were revived and adapted. The versions of Shakespeare made for Davenant and Killigrew were followed by another batch between 1677 and 1683. On the whole, this second group aimed less at spectacular effect than the earlier, reflecting the success of the simpler Drury Lane Theatre over the larger, showier Dorset Garden.

Dryden's *All for Love* (1678) can scarcely be classed as an adaptation, for though influenced to some extent by *Antony and Cleopatra,* it constitutes a fully independent drama. His *Troilus and Cressida*

(1679) draws more heavily on Shakespeare but has some powerful independent scenes. It is the only version of the play that was acted in Britain until the twentieth century, and its preface, "containing the Grounds of Criticism in Tragedy," is an exceptionally interesting document in the history of adaptation. Dryden's objections to Shakespeare's style help to explain the alterations that he and other adapters made to the language of the plays: "The fury of his fancy often transported him, beyond the bounds of Judgment, either in coyning of new words and phrases, or racking words which were in use, into the violence of a Catachresis." Since Shakespeare's time, "the tongue in general is so much refin'd . . . that many of his words, and more of his Phrases, are scarce intelligible. And of those which we understand some are ungrammatical, others course; and his whole stile is so pester'd with Figurative expressions, that it is as affected as it is obscure."

Dryden's specific criticisms of *Troilus and Cressida,* too, are revealing of his canons of taste. While allowing that Shakespeare's "Characters of *Pandarus* and *Thersites,* are promising enough," he complains that

> after an Entrance or two, he lets 'em fall: and the later part of his Tragedy is nothing but a confusion of Drums and Trumpets, Excursions and Alarms. The chief persons, who give name to the Tragedy, are left alive: *Cressida* is false, and is not punish'd. Yet after all, because the play was *Shakespear's,* and that there appear'd in some places of it, the admirable Genius of the Author; I undertook to remove that heap of Rubbish, under which many excellent thoughts lay wholly bury'd. Accordingly, I new model'd the Plot; threw out many unnecessary persons; improv'd those Characters which were begun, and left unfinish'd: as *Hector, Troilus, Pandarus* and *Thersites;* and added that of Andromache. After this, I made with no small trouble, an order and Connexion of all the Scenes. . . . The whole Fifth Act, both the Plot and the writing are my Additions.

In this last act, Cressida protests, truly, to Troilus that she has been true to him. Diomedes tells Troilus that he has been her lover, and as a result, Cressida stabs herself. Troilus, finally persuaded of her innocence, kills Diomedes, is overcome by the Greeks, and falls dead on Diomedes' body. Hector dies offstage.

Clearly, Dryden believed that he had improved on Shakespeare. He was enough of an artist to write a play that had its own validity; it continued in performance until 1734. If his strictures on Shakespeare seem absurdly condescending and uncomprehending to us, it is worth remarking that as late as 1920, G. C. D. Odell could write, "The play as a play is better, I believe, than Shakespeare's, which is hardly a play at all." More recently, Shakespeare's play has been triumphantly vindicated in performance, and its dramaturgy has been illuminated and justified in criticism, while Dryden's adaptation has fallen into obscurity.

Another adaptation that had a considerable period of success is *Caius Marius* (1680), in which Thomas Otway (author of *Venice Preserved,* one of the best Restoration tragedies) grafted the love story of Romeo and Juliet onto an episode of Roman history. Otway had the idea of permitting his counterpart to Juliet to awaken before the death of her lover, so that the two could have a final conversation. Otway's play kept *Romeo and Juliet* off the stage until 1744, and his idea for the death scene survived well into the nineteenth century. Other adaptations were less successful, for varying reasons. Nahum Tate's metamorphosis of *Richard II* into *The Sicilian Usurper* (1681) was suppressed after the second performance because, in spite of the change of setting, it was thought to reflect unfavorably upon the monarchy. John Crowne's two avowedly anti-Catholic plays (1681, 1682) based on *Henry VI* were also suppressed. Tate's *Ingratitude of a Commonwealth* (1682), based on *Coriolanus,* failed in spite of a sensationally violent finale.

Tate is the author of perhaps the most influential and notorious of all the adaptations. In his dedication to *King Lear,* played at Dorset Garden in 1681, Tate tells how he had found the play "a Heap of Jewels, unstrung, and unpolish't; yet so dazzling in their Disorder, that I soon perceiv'd I had seiz'd a Tresure." He shows more ability than Dryden to accept Shakespeare's individual style: "The Images and Language are so odd and surprizing, and yet so agreeable and proper, that whilst we grant that none but *Shakespear* cou'd have form'd such Conceptions; yet we are satisfied that they were the only Things in the world that ought to be said on these Occasions." The play's structure was deficient, but Tate had had the "good Fortune to light on one Expedient to rectifie what was wanting in the Regularity and Probability of the Tale, which was to run through the Whole, a *Love* betwixt *Edgar* and *Cordelia;* that never chang'd Word with each other in the Original. This renders *Cordelia's* Indifference, and her Father's Passion in the first Scene, proba-

ble. It likewise gives countenance to *Edgar's* disguise, making that a generous Design that was before a poor Shift to save his Life."

Tate found that his method required him to make "the Tale conclude in a Success to the innocent destrest Persons." So, in the final scene, Lear presents Edgar with Cordelia: "Take her Crown'd; / Th'imperial Grace fresh blooming on her Brow." Gloucester confers his blessing, Kent adds "Old *Kent* throws in his hearty Wishes too," and Lear suggests to Gloucester:

> Thou, *Kent,* and I, retir'd to some cool Cell
> Will gently pass our short Reserves of Time
> In calm reflections on our Fortunes past.

The play ends with a resoundingly moral couplet as Edgar declares to Cordelia:

> Thy bright Example shall convince the World
> (Whatever Storms of Fortune are decreed)
> That Truth and Vertue shall at last succeed.

Tate's other changes include the total omission of the Fool and the depiction of Edmund's sexual intrigue with Goneril and Regan in a manner characteristic of the age. When not writing in his own dialogue, Tate tends to make a thorough paraphrase of the original rather than tinker with it in Davenant's somewhat halfhearted manner.

Tate's *Lear* has become something of a critical battlefield. It is easily scoffed at for its reductiveness, its simplistic neatness of structure, its evasion of tragedy, and its moralistic triteness. Yet it has been one of the most successful plays in the history of English drama. It continued to be performed (though with an increasing number of reversions to Shakespeare) until William Charles Macready restored the Fool in 1838. Undeniably, Tate's *King Lear* continued to exert an appeal when many other Restoration plays were forgotten. But, while we may grant its success in its own terms, it pales into triviality when compared with its source. Tate would be easier to forgive had he not been so appallingly successful.

The last important group of adaptations dates from the years 1692–1700. The most ambitious as a stage spectacle is *The Fairy Queen,* an adaptation by an unknown hand of *A Midsummer Night's Dream* played at Dorset Garden in 1692. Shakespeare's play is not greatly altered but is rearranged to form a framework for an unrelated series of spectacular scenes marvelously set to music by Henry Purcell, who used no word of Shakespeare: Purcell's score can be heard in concert performance without affording a hint that it has anything to do with Shakespeare. Another, curiously related adaptation is Charles Gildon's *Measure for Measure, or Beauty the Best Advocate,* given at Lincoln's Inn Fields in 1700, in which a greatly simplified version of Shakespeare's play, omitting the lowlife characters, is conflated with Purcell's opera *Dido and Aeneas* (which has words by Nahum Tate). The excuse is that Escalus is presenting Angelo with a four-part masque to celebrate his birthday. The epilogue to this odd work, spoken by an actor representing Shakespeare's ghost, suggests a strong undercurrent of uncertainty, even guilt, about the ethics of adaptation:

Enough, your Cruelty Alive I knew;
And must I Dead be Persecuted too?
Injur'd so much of late upon the *Stage,*
My *Ghost* can bear no more; but comes to Rage.
My *Plays,* by *Scriblers* mangl'd I have seen;

.   .   .   .

Oh! if *Mackbeth,* or *Hamlet* ever pleas'd,
Or *Desdemona* e'er your Passions rais'd:
If *Brutus,* or the Bleeding *Cæsar* e'er
Inspir'd your Pity, or provok'd your Fear,
Let me no more endure such Mighty Wrongs,
By *Scriblers* Folly, or by *Actors* toungs.

The most influential of this second major batch of adaptations was Colley Cibber's *Richard III,* first acted in 1699. This is only about two-thirds the length of Shakespeare's play (admittedly, one of his longest). It has considerably fewer characters and is far more single-minded in its concentration upon Richard himself. Queen Margaret, Clarence, Edward IV, Hastings, the Archbishop, the murderers, and a number of lesser characters are all dropped. The role of King Richard himself is proportionately fattened; it is no coincidence that Cibber adapted the play with himself in mind as Richard. About a third of the play is in Cibber's own words. The rest is borrowed or adapted from Shakespeare: along with the original play, *Henry VI, Parts 1* and *3; Henry IV, Parts 1* and *2; Richard II;* and *Henry V* are all laid under contribution. Cibber's original passages include one or two that have passed into the language and are still sometimes thought of as quotations from Shakespeare: "Off with his head; so much for Buckingham" and "Richard's himself again." Cibber's *Richard III* is in many respects

immeasurably inferior to Shakespeare's. Nevertheless, it had great melodramatic potential and provided a virtuoso vehicle of stunning effectiveness. It became one of the most successful plays of the English theater, supplanting Shakespeare's original until the late nineteenth century, influencing in structure and even in language Olivier's film of *Richard III* (1956) and perhaps still affecting the theatrical image of the play.

By about 1700 the most important adaptations had been made. Minor ones continued to appear, not always successfully. John Dennis, adapting *Coriolanus* as *The Invader of His Country* (1719), claimed to have found that in the original play

we may descry
Where Master-strokes in wild Confusion lie,
Here brought to as much order as we can
Reduce those Beauties upon Shakespeare's plan.

For all his efforts, the new play lasted only three nights. Charles Johnson's *Love in a Forest* (1723) represents a rare attempt to put the romantic comedies back into circulation: it combines parts of *As You Like It* with the Pyramus-and-Thisbe scenes of *A Midsummer Night's Dream.* It had little success. But the established adaptations continued to be played.

If the story so far has been rather of the ways in which some of Shakespeare's texts were adapted than of the manner of performance, this is mainly because accounts of performances in this period are few and far between. Not until the early years of the eighteenth century did theater journalism develop to any appreciable extent: the earliest periodical criticism of drama was written by Richard Steele in the *Tatler* (from 1709) and elsewhere, and its later development was fitful. Still, the major performers even of the earlier period have left enough record for us to be able to gauge something of their impact on audiences.

Unquestionably the leading actor from the early years of the Restoration until his death in 1710 was Thomas Betterton. His range was great; in Shakespeare, he excelled as Othello, Brutus, Henry VIII, Hotspur (in his younger days), Falstaff, and, above all, Hamlet, which he continued to play into his seventies. His acting style appears to have been characterized by restraint, by considerable powers of impersonation, by great vocal control, and by an extraordinary capacity to command the rapt attention of the audience. Thus, Colley Cibber described how "he made the Ghost equally terrible to the Spectator as to himself! and in the descriptive Part of the natural Emotions which the ghastly Vision gave him, the boldness of his Expostulation was still govern'd by Decency, manly, but not braving; his Voice never rising into that seeming Outrage or wild Defiance of what he naturally rever'd." And an anonymous critic records how "when *Hamlet* utters this line, upon the Ghost's leaving the Stage . . . *See—where he goes—ev'n now —out at the Portal:* The whole Audience hath remain'd in a dead Silence for near a Minute, and then—as if recovering all at once from their Astonishment, have joined as one Man, in a Thunder of universal Applause" (*The Laureate,* 1740). Both Betterton's speaking and his movements would probably seem inordinately stylized to us, but it is clear that he could convince contemporary theatergoers of the reality of the passions that he portrayed.

Of all English actors, perhaps the one who seems to have reached the farthest extremes of stylization without altogether forfeiting the respect of audiences is James Quin, who made a great hit as Falstaff in 1720 and remained a leading performer until his retirement in 1751, having spent the closing years of his career in rivalry with the young David Garrick, of whom he declared, "If the young fellow is right, I and the rest of the players have been all wrong." The celebrated engraving of Quin as Coriolanus, which illustrates the plume, full wig, and truncheon that were among the conventional appurtenances of the tragic hero, cannot but seem ludicrous to us.

Quin's extreme of declamatory artificiality induced one of those violent reactions that recur in the history of acting, and the prime agent of reaction was Charles Macklin, famous above all for his Shylock, a role that he first played in 1741. Before then, it had generally been given to low comedians, but Macklin invested it with tragic dignity. Macklin was also a remarkable Iago, giving the character a credible subtlety that transformed not only the role (previously played as a stock villain) but also the play. He was regarded as revolutionary in his naturalism; as a teacher (John Hill records, in *The Actor*),

it was his manner to check all the cant and cadence of tragedy; he would bid his pupil first speak the passage as he would in common life, if he had occasion to pronounce the same words; and then giving them

more force, but preserving the same accent, to deliver them on the stage. When the player was faulty in his stops or accents, he set him right; and with nothing more than this attention to what was natural, he produced out of the most ignorant persons, players that surprized everybody.

Macklin's last appearance as Shylock was at the age of ninety—ten years after the death of Garrick, the great man of the theater for whom he paved the way.

The Age of Garrick

In this period, the history of the theaters is mercifully simpler than during the previous one. Covent Garden had been built in 1732, and the pattern of theatrical monopoly initiated at the Restoration had weakened to a point where, in the 1730s, as many as five companies were performing simultaneously in London. The authority of the lord chamberlain and, under him, the master of the revels had also weakened, and dramatic satire increased, to the discomfort of the authorities. These problems were tackled in the Licensing Act of 1737, which restricted dramatic performances to the patent theaters—Drury Lane and Covent Garden—or to others licensed by the lord chamberlain and which required the licensing of new plays and of additions to old plays.

Drury Lane, which had been ill managed, was restored to an even keel in 1747, when James Lacy entered into partnership with David Garrick. Thomas Davies records that

Mr Garrick and Mr Lacy divided the business of the theatre in such a manner as not to encroach upon each other's province. Mr Lacy took upon himself the care of the wardrobe, the scenes, and the economy of the household; while Mr Garrick regulated the more important business of treating with authors, hiring actors, distributing parts in plays, superintending rehearsals, etc. Besides the profits accruing from his half share, he was allowed an income of £500 for his acting and some particular emoluments for altering plays, farces etc.

This arrangement continued virtually unchanged until Garrick retired in 1776. Covent Garden enjoyed a slightly less stable management but remained generally successful throughout the period, at times offering serious competition to the Garrick regime. Some actors moved from one theater to another, and in emergencies there was even occasional last-minute borrowing, but on the whole they followed independent courses.

The other theater that rose to some prominence in the period is the "little" theater in the Haymarket, built in 1720; in 1766 the entertainer Samuel Foote was granted a special patent allowing him to run a company during the summer season. Performances were occasionally given in other places in the capital; and in the English provinces, Scotland, and Ireland, theater-building developed rapidly. All the great actors played outside London, but London remained the theatrical center.

David Garrick is unquestionably the dominant figure from the time of his sensational London debut in 1741 as Richard III in the minor playhouse in Goodman's Fields. He was not only one of the greatest actors the English stage has ever known but was also a remarkably efficient theatrical manager. He approached more closely to the modern concept of a director than anyone before him, putting on plays with exceptional care for overall effect, and, to this end, became an important technical innovator. He was a prolific writer—perhaps the most successful eighteenth-century playwright next to Sheridan and Goldsmith—and a scholar of English dramatic literature, owning an important collection of early printed plays. He was a cultivated, elegant, self-controlled man who added dignity to his profession.

With Garrick, we come firmly into an age in which the actor was dominant, a state of things that was to persist until the middle of the nineteenth century. It was not an age of great playwriting—far less so than the Restoration, let alone the Elizabethan and Jacobean periods. Yet it was an age in which theater was popular—not for originality among its playwrights, not especially even for spectacle, but primarily for enjoyment of the art of acting. The audiences included many connoisseurs who would see the same plays over and over again, admiring virtuosity, looking forward to their favorite actors' "points"—that is, their moments of particular effectiveness, carefully prepared and, when successful, rewarded by rounds of applause.

And they enjoyed competition. In 1750, for instance, Garrick lost two of his leading performers, Spranger Barry and Susanna Cibber, to Covent Garden, where they were to open together as Romeo and Juliet. Garrick, who had not previously played Romeo, decided to challenge Barry, and announced performances with George Anne

Bellamy as Juliet. For twelve successive nights, from 28 September, *Romeo and Juliet* was played at both the patent theaters, provoking, from one I. H——t in the *Daily Advertiser,* the lines

> Well—what tonight, says Angry Ned,
> As up from bed he rouses,
> Romeo again! and shakes his head,
> Ah! Pox on both your houses!

After the twelfth night Covent Garden yielded the palm to Drury Lane, but it was a close contest. One lady, asked to judge between the respective Romeos, is said to have remarked, "Had I been Juliet to Garrick's Romeo,—so ardent and impassioned was he, I should have expected he would have *come up* to me in the balcony; but had I been Juliet to Barry's Romeo,—so tender, so eloquent, and so seductive was he, I should certainly have *gone down* to him!"

Garrick was a great enthusiast for Shakespeare and was, indeed, a key figure in the movement that turned him into an object of romantic veneration. In 1769 he organized the three-day festival in Stratford-upon-Avon that has, appropriately enough, come to be known as the Garrick Jubilee, since amid all the junketings—the horse races and the fancy dress ball, the oratorio by Thomas Arne, and the ode by Garrick—no line of Shakespeare was spoken. Yet the event was decisive in establishing Stratford as the center of Shakespearean celebration. Without it, there might well have been no Royal Shakespeare Company today. But this was a mere diversion from Garrick's more serious activities. His major contributions to the Shakespearean stage tradition lie in staging, in adaptation, and in acting.

For his time, Garrick was exceptionally rigorous in the rehearsal and presentation of plays. Kalman Burnim's *David Garrick, Director* concerns itself primarily with this aspect of his art, and though Burnim seems to work from a theory that Garrick was above all a conscientious director, and then has to admit that the evidence needed to prove the theory is often inadequate at best, he does effectively demonstrate at least that Garrick's ideals favored well-rehearsed and consistently presented productions. Certainly his contemporaries thought him unusually careful, as Thomas Davies testifies: "Order, decency, and decorum, were the first objects which our young manager kept constantly in his eye at the commencement of his administration. He was so accomplished himself in all the external behaviour, as well as in the more valuable talents of his profession, that his example was greatly conducive to that regularity which he laboured to establish." Davies goes on to praise Garrick's maintenance of punctuality and good discipline at rehearsals and his care and skill in casting, remarking particularly on the presentation of Ben Jonson's *Every Man in His Humour*—significantly, a little-known play on behalf of which Garrick made special efforts in his anxiety to succeed with it.

Garrick disciplined his audiences as well as his performers, and one of his most important reforms was the final banishment of spectators from the stage. The situation that obtained before his reform is vividly described by Tate Wilkinson in his *Memoirs* (1790):

> Suppose an audience behind the curtain up to the clouds, with persons of a menial cast on the ground, beaux and no beaux crowding the only entrance, what a play it must have been whenever Romeo was breaking open the supposed tomb, which was no more than a screen on those nights set up, and Mrs Cibber prostrating herself on an old couch, covered with black cloth, as the tomb of the Capulets, with at least (on a great benefit night) two hundred persons behind her, which formed the back ground, as an unfrequented hallowed place of *chapless* skulls, which was to convey the idea of where the heads of all her buried ancestors were packed.

Obviously no illusion was possible in such circumstances, and equally obviously Wilkinson writes from the point of view of one who seeks illusion when he describes this as "a truly ridiculous spectacle." Yet he admits having "seen occasionally many plays acted with great applause to such mummery," finding this a "strange proof" that "a mind may be led by attention, custom, and a willingness to be pleased without the least aid of probability." Playgoers of the present who have seen Shakespeare played in the round, with no attempt at illusionistic scenery, may be less surprised than Wilkinson was that theatrical success could be achieved in such circumstances. Still, there were problems beyond the breaking of illusion. Wilkinson records, for example, that "Mr. Quin, aged sixty-five, with the heavy dress of Falstaff . . . was several minutes before he could pass through the numbers that wedged and hemmed him in, he was so cruelly encompassed around"; and he notes that on some nights "there would be a group of ill-dressed lads and persons sitting on the stage in front, three or four rows deep," with the result that "a performer on a popular night could not step his foot with safety, lest he either should thereby hurt or offend, or be thrown down amongst scores of idle tipsey apprentices."

Garrick remedied the situation tactfully, first increasing the capacity of the theater (from about 1,268 in 1747 to 2,206 after 1762) so that performers could not complain that their benefit receipts would be diminished by banishing spectators from the stage. Another of his reforms was the introduction in 1765 of new lighting techniques, removing the chandeliers that hung above the stage in full view of the audience, whatever the scene, while increasing the number of candles concealed at the sides of the stage and strengthening the footlights illuminating the forestage, on which most of the action occurred. In stage setting, the most important event of Garrick's management was his employment from 1771 of the Alsatian artist Philippe Jacques de Loutherbourg, whose success with picturesque scenic and lighting effects anticipated the spectacular staging methods of the nineteenth century.

The plays presented at both Drury Lane and Covent Garden during Garrick's career included a high proportion by Shakespeare. Though Garrick often used existing adaptations, he frequently restored passages of the original text. But he also made new adaptations of his own and sometimes added passages of his own composition to the earlier adaptations. The first text for which he was responsible offers an example. In 1744, before he became manager at Drury Lane, he put on *Macbeth.* Since 1700, it had been played some 200 times in London in the Davenant adaptation. Garrick announced that he would play it "as written by Shakespeare," which is said to have provoked Quin into asking, "What does he mean? Don't *I* play *Macbeth* as Shakespeare wrote it?" Garrick consulted Dr. Johnson and William Warburton about dubious points in the text. But he also cut some 270 lines and added some explanatory passages. He substituted a servant for Shakespeare's Porter, omitted the murder of Lady Macduff and her son, greatly abbreviated Malcolm's self-accusations of wickedness, and used some of Davenant's elaborations in the witch scenes.

Garrick was particularly good at death scenes, excelling "in the expression of convulsive throes and dying agonies." Shakespeare failed to provide

Macbeth with a dying speech. Davenant had supplied him with moralistic last words: "Farwell, vain World: and what's most vain in it, Ambition." Garrick filled the gap more amply, in elegiac terms:

> 'Tis done! the scene of life will quickly close.
> Ambition's vain, delusive dreams are fled,
> And now I wake to darkness, guilt and horror.
> I cannot bear it! Let me shake it off.—
> 'Twa' not be; my soul is clogged with blood.
> I cannot rise! I dare not ask for mercy.
> It is too late, hell drags me down. I sink,
> I sink—Oh!—my soul is lost forever!
> Oh!

It is moralistic, guiding the spectators' reactions in a heavy-handed way. To us, it seems obvious claptrap, though with echoes of the dying speech of Marlowe's Faustus. Yet Garrick was so effective in it as to prompt Francis Gentleman to ask, "Who has heard his speech, after receiving his death wound, uttered with the utmost agony of body and mind, but trembles at the idea of future punishment, and almost pities the expiring wretch, though stained with crimes of the deepest die?" Macbeth was one of Garrick's finest roles until 1768, when he gave it up following the death of Hannah Pritchard, who matched him as Lady Macbeth.

Though Garrick's version of *Romeo and Juliet* (1748) is much closer to Shakespeare's play than is Otway's *Caius Marius,* it is still some distance from Shakespeare and was in fact influenced by Otway. In the advertisement to the printed text, Garrick declares that the design of the alterations "was to clear the Original, as much as possible, from the Jingle and Quibble, which were always thought the great objections to reviving it." Here, he echoes Dryden's comments on Shakespeare's language—and, indeed, objections to the conceited wordplay of *Romeo and Juliet* are not uncommon today. Garrick's changes include the omission of Lady Montague and of any mention of Rosaline: Romeo is in love with Juliet from the start. In later versions Garrick introduced an elaborate funeral procession for Juliet, for which William Boyce wrote a choral dirge that was to be popular for many years. Also greatly successful was Garrick's development of Otway's notion of having Juliet wake up in the tomb before Romeo dies, giving them the opportunity for a last conversation. The scene reads badly today, but again there is no doubting that it could be effective in performance, and not only when

Garrick played Romeo. It continued to be played during the nineteenth century; Hazlitt refers to "the last scene at the tomb with Romeo, which, however, is not from Shakespeare, though it tells admirably upon the stage." Much later in the nineteenth century, George Bernard Shaw saw it at one of its late appearances and perhaps helped to hasten its neglect by describing how "Romeo, instead of dying forthwith when he took the poison, was interrupted by Juliet, who sat up and made him carry her down to the footlights, where she complained of being very cold, and had to be warmed up by a love scene, in the middle of which Romeo, who had forgotten all about the poison, was taken ill and died."

Among Garrick's less honorable versions of Shakespeare is his *Winter's Tale* (1756), made up mostly from the last two acts of the original, though introduced by an absurd prologue declaring his "plan, to lose no drop of that immortal man." It succeeded for so long as Garrick played the greatly reduced role of Leontes, usually in a double bill with the much longer *Catherine and Petruchio* (1756, based on *The Taming of the Shrew*), which was regularly acted until 1886 and occasionally later; it, too, was castigated by Shaw. Garrick played *King Lear* with great success from 1742, when he was twenty-five; mostly he used Tate's adaptation, though in 1756 he announced it "with restorations from Shakespeare." He had thought of restoring the Fool but lacked the courage. Though he kept an abbreviated version of Tate's love story as well as the happy ending, he restored many of Shakespeare's lines. As Hamlet, he played mainly in a conventional text somewhat shortened but otherwise not significantly altered. But during the season of 1772–1773 he staged an extraordinary version in which he put into effect his vow "that he would not leave the stage till he had rescued that whole play from all the rubbish of the fifth act." It was not printed until the present century. Garrick also adapted *Much Ado About Nothing* (1748), in which he played a fine Benedick; *A Midsummer Night's Dream* (as *The Fairies,* 1755) and *The Tempest* (1756), both with music by J. C. Smith; and, in the 1758–1759 season, *Antony and Cleopatra,* in which he was assisted by the great editor Edward Capell. Garrick played Antony, but the play was unfamiliar, for it had not been acted since Shakespeare's time. The actor found the role "laborious," and the play had only six performances.

Garrick was not the only adapter of Shakespeare

during these years, though he was the most important. George Colman, for example, made a version (1768) of *King Lear* for the other theater, also restoring some of Shakespeare's lines. The movement to return to Shakespeare's text was slowly gathering impetus. It is ironical that one of the harshest attacks on Garrick as play-adapter should have come from the son of the adapter of *Richard III*, the play in which Garrick made his name. Theophilus Cibber wrote bitterly around 1756 that Garrick's

houses are crowded, for what he designs [deigns?] to give must be receiv'd, it is *Hobson's* choice with the town. . . . *The Midsummer Night's Dream* has been minc'd and fricaseed into an undigested thing called *The Fairies;—The Winter's Tale* mammoc'd into a Droll; *The Taming of the Shrew,* made a farce of;—and *The Tempest* castrated into an Opera. . . . In . . . his absurd prologue to the *Winter's Tale* he tells you

That tis his joy, his Wish, his only Plan
To lose no Drop of that immortal Man!

Why truly, in the aforementioned pieces he does bottle him up with a Vengeance!—He throws away all the spirited Part of him, all that bears the highest Flavour, then, to some of the Dregs, adds a little flat stuff of his own, and modestly palms it off on his Customers—as Wines of the first Growth.

But it was not merely the injudicious who approved. In 1770, Francis Gentleman, in his notable volumes of dramatic criticism, remarked that "no play ever received greater advantage from alteration" than *Romeo and Juliet;* he was no less complimentary about Garrick's revised death scene for Macbeth and concurred, it would appear, with his opinion of *Hamlet.*

Garrick became such a cult figure in his own time that many writers recorded their impressions of him, with the result that we can reconstruct his performances in our imagination with greater confidence than those of any actor before him. Henry Fielding pays him an oblique compliment in *Tom Jones* with Mr. Partridge's reaction to his *Hamlet:* "He the best player! Why I could act as well myself, I am sure, if I had seen a ghost, I should have looked in the very same manner, and had done just as he did—the King for my money; he speaks all his words distinctly, half as loud again as the others—anybody may see he's an actor." Many of the descriptions are simple eulogy, often describ-

ing Garrick's effect on the audience rather than him. Remarkable among these is the tribute paid by Henry Bate in the *Morning Post* (22 May 1776) to one of his last performances of *King Lear:*

The curse at the close of the first act,—his phrenetic appeal to heaven at the end of the second on Regan's ingratitude, were two such enthusiastic scenes of human exertion, that they caused a kind of momentary petrefaction thro' the house, which he soon dissolved as universally into tears.—Even the unfeeling Regan and Gonerill, forgetful of their characteristic cruelty, played thro' the whole of their parts with aching bosoms and streaming eyes.—In a word, we never saw before so exquisite a theatrical performance, or one so loudly and universally applauded.

But the most detailed and vivid accounts of Garrick—or, indeed, of almost any actor—in performance were written by the German philosopher Georg Lichtenberg. There is room here only for an extract from his account of Garrick as Hamlet. On Hamlet's seeing the Ghost,

his whole demeanour is so expressive of terror that it made my flesh creep even before he began to speak. The almost terror-struck silence of the audience, which preceded this appearance and filled one with a sense of insecurity, probably did much to enhance this effect. At last he speaks, not at the beginning, but at the end of a breath, with a trembling voice: "Angels and ministers of grace defend us!" . . . The ghost beckons to him; I wish you could see him, with eyes fixed on the ghost, though he is speaking to his companions, freeing himself from their restraining hands, as they warn him not to follow and hold him back. But at length, when they have tried his patience too far, he turns his face towards them, tears himself with great violence from their grasps, and draws his sword on them with a swiftness that makes me shudder, saying: "By Heaven! I'll make a ghost of him that lets me!" That is enough for them. Then he stands with his sword upon guard against the spectre, saying: "Go on, I'll follow thee!" and the ghost goes off the stage. Hamlet still remains motionless, his sword held out so as to make him keep his distance, and at length, when the spectator can no longer see the ghost, he begins slowly to follow him, now standing still and then going on, with sword still upon guard . . . until he too is lost to sight. You can well imagine what loud applause accompanies this exit. It begins as soon as the ghost goes off the stage, and lasts until Hamlet also disappears.

To us, it is strange to think of an audience applauding lengthily during the action of a play. Enjoyment might seem to be lost in the desire to express admiration of virtuosity. But it is clear that Garrick could exert a mesmeric effect upon his spectators and clear, too, that what they admired most was the impression of naturalness that, with however great a degree of calculation, he conveyed in all his roles.

The Romantic Period

On Garrick's retirement in 1776, his business interests in Drury Lane were transferred to the young Richard Brinsley Sheridan, who remained nominal manager until 1809. John Philip Kemble became the active actor-manager in 1788 but left Drury Lane in 1802 and ran Covent Garden with great success from the autumn of 1803 until his retirement in 1817. Both theaters were twice altered and remodeled, in 1782 and 1792. When Drury Lane re-opened in 1794, its capacity was increased from 2,500 to 3,611; this theater burned down in 1809. Covent Garden had also been destroyed by fire in the previous year; the new building, opened in 1809, also housed over 3,000 spectators. The increasing size of the theaters affected styles of both acting and production. After Garrick died, acting style reverted to the more statuesque and stately, and more spectacular staging methods gradually evolved.

The earlier part of this period is dominated by the Kemble family. John Philip's sister, Sarah Siddons, made an unsuccessful debut as Portia at Drury Lane in 1775; she acted briefly with Garrick during the last four months of his career but then spent six years in the provinces, mainly at York and Bath. Her reemergence at Drury Lane in October 1782 caused a sensation comparable to Garrick's London debut, and before long Joshua Reynolds had immortalized her as the tragic muse; exceptionally for him, he signed the painting, from a desire, as he told her, "to go down to posterity on the hem of your garment." Her brother, John Philip Kemble, succeeded in the same theater, as Hamlet, in 1783. For a quarter of a century, these were the two leading interpreters of Shakespearean roles.

Mrs. Siddons was undoubtedly the greater performer, above all in tragedy. She studied her roles with minute care and imagined them with impressive intensity. A large lady, she must have had colossal emotional power to animate the dignity and grace of her deportment. Hazlitt wrote, "Power was seated on her brow, passion emanated from her breast as from a shrine. She was Tragedy personified." But she could lose herself in a role. J. C. Young described how, as Volumnia in *Coriolanus,*

> she forgot her own identity . . . when it was time for her to come on, instead of dropping each foot at equidistance in its place, with mechanical exactitude, and in cadence subservient to the orchestra, deaf to the guidance of her woman's ear, but sensitive to the throbbings of her haughty mother's heart, with flashing eye, and proudest smile, and head erect, and hands pressed firmly on her bosom, as if to repress by manual force its triumphant swellings, she towered above all around, and rolled, and almost reeled across the stage, her very soul, as it were, dilating and rioting in its exaltation, until her action lost all grace, and yet became so true to nature, so picturesque, and so descriptive, that pit and gallery sprang to their feet, electrified by the transcendent execution of an original conception.

A passage such as this, evocative though it is, is a reminder that we are in an age of consciously fine writing. Essayists such as Charles Lamb, William Hazlitt, and Leigh Hunt found in the theater a subject for their literary talents, and we may sometimes sense in accounts of actors a desire to score literary points akin to the theatrical points beloved of contemporary audiences. But when all allowance has been made for artistic license, it is difficult not to believe that Mrs. Siddons was the greatest of all English actresses in tragic roles. She shone as Isabella in *Measure for Measure,* as Queen Katherine in *Henry VIII,* and above all as Lady Macbeth, a performance to which Sheridan Knowles paid tribute in conversation with the American tragedian Edwin Forrest, who asked him about the sleepwalking scene: " 'I have read all the high flown descriptions of the critics, and they fall short. I want you to tell me in plain blunt phrase just what impression she produced on you.' Knowles replied, with a sort of shudder . . . 'Well, sir, I smelt blood! I swear that I smelt blood!' "

As an actor, John Philip Kemble was less consistently overwhelming in his impact, and his statuesque qualities rendered him liable to gibes such as Hazlitt's complaints that he played Hamlet "like a man in armour, with a determined inveteracy of purpose, in one undeviating straight line," and that his "supercilious airs and *nonchalance*" as Coriolanus "remind one of the unaccountable abstracted air, the contracted eyebrows and suspended chin of a man who is just going to sneeze." But Hazlitt could also appreciate Kemble's merits, finding that his distinguishing excellence was "intensity" and that "in embodying a high idea of certain characters, which belong rather to sentiment than passion, to energy of will, than to loftiness or to originality of imagination, he was the most excellent actor of his time." Like his sister, Kemble could impress not only by his formality but also by flashes of naturalism, as in his death scene in *Coriolanus,* described by Sir Walter Scott:

> The Volscian assassins [approached] him from behind . . . [and] seemed to pass their swords through the body of Coriolanus. There was no precaution, no support; in the midst of the exclamation against Tullus Aufidius, he dropped as dead and as flat on the stage as if the swords had really met within his body. We have repeatedly heard screams from the female part of the audience when he presented this scene, which had the most striking resemblance to actual and instant death we ever witnessed.

It is not only as an actor that Kemble has his place in the history of Shakespeare on the stage. He did much to keep Shakespeare before the public, reviving twenty-seven of Shakespeare's plays in twenty-nine years; he made great efforts to maintain high standards of production; he amassed an important library; and he rethought the acting versions of the plays, publishing his own texts in versions that were long influential. One of his amiable idiosyncrasies was to bestow names upon minor, previously anonymous figures; thus, the outlaws in *The Two Gentlemen of Verona* become Ubaldo, Luigi, Carlos, Stephano, Giacomo, Rodolfo, Valerio, and so on.

Enthusiastic Shakespearean though he was, Kemble was no purist; though he sometimes restored Shakespeare, he also sometimes reverted to adapted texts. For instance, though John Bell's edition of theatrical texts of 1773–1775 gives *The Tempest* with many cuts but with no lines from the Dryden-Davenant adaptation, Kemble, in 1789, used much of the Restoration version. He used Cibber's *Richard III* and Garrick's *Romeo and Juliet.* In 1809 he put back into *King Lear* much of the verse of Tate that Garrick, half a century before, had banished in favor of Shakespeare. He played Coriolanus, probably his greatest role, in a text that

not only was heavily cut but included extended interpolations from a tragedy on the same subject by James Thomson, first given at Covent Garden in 1749.

It was inevitable that the formalism of the Kemble school of acting should be challenged by a swing back to apparent naturalism; and when the challenge came, it was sensational in its impact. The day in January 1814 when Edmund Kean made his debut at Drury Lane as Shylock sounded the death knell for the Kemble school of acting. Kean was unimpressive in stature and often hoarse, especially in the vast recesses of Drury Lane. But in his brief prime, he must have been the most electrifying actor of the English stage, transcending his limitations by the imaginative intensity with which he identified himself with the characters he played. Even late in Kean's career, Leigh Hunt could remark that he could not see him

> without being moved, and moved too in fifty ways— by his sarcasm, his sweetness, his pathos, his exceeding grace, his gallant levity, his measureless dignity: for his little person absolutely becomes tall, and rises to the height of moral grandeur, in such characters as that of Othello. We have seen him with three or four persons round him, all taller than he, but himself so graceful, so tranquil, so superior, so nobly self-possessed, in the midst, that the mind of the spectator rose above them by his means, and so gave him a moral stature that confounded itself with the personal.

Kean had some famous touches of innovative business designed, often, to epitomize his view of the character he was playing. As the dying Richard III, "when his sword is beaten out of his hands he continues fighting with his fist as if he had a sword" (Henry Crabb Robinson); and as Hamlet, at the end of the "nunnery" scene, he returned, having "gone to the extremity of the stage, from a pause of parting tenderness to press his lips to Ophelia's hand." This, writes Hazlitt, "had an electrical effect on the house. It was the finest commentary that was ever made on Shakespear. It explained the character at once (as he meant it), as one of disappointed hope, of bitter regret, of affection suspended, not obliterated, by the distractions of the scene around him!" It is natural that Hazlitt, author of *Characters of Shakespear's Plays* (1817), should have written so much and so memorably about Kean. Both of them demonstrate the romantic fascination with individual character, a fascination that helps to explain the emphasis in this period on the individual actor and the characters he portrayed, even at the expense of the organic unity which, during the same period, Coleridge was analyzing in Shakespeare's plays. (Seen in this light, Coleridge's remark that to see Kean act was like "reading Shakespeare by flashes of lightning" may not be wholly complimentary.)

Kean was at his greatest as strongly characterized figures—Shylock, Richard III, Lear, Othello, Iago, Macbeth. He was less impressive as Richard II and Romeo, perhaps because, as Hazlitt wrote, he was "always on full stretch—never relaxed." The version of *Richard II* in which he played was an odd one devised by Richard Wroughton (1815), in which the queen mourns over the king's body in words adapted from those of the dying Lear ("Pray you, undo my lace . . ."), with a snatch of *Titus Andronicus.* Admittedly, the words had not been spoken in performances of *King Lear* for 150 years, and Kean may have been conscious of the irony in the situation. In 1823 he made an attempt to improve the text of *Lear* and did at least die in the role, though otherwise the text was mostly Tate's. As so often in nineteenth-century versions of the tragedies, the curtain falls immediately on the death of the hero: Kean's last words are "Look there.—Look there," followed by the direction "Gives a convulsive gasp and falls back. He is supported by Kent R. and Edgar L.—The curtain falls to slow music." In 1820 Kean presented a *Coriolanus* freed from the non-Shakespearean portions that were commonly acted (though the playbill announced, "In Act II, An Ovation, in which will be introduced an Ode of Triumph Written by Mr. G. Soane, and composed by Mr. T. Cooke").

Hazlitt and Leigh Hunt, among others, frequently protested against the continuing use of Cibber's *Richard III,* Tate's *Lear,* and Garrick's *Romeo and Juliet,* and new adaptations appeared from time to time, though none of them had the staying power of the earlier ones. A version of *Henry VI* of 1817 is described by Odell as "the very last effort to mutilate Shakespeare, and to make a new play out of the shattered remains of his handiwork," a remark that subsequently proved untrue.

Of course, it is possible to "mutilate Shakespeare" without rewriting him. The cutting and rearranging of a play can falsify it as much as the substitution of new dialogue. And just as, on the whole, Shakespeare's lines were coming to be preferred to those of his adapters, there arose another movement that encouraged the shortening and rearrangement of texts.

Until late in the eighteenth century, Shakespeare's plays had normally been given in costumes of the period in which they were acted (with some essential modifications) and in stock settings. Early in the nineteenth century there grew up the movement to play them in historically accurate costumes against settings elaborately designed to simulate historical reality. Charles Kemble (John Philip's brother) took over the management of Covent Garden in 1822 and in the following year put on a revival of *King John,* with Charles Young as King John and Kemble himself as the Bastard, for which James Robinson Planché designed the costumes. Planché wrote:

> When the curtain rose, and discovered King John dressed as his effigy appears in Worcester Cathedral, surrounded by his barons sheathed in mail, with cylindrical helmets and correct armorial shields, and his courtiers in the long tunics and mantles of the thirteenth century, there was a roar of approbation, accompanied by four distinct rounds of applause, so general and so hearty, that the actors were astonished.

He claims that "a complete reformation of dramatic costume became from that moment inevitable upon the English stage." Increasingly from this time Shakespeare productions were to be characterized by visual elaboration, to a point at which the drama was in danger of being swamped by decorative and archaeological detail. This may have been a form of compensation for the absence of actors of the first rank. From the deaths of Kemble and Kean until late in the century, only William Charles Macready seems to have had anything of their power and scope.

Macready was a careful, conscientious actor rather than a profoundly exciting one, but he was original to the extent that he sought overall consistency and uniformity of characterization rather than the making of a series of effective points; thus, in his amazingly voluminous and self-revealing diaries, he complains of "the prescriptive criticism of this country, in looking for particular points instead of contemplating one entire character." After playing Othello in 1836, he wrote that "the audience seemed to wait for Kean's points, and this rather threw me off my balance." He acted often with Helena Faucit, who wrote a moving account of their playing of the final scene of *The Winter's Tale.*

Macready managed Covent Garden from 1837 to 1839 and Drury Lane from 1841 to 1843, emulating Kemble in his attention to detail and discipline. He had good intentions about Shakespeare's texts, writing in 1838 that he "looked over Shakespeare's plays of *King Richard II* and *King Richard III.* Astonished at the base venality of the disgusting newspaper writers—the wretches—who dare to laud the fustian of Cibber, and tried to keep the many in ignorance by praising his trash called *Richard III.*" His principal achievement here was the final restoration to the stage, in 1838, of something approximating to Shakespeare's *King Lear.* His text is not complete, but it includes no Tate and restores the character of the Fool. Macready was so nervous about this that he almost changed his mind, and he engaged a girl, Priscilla Horton, for the role. He was rewarded by a review from John Forster that said, "Mr. Macready has now to his lasting honour restored the text of Shakespeare, and we shall be glad to hear of the actor foolhardy enough to attempt another restoration of the text of Tate! Mr. Macready's success has banished that disgrace from the stage for ever." Forster continued with a detailed appreciation of the Fool's part in the play and concluded that this "is the only perfect picture that we have had of Lear since the age of Betterton." For all this, there are many cuts and some rearrangements "occasioned," as Odell surmises, "by the necessity for compression under the new stage conditions of scenery frequently changing." The blinding of Gloucester is not represented on stage or even (as in Kemble's version) as happening offstage. Nor does Gloucester jump off the supposed cliff. There are a few interpolated anonymous lines. But at least Tate has been ejected.

Later in the same year Macready produced a *Tempest* free of Dryden and Davenant, which was a great popular success. But Shakespeare's text was far from complete. In the first scene, as *John Bull* put it, a "mimic vessel was outrageously bumped and tossed about on waves that we can liken to nothing save tiny cocks of hay, painted green, and afflicted with a spasm." Ariel, played by a girl, was "whisked about by wires and a cogwheel, like the fairies in *Cinderella.*" The production was played fifty-five times.

Macready withdrew from Covent Garden in 1839, to be succeeded there by Charles Mathews and his wife, Eliza Bartolozzi, better known as Madame Vestris. So far as Shakespeare is concerned, their reign is distinguished mainly by the production of two comedies. *Love's Labor's Lost,* heavily cut, failed in 1839, for there was a riot on the first night because the new managers had closed the shilling gallery. But at least they had attempted to enlarge the repertory by a play that had not been acted, even in adaptation, since the closing of the theaters. And in the following year they gave *A Midsummer Night's Dream,* also in Shakespeare's text, though again with many cuts and with some passages sung instead of spoken (as has been done in our own time).

There are a number of ways in which the early 1840s mark a turning point in the history of Shakespeare on the English stage. The traditional adaptations were at last losing their grip. They continued to exert an influence, if only by reaction; but the only ones to survive this period as the standard acting texts were Cibber's *Richard III,* Garrick's *Catherine and Petruchio,* and Garrick's version of the last scene of *Romeo and Juliet.* There were signs of interest in plays that had previously been rarely, if ever, performed. And in 1843 appeared the Act for Regulating the Theatres.

In his speech on retiring from the management of Drury Lane in that year, Macready had made a plea for the abolition of the monopoly of the patent houses. Drury Lane and Covent Garden were too big for serious performances of Shakespeare. London had grown, and theaters were needed in outlying areas. The new act, in an attempt to improve the state of the drama, permitted any theater to be licensed by magistrates for the performance of legitimate drama. To some extent, this merely regularized an existing situation, but it had far-reaching effects. It turned the serious drama in new directions. In 1847, Covent Garden became an opera house, as it still is. (The theater burned down in 1856 and was replaced by the present building in 1858.) Drury Lane came to be used for large-scale musical and spectacular shows, including occasional productions of Shakespeare. Legitimate drama flourished in smaller theaters. The increasing seriousness and success of original playwriting in the later nineteenth century would not have been possible without the 1843 act. And it encouraged productions of Shakespeare, which, because they could be given in smaller theaters, did not need to coarsen their effects in order to make an impact. For the remainder of the century, Shakespeare production was dominated by actor-managers running their own theaters and companies for most of their careers. The three most important were Samuel Phelps, Charles Kean, and Henry Irving. Developing the methods of Kemble and Macready, they worked in a tradition that put great emphasis on pictorialism.

Samuel Phelps's management (1844–1862) of Sadler's Wells Theatre, in the London suburb of Islington, was a direct result of the 1843 act and a rapid justification of it. In the smaller theater in an unfashionable area, Phelps was able to mount genuine ensemble productions for audiences that were willing to take a serious interest in Shakespeare's plays as works of art rather than as vehicles for virtuoso performances. Only at this time did it become possible to think of Shakespearean productions as interpretations of the plays. Though Phelps himself was a star actor, he subordinated his own performances to the overall effect. As Henry Morley put it, "Although only in one or two cases we may have observed at Sadler's Wells originality of genius in the actor, we have nevertheless perceived something like the entire sense of one of Shakespeare's plays."

Perhaps the most remarkable initial fact is the range of Phelps's repertory. During his eighteen years of management he produced every play in the Shakespeare canon except for the three parts of *Henry IV, Richard II, Titus Andronicus,* and *Troilus and Cressida,* as well as reviving other plays of the period. In 1845 he displaced Cibber's *Richard III* with Shakespeare's. Admittedly, he did not play an unaltered text of this exceptionally long play. The *Times* critic wrote, "There are several liberal omissions, and some parts are transposed, but the construction and march of the play are Shakespeare's." The *Times* also noted with some surprise that "a very different play it is from the common version." Whether it was likely to be more popular with actors was doubted. After all, the actor in Shakespeare cannot—or should not—say, "Off with his head; so much for Buckingham" or "Richard's himself again"—a line that Olivier allowed himself in his film. Phelps did not succeed in banishing Cibber forever; indeed, when he revived the play in 1861–1862 it was in Cibber's text. But he showed a refreshing independence and acted the central role "in the unaffected and level style, so characteristic of this gentleman's performance," as the *Illustrated London News* put it. Also in 1845 he gave *King Lear* in a more genuinely Shakespearean version than Macready had played and with the Fool played by a man, as well as an exceptionally full text of *The Winter's Tale.* His *Macbeth* of 1847 dispensed with the traditional balletic and operatic interpolations in the witches' scenes. In 1849 he

put on the rarely played *Antony and Cleopatra* without additions, and in 1851 he had an unexpected success with *Timon of Athens.*

With *Pericles* in 1854, not performed for two centuries, he had understandable problems; the brothel scenes were not to Victorian taste, and to stage the play at all was adventurous; here he did resort to some rewriting, omitting Gower and adding passages of his own to fill the gap. The two brothel scenes were compressed into one; Morley, a sympathetic critic, wrote that "although the plot of the drama was not compromised by a false delicacy, there remained not a syllable at which true delicacy could have conceived offence." The staging of the last act employed a traveling panorama of the journey from Mytilene to Ephesus.

Phelps's best-remembered production was of *A Midsummer Night's Dream,* in 1853. The play had been badly exploited in most previous productions, which had tended either to concentrate on the comedy at the expense of the poetry or to treat it as a vehicle for musical spectacle. Hazlitt, writing about Frederic Reynolds' adaptation at Covent Garden in 1816, commented despairingly that "poetry and the stage do not agree together." The play's spirit "was evaporated, the genius was fled, but the spectacle was fine: it was that which saved the play." But Phelps triumphantly demonstrated that Hazlitt had been mistaken to generalize on the basis of a heavily adapted version. Henry Morley wrote:

Mr. Phelps has never for a moment lost sight of the main idea which governs the whole play, and this is the great secret of his success in the presentation of it. . . . The scenery is very beautiful, but wholly free from the meretricious glitter now in favour. . . . There is no ordinary scene-shifting; but, as in dreams, one scene is made to glide insensibly into another. We follow the lovers and the fairies through the wood from glade to glade, now among trees, now with a broad view of the sea and Athens in the distance, . . . over all the fairy portion of the play there is a haze thrown by a curtain of green gauze placed between the actors and the audience, and maintained there during the whole of the second, third, and fourth acts. . . . Very good taste has been shown in the establishment of a harmony between the scenery and the poem.

Unquestionably Phelps was working within the pictorial method of presentation dominant throughout the nineteenth century. His success lay in employing pictorial effects with good taste and with a concern that they serve the play. His desire to achieve naturalistic illusion brings him closer to modern epic films than to symbolic productions. He sometimes had to exert considerable ingenuity to achieve his effects economically, as John Coleman demonstrates in his account of *Henry V* when

> in the march-past before Agincourt, the troops defiled behind a "set piece" which rose breast high. Madame Tussaud modelled eighty wax heads—these were fitted on "dummy" figures of wicker work, clad in the costume and armour of the period. Every man of the gallant forty carried two of these figures, one on either side, attached to a sort of frame-work, which was lashed to his waist; hence it seemed as if they were marching three abreast. As they tramped past, banners streaming, drums beating, trumpets braying, the stage seemed crowded with soldiers, and the illusion was so perfect that the audience never once discovered the deception.

As an actor Phelps appears, for all his versatility, not to have been in the highest rank. The middle of the nineteenth century was not a great time for English acting. Edmund Kean's son, Charles, reacted strongly against his father's notorious bohemianism, cultivating a respectability that, however admirable in his private life, was unexciting in the theater. Though his London acting career began in 1827, when he was sixteen, not until 1838 did he emerge from his father's shadow and establish himself as a leading actor. As a performer, he was at his best in gentlemanly melodrama. His place in Shakespearean stage history rests mainly upon his managership of the Princess's Theatre from 1850 to 1859. In some respects, after Phelps he represents a backward step. An antiquarian who reached the dignity of a fellowship of the Society of Antiquaries, he allowed his passion for archaeology and historical research a free rein in his productions of Shakespeare. Understandably, he had a predilection for the English history plays; his first important Shakespeare production, in 1852, was of *King John;* his biographer, J. W. Cole, claimed that its "total personification of Shakespere, with every accompaniment that refined knowledge, diligent research, and chronological accuracy could supply, was suited to the taste and temper of the age, which had become eminently pictorial and exacting beyond all precedent." A less charitable judgment would be that under Kean's management the plays were turned from dramas into museum pieces, offering a didacticism that appealed to theatergoers earnestly intent upon self-improvement.

Certainly spectacular appeal was achieved. His *Henry VIII* in 1855 took advantage, as he admits, "of the historical fact of the Lord Mayor and City Council proceeding to the royal ceremonial in their state barges, to give a panoramic view of London, as it then appeared." *Richard II* also employed a shifting panorama, and it interpolated an elaborate episode portraying York's description of Richard's entry into London, "with scrupulous accuracy," the "music, the joy-bells, the dances, the crowded balconies and windows, the thronging in the streets, the civic processions, the mailed warriors, the haughty *Bolingbroke,* the heart-broken *Richard,* the maddening shouts of gratulations which attend the one, while the other is received with silence." Claiming that between five hundred and six hundred performers, "all moving in trained regularity or organized disorder," took part, Cole remarks naively that this "gave a reality to the play it was never supposed to possess." Certainly it bears witness to Kean's capacities as a stage manager.

But these and similar efforts greatly slowed down the action. In the program for *The Tempest* in 1857, Kean asked "the kind indulgence of the public . . . should any lengthened delay take place between the acts." His appeal was "made with greater confidence" because "the scenic appliances of the play are of a more extensive and complicated nature than have ever yet been attempted in any theatre in Europe; requiring the aid of above one hundred and forty operatives nightly, who (unseen by the audience) are engaged in working the machines, and in carrying out the various effects." Such methods were possible only in an age of cheap labor.

Kean's historical interests impinged on the comedies too. He regaled readers of his voluminous three-paneled program sheets with the information that, for example, the mechanicals' scenes in *A Midsummer Night's Dream* (1856) used "furniture and Tools . . . copied from discoveries at Herculaneum" and that, in *The Winter's Tale,* Autolycus' costumes derived from the *Hamilton Vases* (vol. I, pl. 43) and "from a Vase, engraved in Gerhard's *Auserlesene Vasenbilder,* taf. 166." Kean's productions were immensely popular, but not everyone took them entirely seriously; *Punch* claimed "authority to state that the Bear at present running in Oxford Street in *The Winter's Tale* is an archaeological copy from the original bear of Noah's Ark," and during the run of this play at the Princess's a charming burlesque of both play and production,

William Brough's *Florizel and Perdita*, drew crowded audiences to the Lyceum.

Kean's scholarly instincts did not extend to textual authenticity. Cibber's *Richard III* was good enough for him, and he restored to *Macbeth* the singing and dancing witches of the Dryden-Davenant adaptation. His *Midsummer Night's Dream* omits about 830 of the roughly 2,200 lines; passages intended to be spoken are sung, Puck's role is greatly abbreviated, Titania is allowed only five lines of "These are the forgeries of jealousy," and the play scene is severely shortened, as is the end of the play, where again lines meant to be spoken are sung. Oberon was played by a woman (a long-standing practice), and Puck, by the nine-year-old Ellen Terry. Kean's *Macbeth* (1853) omitted Lady Macduff's scenes with her son, and the Porter scene; there were many cuts, and the last words of the play were Macbeth's "Lay on, Macduff, and damned be him that first cries 'Hold, enough' " (V. viii. 33–34). The final stage directions are "Alarms —Shouts—Fight—Macbeth is slain. Enter Malcolm, Old Siward, Rosse, Lenox, Angus, Cathness, Menteth, and Soldiers, R. Malcolm is raised on a shield in C. Shouts. Flourish." Victorian actor-managers liked to have the last word.

Kean's personal last word—his farewell speech at the end of his management—shows resentment of criticism, which he obviously had difficulty in understanding. He boasted that he had never "permitted historical truth to be sacrificed to theatrical effect" and that in *Henry V* (1859) his siege of Harfleur "was no ideal battle, no imaginary fight; it was a correct representation of what actually had taken place; the engines of war, the guns, fire balls, the attack and defence, the barricades at the breach, the conflagration within the town, the assault and capitulation, were all taken from the account left to us by a priest who accompanied the army,—was an eye-witness, and whose Latin MS is now in the British Museum." He was incorrigible to the end.

French playwrights greatly influenced nineteenth-century English drama, and some French actors also crossed the Channel with success. The most notable in Shakespeare was the bilingual Charles Fechter, who played Othello, Iago, and Hamlet with great success at the Princess's in 1861 and at the Lyceum in 1864. Charles Dickens wrote warmly of the picturesque credibility of his Iago; and George Henry Lewes, finding his Hamlet marred by his French accent, nevertheless thought that he played the comedy "to perfection" and that

"the passages of *emotion* also are rendered with some sensibility."

From Italy came Tommaso Salvini, who played Othello at Drury Lane in 1875 in Italian and in a heavily mutilated text; Henry James thought that "nothing could be finer than all this; the despair, the passion, the bewildered tumult of it," and Stanislavski wrote that "we were in his power, and we will remain in it all our lives, forever." Others (including some of the actresses who played Desdemona) found the passion and the suffering too painfully real. These were virtuoso solo performers; visitors from Germany, the duke of Saxe-Meiningen's company, who played (in German) *Twelfth Night*, *The Winter's Tale*, and *Julius Caesar* at Drury Lane in 1881, impressed rather by the excellence of their ensemble playing, even to the detriment of performances in individual roles.

A powerful English Shakespearean actor of this period was Barry Sullivan, who acted much in the provinces and found a staunch champion in Shaw, who regarded him as the last and one of "greatest of the line of British Shakespearian star actors from Burbage and Betterton to Macready."

Undoubtedly the greatest English actor of the late nineteenth century was Henry Irving, who in 1895 became the first English actor to be knighted. Irving, who had played Hamlet for the first time in 1874, took over the management of the Lyceum Theatre in 1878. There, until the end of the century, he presented a series of Shakespeare productions along with other poetic dramas, such as Tennyson's *Becket;* popular melodramas, notably *The Bells;* and sentimental plays. When Irving went on tour, the Lyceum often continued to house important Shakespeare productions, native and foreign; so far as Shakespeare was concerned, it was the most important London theater of its time. In spite of this, Irving's Shakespearean repertory was small when compared to those of Phelps and even Charles Kean. During most of his regime his leading lady was Ellen Terry, one of the finest of English actresses.

Like some of his great forebears, Irving achieved his triumphs as an actor in spite of natural handicaps. He was not conventionally handsome; he was tall only "when he wanted to be," as Graham Robertson said; he had a tendency to drag one leg; and Henry James wrote of "the strange tissue of arbitrary pronunciations which floats in the thankless medium of Mr Irving's harsh, monotonous voice." But he also had marvelously expressive features, a sardonic sense of humor, dignity, pathos, and a mesmeric control over the audience. He was an interior actor, in the sense that by gesture, facial expression, and intonation he could suggest a character's state of mind. And he had a perfectionist's attention to detail, along with a superb sense of theatrical effectiveness. His acting style was not primarily lyrical or heroic; he did not attempt Richard II; he failed as Romeo, Othello, Coriolanus, and (at least on the first night) Lear; and his Macbeth (which, said Ellen Terry, looked "like a great famished wolf") split opinion. But he had the proper touch of high comedy for Benedick and a marvelously picturesque pathos in Shylock (a role he is said to have played more than a thousand times); he could convey the shifting complexity of Hamlet's interior life and the callous intellectuality of Richard III and Iago. Even Shaw (who confessed to having persecuted Irving for his lack of interest in serious modern drama) wrote that his Iachimo (in *Cymbeline*) was "no vulgar bagful of points, but a true impersonation, unbroken in its life current from end to end, varied on the surface with the finest comedy and without a single lapse in the sustained beauty of its execution."

Powerful though Irving was as an actor, his importance and influence rested no less on his abilities as theater manager and producer. He stated his ideals as a producer in the preface to his acting edition of *The Merchant of Venice* (1880): "I have endeavoured to avoid hampering the natural action of the piece with any unnecessary embellishment; but have tried not to omit any accessory which might heighten the effects. I have availed myself of every resource at my command to present the play in a manner acceptable to our audiences."

Irving employed highly skilled set designers, painters, costume designers, and composers to adorn his productions; in these respects he refined the methods of Charles Kean, but he had a higher sense of theatrical effectiveness than his predecessor. Some of his best moments as an actor were heavily dependent upon his efforts as a producer: perhaps the most famous came in *The Merchant of Venice* when, after the elopement of Jessica and Lorenzo, the curtain fell but rapidly rose again; then "the stage was empty, desolate, with no light but the pale moon, and all sounds of life at a great distance—and then over the bridge came the wearied figure of the Jew." The curtain fell again as Shylock was about to enter the house; in some later performances, he knocked three times at the door,

showing his unawareness that Jessica was no longer there. Ellen Terry wrote that "for absolute pathos, achieved by absolute simplicity of means, I never saw anything in the theatre to compare with" this effect.

Irving often achieved his pictorial effects at the expense of much cutting and rearrangement of the texts. Of his *Cymbeline,* Shaw wrote that "every part is spoiled except the 'governor's.' " Shaw objected, too, to Irving's bowdlerizations: lines were omitted "to please the curates for whom the Lyceum seems chiefly to exist." Alan Hughes's study of Irving shows that he cut almost half of *King Lear* and *Cymbeline,* not much less of Hamlet, nearly 800 lines from *Much Ado About Nothing,* and more than five hundred from such relatively short plays as *The Merchant of Venice, Macbeth,* and *Twelfth Night.* "In a true republic of art," wrote Shaw, "Sir Henry Irving would ere this have expiated his acting versions on the scaffold." A reaction was due, and when it came, Shaw had more to do with it than he admitted. His famous review of Johnston Forbes-Robertson's *Hamlet* in 1897 begins thus:

> The Forbes Robertson "Hamlet" at the Lyceum is, very unexpectedly at that address, really not at all unlike Shakespeare's play of the same name. I am quite certain I saw Reynaldo in it for a moment; and possibly I may have seen Voltimand and Cornelius; but just as the time for their scene arrived, my eye fell on the word "Fortinbras" in the programme, which so amazed me that I hardly know what I saw for the next ten minutes.

Shaw disingenuously concealed from his readers a fact that later scholarship has revealed: he had written a long letter (now lost) to Forbes-Robertson in which he made suggestions about the production, including the restoration of Fortinbras. The result, to judge from Shaw's account, was a "true classical Hamlet."

Other winds of change were blowing. In 1899, Frank Benson, who ran a company that presented most of Shakespeare's plays, mainly in the English provinces, from 1883 to 1919, gave a full text of *Hamlet* (known as the "eternity" version because it lasted so long) at the Stratford-upon-Avon Memorial Theatre, where Benson organized the annual festival (a brief one, in those days) from 1888 to 1916. He repeated it at the Lyceum in 1900, with performances starting at 3:30 and going on at a leisurely pace, with a one-and-a-half-hour break for dinner, until 11:00 P.M. And in 1903, one of Irving's greatest admirers, Gordon Craig, directed and designed a *Much Ado About Nothing* in which his mother, Ellen Terry, played Beatrice, a role in which she had already triumphed with Henry Irving. The designs were revolutionary in their suggestive simplicity; but this was to be the only Shakespeare production with designs by Craig to be seen in Britain.

The pictorial tradition passed from Irving into the hands of Sir Herbert Beerbohm Tree, whose major productions were at Her (later His) Majesty's Theatre from 1897 to 1914; they included a particularly spectacular *Julius Caesar.*

The Twentieth Century

The major reaction to the pictorial style of Shakespeare production was foreshadowed in a freak experiment as early as 1844, when Benjamin Webster, under the guidance of James Robinson Planché, put on at the Haymarket a production of *The Taming of the Shrew* that attempted to reconstruct the conditions of its first performance. The original text was played (Garrick's adaptation was then the standard version) and, we are told, in full, running to three and a half hours. Needless to say, the interior of the Haymarket did not on this occasion look much like our present notion of an Elizabethan theater. The Induction was acted with full scenery. But for the rest of the play, the *Times* reported, "the whole dramatic apparatus [was] only two screens and a pair of curtains." The newspaper's claim that "this revival is really one of the most remarkable instances of the modern theatre" is no exaggeration; it took place, after all, nearly half a century before the discovery of the De Witt drawing of the Swan: but it was not followed up until 1881, when William Poel put on an amateur production of the First Quarto text of *Hamlet,* with himself in the title role, for a single matinée at St. George's Hall. There was no scenery and no intermission (though a curtain rose and fell briefly from time to time), and the performance lasted only two hours. Poel continued to direct plays by Shakespeare and other dramatists in similar conditions for over half a century. In 1895 he established the Elizabethan Stage Society, and gradually, helped by Shaw's championship, the new movement made headway.

Poel was not a textual purist. He did terrible things to *Richard II, Measure for Measure,* and *Coriolanus.* He was something of an eccentric: in his belief that actors should be cast largely for the timbres of their voices, he went so far as to have Thersites played by a woman. But he showed how much could be gained by speaking Shakespeare swiftly, by avoiding the long pauses and textual rearrangements necessitated by realistic scenery, by intelligent use of an apron stage and an upper level, and by concentrating attention on the actors rather than the scenery. He also had a talent for spotting and training newcomers. His *Troilus and Cressida* in 1912, given in a mangled text and Elizabethan dress, was not merely the first fully staged English performance of the play since Shakespeare's time; it also gave Edith Evans her first major opportunity as Cressida and was responsible for her becoming a professional actress.

Even more important for its influence on the future development of Shakespeare productions was Poel's casting, in 1899, of the twenty-two-year-old Harley Granville-Barker as Richard II. Granville-Barker was to take Poel's ideas, purged of their eccentricity, into the mainstream not only of the professional theater but also of Shakespeare criticism and scholarship. His most important productions, at the Savoy Theatre from 1912 to 1914, were of *The Winter's Tale, Twelfth Night,* and *A Midsummer Night's Dream.* He reversed Poel's procedure to the extent that he was less of a purist about design than about texts. He played almost complete texts in a theater in which an attempt had been made to break down the distancing effect of the proscenium arch. While not dispensing with scenery, he formalized it, not permitting it to hinder the forward movement of the play. Costumes and lighting were imaginative—excessively so for conservative critics. Like Poel, Granville-Barker built out an apron stage and encouraged rapid delivery of the lines without unnecessary pauses and interpolated business. He engaged fully professional casts and rehearsed them rigorously. The plays were brushed clean, stripped of conventional accretions, thought out afresh from beginning to end. Though some critics were shocked, others felt they had experienced a revelation: John Masefield considered the *Twelfth Night* "much the most beautiful thing I have ever seen done on the stage."

Granville-Barker is no less important as a theorist than as a practitioner. His *Prefaces to Shakespeare,* mostly published between 1923 and 1947, are among the few critical writings that belong to the history of Shakespeare production as much as to the history of Shakespeare criticism. They consider the plays from the point of view of one whose main concern is to interpret them in the theater. They were largely influential in demonstrating the stage-worthiness of certain plays, such as *Love's Labor's Lost* and even *King Lear,* and in furthering the understanding of Shakespeare's stagecraft in terms of the theaters for which they were written. Barker was not an antiquarian. Like Poel, he saw the need to understand Shakespeare as a man of his time; but he also was aware of the need to translate such understanding into terms that were accessible to the modern playgoer.

In 1914, London acquired a new center for the performance of Shakespeare's plays for the next half century. In April of that year, *Romeo and Juliet* became the first Shakespeare play to to be given at the Old Vic, a theater situated (like the Globe) on the unfashionable, south side of the Thames. Lilian Baylis guided the theater's fortunes. Audiences had an earnestness akin to those that saw Phelps's productions at Sadler's Wells. The full-text *Hamlet* became an annual event. By 1923 all Shakespeare's plays had been produced, many of them by Robert Atkins. The theater acquired its own kind of fashionableness. There, in the 1925–1926 season, Edith Evans played a wide range of roles, including both Portias, Rosalind, Cleopatra, Beatrice, and Juliet's Nurse. In 1929, John Gielgud led the company, scoring a great success, particularly as Richard II and Hamlet (Donald Wolfit was Claudius); in the following season, his roles included Prospero and King Lear (with Ralph Richardson as Caliban and Kent). In 1932, Peggy Ashcroft was the leading lady, playing Imogen, Rosalind, Portia, Perdita, Juliet, and Miranda; the following season saw Charles Laughton as Henry VIII, Angelo, Prospero, and Macbeth; in 1934, Maurice Evans played a string of leading parts; and from 1936 to 1938 Laurence Olivier's roles included Hamlet, Henry V, Macbeth, Iago, and Coriolanus. Some of England's finest twentieth-century actors were cutting their teeth on the great roles, most of which they were to play again, sometimes in more sophisticated productions but not always with greater personal success.

During these years, too, new perspectives were opening elsewhere. In 1923 the Birmingham Repertory Theatre, under the management of Sir Barry Jackson, gave *Cymbeline* in modern dress, following this experiment with similar productions, including a *Hamlet* in 1925, that were seen in London as well as Birmingham. Perhaps the most important modern-dress production between the wars was Michael MacOwan's *Troilus and Cressida* at the Westminster Theatre in 1938. The play had not yet established itself in the repertoire; at its only Stratford production between the wars, in 1936, it had been dismissed as "a museum piece." MacOwan's modern dress gave it immediacy and relevance to a world about to plunge into war.

Experimental methods were in evidence in Stratford-upon-Avon, too, particularly in Theodore Komisarjevsky's six productions from 1932 to 1939. Directorial fantastications included commedia dell'arte stylizations in *The Merchant of Venice* and *The Comedy of Errors;* potent allusions to modern warfare in a *Macbeth* played on a metallic set, with expressionist devices such as "amplifiers drumming out incantations which Macbeth's conscience speaks, and shadows projected for bodies"; and a superimposition of conventions of melodrama and musical comedy on *The Merry Wives of Windor.* Like Granville-Barker, Komisarjevsky was destroying his audience's preconceptions, but in the process he appears often to have substituted theatrical virtuosity and vivid but generalized mood-painting for Granville-Barker's patient exploration of the text. The exception was *King Lear* (1936–1937), played on a severely simple set of stairs and platforms backed by a cyclorama that, when subtly lit, acted as a "vast reflector of mood." For once, Komisarjevsky subjugated himself to the play, eliciting an immensely powerful performance from Randle Ayrton as Lear.

Other actors, too, continued to challenge the supremacy of the director. Donald Wolfit, after playing leading roles, including Hamlet, at Stratford in 1936 and 1937, formed his own company, which played mainly in the provinces, though also in wartime London. A richly characterful actor whose heroic vocal style bordered on the orotund, he scored his greatest successes as Richard III, Iago, Malvolio, Falstaff, and, above all, a supremely pathetic Lear. He gave his last Shakespeare performances in 1953.

The two greatest Shakespeare actors to emerge from the Old Vic of the 1930s were John Gielgud and Laurence Olivier. Their styles were contrasting; each excelled in roles that the other did not even attempt. Gielgud was the supreme lyric actor of the twentieth-century stage. He could be intensely passionate, but the passion was vocal rather than bodily. Probably no actor has been better equipped to play Richard II or Prospero. His Hamlet, which he played many times in various productions between 1929 and 1944, became a classic performance. He conveyed superbly the inward agony of Angelo and Cassius (both at Stratford-upon-Avon) and was a marvelously tortured Leontes in Peter Brook's Phoenix Theatre production of *The Winter's Tale* in 1951. Granville-Barker came out of retirement to help to direct him as Lear at the Old Vic in 1940, and Gielgud played the role again at Stratford in 1950 and 1955. Though he excelled in the inwardness and pathos of tragic roles, Gielgud's lightness of touch in comedy made him a superb Benedick in his own production of *Much Ado About Nothing* (1949, Stratford-upon-Avon, with Anthony Quayle as Benedick; Gielgud played in it from 1950, with Peggy Ashcroft as an exquisite Beatrice).

Olivier was a far more obviously physical actor than Gielgud; his voice was less naturally beautiful, but he made of it a wonderfully pliant, vibrant, and heroic instrument, capable of plangent pathos as well as sardonic irony, bitter invective, rousing ferocity, and anguished agony. He was a virtuoso actor, in the line of Garrick, Edmund Kean, and Irving, excelling in unexpected transitions, athletic excitement, and startling changes of physical appearance. His protean quality is shown in the range of roles he played. In 1935, with the Old Vic, he alternated Romeo and Mercutio with Gielgud in a production adorned also with the Juliet of Peggy Ashcroft and the Nurse of Edith Evans. In 1944, with the Old Vic company at the New Theatre, he first gave his brilliant Richard III. In the next season he played a strongly characterized, virile Hotspur in *Henry IV, Part 1,* and transformed himself into the aged Justice Shallow in *Part 2.* (Ralph Richardson was a great Falstaff.) Lear in 1946 was less successful, and Antony to Vivien Leigh's Cleopatra (1951, Saint James's) though it had marvelous moments did not especially suit him; but his Titus Andronicus, directed by Peter Brook at Stratford in 1955, was astounding in its tragic intensity; this historic production revolutionized attitudes to the play. In the same season, Olivier was a memorable Macbeth and a grotesquely comic Malvolio. In 1959, also at Stratford, Peter Hall directed him as Coriolanus in a performance that encompassed all the character's heroism, hauteur, and bewildered self-examination in the later scenes; to these Olivier added a wry irony, discovering unexpected com-

edy in the tension between the hero's essential nature and the demands that others make of him. The culminating death leap, after which Olivier dangled, as Kenneth Tynan put it, "like the slaughtered Mussolini," set the seal on a performance of searching intensity. No less powerful was Olivier's Othello for the National Theatre Company in 1964, for which he found bass notes in his naturally light voice. This performance, like Olivier's Henry V, Hamlet, and Richard III, is preserved on film.

The Old Vic had been damaged in the war; it reopened in 1950, and in 1953, under Michael Benthall, embarked on a plan to produce all the plays of the First Folio in five years, culminating in 1958 with a *Henry VIII* featuring Gielgud as Wolsey and Edith Evans as Queen Katherine. Stratford-upon-Avon's postwar productions included, along with those already mentioned, some of the early work of Peter Brook. His *Love's Labor's Lost* in 1946 (with the young Paul Scofield as Don Armado) did much to put another neglected play on the map. Scofield and Robert Helpmann alternated as Hamlet in 1948; Godfrey Tearle played Othello in 1948 and 1949; Tyrone Guthrie directed *Henry VIII* in 1949 and 1950; 1951 saw an innovatory production of the second history tetralogy on a quasi-Elizabethan stage with Michael Redgrave as Richard II and Hotspur, Richard Burton as Prince Hal and Henry V, and Anthony Quayle as Falstaff; in 1953, Peggy Ashcroft played Cleopatra to Redgrave's Antony; and in 1958, Redgrave played Hamlet and Peter Hall directed *Twelfth Night* with Dorothy Tutin as a joyously boyish Viola.

The year 1959 was an all-star celebration of the theater's hundredth season: Charles Laughton played Lear and Bottom; Paul Robeson was Othello; Edith Evans gave one of her most gracious and tender performances as the Countess in Guthrie's scintillating production of *All's Well That Ends Well* and also played a formidable but womanly Volumnia to Olivier's Coriolanus. Old and new came together in this season. Alongside the great star actors with a prewar reputation were young performers who were to play a large part in Stratford's future development. Change was on the way, and the main instrument was Peter Hall, who became director of the theater in 1960.

Before this time, the Stratford company was recruited afresh each year. Hall instituted a contract system with the aim of creating a more coherent, semipermanent company. Still more important, he acquired the lease of the Aldwych Theatre in London, believing that actors were more likely to commit themselves to the company if they could be seen in the capital and act in modern plays, which could not be put on in Stratford. Hall also engaged John Barton (at that time a fellow of King's College, Cambridge) with the particular brief of developing the company's verse-speaking.

Although Peter Hall wished to encourage the ideals of ensemble playing, it was a strength of his direction of the company that he neither employed uniform production styles himself nor imposed them on other directors. But there was a new intellectualism in the air, expressing itself in some radical interpretations. Hall's own *Midsummer Night's Dream* (1959) and *Twelfth Night* (1960) were romantically beautiful to look at; there was some coarseness in the handling of the lovers in the *Dream,* but the fairy world was magically evoked, and even an extremely silly Olivia in *Twelfth Night* did not inhibit the full realization of the play's romance.

Perhaps the first truly great production of Hall's regime was the *Troilus and Cressida* that he directed with John Barton, also in 1960. It was set simply but boldly against a bloodshot backcloth, and the action took place in an octagonal pit of white sand. The production was full of marvelous performances—Derek Godfrey's noble Hector, Dorothy Tutin's sensual but vulnerable Cressida, Eric Porter's finely spoken Ulysses, and Max Adrian's lubricious Pandarus—but its triumph lay in its realization of the play's deepest poetic structures. Moments such as Cressida's sifting of sand through her fingers, the black-clad Myrmidons' brutal slaughter of the half-naked Hector, and the final appearance of a decrepit Pandarus breaking the play's time barrier with a frightening immediacy acquired a symbolic resonance; "director's Shakespeare" was triumphantly justified.

Quite different was Michael Elliott's lovely *As You Like It* in 1961, with the young Vanessa Redgrave as a radiant Rosalind and Max Adrian an infinitely melancholy Jaques. In 1962 came Peter Brook's austere *King Lear,* a rethinking of the play that found no easy sympathy for Paul Scofield's king. In the same season Clifford Williams demonstrated what a good play *The Comedy of Errors* is in an uncondescending production that was richly comic because it did not deny the play's serious ground bass.

Perhaps the crowning theatrical achievement of Hall's directorate was the historical cycle that began in 1963 with *The Wars of the Roses,* three plays arranged by John Barton from the three parts of *Henry VI* and *Richard III.* Barton himself wrote about 1,400 lines in episodes that provided a heavily political interpretation of the action. It was too drastic an adaptation for us to feel that we were being given the chance to assess Shakespeare's achievement in the early history plays; but it was a fascinating and powerful piece of political theater and would have been worthwhile if only for the opportunities it gave to Peggy Ashcroft, playing Queen Margaret throughout the sequence. Her taunting of the captured Duke of York (Donald Sinden) held the house in a Siddons-like grip, with a perfect balance between technical control and imaginative identification with the role. In 1964, for the quatercentenary of Shakespeare's birth, Hall and his colleagues added to these plays the later-composed tetralogy *(Richard II; Henry IV, Parts 1 and 2; Henry V)* to provide an epic sequence that, while it may have wrested the plays into a unity that Shakespeare did not give them, nevertheless demonstrated that much is to be gained from experiencing them as a group.

In 1965, Peter Hall directed another strongly political interpretation, this time of *Hamlet,* cutting some 730 lines (less than usual) and with David Warner as a disaffected student prince. The same season saw John Schlesinger's excellent *Timon of Athens,* with Scofield as a commanding Timon.

After Olivier's *Othello,* the National Theatre has had little success with Shakespeare, perhaps partly because of the physical limitations of its Olivier Theatre. Peter Hall's *Hamlet* (1975) and *Macbeth* (1978), both with Albert Finney, and his *Othello* (1980), with Paul Scofield, employed full texts but, eschewing interpretation, lacked excitement. Gielgud scored a personal success as Julius Caesar (1977), and a *Measure for Measure* (1981, in the Lyttelton Theatre) using mainly West Indian actors and transferring the action from Vienna to a Caribbean island was exciting but manipulated the text to increase the happiness of the ending. In 1984, Peter Hall's exciting production of *Coriolanus,* with Ian McKellen, did much to overcome the problems of the Olivier Theatre.

Peter Hall was succeeded as director of the Royal Shakespeare Company in 1968 by Trevor Nunn, with Terry Hands as joint artistic director. During this period the company securely established itself as the principal purveyor of Shakespeare's plays to the British nation, putting on at least five new productions of Shakespeare every year. A few of them have been dull or misguided, but overall the company has been able to sustain a remarkably high standard, which may be attributed partly to its maintenance of a balance between continuity and change of personnel and partly to a willingness to accommodate a wide range of styles in both production and acting. Standards of ensemble have been high; stars have emerged from within the company, but it has also been able to absorb within itself the talents of performers from many different backgrounds. There is space here to mention only some of the company's most outstanding productions of this period.

John Barton's *Twelfth Night* (1969), with Judi Dench as a witty but deeply poetic Viola, fused the play's comic and serious elements with Chekhovian grace. In 1970, Peter Brook returned to Stratford with a production of *A Midsummer Night's Dream* as revolutionary as Granville-Barker's. It was set (as Granville-Barker had said it should be) in a white box. Costumes were timeless: loose satin garments in bright colors. Oberon and Theseus, like Titania and Hippolyta, were played by the same actor. Oberon and Puck swung on trapezes, and Titania descended, sitting on a great scarlet feather. There was rampart sexuality in Bottom's encounter with Titania. The text was complete and was spoken with rapid clarity. The production was self-consciously iconoclastic, theatrically powerful, and, in its closing moments, homiletic. It did little to realize the grace, charm, and humor of Shakespeare's play, but its self-confident assertion of its own values made it a great happening in its own right. It toured the world.

In 1974, the company opened The Other Place, a small, simply equipped studio theater; there, in 1975, Buzz Goodbody directed an outstandingly intelligent version of *Hamlet* that demonstrated how modern dress can help to clarify a play for modern audiences. In the same year, Terry Hands directed Alan Howard as an exhilarating Henry V in the main theater. Howard also played Henry VI in Hands's brave production of the three parts (1977) in much fuller and purer texts than Hall and Barton had used. Hands (in collaboration with his designers) has a capacity to produce outstandingly beautiful stage pictures, finely demonstrated in his *Richard II* in 1980 and his charming *Much Ado* in 1982.

John Barton's *Richard II* in 1973, with Richard Pasco and Ian Richardson excitingly alternating Richard and Bolingbroke, was an intellectually demanding, highly stylized production that combined implicit commentary on the play with a full realization of its poetry. At The Other Place in 1976, Trevor Nunn directed a textually compressed, small-cast version of *Macbeth* that reduced the play's political dimensions but explored the relationship of Macbeth (Ian McKellen) and Lady Macbeth (Judi Dench) with unbearable intensity. In the same season, in the main house, Dench confirmed that she is the finest Shakespearean actress of her generation with a deeply felt Beatrice to Donald Sinden's ebullient Benedick in a production by John Barton that surprisingly illuminated the play's social structure by setting it in British India. Barton's deeply sensitive *Love's Labor's Lost* followed in 1978.

In 1981, Trevor Nunn set *All's Well That Ends Well* in Edwardian times in a wonderfully detailed and sensitive production that brought Peggy Ashcroft back to Shakespeare as the Countess. Nunn also directed both parts of *Henry IV* in 1982 to open the Barbican Theatre, which replaced the Aldwych as the company's London home. The 1980s have seen new directors and actors at work in Stratford. Adrian Noble directed *Antony and Cleopatra,* with a superb performance from Helen Mirren, at The Other Place (1982); Ron Daniels directed some imaginative and vigorous productions in the main house, including an ingenious *Midsummer Night's Dream* using Victorian costumes (1981) and an admirably unfussy *Hamlet* (1984); and Bill Alexander's big, bold production of *Richard III* (1984) used an ecclesiastical setting to ironic effect and had Anthony Sher as a brilliant Richard.

Theatergoers with access to Stratford or London are fortunate in being able to hope for good productions of most of Shakespeare's plays every few years. Texts nowadays are rarely complete, but cutting is usually undertaken responsibly and is freshly thought out for each production. A few plays, notably *King John,* are neglected; others, especially *Cymbeline,* seem generally to defeat their interpreters. Directors and designers sometimes exercise their own creativity at the expense of the dramatist's; the rarest kind of excellence is that which articulates the text with such cunning art that the play gives the illusion of speaking for itself. Actors, too, sometimes obtrude their personalities or their mannerisms between the audience and their roles; but the English stage has many well-trained and experienced performers of small, as well as large, roles who serve Shakespeare with complete integrity. At present, the future of Shakespeare on the English stage seems to depend largely on the Royal Shakespeare Company; but the National Theatre's challenge may soon become more effective, and the plans to reconstruct the Globe on Bankside may provide the stimulus to another Elizabethan revival.

BIBLIOGRAPHY

Shirley S. Allen, *Samuel Phelps and Sadler's Wells Theatre* (1971). William W. Appleton, *Charles Macklin: An Actor's Life* (1960). Emmett L. Avery et al., eds., *The London Stage 1660–1800: A Calendar of Plays, Entertainments and Afterpieces,* 11 vols. (1960–1968). Herschel Baker, *John Philip Kemble: The Actor in His Theatre* (1942). Dennis Bartholomeusz, *Macbeth and the Players* (1969) and *"The Winter's Tale" in Performance in England and America, 1611–1976* (1982). Sally Beauman, *The Royal Shakespeare Company: A History of Ten Decades* (1982). John Bell, ed., *Shakespeare's Plays as They Are Now Performed at the Theatre Royal in London,* 9 vols. (1773–1775). Ralph Berry, "Komisarjevsky at Stratford-upon-Avon," in *Shakespeare Survey,* 36 (1983). Michael R. Booth, *Victorian Spectacular Theatre, 1850–1910* (1981) and "The Meininger Company and English Shakespeare," in *Shakespeare Survey,* 35 (1982). Kalman A. Burnim, *David Garrick, Director* (1961).

Colley Cibber, *An Apology for the Life of Mr. Colley Cibber, Comedian,* Robert W. Lowe, ed., 2 vols. (1889). John William Cole, *The Life and Theatrical Times of Charles Kean, F.S.A.,* 2 vols. (1859). *Cornmarket Acting Versions of Shakespeare's Plays from the Restoration to the Death of David Garrick,* 86 vols. (1969); 2nd ser., H. Neville Davies, ed., 51 vols. (1970–1973). Gordon Crosse, *Shakespearean Playgoing, 1890–1952* (1953). Richard David, *Shakespeare in the Theatre* (1978). Alan S. Downer, *The Eminent Tragedian: William Charles Macready* (1966). David Garrick, *The Plays of David Garrick,* Harry W.

Pedicord and Fredrick Louis Bergmann, eds., vols. III and IV: *Garrick's Adaptations of Shakespeare* (1981). Francis Gentleman, *The Dramatic Censor,* 2 vols. (1770). William Hazlitt, William Archer, and Robert W. Lowe, eds., *Dramatic Essays* (1895), reprinted as *Hazlitt on Theatre* (n.d.). Philip H. Highfill, Jr., Kalman A. Burnim, and Edward A. Langhans, *A Biographical Dictionary of Actors, Actresses, Musicians, Dancers, Managers, and Other Stage Personnel in London, 1660–1800* (1973–). Harold N. Hillebrand, *Edmund Kean* (1933). Charles B. Hogan, *Shakespeare in the Theatre, 1701–1800,* 2 vols. (1952–1957). Alan Hughes, *Henry Irving, Shakespearean* (1981).

William Moelwyn Merchant, *Shakespeare and the Artist* (1959). Henry Morley, *The Journal of a London Playgoer* (1866). Allardyce Nicoll, *The Garrick Stage* (1980). George C. D. Odell, *Shakespeare from Betterton to Irving,* 2 vols. (1920; repr. 1966). Joseph G. Price, *The Unfortunate Comedy: A Study of "All's Well That Ends Well" and Its Critics* (1968). Mongi Raddadi, *Davenant's Adaptations of Shakespeare* (1979). John Ripley, *"Julius Caesar" on Stage in England and America, 1599–1973* (1980). Marvin Rosenberg, *The Masks of Othello: The Search for the Identity of Othello, Iago, and Desdemona by Three Centuries of Actors and Critics* (1961); *The Masks of King Lear* (1972); and *The Masks of Macbeth* (1978). Charles H. Shattuck, *The Shakespeare Promptbooks: A Descriptive Catalogue* (1965). George Bernard Shaw, *Shaw on Shakespeare,* Edwin Wilson, ed. (1961). Robert Speaight, *William Poel and the Elizabethan Revival* (1954) and *Shakespeare on the Stage* (1973). Christopher Spencer, ed., *Five Restoration Adaptations of Shakespeare* (1965).

Hazleton Spencer, *Shakespeare Improved: The Restoration Versions in Quarto and on the Stage* (1927). Arthur Colby Sprague, *Shakespeare and the Actors: The Stage Business in His Plays* (1944); *Shakesperian Plays and Performances* (1953); and *Shakespeare's Histories: Plays for the Stage* (1964). Arthur Colby Sprague and John C. Trewin, *Shakespeare's Plays Today: Some Customs and Conventions of the Stage* (1970). John Louis Styan, *The Shakespeare Revolution* (1977). John C. Trewin, *Shakespeare on the English Stage, 1900–1964* (1964). Stanley Wells, *Royal Shakespeare: Studies of Four Major Productions at Stratford-upon-Avon* (1977). E. Harcourt Williams, *Old Vic Saga* (1949). Jane Williamson, *Charles Kemble, Man of the Theatre* (1970). J. C. Young, *Memoir of Charles Mayne Young* (1871).

Shakespeare in the Theater: the United States and Canada

CHARLES H. SHATTUCK

Shakespeare in the Colonies

By 1774, when the Continental Congress, girding for the Revolution, banned horse racing, cockfighting, plays, and other expensive diversions, at least 180 performances of fourteen Shakespeare plays (or, rather, English adaptations of Shakespeare) had been seen in the colonies. If the records were complete, Hugh Rankin tells us, the number might exceed 500. The plays seen by the colonists, grouped roughly in the order of their earliest performances, were these: in the 1750s, *Richard III, Othello, The Merchant of Venice, King Lear, Romeo and Juliet, Hamlet, Macbeth;* in the 1760s, *Henry IV, Part 1, Catherine and Petruchio, Cymbeline, King John;* in the 1770s, *The Tempest, The Merry Wives of Windsor, Julius Caesar.* If there were hundreds of performances of these, many hundreds more theatrical performances took place, for the colonists were as eager for the newest as for the best.

But plays were played in only six or eight of the colonies. No "chapels of Satan" rose in New England. The Quakers would have kept the devil out of Pennsylvania, but they were overruled by the king in council. The southern colonies welcomed the players, but their population was so spread out that it was not easy to convene large audiences. Trade and population were concentrating in the North, in New York and Philadelphia. If theater was to flourish it must capture those centers, and by 1774 it had done so.

In 1749 a company of comparative unknowns,

led by Thomas Kean and Walter Murray, played briefly in Philadelphia until the religionists expelled them; they then played in New York, Virginia, and Maryland until late 1752, when they disbanded. Apparently Cibber's *Richard III* was the only Shakespeare in their repertory.

Next, in 1752, came the professionals, Lewis Hallam's "Company of Comedians from London" —no famous stars, of course, but several among them well-known actors from London's minor houses, frozen out of employment by sudden reinforcement of the Theater Licensing Act. They had planned this expedition to the New World for a year, and were rehearsed and ready in eight Shakespeare plays, twenty modern plays, and the necessary afterpieces. On 15 September 1752, in Williamsburg, Virginia, they opened with *The Merchant of Venice.* Hallam, manager and low comedian, played Launcelot Gobbo. Mrs. Hallam, mistress of over forty romantic heroines, was an ideal Portia. The Shylock, Patrick Malone, well-schooled in "heavies," was capable even of Lear.

In 1753–1754 the Hallams managed six months in New York, offering *Richard III, Romeo and Juliet,* and *King Lear,* together with favorite modern plays, and ten weeks in Philadelphia until the Quaker opposition became unbearable. They expected a prosperous time in Charleston, South Carolina; but early in 1755 a tidal wave of the Great Awakening, led by the hellfire preaching of George Whitefield, swept them out. Retreating to Jamaica, they joined forces with the Jamaican manager David Douglass.

In 1756, Hallam died of yellow fever. He bequeathed to Douglass his company, his wife, and his son, Lewis. Douglass and Mrs. Hallam married, and in 1758, Douglass led the company back to the mainland. Forewarned of the difficulties but skilled in diplomacy, he circumvented obstacles and sustained this company for sixteen years.

Beginning in 1766, the American Company (so called after 1763) spent nearly four years in the North, mastering New York and Philadelphia. Twice more, after "rest stops" in the South, Douglass returned to confirm his victory. In 1774 he was preparing to renew the campaign when the order came that until the war ended, all playing must cease. Douglass' company disbanded, his great work done.

After the Revolution

After the British withdrew, the younger Hallam and the Irish-born actor John Henry re-formed the American Company and set up shop in New York in an old playhouse that Douglass had built in John Street. But Thomas Wignell, one of their best actors, deserted them, built a magnificent new theater in Philadelphia's Chestnut Street, and stocked it with fresh recruits from England. For some two decades Philadelphia's theater excelled that of New York.

America had to rush to catch up with the flood of plays that the British had created while the colonists were winning the war; and America had also to turn to the British for actors to fill up the new companies that were organizing in every sizable town and city from Boston to Savannah. Hallam and Henry, jealously dividing the best roles between them, were less active than others in recruitment. Their one grand catch, John Hodgkinson of Bath, was their ruination. Hodgkinson offered remarkable credentials, but he was arrogant, Machiavellian, and merciless. He was greedy for roles, said William Dunlap. He despised his American employers and set about to destroy them. He appropriated their roles for himself and their wives' roles for his own wife. He exacerbated the old hostility festering between them. John Henry broke under the strain, sold his share in the company, and went off to die. Hallam held on as co-manager with Dunlap until 1798, and a few years longer as a minor actor. In 1805, Hodgkinson went

south and died of yellow fever. Few lamented his passing.

Wignell's first recruiting expedition netted him a remarkable principal tragedian, James Fennell. Highly educated, rich-voiced, tall, and handsome, Fennell was a great social success, and he satisfied Philadelphia's taste in a wide range of tragic heroes.

A pair of outsized tragediennes came to America in the 1790s. Charlotte Melmoth had left the stage because of increasing obesity and sailed to America hoping to make a living by platform readings. Because of her beautiful voice she was invited to join the American Company. A fine Lady Macbeth, Dunlap says she was "the best tragic actress New York had yet seen." Elizabeth Kemble Whitlock, sister of Sarah Siddons, came to Philadelphia in 1794 and also played in Boston and New York. In a second expedition in 1796, Wignell caught a jewel—one of the loveliest actresses of her generation, Anne Brunton Merry, who was ideally suited for Juliet, Cordelia, Portia, and Ophelia. Aboard the same ship with Anne Merry, Wignell brought a handsome twenty-year-old, Thomas Abthorpe Cooper, honored by most historians as America's first great actor. Cooper, who modeled his acting on the neoclassic style of John Philip Kemble, realized only after his Philadelphia debut (a well-received Macbeth on 9 December 1796) that Fennell claimed all leading roles in tragedy. He thereupon quarreled with Wignell, broke his contract, and scurried off to New York to enlist under William Dunlap, who was about to open the new Park Theatre. There his Hamlet, which he had indeed studied and played well in London, was received rapturously. Dunlap would later declare it "the best acting I ever saw," and John Bernard thought his Macbeth second only to Garrick's. Yet there were reservations: Cooper would stare into boxes and acknowledge acquaintances there, mispronounce words, lapse into rant, forget his part, and substitute lines from another play.

Beyond the Mountains

Well before 1800, thousands of Americans had penetrated the mountains and established young cities in the Trans-Appalachian West. In 1806, Luke Usher of Baltimore converted the upstairs of his Lexington, Kentucky, brewery into a theater, and he built other theaters in Frankfort and Louisville. In 1814, Samuel Drake, an Englishman, brought his family of actors (three sons and three daughters) to become a permanent Kentucky company. He was credited with establishing a golden age of drama in the West.

In 1820, James Caldwell of Virginia took a company to New Orleans, where from the early 1820s he dominated the English-speaking part of the city and most of the towns up the Mississippi. From about 1816, steamboats began to ply the rivers, a phenomenon of vast importance to the development of theater in the South and West. With a superior stock company in New Orleans, Caldwell could lure many major stars, including Shakespeareans, to make the "grand circle" from New York down to Savannah; across the South to Mobile; then to New Orleans (the peak of the journey, at least a two-week stand); up the Mississippi and Ohio by steamer, playing every port city to Pittsburgh; and then overland to New York. Caldwell built two New Orleans theaters, the Camp Street and the St. Charles, the latter called "the only theatre in the United States . . . truly worthy of a large city." Caldwell's main competition was from Noah Ludlow and Sol Smith, who took over the area after Caldwell's retirement. Each wrote a book about his experiences, and these are our major sources of information about early theater in the Mississippi Valley.

There was no theater in California, of course, until 1850, in the wake of the gold rush. From then on, in San Francisco and inland, theaters were built, burned, and rebuilt in a frenzy of activity. The year 1869 was a momentous one for the profession in California; in that year the Union Pacific Railroad and the spacious California Theatre in San Francisco opened.

When Ralph Rusk made a survey of literature of the midwestern frontier (mainly the Ohio and upper Mississippi valleys, 1800–1840), he found that more evenings were given to Shakespeare than to any other playwright. James Dormon found similar statistics in his study of theater in the antebellum South. Both researchers were careful to point out that a seeming popularity of Shakespeare does not mean that frontier settlers were highly sophisticated drama lovers. Like those of the East, frontier audiences preferred tragedies to comedies, and plays like *Richard III, Macbeth,* and *Hamlet* could match or outdo the most exciting modern melodramas in violent actions and mouth-filling, tub-thumping oratory. Furthermore, the major tra-

gedians making the rounds based their claims to greatness on what they could do with Shakespeare, so they tended to play Shakespeare most often.

Dustbin or Gold Mine

For decades after America won independence, its theater remained an outpost of the English theater —often, indeed, a dustbin for performers not wanted in England. Of the 150 or so actors at work in America in 1800, only one—Anne Merry—had stood at the top of the profession in London and could have gone home, had she chosen. But English actors of distinction eventually realized that an American tour might bring both wealth and fame. Between 1810 and 1826 three great actors and a humble fourth who achieved greatness made the test.

When the Park Theatre opened in 1798 it did not, as expected, restore leadership to New York. By 1806, the manager, William Dunlap, bumbled into bankruptcy. Thomas Cooper took over but was no more effective than Dunlap. In 1808 a young speculator, Stephen Price, bought into the management and began to inquire what the public wanted, what they would pay for. They wanted stars. In 1810, Price sent Cooper to England to catch one. When word came back that he was sending George Frederick Cooke, next after John Philip Kemble the most famous actor in England, few could believe it. America did not know that Cooke was a falling star. Old, ill, exhausted, in debt, and awash with brandy, he was susceptible to Cooper's promise of fair terms. His opening as Richard III on 21 November 1810 drew the most packed, excited, and gratified house that the Park management could have hoped for. It was as if New Yorkers had never imagined what "natural acting," driven by cyclonic power, could do to them. By his keen intelligence, powerful voice, and fierce eyes, Cooke overwhelmed audiences with the tyrants and villains he specialized in. That is to say, as long as he was sober. Cooke certainly meant to return to England, but it was not to be. He died midway in his second season, abandoned by audiences, his mind gone, his body ruined by drink.

Edmund Kean, who came in 1820 and was even more famous than Cooke, overwhelmed by brute ferocity; his explosive Shylock in 1814, with its novel readings and stage business, its startling transitions, and its flashes of blinding intensity, had shaken King Kemble on his throne as Cooke could never do. Kean set a new direction to tragic acting in England. In America, as at home, he excited controversy. Sober loyalists of the Cooper-Kemble school of classical dignity objected that his characterizations lacked unity, that his performances were collections of unrelated "points" with long stretches of humdrum between them. The excitable majority saw him as "the most complete actor that ever appeared on our boards."

His season was immensely successful—until the final night. Piqued because he thought his last Boston audience too small to be worth his effort, he refused to return there. Boston was insulted, and the press, formerly warm in its praise of him, rounded on him in blind fury. London, angered by these Yankee attacks on their hero, welcomed him home exuberantly, but following a scandalous love affair, he took refuge in America in 1825. Of course, he should have avoided Boston. But either false humility or hubris drove him there "to apologize for my indiscretions." On 21 December 1825 a mob chased him from the theater and smashed windows, seats, and chandeliers until the police drove them out. It was America's first full-fledged theater riot. Kean stayed in America and Canada through the summer but soon returned to Drury Lane, all his sins forgiven.

The one visitor who clearly profited from a season in America (1826–1827) was William Charles Macready, who, after Kemble's retirement, was England's most earnest, educated, dedicated, and stable tragic actor. The American critics recognized in Macready's acting a total emotional identification with every role, a unified conception of each character, and a clarity of execution. He sacrificed point-making, and when at his bursts of passion applause inevitably broke out, he remained so deeply in character that he seemed unaware of the applause and continued "acting." One critic, with obvious side-glances at Kean, said of Macready, "His acting is not a point, a flash, a flat-scene, and then another point, and flash, and flat again."

Historians make much of Edmund Kean for introducing to America the romantic mode of acting, as against the static classicism of Cooper; and they have little to say of Junius Brutus Booth except to rehash the hundred tales of his eccentricity, drunkenness, and spells of insanity. Booth went to America in 1821, without fanfare and without even an engagement. He went on impulse and, to put it simply, for love. There was a ship in the harbor, and Mary Ann Holmes, the girl he was in love with, told the already married Booth that she was carrying his child. He simply had to find this girl a country hiding place and make what living he could for them by his art. He landed at Norfolk and spent the summer in Virginia, building up a purse and a sheaf of good notices, while Mary Ann waited out her pregnancy somewhere in the South.

On 5 October 1821, Booth opened in New York, at the newly rebuilt Park. Here, as in Baltimore, in Boston, and elsewhere, he was received with great curiosity, good houses, and good or mixed reviews. But the charge, which had begun in London, that he was merely an imitator of Kean, still pursued him. To confute the charge, Booth would sometimes play Richard III in strict imitation of Kean on one night and in his own manner the next, and thus assert the independence of his own interpretation. Those who knew him best and longest emphasized the differences between the two. According to Thomas Gould, Kean would simply pick the points and passages that suited his powers and give them with electric force. But Booth projected whole characters so completely thought out that "no suggestion of the actor's other impersonations mingle with or mar the impression." John Foster Kirk confirms this, claiming that no other tragedian could so clearly discriminate between such similar characters as Richard, Iago, and Sir Giles Overreach (in Massinger's *A New Way to Pay Old Debts*). Booth did not deal in "flashes of lightning" but in conceptions that were "sustained and related." Booth was onstage for thirty years, mad and sane, not only in New York and other major centers but everywhere else—even at the end in far-off California—an exemplar of the romantic mode to a whole generation of fellow performers, exciting audiences of every level of taste and sophistication.

Visitors Young and Fashionable, 1830–1850

After the departure of the meteoric Kean in 1826 and the nobly grave Macready the next year, interest in theatergoing lapsed somewhat among the more cultivated levels of American society. A surfeit of farces, melodramas, and run-of-the-mill performers of standard drama dulled their appetites. There was, nonetheless, a cluster of young English

Shakespeareans whose artistic and social credentials did make them welcome to "society."

Charles Kean, Edmund's son, was not quite twenty in the fall of 1830, when he tried his wings in America. His talents were meager and his repertory small, but the critics were gentle with him. Expectations ran higher when, in 1832, Stephen Price persuaded the Kembles that the father-daughter team of Charles and Fanny could make a fortune in America. But Charles Kemble's success fell short of expectations, for his Hamlet, a model of correctness, failed to excite crowds as Kean's had done. What the audience wanted was Fanny. Because she was not as exquisitely beautiful as Sir Thomas Lawrence's famous sketch of her, she wisely chose power over prettiness to make her first impression. The truth was, as she told her diary, she hated the profession and loathed the thought of a lifetime devoted to the cheap deception of painted canvas and all that went with it. Only for her father's sake did she allow herself to be worshiped onstage and lionized in society. In the spring of 1834 she turned her earnings over to her father and sent him home, staying behind to marry Pierce Butler, a Philadelphia socialite. The visit of the Kembles was indeed good for their purses, and as Francis Wemyss declared, it revived "the prostrate fortunes of the drama in the United States, and . . . made the theatres once more a fashionable place of amusement."

Next came the lovely Ellen Tree, who stayed in America from 1836 to 1839. Not emphatically a Shakespearean at this point, she did open on 12 December 1836 as Rosalind, and she carried Viola, Beatrice, and others in her repertory. In 1839, Charles Kean came a second time, no longer the tyro of 1830 but by now a London star. Kean played in New York, but after a brief run, attacks of bronchitis cut short his engagement. After a cure in Cuba, he returned in time for his April engagement at the Park. Here he was supported by talented actors, with Susan Cushman the Ophelia to his Hamlet and both Susan and Charlotte Cushman supporting his Lear. As Hotspur, he divided *Henry IV* with James Hackett's Falstaff. On 7 May he combined with Charlotte Cushman in *Macbeth.* In summing up Kean's season, the critics confessed to a certain unease about his work. They did not want to subject him to comparison with his late father, yet, they noted, whenever he committed some sound or action reminiscent of his father, the audience responded vociferously. He "did not do *him-self* justice," said the *Knickerbocker* magazine. At times he seemed careless and lackadaisical, at other times unbecomingly violent. And there was "an affectation" in his speaking that "savors more of the gentleman of the drawing-room, than of the artist."

When Kean came again, in 1845, he brought his famous wife, Ellen Tree. Though almost forty years of age (five years older than he), she appears to have been the more attractive of the two. Besides his wife, Kean also brought a grand plan. He had observed how Macready had risen to unquestionable preeminence in the profession not only by promotion of modern drama (especially Bulwer's plays), but also by his uses of Shakespeare. Macready claimed credit, and was generally granted it, for "restoring true texts" and for applying "fit illustration," which meant creating "historically accurate" settings for each play. In January 1844, working with Alfred Bunn at Drury Lane, Kean had followed Macready's example. He got up a marvelous historical reconstruction of Cibber's reworking of *Richard III,* a play that Macready had neglected. Kean brought all the movables—properties, armor, and costumes—with him and restaged the production at the Park on 7 January 1846, with, as Odell says, "a wealth of scenery and degree of historical accuracy never even dreamed of hitherto on the American stage." Unquestionably what New York saw in 1846 was what London had seen two years earlier. Highly successful, it ran three weeks and was revived later.

That was only the beginning of Kean's plan. He would do for America what Macready already did for London. He had employed George Ellis, a Drury Lane prompter, to transcribe for him all the promptbooks he could find of Macready's Shakespeare productions and all he could find of Macready's costume and scene designs. When in the fall of 1846 he staged *King John* in exact imitation of Macready's production, it failed, costing him thousands out of his own pocket. He quarreled with Simpson, the Park manager, broke with the theater, and went off to the South and West to recoup his losses before returning to England.

American Tragedians: The School of Forrest

Native American Shakespeareans of consequence did not appear until the 1820s. The emergence in 1826 of Edwin Forrest was momentous, for it initiated a school of tragic acting that embodied "the vital, burly, aggressive Americanism of the age." A youth of twenty, who had got his training mainly in the West, Forrest made his official New York debut at the new Bowery Theatre on 6 November 1826. The play was *Othello.* Handsome, vibrant, powerfully muscled, and magnificently proportioned, equipped with a voice of immense range, he gave a performance that for sheer excitement recalled the first night of Cooke's Richard sixteen years earlier. Here was an American who could stand up to any English actor. The stockholders of the Bowery instantly rewrote his contract, elevating him to star status.

Forrest's choice of roles was not predominantly Shakespearean. Othello and Lear were right for him, of course—manly heroes of vast stature and rectitude, destroyed from without by foulest means. After his courtroom disaster in 1851, when he sought to divorce his wife on grounds of adultery only to find himself divorced on the same grounds, he played Othello and Lear almost as autobiography. He played Hamlet because any leading tragedian must do so, but Hamlet's dawdling indecisiveness annoyed him. As an exponent of manliness he disliked villains, so he rarely touched Shylock or Iago. He could not convincingly submit to Macbeth's fear of the supernatural.

His favorite roles were fearless revolutionaries, defenders of the oppressed, which might be expected of one who offstage was a relentless defender of "Jacksonian democracy." Philosophically, then, Shakespeare could be of little use to him, because Shakespeare's affinities were with the aristocrats and led him to portray commoners as knaves, fools, and louts. The more passionately Forrest defended the oppressed of the fictional world, the more furious grew his hatred of the upper classes. He resented the American intelligentsia because they preferred foreign art and artists. He resented the intrusion of English actors into America and gradually came to focus his hostility upon one of them, William Charles Macready.

The often-told story of that enmity, erupting in the bloody Astor Place Riot of 1849, need only be sketched here. When Forrest acted in London in 1836, the critic John Forster, known to be Macready's close friend, reviewed him abusively. Although Macready had entertained Forrest with extreme cordiality, Forrest could not fail to suspect that Forster wrote as Macready wished him to. When Macready (now always billed as "The Eminent Tragedian") next came to America in 1843,

he noticed that Forrest's bills now bore the legend "The National Tragedian," as if to invite partisanship. Forrest reciprocated the courtesies that Macready had paid him in London; and, be it noted, at every face-to-face encounter, both men behaved like perfect gentlemen. Yet from Forrest's playbills and hints in certain newspapers about how easy it would be "to drive any actor off the stage," Macready suspected that Forrest or his "fellow patriots" were itching to make trouble. When Macready toured the grand circle, he was not cheered to learn that Forrest was following him everywhere a week later.

Early in 1845, when Forrest made a second try for London, nearly all the critics turned against him, including "Forster." In Forrest's mind, this could only be a conspiracy headed by Forster—who, as a matter of fact, was confined to his quarters with a prolonged illness and so did not write the *Examiner* reviews or attend any theatricals at all during that time. When Forrest played Macbeth, the audience actually hissed him. This, Forrest thought, must have been a claque inspired by Macready, perhaps even led by him. (Macready was in far-off Newcastle, doing a run through the northern provinces.) When Forrest offered his favorite play, *Metamora,* the critics ridiculed both play and player.

In Edinburgh on 2 March 1846, Forrest took a box near the stage for Macready's Hamlet. Just before the play-within-the-play, at "I must be idle," Macready executed a bit of business inherited from Garrick's time, crossing the stage fluttering a handkerchief. Forrest hissed violently, rose, and stalked out. Later he posted a letter to the *Times,* stating firmly, lest anyone doubt it, that he was the hisser and that Macready's *pas de mouchoir* was a desecration of Shakespeare and must be hissed. And thereafter, in curtain speeches throughout England, Ireland, and America, he spread the word that Macready and his toady Forster had conspired to destroy him in England. When Macready arrived in America in the fall of 1848, the battle lines were drawn. In May 1849, when Macready returned from the grand circle to play Macbeth at the Astor Place Opera House, there were two nights of anti-Macready rioting. On the second, when the mob would not disperse, the militia fired on them, killing thirty-one and wounding an unknown number. Two years later Forrest's disgrace in the divorce court further alienated him from that part of the public which he already despised—the upper classes. Yet he still had "his masses" to applaud him two decades longer and remained a great name throughout the country. And far into the "genteel age," many remembered Forrest as the only great American tragic actor.

By the 1830s, when Forrest had established the muscle-and-thunder school of tragic acting, there were superwomen as well as supermen in the American tragic throng. In 1831 a tall and "elegantly moulded" eighteen-year-old girl named Josephine Clifton enjoyed a string of successes in heavy roles at the Bowery. She reminded one critic of Mrs. Siddons; her attitudes were splendid, her countenance commanding, her voice flexible and sweet. Although, as Ludlow puts it, her person steadily "expanded into Brobdingnagian proportions," her fame spread overseas, and in 1834 she was invited to Drury Lane. One London critic's summation was that "the six-foot specimen of transatlantic genius did not make the impression which was anticipated. Her lungs are inimitable and her arms beautifully brawny, but here praise must cease." Back in the States her reputation continued to flourish. It had not been Forrest's custom to carry a leading lady on his tours, but during most of 1842 he took Clifton with him up and down the eastern states. She then weighed in, as he did, at something over 200 pounds. They shared performances and, according to many witnesses, hotel rooms. Forrest's adulterous relations with Clifton were perhaps the most persuasive evidence that turned the jury against him in the divorce trial of 1851. Clifton was spared the embarrassment of the testimony. She had died four years earlier.

Charlotte Cushman, though no friend of Forrest and a finer artist than he, may still be counted on the distaff side of the school of Forrest. Tall, big-boned, broad-shouldered, mannish in features ("my unfortunate mug," she called her face), she became a Shakespearean by accident. Blessed with a strong contralto voice, she trained for opera. But her teacher forced her into soprano roles, and during her first engagement, at New Orleans in 1835–1836, she damaged her voice so badly that her operatic career was ruined. Luckily an old-time actor who remembered Sarah Siddons recognized in Cushman's size and power and in the "woody," husky tones of her speaking voice her potential as an actress in the spoken drama. He trained her for Lady Macbeth. On Shakespeare's birthday, 1836, at New Orleans, she triumphed in the role for which she is best remembered.

But she had much to learn. For the next seven years in northern cities she was reduced to stock status and cast randomly in plays, farces, light musicals, wherever she was needed. She watched and studied major performers—Ellen Tree, for instance, for grace and wit, and at the Park in New York, in the fall of 1837, Forrest, by then a national hero, just home from his successful stand in London. His careful diction was a lesson to her, and his vocal and bodily force showed her how she might advance her own strength beyond her customary restraints.

In Philadelphia, where she moved in 1840, came her great opportunity. When Macready arrived there in 1843, he was so pleased with her Lady Macbeth that he invited her (and paid her expenses) to accompany him to Boston. The Boston manager would not accept her, however, insisting that his own daughter serve as Macready's support. For Cushman this was not disaster but golden opportunity. For ten nights she sat out front, studying Macready's every movement, his reading of every line. It was a kind of master lesson in the most advanced school of Shakespearean acting. By listening to Macready she found in her own voice varieties of pitch and tone, uses of pause, shifts of speed and volume that she had never imagined possible. Above all, she learned from Macready the cheapness of point-making and how much better it was to build a role into a coherent unity.

In 1845 she gambled her savings on a trip to London, for only there, Macready had insisted, could she complete her education in the art. The sole London engagement she could find at the time was at the Princess's to support Forrest, who was returning for his second campaign. But she had not risked everything to play second fiddle to anyone —least of all, after her experience with Macready, to make her first London impression as mere support to Forrest. She opened before him and without him, much to his annoyance, as Bianca in *Fazio,* a role in which she could display the broadest range of passion and histrionic effects. The critics were astounded by her Siddonian power and began hearalding her as "the very first actress that we have." Having made her point, she consented to support Forrest. She wrecked him. On 17 February 1846 the play was *Othello.* Forrest's Othello pleased no one much; Cushman's Emilia was widely credited with saving the performance. On 21 February the play was *Macbeth.* Forrest was hissed and laughed at; Cushman as Lady Macbeth won higher praise than before. She refused to play with Forrest any longer. When he failed and went to the country, she stayed on at the Princess's for eighty-four nights. Her finest achievement in London was her Romeo, with her sister Susan as Juliet. The playwright Westland Marston declared that the ardor of her lovemaking exceeded that of any male Romeo he had ever seen.

In 1847 she played a long stand with Macready at the Princess's, adding to her list of Shakespearean heavies the role of Queen Katharine in *Henry VIII,* which eventually, when she had gentled down the death scene, became, at least for William Winter, her finest role of all. It is a pity that her size, voice, face, and temperament limited her to so few Shakespearean women's roles. In order to extend her repertory she had to turn to Romeo and even occasionally to Hamlet and Cardinal Wolsey. Her final retirement ceremony in New York on 7 November 1874 was the most spectacular in American theatrical history, with speeches, a poem by William Cullen Bryant, a laurel wreath, a torchlit procession led by a band, and fireworks over Madison Square.

The last, and perhaps the most attractive, male representative of the school of Forrest was John McCullough, known to one and all as Genial John, an actor whose name and work hardly exist in popular memory a century after his death. The son of a poor Irish farmer, he came to America at fifteen to seek his fortune. Self-educated, he learned his first Shakespeare from an Irish workman who could recite long speeches from the plays. In 1860 he got an engagement with E. L. Davenport at the Howard Athenaeum in Boston. One day in an emergency at the theater he astonished Davenport by memorizing a long leading role between noon and curtain time, and playing it without book. In 1861, Forrest, aware of McCullough's handsome face, strong build and voice, and reputation for quick study, hired him as leading man. They were a perfect match. For six years he supported Forrest as Iago, Edgar, Richmond, Macduff, and many non-Shakespearean characters. Inevitably McCullough modeled his acting style on that of Forrest, but when they parted in California in 1866, Forrest ordered him to stop being another Forrest, to stay in California, and to build a style of his own. He could not, of course, effect a radical change, especially in the Far West, where audiences still wanted plenty of noise and muscle for their money; but while resembling Forrest and playing mainly his

roles, McCullough gradually adapted them to his own personality, which was as naturally "genial" as Forrest's was bullying. New York did not see the new McCullough (mostly in non-Shakespearean roles) until 1874, two years after Forrest's death. At once the critics busied themselves pigeonholing him. Confirmed Forrestians put him down as only a mild copy; more "modern" critics saw the difference as a sign that "heroic" acting was becoming more civilized, that McCullough's gentler hero spoke to the new times better than had Forrest's brute at the barricades.

In 1877, McCullough studied the Delsartean method with Steele MacKaye and learned further how to discipline and control his power, to emphasize the subtler emotions, and to aim for coherent development of his roles. Only after these studies did he show his developed Shakespearean acting to the East. His improvement astonished them. His Lear and Othello were the most notable for their newfound clarity and rightness of structure. But McCullough had less than a decade to be known as a "national" actor. By 1883 he began to suffer nervous depression and then, like Lear, the agony of knowing he was losing his mind. He died in an asylum in 1885, at the age of fifty-three, his brain destroyed by paresis.

Shakespeare's Comedy to Midcentury

A few days before Edwin Forrest became an overnight star, James Henry Hackett, appearing at the Park as a Dromio in *The Comedy of Errors,* so exactly duplicated every look, gesture, and tone of his opposite number, Jack Barnes (late of London), that the audience, ecstatic in their confusion, could not tell which was which. Hackett, an incredibly gifted mimic, was even then preparing a more amazing feat of mimicry. On 12 December, one week to the day after Edmund Kean's last American performance of Richard III, Hackett played the same role in exact imitation. (There exists a copy of the play in which Hackett recorded every item of Kean's stage business and readings as he had observed them in a dozen viewings of Kean's performance.) His imitation was not a stunt but a genuine re-creation.

Hackett came from upstate New York, knew his country Yankee types well, and made them and other American originals his stock-in-trade, but it is his Falstaff, which he played for forty years, that keeps his name alive. Although he was America's best-loved Falstaff of the nineteenth century, his Falstaff probably would not much gratify a modern audience, for he made a morality of it, insisting on driving home serious lessons. He could be jolly in the farcical scenes, but he was always an example of wickedness to be corrected. He subtitled *The Merry Wives* on the playbill *Falstaff Outwitted by Women* and meant to show "how a couple of merry honest wives met the impudent advances of a vain old coxcomb" and brought about his punishment. In the *Henry* plays the "always moralizing dramatist" meant to teach young men the danger of "becoming corrupted by intimacy with old and vicious company" and to teach courtiers not to minister to the vices of great patrons, "lest they too, like Falstaff, be left to die in despair."

William Evans Burton was born in London in 1804 and received a classical education at St. Paul's School and Cambridge, from which he withdrew in 1825 to join a provincial company of actors. In 1834 he emigrated to Philadelphia and in 1837 moved to New York, where, says Odell, he "became a source of endless joy to untold thousands who regarded him as the supreme comic performer." From 1848 to 1856 he leased the Chambers Street Theatre, thereafter called Burton's, and gathered about him a company of comedians and farceurs. Burton's style is indescribable because it was so utterly protean. Though offstage he looked like a well-fed congressman, once in costume and character he could express through face and voice or mere silence uncountable absurdities. Someone said he could hold an audience convulsed with laughter for fifty minutes without speaking a line.

All the while his other self was a devout Shakespearean. But not until the spring of 1852 did he begin to take his Shakespearean opportunities in earnest. On 29 March he got up *Twelfth Night,* fitting his portly person to Sir Toby Belch. "He was admirably made up," said the *Albion,* "and revelled and rollicked with infinite gusto through the fun set down for him." Nor did he fail to let "the shrewd worldly wisdom peep at times from the full flood of his sottishness." This was a habit of Burton's, deeply ingrained from years of farce: for split seconds to step out of character and with a wink at the audience to invite them to join him in the fun. He was splendidly partnered by the Andrew Aguecheek of Lester Wallack, "the very essence of feebleness and thread-paperism."

From Sir Toby Belch to Falstaff was a natural progression. Burton followed the example of Charles Kean, who in the preceding autumn had staged *The Merry Wives* at the Princess's in London, applying to it the meticulous historical accuracy that would be his principal legacy to the rest of the century. Burton instructed his scene painter, in nine sets, to represent Windsor Town, Windsor Castle, and surroundings exactly as they appeared in the days of Henry IV and informed the audience on the playbill what they were looking at. He suppressed Falstaff's winks and wiggles; taking Sir John's word for it, he played him as a gentleman. The audience was baffled.

On 3 February 1854, Burton reached a peak in his career as a Shakespearean producer and actor. In *A Midsummer Night's Dream,* he was a lively, jolly, conceited Nick Bottom, much admired by his simple fellow artisans for his skills and his authority. Burton went all out for prettiness and historicity, adding, too, all the Mendelssohn music and many dances by fairies and satyrs. He loaded the playbill with information in the Charles Kean manner and published a twenty-four-page pamphlet describing his scenes and costumes and the scholarly authorities on which they were based. In his next production, *The Tempēst* (11 April 1854), Burton claimed to have cleansed the text of the Davenant-Dryden additions for the first time in America. He was, of course, following Macready, who had "restored" the text in 1838. In fact, his stage manager, John Moore, an Anglo-Irish actor and prompter, had brought to America a transcription of Macready's promptbook, so Burton had a well-worked version to guide him in his own restoration.

However small his stage, he managed to achieve some of the spectacular effects obligatory in the nineteenth century: in the opening storm scene a ship tossed among waves until it smashed to bits; Prospero waved his wand and a tree fell, giving him something to sit on; Ariel flew through the air suspended by slender ropes; Juno appeared in a rainbow with a pair of peacocks that spread their tails; and so forth.

The Winter's Tale, which opened on 13 February 1856, ran for several weeks, and was revived a year later, brought Burton's major Shakespearean work to a grand conclusion. Again, as Kean would do with this play two months later, he advertised the historical authenticity of the settings. In 1856, Burton bought Laura Keene's Varieties, where he carried on somewhat rockily through the financial depression of 1857, reviving his old farces and some of his Shakespeare productions and playing host to various starring actors who passed through. In May 1857 he presented the first New York appearance of the young Edwin Booth.

American Tragedians and Foreign Visitors in the Genteel Age

In mid-October 1864, as Edwin Booth was preparing for what became known as his "Hundred-Nights *Hamlet,*" he mentioned to his friend Adam Badeau that about the end of November "I shall be called upon to be genteel and gentle—or rather, pale and polite." Booth, half tongue-in-cheek, happened upon one word that we may take as a label for the years ahead—the Genteel Age. During this age (roughly the final third of the century) America developed a fair number of tragic and romantic Shakespeareans, native-born or at least trained in America. There also came from abroad an increasing number of Shakespeareans, each bringing his own manner of handling the plays. Some came for glory, others for adventure, and all of them for cash.

In the "slow-moving" world before, and even during, the industrial revolution, dramatic forms became ossified into a few sharply defined types—comedy, tragedy, farce, burlesque, for example—and acting, too, hardened into "lines," each line itself becoming conventionalized. Handbooks for expression of the "dramatic passions," their roots in oratorical practice of classical antiquity, proliferated; and the actor who lacked the means to "be" a character would perforce adopt the handbook conventions and go through the standard motions. As George Henry Lewes neatly described the process in England, the conventional actor would do as others before him had done: "His lips will curl, his brow wrinkle, his eyes will be thrown up, his forehead be slapped, or he will grimace, rant, and 'take the stage,' in the style which has become traditional, but which was perhaps never seen off the stage." Because of certain romantic influences in the arts flowing westward from Europe, combined with revulsion against the jingoistic excesses that incited the Astor Place riots, the art of tragic acting in midcentury America was tending toward subtlety, softness, and restraint.

One of the most promising of native-born tragedians was Edward Loomis Davenport. With his handsome face and figure, fine voice, intelligence, and taste, he was capable in his forties of superb performances of the greater tragic roles. Yet somehow—perhaps for lack of executive ability—he never could maintain a position of leadership in the profession. For a decade he worked out his apprenticeship, playing comic Yankees, melodrama villains, mere walk-ons, whatever came his way.

His career began to take shape in the fall of 1846 when Anna Cora Mowatt engaged him as her leading man. His "high moral character, his unassuming and gentleman-like manners," his versatility, and his usefulness as a coach so delighted her that she engaged him for three seasons, the first to tour America, the second and third to play in England. He stayed on in England for seven years, found an English wife (the actress Fanny Vining), and was well regarded by English audiences and critics. For two months in 1850–1851 he supported Macready at the Haymarket in his final run before retirement. During these years he came to admire the English for their diligent rehearsals, so unlike the lackadaisical preparations he had known in American theaters. He hoped someday to impose such discipline upon actors at home.

When he returned in 1854 he played Hamlet and Othello and delighted the critics with the polish he had acquired, his improved taste, and his mastery of technique. For two or three years, as he toured the country in a mainly classical repertory, he maintained the high artistic principles that he had espoused. But in 1857, when he took up management of New York's Chambers Street Theatre, he succumbed to the popular appetite for the topical and trivial; he abandoned actor training. Eventually he realized that he could never lighten "the lump of stupid self-satisfaction we call the profession." He vowed never again to volunteer advice, suggestion, or hint as to reading or stage business or even makeup to any actor in any play of his. He would "demand just one thing, my *cue.* As long as I got the word to speak on, all the rest might go to the devil!" And when he gave up directing his actors, the rehearsals shortened, the actors had more time for beer and pretzels, and soon they began calling him "a good fellow."

Happily, though, his career climaxed and closed in a burst of glory. When Edwin Booth went bankrupt in 1874 and lost his theater, it fell under the control of a pair of commercial managers, Henry

Jarrett and Henry Palmer, who undertook a series of classical revivals. The first and finest of these (27 December 1875) was *Julius Caesar,* and they called in Davenport for Brutus and Lawrence Barrett for Cassius, each man in his finest and long-established role. The scenery from Booth's own earlier production was available, and this, refurbished and expanded, made an eye-filling mise-en-scène. It ran for 103 consecutive performances and then went on the road for a grand total of 222 performances. The Davenport-Barrett combination was perfect in its contrasts: the one massive, slow, and commanding; the other slight, gaunt, swift-moving, and waspish. The quarrel between them in the fourth-act tent scene was one of the most celebrated passages of Shakespeare that the generation knew.

Edwin Booth

"Mr. Booth's *Hamlet* is the perfect expression of the artistic taste of our times. This taste is characterized . . . by the substitution of finish for feeling, elaborateness for earnestness, accuracy for emotion." Thus "Nym Crinkle," in the *World* newspaper the Sunday after Booth's greatest *Hamlet* opened in his own theater on 5 January 1870. Nym Crinkle could never be satisfied with any less potent a tragic hero than Forrest, and Booth was no Forrest. Slight, lithe, graceful, and handsome, Booth won the admiration and affection of American audiences from the mid-1860s until his last season on the stage. His range of roles was limited. Lack of size and weight prevented him from specializing in Macbeth and Othello, though it is clear that under challenge his emotional power quite overcame limitations of stature. And though he was a good companion in a quiet way to a limited number of intimates, sustained displays of geniality on stage embarrassed him; thus, he disliked playing Benedick. So, too, though in his younger days many women swooned in the presence of his Romeo, he came to "hate" lovers and never played Romeo again after the 1869 production that opened his theater. His strong suits were deep seriousness, intellectuality, and a certain engaging melancholy, which were the mainstays of his Hamlet and Brutus; burning passion, which fed many roles (notably Shylock); and a capacity for sardonic, biting humor, which sustained his Iago and Richard III. He was, moreover, praised for his beauty of speech.

For ten years Booth won a reputation (and ultimately defeat) as a manager and producer, and except for William Burton, he was the first important figure in the American theater to emulate the new British system of building up an entire and usually historically accurate mise-en-scène for each play. He had read J. W. Cole's *Life of Kean* (1859), and when he visited England in 1861, he heard much about the glories of Kean's nine-year tenure at the Princess's. In 1864, at the Winter Garden Theatre, he made the scenes and dresses of *Hamlet* (his "Hundred-Nights Hamlet") as authentic to tenth-century Denmark as research made possible. In April 1865 he withdrew from the theater when his mad brother assassinated President Lincoln, but nine months later popular demand drew him back. His first production in 1866, Bulwer's *Richelieu,* was mounted in seventeenth-century French palatial scenery.

His *Romeo and Juliet* was ready to open when on 23 March 1867 the Winter Garden was destroyed by fire. This disaster seems to have inspired Booth rather than depressed him, for he set about at once drawing up plans and raising money for a great "Temple to the Muses," which would not only house his own master productions but would also stand for centuries, like the great theaters of Europe. Booth's Theatre was a marvel for its time. It seated about eighteen hundred in orchestra, galleries, and boxes, with every comfort: perfect sight lines and acoustics, the air warmed and cooled by great fans above the ceiling, the auditorium illuminated by gaslight that could be dimmed or extinguished at the gas table and lighted by electric spark. Behind the curtain was a wholly original system of instant scene-changing, by which sets could be drawn up into, or lowered from, the flies, or thrust up from, and drawn down into, a thirty-two-foot cellarage through slits in the stage floor. Between the cost of the building, the expense of productions, the incompetence of his bookkeeper, and the chicanery of a financial "benefactor," Booth went deeply into debt. When the financial crash occurred in 1874, creditors moved in, and Booth had to declare bankruptcy.

About sixty-five plays were staged at Booth's Theatre during Booth's tenure, of which perhaps ten—including *Romeo and Juliet, Othello, Hamlet, Macbeth, Richelieu, Much Ado, The Winter's Tale,* and *Julius Caesar*—were given full treatment, the rest being decorated from stock. Booth, intent only on the perfection of the art, never counted the cost.

He found, too, that he could not retain a first-rate company. When he got Charlotte Cushman, for instance, she demanded such a salary that there was no profit. He could pay his old friend Lawrence Barrett, who was a star in circuits outside New York, only half what Barrett could earn on the road. As soon as any promising young actor made a noticeable success at Booth's, he went off to better wages elsewhere.

Booth's opener, *Romeo and Juliet,* on 3 February 1869, was a scenic triumph, but the acting, at least on opening night, was scandalously bad. During his tour he had become engaged to marry Mary McVicker and somehow succumbed to the delusion that she was an attractive actress. She was no Juliet. Intelligent, brisk, sharp, and witty, she set up a competition among New York critics to define her deficiencies. And as for Booth, in the "unseemly and crazy excitement of that night," as he put it, he completely lost sense of what he was doing. Later he got control of himself, and the production managed to hold on for fifty-eight nights. *Othello* followed, from 12 April to 29 May (forty-two nights). He led off as Othello, but after two weeks exchanged roles with Ned Adams and played Iago. "We don't like his Othello," said the *Daily Star,* "but go and see his Iago if you have to be carried on a litter—it is the very best of all he has ever done, possibly as he ever will do." Booth's own opinion, which he communicated to H. H. Furness, neatly sums up his new understanding of the role: "I think the 'light comedian' should play the villain's part, not the 'heavy man.'" Of all his productions at Booth's Theatre, *Hamlet* (5 January to 19 March 1870, sixty-four performances) was the most carefully prepared, drew the strongest box office, received the most voluminous commentary, and fixed Booth's American reputation then as "the greatest Hamlet of them all."

In the long run it was good that Booth's loss of his theater prevented any further pursuit of historical accuracy. A decade later in London, Booth came to understand the limitations of his approach when he put his best efforts into Shakespeare in shabby mountings at the Princess's but drew wretched audiences, while across town the public flocked to the fashionable Lyceum to see Tennyson's shabby play *The Cup* dressed up in the fanciest scenic finery that Henry Irving's most skilled scene painters could contrive. He wrote despairingly to William Winter, "The actor's art is judged by his costume and the scenery: if they are not 'esthetic' (God save the mark!) he makes no stir. . . . Chas. Kean, Fechter, & Irving have feasted the Londoners so richly they cannot relish undecorated dishes." He confesses that he had done the same ill work at home "but was fortunately checked, by fire first and afterwards by bankruptcy. I do not regret my losses now—since I've seen the evil results of 'grand revivals.'"

In 1875, Booth suffered a carriage accident that nearly killed him. For days he lay in a coma, and when he recovered, it was found that his left arm was broken. Clumsy surgeons set it badly, rebroke it, and set it again, but he could never use it thereafter. In performance he could gesture only with his right arm, while the left dangled helplessly at his side. On 25 October 1875 he returned to the New York stage under the auspices of Augustin Daly, who mounted his *Hamlet* and other regular plays in simple but decent decors and provided staging for *Richard II,* which Booth had never acted before, and *King Lear,* which he had not touched since 1857, in the standard acting version descended from the seventeenth-century corruption by Nahum Tate, and now was eager to undertake in an "arrangement" of Shakespeare's own text.

In 1876 he toured the South, where he had not been seen in over a quarter of a century, and in the fall of that year he accepted John McCullough's invitation to San Francisco. This was a curious experience, for in the West he played his standard pieces as he had developed them in the East, more and more in the direction of intimacy and delicate suggestion; but the Californians had recently been visited by the "brass-boweled" barnstormer Barry Sullivan and still liked their meat raw. The critics tended to write down Booth's Hamlet as "passable."

In 1883, Booth fulfilled a lifelong ambition to play Shakespeare in Germany. He came home exhausted, not to mention considerably out of pocket, for European excursions cost more than they brought in. And he was discouraged. For two seasons (1884–1886) Booth practically withdrew from the New York scene: he joined the Boston Museum Company, which throughout his professional career he had regarded as almost subprofessional. One more grand tour to replenish his bank account was all he could hope for.

At exactly the right moment his old friend Lawrence Barrett took charge, offering to become his managing partner. Barrett would provide a company, lay out a tour, plan a repertory—and all

Booth need do was act. This tour turned out to be five tours. In the first, in 1886–1887, Booth starred alone, doing 232 performance in sixty cities, and profiting over $212,000; in the second, third, and fifth, Barrett and Booth, "the loving brothers," traveled together, dividing roles in such plays as *The Merchant of Venice, Othello, Julius Caesar, King Lear,* and *Hamlet;* in the fourth season, Booth was teamed with Helena Modjeska. The exhausting but exhilarating routine ended only in 1891 with the sudden death of Barrett and the immediate retirement of America's best and best-loved actor of his time.

Lawrence Barrett

When Lawrence Barrett and Edwin Booth first met in 1857 at Burton's Theatre in New York, there was no question of precedence: Booth, at twenty-four, fresh from his apprenticeship in the West, had determined to make his way as a star, and Barrett, at nineteen, was merely a promising beginner in Burton's stock company. On 12 May 1857, when Booth played Hamlet, Barrett was his Laertes. And so it would always be: Booth as Hamlet, Shylock, Macbeth, and Barrett as Laertes, Bassanio, Macduff. But Barrett's range of roles far exceeded Booth's. Booth hung close to Hamlet, Iago (sometimes Othello), Richard III, Shylock, Brutus, Macbeth, and rarely two or three other Shakespearean roles, and outside Shakespeare, Bulwer's Richelieu and Bertuccio in *The Fool's Revenge.* Barrett played all these Shakespearean roles and as many more. In whatever he played he was expert, efficient, a good acting machine, but rarely endearing and somewhat less than great.

In February 1862, Barrett was with Booth at New York's Winter Garden at the lowest, sorriest time in Booth's whole career. Barrett carried the leads to the end of the season and through Booth's period of mourning and withdrawal from alcoholism, and in the fall of 1863 he was still on hand to play the Ghost to Booth's Hamlet. But this was not progress; he must keep out of Booth's shadow. In a bold move he abandoned New York and bought into the management of the Varieties Theatre in New Orleans. That city provided Barrett unrivaled opportunity to star in all the classic leads and a dozen modern pieces quite outside Booth's repertory or interest. He made himself known and popular in all the river towns from Memphis to

Pittsburgh. In December 1867 he joined John McCullough at Maguire's Opera House in San Francisco; his Hamlet and McCullough's Forrestian roles prompted men of means to build them a theater, the California, so huge and popular that the box office averaged close to a thousand dollars a night.

But this was not enough. Booth's Theatre had opened just two weeks after the California, and the fame of it had spread everywhere. In mid-December, Barrett wrote Booth, proposing "that some arrangement mutually advantageous might be made between us for the future." Booth could hardly have spent much thought on Barrett's vague proposal, for the very next night the curtain would rise on the greatest of all his Hamlets. In August 1870, Barrett sold his California interests and went to New York, not to Booth's but to Niblo's Garden, invited by Jarrett and Palmer for a month-long engagement. In the final week the management offered an all-star company in *Julius Caesar:* Barrett's fiery Cassius against the noble Brutus of E. L. Davenport, and Walter Montgomery, Mark Smith, and Madame Ponisi as major supports. The success was so great that Booth realized it was incumbent upon him to make room for Barrett, though the terms he could offer were pitiably less than Barrett could make on the road. Barrett would begin playing seconds to Booth, and Saturday nights were his to stage plays of his own choosing and take the profits.

Thus did Barrett arrive at his longed-for destination, but late in 1872 he had a bitter falling-out with Booth about who was to perform in the Barrett-acquired play *Marlborough.* Probably Barrett was lucky to be done with Booth, who was financially against the wall. The panic of 1874 hurt Barrett but did not destroy him, while Booth lost everything. In the fall of 1873, Barrett for the first time organized his own road company and played engagements in seventy-five cities east of the Mississippi. He played 248 performances of seven Shakespeare and twelve non-Shakespeare plays and learned the problems of carrying a whole company with him, and his reputation expanded widely. The grand climax of this period was his second call to New York by Jarrett and Palmer, who, having taken over Booth's Theatre and everything in it, proposed to create the *Julius Caesar* of the century. Their success was total. The run of the play, counting its road tours, far more than doubled the record of any Shakespeare in America. About 1880, Barrett and Booth succeeded in ending their old enmity and embarked on the series of coast-to-coast tours referred to above.

Charles Fechter

Charles Albert Fechter, who had been born in London and brought up in France and was one of Paris' leading performers of contemporary melodramas and romances, looked across the channel and decided it was time to rescue the London theater from the chains of convention, first by treating the English to his authoritative reading of modern French plays—in English, of course, which he spoke fluently though with a marked Gallic accent. Having delighted the English and made himself quite at home in London, he astounded everyone in 1861 by offering *Hamlet.* It was his purpose to bring Shakespeare's heroes down to earth from the unreal heights of posture, gesture, and rant. His Hamlet would be colloquial, suave, genteel, at home in parlor and boudoir. Hamlet was the character to start with (and to stop with, as it turned out, for his Othello failed). Hamlet is a gentleman, a courtier, a scholar, a lover, a wit, a good companion. Fechter further made him a dashing, joyous man of the world and startled the spectators with such novelties of line-reading and stage business that few would regret the loss of the moodiness and introversion expected of Hamlet. (Some readings were apparently the result of his imperfect understanding of the language.)

Fechter arrived in New York in the first days of 1870 and set up shop at Niblo's on 10 January. The timing was unfortunate if he intended to astonish with his Hamlet, for just five days earlier Booth had opened his master production of *Hamlet* at his own theater. Fechter bided his time with a month of *Ruy Blas* and *The Duke's Motto.* When Fechter did show *Hamlet* for six nights, the *New York Times* critic denied him "princeliness" and "repose," observed that he acted from "without" rather than from "within"—and finally declared him the best Hamlet he had ever seen! Booth, after all, he said, is only a high-grade eclectic artist, but Fechter is a genius, "the pre-Raphaelite of his art." Henry Clapp, a thoughtful Boston critic, also came down on the side of Fechter. His "genius is manifestly positive and aggressive rather than negative and receptive; he must reproduce Shakespeare, not reflect him." And "a genius like Fechter can neither be desired nor expected to represent the thought of

another mind without changing and coloring it by an alchemy of its own." Fechter persuaded most playgoers to accept the modern theater aesthetic, wherein Shakespeare's play is no longer the central object of interest except to the textual scholar, the literary critic, and the publisher of books for schoolrooms and library shelves. From Fechter to Jonathan Miller, the play is only raw material for the theater artist to convert into whatever pleases him and us, according to what we in our time happen to call "nature" or "reality."

Adelaide Neilson

Adelaide Neilson of England first visited America in 1872 and became by far the most enchanting Shakespearean actress then on the American stage. Americans first saw her as Juliet, the role for which she is best remembered. Critics recorded many of her points: the pretty way she kissed the spot on her hand that Romeo had kissed; her taking of the vial from Friar Lawrence not with a crescendo of terror but a cry of joy; the controlled delirium of the potion scene; and at the moment of death the beautiful action of drawing her dead husband's arm under her head. Year after year her Juliet continued to charm audiences. By 1874, it was noted, she had played Juliet nearly 800 times in England and America, but "she depicts her with as much freshness of color, spirit, and care as if she were her newest creation."

Viola was a role peculiarly fitted to her own personal qualities. As Henry Clapp said of her impersonation, "We can remember no representation of comedy so perfect as this. The spell seemed to be cast over every listener, and to maintain its sway in face and speech long after the curtain had fallen upon the fifth act." A week after *Twelfth Night,* Daly produced *Cymbeline* for her (14 May 1877), and her Imogen, though seen briefly, seems to have embodied and improved upon the best of all her earlier roles. The role obviously called for a vastly greater range of emotion than any other in her repertory.

Tommaso Salvini

Tommaso Salvini was born to play Othello. Not especially tall, he was broad-shouldered and heavy-set, with large features, flashing black eyes, and an amazingly powerful but controllable voice. He could express every emotion within the tragic-heroic range. He certainly belonged to no other range. The great black mustache that he cultivated in his twenties and never removed was a powerful declaration of his heroic masculinity. His greatest attribute was his voice, which Towse of the *Post* called "one of the most powerful, flexible, and mellifluous organs ever implanted in a human throat." It was natural that in 1853, when Giulio Carcano's translation of Shakespeare came into his hands, he fixed upon Othello, the most muscular and soldierly of the tragic heroes, and made a profound study of it. He read Cinthio's novella, studied the history of Venice, and investigated in depth the nature of the Moors, their art of war, religious beliefs, and passions. He came to the play knowing more about the Moors than Shakespeare knew (too much perhaps) or any of the generations of actors since Shakespeare's.

He went to New York first in 1873, and altogether five times down to 1889–1890, and on his first visit performed in fifteen cities, from Boston to New Orleans. At first he brought an all-Italian company; but in 1880 and after, he played in Italian, with an English-speaking company. The mixture of languages annoyed some, but audiences soon realized it was much easier to concentrate on Othello's part and Salvini's playing of it if they did not have to struggle to understand all the other speakers.

Edward Tuckerman Mason, who devoted an entire book to a description of Salvini's performance, emphasized Salvini's "naturalness" and contrasted it to the artificiality of other Othellos. In Nym Crinkle's eyes, and to his vast delight, Salvini had once more revealed Othello in the manner and spirit that Shakespeare intended—not as a priestly protector of marriage laws but as just what certain hostile critics had labeled him, an "elemental ruffian" and a "sweating beast."

Salvini's Lear may have been one of his most attractive roles, but it did not receive the appreciation it deserved. Unlike Forrest and all the other remembered Lears, he laid aside the concept of kingship and command, and, with his penchant for realism, projected the character as, above all, an eighty-year-old man.

Mary Anderson

In the late nineteenth century, the number of women on American stages increased markedly, not only as star attractions but in positions of authority—managing their own companies and directing their own affairs. The greater number came from abroad, for in this, as in other aspects of theater, conservative America followed the leaders. But we had a few of our own. When Booth and Barrett in the 1880s looked over the ranks of male colleagues for someone they could count on to carry forward their tradition, they found none with sufficient vigor, style, and devotion to the classic drama. Failing in their search for dramatic heroes they set their hopes on tall, queenly, divinely fair Mary Anderson.

After various provincial efforts in the South and West, Anderson dared New York in 1877. Her work was raw, but everyone acknowledged her beauty. She possessed, said the *Herald*, "a singularly sweet organ-toned voice." When, in 1883, Henry Irving left his Lyceum in London for his first American tour, manager Henry Abbey invited Anderson to take Irving's place. As a matter of fact, she took the Lyceum for two seasons. The first season she did no Shakespeare but only nineteenth-century plays. The London critics acknowledged her beauty but strove to deride her lack of freshness, spontaneity, and "the divine fire." All season they declared that she had talent but no genius; but somehow they could not affect her popularity, and she became the rage of London.

In her second Lyceum season she chose to do Juliet. The fact that Irving and Ellen Terry had mounted a splendid *Romeo and Juliet* two seasons earlier did not deter her. She began, like a true child of the nineteenth century, by visiting Verona, with an artist to sketch every site that she could possibly use. From these sketches, London's finest scene painters created an authentic Verona on the Lyceum stage. The labor of preparing the staging so exhausted Anderson that she had neither the time nor strength to rethink and rehearse her Juliet as she ought to have done, and on her opening night (1 November 1884) she lapsed into crudities that fresh study could have prevented.

The critics let fly at her. According to the *Saturday Review,* she was all poses and attitudinizing and girlish playfulness when she should be radiant with the glow of passion; she lapsed into an American accent; she could not speak blank verse; her lament over Romeo's banishment was mere rant; she vulgarized scenes by crude stage business; and so on. But when she brought *Romeo and Juliet* to America in the fall of 1885, it was received in high favor.

In America, that autumn, while her *Romeo and Juliet* pleased nearly everyone, her opening with *As*

You Like It (12 October 1885) drew a good many negative critiques. In 1887–1888 she again took the London Lyceum to revive the rarely performed *The Winter's Tale.* And as an even bolder stroke, counting on a couple of lines that mention the resemblance of mother and daughter, she decided to double as Hermione and Perdita (the first actress in modern times to do so). She also cut the play in half, retaining few more than 1,500 of Shakespeare's 3,075 lines. Her bowdlerizing was absurd: she could not make herself say, "The bug which you would fright me with," "strumpet," "first fruits of my body," "the innocent milk," or "the child-bed privilege."

The *Saturday Review* critic asserted that "Miss Mary Anderson has again done what within her lay to bring Shakespeare into disrepute" and prophesied that she would "drive educated audiences from the theatre." He could not, being so right, be so wrong. *The Winter's Tale* became the most celebrated and popular play in Anderson's repertory. In America it was held to be her masterpiece. Even Nym Crinkle thought that "in Hermione and Perdita she has found her metier."

Lillie Langtry

Lillie Langtry, the daughter of an Anglican priest on the isle of Jersey, came into the theater only out of necessity. She lapsed into an unfortunate marriage; became the mistress of Edward, prince of Wales; and carried on a passionate love affair with his nephew, Louis Battenberg, who fathered her child. In 1881, when she returned from Jersey, where she had gone to wait out the birth, she was without money or opportunity. The likeliest market for her assets—beauty, wit, and notoriety—was the stage.

London first saw her in Shakespeare on 23 September 1882, when she presented herself as Rosalind with a scratch company that she was about to take with her to America. Most of the critics treated her sympathetically: not yet a finished artist but a promising one, who would have to be taken seriously after the rough edges were smoothed during her forthcoming season in America.

From 23 October 1882, the day Mrs. Langtry landed in New York, that city was aflame with Langtry fever. On 6 November an audience of the wealthiest and most fashionable assembled to inspect this internationally famous professional beauty. They were disappointed. By 13 November,

her first night as Rosalind, the Langtry fever had broken. Fashion stayed at home and speculators hawked tickets in the street at a dollar apiece. The major critics condemned her Rosalind thoroughly: it was "a great disappointment"; "she reads her lines badly"; "she cannot play Rosalind at all."

During the week of 9 December a Langtry scandal broke upon the town. For several weeks past she had been seen everywhere with a dashing young man-about-town, and word got out that they spent nights as well as days together. When she left New York for her tour of the country, her reputation was so besmirched that it would have sunk another woman. But not this one. Her fortunes battened on gossip and hostility. Wherever she went, often with the young man in tow, crowds stormed the box office. In April 1883 she arrived back in New York with a clear profit of well over $100,000.

During the 1880s she would spend four more seasons in America, drawing many hundreds of thousands of dollars. From the beginning she vowed that she would be recognized not merely as a beauty but as a successful actress; and to the world's rising amazement, she achieved that goal. In her *As You Like It* in February 1889, the *Spirit of the Times* could not imagine "a more charming, piquant, and dainty Rosalind." Her beauty of person and beauty of speech contributed much to her success, of course, and the fact that she was not "actressy" but projected her own wit and personal charm through characters like Rosalind—in short her "naturalness"—surprised and delighted her beholders. As Lady Macbeth, she was unlike Charlotte Cushman in every way imaginable. But many who had come to scoff on 21 January 1889 remained to cheer. It was a "new" Lady Macbeth, one that New York had never imagined. Nor had London imagined it until just three weeks earlier, when Ellen Terry had similarly overturned the common preconception of the role. This was not the traditional virago, bullying her husband to action, but womanly, wifely, and loving, wooing and seducing Macbeth to his course of action, not driving him.

Helena Modjeska

Helena Modjeska was born in Poland, became an actress there, and rose to the top of the profession, but as a Shakespearean she was an American. She came to America with her husband, Karol Chlapowski, Count Bozenta, when she was thirty-six, knowing but a few words of English and very little Shakespeare, even in translation. She went to San Francisco, studied English with a coach for some months, and persuaded John McCullough and Barton Hill, managers of the California Theatre, to give her a hearing. On 20 August 1877 she made a successful debut in Scribe's *Adrienne Lecouvreur* and a few days later played Ophelia and, within a week, Juliet. She played Juliet occasionally from 1878; but not until 1882, and after one season of polishing her English in London, did she offer herself as Rosalind and Viola. Thereafter she added Imogen, Desdemona, Julia, Isabella, and Beatrice. When she joined Booth for a season in 1889, she had to revive Ophelia and study Lady Macbeth and Portia afresh. Later she added Queen Katharine, Cleopatra, and even, briefly, Constance in *King John.*

During her thirty-year American career, she played fourteen Shakespearean roles, exceeding in range as well as number the repertory of any other American actress of her time. And she carried this repertory, along with her many non-Shakespearean roles, throughout the nation. She played in over 225 towns and cities in thirty-nine of the then forty-five states, and in five provinces of Canada. More truly than any other Shakespearean actress of the day, she served the entire country. And of all the many continental actors who came to America in those prosperous times, she was the only one who made herself an American.

Some objection was made to her ineradicable foreign accent. Her voice was as beautiful as a flute, but she could not altogether master the Anglo-American rhythms of speech, especially in the speaking of verse; and often well-known lyric passages came out of her as explanatory prose, for she had got the sense but not the music. On the other hand, her ignorance of Anglo-American points in certain roles was a blessing. She studied the roles for the first time unaffected by stale tradition, and thus passed over many too well expected points and created others no one had ever thought of.

Henry Irving and Ellen Terry

Henry Irving and his leading lady, Ellen Terry, first arrived in America on 24 October 1883 and were heralded by Stephen Fiske, in the *Spirit of the Times,* as "the dramatic event of the week, of the season,

of the century." No actor in history, he said, ever held so high a place on the English stage as Irving held at that moment. Not only was he worthy successor to the great line of English tragedians, but he had also revolutionized all regular methods of company management and the staging of plays. No actor before him had played so many parts (nearly 700, Fiske had been told), played a Shakespearean role for so many consecutive nights (200 nights of Hamlet, 210 of Benedick, 250 of Shylock), or played for so much money.

Hamlet, in which Irving made his first great Shakespearean success, playing it in 1874 for 200 successive performances, long remained his favorite role. In it, he most conspicuously defied playhouse tradition (many would say he defied the art of the play) by imposing on the role his newfound "realism," his "natural treatment and colloquial style." He intended to realize a Hamlet who was no mere playactor or declaimer but a deeply troubled and thoroughly believable human being.

American audiences and critics were much taken with Irving's elaborate scenery and meticulous management but puzzled, to say the least, by his person and performance. Admittedly he was "interesting" and probably brainy, and as the years passed and he came again and again, the assumption grew that he must be a very great actor. But from the beginning there were objections to his physical and vocal eccentricities and mannerisms.

Many Americans were astounded at what they saw and heard when Irving appeared before them. After his opening in *The Bells,* young Harrison Grey Fiske wrote in the *New York Dramatic Mirror:* "Nothing that has been said about Mr. Irving's celebrated 'mannerisms' has exaggerated them. They are almost past belief. His mannerisms . . . consist of a remarkable style of walking and gesticulating, a hitherto unknown perversion of the English tongue, and a delivery which is like no other in the whole world." He remarked that Irving's "utterance is slow and fitful, sentences being pumped out, with evidences of awful effort, in short sections. . . . Stress is laid on the wrong syllables, emphasis is given to wrong words, and the meaning of lines is frequently perverted. . . . The words themselves are often rendered unintelligible by inexplicable mispronunciations." All of this was in line with Irving's insistence on the primacy of the actor, which set him free not only from "the book" but also from tradition.

In *Much Ado About Nothing,* which he played throughout the country in 1883–1884, Ellen Terry always carried off the honors. Irving's Benedick was generally regarded as only tolerable, but Terry's Beatrice was so much loved that Irving would bring *Much Ado* to America twice more, in 1884 and 1893. She, no more than Irving, felt constrained by tradition or by the script, and her Beatrice was a novelty. In Victorian eyes, Shakespeare's Beatrice was a bit "unwomanly," perhaps at times something of a virago, but nothing shrewish or mannish was apparent in Terry's performance. As a Boston critic put it, she had simply reshaped the role so that it was "quite too much like Rosalind, entirely reconstructed on a nineteenth century plan, obviously more feminine and gentle than Shakespeare intended." All the same, he continued, she was "about as bewitching as it is given to any mortal to be upon the stage."

The mise-en-scène of Irving's *Merchant of Venice* had been created at the Lyceum on short notice, and by Lyceum standards it was regarded as comparatively simple (evidently more painted drops than "built scenes"). Yet, up to 1883, American audiences had never been treated to anything so satisfying. "It was the very poetry of the scene painter's and stage manager's art," declared the critic of the Boston *Evening Transcript,* and the *Spirit of the Times* was gratified that the stage was not overcrowded with scenery, properties, or people.

The last Shakespeare production that Irving introduced to America was *Macbeth;* the first-night audience wanted to be enthusiastic, but their attempts fell flat. As expected, Irving's concept of Macbeth ran counter to stage tradition. According to most critics of the day it also violated the text. Irving rejected out of hand the traditional concept of Macbeth as "a good man who has gone wrong under the influence of a wicked and dominant wife," and took to the lecture platform to explain his own concept. Irving so slurred the better elements in Macbeth's nature, as exhibited in the first two acts, that one could not perceive in him any struggle between the powers of good and evil. Terry's Lady Macbeth came off much better. Most critics accepted her joyously. From the wealth of annotation in her rehearsal books we can believe that she thought more deeply about this role than any of her "easier" ones. Of the mise-en-scène of the six Shakespeare productions that Irving brought to America, that of *Macbeth* was praised above all the rest. "It may be doubted," said Jeannette Gilder, "when this tragedy ever before was produced with such pictorial treatment, such appreciation of the spirit of poetry and of fateful portent that pervades it."

American critics argued endlessly about Irving's worth as an actor, but no one doubted his contribution to the theater in his function as a manager. He depended on the most esteemed artists of the day, from Pre-Raphaelites like Sir Edward Burne-Jones to academic neoclassicists like Sir Lawrence Alma-Tadema, to design scenery; the finest scene painters, such as Hawes Craven, William Telbin, and Joseph Harker, to execute the designs; Charles Cattermole and Alice Comyns Carr to design the costumes; and Edward German and Sir Arthur Sullivan to compose the music.

Herbert Beerbohm Tree

One of Irving's young rivals, Herbert Beerbohm Tree, shared with him the belief that what makes the difference between great acting and what Irving would call mere mumming was the projection of the actor's "own humanity": "You cannot imagine a characterless person playing the great characters of Shakespeare.... It requires individuality, to realise the creations of the master brain." It was Tree's boast, confirmed repeatedly by his wife, that he never "studied" a role (never, when undertaking a classic role, looked into the traditional modes in which it had been played) but rather drifted into a role, improvising business and even language as rehearsals proceeded. Needless to say, Tree's "individuality" was very unlike Irving's. Irving was a formidable person—proud, reserved, domineering, aloof. Tree was a companionable person—carefree, playful, dandiacal, whimsical, witty, boyishly eager to please and to be pleased. Tree's biographer Hesketh Pearson says there can be no doubt that Irving was "a far greater actor. Irving enthralled an audience; Tree entertained it."

When Tree began to play Shakespeare in 1889, he chose *The Merry Wives of Windsor* (not, to be sure, a play that Irving would have touched), and in 1892 he undertook *Hamlet.* By 1895 he was ready to follow the Irving pattern of touring with his company in America, but for all Tree's affability, wit, and desire to please, for all his well-advertised candidacy as successor to Irving, he roused little enthusiasm from the American critics. The *New York Sunday Times,* among others, recalled Henry James's assessment of Tree's original London Falstaff as mere scenery: "Why Falstaff's very person was nothing *but* scenery. A false face, a false figure, false hands, false legs—scarcely a square inch on which the irrepressible humour of the rogue could break into illustrative touches."

Tree's Hamlet, which he exhibited at Abbey's a week later, was treated somewhat less harshly, though largely because of its elegant appearance. The American critics had their own terms of dismissal, of which the commonest was "melodrama." Tree had so far yielded to the fashion of musical accompaniment that he had commissioned George Henschel to compose an extensive score, Wagnerian in manner, with a leitmotiv for each important scene and character. The emotional appeal of this music, together with tricky lighting effects, seemed often to play Shakespeare off the stage, to reduce the text to the status of libretto. More damaging still was Tree's inability to conceive and execute a wholly consistent study of Hamlet. Jeannette Gilder, for example, pointed out that he depended altogether on externals. Tree's response to the critical bombardment was characteristically good-humored. He got up a lecture, "Hamlet from an Actor's Prompt Book," which he delivered at Harvard a month later. The opening gambit of his lecture was a half-playful claim for infallibility, based on something like a Socratic chain of inspiration descending from muse, to poet, to performer.

For nearly twenty years Tree kept to London, but in the autumn of 1915, he accepted a call from Triangle-Reliance of Hollywood to make a series of Shakespeare motion pictures. In 1916 he completed a film of *Macbeth.* Unfortunately, though it was handsomely reviewed, it failed so dismally at box offices that the company abandoned plans for further Shakespeares. Meanwhile, he found reason to return to the American stage. The year 1916 was the tercentenary of Shakespeare's death, and since the European nations were totally preoccupied with tearing each other to pieces, it was mainly left to America to do the honors. Tree, eager to participate, arranged with Triangle-Reliance to interrupt his film work to join the New York celebrations.

Tree's first contribution, which opened on 14 March 1916, was a revival of his 1910 production of *Henry VIII,* which he brought from London, lock, stock, and barrel. It was quite in character for Shakespeare's supreme pageant-master to put forward this most flamboyantly pictorial and archaeologically correct production—his ultimate development in what he referred to as "the modern manner." We must avail ourselves of those adjuncts that, in these days, science and art place at the manager's right hand. We must grant him the crowds and armies, the pride, pomp, and circumstance that he calls for everywhere in his work. In order further to achieve this "modern manner," Tree cut *Henry VIII* to the quick, reducing it, as was his wont, from five acts to three, and offering, with just enough language to hold it together, a three-and-a-half-hour banquet of pictures, processions, music, dance, and pantomime.

Henry VIII prospered for six weeks, but on 8 May, having promised New York not only a play but also a festival, Tree laid it by and opened a two-week run of *The Merchant of Venice.* Interest ran high, for New York had never seen Tree's famous Shylock and his Portia was to be Elsie Ferguson, a young actress with an enormous following. Her fans greeted her with an ovation almost embarrassingly long, but then had to settle for something less than a satisfying Portia. Tree got less sympathetic treatment. Never, said one critic, had a New York audience seen the text of the play "so excised, transposed, and otherwise altered to suit the convenience of an actor whose chief efforts are for the sake of spectacular effect." *Life* magazine complained that the impulse toward "realism" got so out of hand that in many passages "the incidental music and the work of the picturesque supernumeraries was permitted to interfere with the real action as interpreted by the speaking characters." It was Tree's cleverness in his own performance that most distracted his best critics and belittled him in their estimation. Whatever the critics' irritation over this business (some did praise it), audiences greeted it with a storm of applause, as if it were the finest passage Shakespeare ever thought of.

To round off his festival, on 25 May, Tree offered his *Merry Wives of Windsor,* which the American critics had treated so scornfully in 1895. Probably remembering the harsh critiques, Tree wanted to prove his Falstaff to Americans after all. During the last twenty years he had played the role happily in London many dozens of times and felt he deserved an American reappraisal. He was right. In 1916 everyone agreed that his Falstaff was far superior to either his Shylock or his Wolsey, and even the insatiable perfectionist Towse found *The Merry Wives* the best in pictorial quality, in ingenuity of stage business, and in faithfulness to text of all of Tree's contributions to the tercentenary. No one at this time quarreled with his outlandish makeup, and apparently over the long years of playing the part Tree had extended his vocal range.

Johnston Forbes-Robertson

Happily for the record of foreign visitors, a near contemporary of Sir Herbert's—less aggressively "theatrical" but, in his one great role of Hamlet, far more gratefully remembered—was Johnston Forbes-Robertson. The son of an art critic, he aspired to a career as a painter, and only by chance drifted into the acting profession. Thanks to his rich voice, handsome face, and natural intelligence, he became much in demand—an "actor's actor"—to play supporting roles. In 1897, when he was forty-four, Henry Irving offered him the use of the Lyceum Theater and urged him to undertake Hamlet. Bernard Shaw, who admired him for his braininess and good taste, counseled him and prophesied his success, for according to Shaw Hamlet is not dominated by the common passions, like Romeo or Othello, but by intellectual passion. He is a thinking hero, "one whose passions are those which have produced the poetry, the art, and the statecraft of the world." True to Shaw's expectation, Forbes-Robertson's Hamlet was accepted at once by London audiences as the ideal Hamlet of the new day.

In 1903 word that Forbes-Robertson would bring his Hamlet to America roused no fever of expectation like that which preceded Irving twenty years earlier. Informed critics and the cognoscenti, of course, were eager for his Hamlet, reputed to be so unlike any other, so picturesque, so untheatrical, sane, beautiful to look upon, so modern in interpretation yet so exquisite in delivery of Shakespeare's poetry. But when he sailed in September 1903, following the advice of American managers based on obscure commercial intentions, he left his *Hamlet* production in storage and brought as his main piece his latest London success, a sentimentalized dramatization of Kipling's *The Light That Failed.* Word was given out that he would postpone Shakespeare until his second visit a year later. But sometime in the early winter Forbes-Robertson dispatched his brother Ian to London to fetch the *Hamlet* sets and costumes from storage. After training his company in their more demanding roles and trying out the production in other cities, he introduced his *Hamlet* to New York on 7 March 1904.

It was not the happiest of opening nights. For some reason the stagehands at the Knickerbocker made a concerted effort to spoil the occasion, bungling the scene changes, cursing and swearing in the wings, wandering in their shirt sleeves in sight of the audience. It was noticeable, too, alas, that most of the actors were unworthy of their Shakespearean assignments. Yet of Forbes-Robertson's performance Adolph Klauber could declare in his *New York Times* review that "it has been accepted by intelligent playgoers everywhere as the one truly great Hamlet of the modern stage," and "the result was such an evening of Shakespearean enjoyment as comes once or twice in a generation." Inevitably there were objections, especially from the older critics. Towse of the *Evening Post* suggested that playgoers schooled in earlier traditions "might be inclined to deny that Mr. Robertson's conception is that of Hamlet at all." Many "old-fashioned folk" will accuse this "nervous, intellectual, impulsive, and essentially modern actor" of committing "a most deplorable sacrifice—of poetic and romantic elevation—in fine, of those very qualities which most enthrall and encourage the imagination." Klauber tells us that Forbes-Robertson

> impersonates in the highest degree the modern feeling for simple and flawlessly human art. . . . As Forbes-Robertson sits in a leather arm chair . . . the thoughtful profile, the melancholy luminous eyes, the simple dignified attitude suggest nothing so much as the Prince of Denmark. On the stage these attributes heighten and kindle under the spell of beautiful thought and gracious human emotion, but they retain their quality of exquisitely modulated lifelikeness. As for his voice—but words fail for that voice, leaving the . . . most opulent dictionary bankrupt. If it is less golden and crimson in its emotional suggestion, it is more than silver. In its moments of repression it mutters sonorously like an organ, and like an organ it swells in passionate utterance with a thousand musical modulations. It caresses, it pleads, it sobs, and it cries out in pain. And every tone is replete with delicate thought and apt meaning.

Forbes-Robertson always believed that Klauber's long and eloquent review was the making of his reputation in America.

Not long after his New York success in 1904, Forbes-Robertson concluded his American tour with a surprising gesture. In 1895, George Pierce Baker had erected a reconstructed Elizabethan stage in Sanders Theatre at Harvard University for a production of Jonson's *The Silent Women;* and for several years he and other members of the Harvard English faculty had been studying Shakespeare and other Renaissance plays in the light of that experiment. When Baker heard that the great Hamlet was coming to America, he invited him to play on "Shakespeare's own stage." Accordingly, after special adjustment of text and stage business and some special rehearsals, on 5 and 6 April 1904 for the first time in America *Hamlet* was performed by professional actors in a setting very like that for which the play was written.

Thereafter Forbes-Robertson came to America frequently, usually bringing his American-born wife, Gertrude Elliott, as his leading lady. He played Hamlet regularly, of course, together with a mixed repertory of modern roles. In 1913 he brought a company of over sixty performers and aides, nine carloads of scenery, and a repertory of eight plays, including *Hamlet.* During this visit he performed two of his Shakespearean roles that few Americans had ever seen. Shylock, which he offered at the Shubert beginning on 21 November, he had played only rarely. Forbes-Robertson's Shylock was more nearly "the Jew that Shakespeare drew" than the more majestic and lofty Shylock of Irving. As H. T. Parker pointed out, year by year Irving built his Shylock into an apotheosis of the finer and nobler traits of the character, while Forbes-Robertson delivered only what he found in the text. He emphasized hatred of Christians and eagerness for revenge.

On 15 December he offered New York his second Shakespearean novelty—Othello, a role that he had played only occasionally since 1897. Most professional observers found that Othello was simply outside Forbes-Robertson's range. Klauber put the case almost as Shaw might have: "Forbes-Robertson . . . is essentially an actor of the intellect, with a sensitive, sympathetic organism capable of very definite and beautiful gradations of emotion. His best effects are produced through processes that suggest a ruling mentality in the man. That is one of the things that makes his Hamlet extraordinary."

After his 1913–1914 tour and a year of rest he returned to America for his farewell, traveling 18,000 miles and playing one- and two-night stands in 118 smaller towns and cities where he had never been seen. It would not do to call Forbes-Robertson the greatest Shakespearean to visit America during the generation before the World War I, for his Shakespearean roles were few. But for his Hamlet alone he may surely be called the finest.

Augustin Daly and the Shakespeare Comedies

Augustin Daly was not an actor but a director-producer. The English artist W. Graham Robertson defined one half of Daly with keen insight: "Daly must have been a great actor who could not act. He was rough and uncouth, with harsh utterance and uncultured accent; a singer without a voice, a musician without an instrument." So he used his performers to do what he could not do. He claimed that there were no stars in his theater, but over the years, he depended on four principal actors: for comic old ladies, Mrs. George Gilbert; for male low comedy, James Lewis; for romantic male leads, John Drew (who abandoned Daly in 1892); and for romantic female leads, Ada Rehan. Nym Crinkle touches lightly on Daly's authority over the physical production in a couple of sentences about Daly's *Midsummer Night's Dream:* "Mr. Daly controls every movement of every actor, every fairy, every super, the angle of every piece of furniture in his production of the *Dream.* There isn't a hairpin that doesn't get its point from him."

His house rules approached the ridiculous in secretiveness. Rehearsals were strictly closed; members of the company were never to be interviewed on any subject whatever. They were even forbidden to walk along Broadway, lest they be recognized and accosted by strangers. No one could bring up a matter of business except in Daly's office, and then only by appointment. No one was allowed to say "Good morning" to him unless he spoke first. And partly by threats, partly by favors, he controlled most of the New York press. William Winter of the *Tribune,* the "Dean" of the critics, was in his pocket. He paid Winter for arranging acting versions of the classics, for vetting versions arranged by others, for writing introductions to his acting versions as printed.

Between 1869, when he first took up management at the Fifth Avenue Theatre, and 1877, when he failed financially, Daly seeded into his busy program a surprising amount of Shakespeare. In 1869 he entertained the English actress Mary Scott-Siddons, whose repertory included *Twelfth Night, As You Like It,* and *Much Ado.* In 1875 he reintroduced Edwin Booth to the stage after his near-fatal carriage accident and, for the only time in his career, put his company to work at Shakespearean tragedy, supporting Booth in *Hamlet* and *Othello,* and setting him up in new productions of *Richard II* and *King Lear.* In 1877, Adelaide Neilson's third

American visit brought him her lovely Viola, Imogen, and Juliet. Besides these, moreover, he produced four Shakespeares with his own company.

After bankruptcy he spent a sabbatical overseas. When he resumed management in the fall of 1879, he held off doing Shakespeare; but in 1886 he began as he had begun in 1872, with *The Merry Wives,* the first of ten Shakespeares with which he would make his reputation in the next dozen years.

William Winter, his dramaturg and literary adviser, spelled out principles of emending plays for the stage which served Daly very well. He began with the pious principle that it was "presumption," it was "sacrilege," to touch even reverently the work of "the divine William." That understood, he proceeded with the "touching" on the basis of these principles: (1) Shakespeare put his works together so poorly for use on the modern stage that we must improve them. (2) It is impossible to act Shakespeare as the text is written; indeed, "a servile fidelity to the original text is not . . . a sign of either good judgment or practical scholarship." (3) Every play must be cut to a playing time of three hours at most. (4) All "foul or vulgar" language must be suppressed. (5) Descriptive passages, which only duplicate what the scene painter can express better, are dispensable. (6) Merely "literary" passages, which impede action, must go.

The Merry Wives of Windsor in 1886 was only mildly successful, the actors in their fancy dresses being altogether too young, brisk, and pretty to match the country town milieu of the play; and after Winter's frenetic bowdlerizing, the text offered little more substance than any Victorian farce. With *The Taming of the Shrew* a year later, Daly enjoyed his first unalloyed triumph. Whereas *The Merry Wives* called for a dozen superb comedians, the life of *The Shrew* depended simply on two —Ada Rehan and John Drew as Kate and Petruchio—and these, evenly matched, were the best pair of romantic comedians that Daly ever owned. Rehan took the honors, of course, from her first entrance—a pillar of fire, "a woman of the passionate red Italian loveliness to which the Venetian school of painting has accustomed us." As Graham Robertson put it, "Not a whit of her shrewishness did she spare us; her storms of passion found vent in snarls, growls, and even inarticulate screams of fury; she paced hither and thither like a caged wild beast, but her rages were magnificent, like an angry sea or a sky of tempest; she blazed a fiery comet

through the play, baleful but beautiful." Whip-cracking Drew took his share of applause, too, driving the play along with the excitement of a chariot race. When Daly took the play abroad, the actors were lionized by all society, perhaps the first American Shakespeare to achieve unequivocal London approval.

If Ada Rehan astonished the world and won its admiration with her Katherine, she won its affection with her Rosalind in *As You Like It.* The role of Orlando had not much to offer John Drew, and after this he left the company; but Rosalind, whether in "the sweetness, the passion, and the buoyancy" of the first act or the "gleeful animal spirits" of the forest scenes, played an unmitigated triumph. In England all the profession, from Helen Faucit to Ellen Terry, and literary figures from Justin McCarthy to Thomas Hardy, poured out their praises. Rosalind was doubtless the most joyous experience of Miss Rehan's professional life.

Not all of Daly's productions were so happy as these, or so free from well-merited objection. His *Midsummer Night's Dream* was little better than a box of ingenious stage tricks. His *Twelfth Night* was an absurd reduction of the play to a prettiness of music, moonlight, and pink roses. His *Tempest* was a clumsily managed set of unworkable devices. His *Merchant of Venice* lacked a Shylock. Again and again he was attacked for butchering texts, for garishness, outmoded methods, crass showmanship, and bad taste; and his relations with the press and with professional rivals were quite in tune with the age of the Robber Barons. But his record cannot be forgotten.

Richard Mansfield

When Booth and Barrett were organizing their tours in the late 1880s, they had considerable difficulty in filling their companies with actors truly capable of supporting their high endeavors. The pickings were slim. As popular taste for Shakespeare and the classics, classically performed, gave ground to taste for new plays, fewer and fewer young persons coming into the profession concerned themselves much with perfecting the histrionic techniques by which Booth and his father before him were judged great. If in America there did emerge from the crowd of mediocrities a reasonably effective and classic-style actor—a Louis James, a James O'Neill, or a Frederick Warde—he would take himself out of the market, assemble his own company, and set off as a star in his own right. And finally the command of the Shakespeare stage in America was often usurped by foreign visitors.

It is doubtful that Booth and Barrett would ever have seriously considered Richard Mansfield, a German-born, English-educated actor who had not yet attempted Shakespeare or even "found himself," except as a popular musical entertainer and character actor in certain spectacular and peculiarly repulsive roles. Yet Mansfield had a remarkable range of talents, and if he had lived a decade longer (and been spared a certain meanness of character), he might finally have fulfilled the Booth-Barrett hopes for the future of classic tragedy. As it was, he played only four leading Shakespeare roles and never touched the great ones. He was handsome enough, not tall but well-built, with a voice of great power.

Mansfield was determined to conquer London and even to outshine Irving, whom he had somehow come to distrust. He would produce Shakespeare and lay plans for a grand revival of *Richard III.* "Colley Cibber was to be entirely discarded, and Shakespeare enthroned once more," Mansfield declared in *Harper's Weekly* as late as 1890, but what he had actually staged was a hodgepodge of Cibber, Shakespeare, and "history." He claimed in a letter to Winter that he had used Cibber's structure, Shakespeare's language, and the "truth" about Richard, duke of Gloucester. The London critics were genuinely impressed by the splendor of the spectacle and by the scholarship that had recreated the architecture, the armor, the dresses, and the manners of the fifteenth century.

But in America the production did not hold. The Boston reviews were sorely mixed. His most powerful advocates in New York went to Boston to welcome him and, of course, sent back glowing reports of the opening night. Ironically, though, certain other critics, after years of complaining about the shabbiness of American stagings of Shakespeare, found that Mansfield's staging was too beautiful, too expensive, too much.

In his *Merchant of Venice,* he would show up Irving's "false" Shylock by opposing to it his own "true" one. "Irving made Shylock a gentleman," he wrote, "but he had his reasons for that. There can be no doubt at all that Shylock was nothing of the kind. . . . I shall make Shylock what Shakespeare evidently intended: a hot-blooded, revengeful and rapacious Oriental Jew." Mansfield deliberately suppressed every call for sympathy, and his Shylock attracted little public interest or critical favor.

Seven years would pass before Mansfield came to Shakespeare again. By 1900 he had at last achieved the recognition that he had so long striven for, that he was indeed America's leading actor, and he was now ready to cap that reputation by once more attempting to treat Shakespeare to an unforgettable revival. He did not choose *Hamlet* or *Othello,* which depended upon acting beyond his power, but, rather, *Henry V,* which could restore the laurels he had won in *Richard III* as a grand *metteur-en-scène.* Since in Mansfield's previous "serious" work he had specialized in villains, it was startling to see him undertake the role of the hero-king, yet it turned out to be an ideal role for him. The core of the role is simple manliness—bold, bluff, resolute. Henry has no subtle inner problems, no doubts or fears. From first to last he is king, always in command. He needs only to hold an army together, win a war, and woo a bride. Henry does not grow, but from scene to scene he changes, he plays many roles, and for an inveterate character actor like Mansfield, he offers a splendid range of opportunities.

The most interesting, though perhaps the least credible, interpretation of Mansfield's performance of Brutus in *Julius Caesar* is that of James Huneker in the New York *Sun.* Although many critics found Mansfield's mannerisms of voice, posture, and movement in this role not only faulty but often ludicrous, Huneker found that through exercise of imagination, all his qualities, good and bad, fused into a novel and splendidly intelligible character. It was his last Shakespeare, and as we look back over his Shakespearean roles, we realize that although major Shakespeareans played these roles, they do not, taken together, constitute the repertory of a major Shakespearean. As a producer of Shakespeare, Mansfield held from first to last to the nineteenth-century philosophy of mise-en-scène and added nothing to it but a certain polish.

Robert Bruce Mantell

Probably the fairest thing to be said about the Scottish-born Robert Bruce Mantell is that theater historians have treated him most unfairly. For fifteen years or so, remotely seconded by E. H. Sothern, he was the leading American performer of Shakespeare's tragic heroes. He played, with varying degrees of success, a round dozen of the heavy

Shakespearean roles, from Romeo and Shylock to Macbeth, Othello, and Lear. Between 1904 and 1919 he visited Broadway nine times, his engagements ranging from two weeks to two months, giving (according to Attilio Favorini's count) some 275 performances of Shakespeare. He crisscrossed the country with his companies, and during his whole career played Shakespeare some 4,900 times. In a generation when fashionable American audiences were turning away from the classics, Mantell maintained a steady audience of Shakespeare lovers, though little mention of his service or his success appears in the history books.

Mantell brought nothing new to the theater: his nondescript sets and costumes bespoke little concern for the niceties of historical research or for beauty of stage decoration, he was no intellectual, and he never acted from Shakespeare's texts, but always from old acting editions—usually Edwin Booth's as prepared and published by William Winter. What he did bring was something half-forgotten during the years since the death of Barrett and the retirement of Booth—Shakespearean tragedy full-voiced and muscular, driven by masculine power.

Richard III was always one of Mantell's best cards, useful to him to the end of his career, its strong, even coarse, histrionic effects providing the actor easy opportunities to catch the attention of and warm up any audience. One would not expect an actor of Mantell's physical dimensions to fit into the commonly held image of Hamlet, but any aspiring tragedian had to submit to the Hamlet test. Mantell had played the part, off and on, for twenty years, but on 6 November he exhibited it to a New York audience for the first time. It was respectfully, even cordially, received. The *Herald* critic called it graceful in attitude and gesture, vocally harmonious, yet lacking in inspiration. Its planning was obvious. But to William Winter, Mantell's very act of undertaking the part was sheer audacity; his execution of it a desecration. Booth had died, and Irving too, and Hamlet died with them. Mantell's "respectable talent and ample experience . . . do not seem to have done him much good."

Mantell's Lear was immensely successful. He was a virile king, said the *Dramatic Mirror,* magnificent in his rages and maledictions in the early scenes, and deeply moving without being maudlin in his final scenes with Cordelia. Though Mantell's style was "old school," he satisfied thousands of New Yorkers by restoring to them Shakespeare's greatest tragedy with undreamed-of intensity and power.

Early in 1907, Mantell took his Shakespeare to Boston, where in three weeks he played eight parts in seven plays and received both handsome compliments and sharp correctives, especially from H. T. Parker and E. F. Edgett of the Boston *Transcript.* Parker, who covered *King Lear,* was well pleased with Mantell's revival of the old-school methods. They reminded him of theatergoing in his boyhood, when one went to the theater simply to see a great actor play Lear. The subordinate characters were scarcely individualized. Unlike most modern actor-managers, Mantell made no attempt to create a Britain of any particular century. The palace halls, the heath, the battlefields were conventional theatrical nowheres, in some semibarbaric time. Unlike most modern actors, Mantell and his company made no attempt to humanize or naturalize the language but took it off the spool, so to speak. It was simply poetry in the theater, every line of it audible and so justly phrased and emphasized as to disclose its meaning. It was a bit artificial, perhaps even stilted, but surprising in that it allowed Shakespeare to speak for himself.

Once in 1906 a dinner companion asked Mantell to comment on the common critical charge that he was an "old-fashioned" actor. He rose to the charge with what satisfied his interlocutor as "an admirable argument":

What else can the acting of Shakespeare be but the acting of the old school? Those are dramas that you can't modernize—and this has been proved time and time again by the failures in Shakespearean roles of modern "naturalistic" performers. . . . In the modern plays one has merely to copy the people in everyday life. Where can you go into the streets or the restaurants or the homes and find a Brutus? . . . Still I do not admit that I am an actor of the old school. The actors of the real old school, if you saw them today, would seem to be devouring the scenery. I am attempting to bridge over the gap, . . . using as much modern method as possible without forfeiting the tragical elevation of the theme and verse.

Mantell then rose from the dinner table, lit a fresh cigar, and said, "I don't want to hurry you, but I've got to play Othello tonight. I have to get to the theatre ahead of time. You see, I'm a conscientious actor, and when I play the Moor I always black all over!"

The Sothern and Marlowe Partnership

It is not the fashion nowadays to idolize E. H. Sothern and Julia Marlowe, to rank them with the Booths, the Salvinis, the Rehans and Modjeskas, whose fame as Shakespeareans preceded theirs. Even in 1909, when they were called upon to dedicate the palatial New Theatre on Central Park West, few New York theater devotees would have held them equal to the glamorous Irving and Terry, whose American visits were of recent memory. Yet they certainly deserved the highest esteem of their contemporaries and deserve now a better remembrance than they enjoy.

When Julia Marlowe was hired now and then as a very young walk-on by the theater managers of Cincinnati, she came to realize that the principal aim of many great actors of the day was not so much to embody the characters they were said to be playing as to "make points"—that is, in tragedy or serious drama, to deliver strong emotional passages so loudly, accompanied sometimes by such extravagant postures of surprising stage business, that the audience would automatically respond with roars of applause. Even more disturbing was to realize that the actors did not understand, and hence could not project, the meaning of the words they were so melodiously intoning. Thus, in her own private study of roles, Marlowe strove to reconcile meaning and music, and she would "keep on until it is right and I know it is right and will stay right." Throughout her promptbooks thousands of "right" words are underscored. And many a time when we find a critic complaining of her "imperfect elocution" or "reading her lines badly," the probable truth is that she was reading the lines correctly but not as the critic was accustomed to hearing them.

The young and inexperienced Marlowe was taken under the wing of an older actress, Ada Dow. In a straightforward business arrangement, Dow accepted a lien on the girl's future income, and in return fed and housed Marlowe for several years while she read, thought, memorized, and taught herself how to act. On 12 December 1887, an impressario named Colonel Robert Miles presented Marlowe for an entire week at the Star Theatre in New York, where she would for the first time reveal her beloved Shakespeare, opening the week with Juliet and closing with Viola, roles that she had been studying and acting to herself, but never to an audience, for years. Of course, there were

faults in these early performances, and most critics were kind enough to mention them in the way of advice, as easily correctable. The critic for the Chicago *Tribune* had acknowledged that she was a novice whose full powers were yet to be developed, but he admired the courage and cheerfulness with which she went about her work: "She was perfectly at her ease, graceful, and quickly intelligent, and never did anything that displeased." She was truly an original, he declared, "infinitely superior to several manufactured actresses of mechanical methods" who had lately been forced upon the public. From observing her Viola, Lyman Glover of the *Herald* concluded that she was possessed of "far more than ordinary dramatic instinct, with a leaning toward comedy altogether delightful in its impetuous and unstudied grace."

It happened just then that Helena Modjeska was retiring for a period of rest, so Marlowe took over her entire supporting company. An excellent group, it was devoted to Madame Modjeska and at first resented taking orders from a young unknown posing as a star after one brief professional season. To expand her Shakespeare repertory, she spent most rehearsal hours in December 1888 directing the company in *As You Like It,* which she intended to offer in Philadelphia. The great event of the Philadelphia season, as Marlowe hoped, was the new Rosalind, who appeared on 3 January. In February she went to Boston, eager to exhibit her Rosalind there. It was well that she did, for her opening night (18 February) garnered her more applause and critical appreciation than any single night in her young career.

By now, quite innocent of the dangers that lay ahead, she knew she must again face New York. She had not played there since her week at the Star two years before, so she was hardly known to the New York public. She arrived in New York on schedule, counting on a success with *As You Like It,* expecting to fill out the run with all her other tried and true plays in repertory order. But in mid-December 1889, Augustin Daly staged *As You Like It*—in his company was the already famous star, Ada Rehan as Rosalind—and it entirely captured the attention of the public and the press. Marlowe did not dare offer her quieter, "autumnal," and comparatively sentimental production in competition with Daly's. Instead, she got out an old-fashioned sentimental piece called *Ingomar* and repeated it night after night for two weeks, losing money all the while. In desperation she opened *As*

You Like It on 27 January 1890, lost more money, and closed it two weeks later. She would not attempt New York again for five years.

In 1891–1892, Marlowe added *Much Ado* and *Cymbeline* to her Shakespeare repertory but not, it appears, very successfully. Yet the season was a prosperous one, and so, too, the next (1892–1893). Her leading man was the talented and ambitious young Robert Taber, whom she made the mistake of marrying. Their billings read "Julia Marlowe Taber and Robert Taber," and this diminished her popularity. At least once she had to go to court to obtain the salary contracted for because a local management contended she had violated her contract by change of name. Many people resented Taber, too, suspicious that he had tricked his way to stardom simply by marrying a star. In 1897, while the Tabers were vacationing in France, a stunning message came to them from the Theatrical Syndicate (which had recently seized total control of theater business in America): they would welcome Miss Marlowe in their houses, but not with Taber as co-star. That was the end of a bad marriage.

Much as she would have liked to return at once to Shakespeare, that would have been vetoed by the Theatrical Syndicate, so she chose *The Countess Valeska,* a romantic melodrama. She toured with it, and when she returned, it was to revive some favorite Shakespeare. But more and more she was being drawn away from Shakespeare. By 1904 she could no longer live without Shakespeare. And there, ready to companion her, was Edward Hugh Sothern. Among the Syndicate gang were a pair of brothers whose vision encompassed art as much as pots of gold, Charles and Daniel Frohman. Charles Frohman took Sothern and Marlowe in hand and planned their future.

Edward Hugh Sothern was the son of the English comedian E. A. Sothern, and at the age of twenty he joined his father to follow the actor's trade. Once he had found his metier, he was a quick study. After a few months with the Boston Museum company learning the elements, he had a brief stint with John McCullough just before McCullough's tragic breakdown. He had been discovered by Daniel Frohman in 1886, and from 1886–1898 he was Frohman's leading man, specializing in light comedy and dashing cloak-and-sword drama. But like many another romantic comedian, he wanted to make his mark in classic drama too. To the astonishment and delight of everyone (except William

Winter) on 17 September 1900, at the Garden Theatre, he staged and played so fine a Hamlet that at first blush many observers were ready to place it among the greatest Hamlets in living memory. He did not press on to further experiments in Shakespeare, perhaps because being comparatively slight of stature he did not see himself in other major Shakespeare roles. In 1904, Julia Marlowe saw Sothern's Hamlet for the first time. Sensing in Sothern not only refined artistry but a professional integrity that was compatible with her own ideals, she at once proposed to Daniel Frohman, still Sothern's manager, that there be a Sothern-Marlowe tour during the 1904–1905 season, doing nothing but Shakespeare. Sothern was flattered, and Frohman and his brother, Charles, were so struck by the novelty and daring of the idea, as well as confident of the quality of the artists, that they offered very generous terms.

Sothern and Marlowe made a perfect team. Marlowe was far more deeply read in Shakespeare and the literature about him, and many years more experienced in Shakespearean acting. But Sothern was an apt, eager, and extremely intelligent pupil, and their working habits were complementary. In the late summer of 1904, Frohman sent them out to Chicago to test three plays: *Romeo and Juliet, Much Ado About Nothing,* and *Hamlet.* This initiation of the Sothern and Marlowe combination in Chicago was an important event in the stage history of Shakespeare in America, and W. L. Hubbard, sensing it, made it plain in his weekly essays in the Sunday *Tribune* called "The Playgoer." It marked the end, he said, of a long drought of classic drama in Chicago. It demonstrated that in Chicago at least, and doubtless throughout the country, an audience, weary of Syndicate-sponsored trash, would welcome a revival of Shakespeare.

After the second season of their partnership—a season of *The Taming of the Shrew, The Merchant of Venice,* and *Twelfth Night*—they separated from Charles Frohman's management. Frohman did not approve of their plan for the third season, which included, besides repetitions of Shakespeare, three modern plays and a London venture. Their parting with Frohman was perfectly amicable, and getting out from under the Theatrical Syndicate was a relief. By shifting allegiance to the Shuberts, the actors expected to improve their opportunities and income. When their third season together ended in London, they realized that the American public had probably seen enough for a while of the limited repertory in which they could costar with fair distribution of honors. So for the 1907–1908 and 1908–1909 seasons, they divided.

In the spring of 1909 they were asked to lead the New Theatre's stock company in all its productions of classic plays, the first step in an attempt to create a national theater. Their first assignment would be to direct and play the leading roles in *Antony and Cleopatra.* Of course, they accepted the invitation, and even agreed to head the company in classic drama for the future. Caught up in the universal euphoria, they failed to recognize that neither of them was right for *Antony and Cleopatra.* It was written into their contract that in all classic plays which they would perform at the New, they were to be responsible for their own stage business. They took this to mean that, as was their custom, they would plan and direct the acting of the whole company, but it turned out that Louis Calvert, the well-known English actor and producer, had been brought over to serve as principal stage director. Eventually Calvert withdrew, and Sothern pulled the company through the rehearsals. But this ugly confusion of authority contributed to the ultimate failure of the New Theatre's opening play. Another impediment to success of the production was overblown scenic arrangements. The production was a failure, and Sothern and Marlowe shouldered their fair share of the blame.

Well before the opening, however, Sothern and Marlowe explained to the management that they would have to separate from the New. They sensed that in spite of all proclaimed intentions this was not a theater for "the people." They organized their own company and went on tour in Shakespeare. Early in 1911, Sothern finally won a divorce from his first wife and in the summer of that year he and Marlowe were married. Thereafter, for the next three and a half seasons they toured regularly and widely, reaching into the South, the Northwest, and even Canada. In January 1914, Marlowe fell ill and had to withdraw for the season. Then World War I broke out, and from 1914 to the fall of 1919, they did not play, Sothern spending most of his time (joined occasionally by Marlowe) entertaining the troops with patriotic recitations and solo scenes from Shakespeare. Thus, they were prevented from joining the cluster of Shakespeareans, English and American, who vied with each other in New York in 1916, celebrating the tercentenary of Shakespeare's death. They returned to the stage in 1919 and played their repertory in all but one season through the spring of 1924, when they retired forever.

Julia Marlowe and her partner and eventual husband Sothern were a brave and devoted pair of artists, who through a troubled and often drab period in our theater struggled to keep Shakespeare alive. Eventually they had the strength and will to break all false managerial bonds and manage themselves. Late in their careers, they even shook free of the overloading of Shakespeare stages, imposed largely by Henry Irving and his generation of foreign visitors. Though never in the forefront of scenographic revolutionaries, they took what was essential from the new schools of "stage decoration" and got back some degree of the scenic simplicities in which Shakespeare could do his own work.

The Interwar Years

As the Marlowe-Sothern partnership was nearing its end, two successors were coming up fast. In 1918, Fritz Leiber and Walter Hampden emerged as very promising Hamlets. Unfortunately, both men have now sunk into obscurity. In fact, a recent history of American acting does not even mention them in the index. Fritz Leiber was associated with Robert Mantell for twelve years (1908–1920) before breaking off to head his own company. In 1928, he was offered the directorship of the newly formed Chicago Civic Shakespeare Society and Repertory Company. The company toured for two years to splendid reviews, but Leiber's management was cut short by the Wall Street crash of 1929, and he retreated to Hollywood to act in movies.

Of greater concern is the historians' neglect of Walter Hampden, whose range, skills, and critical reputation far surpassed those of Leiber's. In 1918 he played so splendid a Hamlet at the Plymouth Theater, under Frank McEntee, that critics likened him to Forbes-Robertson and Edwin Booth. In 1921, Towse of the New York *Evening Post* proclaimed Hampden to be "the head of all living American tragedians." In the fall of 1925, he opened Hampden's Theatre, becoming America's only remaining actor-manager.

In 1920, the distinguished director Arthur Hopkins, together with the rising new stage designer Robert Edmond Jones, contemplated renewing Shakespeare productions by coopting to their service the Barrymore dynasty. They began with John, already an established matinee idol, in the role of Richard III. With barely six weeks to go to opening night, John began speech lessons with Margaret Carrington to improve the tonal quality of his voice. Ned Sheldon prepared a new version of the play, restoring Queen Margaret and prefacing Shakespeare's *Richard III* with several scenes from *Henry VI.* Jones's set, suggestive of the Tower of London, was reported to be one of his finest. The entire production—acting, staging, directing—astounded the critics. Unfortunately, it closed only a month after it opened when Barrymore suffered a nervous breakdown.

The next Hopkins-Jones project, in 1921, was with Lionel Barrymore in *Macbeth.* It was the season's greatest disappointment. Lionel Barrymore's acting was a total failure, and the production was described by Defoe of the New York *World* as "a total misconception of the play and a complete misapplication of the theater's modern method of decorative art."

On 16 November 1922, Hopkins and Jones finally found their one Barrymore-Shakespeare triumph—John Barrymore's Hamlet. This production would fill one season, open a second tour, and be reconstructed in 1925 to make a stand in London. Although there have been greater Hamlets before and after this in America, the applause and acclaim for Barrymore's performance still drown out the rest. The production was a personal triumph for Barrymore. He unconventionally pulled the teeth of the character, suppressing the bitterness and bawdiness, and made Hamlet the perfect gentleman. He was prosaic in his delivery and incredibly slow. Nevertheless, glamour swirled around the production and it was popularly regarded as a masterpiece.

Unhappily, Hopkins and Jones committed to one more Barrymore. Ethel Barrymore was brought out in *Romeo and Juliet* on 27 December 1922. It was a failure. The setting, the lights, and the acting were disasters. Miss Barrymore spoke in a bated, husky monotone. There was not one youthful, romantic, or loveswept note in any of her speeches or gestures. Another reason for its failure was the rush to get it on the stage in advance of the rival production with Jane Cowl and Rollo Peters, which throbbed with vitality.

Thus, the "Barrymore experiment" ended. A few years later, however, Ethel redeemed herself as a fine Portia and Ophelia with Walter Hampden;

neither John nor Lionel attempted Shakespeare on stage again. Yet the productions made their mark. Jones's scenic practices developed the principle that "less is more" and showed how to clear the stage for the actor.

The early 1930s produced two or three minor events, but one effort that got the attention of Shakespeare enthusiasts was the establishment of the new Shakespeare Theatre in New York, in 1932. Under the loving eye of Percival Vivian, it survived only two years in the face of the economic depression. But during that time, the Shakespeare Theatre received many favorable notices, albeit for its ideals more than its productions.

The *Romeo and Juliet* of Katharine Cornell was the first great event of the mid-1930s. She had never aspired to playing Shakespeare, and her unstudied portrayal of Juliet was heralded by many as the Juliet of that generation. Directed by Guthrie McClintic, her husband, the production toured widely, featuring Basil Rathbone as Romeo during the first season and Maurice Evans during the second season. Grenville Vernon wrote in *The Commonweal* that it was "a performance which glorified neither the star, the actors, nor the director, but all three together, and therefore the play." In another enormously popular production, America's best-loved comedians, Alfred Lunt and Lynn Fontanne, starred in 1935 in *The Taming of the Shrew.* Brooks Atkinson of *Theatre Reviews* described it as "most exceedingly low and most exceedingly funny." It arrived on Broadway at a time when Shakespeare was scorned by most theatergoers as grim and academic.

Stimulated perhaps by these two great successes, there seemed to be a sudden rebirth of interest in Shakespeare, especially when the productions were conceived with special ingenuity. A particularly successful example was Orson Welles's "voodoo" *Macbeth.* Set in Haiti, it opened in Harlem in 1936 with an all-black cast. The reviews were favorable if somewhat patronizing. *Commonweal* spoke of the actors' "musical voices," which were hindered by their limited "comprehension of the Shakespearean spirit and . . . reading of blank verse."

In 1936, New York and Boston were treated to two different productions of Hamlet, one with John Gielgud and the other with Leslie Howard. The concurrent productions, both with such notable actors, drew unavoidable comparisons. The consensus of reviewers was best stated by Richard Watts, Jr., of the *New York Herald-Tribune:* "Mr. Gielgud's portrayal is far more distinguished and moving, but his production is not as striking and handsome as that which Mr. Howard has devised." One critic suggested "hitching Gielgud's performance to Howard's settings."

The year 1937 witnessed one of the most celebrated flops in history. The opening line of John Mason Brown's *Post* critique of Tallulah Bankhead in *Antony and Cleopatra* says it all: "Tallulah Bankhead barged down the Nile last night as Cleopatra—and sank." It was said by one critic that the frank skeptics were the least disappointed.

The very next night after Tallulah's disaster, Broadway found something to cheer about. On 11 November 1937 Orson Welles of the Mercury Theater displayed his unforgettable *Julius Caesar*. It was played on an absolutely bare stage, and in modern dress. The costumes of Caesar's party were military, and significantly their shirts were brown. Here was a bold political statement. Caesar was Mussolini, and the production was an attack on modern fascism. The exuberant critical response confirmed Welles's brilliance as a director.

A new chapter in the history of Shakespeare's plays on the American stage began with the production of *Richard II* at the Saint James Theatre early in 1937. It was performed with Maurice Evans, a brilliant English actor, as Richard, under the direction of the then little-known Englishwoman Margaret Webster. It was Webster who directed most of the truly first-rate Shakespearean productions of the next several years, including the Evans production of *Hamlet* (1938); *Twelfth Night,* with Evans and Helen Hayes (1940); *Macbeth,* with Evans and Judith Anderson (1941); and a deeply moving *Othello,* with Paul Robeson (1943). In 1945 came *The Tempest* and in 1946 *Henry VIII,* this last produced by the American Repertory Theatre, with Eva Le Gallienne as Katharine and Walter Hampden as Wolsey. Webster was the toast of American critics. Brooks Atkinson called her the "finest director of Shakespeare this town ever had." John Mason Brown called her a genius. Her approach to Shakespeare was scholarly and straightforward. Deploring gimmicks, she adhered fastidiously to the text and, insofar as time and the talents of her performers warranted, "let Shakespeare do his work." Yet being supremely theaterwise, she knew exactly when to yield principle in order to get superb results. Of Paul Robeson she once said, "Is it possible to have a great Othello who is not a good Othello?" The record shows what sacrifice of verse-speaking she permitted Robeson while helping him to create the greatest Othello the American stage had ever produced.

Evans and Webster ended their association when Evans was drafted into the United States Army in 1940. While in service, Evans produced a cut-down version of *Hamlet,* which became known as the "G.I. version," and played it in army camps across the country and all over the Pacific. In 1945 the New York public and critics were delighted to receive his Hamlet performance again, even in this much-shortened form.

The Postwar Years

During World War II there was very little Shakespeare of import produced. But in 1946, the Old Vic, led by Laurence Olivier and Ralph Richardson, brought a repertory of great plays to New York, signaling a renewal in our theater of classic drama of the highest quality. Their plays were Shakespeare's *Henry IV, Parts 1 and 2,* Chekhov's *Uncle Vanya,* Sophocles' *Oedipus Rex,* and Sheridan's *The Critic.* Richardson's Falstaff and Olivier's Hotspur and Justice Shallow were the finest within memory for most American theatergoers. And Olivier's Oedipus and Mr. Puff, both in an evening, marked a peak of achievement in Olivier's career. This 1946 visitation may be remembered, too, as the first of a stream of British Shakespeare productions that continue to flow to us still almost annually.

In 1947, Donald Wolfit, the last of the old-time actor-managers, brought his English Company and repertory to New York for three weeks. For playgoers whose memories reached back to the days of Sothern and Marlowe, Mantell, and the like, the Wolfit visit stirred nostalgic. Of far greater moment that year, however, was the fact that our "greatest American actress," Katharine Cornell, whose only other Shakespeare had been her *Romeo and Juliet,* brought into New York (after testing in the country) an extraordinarily beautiful *Antony and Cleopatra.* With Godfrey Tearle as an ideal aging Antony, and a faultless supporting company, this Shakespeare has perhaps never been surpassed by an American company on Broadway.

Two imports, one from England and one from Hollywood, failed to live up to expectations. In 1948 Michael Redgrave and Flora Robson appear to have undone *Macbeth* by histrionic overdoing. In

1950 the much-loved film actress Katharine Hepburn made her Shakespearean debut as Rosalind in *As You Like It,* but though she was lovely to look at, her voice was not well suited to the role. And in 1950 the play itself had not much chance with the hypersophisticated critics of the day. "This pastoral potboiler," wrote one of them, "was one of the dullest and silliest plays a man of genius ever wrote."

In 1951 England sent us a remarkable experience—a double production of Shaw's and Shakespeare's Cleopatra plays, starring Olivier and Vivien Leigh. The production had originated in London for the Festival of Britain. The set was constructed on a revolving stage with Roman columns on one side and Egyptian columns on the other. The critics praised the production for the most part, and they enjoyed the unique opportunity to measure the contrasting values and points of view of Shaw and Shakespeare. The Ziegfeld Theater was too vast a house, however, for the delicate voice and figure of Miss Leigh, and, as frequently happened during their professional association, Olivier tended to mute his effects so as not to overpower hers.

In 1954, the rarely performed *Coriolanus,* with Robert Ryan, was brought to the stage by John Houseman at the Phoenix and was well received. Two years later, after a nine-year absence from the American stage, Orson Welles appeared in New York in his own production of *King Lear.* With his size, voice, and sense of command, it seemed inevitable. In London a year earlier, in a sort of Pirandellian warm-up to his performance of Ahab in a stage adaptation of *Moby Dick,* he rumbled a minute or two of Lear's opening lines, and the effect was thrilling; but two hours and more of the unrelieved rumble bred monotony. Because of his splendid reputation as a film actor (abetted by the fact that he played King Lear in a wheelchair, having broken his leg just before the opening), reporters and critics covered his appearance extensively, but their judgments on artistic grounds did not add up to success.

Beginning in 1954 we were treated to a series of visitations by London's newly reorganized Old Vic. In 1953 Michael Benthall was appointed to oversee a scheme to present every play in the Folio within five years. From time to time he exported the results. The first to come, in 1954, *A Midsummer Night's Dream,* was a mistake. Vastly overproduced, its thirteen tons of scenery could be accommodated

only on the stage of the Metropolitan Opera House. If the acting of Moira Shearer, Robert Helpmann, Stanley Holloway, and others was acceptably modern, yet the orchestra of sixty playing the whole of the Mendelssohn music, the crowds of extras, the old-fashioned special effects, the cumbersome wing-and-drop woodlands spoiled the charm of the play for most beholders.

Thereafter, the Old Vic learned to travel light, bringing more plays at a time with better actors and far less baggage. In the fall of 1956 we received *Richard II, Romeo and Juliet, Macbeth,* and the famous Edwardian *Troilus and Cressida* by guest-director Tyrone Guthrie. This and the next company were not confined to New York but toured from coast to coast, bringing brightly conceived productions to communities long starved for Shakespeare. In the fall of 1958, the Folio project being completed, they brought us *Twelfth Night, Hamlet,* and *Henry V.* Soon thereafter the Old Vic, as an organization, ceased to exist and the building became the temporary home of the newly established National Theatre.

Brooks Atkinson could describe the Old Vic of that generation as "a genuine twenty-four carat repertory company with a distinguished tradition"; but other critics, of jaded appetites, complained that the company's work was too studied, too lacking in passion. These objectors failed to recognize that this was a talented but young company, learning their trade, so to speak, by the formidable experiment of working through the entire Shakespeare canon. Looking back over their numbers we find such now well-known names as John Neville, Claire Bloom, Paul Rogers, Richard Burton, Charles Gray, Jeremy Brett, and Keith Michell, among many others.

In 1958, producer Joseph Papp took Shakespeare to New York's Central Park with fine productions of *Othello* and *Twelfth Night;* he has been providing free "Shakespeare in the Park" ever since. Papp has produced every Shakespeare play, some of them many times over, and introduced a number of now-famous performers to New York audiences. In 1972, his summer production of a ragtime-era version of *Much Ado About Nothing* enjoyed a successful run on Broadway and was eventually produced for television. Also that year, Papp's production of *Hamlet* with Stacy Keach received much critical acclaim.

To honor Shakespeare's four-hundredth birthday in 1964, John Gielgud directed a *Hamlet* featuring Richard Burton, and the Royal Shakespeare Company sent us Peter Brook's *King Lear* with Paul Scofield and Clifford Williams' *Comedy of Errors.* Gielgud had the unhappy notion of presenting his play in randomly chosen modern dress, as if it were a play in rehearsal. It was his wish to strip the play of "all extraneous trappings," unencumbered by scenery, decorative properties, or any suggestion of historical period. But from the opening New York street accents of Bernardo and Francisco, the historical period was set: it was here and now, and it was indeed a rehearsal, not yet ready to show the public. Burton's Hamlet was tragic only in the sense that Burton's career was a tragic waste, never more apparent than here. Equipped with splendid physique, face, and voice, he ought to have led the Shakespeareans of his generation, but even in his Old Vic days he fell short of expectations as Henry V and Hamlet. His 1964 performance was tentative, inconsistent, uncertain of technique or purpose. Many critics concluded that the honors, such as they were, all went to the Polonius of Hume Cronyn.

Of the *King Lear,* on the other hand, there was no question that the firm directing hand of Peter Brook was in charge, nor that the merciless dehumanization of Lear's world was derived from the Polish interpreter of Shakespeare, Jan Kott, nor that the scenic barrenness and harsh white lighting owed more than a little to the alienation theories of Bertolt Brecht. Brook even deleted the few redemptive lines of the text, and no one could doubt that he meant the play to express relentless cruelty.

In 1971, the RSC sent us another astonishing work by Peter Brook, his reduction of *A Midsummer Night's Dream* to what the London *Times* called its genuine essences, its platonic form. Gone were the marble palace of tradition, the verdant forest, the gauzy fairies, and every item of literal "reality." The stage was a white-walled room, lighted with white light, containing ladders, swings, trapezes, and coils of wire in lieu of trees. The characters were circus acrobats and clowns. Of course it was controversial, breeding reams of letters to the editor. But even those critics who could not quite approve of so far-fetched a translation of Shakespeare had to admit the production was dazzling.

The RSC came to the Brooklyn Academy of Music in 1974 with *Richard II,* directed by John Barton. Richard Pasco and Ian Richardson alternated in the roles of Richard and Bolingbroke. It visited Brooklyn again in 1975 with *Love's Labor's Lost,* to a typically respectful reception, and again in 1976 with *Henry V* (starring Alan Howard), which received more unqualified praise than any other RSC production since Brook's *King Lear.* Even John Simon declared that "Alan Howard is a superlative Henry, and the daring that he has found in the role is beautifully matched by the actor's own choices." It was to Simon "a revelation of what it is like to be in the theater in a country where theater is still revered as one of life's centralities."

The next few years produced very little Shakespeare of note other than Papp's productions and occasional visits from British troupes. In 1979, Al Pacino played *Richard III* to enthusiastic audiences and scornful critics, and 1980 saw the birth of the Brooklyn Academy of Music Theatre Company, with David Jones, formerly of the RSC, as director. The company opened its first season with *The Winter's Tale.* Critics were gentle and polite to the new company, although there were few memorable moments in the production. The company's second Shakespearean production, *A Midsummer Night's Dream* in 1981, was a dismal failure.

A month before the *Dream* collapsed in Brooklyn, an even more startling disaster struck at Lincoln Center. The Vivian Beaumont Theater had been dark for three years when a new organization called the Lincoln Center Theater Company, its producer Richmond Crinkley, took it over. Crinkley persuaded the celebrated opera director Sarah Caldwell, who had never directed a play, to undertake *Macbeth.* He even provided her with an actor to play the lead, a young man whose only previous accomplishment of note had been to star in Crinkley's production of *The Elephant Man* a year or so earlier. Miss Caldwell's favorite stage designers provided her what one critic called "an obstacle course" of metal ladders and staircases (one of them spiral) reaching up to a catwalk crossing the stage some fifteen feet above floor level—where, in fact, several important passages were performed. Such ill-advised combinations of inexperience and dubious talent, along with Miss Caldwell's penchant for inserting tableau scenes (Duncan's banquet, the Macbeths' coronation), doomed the experiment from its inception.

In 1982, the Midlands Britisher, Nicol Williamson—whose revolutionary angry-man Hamlet in 1969 had split critical opinion down the middle (it was the best Hamlet of our time, or it was the worst)—now at the Circle in the Square, directed himself in his own production of *Macbeth,* to much the same critical end. As an aggressive and deliberately antagonistic personality he could not escape squabbles among the critics—more against him than in favor, and since he had no director there was no one to dissuade him from imposing on the play an irrelevant transition from piety (much ado about the crucifix) to devil-worship. Few people made much sense of it.

There is one more triumph to record. Simultaneously with Williamson's ill-conceived *Macbeth* there arrived at the Winter Garden the best *Othello* since the Webster-Robeson *Othello* of 1943. It came into town after many troubles on the road—changes of directors, of casting, of technical effects—but except for an inadequate Desdemona (the third actress to be tried), the overall effect was an evening of intense excitement. This was James Earl Jones's sixth attempt at Othello, and he seemed at last—with his massive body, voice, and authority, and with the stimulus of a brilliant Iago—to fill the role. Christopher Plummer explored every dimension of Iago's malevolence with utmost cunning. In vocal range, facial expression, and body language, he was at once the honest friend, the upright soldier, and the ideal ensign—and the devil incarnate. None of his victims (save Emilia) could doubt his devotion to them or suspect him of deceit. The swiftness and energy with which he destroyed them simply mesmerized the audience.

Shakespeare Festivals

If there is precious little Shakespeare on Broadway, and the best of that mostly imported, the nation is awash in Shakespeare made-in-America. For the year 1979 the *Shakespeare Quarterly* (summer, 1980) carried reviews of 135 productions from Maine to the West Coast, covering nearly every play in the canon. Of these productions, forty were reported from school drama departments or temporary groups; ninety-five from established and ongoing organizations, most of them using the word "festival" in their titles. The usual number of productions by a company was two or three. Of the quality of these festival theaters one cannot generalize. But the public wants Shakespeare, and the theaters thrive. To take a single example, the Oregon Festival (the oldest), a non-Equity company situated far from any population center, operates four theaters and plays to 90 percent capacity. Peo-

ple go hundreds of miles to that small town of Ashlands because it's Shakespeare, and it's good.

In 1950 Lawrence Langner of Theatre Guild, Inc., decided that the United States should have its own professional Shakespeare theater near to New York, the center of actor talent and home of huge audiences. The name of Stratford, in Connecticut, seemed a happy omen, so he built his theater there, but a name was not enough. The theater, handsome from without, was ill-planned within, equipped with a stage that has cost endless experiments to make it work effectively. Few New York actors were trained to handle classic drama, and from the first, only the occasional English or Canadian actor got critical approval for verse-reading. The first director, Denis Carey, spoiled his first (1955) season with dull productions of *Julius Caesar* and *The Tempest.* John Houseman improved the directing, bringing off an excellent *All's Well That Ends Well;* and there were such early successes as Philip Bosco's Coriolanus and Morris Carnovsky's Shylock, Prospero, and King Lear. But too often, young directors substituted gimmicks for interpretation (*Troilus and Cressida* became the American War Between the States), and Broadway actors plastered Broadway tricks over the characters they were playing. Morale so declined that by 1964, the Shakespeare quatercentenary, when a hundred Shakespeareans met there to celebrate, the director of *Hamlet,* his star, and his Ophelia decamped shortly before the event and their work was finished by substitutes.

Attendance dwindled, debts rose, and in the mid-1970s with the death of Joseph Verner Reed (who is said to have bankrolled much of the losses) drastic measures were called for. The theater went dark in 1977, opened again under different management in 1978, and persists erratically, its initial high hopes forgotten.

The Stratford (Ontario) Shakespeare Festival is credited by many critics with producing the most important Shakespeare in North America. The idea of holding a festival of Shakespeare's plays in Canada was conceived by Tom Patterson, a Stratford-born journalist. His first move was to invite Sir Tyrone Guthrie to come to Canada, visit Stratford (and its Avon river), and advise on the organization of a Shakespeare festival comparable to the English one. Guthrie, who longed to build a theater fit for Shakespeare, leaped at the opportunity. He persuaded the committee that Patterson had assembled in Stratford that they must begin with a stage—one devised by him and his designer Tanya Moiseiwitsch. It was to be unlike any stage they had ever known—simply a long, broad open platform, a wall with appropriate entrance doors at the back of it, the audience in a half circle around it. No proscenium arch, no curtain, no scenery. Not even a building to cover it, since the time was short for the proposed opening: they would cover it with a tent.

Guthrie agreed to direct the first seasons (1953–1955), bringing over Alec Guinness to open the theater with *Richard III,* and Irene Worth for Helena in *All's Well.* By one miraculous last-minute save after another, all came together as Guthrie planned it, and the Stratford Shakespearean Festival (later shortened to the Stratford Festival) was under way. The tent lasted for four seasons; in 1957, the festival being assured of permanence, they built the magnificent, permanent, tent-like structure that houses it now.

Guthrie brought Michael Langham to succeed him in 1956. Twelve years later Langham turned over the reins to Jean Gascon, a flamboyant actor and the creator of Le Théâtre du Nouveau Monde in Montreal; and Gascon brought on as a codirector John Hirsch from Winnipeg. In 1975 a young English director, Robin Phillips, succeeded to the overall management.

Many splendid actors have joined the company and gone on elsewhere, but there has always been, at any given time, a "family" there—a set of actors who have played together for enough years to know the place, the plays, and each other. During Robin Phillips' five years, for instance, one could count on finding these: William Hutt, Douglas Rain, Martha Henry, Tom Kneebone, Frank Maraden, Marti Maraden, Pat Galloway, Mia Anderson, Jackie Burroughs, Richard Monette, Nich-

olas Pernell, Hume Cronyn, and Jessica Tandy, Brian Bedford, and Maggie Smith. But in 1980 the sky fell in.

Phillips was leaving, and the governing board of thirty (mainly citizens and professional men of Stratford and Toronto, the chairman one Robert Hicks, a Toronto lawyer) could not agree where to turn. The theatrical profession of Canada was demanding that the position be filled by a Canadian; chairman Hicks was determined that they engage the famous British director John Dexter. In the midst of the controversy they settled on a compromise: the directorate for two years should be undertaken by a quadrumvirate—Martha Henry, the dramaturg, another actor, and a designer. This "Gang of Four" went seriously to work, laid out their plans, submitted them, and had them accepted. Within a month they were told to forget it, that the board was securing Dexter.

Of course the four resigned from the theater, and with them William Hutt, Douglas Rain, and a large contingent of the "family." Nor would they ever return until the impossible occurred: full restitution of their losses and a public apology.

Nor did the board get Dexter. His appointment was prevented by the minister in charge of immigration, who refused to issue a work permit. Eventually they hired John Hirsch of Winnipeg, who took over the crippled company and tried valiantly to rebuild it. His successor will be John Neville, the leading young actor at the Old Vic in the 1950s, since then director of various English theaters, and lately of the theater in Halifax. The future of the Stratford Festival of Canada is problematic, but surely its three decades of sound foundation-work will not be allowed to crumble. It is Tom Patterson's dream, Tyrone Guthrie's noblest monument, Canada's national treasure.

661

Shakespeare as a World Figure: Translation and Performance Around the World

ANNE PAOLUCCI

When Shakespeare first acquired his reputation as a world figure in literature, the term had a much narrower meaning than it has today. In using it today, we must increasingly have in mind the entire world, including the Middle East, South and East Asia, Latin America, and Black and Muslim Africa, as well as all of Europe and the far-scattered lands of the English-speaking peoples.

In 1963, Louis Marder noted that Shakespeare's plays had been translated into at least sixty-eight languages and that more than 105 nations had sent their flags to be unfurled in celebration of Shakespeare's birthday the year before at Stratford-upon-Avon. In his thirty-five-page review of Shakespeare's foreign reputation, Marder limited himself to Germany, Scandinavia, France, Italy, Central Europe, Russia, and the Orient, allotting twenty pages to Germany and France, eight to the rest of Europe, and three to the Orient. That narrowly focused emphasis was a reminder that when Shakespeare first attained the status of a world figure, all it meant was that he had come to be regarded as such by the major literary critics of four nations: England, France, Germany, and Italy. Those four nations had reached a critical consensus by the last quarter of the nineteenth century. After that, the rest of Europe rapidly fell into line. In those days, the attitudes of the United States and Russia counted for little in this respect, since England still spoke authoritatively in cultural matters for all of the English-speaking peoples and Russia's European cultural status was still peripheral. But, for reasons that remain difficult to formulate, Spain's attitude, too, counted for little, even though, with Cervantes, Lope de Vega, Tirso de Molina, and Calderón, her golden age of the same decades had produced a theater that, in the dynamism of its growth, was surely the equal of Elizabethan England's.

Once the consensus was reached in the major nations, criticism of Shakespeare, which had established him as the greatest poet-dramatist of the modern world, rapidly gave way to Shakespeare scholarship, which is something very different. Germany took the lead. A scholarly German Shakespeare Society was founded in 1864, the year of the tercentenary celebrations, and in 1865 it began publication of its prestigious annual, the *Shakespeare-Jahrbuch,* which kept track of Shakespeare's fortunes everywhere. Half a century later, two German professors of English at Leipzig University, Walther Ebisch and L. L. Schücking, compiled the first nearly comprehensive *Shakespeare Bibliography* (1931), to which they added a supplement in 1937. Then came Gordon Ross Smith's *Classified Shakespeare Bibliography 1936–1958* (1963), which dwarfed its predecessors while making use of the same system of classification. Ebisch and Schücking had been considered by Ronald Berman especially valuable "for its listing of continental scholarship"; Berman characterizes Smith's work as covering many things, "from the problems of Turkish translation of Shakespeare to the acting of Jean-Louis Barrault."

The system of classification in the Ebisch-Schücking and Smith volumes is itself a major contribution to Shakespeare scholarship, as a glance at Smith's table of contents demonstrates. In its divisions, which cover Shakespeare's influence outside of England, translations, and the staging of his plays in foreign lands (among many other topics), scores of countries are specified, as well as the major writers who have been influenced, most of the translators, and the leading directors and performers. The longest lists are for the major Western nations; but Portugal and the East European nations are accorded their due, as are Japan, Greece, and Turkey. Under translators, for instance, Braga, Bragança, Pennafort, and Silva Ramos are listed for Portugal; Burian, Derin, Givda, and Sevin for Turkey; Fukuda, Mikami, and Sawamura for Japan; Carthaios and Rotas for Greece; and itemized translations are indicated also for Rumanian, Serbo-Croatian, Slovene, Czech, Slovakian, Macedonian, Bulgarian, Albanian, Gaelic, several languages of India, Esperanto, Hebrew, Yiddish, Hungarian, Finnish, Indonesian, Chinese, and "Miscellaneous Oriental and African."

Since 1958, the task of compiling a comprehensive bibliography with adequate coverage of translations, foreign performances, and studies in foreign languages has become increasingly difficult. In their *Selective Bibliography* (1975), James G. McManaway and Jeanne A. Roberts apologize for the limitations they had to impose in this regard, which, as they said, were "much to be regretted, for the reading, enjoyment, and theatrical production of Shakespeare is now worldwide." The editors did, however, include separate listings of sixteen articles from the excellent 1956 issue of *Shakespeare-Jahrbuch* (vol. 92), which surveyed the progress of Shakespeare translation in many lands. (It should be noted that, since 1964, there have been separate East German and West German Shakespeare yearbooks.) But for a fair sense of the flow of Shakespeare translations and stagings around the world, most valuable are the theater surveys and annotated bibliographies published annually in *Shakespeare Quarterly, The Year's Work in English Studies, Shakespeare Survey, Shakespeare Studies,* and specialized periodicals like Japan's *Shakespeare Translation.*

The last-named periodical, published annually under the auspices of Seijo University in Tokyo, was a fortunate outcome of the first World Shakespeare Congress that met in Vancouver, Canada, in August 1971. Reports to the congress by the chairmen of several of its investigative committees—on international cooperation, bibliography, new research methods, and translation—had emphasized the need to find ways of dealing "with the growing complexity of Shakespeare research and theatre activity" on a global scale. One thing the reports revealed, quite incidentally, was that much of the initiative in working toward international cooperation on bibliography and translation problems was being taken by Japanese scholars, who seemed to be assuming in the late twentieth century something like the responsibilities that German Shakespeare scholars had assumed in the late nineteenth century. The committee on translation, for instance, had four members, representing France, India, Germany, and Japan, and a Japanese chairman. The chairman reported that there had been indeed "a wide difference" of attitudes among the members about Shakespeare translation, the divergences being "especially noteworthy" between the statements of the European members and the Asian, reflecting the "wide differences" in linguistic and cultural backgrounds. Reviewing those differences, the chairman said:

Germany would be accredited with the oldest history in Shakespeare translation, having her own problem, however, which is that German translation has tended to become stereotyped, as the result of the cumulative efforts. French translations, from the nature of the language, cannot avoid the tendency to become longer than the original. India has also a fairly long history of Shakespeare translation. However, the peoples of India are still in great need of standard translations in various dialects. Japan has no less serious problems. In the case of the Japanese translation, perhaps we might even say that "translation" is not the right word for the kind of work involved and the result thereof, the reason being that, because of the nature of the language, there is such a wide range of choice for the equivalent and the parallel to the original and the entire business is left to the free choice of the translator.

(Leech and Margeson, 1972)

The two things on which the committee members unanimously agreed were "that Shakespeare should be global, not the sole possession of those whose native tongue is English," and that "word-for-word translation is the most appropriate style for the new Shakespeare translation"—the latter having been determined by what the chairman called an "unexpected convergence" of opinion.

The two Japanese members of the committee proceeded shortly thereafter to found *Shakespeare Translation.* After publication of its fifth annual issue, the periodical received a glowing notice in *The Year's Work in English Studies* (volume 59, 1979). David Daniell reviewed the contents of the first five issues at some length, noting that each volume to date had combined articles surveying the state of Shakespeare translation in scores of countries around the world with essays focused on problems of translation in general or on the specific difficulties involved in translating particular plays or scenes for performance. The first issue (1974) included H. W. Donner's "Some Problems of Shakespearean Translation" and Jürgen Wertheimer's "Text Type and Strategy of Translation," as well as articles dealing with problems of translating scenes into Japanese, Hindi, Bengali, and Korean. In the second issue (1975), there were articles on the first Greek Shakespeare translation, which dates from 1818; a comparison of Spanish translations of *Hamlet,* focusing on the soliloquies; and a fascinating discussion by Jagannath Chakravorty on the "problems of getting *Lear*'s storm-scene into Bengali, Hindi and Marathi." Chakravorty is represented also in the third issue (1976), offering a modern Indian view of the relative advantages and disadvantages of translation in verse and prose. Important for its rarity is the article in the same issue on early Arabic Shakespeare studies and translations. Portuguese and Greek translations are surveyed in the fourth issue (1977), along with articles on problems of translating specific plays into Chinese, Japanese, Russian, and German. Of the fifth issue (1978), Daniell notes that it is a memorial both to the founder of *Shakespeare Translation,* Toshiko Oyama, and to T. J. B. Spencer. It contains a comparison by Rudolf Stamm of six German versions of one scene from *Hamlet* (III. iv. 1–32); an Italian approach to problems of translating Shakespeare by Giorgio Melchiori; reviews of the state of translation into Hungarian, Hindi, and Japanese; plus a "charming essay," as Daniell puts it, "by Olga Akhmanova and Velta Zadornova from Moscow," which "deals with the problem of getting quotations across in another language." "This entire series," Daniell concludes, "is already very distinguished, and handsomely produced; it is of great importance." In their *ECCE Translator's Manual* of 1980 (ECCE stands for English-Chinese

Chinese-English), John J. Deeney and Simon S. C. Chau also accord *Shakespeare Translation* the highest praise, noting that it is the "only journal devoted to the discussion of the translation of Shakespeare into other languages . . . with contributions from all over the world."

There is a vast difference between the idea of deliberately encouraging word-for-word translation, as a lowest common global denominator, and the impulses that motivated the Germans of Goethe's time. Still, the major extensions of Shakespeare's fame outside of England have been the work of nations more or less addicted to translating as a way of developing their own national literary cultures. When the earliest of Schlegel's Shakespeare translations began to appear, the poet Novalis (Friedrich von Hardenberg) observed in a letter of praise: "We Germans have been translating for a long time, and the desire to translate appears to be a national characteristic. . . . Your Shakespeare is an excellent canon for the scientific observer. Except for the Romans we are the only nation which has felt the urge to translate so irrepressibly and whose culture owes so immeasurably much to translation. Hence the many analogies between our literary culture and that of the later Romans" (Lefevere). The Armenians have advanced a similar reputation for themselves as a translating people; and now it appears to be the turn of the Japanese—the most open to foreign influences, at least superficially, of all the major Asian nations.

The following survey will review first how Shakespeare's fame was securely established initially in Europe, and how the critical appreciation of his works gradually gave way, after consensus was reached, to scholarship. It is a process that begins with Voltaire's initial appreciation, imitation, and criticism of England's national poet and that ends with Benedetto Croce's "criticism of the history of Shakespeare criticism," which has made it relatively easy, ever since, to distinguish between genuinely literary or poetic criticism and postcritical scholarship, or scholarly shadow-boxing, as T. J. B. Spencer preferred to call it. That will be followed by a brief account of the rapidly broadening base of Shakespeare's fame to include most of the non-English-speaking peoples of the world. Western scholarship, and particularly the teaching of Shakespeare to non-Westerners in the major universities of the English-speaking nations, greatly encouraged the extension of Shakespeare appreciation around the world; far more important has been the consequent burgeoning of translations, adaptations, imitations, and more or less faithful performances almost everywhere. A conclusion will consider briefly why Shakespeare has in fact so easily outstripped all the other great writers of the West —some of whom, like Dante and Homer, are surely his equals in poetic power—in the universality of his appeal.

Reception in Europe: From Voltaire and Lessing to Tolstoy and Croce

During his lifetime, and for more than a century after his death, Shakespeare remained virtually unknown outside his homeland. War raged between England and Spain through much of that time, and it inspired great literary activity in both lands. France, however, took little notice of the literary activity, being too busy trying to impose its own hegemony on the rest of Europe. It may be that the flowering of drama in England happened too quickly for foreigners to be caught up in its influence. At any rate, by 1630, as C. M. Haines observes in his *Shakespeare in France* (1925), it was too late; the French neoclassicists, led by Jean Mairet, had swept the field. Whatever impulse a Corneille might have felt to follow the example of the English or Spanish stage was rapidly overcome. Not until a century later could Shakespeare begin to find an appreciative audience on the French-dominated Continent; and to receive serious recognition even then, he had to wait, as Haines put it, "for the youthful enthusiasm of his bitterest enemy— Voltaire."

Voltaire was not the first Frenchman, or European, to read Shakespeare or to express an opinion about him. Still, it is he who must be credited with having introduced England's national poet to the Continent. Voltaire had read Shakespeare during his years of exile in England (1726–1729). Back in France, he wrote plays of Shakespearean inspiration and much criticism, in prefaces to his plays, in an essay on epic poetry, and in his *Lettres philosophiques*. He initially said of Shakespeare almost exactly what English admirers and critics from Ben Jonson to John Dryden and Alexander Pope had been saying: namely, that Shakespeare was a natural genius, a great writer despite the fact that he "lacked art" and too often let his fancy drive him

beyond the bounds of judgment. But whereas those English critics who applied the neoclassical standards almost invariably apologized for having to do so, Voltaire did not apologize. For him, any suggestion that Shakespeare's natural genius could possibly have raised him to heights of art worthy of comparison with Corneille or Racine was to be flatly rejected. One could say that Shakespeare was indeed a creator of the English stage, provided one added quickly that he was also its ruin—in support of which judgment Voltaire wrote: "There are such beautiful, such noble, such dreadful Scenes in this Writer's monstrous Farces, to which the Name of Tragedy is given, that they have always been exhibited with great Success. . . . Most of the modern dramatic Writers have copied him; but the Touches and Descriptions which are applauded in *Shakespeare,* are hiss'd at in these Writers" (Kermode).

Dryden had come close to saying the same thing. He had argued—as T. S. Eliot has pointed out— that the possibilities of writing in Shakespeare's mode had been exhausted, that those who persisted in using that mode could only damage Shakespeare's reputation and deprive English literature of a serious future. With that notion Voltaire fully agreed. But as time passed and fairly good translations began to appear, Shakespeare gained admirers in France who did not fear what Dryden feared, since translations can easily give new life to an exhausted mode of writing. Some French translators in fact began to praise Shakespeare with far less reserve than Voltaire thought proper. In 1760, a suggestion that Shakespeare might conceivably rank higher than Corneille as a tragedian drew an angry retort from him. A climax of resentment was reached in 1776, when the first two volumes of the projected twenty-volume translation by Pierre Letourneur appeared. A dedicatory letter by Letourneur said of Shakespeare: "Never did a man of genius penetrate more deeply into the abysses of the human heart nor cause passions to speak the language of nature with greater truth." Voltaire was indignant. Letourneur, he said, was trying "to make us look upon Shakespeare as the only model of genuine tragedy." To the comte D'Argental, he wrote with deep resentment: "It is I who was the first to show the French some pearls which I had found in his enormous dung-hill. I did not then expect that one day I should contribute to trample under foot the crowns of Corneille and Racine in order to adorn the brow of a barbarian stageplayer" (Marder).

By that time, critics in many lands were responding to Voltaire's excesses. In England, there had been Samuel Johnson's *Preface* of 1765, which "trampled heavily on Voltaire," as R. W. Babcock puts it in *The Genesis of Shakespeare Idolatry: 1766–1799* (1931), where he documents what a "lost battalion" of English critics did for Shakespeare immediately following publication of that preface. Soon an Italian response was made by Johnson's friend Giuseppe Baretti, editor of the notorious *Frusta letteraria* (The Literary Lash). He came to Shakespeare's defense with the fervor of a convert. Baretti had criticized Dante for offending classical tastes with his medieval barbarism; yet when he had mastered English in Johnson's company—compiling a still-authoritative *Dictionary of the English and Italian Languages*—he put aside all of that and wrote in French his caustic discourse on Shakespeare and Voltaire, which was published in London in 1777.

The most important response to Voltaire in those days came from Germany, in the work of Gotthold Ephraim Lessing. His *Hamburgische Dramaturgie,* published serially (1767–1768) and as a book (1769), contained a devastating critique of Voltaire and high praise of Shakespeare, as part of a discussion of *Richard III.* Almost a century later, the eminent scholar Georg Gottfried Gervinus would not hesitate to say in his *Shakespeare Commentaries* (1850): "The man who first valued Shakespeare according to his full desert was indisputably Lessing. . . . The English editors and expositors of his works were yet under the Gallic yoke, when Lessing cast aside the French taste and the opinion of Voltaire, and with one stroke . . . transformed the age" (Halliday, 1958).

Lessing influenced Johann Gottfried Herder, who, in turn, rescued Johann Wolfgang von Goethe from the so-called tyranny of French classical models. Goethe had started out a thoroughgoing Francophile; guided by Herder he became a thoroughgoing Germanist and ended up, finally, a champion of what he called world literature *(Weltliteratur),* with respect to which, in his view, national boundaries would no longer matter. Goethe was by no means so foolish as to imagine that divided Germany's great neighbors—France, England, Spain—were about to abandon their age-old national pride. All three had produced their literary giants only after they had affirmed themselves as nation-states. Their literary flowerings had been manifestations of their national aggrandizements, in which national boundaries had counted a great deal. Dante had inaugurated Italy's great literature at a time when it was even more divided than the Germany of Goethe's day. But Dante had clearly established himself as an imperial and therefore universal poet, writing in the language of imperial administration and universal Christianity, as well as in his native vernacular; and as a vernacular poet, he had been very conscious of playing a creative rather than an imitative role.

The case of German literature in Goethe's age was very different. The other major vernacular literatures of Europe had already had their flowerings, so there was no alternative for the Germans but to borrow and imitate. What occurred was simply a shift from stifling dependence on the French for literary models to a somehow liberating dependence on the English. Fortunately, when they turned to the English for guidance, the Germans found the towering figure of Shakespeare to make them feel gloriously at home. Before long, their own literature experienced a belated flowering. Foreign critics were soon hailing Goethe as a German equivalent of Dante as well as of Shakespeare, and the new writing that surrounded him was almost universally accorded a status of virtual equality with the long-established European literatures. And there was no doubting that the taking up of English models had inspired the great renewal. "Our novels, our plays," Goethe could proudly say in his late years, "from whence have we received them, if not from Goldsmith, Fielding, and Shakespeare?" Pride could enter into it because, by then, the currents of English-German literary influence had ceased to be one-sided. In 1824, Thomas Carlyle had published a translation of Goethe's great novel *Wilhelm Meisters Lehrjahre,* with its already widely debated interpretation of the character of Hamlet; and in the following year his much-praised biography of Friedrich Schiller had appeared. That, perhaps more than anything else, had prompted Goethe to exclaim: "It is splendid that we now, because of the lively interchange among French, English, and Germans, have come to a point where we can correct each other. This is the great benefit which results and will continue to result from world literature." Carlyle, he had gone on to illustrate, was proving himself a more insightful interpreter than the Germans of some of Germany's major works, even as some of the Germans had proved to be better interpreters of Shakespeare and Byron than the English (Jost).

WILLIAM SHAKESPEARE

Goethe had begun reading Shakespeare in 1770. In his panegyric for the celebration of Shakespeare's name day in Strassburg on 14 October 1771 *(Zum Shakespeares Tage),* he described his first impressions: "The first page of him I read made me his for life, and when I was done with the first work, I stood like one born blind to whom a magic hand gives sight instantaneously . . . ; all was new, unknown, and the unwanted light pained my eyes" (Neff). From that moment on, he knew he would abandon the regular theater with its shackling unities of place, action, and time: "I knew myself to be free." That same year, he wrote a draft of *Götz von Berlichingen,* the play that at once established his reputation as "Germany's Shakespeare" when published in 1773 and performed in 1774. A translation of *Julius Caesar* by C. W. Borcke had appeared as early as 1741. Goethe, however, initially read Shakespeare in the translations of the plays that C. M. Wieland published between 1762 and 1766, all of which were in prose, except for *A Midsummer's Night Dream.* There followed in the period 1775–1782 a new prose translation of all the works by J. J. Eschenburg. And finally, out of the atmosphere of Goethe's own *Sturm und Drang,* came the first translation of genius, produced by August Wilhelm von Schlegel, who himself translated sixteen plays between 1797 and 1801 and added a seventeenth in 1810. The complete edition that resulted, with the collaboration of Graf Wolf von Baudissin and Dorothea Tieck, appeared in the period 1823–1829, in nine volumes edited by Johann Ludwick Tieck. That edition quickly superseded the translations of J. H. Voss, published between 1818 and 1829.

As for performances, it is known that prose adaptations of some early plays of Shakespeare were included in the repertories of English actors traveling in Germany in the late-sixteenth and seventeenth centuries, and that several German plays based on Shakespeare were also performed. But it was the Schlegel-Tieck translations that secured Shakespeare's triumph on the German stage. Goethe himself had produced Schlegel's version of *Julius Caesar* in 1803. Thereafter, a time was soon to come when it could be said that *unser* (our) Shakespeare was being performed more frequently on the German stage than in the playwright's native England.

Goethe's claim that German critics might already have outstripped the English as interpreters of Shakespeare could hardly have gone unchallenged in Shakespeare's homeland. The ideal of *Weltliteratur* might suit a Goethe in fragmented Germany, but William Hazlitt was quick to "confess" in his *Characters of Shakespeare's Plays* (1817) that "some little jealousy of the character of the national understanding was not without its share in producing the following undertaking, for 'we were piqued' that it should be reserved for a foreign critic to give 'reasons for the faith which we English have in Shakespeare'" (Halliday, 1958). The foreign critic was A. W. von Schlegel, whose "very admirable Lectures on the Drama" were, Hazlitt acknowledged, "the only work which seemed to supersede the necessity" of an attempt like his own. Two years earlier, in his *Essay, Supplementary to the Preface,* William Wordsworth had summed up the state of Shakespeare's European reputation: "At this day the French Critics have abated nothing of their aversion to this darling of our Nation. . . . The most enlightened Italians, though well acquainted with our language, are wholly incompetent to measure the proportions of Shakespeare. The Germans only, of foreign nations, are approaching towards a knowledge and feeling of what he is. In some respects they have acquired a superiority over the fellow-countrymen of the Poet" (Halliday, 1958).

Coleridge took strong exception to those words, complaining bitterly against the readiness of many English critics either to claim for themselves the startlingly new things that he had long since said about Shakespeare's genius, or worse, as in Wordsworth's case, to attribute the merit of them "to a foreign writer, whose lectures were not given orally till two years after mine, rather than to their countryman." Somewhat in the fashion of Voltaire, at his most resentful, Coleridge appeals "to the most adequate judges . . . whether there is one single principle in Schlegel's work (which is not an admitted drawback from its merits), that was not established and applied in detail by me" (Halliday, 1958).

Still, by and large, the English welcomed the German confirmation of their view of Shakespeare. Thereafter, the reserve that had kept their praise this side of idolatry for so long was abandoned, and the same soon occurred in the rest of Europe as well. Shakespeare idolatry has been a much-studied subject. Robert Babcock repeatedly cites C. M. Haines's *Shakespeare in France: Criticism, Voltaire to Victor Hugo* (1925) as indispensable for the period down to Voltaire's death. But it is valuable also for its account of the next hundred years, during which, after having been ignored in France for a century and then despised for a century, Shakespeare came to be adored for a century. Haines abruptly ends his study with the year 1870, because the position of French criticism thereafter is "that enunciated by Hugo" in his book on Shakespeare that appeared in 1864, the tercentenary year. With that book, says Haines, Victor Hugo proved himself to be France's version par excellence of the "pure devotee of Shakespeare, who is found in every modern country and who puts aside nationality before the universality of England's poet." Criticism can do no more, says Haines; and he concludes: "As the knowledge of Shakespeare advances, and as the opinion of different nations about him tends to arrive at a common position, criticism becomes merged into scholarship. . . . Hence it can be no part of the present inquiry to consider in detail the work of French scholars upon Shakespeare in recent years."

It should be noted that Haines's study and Babcock's are very convincingly updated in *The Persistence of Shakespeare Idolatry: Essays in Honor of Robert W. Babcock,* edited by Herbert M. Schueller and published in 1964, the quatercentenary year. Among the essays on English Shakespeare criticism before and after the period examined by Babcock, the volume includes Henri Peyre's "Shakespeare and Modern French Criticism" and Hermann J. Weigand's "Shakespeare in German Criticism," each of which is a masterful introduction to its subject. Professor Peyre recalls that "between 1885 and 1920 or so," French criticism reacted rather harshly against the romantic enthusiasm for Shakespeare that culminated in Hugo's book—"le dernier beau cri" of that enthusiasm, as Pierre Brunel would call it in his *Claudel et Shakespeare* (1971). But Peyre notes also that mid-twentieth-century French criticism had already reversed that antiromantic verdict; that "many a monograph should be written on Shakespeare's translators since 1850 or since 1900," as well as "on the staging and success of varied Shakespearean plays"; and that today the "startling discovery would probably be made that no city has seen more of Shakespeare's plays performed (since 1920 even the comedies and the histories) and with more ingeniousness and more art than Paris since 1920—not even New York, Berlin or London." He will concede only that "France has no equivalent to Friedrich Gundolf's classical work of 1911 on *Shakespeare und der deutsche Geist* [see Professor Weigand's assessment

of the 1928 edition, in the same volume]; nor did she ever have such two superb translators as Schlegel and Tieck." Of André Gide's much-discussed translation of *Hamlet,* done for the 1946 production by Jean-Louis Barrault, as also of his version of *Antony and Cleopatra,* Peyre does not hesitate to say that it was done "with far less skill than is too generously granted him by some critics." For an exciting reevocation of the powerful impression that Shakespeare made on the leading French poets, critics, painters, and composers of the nineteenth century, from Mme. de Staël, Chateaubriand, Stendhal, Delacroix, and Berlioz to Baudelaire, Mallarmé, and Laforgue, see Rosette Lamont, "The 'Hamlet-Myth' in Nineteenth-Century France" *(Council on National Literatures/Quarterly World Report,* 1982).

In his *Shakespeare in Italy* (1916), Lacy Collison-Morley had drawn the same conclusion that Haines would later draw with regard to France. In Italy, the reversal in Shakespeare criticism that had started with Baretti's polemic of 1777 reached its culmination in Alessandro Manzoni, Italy's greatest novelist—whose *I promessi sposi* (The Betrothed) "has probably had more influence in Italy than any other novel in any other land"—and Francesco De Sanctis, her greatest literary critic. Except for the comedies of Niccolò Machiavelli and Carlo Goldoni and the thoroughly theatrical rather than literary commedia dell'arte of the overlapping centuries, Italy, until the days of Luigi Pirandello, had consistently failed to produce a significant drama. Thus, having no celebrated dramatists of its own to defend against the claims of the English champions of Shakespeare, the Italians could follow the example of the German romantics rather than that of Voltaire. Goethe's very Shakespearean *Götz von Berlichingen* and the Shakespeare criticism of A. W. von Schlegel in fact inspired Manzoni to write his own romantic tragedies, *Il Conte di Carmagnola* (1816–1820) and *Adelchi* (1822), even as Goethe's *Werther* had inspired Manzoni's contemporary Ugo Foscolo to write his *Last Letters of Jacopo Ortis* (1798–1802). Manzoni read Shakespeare in the French translations of Letourneur. Even in imitating Shakespeare, however, Manzoni (like all of Italy's so-called romantic poets, including Giacomo Leopardi as well as Foscolo) remained at bottom a classicist, at least to the extent of not mixing comedy and tragedy in the same play. In his epic novel, however, he would later in fact "give full rein"— as Collison-Morley notes—"to the delightful humour which he had excluded so severely from his plays."

Most notable among Manzoni's writings on Shakespeare is a treatise-length letter (1820) in French on the "unities of time and place in tragedy," which includes an extended comparison of the dramatic characterizations of Shakespeare's Othello and the Othello-inspired hero of Voltaire's *Zaïre.* (Passages quoted below are translated into English by the present writer, from the original French version of the letter that appears in Manzoni's *Opere,* M. Barbi and F. Ghisalberti, eds. [1943].) Because of his apparent violation of the unity of time, what Shakespeare permits us to see in his *Othello,* says Manzoni, is "suspicion conceived, combated, cast out, yet returning with new incentives, stirred up and manipulated by the diabolical artifices of a perfidiously false friend: and one sees this suspicion—explored through stages each as terrible as it is true to life—finally raised to certitude." Voltaire, instead, respecting the unities, is constrained to try to show how a hero who starts out in the morning as a benign protector and suitor can be driven to murderous jealousy in twenty-four hours. Manzoni writes also of Richard II and Macbeth, observing that to force such characterizations into the straitjackets of the unities amounts to submitting them to visible torture. And, having mentioned torture, Manzoni wittily alludes to the great work of his grandfather, Cesare Beccaria, which had led to the abolition of torture throughout Europe. Playing lightly on the basic terms of the debate over the unities, he says: "Error itself, in fact, will in no place and in none of its shapes let itself be rooted out in the course of a single day. Torture, for instance, survived for some time after the immortal treatise *On Crimes and Their Punishments* appeared. One would have to be very impatient and egotistical, therefore, to complain of the tenacity of literary prejudices."

Manzoni read Shakespeare in French; but soon Michele Leoni's Italian versions began to appear in fourteen volumes (1819–1822). Then came Carlo Rusconi's complete edition of 1839, followed in that same year by the first of Giulio Carcano's versions, long considered the best, which were finally published as a whole in twelve volumes (1875–1882). Since then, many poets, playwrights, and scholars have tried their hand, including Mario Praz (who edited the complete works in 1961), the eminent scholar E. Chinol, and Nobel Prize-winning poet Salvatore Quasimodo, whose *Tempest* is highly praised.

A series of great Italian actors and actresses took these translations to the stage starting in the 1840s. These included Gustavo Modena and his pupil Ernesto Rossi, the brilliant Adelaide Ristori, and, greatest of them all, Tommaso Salvini. Carmelo Bene, making revolutionary use of the resources of television, is a worthy continuator of that tradition of acting today. Yet, Italy's greatest contributions to staged appreciation of Shakespeare have undoubtedly been the operas *Otello* (1887) and *Falstaff* (1893) of Giuseppe Verdi. The libretti of Arrigo Boito are dramatic works of art in their own right; and Verdi's music, especially in *Falstaff,* gives one a new sense of the meaning of dramatic catharsis, for comedy as well as tragedy.

The inevitable turn from Shakespeare criticism to Shakespeare scholarship in Italy had its beginnings with Francesco De Sanctis, who was a literary historian as well as a great critic. De Sanctis, like most Italian critics since, was profoundly influenced by Georg Wilhelm Friedrich Hegel, rather than Goethe or Schlegel. His debt to Hegel is one that he shared with Vissarion Belinski in Russia and Hippolyte Taine in France, and even more with A. C. Bradley in England. In Hegel's pages on Shakespeare, De Sanctis found what Bernard Bosanquet, the great English historian of aesthetics, and Bradley were later to find; and it enabled him to set Shakespeare beside Dante as the two towering poets of the romantic art of the Christian-modern world, as distinguished from the classical art of Greece and Rome and its European Renaissance revival.

The De Sanctis–Bosanquet view of Dante and Shakespeare has been reinforced by Francis Fergusson's observations in *Trope and Allegory: Themes Common to Dante and Shakespeare* (1977), where, as against the "fashionable view that Shakespeare was an uncommitted skeptic," Fergusson joins Bosanquet in affirming that Shakespeare and Dante were "writing out of the same context." But it is T. S. Eliot, not directly under Hegel's influence (he regretted later that he had not been), who perhaps best formulated the Bosanquet-Hegelian view of the achievement of Dante and Shakespeare. In words that come very close to what De Sanctis had written a half-century before, Eliot said in 1929: "Take the *Comedy* as a whole, you can compare it to nothing but the *entire* dramatic work of Shakespeare. The comparison of the *Vita nuova* with the *Sonnets* is another, and interesting, occupation. Dante and Shakespeare divide the modern world between them; there is no third. . . . Shakespeare gives the greatest *width* of human passion; Dante the greatest altitude and greatest depth. They complement each other. It is futile to ask which undertook the more difficult job."

It is important to stress such Anglo-Germanic formulations of a Dante-Shakespeare link on the highest levels of poetic art, because without them it might have been very difficult indeed for Shakespeare to attain the same high level of acceptance in Italy that he had already gained in Germany and was gaining in France at the time of De Sanctis. De Sanctis was aware of how much Italy owed the German and English romantic critics (and the Americans of Longfellow's time as well) for its own nineteenth-century Dante revival; and it seems almost as if he wished to pay back a vast debt of gratitude when, at the climax of his long analysis of Dante's genius for rapid characterizations in the *Inferno,* he wrote an often quoted passage that ends with a two-word bombshell. Dante, De Sanctis has been saying, manages to call all the infernal dead back to life with masterful strokes, so that they can be seen in their characteristic acts. But it is clear that their vitality is too intense to sustain a merely temporal existence. Dante has caught their vitality concentrated in a point of no dimension, a point of pure will, which is to be the placeless place, as it were, of their eternal life-in-death. At that moment De Sanctis interrupts himself to draw a seemingly historical link, for which Benedetto Croce will later not forgive him. De Sanctis says: "Those mighty figures, stiff and epic as statues there upon their pedestals, are awaiting the artist who shall take them by the hand and cast them into the whirlpool of life and make them dramatic. And the artist was not an Italian: he was Shakespeare [*fu Shakespeare*]" (Collison-Morley).

Those words were written in the late 1860s, at just about the time that Victor Hugo was completing his book on England's national poet—the first work in French criticism, as C. M. Haines observed, to accord Shakespeare "absolute primacy in the world's art, alongside Homer and Dante, in that height which, as Hugo says, 'is the region of equals.' " After that, in Italy as in France, criticism of Shakespeare, with only rare exceptions, gives way to scholarship.

Shakespeare's reception in Russia followed a pattern very like that in Italy, with the Russians initially reading him in French or German versions and basing their first translations on such versions. Unfortunately, Leo Tolstoy's notorious essay on "Shakespeare and the Drama" (1906)—which

Morris Weitz refers to in *Hamlet and the Philosophy of Literary Criticism* (1964) as "the most vehement denunciation every written"—has drawn so much attention to itself as almost entirely to eclipse the previous history of Russian criticism. In fact, scholars have repeatedly stressed that the essay "represents a complete contrast to all the evaluations" of the main tradition before and since. R. H. Stacy makes the point in his history of *Russian Literary Criticism* (1974), reaffirming what Louis Marder had said in 1963, namely that the "disproportionate fascination" of the Soviets with Shakespeare "has a long history." Shakespeare became a favorite, in Marder's words, "as soon as Russian eyes opened to the culture of the West."

D. S. Mirsky observed in 1926 that Alexander Pushkin's *Boris Godunov* (1825) was a "first essay in Russian romantic—Shaksperean—tragedy as opposed to the hitherto prevalent French forms." When the play was performed the following year in Moscow, "it was acclaimed as [Pushkin's] masterpiece by the young idealists whose idols were Shakspere (a German Shakepere) and Goethe"; but the performance of Nicholas Palevov's translation of *Hamlet* in 1838, Mirsky observes, marked a turning point in Russian literary history. With Paul Mochalov in the title role, that *Hamlet* played to packed houses. Then came a long review-essay on "Mochalov in the Role of Hamlet" by Russia's first great literary critic, the Hegelian Belinski, which, in Marder's words, "treated Shakespeare as an integral part of the Russian dramatic and literary scene." The idealists, Mirsky wrote, "found in Hamlet a fellow spirit, while the rest of the audience were carried away by the romantic beauty of the dialogue, and still more by the inspired acting of Paul Mochalov, Russia's great romantic tragedian."

Translations came rapidly after the 1830s. The first Russian version of the complete works was a collaborative effort edited by the poets A. N. Nekrasov and N. Gerbel in 1865. P. A. Kinshin's edition appeared in 1893. Major Russian dramatists, poets, and novelists from A. N. Ostrovsky to Boris Pasternak have produced translations, and in 1950 there appeared a now standard eight-volume edition published by the leading Soviet Shakespeare critic, Aleksander A. Smirnov (with A. Anikst). From an ideological standpoint, it is no doubt fortunate that Marx left little specific guidance for a Marxist interpretation of the plays, having limited his own discussion to the discourses on gold in *Timon of Athens.* What Marx says there about Timon's misanthropy he owes to Hegel, though it is turned "upside down," as he liked to say. Still, on whatever grounds, Shakespeare has triumphed in the Soviet Union, where tens of millions of copies of his plays have been published in the more than "twenty-eight languages spoken by the various peoples." As Roman Samarin noted in 1965, after "the whole Soviet Union had celebrated the four-hundredth anniversary of Shakespeare's birth," that celebration marked a "red-letter day in the calendar of a country in which Shakespeare has truly found a second home." Certainly, as Irene R. Makaryk summed it up in 1982, "Shakespeare is undoubtedly the most popular and most revered foreign dramatist in the Soviet Union."

When Tolstoy wrote his critique of 1906, A. C. Bradley had already published his lectures on *Shakespearean Tragedy* and was about to publish in his *Oxford Lectures on Poetry* (1909) those on "The Rejection of Falstaff," "Shakespeare's Antony and Cleopatra," "Shakespeare the Man," "Shakespeare's Theatre and Audience," and "Hegel's Theory of Tragedy." In those lectures, Bradley brings to completion what Coleridge and Hazlitt had started, namely, a total absorption into English Shakespeare criticism of the German romantic view of England's national poet. Quite fittingly, therefore, in locating Bradley's place in the fourth of his *Four Centuries of Shakespearian Criticism* (1965), J. Frank Kermode has written: "At the gates of the century stands the still gigantic figure of Bradley. Bradley was a Hegelian, but there is no reason why this should trouble the reader." The same can be said of most of the many other Hegelians, ranged to the left and right of Bradley, who have been producing Shakespeare criticism in many lands. The point is that, like Aristotle (and in as many fields), Hegel has generated all sorts of disciples, with F. H. Bradley, A. C. Bradley, Bosanquet, W. H. Pater, J. A. Symonds, John Dewey, and Bertrand Russell ranged in the middle; Giovanni Gentile (and Croce, too, for a time) and scores of disciples extending to the right; and an endless stream of Marxists, penetrating deeply into every quarter of the modern world, on the left. Of all these, Croce is really the only one who ranks as a first-rate Shakespeare critic, comparable (though of an altogether different frame of mind) to A. C. Bradley. Croce devoted himself, in all fields, to what must be called a criticism of the history of criticism. Accepting the view that genuine criticism of Shakespeare ended in Europe around 1870, he quite deliberately took up the task of separating the wheat from the chaff in the legacy of Shakespeare studies. And it is with full appreciation of Croce's service in this regard that F. E. Halliday cites him again and again in *Shakespeare and His Critics* (1958), as well as in *A Shakespeare Companion: 1564–1964* (1964). In the first of those volumes, Halliday uses Croce's well-defined terms to distinguish the various literary and nonliterary approaches to Shakespeare, and in the latter he briefly sums up Croce's contribution: "His criticism of Shakespeare in *Ariosto, Shakespeare and Corneille* is an analysis of his poetical personality, of the character and development of his art, and a protest against the irrelevance of the biographical, objectivistic, exclamatory and realistic schools of Shakespearean criticism."

Under Hegel's influence, A. C. Bradley had in fact adopted a perspective in *Shakespearean Tragedy* very similar to Croce's. In the opening sentences of his introduction, he says, indeed, that he means to ignore the history of English literature and of drama in general, avoid comparisons with other authors, leave untouched questions about his life and character, about texts, sequences, and sources, and even pass over in silence what might be called poetry in the restricted sense that identifies it with the "beauties of style, diction, versification." Yet he departs from Croce and holds firmly to Hegel in taking very seriously the concept of genre, which distinguishes three "voices" of poetry: epic, lyric, and dramatic. His object in the book, Bradley specifies, is "dramatic appreciation: to increase our understanding and enjoyment of these works as dramas. . . . For this end all those studies that were mentioned just now, of literary history and the like, are useful and even in various degrees necessary. But an overt pursuit of them is not necessary here." Indispensable, on the contrary, is long familiarity with the plays, and "that native strength . . . and habit of reading with an eager mind which," Bradley concludes, "make many an unscholarly lover of Shakespeare a far better critic than many a Shakespeare scholar."

Bradley thus attached himself to the main line of Shakespeare criticism that triumphed first among the German and English romantics, but eventually also in France. Even in the days of Victor Hugo, as Haines observed in 1925, the French could never wholly abandon their artistic preference for the classical. Yet they certainly rose finally to heed the challenge posed by Hippolyte Taine. As Haines reports it: " 'Ascend the stage,' says Taine, 'and contemplate the whole scene: . . . do you not see the poet behind the crowd of his creatures?' Yes, replies Alexandre Dumas—in the phrase which I have already called the noblest appreciation of Shakespeare ever contained in a single sentence—for 'After God, Shakespeare has created most.' "

"Triumph and Tyranny" in the Neglected and Emergent National Literatures

In his British Academy lecture of 1959 on "The Tyranny of Shakespeare," T. J. B. Spencer argues that, once that tyranny was established, early in the nineteenth century, all efforts to lift it were foreordained to fail. Spencer cites Walter Scott, Matthew Arnold, Walter Bagehot, Tolstoy, and G. B. Shaw as challengers of that tyranny before his own time. And then he adds: "Our most famous living poet, forty years ago, slipped into a paragraph the statement that Shakespeare's most popular tragedy is 'most certainly an artistic failure.' But the response to this challenge has been disappointing." Even the French, to whom "we have hitherto been able to look for a disillusioned and eccentric view of Shakespeare's merits," says Spencer at the close of his tour de force, have "capitulated, and the modern French criticism is among the best. No, the spectacle afforded by modern criticism is the shadow-boxing of rival bardolators. Shakespeare is a dead issue. The resistance to his magnificent tyranny is over; and with it has gone something of the vigour and excitement and courage of Shakespeare criticism."

That Shaw or Eliot should have resorted to literary ruses to restore some of the old excitement to Shakespeare criticism in the English-speaking world—as Croce had tried to do for Europeans generally—could hardly occasion surprise, though it would have been surprising indeed had such ruses succeeded. What was needed was rather a repetition of what had happened in Germany in Goethe's time, when Shakespeare was first perceived as a great "English mirror" in which other peoples could see their own established, neglected, or even emergent national literary identities sharply reflected or shaping themselves for the first time.

And that has in fact been happening in our own time. Most Asians, Africans, and Latin Americans who study Shakespeare probably do so at first at a university where the tyranny of Shakespeare reigns unchallenged and where most of those who teach and publish are indeed engaged in shadow-boxing. Still, as compared with the folks back home, the chief writers in the non-English-speaking lands outside Europe can approach Shakespeare with considerable liberty. They can feel free to treat a translated Shakespeare as their own contemporary, as Goethe had urged his fellow Germans to do; and if they have the requisite talent, the results can be refreshing.

David Daniell makes the point in his Shakespeare bibliographical survey for *The Year's Work in English Studies* (volume 61, 1980). "The *New Swan* Shakespeare," he writes, "now includes a *Tempest* of unusual interest, as it is edited by the distinguished Nigerian scholar Michael J. C. Echeruo, who has a refreshingly different view." That view has to do with an anticolonialist interpretation. It is indeed refreshing to be told by Echeruo that "Shakespeare's readers now include Americans, Japanese, Indians and Africans" who bring "not only new interpretations based on the experience of a new set of readers, but cruel deductions arising from the evidence which the play offers of prejudices and attitudes meant originally only for true English ears." The scholarly Nigerian editor notes more particularly that "many African and Black American writers have taken their cue from Caliban" in appraising the fate of the Mirandas of the world. Daniell calls it a "pity" that Echeruo "had not the space to develop such matters beyond a following paragraph."

In Goethe's day, the celebration of Shakespeare by foreigners tempted some of them to imagine that such transnational appreciation augured the start of an epoch of *Weltliteratur*. Marxist critics, who envision the advent of a stateless, nationless, and classless world community, can still be found suggesting something of the sort; but the more likely pattern is the opposite. The reception of Shakespeare today is primarily a national literary-linguistic challenge, as foreign scholars in the field have been insisting for decades. In a talk, published in 1979, on modern Indian responses to Western literature, R. K. DasGupta notes, for instance, that, although modern India readily acknowledges that Shakespeare was a "much profounder poet than Kalidasa, the greatest Sanskrit dramatist," that did not mean that living writers of modern India could meaningfully take Shakespeare as a model. Rabindranath Tagore, the first Far Eastern Nobel laureate in literature, said he "found Shakespeare too agitating to produce the joy one expected from great poetry." That comes close to Tolstoy's attitude. But DasGupta has in mind the need to explore the fact that ancient India, like the ancient Hebrews, produced neither true tragedy nor true comedy in the Western sense. French critics of Shakespeare, we are reminded, sound French, even as German critics sound German, and English critics English. For too long, unfortunately, modern Indians have tried to sound English in writing about Shakespeare. There may come a significant change, DasGupta concludes, when Indians finally "shed English as the medium of our higher studies in Western literature."

Making a similar point in "Comparativisation: The Example from China" (1979), John J. Deeney admonishes Western and Chinese comparatists alike that, in trying to communicate what we most treasure in our great authors, East and West, perhaps "more attention could be paid to a 'contrastive literature' approach, especially when contrast could be more instructive than comparison." Simon S. C. Chau, a frequent collaborator of Denney's in Chinese translation projects, has made the same point most emphatically in "The Nature and Limitations of Shakespeare Translations" (1980): "Since the first Chinese translation of Shakespeare appeared in 1903," Chau informs us, "the task of rendering Shakespeare into Chinese has been followed up by no less than forty translators, many of whom are distinguished poets, writers, scholars and dramatists in their own rights." The first edition of the complete works in Chinese, by Liang Shih-ch'iu, appeared in 1969, though by then many individual plays had been repeatedly translated. While acknowledging that there are basic cultural barriers to wide appreciation, regardless of the accuracy of translations, Chau concludes optimistically that a time may yet come when a Chinese audience— even on the mainland—may feel "perfectly at home with the Elizabethan-style apron stage, and be as familiar with Hamlet, Lear and Falstaff as was the Globe audience."

Modern Japan has apparently been more determined than any other Asian nation to accept the achievements of the West (and even to vie with it) in all fields, including that of Shakespeare studies. Beneath an actively receptive surface, painful moments are occasionally revealed. In "Shakespeare and the Modern Writers in Japan: Translation and Interpretation by Shōyō, Ōgai, and Sōseki," published in *Shakespeare Translation* (1980), Yoshiko Kawachi informs us that, though there were earlier references to Shakespeare in Japanese, the first translation of a play—*Julius Caesar*—dates from 1883. It was published in a newspaper and appears to have served a political end. The same can be said of Shōyō Tsubouchi's version of the play published the following year. But Shōyō Tsubouchi—who, like Ōgai Mori and Sōseki Natsume, is famous enough to be known by his first name—went on to translate the complete works of Shakespeare during the period 1909–1928.

Shōyō made himself a Shakespeare scholar without journeying to the West. Ōgai, on the other hand, went to study in Germany when he was relatively young; while Sōseki, at a more advanced age, went to England. Ōgai appears to have enjoyed his time abroad, though he complained at least once of German professors who disparaged his native land. Of his stay in England, Sōseki later wrote: "I lived unpleasantly in London for two years. I took my wretched place among the English gentlemen, as if I had been a shaggy dog surrounded by a pack of wolves." Yet it was in Shakespeare that he seems to have found an objective correlative for a particularly melancholy mood. "Walking around the Tower of London," Kawachi writes, "he imagined the scenes of *Richard III* in which the two young princes were murdered." Sōseki eventually succeeded to Lafcadio Hearn's post at Tokyo University. These three writers, our author concludes, responded differently to Western influences; "but Shakespeare enriched their literary accomplishments, and played an important part in their efforts to modernize Japanese literature."

Far more complex and difficult is an assessment of the prospects of full appreciation of Shakespeare among Black Africans and Arab Muslims. In Africa, with its many tribal tongues, its ancient Amharic literary tradition in Ethiopia, and its English-, French-, Portuguese-, and Arabic-speaking elites across the continent, translating Shakespeare into the native languages is still more or less a diplomatic challenge. President Julius Nyerere of Nigeria has said that he translated *Julius Caesar* (and *The Merchant of Venice*) into his native Swahili in order to show the world the true cultural potential of what is now Nigeria's national language. Sol T. Plaatje, on the other hand, appears to have translated Shakespeare into his native Setswana as a trial of his personal literary competence. On another level, there is the case of the Zulu writer K. E. Masinga, who, as Tim Couzens reports, was hired as the first Zulu broadcaster for South African radio in the early 1940s. He had initially been allotted only five minutes. To prove that he deserved more time, he began translating and broadcasting bits of Shakespeare. "I translated Shakespeare," he has said; "I dramatized Shakespeare; I called the people, the artists, I trained them and Shakespeare was heard for the first time over the air by the Zulus. They were surprised when they heard something like *The Comedy of Errors;* they were dumbfounded when they heard *Romeo and Juliet.*" Masinga's air time was extended, and it is said that he eventually translated and produced at least nine Shakespeare plays, "some of which may still be preserved on glass records" (Heywood).

Since his works have been translated into French and Portuguese, Shakespeare comes easily to Black Africans who speak and write those languages and English. In "Shakespeare and the Living Dramatist" (*Shakespeare Survey,* 36, 1983), Wole Soyinka, the noted Nigerian playwright and Shakespearean, who writes in English, but with a strong local flavor and idiom, contrasts the responses to Shakespeare of Arab Islam and Black African Islam. He observes that "between 1899 and 1950, some sixteen plays of Shakespeare had been translated and/or adapted by Arab poets and dramatists," and that "there will have been others by now because even the government of the United Arab Republic, fed up with the number of embarrassingly inaccurate and inelegant translations, set up a committee to produce a scrupulous and complete translation of Shakespeare's works." By the quatercentenary year, Soyinka says, the Arab fascination with Shakespeare had already reached the point of a claim, advanced by M. M. Badawi in "Shakespeare and the Arab World" (*Cairo Studies,* 1964), that Shakespeare—as Soyinka sums up and paraphrases —"was in fact an Arab," that his "real name, cleansed of its anglicized corruption, was Shayk al-Subair"—as Arabic a name "as any English poet can hope for." Turning from the Arabs to the Blacks of Islamic Africa, Soyinka hastens to note the absence as yet of any claim that Shakespeare might have been a Black Muslim, even though his works (despite an affinity of their language with classical Arabic) have had on Black Africa something like the culturally liberating effect that they had on the Germans of Goethe's time.

Despite its current fascination with Shakespeare (no doubt perceived in part as a diplomatic challenge), the Arab world, unlike the civilizations of the Far East, has had no literary tradition to prepare it for modern drama and Shakespeare. In Iran and in the strongly Christianized parts of Lebanon and Syria, there have been "passion play" traditions and related entertainments; but it cannot be said that the modern theater in the Islamic lands in any sense developed out of such traditions. Among the major Islamic peoples, only the Turks, who took the faith of the Islamic Arabs by conquest—and have always therefore felt freer about discarding elements that have proved too restrictive politically, like the Arabic script, for instance—have actually abandoned themselves fully to the theater in the Western sense and to Shakespeare in particular. But the Turks, too, have had intermediaries, in westernized Jews and, much more important, in the Christian Armenians of the vast Armenian diaspora.

Rather than plunge into the complexities of research in this vast new area, it will best serve our purpose to glance at a segment of the New York Shakespeare Summerfest of 1981. The three-month event featured lectures, musical interludes, dance, dramatizations of parts and stagings of entire plays, and films and workshops in scores of locations in the metropolitan area. At its core was an exhibit of materials from the collection of the Folger Shakespeare Library in Washington, D.C. A program titled "Shakespeare and the World" gave weekly presentations on "Shakespeare and the Afro-American Community," "Shakespeare and the Hispanic World," "The Greek Meets the Elizabethan," "Shakespeare's Germany: Plays, Poetry, and Music," "Shakespeare in Japan," "Shakespeare and the Armenian Theater," "The 'Hamlet-Myth' in Nineteenth-Century France," "The Many Faces of Love: Shakespeare's Italy," "Shakespeare in Russia: Excerpts from Poetry, Fiction, and Music," "Shakespeare in the Yiddish Theater," and "Shakespeare on the Turkish Stage." To integrate the whole, the directors had been asked to emphasize how the people they represented had met the challenge of "receiving" Shakespeare—a challenge aptly summed up by the Armenian poet-critic Hovannes Toumanian: "Shakespeare has become a criterion by which to determine a nation's cultural standards." The German, French, Italian, and Russian programs stressed characteristic national responses rather than translations. France's presentation, for example, culminated in a dramatic reading of Laforgue's lampoon of Hamlet. The Greek, Hispanic, Turkish, Yiddish, and Armenian groups, on the other hand, chose passages for bilingual representation that served to show the capacities of their languages and performers to express the best of Shakespeare, while singling out the parts of the plays that seemed to come closest to expressing their own most prized national or ethnic characteristics. And with a hardly less characteristic emphasis, the Japanese program was structured around a showing of the 1957 film *Throne of Blood* (A. Paolucci).

The first program, "Shakespeare and the Afro-American Community," started with an address by Errol Hill on "Black American Actors in Shakespeare." In reviewing the long-obstructed struggle to make Shakespeare a possession of American Blacks, Professor Hill reminded his audience of the achievement of the great Black American Shakespearean Ira Aldridge, who, having been denied a comparable opportunity in the United States, went abroad to triumph in Shakespearean roles not only in England but all across Europe and beyond. (Later, in the Turkish program, Tunc Yalman, its director, recalled that the "first performances of Shakespeare to be heard in Istanbul in the English language were presented by the American Black actor Ira Aldridge in 1866. Aldridge appeared as Shylock in *The Merchant of Venice,* as well as in the title roles of *Othello* and *Macbeth.*")

As native English-speakers, Errol Hill noted, American Blacks in the theater found Shakespeare's language irresistible. But that they should have struggled so long to play the great roles in the Broadway theaters (as Paul Robeson finally did with *Othello* in 1943) surely gives some support to Montgomery Gregory's observation that Shakespeare "was the first dramatist to appreciate the 'intriguing opportunities' in the life of the darker races." Hill suggested that Shakespeare, as a dramatist, was sex-blind as well as color-blind, creating female roles that could be played by men, to be sure, but also male roles that could be played by women. That the roles of Othello, Lear, Shylock, and Macbeth should have remained closed to Black actors—after white actresses on the French, Italian, German, Armenian, and English stages had played great male roles—was intolerably out of line, Hill insisted, with the spirit that animates the plays. Pointing in a parallel direction is James Baldwin's

account of why, having repudiated his white literary heritage, he "stopped hating Shakespeare." In Shakespeare's "bawdiness," he says, he had found the "ineffable force which the body contains, which Americans have mostly lost, which I had experienced only among Negroes, and of which I had been taught to be ashamed" (Roucek and Kiernan).

The program on "Shakespeare and the Hispanic World" focused at first on the historic Anglo-Hispanic hostility, which has so long delayed appreciation of Shakespeare among Spanish speakers. Later, in both performance and discussion, the program suggested anti-Spanish as well as anti-English (anti-European) interpretations of *The Tempest,* and it ended with readings from *Troilus and Cressida* that made them sound like Quixote–Sancho Panza dialogues out of Cervantes. The Greek dramatic readings made vivid the differences between Shakespeare translations into the classical (Katharevusa) and popular (demotic) varieties of modern Greek, which are still vying for primacy in Greek education. The Turkish and Armenian programs offered impressive reminders of how closely linked—despite the fierceness of current feelings—the two peoples have been in their appreciation of Shakespeare. A major difference, to be sure, has been the fact that, since the rise of Kemal Ataturk, the Turkish reception of Shakespeare has had strong governmental support. In Tunc Yalman's words: "With the impetus provided by Ataturk's cultural reforms, theatre in Turkey took giant strides. A highly gratifying aspect of its evolution is the Turkish passion for Shakespeare. With the exception of a handful of countries with an ingrained theatre tradition, Turkey has enjoyed more presentations of the tragedies and comedies, and has probably maintained a higher level of Shakespeare production than the rest of the world."

The Armenians have not known anything like that sort of support for their long literary-theatrical romance with Shakespeare—though some of the Soviet Union's largesse for Shakespeare studies does indeed reach Soviet Armenia. But even so, the presentation on "Shakespeare and the Armenian Theater" took up without hesitation the challenge of the truly great characterizations of the greatest plays. Before it was over, the "passionate enthrallment" of the performers with their parts had fully communicated itself to the audience. A translating people par excellence since their alphabet was invented, the Armenians have truly made Shakespeare their own. The leading Soviet-Armenian critic, Rouben Zarian, thus aptly summed up the relationship in a London address of 1965: "To say that Armenian writers were intensely fond of Shakespeare would be by far an understatement. . . . Shakespeare was to them a typical example of how a writer, altogether true to the realities of his time, could maintain his force and influence undiminished centuries later. He was confirmation of the great truth which says that to be national is indeed to be universal." For an excellent survey of Shakespeare translations and productions in Armenian, see Nishan Parlakian, "Shakespeare and the Armenian Theater" (*CNL/QWR,* 1982).

Conclusion: A Key to Shakespeare's Contemporary Universality

Some ten years before T. S. Eliot issued his notorious "challenge" about *Hamlet* in 1919, A. C. Bradley had published a Hegelian-inspired lecture on "The Rejection of Falstaff," in which he seemed to say of Shakespeare's greatest comic figure what Eliot was later to say about Hamlet. Eliot's charge was that *Hamlet* must be declared an "artistic failure" because, in attempting to characterize its hero, Shakespeare had simply "tackled a problem which proved too much for him." Bradley had earlier said that "in the creation of Falstaff," Shakespeare had "overshot the mark," had "overreached himself," had indeed let himself be "caught up on the wind of his own genius, and carried so far that he could not descend to earth at the selected spot."

The parallels are obvious. The difference is that, under Hegel's influence, Bradley does not judge the result of Shakespeare's having "overreached himself" an artistic failure. Instead, he supplies us with a response to Eliot's challenge of the sort that Eliot himself (as T. J. B. Spencer apparently read him) may have wished to provoke. We realize, by the end of Bradley's lecture, that he has been intending the highest praise, recognizing that, in overreaching himself, Shakespeare was pressing his art beyond the limits of the strictly classical ideal— that of Nietzsche's *adäquate Objektivation,* of Eliot's "objective correlative"—to the transcendent heights of truly romantic art.

Here we should remind ourselves that when the German romantics were closing ranks with the English against the excesses of Voltaire, they were also developing a new aesthetics, the purpose of which was to do philosophical justice to every kind of art that has ever been seriously valued, whether in the Far East, the Near East, or Europe, whether in ancient, medieval, or modern times. That new aesthetics, with its reevaluations of Gothic architecture, Dante, and Shakespeare, reached its culmination in the vast Hegelian system of fine art. Its impact on English criticism was made through the philosophic labors primarily of Bernard Bosanquet, but also of the brother of A. C. Bradley, the same F. H. Bradley about whom Eliot would later write his Harvard doctoral dissertation.

With respect to drama, Hegel's aesthetics reinterprets Aristotle's poetics to permit it to include the experience of the Oriental peoples and modern Europeans. Of its theory of tragedy in particular, A. C. Bradley did not hesitate to say that, since Aristotle, the "only philosopher who has treated it in a manner both original and searching is Hegel." And as for comedy, Bradley points explicitly to Hegel's notion of the highest possible attainments of romantic art when he says of Falstaff's "freedom of soul" as a dramatic creation that it is "a freedom illusory only in part, and attainable only by a mind which had received from Shakespeare's own the inexplicable touch of infinity which he bestowed on Hamlet and Macbeth and Cleopatra, but denied to Henry the Fifth."

At the heart of Hegel's aesthetics are the concepts—by no means original with him—of symbolic, classical, and romantic art, each defined in terms of the diverse possible relations of content to form. In symbolic art, which can rise to the restless heights of the sublime, content and form are reciprocally inadequate: an idea inadequately grasped is given an inadequate objective form; and the result, at best, remains tremulously insecure on both counts. In classical art, as the Greeks perfected it, an idea grasped with complete intuitive adequacy is given comparably adequate or ideal expression. Romantic art returns to something like the reciprocal inadequacy of symbolic art: artistic intuition is now, however, raised to a level that is more than adequate—to that of the transcendent God of the Jews or Neoplatonists, for instance—so that the artist is obliged to overreach himself in trying to give it objective expression. Epitomizing the distinctions in a formula as profound as it is brief, Hegel says: "Symbolic art *seeks* the perfect unity of inner meaning and external shape which classical art *finds,* . . . and which romantic art *transcends*" (H. Paolucci).

Romantic art's first great age ended with Dante. Then came the Italian classical Renaissance, which threw the preceding age into almost total eclipse. Beneath the surface, the forces that had produced the Gothic cathedrals as well as Dante were still operative; but post-Renaissance neoclassical theories of art sought quite deliberately to harness and discipline them, like unruly giants, for beauty's sake. Yet, as Dryden complained, we who insist on the need for such discipline are not giants. The giants were the Shakespeares, Dantes, and Homers, who cannot be the subjects of rules; for they give rules and even then cannot be bound by them, being, as the Roman jurists used to say, *legibus solutus* (not bound by the laws). Romantic art had its resurgence in the age of Goethe in Germany and then in England and on the rest of the Continent, when Shakespeare was perceived as having brought its first age to a tardy Nordic culmination. The characteristic relation of content and form is here that of transcendence, with the artist protesting, as Dante does in his *Paradiso,* that what he has intuited is too much for his memory, while what he remembers is too much for his words. Art itself is thus torn internally (Eliot saw this with clarity) in its yearning to express the profoundest depths or greatest heights of human experience. Hegel's word for it is *Zerrissenheit* (tornness), of which the central image is that of the transcendent divinity of the Neoplatonists, Jews, and Muslims literally torn in the flesh upon the cross, at once foolishness to the Greeks, as St. Paul says, and a stumbling block to the Jews. Art can have a future in our prosaic age, Hegel insisted, only in its romantic form; but it is a form that makes intelligible, in its "tornness," all that the art of the East has traditionally sought as well as what the Greeks believed themselves to have found. A sense of art's self-transcendence as art, which the European romantics experienced in their reading of Shakespeare, is perhaps what has begun to have a comparably powerful appeal to non-Europeans, prompting them not only to study his plays but also to translate and perform them in their own languages. In its self-transcendence art shows itself, finally, to be truly universal.

Yet in Shakespeare, as compared with Dante, there is another dimension that needs to be indicated. What Shakespeare's art transcends as its loftiest content is an experience of nationhood with which all the peoples of the world can fully identify themselves today as never before. Shakespeare wrote during England's great age of discovery, with the results of which he shows a vast and largely sympathetic acquaintance. In this respect, Cumberland Clark's *Shakespeare and National Character* (1932) deserves to be better known. Its review of Shakespeare's "knowledge and literary use" of the distinctive "characteristics of the different peoples of the world" makes it obvious why Shakespeare's works seem to mirror so much more of the world's infinite variety than is reflected in Homer or even in Dante. Shakespeare is thoroughly English, to be sure; but he gives us a realistic sense of English nationhood that is clearly a prototype of all nation-making, in which all who read him or see him performed on stage in any language can find a model for themselves. Addressing himself to this theme in 1823, Hegel said: "Shakespeare's tragedies and comedies . . . have been attracting an ever wider public because, despite their very strong national emphasis, the universal human interest in them is incomparably stronger. . . . Shakespeare's works have gained entrance everywhere except where national conventions of art are too narrow and specific" (H. Paolucci).

A similar point has recently been made, but with a very practical emphasis, by Ralph Berry in his introduction to *On Directing Shakespeare: Interviews with Contemporary Directors* (1977). Berry limited himself in those interviews to major Anglo-American and European directors—Jonathan Miller, Konrad Swinarski, Trevor Nunn, Michael Kahn, Robin Phillips, Giorgio Strehler, and Peter Brook —but what the interviews stressed about performances is of universal application. In his words: "Every production of Shakespeare presupposes a national group which is the predominant audience." A summer production at Stratford, or at some Shakespeare festival centers in the United States or Canada, may indeed "play to a largely international audience"; but, as Berry insists:

my essential point remains. . . . The meanings latent in the text have to be actualized with that audience in mind. A *Coriolanus* founded on the overtones of an English public school upbringing is a perfectly valid conception, for an English audience. To an audience unfamiliar with English ways these particular meanings would fail to resonate; but there are always alternatives. The militaristic side of Coriolanus' upbringing finds echoes in the social structure of many nations and tribes, but happens not to be a strong English tradition. Even so simple a term as "soldier" needs a specific (and not a generalized) audience before it can satisfactorily be defined. (Consider what "soldier" connotes to a Japanese, a Swede, a German, an American.) The point is that the meanings are not lexical absolutes, to be animated by the players. Meanings are generated by community and history; the audience participates in and establishes them. The audience does not, as it were, blankly spectate at a set of visual and aural images. Thus the director has to enter into that audience's bloodstream, to be aware of the images that compose the present and the past of the community—its felt history, that is to say.

Adaptation of Shakespeare performances to historically determined traditions has affected the staging of the plays in England itself, through the centuries, as well as in the United States, Canada, Australia, and the other English-speaking lands that have developed or are in the process of developing distinctive national characters despite the shared language. Many other languages—Portuguese, Spanish, Dutch, Arabic, Urdu-Hindi, Bengali, Chinese—are now shared by manifestly diverse nations. Moreover, much of what is directly communicated in dramatic performance is, to begin with, nonverbal, so that, when we read a review in our own language of a Shakespeare performance in East or West Germany, Sweden or Finland, Moscow or Rome, Paris or Tel-Aviv, Portugal or Brazil, it hardly distracts us at all not to be told very much about the words. Thus, in reporting on Shakespeare productions in West Germany for the *Shakespeare Quarterly*'s annual review (1983), Wilhelm Hortmann and Klaus Bartenschlager both criticize the essentially nonverbal impressions left on them by Peter Palitzsch's "altogether unsuccessful *Othello*" at the Residenztheater in Munich, of which Hortmann says more particularly that, in a "reductionist" mood, Palitzsch's purpose was apparently to work off his "ideological grudges in acts of aesthetic revenge," obliterating the "inner accord between the noble Moor's moral and martial stature and his unconditional love" simply by "cutting out the first act and dispensing with Venice altogether." Hortmann hails Klaus Michael Grüber's *Hamlet,* in an uncut version staged at the new thirty-five-million-dollar Schaubühne in Berlin, as "undoubtedly, the chief Shakespeare event" of the year, even while acknowledging that the "size of the stage dwarfed the figures physically" and that "what remained" finally was the "image

of the play as a nostalgic artefact . . . a most beautifully embalmed corpse, the monument of its own magnificence." Klaus Bartenschlager contrasts Palitzsch's *Othello,* instead, with Ernst Wendt's production of *As You Like It* on a virtually bare stage in Munich's Kammerspiele. He dwells on the tempo and rhythm of the dialogue, noting that it gave one an impression of hearing Albee or Beckett and admonishing that, quite obviously, "Shakespeare's bantering could not be turned into Beckett with impunity." Only parenthetically are we told that the translation was mostly Schlegel's; it was far more significant, theatrically speaking, that long passages were in fact "spoken in English." The critic ridicules the effect; yet one would guess that the spectacle as a whole—not less than the Palitzsch *Othello* and the Grüber *Hamlet*—mirrored an important facet of the developing national characteristics of a painfully divided modern Germany. On the nonverbal elements in literature, René Wellek has aptly written: "Motifs, themes, images, symbols, plots, and compositional schemes . . . as well as qualities such as the tragic or the comic, the sublime or the grotesque, can be and have been discussed fruitfully with only a minimal or no regard to their linguistic formulations." If that were not so, the very notion of translation would be inconceivable. In fact, millions of readers today know and appreciate the works of the truly great writers—from Homer and Virgil to Dante, Shakespeare, Goethe, Tolstoy, and Dostoevsky, among many others—in translations that "hardly convey even an inkling," as Wellek puts it, "of the peculiarities of their verbal style."

Wellek does not deal explicitly with what performance adds to translations of plays, but his comments on the filming of novels and plays are relevant. Silent films were "often comprehensible and aesthetically effective," he reminds us, "without recourse to subtitles"; and films generally are sufficient proof in themselves that the "devices and techniques of literature can be transferred into a nonlinguistic medium." Hegel argues this point with directness: performances of plays constitute a crowning achievement—the synthesis of all the arts, with architectural and pictorial sets, and with performers (like sculptured figures of living flesh) whose cadenced speech is the loftiest musical expression of the pulsating life of thought and feeling. And when they happen to be performances inspired by the texts of Shakespeare, translated or in the original, T. S. Eliot's words on greatness in literature certainly become more relevant. "The 'greatness' of literature," Eliot wrote, directing his remarks against an extreme tendency of formal criticism in his day, "cannot be determined solely by literary standards; though we must remember that whether it is literature or not can be determined only by literary standards."

BIBLIOGRAPHY

Robert W. Babcock, *The Genesis of Shakespeare Idolatry: 1766–1799* (1931). Ronald Berman, *A Reader's Guide to Shakespeare's Plays* (1965). Ralph Berry, *On Directing Shakespeare* (1977). A. C. Bradley, *Shakespearean Tragedy* (1904) and "The Rejection of Falstaff," in *Oxford Lectures on Poetry* (1909). Simon S. C. Chau, "The Nature and Limitations of Shakespeare Translation," in William Tay, Ying-hsiung Chou, and Heh-hsiang Yuan, eds., *China and the West: Comparative Literature Studies* (1980). Cumberland Clark, *Shakespeare and National Character* (1932; repr. 1972). Lacy Collison-Morley, *Shakespeare in Italy* (1916). Benedetto Croce, *Ariosto, Shakespeare and Corneille,* Douglas Ainslie, trans. (1920). David Daniell, "Shakespeare," in *The Year's Work in English Studies,* 59 (1978) and 61 (1980). R. K. DasGupta, "Indian Responses to Western Literature in the Nineteenth and Twentieth Centuries," in *Proceedings of the Seventh Congress of the International Comparative Literature Association* (1979).

Phanuel Akubueze Egejuru, *Towards African Literary Independence: A Dialogue with Contemporary African Writers* (1980). T. S. Eliot, *Selected Essays: 1917–1932* (1932; rev. 1964). Montgomery Gregory, "The Drama of Negro Life," in Addison Gayle, ed., *Black Expression* (1969). C. M. Haines, *Shakespeare in France: Criticism, Voltaire to Victor Hugo* (1925). F. E. Halliday, *Shakespeare and His Critics* (1949; rev. 1958) and *A Shakespeare Companion: 1564–1964* (1964). Christopher Heywood, *Aspects of South African Literature* (1976). Wilhelm Hortmann, "Shakespeare in West Germany," in *Shakespeare Quarterly,* 34 (1983). François Jost, *Introduction to Comparative Literature* (1974). Yoshiko Kawachi, "Shakespeare and the Modern Writers in Japan: Translation and Interpretation by Shōyō, Ōgai, and Sōseki," in *Shakespeare Translation,* 7 (1980). J. Frank Kermode, ed., *Four Centuries of Shakespearian Criticism* (1965). Rosette Lamont, "The 'Hamlet-Myth' in Nineteenth-Century France," in *Council on National Literatures/Quarterly World Report,* V (1982). Jacob M. Landau, *Studies in the Arab Theater and Cinema* (1958). Clifford Leech and J. M. R. Margeson, eds., *Shakespeare 1971: Proceedings of the World Shakespeare Congress* (1972). André Lefevere, *Translating Literature: The German Tradition from Luther to Rosenzweig* (1977).

James G. McManaway and Jeanne A. Roberts, *A Selective Bibliography of Shakespeare* (1975). Irene R. Makaryk, "Soviet Views of Shakespeare's Comedies," in *Shakespeare Studies,* 15 (1982). Louis Marder, *His Exits and His Entrances: The Story of Shakespeare's Reputation* (1963). D. S. Mirsky, *A History of Russian Literature* (1949). Emery Neff, *A Revolution in European Poetry: 1660–1900* (1940). Anne Paolucci, ed., "Shakespeare and the World," special issue of *Council on National Literatures/Quarterly World Report,* V (1982). Henry Paolucci, *Hegel on the Arts* (1979). Nishan Parlakian, "Shakespeare and the Armenian Theater," in *Council on National Literatures/Quarterly World Report,* V (1982). J. S. Roucek and Thomas Kiernan, *The Negro Impact on Western Civilization* (1970). Roman Samarin and Alexander Nikolyukin, eds., *Shakespeare in the Soviet Union,* Avril Pyman, trans. (1966). Herbert M. Schueller, ed., *The Persistence of Shakespeare Idolatry: Essays in Honor of Robert W. Babcock* (1964). T. J. B. Spencer, "The Tyranny of Shakespeare" (1959), in Peter Alexander, ed., *Studies in Shakespeare* (1964). R. H. Stacy, *Russian Literary Criticism* (1974). René Wellek, *Discriminations* (1970). Tunc Yalman, *Shakespeare in Atatürk's Turkey* (1981). Rhowben Zaryan, *Shakespeare and the Armenians,* Haig Voskerchian, trans. (1969).

Shakespeare on Film and Television

JACK J. JORGENS

Shakespeare on Film

Shakespeare has generated some truly exotic manifestations on the movie screens of the world. It was inevitable in the era of the silent film that his plays would undergo significant changes, since a large part of the movie audience was barely literate, the movies were far more business than art, and Shakespeare's poetry and prose were absent except in the interspersed titles. When filmmakers gave in to the impulse to modernize, burlesque, or go the Bard one better, extraordinary metamorphoses resulted, such as *Romeo and Juliet at the Seaside, The Jewish King Lear,* and *When Macbeth Came to Snakeville.* History, Shakespeare's sources, and the overheated imaginations of filmmakers often shaped the moving shadows on the screen more than anything Shakespeare ever wrote, but the names were not changed to protect the innocent.

After the coming of sound, Shakespeare was fused with other arts: opera, in the many Russian films based on Nicolai's *Merry Wives of Windsor* and Verdi's *Macbeth* and *Otello;* ballet, in George Balanchine's *A Midsummer Night's Dream* (1967), with Edward Villella and Suzanne Farrell, and Kenneth MacMillan's *Romeo and Juliet* (1966), with Rudolf Nureyev and Margot Fonteyn; and the Broadway musical, in *Kiss Me Kate* (1953), *West Side Story* (1961), and *The Boys From Syracuse* (1940). Shakespeare has been married to many film genres. We have had *The Tempest* as science fiction (*Forbidden Planet,* 1956), *Macbeth* as a gangster film (*Joe*

Macbeth, 1955), and *A Midsummer Night's Dream* (1959) as a brilliant puppet film by the Czech master Jiri Trnka. Scenes from Shakespeare abound in "backstage" films like *The Prince of Players* (1955), *Kean* (1956), and *A Double Life* (1947), where jealous conflicts onstage merge with those offstage. Richard Dreyfuss' hilarious rendition of Richard III as a flamboyant homosexual in *The Goodbye Girl* (1977) is a delicious parody of the outlandish distortions of Shakespeare in the 1960s by stage directors desperately in search of the original. Some of the world's best filmmakers have worked variations on Shakespeare's stories, as in Claude Chabrol's *Ophelia* (1963), Woody Allen's *A Midsummer Night's Sex Comedy* (1982), and Paul Mazursky's *The Tempest* (1982).

Regrettably, this survey is limited to full-length works readily available in English (with some extraordinary exceptions) and to works that are close enough to Shakespeare's plays to have some interpretive value. Since television is like the water running under Tower Bridge—fleeting, abundant, plagued by sameness, critically ignored, and seldom preserved—television versions of Shakespeare will receive considerably less emphasis than film versions. The survey will not deal with the plentiful educational films about the works of Shakespeare. For those, see the bibliography for Andrew McLean's *Annotated Bibliographies and Media Guide for Teachers* and Barry M. Parker's *Folger Shakespeare Filmography.*

Shakespeare on Silent Film. The hundreds of

Shakespeare films made between 1899 and the advent of sound have been chronicled in detail in one of the most astonishing pieces of film scholarship ever compiled, Robert Hamilton Ball's *Shakespeare on Silent Film* (1968). The first recorded Shakespeare film showed a brief scene of Herbert Beerbohm Tree as King John signing Magna Charta (a scene that does not occur in Shakespeare's play). Soon dozens of other snippets from the plays and radical condensations of Shakespeare's plots appeared. In the teens, filmmakers became more ambitious. Enrico Guazzoni, responsible for the massive Italian *Quo Vadis?* (1912), unleashed two huge spectacles: *Antony and Cleopatra* (1913) and *Julius Caesar* (1914). The latter, made in eighteen months with a cast of twenty thousand, adhered only vaguely to Shakespeare.

Johnston Forbes-Robertson may have tried to remain faithful to the text and the idiom of the stage in *Hamlet* (1913), but Frederick Warde in *Richard III* (1913) suited popular tastes better. A playbill (not necessarily factually reliable, according to Ball) reads, "A Feature Costing $30,000 to Produce . . . / 1500 People, 200 Horses / 5 Distinct Battle Scenes. A Three-Masted Warship, Crowded with Soldiers, on Real Water. Architecture, Costumes, Armor, All Historically Correct in Every Detail." Between reels, Warde lectured and read passages from the play.

The most famous names of the age played in silent-film versions of Shakespeare's works: Sarah Bernhardt, Mounet-Sully, Frank Benson, Ermete Novelli, Ruggero Ruggeri, Francesca Bertini, Henny Porten, Clara Kimball Young, Harry Baur, Beverly Bayne, and Theda Bara, among others. *Hamlet* (1920), made in Germany by Svend Gade and Heinz Schall, features the famous Danish actress Asta Nielsen in the title role. In this film, Horatio, embracing the dying prince, discovers that "he" has breasts. Hamlet is a woman who has loved Horatio all along (Gertrude had disguised the sex of her daughter to assure her succession). *Othello* (1922), made in Germany by Dmitri Bukhovetsky, features Emil Jannings as a primitive, animalistic Othello and Werner Krauss as Iago. Ball describes the film fairly as "a bald and not very well told story of primitive passions without nobility, romance, or poetry," plagued by bad acting and editing and by too many titles.

It is testimony to Shakespeare's strong story lines and theatrical sense that so many spectators of that day found power in these versions of his works, stripped as they are of poetry and dialogue. But to modern viewers, most silent films of Shakespeare's works are of marginal artistic value. It was only with the coming of sound, when the word could harmonize with, and play off, the image, that the art of Shakespeare on film came of age.

The 1930s. The first four Shakespeare "talkies" in English were *The Taming of the Shrew* (1929), directed by Sam Taylor; *A Midsummer Night's Dream* (1935), directed by Max Reinhardt and William Dieterle; *Romeo and Juliet* (1936), directed by George Cukor; and *As You Like It* (1936), directed by Paul Czinner. *The Taming of the Shrew,* made in both silent and sound versions, features a heated battle between Douglas Fairbanks and Mary Pickford (who were not getting along very well in private life either). The emphasis is on the farce, and a broad wink from Pickford in her concluding speech lets everyone know that her capitulation is a farce too.

Romeo and Juliet was the brainchild of Irving Thalberg at Metro-Goldwyn-Mayer (MGM), who in this film suffocated the talents of one of the finest actors' directors in American film, George Cukor. Enormous research into the historical background, a pious attitude toward the text, and plush MGM costumes and sets did nothing to alleviate the blandness of middle-aged Leslie Howard and Norma Shearer in the leading roles, although John Barrymore hamming it up as Mercutio, Basil Rathbone as Tybalt, and Edna May Oliver as the Nurse are delightful to watch. The enterprise as a whole sinks under the weight of visual decorativeness, static images, and gentility.

As You Like It suffers from the mismatch of a handsome but pale and stiff young Laurence Olivier with a sly, charming, and mobile Elisabeth Bergner, whose lines are delivered in a thick Austrian accent. Gone for the most part are Touchstone's earthy humor and Jaques's cynical poses, leaving nothing to offset the cute cottages, pastoral scenes, and herds of sheep. Gone too are the quickness and playfulness so characteristic of Shakespearean comedy. As in all Shakespeare films of the 1930s, the images and actions drag—ironically, at a time when fast, sophisticated dialogue comedies with complicated plots by directors like Ernst Lubitsch, Howard Hawks, and Preston Sturges were big hits. Directors of Shakespeare films tended to simplify speeches and plots and to slow everything down. It was not until after World War II that a lively pacing of words, actions, and images finally came together.

Max Reinhardt had staged *A Midsummer Night's Dream* extravagantly many times. His film, codirected with William Dieterle, is an altogether outrageous, audacious pastiche of Shakespeare and Hollywood. Warner Brothers had been criticized by the censors for the violence of gangster movies and for Mae West's racy remarks, and the studio wanted a classic to improve their image. In the process, they produced by far the most entertaining Shakespearean film of the period. The film boasts an amazing cast: tough-guy Victor Jory as Oberon in black sequins and antlers; shapely, beautiful, and blonde Anita Louise as Titania; Ian Hunter as a standard British Shakespearean Theseus (the English critics liked him); and Verree Teasdale (playing in sighing, fist-to-forehead style) as a melancholy Hippolyta. The directors cast crooner Dick Powell as Lysander, Olivia de Havilland as a spunky, college-girl Hermia, Mickey Rooney as a mischievous Puck, and Nini Theilade as the First Fairy. The shimmering, balletic production numbers choreographed by Theilade and Bronislava Nijinska look suspiciously like Busby Berkeley creations. Warner Brothers comedians played the rustics: Joe E. Brown as Flute and (a stroke of casting genius) James Cagney as Bottom, a hilarious blend of union weaver, Chicago hood, and Ugly Duckling. Billy Barty played a diminutive Mustard Seed, and Kenneth Anger played the Indian Boy.

The sets are lavish: swirling pillars and shiny floors in the palace; a shadowy workshop with lots of tools; a forest full of fairies dancing up and down moonbeams; gnome orchestras; deer, owls, frogs, birds, and unicorns; and lush grass, pools, fog, and giant trees drenched in moonlight and as much Mendelssohn as Erich Korngold could orchestrate. This *Dream* has its angry critics who lament the loss of much of the verse and who object to the insertion into a patently English fantasy of so many Germanic and American clichés. But the film also has its fans. The eminent scholar G. Wilson Knight wrote in 1936, "I was impressed by the way in which the producer brought, *what is in the poetry,* the nightmarish fearsomeness of the woods and its wild beasts. . . . I liked Oberon on his horse."

The 1940s and 1950s. It was Laurence Olivier who first demonstrated that a Shakespearean film could be both a popular and an artistic success—a good movie and good Shakespeare. He directed and starred in *Henry V* (1944), made in vivid color with spirited music by William Walton. The film brims over with high spirits, bustles with activity, and is unafraid of Shakespeare's language, which ranges far beyond the usual realistic film dialogue. The film slights the darker sides of the play and its hero, but Olivier's interpretation is in tune with the nationalistic feelings of Englishmen engaged in a life-and-death struggle with Hitler's Germany. C. A. Le Jeune said, "What Shakespeare wrote in *Henry V,* and what the film has splendidly caught in its own fashion, is a fanfare; a flourish; a salute to high adventure; a kind of golden and perennially youthful exaltation of man's grim work."

To watch *Henry V* today is to look at English theater and history as though through a prism: we see Henry, the theatrical hero of medieval England, storming France and winning against all odds; Richard Burbage, the greatest actor of the Elizabethan age, playing Henry at the Globe and speaking the glorious lines of England's finest poet-playwright at the height of the English Renaissance; Olivier, the rising star of the English stage, playing the royal conqueror to an England summoning up its forces for an invasion of Nazi-occupied France in 1944. *Henry V* is a film of old values. As Harry Geduld says, it "is, ultimately, a movie about the strengths of discipline, determination, leadership and union in a common cause, and the hollowness of arrogance, ostentation and indecision." The film is stylistically playful and fluid in a Shakespearean way, as too few film adaptations have been. It begins with a robust re-creation of the Globe with its frankly theatrical stage and costumes. The actors play to a lively audience made up of all classes in Elizabethan England. The audience noisily responds to the actors' blunders, bawdy jokes, and high-flown rhetoric in a manner unknown to the tame audiences of today. Olivier then moves out of this historical re-creation into two other interestingly contradictory styles. One is the style of the costume picture, an "opening out" of the play into a world of heightened realism that culminates in the battle of Agincourt, with a splendid charge on horseback, hundreds of extras, and Eisensteinian cutting and compositional conflict. The other is a blend of nineteenth-century theatrical artifice with canvas backdrops and elaborate sets that recall the flat compositions, distorted perspective, and bright colors of medieval manuscript il-

42 and 43. Two scenes from the film *Henry V* (1944), directed by Laurence Olivier.

luminations. After this clash of styles, which echoes the conflict of bluff, plain-speaking Englishmen with foppish, blustering Frenchmen, the film leaves the film illusion of Henry's story for a return to the documentary re-creation of Shakespeare's Globe and its audience.

In *Hamlet* (1948), Olivier found a character unlike men of action such as Orlando and Henry V. At the beginning, as the camera moves down toward the murky castle from a dizzying height, Olivier announces his interpretive emphasis:

> So oft it chances in particular men
> That through some vicious mole of nature in them,
> By the o'ergrowth of some complexion
> Oft breaking down the pales and forts of reason,
> Or by some habit grown too much: that these men
> Carrying, I say, the stamp of one defect,
> Their virtues else—be they as pure as grace,
> Shall in the general censure take corruption
> From that particular fault.

Then, as the camera booms in on soldiers carrying Hamlet's body up to the ramparts, he adds, "This is the tragedy of a man who could not make up his mind."

Yet, this clash between Olivier's talent for playing men of action and his conception of Hamlet as an indecisive poet makes the film interesting. Mary McCarthy wrote:

> Sir Laurence Olivier's is the only *Hamlet* which seizes this inconsecutiveness and makes of it an image of suffering, of the failure to feel steadily, to be able to compose a continuous pattern, which is the most harrowing experience of man. Hamlet, a puzzle to himself, is seen by Olivier as a boy, whose immaturity is both his grace and his frailty. This uncertainty as to what is real, the disgust, the impulsiveness, the arbitrary shifts of mood, the recklessness, the high spirits, all incomprehensible in those middle-aged, speechifying Hamlets to whom our stage is habituated, here become suddenly irradiated.
>
> (Eckert)

In this film, Olivier takes a heavily psychological view of the prince. Freud wrote in *Interpretation of Dreams* that Hamlet "is able to do anything—except take vengeance on the man who did away with his father and took that father's place with his own mother, the man who shows him the repressed wishes of his own childhood realized." This assess-

ment, with which Olivier would appear to agree, strikes most critics today as a reductive view of a complicated character. Olivier's execution is often heavy-handed. The camera obsesses over Gertrude's bed, shows a symbolic castration as Hamlet drops his dagger into the sea at the "To be, or not to be" soliloquy, and dwells on phallic cannons, pillars, and towers, as well as vaginal hallways and curtains. Yet the shadowy, echoing castle, stripped of the spectacle of color of *Henry V,* is a powerful and appropriately dreamlike setting that serves to focus attention on the characters and their words. This economy of the stage, making a throne or a staircase or a wig resonate, letting the poetry paint images in our imaginations, contrasts vividly with the adaptations of directors—such as Franco Zeffirelli—that seem burdened with irrelevant detail.

Critics who dismiss Olivier as a film director ignore his ability to create distinctly cinematic solutions to the artistic problems Shakespeare poses for the screen. The ghost of Hamlet's father, for example, though appearing on the screen, is also embodied in the moving camera that observes the action from high angles, prowls broodingly along corridors, and circles behind the principal characters as they watch the play-within-the-play. Light makes scenes and characters appear and disappear in the darkness like ideas in Hamlet's (or Shakespeare's) mind. Olivier's impulse to simplify the story is bothersome: he rearranges scenes to make the tangled action more logical and eliminates Fortinbras, Rosencrantz, and Guildenstern, among others, to cut the film's length. But he did tackle the problem of finding a style suitable for this play, disregarding the expectations of audiences conditioned by film realism. In the context of film history, *Hamlet* is a very original work.

In *Richard III* (1955), again Olivier plays a dominant central role, making the other characters all but disappear and stressing the individual at the expense of the historical and social contexts. (Olivier cut the perpetually railing Margaret and, with her, the background of the *Henry VI* plays.) Again blatant theatricality and artificiality run counter to screen realism, pulling cinema toward theater rather than theater toward cinema. Again the film demonstrates a reverence for words, even if they are not always by Shakespeare in the order in which he wrote them. Again Olivier makes some concessions to the mass audience, cutting the difficult, expansive character of Richard and breaking up the seduction of Anne into two scenes so as not

44. The final scene from *Hamlet* (1948), directed by Laurence Olivier.

to strain credulity. What is new about *Richard III* is the pervasive black humor of a Renaissance wolf gleefully mowing his way through medieval sheep. Olivier the matinee idol—frolicking with a limp, a withered hand, and a hump on his back—is devilishly charming. As he gives us sidelong glances from beneath his jet-black wig, it is impossible to separate Richard's relish in doing evil from Olivier's relish in the wicked irony and dark farce of the role.

In design the film harks back to the colors of *Henry V.* The bloody reds, ominous shadows, and compressed, composite set (each room seeming only steps from the others) function as constant reminders of the hysteria of Richard's victims, who have no hope of escape. Driven out of this maze

45. Laurence Olivier and Claire Bloom in a scene from *Richard III* (1955), directed by Olivier.

into nature, Richard is weakened by nightmares about his victims. He is killed not in individual combat as in Shakespeare but by a horde of soldiers who butcher him as if at a boar hunt. Richard has shattered all rituals of loyalty, love, and religion. Now, Olivier implies, a much more primitive ritual is enacted to purge England of a plague of violence.

Next Olivier tried to raise money for a film of *Macbeth,* which theater critics of the 1950s had called his greatest performance, but he failed. Though he would act in more films and in television versions of Shakespeare, his career as a director of Shakespearean films was over.

The other pioneer who explored the creative possibilities of the Shakespeare film was Orson Welles, whose experience in radio drama, theater, and motion pictures and love of Shakespeare made him ideally suited for such an undertaking. Welles termed his first effort, made at Republic in 1948, "an expressionist *Macbeth,*" not a straight rendition but "a violently sketched charcoal drawing of a great play." The result is an interesting disaster. The sound track is a jumble of Scottish, British, and American accents; the cutting (done in Welles's absence) is chaotic, and the performances are weak.

A new character called the Holy Father (Alan Napier) was intended to heighten the contrast between the Christian forces of good and the pagan forces of evil at the core of the film.

What redeems this *Macbeth* is sheer visual creativity, images that capture Macbeth's nightmarish inner world as he cuts himself free from humanity. Fear, guilt, sleeplessness, and alcohol distort everything. The cave walls sweat. Withered branches and crosses on which are mounted heads of traitors are silhouetted against a smeared gray sky. Swirling fog fills the screen as Macbeth speaks his "To-morrow, and to-morrow, and to-morrow" speech. The witches mold a figure out of wet clay and mockingly crown it king. Lady Macbeth embraces Macbeth at the moment the huge blade of the executioner's ax falls on Cawdor's head. The body of the dwarf Seyton, who has hung himself from a bellrope, slowly sways back and forth ringing the alarm bell with disturbing, soft irregularity. From above, the camera fixes Macbeth against Rorschach-test floors. A sword passes before the eyes of a voodoo doll as Macbeth hallucinates a dagger. Macbeth's blurred, warped image is reflected in a metal shield. Lady Macbeth's bloody hand is spread out in the foreground of a shot, seeming larger than her whole body. Such visceral images represent Welles's first attempt to match in his own medium the power of Shakespeare's poetic images.

Of the three lead roles in Welles's *Othello* (1952) —Welles's noble Moor, Suzanne Cloutier's angelic Desdemona, and Michael MacLiammoir's sexually envious Iago—MacLiammoir's is the most interesting. This is neither Iago as devil nor Iago as passionate, melodramatic villain, but a bland, passionless man gnawed at by his impotence, manipulating other people's weaknesses like a bored mechanic. The best performance is not by the actors, but by the camera, which creates stunning images and a dense texture of screen poetry matched in Shakespeare films only by Kurosawa and Kozintsev.

Welles contrasts Venice with Cyprus, pitting sophisticated tracery, arches, and piazzas, ornately ordered staircases, and glassy, still canals against a primitive, brutal fortress with vast ramparts lashed by an angry sea. The luxury, art, and Christianity of Venice give way to the spartan military life and pagan imagery of Cyprus. Welles emphasized a second thematic dialectic in his German television film *The Making of Othello:* the clash of the heroic, romantic style of Othello with the dark, twisted style of Iago. The imagery surrounding the Moor, like his language, is on an epic scale: ships and plumed troops; low-angle shots of grand architecture; sunshine, sky, and sea; banners flying and cannons firing; and crowd scenes. The style that is used for Iago is made up of distorted reflections, tortured compositions, elliptical editing, vertiginous camera movements, shadows, and labyrinths.

While the film fractures the narrative at the beginning—so much so that Welles resorts to voice-over narration to explain what is happening—the dominance of the elements associated with Iago

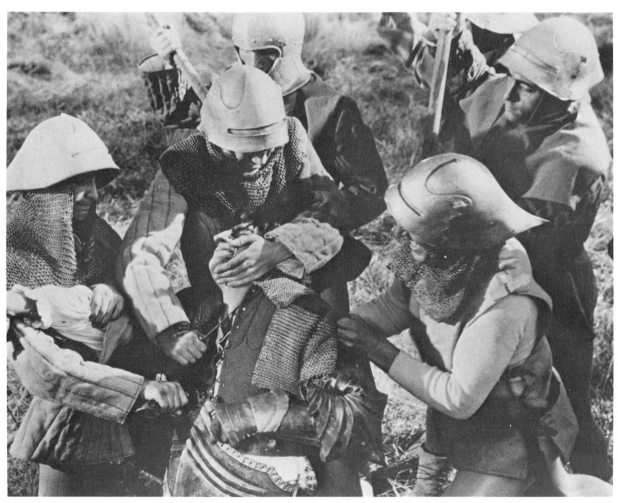

46. Laurence Olivier in the death scene from *Richard III.*

688

47. (Right) Suzanne Cloutier and Orson Welles in a scene from *Othello* (1952), directed by Welles. 48. (Below) Orson Welles as the Moor on the steps of his fortress in Cyprus, from *Othello*.

over those used for Othello marks the inexorable progress of the tragedy. Sound in the film is similarly uneven, blending inaudible and badly synchronized dialogue with an imaginative use of audio collage that Welles learned in radio in the 1930s.

In contrast to Welles's visual fireworks, *Julius Caesar* (1953), produced by John Houseman and directed by Joseph Mankiewicz, is visually static and tame, apparently imitating Roman friezes and oddly lacking in detail, given its avowed intention to echo the fascist rallies of Hitler and Mussolini. But surrounding Louis Calhern as Caesar—a small man inside a large body, a man rigid not out of strength but out of fear—is a remarkable trio: James Mason as Brutus, John Gielgud as Cassius, and Marlon Brando as Antony.

Mason's Brutus is a man of integrity and principle who acts out of love for Rome. But he is a naive idealist, lost in the ambiguous, shifting political quagmire of the real world. He is never able to accept the necessity of Caesar's death, never sure what he should have done. Gielgud's Cassius is a narrow but intense, nearsighted man driven by feelings of jealousy and inferiority, a born follower who overcomes his weakness by blustering. Sometimes he is cool and cunning, but under pressure he becomes fatally rash. He thinks he wants power, but all he really wants is death. Brando's Antony is utterly ruthless, a Machiavellian's Machiavelli easily shifting his persona from loyal friend and follower of Caesar to cunning orator, to dangerous enemy. Above all, Brando conveys a sense of danger, a feeling of unpredictability and impending violence that marks him as Caesar's successor.

Outside the English-speaking world, the finest film translation of Shakespeare is Akira Kurosawa's Japanese version of *Macbeth,* called *Throne of Blood* (1957), with Toshiro Mifune as Washizu (Macbeth) and Isuzu Yamada as Asaji (Lady Macbeth). Kurosawa abandons Shakespeare's poetry and dialogue and recasts the dramatic structure; yet he preserves the essence of the story. An ambitious samurai warrior, urged on by his wife and by supernatural beings, murders his feudal lord and rules (and is ruled) by fear until he is destroyed.

A labyrinthine forest surrounds the lord's castle, serving as a metaphor for both the moral confusions of civil war and the emotional turmoil within Washizu. In the Forest Spirit, a calm white-faced figure who is amused by the refusal of men to face their desires, the warriors Washizu and Miki meet a creature they are ill-equipped to understand. She is "helpless," passive, and static; they are armed, aggressive, and violent. She sits in a flimsy stick hut; they serve a lord whose mighty castle has never been defeated. They ask questions about the future; the Spirit answers by disappearing and leaving the warriors among heaps of bones.

Kurosawa tells the Macbeth story in flashback, beginning at a time when the huge forest castle has been destroyed. Fog rolls over the empty hills. A marker records Washizu's rebellion, which succeeded and failed long ago. A chorus sings, "Behold, within this place now desolate stood once a mighty fortress, lived a proud warrior murdered by ambition, his spirit walking still. Vain pride, then as now, will lead ambition to the kill." This thrust into the past, plus the film's extreme detachment from its central character, make for a colder, much more ironic work than Shakespeare's. Our fascination with Shakespeare's murderer, our astonishment at his imagination, and our pity for his suffering are gone. Kurosawa looks down like a distant, uncaring god on a hero ironically trapped in a web of perfect aesthetic forms.

Kurosawa makes visual the key themes of Shakespeare's play. Hideous bloodstains smear the walls of a traitor's room and a messenger refuses to die after Washizu stabs him in the neck. Washizu's fortress is invaded by birds as his enemies cut down the trees in the forest. And at the end, the forest moves in slow motion to ominous, low musical notes toward Washizu, fulfilling the Spirit's prophecy and turning his men against him. The sterility of the Macbeths is made literal. Asaji becomes pregnant, giving Macbeth further reason to be ambitious. But when the child is stillborn, Asaji goes mad (destroyed from within like Washizu). One of the most harrowing moments in the film is when Washizu watches Asaji continue to wash imaginary blood from her hands after he has taken away the bowl of water.

Toshiro Mifune plays Washizu with tremendous ferocity. The warrior is at home neither in the tangled forest nor in the cool, geometrical interiors of the fortress. He is always in motion, anxious, panicked, racked with doubt while his wife plays on his fears and while ambition taunts him. Finally, death comes from hundreds of arrows. In a final grotesque gesture of defiance, he stumbles down a flight of stairs, staggers toward his men, and tries to draw his sword before falling to the ground. The fog sweeps in, the fortress is gone, and the chorus chants again.

Other foreign directors tried their hand at Shakespeare in the 1950s, though not with such impressive results. Renato Castellani's *Romeo and Juliet* (1954), with Laurence Harvey and Susan Shentall, is an Italian film in English. The rich color and elegant settings in Verona, Siena, and Venice make the work visually beautiful. Unfortunately the architectural backdrop is richer and more expressive than the actors, and the story moves with fatal slowness. In a failed attempt to compensate, the director has poured conventional movie music over the remains of the text like syrup over a questionable dessert.

The Soviet Union has produced, among others, *Othello* (1955), directed by Sergei Yutkevitch and overacted by Sergei Bondarchuk and Irina Skobtseva; *Twelfth Night* (1955), directed by Jakow Frid; *Much Ado About Nothing* (1956), directed by L. Samkovoi; and *The Taming of the Shrew* (1961), directed by Sergei Kolossov. Done in heavy, slow, operatic style with elegant color and elaborate sets, these films have had little impact on Western audiences.

Franz Peter Wirth's *Hamlet* (1960), made in Germany and dubbed in English, with Maximilian Schell as Hamlet, is acted against a fixed, bare theatrical set of heavy timbers. Hans Caninberg overplays Claudius as an oily, slit-eyed sewer rat, but Schell's performance is a vigorous and sensitive one.

The 1960s. The social upheavals and artistic experiments of the 1960s and early 1970s prompted filmmakers to find Shakespeare the radical behind Shakespeare the establishment icon. Russian film director and Shakespeare scholar Grigori Kozintsev gave the world a wonderful gift for Shake-

49. Toshiro Mifune (r.) as Washizu meeting the Forest Spirit in a scene from *Throne of Blood* (1957), directed by Akira Kurosawa.

50. The death scene from *Throne of Blood.*

speare's four-hundredth birthday, a magnificent wide-screen, black-and-white film of *Hamlet* (1964), starring Innokenti Smoktunovski. Using Boris Pasternak's prose translation, Kozintsev followed Welles in trying to translate the poetry into the language of the screen. A screen version, Kozintsev said in a 1972 essay, "shifts the stress from the aural to the visual. The problem is not one of the aural to the visual. The problem is not one of finding means to speak the verse in front of the camera, in realistic circumstances ranging from long-shot to close-up. The aural has to be made visual. The poetic texture has itself to be transformed into a visual poetry, into the dynamic organisation of film imagery." His *Hamlet* is a cinematic poem of stone, iron, fire, sea, and earth. In 1966 he wrote:

Stone: the walls of Elsinore, the firmly built government prison, on which armorial bearings and sinister bas-reliefs had been carved centuries ago.

Iron: weapons, the inhuman forces of oppression, the ugly steel faces of war.

Fire: anxiety, revolt, movement, the trembling flame of the candles at Claudius's celebrations; raging fiery tongues (Horatio's narrative about the ghostly apparition); the wind-blown lamps on the stage erected for "The Mousetrap."

Sea: waves, crashing against the bastions, ceaseless movement, the change of the tides, the boiling of chaos, and again the silent, endless surface of glass.

Earth: the world beyond Elsinore, amid stones—a bit of field tilled by a ploughman, the sand pouring out of Yorick's skull, and the handful of dust in the palm of the wanderer-heir to the throne of Denmark.

The opening images set up a dialectic of life and death, fixity and change (a torch burning against rock, the shadow of the fortress on the sea), that is carried through the rest of the film. No other Shakespearean film has so many memorable and significant images: Ophelia's soft, young body encased in an iron corset and walked through mechanical dance steps like a windup doll by crones dressed in black; Hamlet poised on the cliff between sky and sea; spies hiding behind each curtain and door; a cold fireplace; empty chairs that remind us of their owners; billowing tapestries and curtains symbolically linked with death.

Underlying this imagistic pattern is a Marxist-humanist view of the play. Kozintsev relates the sickness of the court of Elsinore to the clash between Renaissance ideals and the ruthless accumulation of capital, between the professed nobility of man and contempt for the individual in the name of the state. Claudius' court, where the tactics for keeping control are all too familiar to citizens of nineteenth- and twentieth-century Russia, is characterized by "callous emptiness. The noble and the spiritual have vanished from life." Hamlet confronts the malaise of a whole age, not (as in Olivier's film) his own psychological problems.

Olivier and Welles again turned to Shakespeare: Olivier in a film of *Othello* (1965), directed by Stuart Burge and based on the fine National Theatre production directed by John Dexter, and Welles in his 1966 recasting of the Henry IV plays, *Chimes at Midnight* (also known as *Falstaff*). Each film has scenes of stunning power, yet each is flawed. Together they illustrate the unhappy degree to which insufficient time, money, and techni-

cal consideration can affect the quality of a Shakespeare film.

Othello ought to have been a great film. The portrayals are extraordinary: Olivier's Othello is a savage, sensual, powerful black general; Maggie Smith's Desdemona is a daring, beautiful, strong, loyal wife; and Frank Finley's Iago is a cunning, blunt, ambitious, perverted soldier. The technique chosen to transpose the stage production onto the screen was to rebuild the theatrical set in a film studio and to shoot in the style of television—that is, to take repeated run-throughs of the action with several cameras at varying angles and with various lenses in order to give the editor the choice of cutting from one shot to another. Most of the blocking and gestures of the stage production were preserved intact. But this is not the way good films are made. A stage production can serve only as raw material for translation into a new medium. The power of cinema derives from placing one camera in precisely the right location, lighting the image for that angle only, and blocking the gestures and movement for the greatest visual beauty and energy for that shot and for that dramatic moment. Multiple-camera technique is cost-effective, but it involves fatal compromises. Tantalizing proof of what a remarkable film we might have had can be seen in the searing photographs of the theater production by Angus MacBean in Kenneth Tynan's souvenir book *Othello: The National Theatre Production*. As it is, the film seems too long and is full of boring imagery.

Denied Hollywood craftsmanship and machinery, distrusted by the money people who allow directors to practice this most expensive art, his energies and concentration scattered, Orson Welles performed a miracle by merely finishing *Chimes at Midnight*. Lacking the resources to concentrate on every scene, he chose to focus on the big scenes. The result is a roller-coaster film with extraordinary highs and lows. John Gielgud gives perhaps his greatest screen performance as guilt-ridden, dying Henry IV, tormented by his wayward son, sleeplessly looking out at his kingdom from his cold, dark castle. Welles's Falstaff is less funny than touching and melancholy. Sitting drunk before a fire with old Shallow and Silence, he listens to lies about the past and hears of the many who are dead; his poetic reflection ("We have heard the chimes at midnight, Master Shallow") captures the late-night musing of old age perfectly.

The battle at Shrewsbury is the pivot of the film,

transforming "Merrie Englande" into a world of ruthless, treacherous men. It opens with the chivalric splendor of horses and banners, shifts tones as Falstaff in spherical armor comically flees this way and that, settles into rapid moving shots of the grim labor of war until both sides are covered with mud, and climaxes with the single combat of Hal and Hotspur. It is one of the greatest battle scenes in film history.

Finest of all the film's scenes is the rejection of Falstaff, a perfect marriage of theater and cinema: Falstaff rushing through the wintery landscape to reap his rewards; Falstaff breaking through the crowd to cry out and to see his beloved Hal, shocking all who observe and halting the royal procession; the rows of banners behind Hal as he ruthlessly brings Falstaff to his knees with banishment; Falstaff's smile as he understands why Hal must renounce him. When Hal walks off into the misty rows of banners, followed by his soldiers (with no background music, only the sounds of feet and armor), Falstaff is left dwarfed by a huge tower in the background: "Master Shallow, I owe you a thousand pound."

51. John Gielgud as Henry IV, in a scene from *Chimes at Midnight* (1966), directed by Orson Welles.

The film's flaws are many. Scenes are weakly constructed and played. There are problems with the quality and synchronization of the sound (an irony, since Welles is a master of film sound). There were difficulties at the Spanish laboratory, which could not print the film with the texture of old photographs that Welles wanted. The humor lags. But none of these can take away from the splendor of the film's best scenes.

Franco Zeffirelli's instincts for the commercial and the spectacular made his two Shakespeare films, by contrast, much more widely seen and known. *The Taming of the Shrew* (1966) features the domestic warfare of Richard Burton and Elizabeth Taylor, Michael Hordern as Baptista, Cyril Cusack as Grumio, and Michael York as Lucentio. The film opens at a saturnalian festival in Padua—with bawdy songs, a lively "corpse" tossed in the air by members of a mock funeral procession who cavort through the streets, sacrilegious pig-faced bishops, and ugly kings and queens. This new saturnalian frame goes deep to the roots of all dramatic comedy and announces a theme of importance to Zeffirelli's interpretation of the play—the theme of rebellion. The struggle of the central couple is a messy kind of mutual therapy. In Padua, where students are

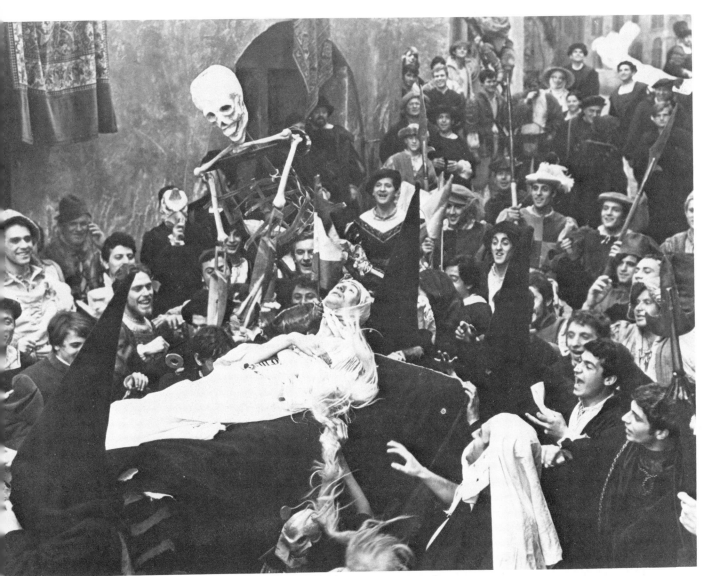

52. A mock funeral procession from the opening scene of *The Taming of the Shrew* (1966), directed by Franco Zeffirelli.

more interested in love than books, lovers school each other. Hero and heroine make each other more interesting and imaginative. Petruchio, the drunken, greedy lout, becomes Petruchio, the witty, gentle man. Katherina, the violent "shrew," jealous of her sister, sexually frustrated, a spoiled rich girl, becomes Kate, the generous, loving, playful, happy wife. It is a rough passage, but they both enjoy it.

The larger context of this battle of the sexes is more important than in traditional productions. From the opening revels it is plain that Petruchio and Kate are the Lord and Lady of Misrule. They are leaders of a rebellion against the conformity and repression of Paduan society, a comic oedipal revolt against the fathers. Their pagan wedding makes a mockery of orthodox religious ritual. Petruchio, in preposterous costume, falls asleep after gulping down the holy wine to toast his new bride. The film is a carnival of farcical, festive destructiveness, much of it aimed at the luxuries and structures of Padua. Materialism is an enemy to true love. Paduans are trapped in rigid roles, and if in comedies of the green world, as Northrop Frye calls Shakespeare's romantic comedies, a new society crystallizes around the hero and heroine, part of the freedom offered by the new regime is the freedom to be more than a comic type. Petruchio's country house, littered though it is with dust and louts, is a symbol of his refusal to be absorbed into society.

Not everyone likes Zeffirelli's operatic style of filmmaking. His spectacular scenes, heavy use of background music, and broad comic effects are obvious attempts to play to mass audiences. He allows a laziness in Richard Burton, whose dumb hearty laugh can drive viewers to distraction. And he is capable of shameless sentimentalizing, as when Kate watches through stained glass as Petruchio announces the wedding to her father. But Zeffirelli is a thoughtful director, and his instinct for playing to the pit is not as foreign to the spirit of Shakespearean drama as purists might claim.

Zeffirelli's enormously popular *Romeo and Juliet* (1968), with Leonard Whiting as Romeo, Olivia Hussey as Juliet, Michael York as Tybalt, and John McEnery as Mercutio, displays the same mix of broad effects and interpretive insight. As in Castellani's 1954 version, setting plays an important part, but here the hot, dusty squares and lavish Renaissance rooms do not overshadow the story or slow it down. A driving energy propels the film forward, toward its fatal conclusion.

Zeffirelli shows little sensitivity to Shakespeare's verse. He is more interested in what he calls "the poetry of human relationships." Though he sometimes leans toward caricature, at least the characters have life. Young, aristocratic Lady Capulet, uncomfortable at having such a mature daughter, is embarrassed by her coarse, older merchant husband and is strongly attracted to her handsome, young nephew Tybalt. She is much more vividly portrayed than in most productions. Mercutio's streaks of madness, self-destructiveness, and jealousy are supported by the text, and the inventiveness of his gestures (mimicking various characters, placing a shroudlike handkerchief over his face, hoisting the Nurse's skirts) matches his verbal inventiveness well.

The depiction of Romeo and Juliet as young teenagers works beautifully in the first half of the film. They are impetuous, hungry, silly, always in a hurry. The core of Zeffirelli's interpretation of the play, first seen in his Old Vic production in 1960, is the clash between generations, a theme well-attuned to movie audiences in 1968. The old talk; the young act. The old take their time and deliberate; the reckless young are in a big hurry to do everything, even to die. The old worry about money, status, and power; the young play deadly games in the town square. Neither generation understands the other.

The director shifts styles halfway through the story. After Mercutio's death the shots become less busy, the light and bright colors drain away, and Verona becomes a cemetery. Too late the old discover their own ignorance and learn the price of their rivalry. Regrettably the two lead actors do not meet the demands of their final scenes. In the play, Romeo and Juliet are tragic figures; they know that they have lived whole lives in a few weeks and how they have collaborated with fate in destroying their lives. In the film they do not grow up, but are merely pathetic. We pity them for their pain and loss; but we do not revere them, because they have not attained tragic awareness.

Not all the films of the 1960s are so distinguished. Stuart Burge's *Julius Caesar* (1970), with Charlton Heston as Antony, Jason Robards spectacularly miscast as Brutus, Richard Johnson as Cassius, John Gielgud as Caesar, and Richard Chamberlain as Octavius, is a classic lesson in how not to do it.

The 1970s and 1980s. The early 1970s seemed to promise a continuation of the surge of the 1960s

53. Mercutio playfully hoisting the Nurse's skirts in a scene from *Romeo and Juliet* (1968),
directed by Franco Zeffirelli.

with films by three major directors: Peter Brook, Grigori Kozintsev, and Roman Polanski. In contrast to Burge, who attempted to record a powerful stage production in his 1965 *Othello,* Brook in *King Lear* (1970) used his extraordinary Royal Shakespeare Company production as raw material for a new work in a new medium. Stylistically, the film has a raw, primitive quality: dark, grainy black-and-white images with occasional blasts of intense light; prolonged silences in place of music; camera work that makes use of intense close-ups and shallow depth of field for a minimal reliance on spectacle. Ragged elliptical editing, out-of-focus shots, discordant compositions, and hallucinatory visions force the spectator to experience the disorientation and obscured sight of Lear and Gloucester as they are driven onto the snowy heath.

Brook's interpretation was heavily influenced by Jan Kott's essay "King Lear, or Endgame," in *Shakespeare, Our Contemporary,* as well as by Jerzy Grotowski's demand for a "theater of cruelty" that strips the stage of ornament and returns to the violent mythic roots of theater. Dressed in animal skins and living in a crude fortress, the characters seem close to cavemen. Theirs is a survival culture without arts, books, music, and civilized comforts. Brook strips away much of Shakespeare's poetry and aspires to a text of "nothing." The performances by Paul Scofield as Lear and Irene Worth as Goneril are fierce but muted, disappointing critics who looked for grand Shakespearean acting with sweeping gestures, dramatic crossings and re-crossings, and vocal virtuosity. Brook cares little for audience comfort. The fractured exposition and

54. Jack MacGowran (l.) as the Fool and Paul Scofield in a scene from *King Lear* (1970),
directed by Peter Brook.

the sketchy presentation of the Edmund-Edgar sub-plot make the story almost impossible to follow for those who do not already know it. The violence is blunt and shocking. The Fool provides little relief from the consistently grim tone, and the ending provides no catharsis, burdening the audience with the full weight of the destruction of the royal family, meaningless suffering, and apocalypse in nature. But granted the editing of Shakespeare's play and its lack of entertainment value, Brook's *King Lear* remains an extraordinary achievement, one of the most powerful of all Shakespearean films.

Kozintsev's *King Lear* (1970) is both a complement and contrast to Brook's bleak film. Kozintsev's is a Christian-humanist vision, stressing Lear's progress from blindness to sight, from pride and anger to love. The strongest scenes in Brook's film are those of violence and suffering, with the magnificent exception of the tender scene with the mad Lear and the blind Gloucester on a rocky beach; the most gripping moments in the Russian film are those of recognition, repentance, and forgiveness

that culminate in the beautiful, moving reconciliation of Lear and Cordelia, surrounded by Edmund's brutal soldiers. Kozintsev's work is made in the romantic, epic Russian style, with flames burning along the walls of a gigantic fortress; an elaborate, stunning musical score by Dmitri Shostakovich; exciting fight scenes, including a prolonged final duel between Edmund and Edgar (in Brook's film it was a long circling followed by one sudden blow); and elaborate displays of royal followers and wealth. Brook's work is subjective, interior, and solipsistic. Kozintsev places Lear's fall in a social context. Masses of peasants suffer from the civil war. When Lear is driven out onto the roads, he joins hundreds of other homeless wanderers—cold, hungry subjects whom Lear has ignored in the splendid czarlike isolation of his castle.

In the Russian *Lear,* the Fool (Oleg Dal), thin and with a shaved head, provides more savage as well as more playful humor than the older, more subdued Fool in the Brook version. Far from Scofield's huge, static granite-faced ex-soldier, Lear as played by Yuri Jarvet is a dignified, small, elf-faced

55. (Above) Valentina Shendrikova as Cordelia and Yuri Jarvet in a scene from *King Lear* (1970), directed by Grigori Kozintsev. 56. (Right) Oleg Dal in the closing scene of Kozintsev's *King Lear.*

699

man with a shock of white hair; he is volatile, mobile, and demonstrative. Kozintsev gives his actors the big gestures that Brook avoided. Edmund hurls a stone defiantly at the sky at the end of his "Gods, stand up for bastards" speech. Goneril kisses the corpse of Cornwall hard on the lips before hunting out Edmund and stripping off his coat. At the end, the Fool sits amid the rubble playing his flute until he is kicked aside by passing soldiers. To be greeted in the same year by two such magnificent and magnificently different versions of a great tragedy was a remarkable event.

Roman Polanski's *Macbeth* (1972), with Jon Finch and Francesca Annis as an unusually young pair of Macbeths, is an upsetting, powerful film. Said literary adviser Kenneth Tynan, "It makes no sense to have Macbeth and Lady Macbeth performed by 60-year-olds and menopausals. It's too late for them to be ambitious." Building outward from this casting, Polanski constructed a thematic pattern of beauty and ugliness: a fair, young witch and two foul ones, a beautiful landscape and the ugly remains of battle, and domestic happiness in MacDuff's house followed by grotesque violence. Polanski says of Macbeth, "His acts are very primitive but his thoughts are very sophisticated" (*Times* [London], 28 February 1971).

Brutality seems all too usual in so primitive a setting. The weak naturally fall to the strong and the butchering of animals extends easily to the butchering of people. Macbeth's tortured imaginings seem precursors of another world. The opening images powerfully state the themes of the story. A lurid pink-orange dawn evolves to the flat light of day, establishing a world of half-light. The tidal flat is neither land nor sea. Nature equivocates. Images anticipate the patterns that will pervade the film: a witch's crooked stick foretells penetration and rape; a rope, a dagger, blood, and a severed hand are buried in the sand; apparitions disappear into the fog.

The violence of this *Macbeth* is especially disturbing, because it is so often linked with eroticism (rape; the fascination and excitement of Lady Macbeth at the baited bear; Macbeth's sitting astride Duncan, stabbing him again and again) and because it is so frequent, bloody, and prolonged. To those who objected, Polanski responded that the truly pornographic violence is the "clean" kind on television. "If you don't show violence the way it is, I think that's immoral and harmful. If you don't upset people, then that's obscenity" (quotes by Bernard Weinraub, *New York Times Magazine*, 12 December 1971).

Macbeth is often viewed as a ritual cleansing, a return to natural and moral order, health, and justice. In Polanski's interpretation, the new order is tainted by the old. Ross, who plays an active role in Macbeth's regime and ultimately betrays him, crowns Malcolm king. The end circles back to the beginning. Malcolm's limping, envious brother Donalbain rides in the rain to visit the rock dwelling of the witches with the same discordant bagpipe music playing as when Macbeth visited them. The cycle of violence will begin again.

A few more Shakespearean films were made in this period. Charlton Heston played a creditable Antony in an otherwise ordinary *Antony and Cleopatra* (1973) directed by Heston. And Derek Jarman directed an energetic, bizarre version of *The Tempest* (1980) described as follows by J. Hoberman in the *Village Voice* (24 September 1980):

Prospero, sourly played by avant-garde playwright Heathcote Williams, presides over a ramshackle, furniture-crammed, candle-lit abbey where the floors are covered with straw and the walls with occult doodles. Ariel looks as wasted as a David Bowie spaceman, while a rather hearty Miranda wears her hair in bedraggled feather-and-pearl encrusted corn-rows. Caliban is played by the blind mime Jack Birkett, and with his massive bald head and steam-shovel mouth (slobbering raw eggs or emitting a high-pitched giggle), he looks like one of Chester Gould's larcenous gargoyles and, indeed, manages to steal the film.

Miranda delivers her "Brave new world" speech to romping young sailors, the music is raucous, and the film ends with a "goddess" in a yellow butterfly suit singing "Stormy Weather."

But for all practical purposes, the making of feature-film versions of Shakespeare stopped in 1972. Rumors circulate of producers and directors trying to get projects off the ground, but nothing happens. We can blame it on the soaring costs of filmmaking or on the takeover of the studios by large corporations. We can point to the training and interests of young directors and actors who, unlike Olivier, Welles, Kozintsev, Brook, and Polanski, have little experience in the theater and no knowledge of Shakespeare. It may be symptomatic of the conservatism and artistic timidity of the times. Whatever the reason, the energy to produce Shakespeare has shifted to television, a medium less well suited to his plays.

Shakespeare on Television

Television productions of Shakespeare are less highly regarded and have received much less critical attention than have film versions. This may have to do with differences between the two media: small-screen television is dwarfed by the large scale, sharpness, brilliant color, and sophisticated sound tracks of feature films. Television affords far fewer opportunities for the visual translation so important to film directors. The intimate nature of television, which renders close-ups and small scenes well, in theory allows for a greater emphasis on the poetry and the actor's performance. But in practice it often makes for a kind of bland, neutral presentation less striking in conception and less original in interpretation than in the best films.

The discrepancies may have to do with money. Television budgets seldom allow anything but cramped, threadbare studio productions with little rehearsal time, second-rate casts, and minimal advertising. First-rate directors with a real knowledge of Shakespeare seldom direct Shakespeare for the television screen. Performances that might be electrifying in the theater drop in temperature precipitately when rendered by directors who grind away at their scenes with three cameras and who lack the skills in precise camera placement, composition, and cutting of Polanski, Kozintsev, Brook, or Welles.

Television is a transient medium. Unlike films, which continue to be available, television programs are seldom shown again and often are thrown away or erased. Most of those that survive are unavailable to any but the most dogged researchers, and contractual snarls often prohibit showing them in public. There exists no archive where one can view more than a few of the television versions of Shakespeare's work.

In the United States, pioneers of the nerve-racking medium of live, multiset television drama, like the pioneers of silent film, tackled Shakespeare with great fervor. There was an adaptation of *Julius Caesar* (imitating in its modern dress the famous Welles-Houseman Mercury Theater production of 1937) on CBS's "Studio One" (1949); a production by The Players of *Macbeth* on "NBC Repertory Theatre" (1949); and Charlton Heston and Judith Evelyn in *Macbeth* on "Studio One" (1951). Maurice Evans appeared in a series of "Hallmark Hall of Fame" productions, including *Macbeth* with Judith Anderson (1954), *Hamlet*

(1953), *Richard II* (1954), *The Taming of the Shrew* with Lilli Palmer in 1956, and *Twelfth Night* (1957). A young Susan Strasberg played Juliet on the "Kraft Television Theatre" (1954), and viewers saw Claire Bloom and John Neville in an Old Vic *Romeo and Juliet* (1957).

Three better versions shot on film but clearly tailored for television, stressing close-ups and made on small budgets, are worth noting. In Frank Dunlop's *The Winter's Tale* (1966), adapted from an Edinburgh Festival production, Laurence Harvey as Leontes, Jane Asher as Perdita, and Moira Redmond as Hermione give competent performances, but the imagery, as is so often the case in television adaptations, is unmemorable. Peter Hall's *A Midsummer Night's Dream* (1969) features David Warner as Lysander, Diana Rigg as Helena, Helen Mirren as Hermia, Ian Richardson as Oberon, Judi Dench as Titania, Iam Holm as Puck, and Paul Rogers as Bottom. In this oddly muted, unfestive production, the courtiers and their eighteenth-century country house are insufferably bland. But the rustics have real life, and once we are out in the wet greenery, creative cutting and camera work make the film interesting to watch. *Hamlet* (1969), directed by Tony Richardson, has Nicol Williamson as Hamlet, Anthony Hopkins as Claudius, Judy Parfitt as Gertrude, and Marianne Faithful as a lascivious Ophelia incestuously involved with Laertes. Shot at the Roundhouse Theater, it is acted out largely against limbo darkness. Williamson's nasty, snarling, nervous, intellectual Hamlet is the center of interest. He is disgusted by his drunken, bloated uncle and sensual mother and despairs of a world that will accept them as royal leaders in place of his father. Would that his intensity had saturated the production as a whole.

While regional theaters in the United States have been unwilling or unable to mount television versions of their productions, Joseph Papp and his New York Shakespeare Festival mounted two interesting productions: a bubbly Roaring Twenties version of *Much Ado About Nothing* with Sam Waterston and Kathleen Widdoes, which may be the best production of a Shakespeare comedy ever done on television, and a competent *King Lear* with James Earl Jones.

In England, Shakespeare was also a staple of early television. From 1946 to 1952, the BBC produced *As You Like It, Romeo and Juliet, Hamlet, Macbeth, Othello, King Lear, Richard II, Henry V, The Merchant of Venice, Twelfth Night, Julius Caesar,* and

King John. The 1960s saw three distinguished series: *An Age of Kings* (1961), directed by Peter Dews, consisted of fifteen one-hour segments based on the *Richard II* and *Henry VI* tetralogies; *The Spread of the Eagle* (1963), in nine segments, was based on *Coriolanus, Julius Caesar,* and *Antony and Cleopatra;* and *The Wars of the Roses* (1965), in three three-hour segments, was based on the Royal Shakespeare Company production by Peter Hall and John Barton, starring Peggy Ashcroft, David Warner, Roy Dotrice, Ian Holm, and Donald Sinden. The two notable British productions of the 1970s were Jonathan Miller's wonderful National Theatre production of *The Merchant of Venice* with Olivier as Shylock and Trevor Nunn's fine version of *Macbeth.*

The most ambitious effort, though, was by the British Broadcasting Corporation, which in 1979 boldly launched a six-year project to produce the entire canon with the sponsorship of three American corporations, Exxon, Metropolitan Life, and Morgan Guaranty Trust. The plays are shown in the United States by the Public Broadcasting System and are distributed by Time-Life. Given painfully small budgets, which allowed only a week of shooting time for each play and prevented the hiring of the best available actors (a policy of no Americans rankled), no one expected that the series would live up to its media-hype claims to be a definitive Shakespeare. Nevertheless, producers Cedric Messina, Jonathan Miller, and Shaun Sutton managed to find some enterprising new talent and produced several competent and a few excellent versions. The comedies did not fare well at all, lacking as a whole the playfulness and spontaneity of good live performances. It seemed as though a blanket of BBC conservatism and the sterile atmosphere of a television studio without an audience constrained even strong comic talents like Helen Mirren as Rosalind, John Cleese as Petruchio, Michael Hordern as Prospero, and Alec McCowan as Malvolio. The tragedies suffered from the absence, with a few exceptions, of the leading actors of the National Theatre and Royal Shakespeare Company. Patrick Rycart and Rebecca Saire as Romeo and Juliet, Ron Cook as Richard III, Michael Hordern as King Lear, and Anthony Hopkins as Othello made game efforts but missed the mark. On the other hand, the cast of *Julius Caesar* performed well, Nicol Williamson as Macbeth was quite good, and Derek Jacobi performed a creditable Hamlet and a superb protagonist in *Richard II,* which was probably the best production of the whole series, directed by David Giles.

Surprisingly, the best work came in the minor plays and in the histories. Kevin Billington's production of *Henry VIII* was elegant and assured, with John Stride as Henry and Timothy West as a wonderful, brooding Cardinal Wolsey. Desmond Davis' *Measure for Measure* was excellent, with Tim Pigott-Smith as Angelo, Kate Nelligan as Isabella, John McEnery as Lucio, and Kenneth Colley as the Duke. David Giles's *Henry IV* tetralogy, especially *Part 1* with Jon Finch as Henry, Anthony Quayle as Falstaff, David Gwillam as Hal, and Tim Pigott-Smith as Hotspur, was very watchable.

But expectations are high for Shakespeare in performance, and the BBC may have undertaken too much. Too many viewers came away from the less skillful productions in the series with the feeling that Shakespeare's plays are boring. More experimentation, more invitations to directors of the imaginative quality of Peter Brook, more selectivity might have prevented this. And through no fault of its own, the series has all but wiped out others, including Paul Bosner's Saint George's Theatre project, which began with a creditable *Romeo and Juliet,* and it has made new feature-film versions unlikely for a while. The retrenchment of the arts channels on American cable television makes it unlikely that much Shakespeare will be offered there, unless enterprising theaters like the Mark Taper Forum in Los Angeles produce something.

Yet there is hope. Michael Elliot's 1984 production of *King Lear* for Grenada Television, with Olivier as Lear, John Hurt as the Fool, and Diana Rigg as Regan, is a fine effort and may spur other producers to take the plunge. On the front lines of the battle between the word and the image, saturated in the paradoxes of centuries-old modernity and metamorphosis from one medium to another, teased by the hunger of mass audiences for good drama, producers and actors of Shakespeare will always be drawn to the screen.

BIBLIOGRAPHY

Robert Hamilton Ball, *Shakespeare on Silent Film* (1968). Peter Brook, "Shakespeare on Three Screens," in *Sight and Sound* (Spring, 1965). Charles W. Eckert, ed., *Focus on Shakespearean Films* (1972). John Fuegi, "Explorations in No Man's Land: Shakespeare's Poetry as Theatrical Film," in *Shakespeare Quarterly,* 23 (1972). Harry Geduld, *Filmguide to "Henry V"* (1973). Jack J. Jorgens, *Shakespeare on Film* (1977). Grigori Kozintsev, *Shakespeare: Time and Conscience* (1966) and *"Hamlet* and *King Lear:* Stage and Film," in Clifford Leech and J. M. R. Margeson, eds., *Shakespeare, 1971* (1972).

Joseph McBride, *Orson Welles* (1972). Andrew M. McLean, *Shakespeare: Annotated Bibliographies and Media Guide for Teachers* (1980). Roger Manvell, *Shakespeare and the Film* (1971). Gerald Mast and Marshall Cohen, eds., *Film Theory and Criticism* (1974). Peter Morris,

"Shakespeare on Film," in *Films in Review* (March, 1973).

James Naremore, *The Magic World of Orson Welles* (1978). Barry M. Parker, *The Folger Shakespeare Filmography* (1979). Donald Richie, *The Films of Akira Kurosawa* (2nd ed., 1970). Kenneth Tynan, ed., *"Othello": The National Theatre Production* (1967).

Literature Film Quarterly has published many articles and special issues on Shakespeare on film. *Shakespeare on Film Newsletter* is a valuable resource. The annual bibliographies of *Shakespeare Quarterly* and *PMLA* list articles and reviews of interest.

Shakespeare's Reputation— Then Till Now

GERALD EADES BENTLEY

About Shakespeare's reputation during his own time many misleading and even false statements have been popularly accepted because made by reputable critics and scholars. In the nineteenth and early-twentieth centuries the admiration for the dramatist was so fervent that critics were certain that his genius must have dominated his own time, and they have looked for evidence to prove that it was. One famous scholar said in 1916:

> In his own day Shakespeare was one of the best-known figures in England. He was held in high esteem, both as a man and as a poet, while in his capacity of dramatic author he was not only immensely popular, but was rated at something like his true value by most persons of taste and judgement.
>
> (George Lyman Kittredge, *Shakespeare: An Address*)

Perhaps this declaration, though untrue, may be excused because it was made before a popular audience at a birthday celebration—an occasion not notable for restraint or for criticism of the birthday child.

Even more misleading and much more culpable is the statement made by Augustus Ralli in his ambitious survey *A History of Shakespearian Criticism:*

> The general average estimate of the century [1598–1694], however, was that Shakespeare was England's greatest . . . —perhaps the world's greatest poet, because in drama he rivalled, if not surpassed, the Greek tragedians and the Latin comedians, and his stream of narrative verse flowed as smoothly as Ovid's.

Far from being the "general average estimate of the century," the specific estimates of this declaration are based on only two allusions of Shakespeare's time (out of more than fourteen hundred allusions to Shakespeare now known from these years). One source is Ben Jonson's unique panegyric to Shakespeare printed in 1623 in the First Folio. The other comes from Francis Meres's *Palladis Tamia* (1598). This publication is really one of the commonplace books so popular at the time, a book into which Meres copied hundreds of passages he wanted to remember. The references to Shakespeare come from a sixteen-page section of this six-hundred-page collection. The section is headed "A Comparative Discourse of Our English Poets with Greek, Roman, and Italian Writers" and is clearly designed to raise the status of English writers. Among the British authors proudly cited and compared by Meres are John Harding, Charles Fitz-Jeffries, Michael Drayton, Samuel Daniel, William Warner, Matthew Roydon, Thomas Watson, George Peele, Lord Buckhurst, Doctor Leg, Doctor Edes, Edward Ferris, the Earl of Oxford, George Gascoigne, Anthony Munday, Henry Porter, and Richard Hathaway, as well as Shakespeare.

Once the reader is acquainted with the nature of Meres's publication of 1598 and has seen some of his selections of other praiseworthy writers, the significance of Ralli's assertion is greatly reduced. Like many other examples of Shakespeare criticism, these popular statements of Kittredge and Ralli illustrate the distorting effect of the almost irresistible temptation to foist the standards and conditions of our own time onto Shakespeare's.

1590–1642

Any understanding of Shakespeare's reputation must begin with the recognition that there are, and always have been, two branches of this reputation: Shakespeare in the theater and Shakespeare in the study, or the actors' Shakespeare and the readers' Shakespeare. Because of the disappearance of the vast majority of all theater records for the years before 1660, Shakespeare's reputation with audiences is much more difficult to assess than his reputation with readers.

The opinions readers have held of Shakespeare as a dramatist and poet can be elicited by collecting and assessing the written references to him and to his work in the last years of the sixteenth century and the entire seventeenth century—not just the two or three abnormal allusions used by Kittredge and Ralli, but all the allusions that have been discovered in the books and extant manuscripts of the time. These allusions have been collected in John Munro's *Shakespere Allusion-Book* and G. E. Bentley's *Shakespeare and Jonson*.

Many hundreds of allusions made to the dramatists of the time have been noted. The period was one of a fantastic outpouring of plays: more than three hundred English playwrights wrote more than 1,500 plays during the reigns of Elizabeth I, James I, and Charles I. Some wrote only one or two plays, but several were quite prolific. Thomas Heywood wrote more than 220 plays, Thomas Dekker about 64, Philip Massinger 55, Henry Chettle 50, James Shirley 38, Thomas Middleton 31, and Ben Jonson 28. In such company Shakespeare's output of 38 plays does not seem remarkably large.

In this great spate of writings, a few playwrights stand out in the recorded estimation of readers of the time whose opinions have been preserved in allusions. Most frequently noted and often praised were the three who were sometimes called the triumvirate, Ben Jonson, William Shakespeare, and the collaborators John Fletcher and Francis Beaumont, considered as one. Thus, Owen Feltham wrote for the memorial volume *Jonsonus Virbius* (1638):

And should the Stage compose herself a crown
Of all those wits which hitherto sh' as known:

Though there be many that about her brow
Like sparkling stones, might a quick luster throw:
Yet Shakespeare, Beaumont, Johnson, these three shall
Make up the gem in the point vertical.

Similarly Edward Phillips wrote in his *Theatrum Poetarum* (1675):

John Fletcher, one of the happy triumvirate (the other two being Jonson and Shakespeare) of the chief dramatic poets of our nation, in the last foregoing age, among whom there might be said to be a symmetry of perfection, while each excelled in his peculiar way.

These three dramatists are most often mentioned and praised by writers of the time whose allusions have been preserved in print or in manuscript. Of the three, Jonson and Shakespeare are cited or quoted more often than Beaumont and Fletcher, and of the three leaders, Ben Jonson and his works are more often praised, quoted, or merely mentioned than Shakespeare's (Bentley, *Shakespeare and Jonson*).

To the modern reader this preference may be astonishing, but to the student of Elizabethan, Jacobean, and Caroline history and literature it should not be. For educated men of the time (and nearly all literary allusions were written by educated men), the accepted standards were classic. How could it be otherwise when all their education, from grammar school through the universities, had been in Latin, the "universal language"? Jonson tried to follow classic standards; Shakespeare did not.

In the allusions of the seventeenth century the plays most often mentioned are Jonson's *Catiline, Volpone, The Alchemist, The Silent Woman, Sejanus,* and *Bartholomew Fair,* each of them referred to more frequently than *Hamlet, Othello, Macbeth,* or any other play of Shakespeare. The play most often praised in the century was not *Hamlet* or *Lear* but *Catiline,* which is lauded or mentioned with respect three times as often as *Hamlet* and eight times as often as *Lear* (Bentley, 1965). Robert Baron, in introducing his own play *Mirza* (1647), wrote, "not without the example of the matchless Jonson, who, in his *Catiline* (which miraculous poem I propose as my pattern) makes Sylla's Ghost persuade Catiline to do what Hannibal could not wish." In his commendatory verses published in the edition of *Mirza* to praise (grossly overpraise) that play, Robert Hills wrote:

Meantime, who'll number our best plays aright
First *Catiline,* then let him *Mirza* write,
So mix your names: in the third place must be
Sejanus, or the next that comes from thee.

Jonson's great contemporary prestige is also shown by the honors bestowed upon him: he was granted a pension for life by the king, making him the recognized dean of letters in his time; among the eighty-four "able and famous laymen" proposed to King James for a British royal academy, the only dramatists are Ben Jonson and George Chapman; Jonson was given honorary degrees by both Oxford and Cambridge; the year after his death a volume of poems in his honor was published, *Jonsonus Virbius;* and he was buried in Westminster Abbey. None of these honors or their equivalents was bestowed upon Shakespeare. Again we are reminded that standards and conditions change; to assume that our standards prevailed in other ages is to pervert our understanding of Shakespeare in his time.

These numbers and examples are enough to show that though Shakespeare was well known and admired among the readers of his time, he was not "rated at something like his true value by most persons of taste and judgement." Even more unfounded is Ralli's statement about "the general average estimate of the century." It may be the estimate of the twentieth century, but it certainly was not the judgement of the writers who were Shakespeare's contemporaries and successors in the seventeenth century. Shakespeare's reputation among readers is not difficult to assess; the material for such an assessment may be laborious to assemble, but it is available. Quite different is the task of assessing Shakespeare's reputation in the theater. One would like to believe that as a dramatic author he was esteemed as highly as Kittredge asserted.

Very few records from Elizabethan, Jacobean, and Caroline theaters have survived out of the many thousands that must have been made for the twenty or so London playing places known to have been used in these reigns (Harbage, *Annals*). The most extensive set of theatrical records surviving is that made by the theater magnate Philip Henslowe in the 1590s and the first decade of the seventeenth century. This treasure trove of production information contains hundreds of records of plays bought from dramatists, costumes and properties purchased, money loaned to acting companies and to individual players, receipts from the performance of individual plays at Henslowe's playhouses, and other theatrical transactions. All the accounts, of course, pertain to theaters Henslowe owned or had an interest in. Unfortunately Henslowe recorded no dealings with Shakespeare or with his company, the Lord Chamberlain–King's Men. This troupe offered the chief competition for Henslowe's enterprises. Henslowe's "diary" (actually an account book) tells us a great deal about the theater business in his time but nothing about Shakespeare or the popularity of his plays.

No other extant theatrical records of the time even approach Henslowe's in copiousness, but there are a few documents that give some hints of Shakespeare's reputation in the theater. Probably the most comprehensive of these more meager accounts are the records of command performances at court. Elizabeth, James I, and Charles I, through their office of the Master of the Revels, ordered various London companies to produce specified plays at court, especially on All Saints' Day, St. Stephen's Day, St. John's Day, Innocents' Day, New Year's Day, Twelfth Night, Candlemas, and throughout Shrovetide. During Elizabeth's reign, court performances were ordered from three to eleven times a season; James and Charles were more extravagant. From the formation of the Lord Chamberlain's company by 1594 to the end of court performances at the beginning of the civil war, Shakespeare's company was called to perform at court over six hundred times—far more than any other company. How many of the plays performed by this troupe were Shakespeare's we cannot tell, for usually the accounts record only the name of the company and the amount paid. Of the few court records before 1616 in which plays are named, eighteen record a play by Shakespeare, but there are 180 performances by the company of unnamed plays. From 1616 to 1642, a larger number of records name plays; in these later years, however, when plays are more often named, only ten Shakespearean plays are noted but about forty of the plays written by Beaumont and Fletcher are mentioned. In these years the productions of Beaumont and Fletcher appear to have been more in demand at court than Shakespeare's, but one must remember that even in these years there are more than 200 recorded performances by the King's Men in which the play is not named (Bentley, *Jacobean and Caroline Stage,* I, 94–100, and VII, 16–128).

Another inadequate source for information about plays produced is to be found in the diary and accounts of Sir Humphrey Mildmay (*Jacobean and Caroline Stage,* II, 673–681). Sir Humphrey was the oldest surviving son of Sir Anthony Mildmay and the grandson of Sir Walter Mildmay, Chancellor of the Exchequer to Queen Elizabeth and founder of Emmanuel College, Cambridge. Sir Humphrey was less active in public affairs than other members of his family; he concerned himself chiefly with the management of estates in Essex and Somerset and with the social pleasures of London. His diary and account book covers the period January 1631/32 to November 1643. In this period of eleven years, he notes his attendance at fifty-seven plays and four court masques—further evidence of the popularity of plays in London. Popularity must not, however, be assumed to include respect, as it so often has been. Sir Humphrey clearly felt a little guilty about his fondness for plays. Several times his note of a visit to a theater is accompanied by phrases such as "was idle," "loitered all the day," "I lost the whole day," and "I loitered att a play."

Though Mildmay generally records his expenditures for these theater visits, he mentions the title of the play he saw only twelve times; he mentions the Blackfriars theater fourteen times, the Globe four times, and the Phoenix, or Cockpit, three times. Four other visits to the Blackfriars can be inferred from the name of the play seen. Since the Blackfriars and Globe were theaters owned and operated by the King's Men, that troupe was clearly his favorite. Of the twelve plays Sir Humphrey named, four had been written by John Fletcher, three by Ben Jonson, two by William Davenant, and one each by Shakespeare *(Othello),* James Shirley, and Lodowick Carlell. Again the evidence is disappointing because of its incompleteness, but such as it is the records of Sir Humphrey's theater attendance suggest that he preferred performances of the plays of Fletcher and Jonson to those of Shakespeare.

Publication records may show something of theatrical success, since the printers must have needed some assurance that a quarto would sell before they invested in paper, ink, and labor. Even so, the evidence is slippery because successful troupes like the Lord Chamberlain–King's company preferred to keep their plays out of print to avoid theft by rival companies (Bentley, 1971).

Before about 1610 the power of the acting companies to forbid the plays they owned to the publishers was rather feeble, but after 1609 the King's Men managed to keep most of Shakespeare's com-

positions out of print until the sharers arranged to bring out the First Folio (1623). By that time the King's Men so dominated the London theater that they could persuade the lord chamberlain to forbid other acting companies and the printers to steal their plays. There are three letters of 1619, 1637, and 1641 from the lord chamberlain to the master and wardens of the Stationers' Company forbidding any printer to publish any of the plays of the King's Men without the consent of the players.

In the years before 1609, sixteen Shakespeare plays were printed in cheap, badly edited quartos, more quartos than for any other playwright, though Thomas Dekker, Jonson, John Marston, George Chapman, and Thomas Heywood each had nine to twelve offered for sale. Certainly these figures show theater popularity before 1609, for usually popularity with audiences furnished the only promise of sales available to publishers. But there were exceptions. For example, several dramatic publications in these years were masques, which were assured of sales because of the prestige of their magnificent presentations at court; the number of Marston publications is partly explained by the fact that most of them had been performed by boy companies, which were forced out of business and whose managers would therefore sell their repertories cheap; the same applies to several Chapman publications.

These extant publication records seem to show that Shakespeare's plays were quite popular with the London audience before 1610. The later, very spotty performance records suggest that Jonson and Beaumont and Fletcher were more in demand than Shakespeare, at least with the audience at court and in the private theaters like Blackfriars. There is almost no extant testimony as to which dramatists were in greatest demand at the more plebeian theaters like the Globe, the Fortune, and the Red Bull. Thus in spite of the paucity of theater records, there are suggestions that in the playhouses Shakespeare's plays seem to have been quite popular before 1610 but less so in the later years of James I and during the reign of Charles I.

The year 1642 marks the end of the period of Shakespeare's theater. In September of that year, after King Charles had fled his capital and civil war had become inevitable, the Lords and Commons, meeting together, passed a solemn ordinance:

Whereas the distressed state of Ireland, steeped in her own blood, and the distracted state of England threatened with a cloud of blood by a Civil War call for all possible means to appease and avert the wrath of God . . . and whereas public sports do not well agree with public calamities nor public stage plays with seasons of humiliation this being an exercise of sad and pious solemnity and the other being spectacles of pleasure too commonly expressing lascivious mirth and levity; it is therefore thought fit, and ordained by the Lords and Commons in the parliament assembled that while these sad causes and set times of humiliation do continue public stage plays shall cease and be forborne.

There followed eighteen years in which there were no legitimate presentations of plays in London. There were a few bootleg performances, usually broken up by soldiers, but none of the old companies could support themselves. Various writers made short skits from Jacobean and Caroline plays, which seem to have been produced about the country at gatherings such as fairs. The most that is known of these interregnum pieces comes from a collection published in 1662 called *The Wits,* or *Sport upon Sport.* Something of theatrical reputations from 1642 to 1660 is shown by the plays from which these "drolls" and playlets have been derived: sixteen of them are taken from plays by Beaumont and Fletcher, two from Shakespeare's plays *(Henry IV, Part 1,* and *Hamlet)* two from Shirley, one from Jonson, and thirteen from obscure or little-known writers. Another suggestion of theatrical popularity is to be seen in the frontispiece of *The Wits.* This fascinating picture shows a stage with seven droll characters on it; presumably these characters were popular ones. In the forefront are Falstaff with a wine cup and his friend the Hostess. Among the other characters are the Changeling from Thomas Middleton and William Rowley's play of that name.

The popular appeal of Falstaff implied by his prominence in the group of characters agrees with the great number of allusions to him in the literature of the seventeenth century. He is named from two to three times as often as any other character of Shakespeare or Jonson—five times as often as Hamlet (Bentley, *Shakespeare and Jonson*).

The Restoration Period

After King Charles II returned to his father's throne in 1660, the London theater was radically changed. In the days of James I and Charles I, the drama had been fantastically popular in the capital:

four theaters that had run in competition (the Globe, the Swan, the Fortune, and the Red Bull) had very large capacities; the private theaters (the Blackfriars, the Phoenix, and the Salisbury Court) each had about one-quarter the capacity of the public playhouses. After a few years of makeshift use of old theaters and modified tennis courts, Restoration players settled down to two theaters that ran in competition, both of them with the approximate capacity of the old Blackfriars and Phoenix. Even so, there were not enough patrons to fill both small houses on the same day; if one had a popular hit, the other could expect only a starvation audience—and this in spite of the fact that the population of London was greater than it had been in the 1630s and 1640s.

The plays performed in the newly tolerated theaters were at first mostly revivals of Jacobean and Caroline plays that were available in print. Especially popular were the plays of Beaumont and Fletcher. John Dryden, whose experience with the Restoration stage was very extensive, wrote in his long piece of dramatic criticism published in 1668, *An Essay of Dramatic Poesy:*

> Their plays [Beaumont and Fletcher's] are now the most pleasant and frequent entertainments of the stage, two of theirs being acted through the year for one of Shakespeare's or Jonson's; the reason is because there is a certain gaiety in their comedies and pathos in their more serious plays which suits generally with all men's humours. Shakespeare's language is likewise a little obsolete, and Ben Jonson's wit comes short of theirs.

Even if Shakespeare's plays did not draw so well as Beaumont and Fletcher's, they were evidently still current in the early Restoration playhouses.

Dryden wrote from the viewpoint of a popular and influential dramatist. The audience may be represented by Samuel Pepys, whose diary shows that he was a very frequent playgoer in the 1660s of which Dryden wrote. Happily the diary of Pepys for the 1660s is much fuller and more informative than that of Sir Humphrey in the 1630s. Pepys's records of his theater attendance agree roughly with Dryden's assessment of popularity. In the 1660s, Pepys saw about seventy performances of twenty-seven Beaumont and Fletcher plays, thirty-seven performances of twelve Shakespearean or semi-Shakespearean plays, and twenty-two performances of six plays by Ben Jonson. Not all the

Shakespeare plays that Pepys saw, however, were pure Shakespeare. *Measure for Measure, Macbeth, The Taming of the Shrew,* and *The Tempest* were rewritten during the decade, and it is not always apparent when Pepys saw the original and when he saw the alteration for the Restoration audiences.

Perhaps a little more about Shakespeare's Restoration reputation can be suggested by Pepys's occasional critical comments. Though he saw *Hamlet* six times, it is clear that he admired most the acting of Thomas Betterton. Of *Macbeth,* Pepys said on 7 January 1666/67 that though he had seen the play only ten days before, it "yet appears a most excellent play in all respects, but especially in divertisements, though it be a deep tragedy; which is a strange perfection in a tragedy, it being most proper here, and suitable." And three months later he comments, "We saw *Macbeth* which, though I have seen it often, yet is it one of the best plays for a stage, and variety of dancing and music, that ever I saw." The final words of this comment make it apparent that what Pepys saw was Davenant's alteration of Shakespeare's tragedy.

Of *A Midsummer's Night's Dream* he says, "It is the most insipid ridiculous play that ever I saw in my life." When he saw *Romeo and Juliet* on 1 March 1661/62, he said, "It is a play of itself the worst that ever I heard in my life, and the worst acted that ever I saw these people do, and I am resolved to go no more to see the first time of acting, for they were all of them out more or less." And finally, of the revision of *The Tempest* by Davenant and Dryden, he said on 13 November 1667, "Saw *The Tempest* again, which is very pleasant, and full of so good variety that I cannot be more pleased almost in a comedy, only the seamen's part a little too tedious."

These comments indicate that though several of Shakespeare's plays were still being performed in the 1660s, the managers found that modifications were needed if the subjects of Charles II were to be attracted to their theaters, and contemporary dramatists provided such alterations. Davenant provided alterations for *Measure for Measure, Macbeth,* and *Hamlet;* Dryden, for *The Tempest, Antony and Cleopatra,* and *Troilus and Cressida;* Nahum Tate, for *King Lear, Richard II,* and *Coriolanus;* John Lacy, for *The Taming of the Shrew;* Thomas Shadwell, for *Timon of Athens;* Edward Ravenscroft, for *Titus Andronicus;* Thomas Otway, for *Romeo and Juliet;* John Crowne, for *Henry VI, Part 2,* and *Part 3;* Thomas D'Urfey, for *Cymbeline;* and there were

a number of others. Some of these alterations are so radical as to make Shakespeare's drama a quite different play. Tate rewrote *King Lear* to make a love affair between Cordelia and Edgar a central element in the tragedy, and it was this love affair that made Cordelia give an unsatisfactory answer to her father in the first scene. Tate cut the Fool out of the play entirely, restored Lear to his throne at the end, and allowed Cordelia and Edgar to marry and live happily ever after.

The Tempest as revised by Davenant and Dryden in 1670 added a younger sister for Miranda and a young man named Hippolyto who had never seen a woman. To balance Caliban, they added a female monster, Sycorax, and to balance Ariel, a female sprite called Milche. Also introduced into *The Tempest* by these revisers were a number of dances, songs, and people flying through the air.

Later Colley Cibber brought out a version of *Richard III* that contains about one thousand lines by Cibber and less than one thousand by Shakespeare. Even Shakespeare's thousand lines contain a number lifted from *Henry VI, Richard II, Henry IV,* and *Henry V.* Hastings, Margaret, Clarence, and Edward IV are all omitted from Cibber's popular version.

Other revisions really produced a new play, like Dryden's *All for Love* (from *Antony and Cleopatra*) and Thomas Otway's *The History and Fall of Caius Marius* (a combination of *Romeo and Juliet* and Plutarch's *Life of Marius*). Whatever the alterations, they furthered the tendency to make one Shakespeare for the stage and one for the study. This radical separation continued for more than two hundred years; it was not until the late nineteenth century that producers began to bring productions closer and closer to the texts that had appeared in the First Folio, and even in the 1980s the plays one sees in our theaters are seldom the unaltered texts that Heminges and Condell passed on.

The divergence between the theatergoers' Shakespeare and the readers' Shakespeare increased during the Restoration. In the playhouse, the revisions by Davenant, Dryden, Tate, Lacy, Ravenscroft, Otway, Crowne, D'Urfey, and others more and more superseded the plays as they had appeared in the First Folio. But for readers the plays were available as they had been issued in 1623. In 1663 the Third Folio appeared, reprinting the thirty-six plays of the First. To a second issue of this folio in 1664 seven new plays were added. These seven plays are commonly known as the

Shakespeare apochrypha: plays considered today almost surely to be not by Shakespeare, but attributed to him erroneously by various early printers. Their inclusion in the second issue of the Third Folio suggests that the publishers thought that Shakespeare's name would sell plays. Another edition of the folio in 1685 also includes these seven plays. In these collections readers found the plays not as they generally appeared on the contemporary stage but as Heminges and Condell had presented them to readers forty and seventy years before.

The most notable comment on Shakespeare in the early Restoration is found in Dryden's *Essay of Dramatic Poesy:*

> To begin, then, with Shakespeare. [H]e was the man who of all modern, and perhaps ancient poets, had the largest and most comprehensive soul. All the images of Nature were still present to him, and he drew them not laboriously, but luckily; when he describes any thing, you more than see it, you feel it too. Those who accuse him to have wanted learning give him the greatest commendation: he was naturally learned; he needed not the spectacles of books to read Nature; he looked inward, and found her there. I cannot say he is every where alike; were he so, I should do him injury to compare him with the greatest of mankind. He is many times flat, insipid, his comic wit degenerating into clenches, his serious swelling into bombast. But he is always great when some great occasion is presented to him; no man can say he ever had a fit subject for his wit, and did not then raise himself as high above the rest of the poets, *Quantum lenta solent, inter viburna cupressi.*

Just before a long analysis of Ben Jonson's *The Silent Woman,* Dryden continues:

> If I would compare him [Ben Jonson] with Shakespeare, I must acknowledge him the more correct poet, but Shakespeare the greater wit. Shakespeare was the Homer, or father of our dramatic poets; Ben Jonson was the Virgil, the pattern of elaborate writing; I admire him, but I love Shakespeare.

In the year of the publication of *An Essay of Dramatic Poesy,* 1668, Dryden was made poet laureate, and for the next three decades he continued to be one of the most respected playwrights. Praise of Shakespeare by so conspicuous a public figure was sure to influence popular opinion; such praise continued to increase until, in the 1690s, there are more allusions to him than to Jonson. Though the old triumvirate of Beaumont and Fletcher, Jonson, and Shakespeare continued frequently to be mentioned, Shakespeare was coming to be recognized as the greatest English dramatist. Dryden continued to praise him and to consider him England's greatest. He said in his "Grounds of Criticism in Tragedy," prefaced to the 1679 edition of his *Troilus and Cressida, or Truth Found Too Late:*

> The poet Æschylus was held in the same veneration by the Athenians of after ages as Shakespeare is by us . . . our reverence for Shakespeare [is] much more just than that of the Grecians for Æschylus.

The Early Eighteenth Century

In the early eighteenth century came a notable event testifying to Shakespeare's burgeoning reputation. This was the appearance in 1709 of the six-volume edition of Shakespeare's plays prepared by Nicholas Rowe, the first edition of the plays that had been really edited. These six volumes constituted the most elaborate collection issued so far, but many features went further and implied Shakespeare's preeminent reputation. Not only had Rowe devoted many months of work to the preparation of the plays; he also treated them as the masterpieces of a great genius. In addition to one illustration for every play, each volume has a symbolic frontispiece showing Shakespeare with the laurel and accompanied by the Graces and the Muses.

For his edition Rowe prepared the first proper life of Shakespeare ever written, and he was more scrupulous in what he set down than many of his successors in the eighteenth and nineteenth and even the twentieth centuries have been. With this biography—which was part of his introduction—Rowe included a certain amount of criticism, some original and some quoted from Dryden and Jonson, plus a good selection from other critics. Rowe's life was used by most eighteenth-century editors, sometimes with acknowledgments and sometimes without. Alexander Pope pretended that the life in his edition of 1725 was a new one, and most readers believed him. Actually it is only Rowe's biography very cleverly cut up and rearranged.

Rowe's work deserves fuller attention because of the great influence it has had on all later editions of the plays and on Shakespeare's reputation. Some of this influence has been good and some of it bad.

The foundations of Rowe's work had been the seventeenth-century folios. The three later ones had been reprints of the First Folio with minor corrections and, in the last two, the addition of the seven apocryphal plays. These texts were records of the plays as Heminges and Condell had used them in the Jacobean Globe and Blackfriars. They were plays prepared for Elizabethan and Jacobean stages —i.e., a placeless theater with no scenery, a theater in which the setting for most scenes was ignored: many scenes occurred no place.

During the Restoration years, the players had begun to use crude scenery; they assumed that a place must have been intended for each scene, though they could not always show it to the audience. That was a radical departure from Elizabethan practice as known from theater studies and as reflected in the folios. In none of the plays as Heminges and Condell prepared them is there any indication of the location of the scenes such as most modern readers assume. In the folios the texts do not carry even the simple statement that appears at the beginning of some of the quartos, such as "The scene Rome."

In the folios most of the plays are not consistently divided into acts and scenes: some are divided into acts only; in the comedy section there is a fairly thorough, though not precise, division into acts and scenes; in the history section some plays are divided and some are not; none of the tragedies has consistent act and scene divisions. *Hamlet,* for instance, is divided into acts and scenes as far as the second scene of the second act, and all the following three and one-half acts are undivided as if that last part of the play were one long scene. Six of the plays in the folios have no act and scene divisions at all.

With a very few exceptions, the plays in the folios have no stage directions of the literary type. For only eight of the thirty-six plays are dramatis personae given. In addition to these variations from the usual features of modern texts, the First Folio has many hundreds of proofreading errors, such as *hot* for *not* and *one* for *none.* Other proofreading errors are not so obvious, and though it is easy enough to see that the First Folio text does not make sense at certain points, nobody has yet discovered exactly what went wrong and what Shakespeare intended.

The first man to make a serious and conscientious effort to edit the plays for the readers of his time, to correct as many mistakes as possible, and to provide the apparatus that most readers require was Nicholas Rowe. His efforts mark a new stage in Shakespeare's developing reputation. He prepared the first modern edition of Shakespeare. His edition included forty-three plays, the thirty-six of the First Folio plus the seven apocryphal plays added to the second issue of the Third Folio in 1664 and repeated in the Fourth Folio. Rowe was not what would now be called a fine editor, but he was the best of his time—and better than many of his successors—and he made more legitimate corrections of the texts as found in the folios than any other editor ever has. Many of Rowe's corrections were sound and have been retained in most editions in the 276 years since. Rowe carefully broke each play into acts and scenes; made a list of dramatis personae to precede each drama; and added entrances and exits, many of which had been omitted or misplaced. Rowe also changed the sixteenth-century punctuation to eighteenth-century punctuation.

Unfortunately, the theater for which Rowe wrote his own plays and in which his readers saw Shakespeare's was a type of playhouse more like our own than like the Elizabethan Globe. Since painted sets were regularly used at Drury Lane and Covent Garden, Rowe designated the places in which he thought the scenes of Shakespeare's plays were intended to take place.

Unfortunately, Rowe's chosen settings involved a violent contradiction of the principle that governed Shakespeare and his contemporary dramatists when they wrote for the Elizabethan public theaters. Theirs was a drama of persons, not a drama of places; the actor was paramount, and his background only occasionally significant. In the majority of scenes in Elizabethan and Jacobean plays the audience is expected to concentrate on words and action and to ignore the place of action. When Rowe and succeeding editors in the eighteenth century concluded that they must nominate a place for each episode in every play, they read through the text carefully, looking for possible hints of place, and then wrote in their discovery at the head of the scene as its setting.

The play was always distorted by these additions and sometimes seriously mutilated, as *Antony and Cleopatra* was. Rowe divided it into twenty-seven scenes, and following his lead, Sir Thomas Hanmer in his edition of 1744 further divided it into forty-two scenes, carefully numbered and located. These misguided revisions have been followed by nearly all editors down to our own time, breaking into fragments the flowing action Shakespeare had planned and making the play extremely difficult to stage as well as irritating and confusing to the conventional modern reader who tries to shift the imagined background thirty or forty times as he reads the tragedy.

The Late Eighteenth Century

Rowe's volumes showed Shakespeare's popularity with readers at the beginning of the eighteenth century. Even more striking is the series of multivolume editions that readers continued to absorb during the next ninety years. There was a second edition of Rowe in 1714; six volumes edited by Alexander Pope in 1725; the very superior edition of Lewis Theobald in 1733; in 1743/44, the six volumes of Sir Thomas Hanmer; a revised version of Pope's edition by William Warburton in eight volumes in 1747; Samuel Johnson's edition in 1765 with its famous prefaces in eight volumes; in 1773, Johnson's edition revised by George Steevens in ten volumes; in 1785, another edition of Dr. Johnson's work revised and augmented by Isaac Reed; and finally, the best text of the eighteenth century, prepared by Edmond Malone and issued in ten volumes in 1790. Malone was the first truly great Shakespearean scholar; the revised edition (1821) of his Shakespeare in twenty-one volumes is one of the great editions and is still used by serious scholars. This list is not a complete measure of the eagerness of eighteenth-century readers to have copies of Shakespeare's plays, for several of these sets were quickly reprinted to keep up with the heavy demand.

A number of these collected editions had critical prefaces asserting Shakespeare's distinction. In 1712, John Dennis published "An Essay on the Genius and Writings of Shakespeare," in which he said, "Shakespeare was one of the greatest geniuses the world e're saw for the tragic stage." In 1725, Alexander Pope published another essay as the preface to his edition. Though Pope was not a scrupulous editor, his admiration for Shakespeare is clear. Shakespeare's plays did not conform to all of Pope's standards, but Pope appreciated many of the aspects of his genius:

> But every single character in Shakespeare is as much an individual as those in life itself; it is as impossible to find any two alike; and such as from their relation or affinity in any respect appear almost to be twins will upon comparison be found remarkably distinct. To this life and variety of character we must add the wonderful preservation of it, which is such throughout his plays, that had all the speeches been printed without the very names of the persons, I believe one might have applied them with certainty to every speaker.

Shakespeare's reputation in the theater was also rising during the eighteenth century, as indicated by the performance records, which are much more available for the London playhouses in these years than they are for the earlier periods. In the first decade of the century, though the records are less complete than in the later decades, about 8 percent of the play performances known were of plays by Shakespeare. The percentage rises nearly every decade until Shakespeare's plays made up more than one-quarter of all those produced in the 1740s. In the last half of the century, out of twenty-two thousand performances known, nearly four thousand were by Shakespeare. The plays most frequently presented were *Hamlet, Macbeth, Richard III, Romeo and Juliet, Othello, King Lear, Henry IV, Part 1, The Taming of the Shrew, The Merchant of Venice,* and *The Tempest.* It is notable that the tragedies were more popular than the comedies. Not all the plays were performed unaltered; though *Hamlet* was usually presented approximately as Shakespeare had written it, as were *Othello, Henry IV, Part 1,* and *The Merchant of Venice,* others were altered, sometimes radically, as were *Richard III, The Taming of the Shrew, King Lear,* and *The Tempest.*

The Shakespeare Jubilee

But the most striking evidence of Shakespeare's great reputation in the late eighteenth century was the Shakespeare Jubilee at Stratford in 1769. By the middle of the eighteenth century, Shakespeare had become so widely known that the citizens of Stratford-upon-Avon decided that it would be well for the town to show more pride in its most famous son. The Stratford corporation wanted a statue of Shakespeare for its rebuilt town hall and approached David Garrick for help. They made him an honorary burgess of the town. Since the town burgesses wanted to attract attention, Garrick was an ideal selection for them, for he was not only the most famous and influential actor of his time but was a master of publicity. During his long and spectacular career Garrick had dominated the London stage. For years he had been actor-manager of the Drury Lane Theater; he had produced twenty-seven of Shakespeare's plays and had acted in most of them. He soon dominated the preparations for Stratford's festival.

The town built a special hall called the Amphitheatre or the Booth, and elaborate preparations for a grand celebration were developed. They planned three evenings of fireworks and ordered special lights; transparent pictures were painted and set up along the banks of the Avon; cannon were placed for salutes; a medal was struck in gold, in silver, and in copper; mulberry-wood souvenirs of all sorts were prepared, all claiming to be carved from the wood of the mulberry tree that had grown in Shakespeare's garden. A grand ball and a masquerade were planned, and tickets were sold in London. A parade of costumed Shakespearean characters with chariots and pageants was arranged; Garrick wrote an ode that he would deliver himself.

The three-day jubilee began with a cannonade and bells at six o'clock on the morning of the first day. As the festivities continued there were breakfasts, parades, an oratorio, a grand ball in costume; odes were read and orations delivered. Some of the masquerade costumes became notorious, especially James Boswell as a Corsican chief.

For days the London newspapers and magazines were full of reports of the Stratford events. These included some ridicule and gave rise to a newspaper feud between Garrick's friends and his enemies. Though some of the events were ridiculous, all reflected the universal acclaim of Shakespeare. Finally, the two principal London theaters, Drury Lane and Covent Garden, each staged extravagant entertainments that purported to be the great jubilee as it had been originally planned. There were frequent stagings of these spectacles; at Drury Lane, Garrick's version had ninety performances and became the talk of the town. Heavy rains and inadequate housing and eating facilities had made the great jubilee rather a fiasco at Stratford. Some people called it "Garrick's Folly," but the outpouring of enthusiasm and veneration of Shakespeare before, during, and after the jubilee makes it something of a landmark in the history of Shakespeare's reputation.

The Nineteenth Century

In the last two or three decades of the eighteenth century and the first few of the nineteenth, praise of Shakespeare became so extravagant that R. W. Babcock said these years marked *"The Genesis of Shakespeare Idolatry."* The magazines printed many pages of fulsome praise: Martin S. Sherlock wrote in the *European Magazine* in 1786, "Shakespeare possessed, in the highest degree of perfection, all the most excellent talents of all the writers that I have ever known." In his famous "Essay on the Dramatic Character of Sir John Falstaff," Maurice Morgann wrote in 1777:

> When the hand of time shall have brushed off his present Editors and Commentators, and when the very name of *Voltaire,* and even the memory of the language in which he has written, shall be no more, the *Apalachian* mountains, the banks of the *Ohio,* and the plains of *Sciola* shall resound with the accents of this Barbarian: In his native tongue he shall roll the genuine passions of nature; nor shall the griefs of *Lear* be alleviated, or the charms and wit of Rosalind be abated by time.

A large collection of such fulsome praise could be gathered, but more popular testimony to Shakespeare's eminence is to be seen in the scores of editions of the plays that the public absorbed throughout the English-speaking world. On a slightly less popular level, many hundreds of critical analyses and commentaries were distributed in books and periodical essays: "Remarks on the Plays of Shakespeare," "Notes upon Some Passages in Shakespeare," "Comments on the Commentators on Shakespeare," "Studies of Shakespeare," and William Hazlitt's "Characters in Shakespeare's Plays."

Adaptations of Shakespeare for special readers appeared; perhaps best known is the much reprinted volume of children's synopses *Tales from Shakespear* (1807), by Charles and Mary Lamb, and *Specimens of English Dramatic Poets, Who Lived About the Time of Shakespeare: with Notes* (1808), by Charles alone. Among the most amusing of such adaptations is Thomas Bowdler's *Family Shakespeare* (1807), an expurgated edition for a prudish generation. Shakespeare lived in a much more permissive age, and his plays are full of vulgarisms, profanity, sexual allusions, and references to natural functions. The amusing aspect of Dr. Bowdler's expurgation is the number of such allusions that he failed to recognize (as is evident from Eric Partridge's *Shakespeare's Bawdy,* 1947). The century also saw a burst of sentimental fiction about the Bard, such as *The Girlhood of Shakespeare's Heroines,* and sentimental collections or extracts, like *The Sweet Silvery Say-*

ings of Shakespeare on the Softer Sex and Cupid's Birthday Book; One Thousand Love-Darts from Shakespeare.

Another aspect of the growing enthusiasm for the Swan of Avon was the formation of many Shakespeare societies in London, Oxford, Cambridge, Edinburgh, Birmingham, and in Philadelphia, New York, Boston, and eventually in smaller cities and towns all over Great Britain, America, and Germany. Many of these societies were little more than reading groups with occasional lectures, but some, like the Shakespeare Society of London and the New Shakespere Society, were scholarly groups with publishing programs.

Not only were the plays published singly or in sets and collections in English-speaking countries, but translations into German, French, Swedish, Portuguese, Hungarian, and other languages appeared. Picture books of Shakespearean characters and scenes were compiled; scores of oil paintings of Shakespearean scenes (mostly imaginary) and actors and actresses costumed for his roles were prepared; his name and the names of his characters and plays were used as trademarks.

In the theaters of the nineteenth century enthusiasm was apparent, but the discrepancy between Shakespeare in the study and Shakespeare in the playhouse became even more pronounced. Most of the Shakespearean critics and commentators were dissatisfied with the performances they saw, and some found them contemptible. William Hazlitt, an active theatergoer, said, "We do not like to see our author's plays acted, and least of all *Hamlet.* There is no play that suffers so much in being translated to the stage," revealing that he conceived of Shakespeare as primarily a writer for the study. Again Hazlitt wrote, "The manner in which Shakespeare's plays have been generally altered, or rather mangled, by modern mechanists, is in our opinion a disgrace to the English stage."

It is not difficult to understand the nineteenth-century critics' dissatisfaction with performances. The London picture-frame stage of their time encouraged a type of production quite wrong for Elizabethan plays. The theater of Macready, Kean, Phelps, Ellen Terry, Henry Irving, and Beerbohm Tree was a theater of place, of spectacle, and of the star system. In a huge playhouse, dazzling sets were erected, plays were altered to emphasize the star parts, and actors were trained to enhance the prominence of the star. Elaborate mechanical devices were developed. Gas lighting illuminated the spectacle and emphasized the separation between stage and auditorium, a separation that Elizabethan playwrights had minimized. In such theaters the more subtle effects of many Shakespearean lines and groupings were destroyed. No wonder Charles Lamb said, "It may seem a paradox, but I cannot help being of opinion that the plays of Shakespeare are less calculated for performance on a stage than those of almost any other dramatist whatever" (*On the Tragedies of Shakespeare,* 1818). And George Bernard Shaw called the Shakespeare performances of his youth "bardicide."

But for many of the Victorian audiences these elaborate and spectacular productions had a strong appeal. Shakespeare's plays in the great Victorian theaters were not so dominant as they had been, but the greatest actors owed much of their fame to their performances of his roles: Kean as Hamlet and Richard III; Macready as Henry IV and Shylock; Phelps as Macbeth; Irving as Shylock and Macbeth; Sarah Siddons as Lady Macbeth; Ellen Terry as Beatrice; Mary Anderson as Juliet; Fanny Kemble as Juliet and Beatrice; and Charlotte Cushman as Romeo [sic].

Production of Shakespeare's plays began in Australia in 1843; many of the English Shakespearean actors like Macready, Kemble, and Kean toured, and most of the chief American actors owed much of their reputations to their interpretations of his characters: Edwin Booth as Hamlet, Mary Anderson as Juliet, Edwin Forrest as Othello.

Reform in Production

Near the end of the nineteenth century the protests of the critics and scholars and a few of the managers and actors against the mutilation of the plays in performance began gradually to have an effect. Led by William Poel and eventually seconded by George Bernard Shaw, Gordon Craig, Nugent Monk, Harley Granville-Barker, and Sir Barry Jackson, more and more people began to see that Shakespeare had written primarily for the theater and not for readers. His plays had indeed been planned for the stage. They had not needed to be adapted for performance as so many had assumed; they had to be adapted for readers.

In the twentieth century this crusade to return production of the plays to something like the principles Shakespeare had followed brought many intellectuals back to the theater, and devotion to Shakespeare on the stage increased tremendously. This devotion was expressed partly in the foundation of scores of local theaters devoted primarily to Shakespeare. Festivals and Shakespeare seasons became annual events in countless cities and towns in Great Britain and North America and as far afield as Tokyo. Productions proliferate in schools and colleges, especially in England where the performance of a dozen or more plays of Shakespeare in one university in one year is not uncommon. Theaters have been built with features approximating those of the Globe in places such as Sheffield; Norwich; Chichester; Liverpool; Stratford, Ontario; Ashland, Oregon; Minneapolis; and San Diego.

The burgeoning of Shakespeare's international reputation in the twentieth century is also attested by the plethora of books and articles that pour every year from the presses of dozens of nations, including all the English-speaking countries as well as Russia, Japan, Germany, France, Belgium, Holland, Scandinavia, India, Poland, and Portugal. There are now at least a dozen different periodicals devoted wholly or primarily to the publication of articles about all aspects of Shakespeare's works, his life, his technique, his influence, and his environment. In 1980 the Shakespeare bibliography listed over twenty-five hundred such books, articles, and reviews published in a single year in many languages (Harrison T. Meserole and John B. Smith, "Shakespeare: Annotated World Bibliography for 1980" in *Shakespeare Quarterly,* 329). A large number of these books and articles were trivial, and too many were downright silly; but the fact that hundreds of authors had written these pieces and that scores of editors had published them is clear evidence of the phenomenal reputation of Shakespeare. Today his reputation as the world's greatest dramatist is acknowledged in all English-speaking countries and in many others whose language is not English.

BIBLIOGRAPHY

Joseph Quincy Adams, ed., *The Dramatic Records of Sir Henry Herbert, Master of the Revels, 1623–1673* (1917). R. W. Babcock, *The Genesis of Shakespeare Idolatry, 1766–1799* (1931). Bernard Beckerman, *Shakespeare at the Globe, 1599–1609* (1962). Gerald Eades Bentley, *The Jacobean and Caroline Stage,* 7 vols. (1941–1968); *Shakespeare and Jonson: Their Reputations in the Seventeenth Century Compared,* 2 vols. (1945; repr. as one vol., 1965); and *The Profession of Dramatist in Shakespeare's Time, 1590–1642* (1971). David Bevington and Jay L. Halio, eds., *Shakespeare: Pattern of Excelling Nature* (1978).

E. K. Chambers, *The Elizabethan Stage,* 4 vols. (1923). Marchette Chute, *Shakespeare of London* (1949). Harley Granville-Barker, *Prefaces to Shakespeare,* 2 vols. (1946–1947) and *More Prefaces to Shakespeare* (1974). W. W. Greg, *The Shakespeare First Folio: Its Bibliographical and Textual History* (1955). Alfred Harbage, *Annals of English Drama, 975–1700* (1940; rev. by S. Schoenbaum, 1964) and "Shakespeare and the Myth of Perfection," in *Shakespeare Quarterly,* 15 (1964). Charles Beecher Hogan, *Shakespeare in the Theatre, 1701–1800,* 2 vols. (1952–1957). Leslie Hotson, *The Commonwealth and Restoration Stage* (1928).

Francis Meres, *Palladis Tamia,* Don Cameron, ed. (1931). John Munro, ed., *The Shakspere Allusion-Book* (1909; issued with a preface by Sir Edmund Chambers, 1932). G. C. Odell, *Shakespeare: From Betterton to Irving,* 2 vols. (1920; repr. 1963). Augustus Ralli, *A History of Shakespearian Criticism,* 2 vols. (1932). S. Schoenbaum, *William Shakespeare: Records and Images* (1981). Arthur Colby Sprague and J. C. Trewin, *Shakespeare's Plays Today* (1970). Johanne M. Stochholm, *Garrick's Folly: The Shakespeare Jubilee of 1769 at Stratford and Drury Lane* (1964).

Shakespearean Scholarship: From Rowe to the Present

J. PHILIP BROCKBANK

Shakespearean scholarship has for over 300 years endeavored to recover and to describe Shakespeare's scholarship. Its history may appropriately begin and end, therefore, with *Love's Labor's Lost,* in which the King of Navarre tells Berowne that "study's godlike recompense" is "that to know which else we should not know," and Berowne retorts, "Things hid and barred, you mean, from common sense?" (I. i. 55–58). The young men of Navarre hope to become "heirs of all eternity" (I. i. 7), and through them Shakespeare expresses both the poignancy and the absurdity of Renaissance academic aspirations. Scholarship is systematic study, meant to retrieve, sustain, and advance the understanding of the past. It allows us to look outside the boundaries of our ordinary perceptions, to extend our experience in time and space, to be as old in knowledge as the story of civilization allows. But its pursuit, Shakespeare's plays tell us, can make us melancholy, vain, and blind; and its results can be disappointing. "Small have continual plodders ever won," says Berowne, "save base authority from others' books" (I. i. 86–87).

Throughout *Love's Labor's Lost* the virtues of poet, pedant, courtier, and lover contend entertainingly with their follies, in ways that illuminate Shakespeare's own responses to scholarship and scholarship's later responses to Shakespeare. In the play the cultivated courtiers mock the rustic worthies, but their own verses are exposed to the critical discourse of the curate and the schoolmaster. Shakespeare shows himself well disposed toward the Renaissance endeavor to make the new languages of Europe emulate the accomplishments of the ancient ones and to achieve, by art and study, the effects of natural and graceful spontaneity. But he also knows what can go wrong in the domains in which the imaginative life of the past is carried into the future—in the academy, in the life-style of the court, in the language of poetry, in the schoolroom, and in the theater.

From the First Folio to Steevens

Even in his lifetime Shakespeare, like the ancients, was culled for "learned, grave and wittie sentences" in order that, as one hostile reader put it, "certain methodicall heads" should (like Holofernes) be able to "rime upon any occasion at a little warning" (Baldwin, I, 26). The publication in 1623 of the First Folio, with its memorial tributes, changed the perspectives of Shakespeare's reception. His fellow actors, John Heminge and Henry Condell, were his first editors; and his most learned rival, Ben Jonson, acclaimed his ascendancy over Aeschylus and Aristophanes. As they receded into the past the plays came to depend less on the live theater and more on the minds and purses of the "great variety of readers" to which they were now addressed. The Folio was reprinted in 1632, 1663, and 1685; each modernized and "corrected" its predecessor and each admitted a crop of new errors; the 1664 impression of the Third Folio added

Pericles and six apocryphal plays to the original thirty-six. A full understanding of the making of the Folio and the transmission of its text has been attained (perhaps still imperfectly) only in the scholarship of the twentieth century; but a significant start, in intention if not in accomplishment, was made by Nicholas Rowe in 1709. His edition was published in six octavo volumes by Jacob Tonson, an early promoter of the Shakespearean book trade. Keeping up the tradition of courting patronage, Rowe dedicates his work to the duke of Somerset and tells him he has compared "the several editions" and given "the true Reading as well as I could from thence." He claims to have done the job "pretty carefully" and to have "render'd very many Places Intelligible, that were not so before."

In fact, Rowe followed the usual practice of basing his text upon the most recent edition (Fourth Folio), and his use of the earlier folios is casual and unsystematic. He made some use of quarto readings in *Henry V* and *King Lear,* but for the most part his interventions were, like those of earlier scribes and press editors, modernizations and clarifications meant for the convenience of the modern reader. He edited Shakespeare in the same way as he prepared his own plays for publication—listing the characters, dividing the scenes, tidying up the exits and entrances; but the conventions he established and the minute judgments he made (without, in Samuel Johnson's phrase, "the pomp of notes") have left a deep impression on editorial tradition.

Yet Rowe's work represents an end as well as a beginning. Since the death of Shakespeare the theaters had closed (1642–1660) and had reopened under a different cultural dispensation; an experience of Shakespeare had to be more deliberately recovered, for it was no longer an everyday inheritance. But there were continuities, too, and Rowe writes "Some Account of the Life of Mr. William Shakespeare" out of a fading oral tradition and the table talk of his contemporaries. "How fond do we see some people of discovering any little personal story of the great men of antiquity!" —Rowe gracefully indulges that curiosity with the help of the actor Thomas Betterton, who is said to have visited Stratford for that purpose. Rowe, like his predecessors in literary criticism and gossip, mixes anecdote, fact, and opinion in a fluent, conversational prose. Thomas Fuller's *History of the Worthies of England* (1662) speaks of Shakespeare as a worthy of Warwickshire, but he makes no con-

nections between the life and the art other than an amusing comparison of Jonson's wit to "a Spanish great Gallion" and Shakespeare's to "an English man of War." Jonson was "built far higher in Learning," but Shakespeare, "lesser in bulk, but lighter in sailing, could turn with all tides, tack about and take advantage of all winds, by the quickness of his wit and invention." Some twenty years later John Aubrey, in a manuscript not adequately edited until 1898, set down (perhaps on the authority of the actor William Beeston) the story that Shakespeare, said to be a butcher's son, when he killed a calf would do it in "a high style, and make a speech." He adds that Shakespeare "understood Latine pretty well; for he had been in his younger years a Schoolmaster in the Countrey."

These are flimsy evidences compared even with Rowe's gleanings from the papers that William Davenant had collected, and they testify to the paucity of the tradition on which Rowe had to build. As he says, "The character of the man is best seen in his writings." His own judgment of the character of the work is poised and generous but not free from condescension to the literary culture of Shakespeare's time: "We are to consider him as a man that lived in a state of almost universal licence and ignorance: there was no established judge, but every one took the liberty to write according to the dictates of his own fancy." Yet Rowe had more than an inkling of the distinctive powers of Shakespeare's "fancy." Had his knowledge of the ancients been more "correct," he says, "the regularity and deference for them, which would have attended that correctness, might have restrained some of that fire, impetuosity, and even beautiful extravagance which we admire in Shakespeare." At the same time Rowe admired (and followed) the chronicle reading that had gone into the making of the history plays:

> What can be more agreeable to the idea our historians give of Henry the Sixth, than the picture Shakespeare has drawn of him! His manners are every where exactly the same with the story; one finds him still describ'd with simplicity, passive sanctity, want of courage, weakness of mind, and easy submission to the governance of an imperious wife, or prevailing faction: though at the same time the poet does justice to his good qualities, and moves the pity of his audience for him, by shewing him pious, disinterested, a contemner of the things of this world, and wholly resigned to the severest dispensations of God's providence.

This is the language of informed judgment, showing, with economy of phrase, a sharply focused response to the complexities of both the history's disclosures and the play's effects; few later accounts of the play can match its brevity and precision, yet it could serve as the basis for a wide-ranging and scholarly account of its significance. Later scholars (including John Dover Wilson) have been almost as reluctant to believe Shakespeare capable of reading the chronicles in English as Rowe believed him incapable of reading the *Menaechmi* in Latin.

Revised versions of Rowe's edition appeared in 1709 and 1714, and it was succeeded by Alexander Pope's in 1723. Tonson's records show that Rowe had been paid £36.10s; Pope received £217.12s, for six handsome volumes offering a more intrusive service to readers, discriminating with quotation marks passages of particular excellence, and confining to the foot of the page those lines he thought unworthy of Shakespeare. Pope was a scholarly poet but not a scholarly editor; he kept the civilization of his day in touch with Horace, but he understood neither the language nor the theater of Shakespeare's time: "It must be allowed that Stage-Poetry of all other, is more particularly levell'd to please the *Populace,* and its success more immediately depending upon the *Common Suffrage.*" "Wit grew polite, and numbers learned to flow," said Pope of the English Augustans, and he attempts to transpose Shakespeare into the same key. From *Love's Labor's Lost* he relegated the third line ("And then grace us in the disgrace of death"), no doubt because he thought it a vulgar clench, together with some 200 others, including the quibbles on "l'envoy" and "salve," on "shooting," and on "A good lustre of conceit in a turf of earth." Where he might reasonably have excised lines apparently repeated in Berowne's speech at IV. iii. 284–360, he is content to set 322–333 in commendatory quotation marks.

Pope's prefatory tribute to Shakespeare finds him "not so much an Imitator, as an Instrument, of Nature; and 'tis not so just to say that he speaks from her, as that she speaks thro' him." He thinks the differences between Shakespeare and Jonson exaggerated by "the spirit of opposition" and makes a different distinction: "There is certainly a vast difference between *Learning* and *Language.* How far he was ignorant of the latter, I cannot determine; but 'tis plain he had much Reading at least, if they will not call it Learning." Pope submitted to Tonson a copy of Rowe that had been exten-

sively corrected from the quartos as well as impertinently refined by the man of taste. He also reprinted Rowe's "Some Account of the Life," subjecting it to a good deal of silent editing. He did not make use of the engravings, many of which mediate between the traditions of the stage and those of the visual arts, that Rowe had interspersed in the plays.

While Rowe appears to have been free from what Shakespeare's Jaques called "the scholar's melancholy, which is emulation," the same cannot be said either of Pope or of the next editor in the line, Lewis Theobald. Edward Capell says of Theobald:

> He declaims vehemently against the work of his antagonist: which yet serv'd him for a model; and his own is made only a little better, by his having a few more materials; of which he was not a better collator than the other, nor did he excel him in use of them; . . . in what he has done that is conjectural, he is rather more happy; but in this he had large assistances.

In his table of editions collated, Theobald sets Pope's alone under "Editions of no Authority," but he consistently worked from it and acquiesced in many of its errors and idiosyncrasies. In his preface Theobald hopes that "by the addition or alteration of a letter or two" he has restored to Shakespeare "both sense and sentiment." His successful emendations owe much to what he called "literal criticism" and to a surprising sensitivity to certain properties of Shakespeare's language: "his peculiar manner of thinking, and as peculiar a manner of cloathing those thoughts." In *Antony and Cleopatra* his literal emendations include fertile (F fore-/tell) I.ii.37; bear (F beate) II:vii.110; *Justeius* (F *Iusteus*) III.vii.72; deputation (F disputation) III.xiii.74; discandying (F discandering) III.xiii.165; dislimns (F dislimes) IV.xiv.10; autumn 'twas (F *Anthony it was*) V.ii.87. Of these "discandying" followed, and "autumn 'twas" coincided with, conjectures by the Cambridge scholar Styan Thirlby; while the name Justeius, with others, was a correction out of Plutarch's *Lives.*

Theobald also undertook to support his corrections and conjectures of Shakespeare "by parallel passages and authorities from himself, the surest means of expounding any author whatsoever." Shakespeare and his contemporaries were said to have had "a wonderful affection to appear learned. . . . They declined vulgar images, such as are immediately fetch'd from nature, and rang'd thro' the circle of the sciences to fetch their ideas from thence." No longer regarded, in Milton's phrase, as "fancy's child" and left to "warble his native woodnotes wild," Shakespeare's recondite art became the theme of footnotes through which, as Johnson had it, "the mind is refrigerated by interruption." Theobald found little that was recondite in *Love's Labor's Lost,* said the play was "a very bad one," and emended "school of night" (IV. iii. 250) to William Warburton's "scowl of night"; in the same play he tidied up the misassignments of speeches in IV. ii, on which Rowe had made a start.

Theobald's seven-volume octavo, published in 1733, was reissued in eight volumes in 1740, and its 11,360 copies earned him £652. The Shakespearean book trade was flourishing, and at the upper end of the market Sir Thomas Hanmer's edition, even more splendidly produced than Pope's quartos, appeared in six volumes (1743–1744). Capell was to say of it that "the publisher disdains all collation of folios, or quartos; and fetches all from his great self, and the moderns his predecessors." He added, however, "that as his conjectures are numerous, they are oftentimes not unhappy." It was Hanmer who found "pannelled" in the Folio (*Antony and Cleopatra,* IV. xii. 21) and left "spaniel'd" in the text. In Hanmer's edition, which is based on Pope's, more passages are "thrown to the bottom of the page," but beauties are no longer distinguished by quotation marks. Pope's and Rowe's prefaces are reprinted from Pope's edition, the plays are "Adorned with Sculptures" by Hubert François Gravelot, and the editor offers an occasional note of his own, as when he objects in *Love's Labor's Lost* (V. ii. 572) to the *"wretched quibble upon the words* Ajax *and* A jakes."

William Warburton, bishop of Gloucester, had already made an impression on Shakespeare's text before he published his own edition (again based on Pope and therefore on Rowe) in 1747. Johnson found in his commentary "that precipitation which is produced by consciousness of quick discernment" but allowed him the veneration due to "genius and learning." Thomas Edwards, in his *Supplement to Mr. Warburton's Edition of Shakespear* (1748, reissued as *The Canons of Criticism,* 1750), was less magnanimous, as more rigorous modes of analysis began to displace the confidences of cultivated readers. Those confidences should not be undervalued, and Johnson himself was among the last to display them.

In the preface to his eight-volume, 1765 edition (again from the house of Tonson) Johnson charged Pope with thinking "more of amputation than of cure," attributed Theobald's reputation to "the good luck of having Pope for his enemy" ("so easily is he praised, whom no man can envy"), and blamed Hanmer for failing "to suspect a critick of fallibility." Significantly, in his brief commentary on *Love's Labor's Lost* he allows himself to be expansive about Nathaniel's words to Holofernes: "Your reasons at dinner have been sharp and sententious, pleasant without scurrility, witty without affection, audacious without impudency, learned without opinion, and strange without heresy" (V. i. 2–6). "It is very difficult," says Johnson, "to add any thing to this character of the school-master's table-talk, and perhaps all the precepts of Castiglione will scarcely be found to comprehend a rule for conversation so justly delineated, so widely dilated, and so nicely limited." The continuity of Johnson's style with that of Nathaniel is more than accidental, for Johnson's edition has the virtues of good table talk and, in that respect, looks backward toward the Renaissance rather than forward to the bibliocritical sciences.

Johnson's text was assembled with care and was the best that had yet been published, but the edition is now valued for its weighty and vivacious preface and for its deftly formulated paraphrases and lexical glosses, which themselves testify to the scholar's control of the expressiveness of the language. He took over much of Theobald's commentary but purged it of its bad manners: "The exuberant excrescence of diction I have often lopped, his triumphant exultations over Pope and Rowe I have sometimes suppressed, and his contemptible ostentation I have frequently concealed." But he did not keep back all the evidence of academic vacuity: "I have in some places shewn him, as he would have shewn himself, for the reader's diversion, that the inflated emptiness of some notes may justify or excuse the contraction of the rest."

Shakespearean learning was not the exclusive property of the editors. Richard Farmer kept up the more convivial traditions of scholarship by entertaining "the Shakespeare gang" at Emmanuel College, Cambridge. Johnson himself spent a "joyous evening" there in February 1765, before Farmer published *An Essay on the Learning of Shakespeare* (1767). Farmer was well acquainted with the work of Shakespeare's main and secondary editors, and with his many critics and apologists, including Charles Gildon (who had appended a seventh volume of *Poems,* based on John Benson's version, to Rowe's edition in 1710), George Sewell (who had added a seventh volume to Pope's 1725 edition, including another bad text of the poems, and a history of the stage), and John Upton (the author of *Critical Observations on Shakespeare,* 1746). Farmer, himself a tutor in classics, seems often to speak with the voice of Johnson or with that of John Hales, fellow of Eton, the schoolmaster talked of by Dryden and by Rowe, who upon any topic finely treated by the ancients undertook "to shew something upon the same subject at least as well written by Shakespeare."

Farmer did not deny Shakespeare's classical status, but he insisted on its English and romance foundations. He challenges Pope's comparison of Jonson's copyings of Cicero in *Catiline* with Shakespeare's borrowings from Plutarch in *Coriolanus,* by demonstrating Shakespeare's word-for-word dependence on North's English text. For Timon's speech "The sun's a thief" (IV. iii. 432–445) he finds analogues not only in Anacreon but also in Pierre de Ronsard ("La terre les eaux va boivant"). He recalls Shakespearean commentators to the importance of such works as Richard Tarlton's *Jests* (1638) and Thomas Nash's *Pierce Penilesse* (1592), and to "the vulgar romances of the age." Theobald, whose preface to Shakespeare had included a display of his capacity for "literal criticism" upon Greek texts, had published a play, *Double Falsehood* (1728), which he claimed to have revised from an original manuscript "above sixty years standing." Farmer observed that "sometimes a very little matter detects a forgery" and shows that in the play the word *aspect* is accented on the first syllable, "as it never was in Shakespeare's time." He attended with enterprising vigilance to the minutiae of Shakespeare's reading; he showed that where Richard III speaks of Richmond "long kept in Britain at our mother's cost" (V. iii. 325), Shakespeare had been misled by Holinshed's mistranscription of Edward Halle's "brother's."

Pope said that judging Shakespeare by Aristotle's rules was "like trying a man under the Laws of one Country who acted under those of another"; Farmer invited scholars to trace the clues of Shakespeare's imagination through Elizabethan rather than Greek and Roman labyrinths. Of ancient Pistol's motto, "Si fortuna me tormenta, spero contenta" (*Henry IV, Part 2,* V. v. 97), he remarks that "Sir Richard Hawkins, in his voyage to the South-Sea, 1593, throws out the same jingling distich on the loss of his pinnace" and adds that it is found

again in Anthony Copley's *Wits, Fits and Fancies* (1595). It is perhaps significant that Matthias Shaaber, the New Variorum editor of the play, was unable to find the Copley passage referred to. Like his fellow Shakespearean gangster, George Steevens, Farmer was probably relying on a prodigious memory.

In a note to *Love's Labor's Lost* (IV. iii) Steevens tells us that "Shakespeare, in one of his other plays, uses *night of dew* for *dewy night,* but I cannot at present recollect, in which." It was not merely that they worked without concordances and the information retrieval systems with which we are now familiar, but also that they assumed that understanding flourished only in the scholar's sentience, in the individual's perception, not in an impersonally aggregated body of knowledge. The pleasure and obligation of conversing with other readers and playgoers remained, however, and editions (like table talk) were part of the civilized discourse. In the closing decades of the eighteenth century, scholarship grew less polite, even when it was no less cantankerous.

Edward Capell's edition, published, without its commentary, in ten volumes in 1767–1768, was the first of the new order. In spite of a frolicsome opening sentence comparing Shakespeare to an ostrich that "drops her egg at random, to be dispos'd of as chance pleases," Capell took his incubatory duties very seriously and spent twenty-four years preparing his collations and text. Under the patronage of the duke of Grafton he had been appointed deputy inspector of plays in 1737, but unlike his editorial predecessors he was not himself an aspiring poet or playwright. His approach was that of the bibliographer and historian, and his library, which passed to Trinity College, Cambridge, was ample enough to serve as the basis for the *Cambridge Shakespeare* (1863–1866). Of his commentary Johnson said that he "gabbled monstrously"; and his emendations were sometimes insensitive. He was nevertheless disciplined and rational in his treatment of the text, and he anticipated some currently acceptable editorial procedures. Recognizing, for example, that Shakespeare makes Berowne repeat himself, he cut fifteen lines from the long speech in *Love's Labor's Lost* (IV. iii. 294–299, 307–314). Of subsequent editors, Alexander Dyce (1857) first followed his cuts, but the Cambridge editors retained the repetitious infelicities on the ground that "we would lose no drop of the immortal man'" Capell kept Theobald's "prisons" for F's "poysons" (IV. iii. 300), however, and generally respected the literal interventions of his forerunners. He broke decisively from the style and method of Rowe's preface and looked forward to a fuller account of Shakespeare's professional life, based on the systematic study of the text and documents. He would not have the biographer and the historian swallowed up by "the critick and essayist."

Rival tendencies seem to converge in the several editions for which George Steevens shared responsibility with Johnson and Isaac Reed. Educated at Eton and King's College, Cambridge, Steevens was described by Johnson as an "ingenious gentleman"; he appended to the 1773 edition the essay on Shakespeare's learning by the comparably ingenious Cambridge don Richard Farmer. He mocked Capell's edition but was accused by John Collins in 1777 of stealing from it. He compromised wide and lively erudition by lapses into carelessness, inconsequence, or plain mischievousness. He saw that commentaries must grow ampler before they could afford to grow shorter: "Such as would be acquainted with the propriety of Falstaff's allusions to stewed prunes, should not be disgusted at a multitude of instances, which, when the point is once known to be established, may be diminished by any future editor." In later editions he annotated improprieties under the misappropriated names of two clergymen, John Collins and Richard Amner.

Malone

In the 1773 "Advertisement to the Reader" Steevens pays a generous tribute to Jacob Tonson (grandnephew of Pope's publisher), who had died in 1767: "He was willing to admit those with whom he contracted, to the just advantage of their own labours; and had never learned to consider the author as an under agent to the bookseller." William Jaggard's *Shakespeare Bibliography* records nearly eighty eighteenth-century editions and issues up to 1793, when the *Universal Magazine* reported that "one hundred and fifty thousand pounds have lately been devoted towards splendid editions" of Shakespeare's works. The market was still expanding and diversifying.

Steevens in 1766 had published twenty plays of Shakespeare, "Being the whole number printed in quarto during his life-time, or before the restoration; collated where there were different copies,

and publish'd from the originals." But the most austere and systematic critical apparatus was provided by Charles Jennens in editions of five plays, starting with *King Lear* in 1770. The slow accretions of textual evidence, the more hectic proliferation of opinions and observations, and the aggregated curiosity of a wider public were beginning to shape the demand for editions composed upon the variorum principle. Like that of 1773, the 1778 Johnson and Steevens edition, now revised and edited by Isaac Reed, included "the corrections and illustrations of various commentators" and added "An attempt to ascertain the order in which the plays attributed to Shakespeare were written" by Edmond Malone. Malone published supplements and appendices to this work in 1780 and 1783, before bringing out his own edition in 1790. To earlier prefatory material, including the essay on the chronology, he added "An Essay Relative to Shakespeare and Jonson"; "A Dissertation on the Three Parts of *King Henry the Sixth*"; and "An Historical Account of the English Stage."

Rowe and Theobald had both abandoned careers in law in order to do creative and editorial literary work. Malone brought his legal abilities to the center of Shakespearean studies. He came to England in 1777 after practicing as a barrister in Ireland, and he was quick to cultivate a London literary circle that included Edmund Burke and James Boswell. His 1790 preface opens with sustained quotations from Johnson, but his own interests and procedures took him in a very different direction. In spite of Johnson's "perspicuity and vigour" some of the positions he laid down "may be controverted," and to prove his points Malone had to "go into long and minute discussion." Although he had by this time quarreled with Steevens, he reprints the 1773 "Advertisement" and, like his former partner, does much to recall scholarship to "ancient English literature" and to the writing of Shakespeare's contemporaries. Some who ought to have found his work challenging found it dull. Horace Walpole, for example, thought it "the heaviest of all books" and its commentary "an extract of all the opiate that is spread through all the bad playwrights of that age."

Malone reprinted Rowe's preface but overwhelmed it with footnotes. He used his professional training to good effect upon the records of the Court of Chancery, and he visited Stratford and Worcester to consult local records. He was less concerned with assimilating Shakespeare's plays into the civilization of the eighteenth century than in returning them to that of Shakespeare's lifetime. But the past, re-created from the sort of evidence to which lawyers habitually attend, does not readily compose itself into a "civilization." In response to Rowe's observation that Shakespeare's grand-daughter "died without issue," Malone supplies three pages of notes that include a copy of her will "extracted from the Registry of the Prerogative Court of Chancery." We are sometimes made to feel that the solicitor's records are not, after all, coextensive with the history of imaginative literature.

Yet records can be made to serve imaginative ends, and they do so in Malone's "Historical Account of the English Stage." It takes its starting points from earlier work, including Thomas Warton's *The History of English Poetry* (1774–1781), but it makes fresh use of printed and manuscript sources and, without condescension, traces the history of the stage "from its first rude state to the period of its maturity and greatest splendour"—the period, that is, of the Globe and the Blackfriars, not that of Drury Lane. Malone supposes performances at the Globe to have been "chiefly for the lower class of people; those at Blackfriars, for a more select and judicious audience," and as evidence quotes the prologue to James Shirley's *The Doubtful Heir.*

Malone raised most of the questions that have since beguiled students of Shakespeare's theater, and his answers were always carefully argued and supported. His essay on the chronology of the plays proved the foundation for later inquiries, and its method was judiciously systematic without being mechanical. He argues that the first draft of *Love's Labor's Lost* was written "in or before 1594" and that "some additions were made to it between that year and 1597, when it was exhibited before the Queen." His evidence includes the entry in the Stationers' Register, the allusion in Francis Meres's *Palladis Tamia* (1598), and the reference to Bankes's horse, a story told in Richard Tarlton's *Jests;* but he also takes account of "the frequent rhymes . . . its imperfect versification, its artless and desultory dialogue, and the irregularity of the composition." In his first version he attributed *The Winter's Tale* to the same season, totally misled by what he took to be the objective evidence of an entry in the Stationers' Register that in fact referred to another work, *A Winter-Night's Pastime;* he changed his mind and moved the play to 1604, on the grounds that it lacked rhymes, was not mentioned by Meres, and was designed in sequel to *Henry VIII* as "indirect apology" to the queen's mother, Anne Boleyn. His reason for not assigning it to Elizabeth's reign was that (as William Blackstone pointed out) Camillo's refusal to kill a king (I. ii. 354–361) would have embarrassed the assassin of Mary Queen of Scots.

Here and elsewhere we may doubt the adequacy of Malone's experience of the plays and wonder at the legal disposition to interpret art through documents and court politics. In his handling of the texts as documents, however, Malone made many advances. He illustrates the "gradual progress of corruption from *Richard II* (II. ii. 3), where Q1 (1597) reads "life-harming heaviness," Q4 (1608) has "halfe-warming," and the Folio mistakenly emends to "selfe-harming," and he pursues many such trails throughout his work.

From Boswell to the New Variorum

At Malone's death in 1812 his papers were passed to James Boswell (son of the biographer), and many of their findings were incorporated in the twenty-one-volume variorum edition of 1821. In 1803 Isaac Reed edited what he called the fifth edition of Johnson and Steevens. Under one convention the editions of 1773, 1778, and 1785 are referred to as Variorum; but under another, slightly more appropriate, Reed's editions of 1803 and 1813 are called the First and Second Variorum, and Boswell's the Third. From one point of view the growth of the variorum is evidence of what T. S. Eliot called "the common pursuit of true judgement," but from another it is an episode in the history of hubbub. Malone in 1790 appended to *Love's Labor's Lost,* as a comment on "This child of fancy, that Armado hight" (I. i. 167), a long note by Warburton on romances of chivalry together with a long dissenting comment from Thomas Tyrwhitt. Malone expresses the hope that "Dr. Warburton's futile performance, like the pismire which Martial tells us was accidentally encrusted with amber, will be ever preserved, for the sake of the admirable comment in which it is now enshrined."

Reed's 1803 Variorum is an orderly and self-effacing display of the findings and opinions of a century, he himself not presuming "to imagine himself capable of adding any thing to so exhausted a subject." In his 1821 advertisement Boswell found that "among the defects of the later editions of Shakespeare, may be reckoned an exuberance of comment"; his edition shows more consideration for readers than most of the variorums. It is also sensitive to the emergence of a European Shakespeare. Eighteenth-century commentators often found it necessary to meet French skepticism about Shakespeare ("C'est une belle nature," said Voltaire to Walpole, "mais bien sauvage"), but in the nineteenth century they were to be exposed to exotic encomia. "Even in France," says Boswell, "which has always been remarkable for a bigoted attachment to its own literature, a tardy and unwilling tribute has been paid to the genius of Shakespeare." It was from Germany that the strangest ideas were visited upon the English: "We are bound particularly to notice M. Schlegel . . . sometimes perhaps too refined; and too enthusiastick for our colder and more didactick style of criticism; there is, occasionally, too much metaphysical curiosity in his analysis; he is inclined to make Shakspeare, who wrote for the people, too much of a poetical mystick." Both French and German traditions of intellectual inquiry have in our own time made a powerful impact upon Shakespearean scholarship, but in Victorian England and in America, European thought found its way into those areas of Shakespearean criticism that owed most to the romantic movement and to philosophic idealism. Some of the effects are made visible in the New Variorum, whose publication under Horace Howard Furness began in Philadelphia in 1871.

But in the meantime scholarship in the wake of Malone was kept up in London by the Shakespeare Society (1840–1853), under the sway of John Payne Collier and including in its membership Charles Knight, James Orchard Halliwell (later called Halliwell-Phillipps), George Lillie Craik, and Alexander Dyce. The society began well, with the publication of Dyce's edition of *Sir Thomas More,* and followed it with many other plays and collections of documents, including Peter Cunningham's *Revels at Court,* plays by Thomas Heywood and Antony Munday, and *Early Prose and Poetical Tracts* of the reign of Elizabeth. Unfortunately there was a worm in the bud. Collier had been a law student at the Middle Temple before working as a reporter for the *Times.* After reading Spenser he wrote a poem, "The Poet's Pilgrimage," which was admired by Wordsworth but rejected by a bookseller with the advice that it be turned into prose. Like other forgers, he was a frustrated creator. In

February 1795 Samuel and William Ireland had exhibited Shakespearean love letters, his profession of faith, various documents later published as *Miscellaneous Papers and Legal Instruments,* and a lock of hair. William had begun by copying a facsimile Shakespeare signature in Malone's edition, and it was Malone who decisively exposed the whole enterprise.

Collier worked more subtly and shared something of Malone's knowledge of documents and palaeography. His three-volume work, *The History of English Dramatic Poetry to the Time of Shakespeare; and Annals of the Stage to the Restoration* (1831), had proved his mastery of the authentic material and won him the respect of scholars. His meddlings with the Egerton and Dulwich papers were therefore the more insidious. An authentic illustration of *Titus Andronicus* at Longleat, for example, carries annotations ascribing it to Henry Peacham and a scene number that Collier used for his edition of the play. Many forged marginalia in a copy of the Second Folio, known as the Perkins Folio, served as Collier's authority for *Notes and Emendations* (1852) and for much in his own 1853 edition. The resulting controversy led to the breakup of the Shakespeare Society. By 1860 most of the forgeries had been brought to light, including passages in lectures by Coleridge that Collier claimed to have reconstructed from his own shorthand notes; these were challenged by Andrew Edmund Brae in an anonymously issued pamphlet called *Literary Cookery* (1855).

Collier was trying to appease real appetites. The hunger for a past that satisfied the imagination had moved many who should have known better to swallow the Rowley fabrications of Thomas Chatterton. William Ireland made a pilgrimage to Bristol in tribute to Chatterton, the pathos of whose life had inspired Wordsworth, Coleridge, and Keats, and he made forgery a manifestation of romanticism. It might be said of Collier that his romanticism contaminated his scholarship.

Halliwell-Phillipps had been embarrassed by the activities of Collier but also, in the best sense, inspired by them. His own contributions to documentary scholarship are still not fully assimilated. He returned to the Stratford documents and extensively corrected Malone's transcriptions. "In many instances," says Schoenbaum, "his texts are the fullest ever published." He gives four pages to the records of 1598 in which Shakespeare is listed as the holder of ten quarters of malt. The effect of much of his work is to frame the still shadowy portrait of the Warwickshire worthy. But he is not totally inattentive to the plays. In his *Memoranda on Love's Labour's Lost, King John, Othello and on Romeo and Juliet,* published in 1879 but written in 1855, he remarks that "a complete appreciation of *Love's Labour's Lost* was reserved for the present century, several modern psychological critics of eminence having successfully vindicated its title to a position amongst the best productions of the great dramatist," and he goes on to name Coleridge. His documentary scholarship keeps itself at a safe distance from criticism but adds five pages to the notes and the picture of a dancing horse that Malone had already contributed in annotation of Moth's allusion to it in I. ii. 52. After a sympathetic discussion of Capell's excisions from IV. iii. 294–314, he gives his views on verse tests and finds them "seldom of decisive use excepting when they are made entirely subservient to arguments founded on the more positive criteria of dramatic power and characterization."

It is therefore not entirely true that Halliwell-Phillipps' Shakespeare is merely the man of property. "The unphilosophical biographer," says Schoenbaum, "has paused before this likeness of a plump, well-fed, middle-aged citizen, and he has come away persuaded that his subject was much as other men." Halliwell-Phillipps himself played the property market; he was accused of abstracting manuscripts from Trinity College, Cambridge, and selling them to a dealer, and he released his published transcriptions on a scale small enough to maintain their rarity value.

The New Shakespere Society was founded in 1874 by Frederick James Furnivall in order, "by a very close study of the metrical and phraseological peculiarities of Shakespere, to get his plays as nearly as possible into the order in which he wrote them," but such study was to serve a more comprehensive purpose, an understanding of "the progress and meaning of Shakespere's mind." The word *progress* has its distinctive period flavor. The more we study Shakespeare, proclaims Furnivall in the society's *Transactions* of 1874, "the better England will be"; he was introducing the society's first paper, by the Reverend Frederick G. Fleay, "On Metrical Tests as Applied to Dramatic Poetry." It includes its own progressive manifesto:

Our analysis, which has hitherto been qualitative, must become quantitative; we must cease to be empirical, and become scientific: in criticism as in other matters, the test that decides between science and empiricism is this: "Can you say, not only of what kind, but how much? If you cannot weigh, measure, number your results, however you may be convinced yourself, you must not hope to convince others, or claim the position of an investigator; you are merely a guesser, a propounder of hypotheses."

Fleay's mimicry of the styles of a half dozen of Shakespeare's contemporaries proves him to be not without literary sensitivity; but his determination to quantify, to subdue the subjectivities of perception to the objectivities of fact, was characteristic of the new scientism.

For Auguste Comte, its prophet, the progressive process of history moved from the poetic age, through the ages of metaphysics and reason, to the positive age—the age of fact. His confidence in the power of fact was itself, skeptics might say, poetic and metaphysical, even apocalyptic. And it proved infectious. "In the great European republic," said George Henry Lewes, in his exposition of Comte's philosophy of the sciences, "the impulse of new social elements constituted an universal movement of partial recomposition, destined to concur with the simultaneous movement of political decomposition, in order to evolve from their inevitable combination the final regeneration of Mankind." Such a faith took Gradgrind into the schoolroom of Dickens' *Hard Times* and Fleay into the New Shakespere Society. Once the facts were recognized they would recompose themselves in a new enlightenment: analysis would yield synthesis, disintegration give place to a true reintegration, deconstruction to reconstruction.

Furnivall's program for the society owed much to an article contributed by James Spedding, the editor of Francis Bacon's works, to the *Gentleman's Magazine* for August 1850, "On the Several Shares of Shakespere and Fletcher in the Play of *Henry VIII*," which was appended to the *Transactions* of 1874. Spedding's paper was primarily addressed to the reader's judgment and the listener's ear; its tabulations are meant to reassure the convinced and alert the skeptics. Fleay was the first of the "disintegrators," who tried to redistribute the plays between collaborating authors on evidence that could be called to precise account. His most formidable successor was the rationalist and parliamentarian John Mackinnon Robertson.

A very different kind of preoccupation was promoted by two papers read later in 1874 to the New Shakespere Society by Richard Simpson: "The Political Use of the Stage in Shakespere's Time" and "The Politics of Shakespere's Historical Plays." With greater tact and precision than his predecessors (Warburton, Walpole, and Malone) Simpson holds the political allusiveness of the plays in a more convincing perspective and with great economy of line. He says of *King John* that while it borrows its plot from *The Troublesome Raigne*, "the political tendency of the old play is entirely suppressed," and attention diverted from Henry VIII's struggle with the church to Elizabeth's treatment of Mary Queen of Scots.

Furnivall encouraged both minute investigation and comprehensive interpretation. He wrote prefaces to the English version of G. G. Gervinus' *Commentaries* (1874), and he edited a forty-three-volume series of quarto facsimiles (1880–1891). He admired Gervinus for taking a broad view of Shakespeare, and he helped Edward Dowden (*Shakespere: A Critical Study of His Mind and Art*, 1875), vice-president of the society, to do the same. Of August Wilhelm von Schlegel's dramatic lectures Gervinus said that they testified "to poetic delicacy and sensibility; all is fair, alluring, inspiring—a panegyric of a totally different kind to the criticising characteristic of the English expositors." Dowden, too, cultivated delicacy and sensibility. "The true question to ask respecting a book," he says, quoting Whitman, "is, *Has it helped any human soul?*" But English expositors continued to ask smaller questions, and answers (or further questions) continued to accumulate.

Furness inscribed his New Variorum *Romeo and Juliet* in 1871 to "The Shakespere Society of Philadelphia." In the nearly fifty years since Boswell, he says, "criticism has made great progress, . . . Shakespeare has never had critics who brought to their task greater learning, keener critical sagacity and more reverential love than have been shown by his more modern editors." He showed a similar confidence in the new techniques of reproduction, collating the four quartos from Ashbee's facsimiles, and the First Folio from Staunton's photolithograph. He appends selections from the critics, deliberately giving more space to the French and German than to the English, but allowing himself to remark that "occasionally the demand made by German commentators upon our admiration a little outruns our ability to meet it." He exercises patience and good sense in assembling a miscellany of observations; but while many curiosities are satisfied, his method does little to vindicate the nineteenth century's faith in incrementally advancing knowledge.

Edmund Chambers and the Documents

Another kind of variorum enterprise was at the same time under way in the New Shakespere Society. Its purpose and history are described by the title page of its final public appearance in 1932: *The Shakespere Allusion-Book: A Collection of Allusions to Shakespere from 1591 to 1700 . . . Originally Compiled by C. M. Ingelby, Miss L. Toulmin Smith, and by Dr. F. J. Furnivall, with the Assistance of the New Shakespere Society; Re-edited, Revised, and Re-arranged, with an Introduction, by John Munro (1909), and Now Reissued with a Preface by Sir Edmund Chambers*. But Chambers' introduction makes it ironically clear that all that collaborative effort is already superseded. He reports that Richard P. Cowl had collected two or three hundred more allusions to *Henry IV* alone—the project was passing beyond the scope of a book. In 1948 James McManaway remarked that at the Folger Library "the search for early references to Shakespeare continues, but it is rarely possible to add to the 5,000 or more titles already in the Library."

Other endeavors of the time have found a more finite outcome. In his *Memoranda Intended for the Use of Amateurs*, published in 1884 to assist Shakespearean researchers in the Public Record Office, Halliwell-Phillipps supposes that "it would take a hundred people more than a hundred years to go through the records exhaustively." Some of his leads were followed. Charlotte Carmichael Stopes (*Shakespeare's Family*, 1901) included some authentic new material in her often girlish and gossipy account of "an interesting Warwickshire gentleman" and his neighbors. But an American rival, Charles William Wallace, and his wife proved much more successful. In an article contributed to *Harper's Monthly Magazine* (March 1910) he claimed to have searched "some million of documents" before discovering the twenty-six pertaining to the Belott-Mountjoy suit, nine of which mention Shakespeare. The research, showing that Shakespeare in 1612 had only vague memories of a marriage he had encouraged about eight years earlier, tells us more about the Huguenot tradesman and his apprentice than about the poet and playwright.

But these documents, with other findings, connecting Shakespeare with the Blackfriars and the Globe in 1615, occasioned much public discussion, alighting on such questions as the possibility that Milton might have seen Shakespeare in Bread Street. Leslie Hotson, again in the wake of Halliwell-Phillipps, published his account of Shakespeare's quarrel with William Wayte (*Shakespeare versus Shallow,* 1931) and argued that Shallow and Slender in *The Merry Wives of Windsor* were mockeries of Wayte and William Gardiner. In *I, William Shakespeare* (1937) Hotson traced a connection between Leonard Digges, who contributed verses to the First Folio preface, and Thomas Russell, an overseer of Shakespeare's will. His creative imagination won a response from the records, and he showed great skill in making stories and structures from the debris of fact. His account of *The First Night of "Twelfth Night"* (1954) overstates an interesting case by insisting on too direct and circumstantial a connection between fact and fiction.

Edgar I. Fripp followed in Halliwell-Phillipps' tracks but colored his evidence with a more serene and cultivated image of Shakespeare the man. He is sensitive to the plays, and his major work, the posthumously published, two-volume *Shakespeare, Man and Artist* (1938), comes up to the expectations awakened by one of its opening sentences: "He was reared in romantic woodland country, rich in historical buildings and associations, the home of an aristocracy still 'worshipful,' hardworking, and serviceable to the State." He sees *Love's Labor's Lost* as a genial court satire, distantly but distinctly related to English dealings with Henry of Navarre, and thinks "the Queen would appreciate the loss of Love's labour, and the dispatch of the men about their business." But "Stratford predominates over the Court. At every turn we are reminded of the Poet's native country, his boyhood and schooldays, games and lessons, . . . the forest and deer of Arden."

Fripp belongs to a nineteenth-century tradition, initiated by Furnivall, Edward Dowden, Georg M. C. Brandes, and others who made of Shakespeare's life and art a kind of pastoral symphony. The characteristic temper of twentieth-century scholarship in its first phase is expressed and determined by Edmund K. Chambers in *William Shakespeare, A Study of Facts and Problems* (1930): he values the facts but does not believe that a revelation is at hand. His biographical account is divided into sections dealing with Shakespeare's origin, the stage in 1592, and Shakespeare and his company. His Shakespeare is a professional actor and playwright,

not conspicuously a Warwickshire gentleman. Chambers' handling of problems of authenticity and chronology, and his account of our state of knowledge of the plays and poems, remain authoritative; they are a necessary starting point. The records and allusions printed in the second volume remain useful, and its metrical tables have yet to be displaced by a more sensitive equivalent.

Shakespeare's Sources and Reading

Chambers deals briefly with the known sources for each play, but it has been left to others to further the work initiated by Gerard Langbaine in *Momus Triumphans, or the Plagiaries of the English Stage Expos'd* (1687). Charles Gildon, William Oldys, and Richard Farmer contributed findings that were assimilated into editorial tradition, but the first major collection of source material was the three-volume study by Charlotte Lennox, *Shakespeare Illustrated, or the Novels and Histories, on Which the Plays of Shakespeare Are Founded, Collected and Translated from the Original Authors. With Critical Remarks* (1753–1754). In 1831 Karl Joseph Simrock, a German poet and professor, published *Quellen des Shakespeare in Novellen, Märchen und Sagen*. J. P. Collier's two-volume *Shakespeare's Library* (1843) claimed that its contents were "Now first collected and printed"; it was extended to six volumes by William C. Hazlitt in 1875. Geoffrey Bullough's *Narrative and Dramatic Sources of Shakespeare* was published in eight volumes from 1957 to 1975. When he began work, he said, " 'Source-hunting was disparaged as futile," for those were the days "of textual revisionism," bibliographical discovery, psychoanalytic plumbing, and symbol-clashing, all useful as well as fashionable activities." His aim was "not to discover new sources but to make those already known accessible to Shakespeare lovers, and in the introductory essays to indicate (however distantly) the imaginative process informing his dramatic structures" (*Narrative and Dramatic Sources*, VIII, p. vii).

Much source material has been assimilated into the major editions, including Edward Capell's *Notes and Various Readings to Shakespeare*, 3 (1783), Halliwell-Phillipps' edition of 1853–1865, and the New Variorum. Shakespeare's reading was wider than any collection of sources and analogues suggests. "The critics plough," said the critic Walter Raleigh, "where Shakespeare danced." Matthew W. Black, in the New Variorum *Richard II* (1955), assembles source material from six chronicles (including Créton's *Histoire* and Le Beau's version of *Chronique*), a verse history, and an old play. Langbaine in 1691 invited his readers to look for the plot in ten chronicles, but John Dover Wilson in his editions of *Henry VI* (1952) and *Richard II* (1939) built a number of hypotheses—some ingenious to the point of absurdity—on the assumption that Shakespeare was not one to waste his time reading. As Black observes, "Many of the passages which remained most accurately in Shakespeare's memory are in the marginal notes or at the foot or head of a column in the 1587 edition of Holinshed." He pictures "a masterly process of skimming, in which the dramatist took what suited his purpose." Our attitude toward Shakespeare's sources is critically dependent upon our understanding of "the poet's eye in a fine frenzy rolling," upon "the quick forge and working-house of thought."

Among twentieth-century contributors to our knowledge of Shakespeare's metamorphic reading capacities may be named Henry R. D. Anders (*Shakespeare's Books,* 1904), Ashley H. Thorndike ("Shakspere as a Debtor," 1916), Virgil K. Whitaker (*Shakespeare's Use of Learning: An Inquiry into the Growth of His Mind and Art,* 1953), and Kenneth Muir. The first volume of Muir's *Shakespeare's Sources,* dealing with the comedies and tragedies, appeared in the same year as Bullough's first volume; a change of plan led to a revised and extended version, *The Sources of Shakespeare's Plays* (1977). He includes many illustrations of the way in which Shakespeare's general reading "is woven into the texture of his work." With or without recourse to theories of "reception" and "intertextuality," attention to Shakespeare's sources has increased our awareness of the dependence of a reader's or playgoer's perceptions upon his own literacy.

Both Bullough and Muir begin by acknowledging the value of Thomas Whitfield Baldwin's compendious and agreeably discursive two-volume work, *William Shakspere's Small Latine and Lesse Greeke* (1944). Bullough's first source text is *The Menaechmi* of Plautus, but it is given in the English translation of 1595 by William Warner, first pointed out by Farmer, which was almost certainly published after *The Comedy of Errors* was written. It is not that Bullough doubts Shakespeare's ability to read Latin, but he quite rightly doubts that of his own readers. In the perspectives of history, Baldwin's work looks like a response to Farmer's *Essay;* it suggests that Shakespeare's classical learning was

owed to his petty school and grammar school education. While there is no documentary proof of his having attended the Stratford grammar school, the hypothesis is consistent with the evidence of the plays.

Shakespeare's treatment of the comedy of scholarship in *Love's Labor's Lost* appears to recall his own experience as a pupil and perhaps—if Aubrey's report that he was a schoolmaster in the country is to be trusted—as a tutor. He seems to describe his own natural aptitudes as a poet even as he makes fun of Holofernes' flaunting of them (IV. ii. 63–69). The "figures," "motions," and "revolutions" of the poet's "foolish extravagant spirit" have proved intractable to systematic pedagogy. Yet Shakespeare's comedy requires that critical distinctions be made and informed judgments cultivated. "Holofernes," says Baldwin, "has brought the whole background of grammar school poetical teaching to bear upon Berowne's poetical missive." A lively memory for what he read at school, a readiness to use translations when they were available, and a preparedness to engage as best he could with Latin, French, and Italian texts when he had to account well enough for what is to be found in the "learning" of the plays. But this way of putting it should not lead us to underestimate the range and depth of Shakespeare's engagement with the classical past.

"The 'timeless present,'" said Ernst R. Curtius in *European Literature and the Latin Middle Ages* (1953), "which is an essential characteristic of literature means that the literature of the past can always be active in that of the present"; and he instances Homer in Virgil, Virgil in Dante, Plutarch and Seneca in Shakespeare. Plutarch's presence was mediated through Thomas North's English (and Amyot's French); Ovid's *Fasti* (the source of *Lucrece*) Shakespeare knew at firsthand; and it is probable that a schoolboy's memories of Quintilian found their way into the mouth of Holofernes, whose own name and conception were owed (says Malone) to Rabelais. Shakespearean scholarship is growing reconciled to the multiple and miscellaneous nature of Shakespeare's sources.

Diversifying Interests

It finds it rather less easy to manage its own diverse dispositions and interests. Already in the nineteenth century the space was widening between the demands of the specialists, the general public, and the schoolroom. Charles Knight and others addressed themselves to a wide range of readers, the researchers in the societies talked to each other, and toward the end of the period, editors, including Chambers, John Churton Collins, and Arthur Wilson Verity, were preparing special editions for schools. Of the Shakespeare societies of Europe and America, only the Deutsche Shakespeare-Gesellschaft survived to flourish in the twentieth century, partly, no doubt, because Shakespeare studies were being actively promoted in the German universities when the society was founded at Weimar in 1865. Important studies of *Richard III,* for example, were published by Wilhelm Oechelhäuser in the *Jahrbuch* (1868) and by George Bosworth Churchill in *Palaestra* (1900), the latter work having started as a dissertation at the University of Berlin. The periodical of the Shakespeare Society of New York, *New-Shakespeareana,* outlived the society but ceased publication in 1912.

The *Shakespeare Association Bulletin,* with its annual classified bibliography, ran from 1924 to 1949 before becoming, in 1950, the *Shakespeare Quarterly,* published by the Folger Shakespeare Library. Its annual bibliographies offer the most comprehensive guide available to the continuing flow of ideas and apprehensions "nourished in the womb of pia mater," but they come from many different cultures and have been designed to serve many different purposes. The hospitality of the great libraries, including the Folger Library, the Huntington Library, the Munich Shakespeare Library, and those of London, Oxford, Cambridge, and Birmingham, has afforded some opportunity for that international community of scholarship that was so highly prized in the Renaissance. But few would deny that academic exigencies and career prospects have generated much of the "scholarship" of our own time, and (to adapt Johnson's words) it is not very grateful to consider how little the succession of scholars has added to their author's power of pleasing.

Shakespeare Survey was first issued in 1948 under the sponsorship of the universities of Birmingham and Manchester, the Shakespeare Memorial Theatre, and the Birthplace Trust, under the editorship of Allardyce Nicoll. Its themes and its selection of material have been partly shaped by its traditional connection with the once annual, now biennial, International Conference of the Shakespeare Institute of the University of Birmingham

(founded by Nicoll in 1951). From time to time it publishes surveys of the current state of scholarship and criticism in various fields. The first issue, significantly, centered on the theater of Shakespeare's time. Nicoll was eager to create occasions, in talk and in print, on which scholars from all over the world might discuss the plays in performance. In a revealing article in the second issue, however, Hardin Craig, writing on "Trends of Shakespeare Scholarship," speaks from the confidence of scholarship's ascendancy over the theater and, indeed, over criticism:

> Whatever interesting things may be read into Shakespeare by imaginative critics and stage directors, there is no doubt, in the minds of scholars at least, that Shakespeare's own meaning is the greatest of meanings and is the one the world needs. . . . It is my hope that the Shakespeare Memorial Theatre will more and more take upon itself the task of achieving correctness in the interpretation of Shakespeare's plays.

Few would endorse those sentiments now. We have become too keenly aware of the dependence of our perceptions upon our predispositions, and while scholarship and criticism may help us to change our predispositions, we cannot, in Collingwood's phrase, do more than "meet the past halfway."

In 1964, the *Shakespeare Newsletter* (no. 76), under the editorship of Louis Marder, presented "A Synoptic View of the Past, Present and Future of Shakespearean Scholarship and Criticism." It makes many proposals that grow naturally out of the preoccupations of the past. Muir, for example, invites Shakespeareans (perhaps at the Folger or at the Shakespeare Institute) systematically to comb all the books published in England before 1613 and all the foreign-language works that were accessible to Shakespeare. Ten scholars, he supposes, could get through the English books in seven years, but the foreign ones would take longer. In fact, a chronological index of the short title catalog (STC) items was prepared at the institute under Nicoll's guidance and a series of doctoral theses prepared on books and their readers. Their findings, however, are not readily related to Shakespeare's poems and plays.

Neither Hilton Landry's projections for a well-annotated edition of the Sonnets, nor Hilda Hulme's musings on the forms that the study of Shakespeare's language might take (both in the

1964 *Newsletter*), quite anticipate Stephen Booth's remarkable analytical commentary in his edition of the Sonnets (1977). It "is designed," says Booth, "not only to help a twentieth-century reader to a Renaissance reader's understanding of Shakespeare's idiom but also to answer academic questions about how the sonnets work—how they achieve the clarity and simplicity most of them have from the unstable and randomly dynamic locutions they employ." The early Arden editions (1899–1937) of Shakespeare profited much from the participation by some of their editors in the preparation of the *Oxford English Dictionary,* with its rich inheritance from nineteenth-century philology. Booth's perception of the Sonnets is owed at once to his attentiveness to the Renaissance evidence and to his twentieth-century consciousness of the subliminal dynamics of the language. That is as it should be; it is part of the process through which the "timeless present" of scholarship is created.

A different impulse of scholarship is at work in Bernard Spivack's *Shakespeare and the Allegory of Evil* (1958), subtitled *The History of a Metaphor in Relation to His Major Villains.* Spivack follows L. L. Schücking and Elmer E. Stoll in that he insists on the unambiguous character of Shakespearean soliloquy: "The Elizabethan soliloquy is the truth itself." But his method of investigation, rather than put this claim to the test, assumes it as an axiom. Spivack illuminates much in the medieval dramatic tradition that has gone into the making of *Othello,* but he fails to recognize that the play is in a line of heroic plays as well as a line of moralities and that the nuance of soliloquy has by this date a complex history in Shakespeare's own theater. To understand the possibilities it is not enough to read the plays and to reflect on them; they must be experienced in the theater.

Scholars have been slow to recognize that the play in performance is not merely an animated reading. Because its demands on the spectator can be both intimate and communal (in varying proportions), and because it can either expose him to the joys and stresses of uncertainty or allow him the privilege of the gods to look down upon the human scene, the play can make—and does make—fundamental differences to our understanding of human psychology and society. The reflections of Alfred Harbage and Richard Hosley (in *Shakespeare Newsletter,* no. 76) are therefore of particular interest. Harbage notices the continuing tension between those who want simplicity of Elizabethan staging and those who resist the idea; he hopes the dispute will be resolved in favor of simplicity in the light of further study of Walter Wilson Greg's two-volume *Dramatic Documents from the Elizabethan Playhouses* (1931) and of the plays themselves. Hosley wonders about the prospect of designing "new stage forms that will adapt what we conceive to be the essential characteristics of the Elizabethan stage to the needs of twentieth-century production."

Practical questions may well prove to have great historical and ideological significance. The "penny plain" conception of the Elizabethan theater brings to bear upon the fragmentary evidence (the copy of the lost De Witt drawing, the Fortune contract) convictions in line with those of Malone and Pope, about its essentially popular character. The "tuppence colored" account enlists the traditions of symbolic architecture and public pageant. George R. Kernodle (*From Art to Theatre,* 1944) traces form and convention in the Renaissance from classical and medieval sources into the theaters of Spain, Italy, and the Netherlands. Unfortunately the English evidence is sparse, and Kernodle's own speculative reconstruction of the basic pattern of the Elizabethan stage is quite without that unity of style and proportion for which he gives so much evidence elsewhere. Proportion is consistently adduced in John Orrell's *The Quest for Shakespeare's Globe* (1983), which he believes to have been constructed by the *ad triangulum* and *ad quadratum* methods, using a three-rod measure. His findings are based on an analysis of the Bankside panoramas that takes account of the properties of the topographical glass used in their making. They have been assimilated into the designs made by Theo Crosby for the projected reconstruction of the first Globe at Southwark. Richard Hosley, Walter Hodges, and others have worked on a similar project for the second Globe in Detroit. It seems probable that, while the tiring-house façade in the Southwark reconstruction will be consistent with the evidence of the Swan drawing, it will take its rhythms and proportions from analogues in the hall screens of contemporary houses. The theater may therefore represent a convergence of formal and informal traditions, allowing ease of movement between Westminster and Eastcheap, and between remote spectacle and intimacy.

Evidence accumulating in the Malone Society's collections of documents for the Lord Mayor's processions and the midsummer shows suggests that formal allegory was an active ingredient of popular festival. Robert Weimann's *Shakespeare and the Popular Tradition in the Theater* (1978) is subtitled *Studies in the Social Dimension of Dramatic Form and Function* and is suggestive of many of the ways in which the shapes and forms of play, theater, and community interrelate.

Scholarship may now take opportunities to attend simultaneously to what is ordinary and what is extraordinary in the art and life of the Renaissance. In an account of *Shakespeare's Lives* that wittily exposes the imperfect objectivity of research, Samuel Schoenbaum questions the validity of Frances Yates's *A Study of "Love's Labour's Lost"* (1936), which supposes that Shakespeare was intervening on the side of Essex and Southampton against the Raleigh faction, whose poet (in "the school of night") was Chapman: "What sort of audience, one wonders, could have grasped more than a small fraction of these workings of faction? An audience, one suspects, consisting primarily of Miss Yateses." The question, "What sort of audience?" can receive many kinds of answers, including Ann Jennalie Cook's *The Privileged Playgoers of Shakespeare's London, 1576–1642* (1981). Audiences are very variously composed. When *The Tempest* was performed at court in 1611 its audience could well have included Fulke Greville, who had once dined with Giordano Bruno, and Isaac Casaubon, who had enjoyed the patronage of Henry of Navarre and had become a favored talker at the king's table. Those who were, like Prospero, in "liberal arts without a parallel," might have been spectators to the same play (if on different occasions) as that seen by sailors from Southwark, the mates of Stephano and Trinculo. To postulate both kinds of audiences is a way of disengaging ourselves, however imperfectly, from our current dispositions.

Among modern scholars, Muriel C. Bradbrook has cultivated the art of moving gracefully between the refinements of courtly styles and the energies and exigencies of the popular theater. But there is no routine way of assimilating and integrating the perceptions of sociologists, iconologists, demographers, psychoanalysts, and intellectual and social historians, as they converge upon Shakespearean studies. *King Lear,* for example, can be seen in the light of the *prisca theologia* and the *deus absconditus* expounded by William R. Elton in *King Lear and the Gods* (1966); but the scholar must also come to terms with the accounts that Charles J. Sisson gives from the records of contemporary real-life analogues of Lear's story (*Shakespeare's Tragic Justice,* 1961). Similarly, an editor annotating Helena's reference to the "triple eye" (*All's Well,* II. i. 108) must be prepared not only to explain "triple" as "third" but also to recognize that the phrase looks one way toward a quibble on virginity and another way to the figure of Prudentia in Dante (*Purgatorio,* XX. 130–132) and in Chaucer's *Troilus and Criseyde.* The point is not that Shakespeare read Dante but that both poets explored the possibilities of the metaphor latent in the derivation of "Providence" from *providere.*

A readiness to explore Shakespeare's thought in the context of the European Renaissance seems likely to take Shakespeare studies into a less provincial phase. The French publications *Cahiers Élisabéthains,* edited at the University of Montpellier, and the *Actes du Congrès,* from the Société Française, are attentive to the Renaissance while responding to current movements in literary theory. Richard Marienstras' *Le proche et le lointain* (1981) uses many of the insights of modern anthropology "sur Shakespeare, le drame Élisabéthan et l'idéologie Anglaise aux XVIe et XVIIe siècles."

In India, in Japan, and in the Islamic world, new continuities and relations are being fostered between Shakespeare's work and apparently exotic cultures. Different potentials of Shakespeare's art are manifest when, for example, his comedies are read alongside classical Indian stories, such as Kalidassa's *Sakuntula.* The Shakespeare Society of Japan publishes *Shakespeare Studies* (Tokyo), and *Hamlet Studies* is published from New Delhi.

Ideology has now displaced *world picture,* which once translated *weltanschauung.* Most university and school teaching after World War II was dominated by Theodore Spencer's *Shakespeare and the Nature of Man* (1942) and by its elegant, brief counterpart, Eustace M. W. Tillyard's *Elizabethan World Picture* (1943). Tillyard took the view that a period is best understood from its secondary writings, which make explicit the assumptions on which the great works of the time rest. He makes much of the degree speech of Ulysses without overexposing it to the wit of Thersites, and in *Shakespeare's History Plays* (1944) he returns Shakespeare to the confidences of Edward Halle's Tudor myth without dwelling on Clarence's reflections on the indirect and crooked ways of the chronicle providence. Recent studies have been more attentive to the stresses and instabilities of the age of Shakespeare. Our ideologies help to form our response to theirs.

In the present climate of thought, scholarship is

unlikely to forego its interest in the diachronic processes of the past, but it seems likely to accept the covert invitation of current theory to interest itself in synchronic and autonomous structures of image, thought, and feeling that have taken shape in cultural conditions that are not chronologically or consecutively related. Madeleine Doran, in *Endeavors of Art* (1954), takes as her starting point Heinrich Wölfflin's *Principles of Art History* and attempts to analyze dramatic modes of vision in the light of that work. Further exercises, of sharper focus, might be undertaken on the same lines. Shakespeare, for example, may not have been acquainted with Botticelli, but both used the *Fasti* of Ovid, and it might be shown that they shared a mode of vision. Two periodicals, *Representations,* founded in 1983, and *Word and Image,* founded in 1985, are likely to break new ground in this area. (See, for example, Stephen Greenblatt's study of Dürer's treatment of the Peasants' Revolt and Shakespeare's handling of the Cade scenes of *Henry VI.*)

Whatever the relativities of other areas of Shakespeare scholarship might be, the advances of the textual analysts may be supposed more absolute. Bibliographical studies grow more refined (see, for example, Peter W. M. Blayney's *The Texts of "King Lear" and Their Origins,* vol. 1, *Nicholas Okes and the First Quarto,* 1982), but the need to make judgments will remain, and it is unlikely that the text recovered by one generation will wholly satisfy that of another. It will continue to be openly or covertly—or even grossly—modernized; yet not only professional scholars but also playgoers, players, and readers will continue to require access to the authentic texts. How are these to be provided? By annotated facsimiles or by the genesis, on statistical principles and with the aid of a computer, of synthetic old-spelling texts? It is another question that will meet with various answers. But Berowne's words, even in the unprocessed First Folio text, are likely to remain intelligible for a long time to come:

> Learning is but an adiunct to our selfe,
> And where we are, our Learning likewise is.

BIBLIOGRAPHY

There is no comprehensive history of Shakespearean scholarship, but the bibliographies provide its material, and certain studies deal with aspects of the history.

Bibliography. Walter Ebisch and Levin L. Schücking, *A Shakespeare Bibliography* (1931) and *Supplement (1930–1935)* (1937). Gordon Ross Smith, *A Classified Shakespeare Bibliography, 1936–1958* (1963). George Watson et al., eds., *The New Cambridge Bibliography of English Literature,* 5 vols. (1969–1977).

History. Robert W. Babcock, *The Genesis of Shakespeare Idolatry, 1766–1799* (1931). Thomas Whitfield Baldwin, *William Shakspere's Small Latine and Lesse Greeke,* 2 vols. (1944). Edmund K. Chambers, *William Shakespeare: A Study of Facts and Problems,* 2 vols. (1930). Augustus Ralli, *A History of Shakespearian Criticism,* 2 vols. (1932). Samuel Schoenbaum, *Shakespeare's Lives* (1970). David Nichol Smith, ed., *Eighteenth-Century Essays on Shakespeare* (1903; rev. 1963). Virgil K. Whitaker, *Shakespeare's Use of Learning: An Inquiry into the Growth of His Mind and Art* (1953).

Shakespearean Criticism

ARTHUR M. EASTMAN

The history of Shakespearean criticism can be divided into three phases. In the seventeenth and eighteenth centuries, dominated by neoclassical values, critics saw Shakespeare at first as the noble savage, nature's artless child; then, as the era waned, his irregularity waned with it, his art found its roots in nature, and his judgment was discovered to be no less mighty than his genius. In the nineteenth century, roughly from Samuel Taylor Coleridge to Andrew Bradley, Bardolatry bloomed. Attention, often reverent, focused on the plays' unity, now perceived to be organic, and on the characters, who were regarded as complex and subtly true to life. In the twentieth century Shakespearean criticism has proliferated extraordinarily. And while there are thousands of works of this criticism, it has had no single, main line of direction, as in the preceding eras, unless it be attention to the word and the image. Instead abundant attention has been devoted to the Shakespearean text; to the Shakespearean stage and its audience; to the literary and theatrical conventions of Shakespeare's day; and to his social, political, and spiritual milieu. Approaches have multiplied: historical, bibliographical, New Critical, anthropological, psychoanalytic, and feminist.

Early Criticism

"He was not of an age, but for all time! . . ./Nature herself was proud of his designs,/And joy'd to wear the dressing of his lines!" So wrote Ben Jonson in the preface to the First Folio (1623). "To th' shame of slow-endeavoring Art," wrote John Milton in 1630, Shakespeare's "easy numbers flow." For John Dryden, Shakespeare imparted "to Fletcher Wit, to laboring Jonson Art . . . And is that Nature which they paint and draw." In Dryden's view, "all the images of Nature were still present to him, and he drew them, not laboriously, but luckily . . . he needed not the spectacles of books to read Nature; he looked inwards, and found her there." Joseph Addison (1714) found in Shakespeare "all the seeds of poetry."

To be the poet of nature meant to critics of the seventeenth and eighteenth centuries the power of creating, representing, and moving, an ease in generating words, images, and numbers. It meant giving us the characters we know in this world with such compelling vividness that king and counselor, clown and jester, coward and soldier, queen and common slut live before us. It meant, in Samuel Johnson's famous phrase (1747), exhausting worlds and then imagining new—the woods outside Athens, the golden realm of Belmont, the enchanted isle of *The Tempest*—and in them such characters as the naked eye sees not, witches, ghosts, Caliban, Puck, Titania, Cobweb, and Mustardseed. And always it meant moving us, most especially our passions, so that, as Alexander Pope remarked (1725), "the heart swells, and the tears burst out, just at the proper places."

"Yet must I not give Nature all," continued Jonson in the tribute quoted above, "thy Art, / My gentle Shakespeare, must enjoy a part. / For though the poet's matter, Nature be, / His Art doth give the fashion." Jonson's balanced image of Shakespeare—born in nature, made by art—found few echoes in the following decades. To critics of the neoclassical persuasion Shakespeare was more an extravagant and erring stranger in the realm of art than one to the manner born. In an argument that Dryden had sounded before him, Addison and Pope after, Nicholas Rowe (1709) wrote:

> If one undertook to examine the greatest part of [Shakespeare's tragedies] by those rules which are established by Aristotle, it would be no very hard task to find a great many faults: but as Shakespeare lived under a kind of light of mere nature, and had never been made acquainted with the regularity of those written precepts. . . . we are to consider him as a man that lived in a state of almost universal license and ignorance.

Shakespeare's sins against art fell under several headings. One was theatrical barbarism, the practices that Jonson had long before scoffed at: choruses wafting audiences over the Channel, gods descending from a machine, clumsy sound effects, and stage armies no more fleshed out than Falstaff's moldy recruits. A second was generic impurity, the mixing of tragedy with comedy, low characters with high, and the violations of the unities of time, place, and action. A third was non- or misinstruction. Thomas Rymer (1693) waxed jocular at the lessons to be learned from *Othello,* as that "this may be a caution to all maidens of quality, how, without their parents' consent, they run away with Blackamoors." More commonly, the sin was the violation of poetic justice, of failing to punish the evil characters and reward the virtuous. "Cressida is false," grumbled Dryden, "and is not punished." John Dennis complained (1712) of "the good and the bad . . . perishing promiscuously in the best of Shakespeare's tragedies"; "there can be either none or very weak instruction in them." A final catchall category of Shakespeare's artistic sins includes violations of various sorts of decorum, as of characterization and language. Voltaire (1749) found Claudius unregally fond of drink; Dennis deplored that Menenius, though a senator, is presented as a buffoon; and Iago, though a soldier, and hence by nature "open-hearted, frank and plain dealing," was seen by Rymer as "a close, dissem-

bling, false, insinuating rascal." Again, there were the abominations of Shakespeare's style. "The fury of his fancy often transported him beyond the bounds of judgment," Dryden wrote, "either in coining of new words and phrases, or racking words which were in use, into the violence of a catachresis." And Pope thought so ill of much of the language of the plays that he demoted many passages to the foot of the pages of his edition (1723–1725) as manifestly corrupt or the interpolations of the players.

Samuel Johnson's edition of Shakespeare (1765) undertakes judiciously to review prior judgments about Shakespeare. In its preface it offers passages of high praise and of energetically particularized indictment. "Nothing can please many, and please long, but just representations of general nature," says Johnson. Shakespeare is "the poet of nature; the poet that holds up to his readers a faithful mirror of manners and of life. . . . His persons act and speak by the influence of those general passions and principles by which all minds are agitated, and the whole system of life is continued in motion." Shakespeare's drama "is the mirror of life . . . he who has mazed his imagination, in following the phantoms which other writers raise up before him, may here be cured . . . by reading human sentiments in human language; by scenes from which a hermit may estimate the transactions of the world, and a confessor predict the progress of the passions." Most especially Johnson found Shakespeare naturally gifted in comedy (as had Jonson, Rymer, and Rowe) and in "a conversation above grossness and below refinement, where propriety resides," in a language, in other words, that is consonant with the genius of the English tongue.

The praise thus lavished on Shakespeare is followed by a bill of particulars sharply identifying most of the complaints of Johnson's critical predecessors: absence of moral purpose; loosely framed plots; careless final acts; anachronisms and comparable improprieties; self-entangling and coarse wit; tedious, mean, and obscure tragic passages; weary narrations and cold declamations; unwieldy sentiments; inflated trivialities; pathos refrigerated by conceits and equivocations; and the quibble, "the fatal Cleopatra for which he lost the world and was content to lose it." We are dealing with taste here, most especially taste attending to a style that Matthew Arnold almost a century later blamed on "an irritability of fancy." But Johnson's personal indictment was expanded feelingly: "His first defect is that to which may be imputed most of the evil in books or in men. He sacrifices virtue to convenience, and is so much more careful to please than to instruct, that he seems to write without any moral purpose.''

David Nichol Smith (1916) rightly says that Johnson was the last of the great judicial critics who, like Dryden, regarded Shakespeare as a fellow author, a man who wrote for a living. Thereafter, to use R. W. Babcock's term (1931), we enter the era of idolatry. The virtue proclaimed and defined by critics and others had begun, like a balloon tugging at its moorings, to lift Shakespeare into higher realms. Two means were used: invalidating or dismissing the rules of art that Shakespeare had putatively broken and exalting those natural gifts that he had always been acknowledged to possess.

As to dispensing with the rules, there was a long, strong native objection to many of them, first because they were rules—and, hence, as Jonathan Swift and Johnson saw, inimical to the native Britisher's anarchic genius—and second because they were French, with all the effete preciosity that such a pedigree could suggest. Theater audiences gave their approval to Shakespeare's violations of the unities of time, place, and genre, however their educated betters might grimace. Though noses rose at coarseness, there seemed always enough of Polonius in a British audience to appreciate the jigs and bawdry, always enough of the commoner not to resent the mingling of kings and clowns. Johnson scoffed at Rymer, Dennis, and Voltaire for their strictures on Shakespeare's violation of the purity of character types, calling them "the petty cavils of petty minds," since "Shakespeare always makes nature predominate over accident . . . and preserves the essential character." With such claims, one cable tethering Shakespeare to mortality was cut. Another was sheered when Johnson joined Dryden in validating the mixing of comedy with tragedy, for though, as he concedes, "this is a practice contrary to the rules of criticism, . . . there is always an appeal open from criticism to nature." The mixed drama is faithful to the drama's legitimate functions of instructing us, for it is faithful to sublunary nature, and of pleasing us, for our moods are quicksilver, our attention is fleeting, and our greatest pleasure derives from variety. Johnson cuts an even stronger cable when he strikes against the unities of time and place. These derive from the notion that the spectator in the theater is deluded, thinking the

stage Rome or Alexandria, the actor Claudius or Lear. But the theater offers us not reality but imitation. Like pictures or fictions, it affects us by make-believe; and we are moved, not because what we witness actually is reality but "from our consciousness of fiction; if we thought murders and treasons real, they would please no more."

Although many of the complaints against Shakespeare had had to do with his style, its "beauties," as the eighteenth century liked to call them, had been early recognized and often extracted. Charles Gildon had included a collection of them in his *Complete Art of Poetry* (1710). In the margin of his edition, Pope had distinguished "some of the most shining" passages—the Nurse's tale of Juliet's fall, for example, or Mercutio's celebration of Queen Mab. In 1752 William Dodd published *The Beauties of Shakespeare,* guaranteeing Shakespeare an elocutionary canonization yet to be revoked. Recognition of Shakespeare's stylistic genius came, too, from Thomas Gray ("Every word is . . . a picture," 1742) and from Joseph Warton, who argued (1753) that in the single line, "O me, my heart, my rising heart! But down!" (*King Lear,* II. iv. 116) "the dreadful conflict of opposite passions with which [the mind] is agitated are more forcibly expressed, than by the long and labored speech . . . that Rowe and other modern tragic writers would certainly have put into his mouth." In the notes to their editions of Shakespeare, particularly in the glossarial notes that removed the tarnish of lexical and grammatical obscurity, Lewis Theobald early (1733) and Johnson most powerfully in midcentury (1765) helped open the poet's language to understanding and appreciation. In their editions George Steevens (1773, 1778, 1793) and Edmond Malone (1790) continued and intensified the illumination.

Even in his indictment of Shakespeare for sacrificing virtue to convenience, for writing more to please than to instruct, and for writing without moral purpose, Johnson is turning away from the insistence on poetic justice formerly required by Dryden, Rymer, Dennis, and others. This in itself was emancipating, as it permitted attention to be focused not on a mechanical rule but on the meanings or visions communicated in the plays. As Johnson says, from the plays "a system of social duty may be selected, for he that thinks reasonably must think morally." Increasingly, critics found moral wisdom in the plays, not only in their casual axioms and aphorisms but, more important, in their penetration to the springs of character and hence to the laws undergirding human behavior. Johnson himself had contributed to this expanding dimension of Shakespearean criticism in sharp profiles of Falstaff, Polonius, Emilia, and Iago. Others carried on, at increasing length, with increasing infusions of perspicacity and fervor: Thomas Whately with *Remarks on Some of the Characters of Shakespeare* (1785), William Richardson with *Philosophical Analysis . . . of Some of Shakespeare's Remarkable Characters* (1774), and none more profoundly, or happily, than Maurice Morgann in his inspired *Essay on the Dramatic Character of Sir John Falstaff* (1777).

Falstaff is indeed a splendid specimen for analysis, but Morgann's concern extends beyond the fat knight "to the arts and genius of his poetic-maker, Shakespeare, and through him sometimes, with ambitious aim, even to the principles of human nature itself." Space permits only the briefest summary: Human sensibility operates by principles different from those of reason. It takes mental impressions, often from the minutest of circumstances. It values the deed as it values the doer. It loves or hates at first sight. So Shakespeare works upon us, scattering "the seeds of things, the principles of character and action, with so cunning a hand yet with so careless an air, and, master of our feelings, submits himself so little to our judgment, that every thing seems superior." Our understanding tells us that Falstaff is a coward, but Shakespeare affects us by so many delicate, almost invisible impressions that we feel the knight superior to his surroundings, master of his fate, able to play the coward because in fact he is none. There is much more, equally discriminating, worked out in the presentation of Falstaff's dramatic character and sensitively quickening our pulses. Morgann's great essay fully prepares us for that romantic Bardolatry that Coleridge incorporates at the nineteenth century's beginning and that Bradley monumentalizes at its end.

Romantic Criticism

In an important sense, the great flowering of criticism we associate with Coleridge, Charles Lamb, William Hazlitt, and their peers has important German as well as English roots. Gotthold Ephraim Lessing had mocked Voltaire and the whole French neoclassical castle of criticism in his *Hamburgische Dramaturgie* (1767–1769), very much as the lad in Hans Christian Andersen's story exposed the naked emperor. He poked fun at Voltaire's ghost, which, against spectral manners, reveals itself in daylight. Gallantry, not love, inspired Voltaire's tragedy *Zaïre;* "I know but one tragedy at which love itself has labored and that is *Romeo and Juliet.*" And stepping across the critical chasm that had so long obtained between nature and art, Lessing asserted "that not every critic is a genius, but every genius is a born critic. He has the proof of all the rules within himself."

In his journal *Hamburgische Dramaturgie* Lessing gave little space to Shakespeare. Forty years later August Wilhelm von Schlegel gave great space in his *Über dramatische Kunst und Literatur* (1809–1811). In these lectures are to be found, as in Johnson's notes or Morgann's *Essay,* hosts of sharp psychomoral perceptions, as of "the heartless littleness of Octavius," the blending in Hotspur of "rude manners, arrogance, and boyish obstinacy," Hamlet's occasional "malicious joy" and his being "a hypocrite towards himself." More important is Schlegel's grand division between two kinds of equally worthy art, the classic and the Gothic or romantic, Sophocles the chief exponent of the former, Shakespeare of the latter. One is pagan, the other Christian; one finite, the other infinite; one expressive of enjoyment, the other of desire; one focusing on the present, the other on the past and future. Gone from Schlegel's thinking is the myth of a lost literary Eden, and the point of comparing Shakespeare to the ancients is not to condemn him but to appreciate him more fully.

Schlegel's radical definition of the romantic derives as much as anything else from Shakespeare's practice. He recognizes appreciatively a multiplicity of materials, a fusion of opposites, and a series of structural devices to intensify or satirize: the framing by Theseus and Hippolyta of the stories of the other lovers in *A Midsummer Night's Dream,* the expansion of the vision of war provided by the Choruses in *Henry* V, the setting off by its end-stopped couplets of "The Mousetrap" in *Hamlet,* the paralleling of plots (both high, as in *King Lear,* and high and low, as in *Henry IV, Part 1*). The single principle inspiring these several elements is that of organic form:

Organical form . . . is innate; it unfolds itself from within, and acquires its determination contemporaneously with the perfect development of the germ. . . . In the fine arts as well as in . . . nature . . . all genuine forms are organical, that is, determined by the quality of the work. In a word, the form is nothing but a significant exterior, the speaking physiognomy of each thing.

As for Lessing—but with many more and more powerful arguments—art is not separate from nature; it is nature. Genius and judgment in the greatest of art, in Shakespeare, are one.

Inevitably, one must say of Coleridge much of what one says of Schlegel. Though his lectures, given in the same year as the German's, were never formally published, they were repeated again and again over the years and exist for us largely in his own notes and those taken by others. (Coleridge's *Shakespearean Criticism* was edited in two volumes by Thomas Raysor in 1930.) Coleridge, like Schlegel, repudiates the ancient opposition between nature and art, genius and judgment: "No work of true genius dare want its appropriate form. . . . As it must not, so neither can it, be lawless! For it is even this that constitutes genius—the power of acting creatively under laws of its own origination." The plays are organically unified—unified in feeling, in character, and in impression—the product of a mind, an imagination, ever and infallibly generating new insights into humanity. "If we do not understand him, it is our own fault or the fault of copyists and typographers." And Shakespeare found those characters, whose analysis in brief or at length remains one of Coleridge's chief legacies, not by observation but by meditation. Shakespeare "had only to imitate certain parts of his own character, or to exaggerate such as existed in possibility, and they were at once true to nature, and fragments of the divine mind that drew them." To Coleridge we owe the etched delineations of "the motive-hunting of motiveless malignity" in Iago; "intellectual power deserted by all grace, all moral principle, all not momentary purpose" in Thersites; "the mock fortitude of a mind deluded by ambition" in Lady Macbeth; "the prevalence of the abstracting and generalizing habit" of mind in Hamlet. Even more important, Coleridge provides extended and sensitive running commentaries on such plays as *Romeo and Juliet, Hamlet,* and *Lear* and on the psychic twistings and turnings of their central figures.

Coleridge justifies Shakespeare's anachronisms and validates his putative immoralities and obscenities: "Shakespeare always makes vice odious and virtue admirable"; he keeps "at all times the high road of life" and develops a reverential attitude toward him rarely abandoned since Coleridge's death. Finally, to the enormous advantage of all subsequent criticism, whether Shakespearean or more general, Coleridge provides new critical terms or definitions, as of the different kinds of imagination or fancy or of that willing suspension of disbelief that we experience in the Shakespearean theater.

Goethe, who found in the "lovely, pure, noble and most moral" Hamlet a character that "sinks beneath a burden which it cannot bear and must not cast away" (*Wilhelm Meister's Apprenticeship,* 1824), pays tribute to Shakespeare's associating with "the World-Spirit," to his psychological and aesthetic sensitivity, and to his power of achieving the aesthetic ends of comprehension, variety, and vividness of detail (*Shakespeare ad Infinitum,* 1813–1816). Goethe attributes to each play a unifying idea: in *Coriolanus,* resentment of the lower classes who refuse to recognize the superiority of their betters, or, in *Julius Caesar,* the patricians' unwillingness to have a monarch. Further, Goethe perceives Shakespeare's plays as presenting in unparalleled excellence the conflict between necessity and will, between all that determines a character's conduct from without (the conspirators in *Julius Caesar,* for example, or the Ghost in *Hamlet* and the Witches in *Macbeth*) and such freedom as derives from within. For all this praise, Goethe finds cause for censure as well. If Shakespeare is foremost among the world's poets, he falls behind other dramatists. "Shakespeare's whole method," which is half narrative, enormously broad in scope, and appealing through its poetry to the mind's eye, "finds in the stage itself something unwieldy and hostile."

Charles Lamb is famous for insisting on this point. We know now how far the theater of the late-eighteenth and all of the nineteenth century was from that of the Elizabethans, but of this the romantics were ignorant. Goethe yearned for the theater in the mind. Later, on his stage, Lamb saw royal robes with ermine and pearls but knew that he was unconscious of such trifles as he read. He objected to painted backdrops, to the clichés of gesture, and to actors turning speech into oratory. "To see Lear acted—to see an old man tottering about the stage with a walking-stick, turned out of doors by his daughters in a rainy night, has nothing in it but what is painful and disgusting" (1811). Not for a century more would stage and Shakespearean play begin to come together again as they had in Elizabethan and Jacobean London. But not all critics of the theater responded to its performance as did Lamb.

Hazlitt, perhaps the finest theatrical reviewer of his time, relished the addition of gesture to speech, as of Sarah Siddons' rubbing her hands in the nightwalking scene in *Macbeth* or of Edmund Kean's Richard III, fighting "like one drunk with wounds." But Hazlitt's *Characters of Shakespear's Plays* (1817) is dedicated to Lamb and treats the characters as essentially independent of the stage. It is an enthusiastic analysis of the plays, their personages, and their principal speeches. Hazlitt does not rank with Coleridge or Schlegel, but he sees the plays clearly, has a flair for the one-line characterization—Hamlet is "the prince of philosophical speculators," "Shylock is a good hater," Bottom "is the most romantic of mechanics," "Romeo is Hamlet in love," "Iago is an amateur of tragedy in real life"—and brings to his criticism a rich sense of the radiating harmonies deriving from analogy.

In America, Edgar Allan Poe wrote a useful if little-remembered rejoinder to Hazlitt's praise of Shakespeare's characters. They are not, said Poe in 1845, people; they are *dramatis personae,* phantoms, and are inconsistent not out of their own ambivalent psychologies but from "the whims and vacillations—the conflicting energies and indolences of the poet." One thinks back eighty years to Johnson's indictments.

In the same year (1817) as Hazlitt's book, John Keats used a term about Shakespeare that has become a critical commonplace: "negative capability . . . when man is capable of being in uncertainties, mysteries, doubts without any irritable reaching after fact and reason; . . . with a great poet the sense of beauty overcomes every other consideration, or rather obliterates all other considerations."

Thomas DeQuincey is perhaps unduly famous among Shakespeareans for one essay, "On the Knocking at the Gate in *Macbeth*" (1823), an attempt to explain why the knocking "reflected back upon the murderer a peculiar awfulness and a depth of solemnity." For a moment Macbeth and Lady Macbeth have been isolated from humanity, dehumanized in the midnight hour, frozen as it were. Then reaction sets in. The darkness passes, the knocking is heard, "the human has made its reflux upon the fiendish," and we "become profoundly sensible of the awful parenthesis that had suspended the goings-on of the world in which we live."

Like Coleridge at his most excessive ("O what great men hast thou not produced, England, my country"); like DeQuincey in his peroration, "O mighty poet! Thy works are not as those of other men"; like Ralph Waldo Emerson, whose Shakespeare outsees all sages, outloves all lovers, and is more inscrutably wise than Plato; and like Herman Melville, who wrote that "if another Messiah ever comes 'twill be in Shakespeare's person"—Thomas Carlyle in "The Hero as Poet" (1840) waxes idolatrous rather than critical. "Alas," he cries, "Shakespeare had to write for the Globe Playhouse: his great soul had to crush itself, as it could, into that and no other mould." Shakespeare's art is not artifice but nature. He is a prophet; he is an English king.

Three (perhaps four) Victorian critics deserve special mention. Although Augustus Ralli records (1932) that Georg Gottfried Gervinus "has been called a second Dogberry who bestowed all his tediousness upon the world," James Russell Lowell, Edward Dowden, Walter Pater, and A. C. Bradley all praised him or derived perceptions from his commentaries (1849–1850). Like his predecessors, Gervinus had penetrating observations to make of the characters: Henry IV as "rather a master of concealment than in dissimulation," Claudio as surrendering "himself to every momentary impression," Hamlet as a civilized man emerging from a barbarian world, whereas Macbeth is a barbarian in a civilized world. More systematically than his precursors, Gervinus attempts to define Shakespeare's "system of morality," finding it to build foursquare on these concepts: activity, the idea that man must use his powers of action, as Richard II, Hamlet, and Antony do not; self-government by reason and conscience; moderation, as exhibited in Henry V or the York of *Richard II;* and relativity, the dependence of conduct on circumstance and motive. In its application Gervinus' system seems arbitrary, somewhat mechanical, militaristic, and anti-Christian; but the effort is in a direction that engaged others, often fruitfully. Finally, like his precursors, Gervinus finds the plays richly integrated and traces in each the changes and variations worked upon a leading idea, as of "a vain desire for fame in all its forms" in *Love's Labor's Lost* or the ways in which man relates to property in *The Merchant of Venice.*

Edward Dowden in *Shakespere: A Critical Study of His Mind and Art* (1875) and again in his primer, *Shakespere* (1877), set himself, as had Gervinus, better to know the author as well as the plays. William Wordsworth had considered Shakespeare to have unlocked his heart in the sonnets; Robert Browning, in his poem "House" (1876), mocked the idea. Coleridge, professing that Shakespeare derived his characters from introspection, opened on auctorial analysis a gate through which he chose not to pass. Dowden, however, inferred from the plays a life of four periods to which, in his primer, he gave titles: "In the workshop," "In the world," "Out of the depths," and "On the heights." Misleading and sentimental as these titles are, they constitute in all probability reactions to two strikingly different versions of Shakespeare: on the one hand, the man of business, hinted at by Pope, who "for gain, not glory, wing'd his roving flight" and who was celebrated by Samuel Smiles of *Self-Help* (1859), and, on the other hand, the extravagantly, impetuously passionate, disorderly, and conscienceless genius of hedonism conjured up by Hippolyte Taine (*Histoire de la littérature anglaise,* 1863). In his larger work, moreover, Dowden, who deals with many of the plays most sensitively, attempts to get to the heart of their author's mystery:

> Shakspere lived and moved in two worlds—one limited, practical, positive; the other a world opening into two infinites, an infinite of thought, and an infinite of passion. He did not suppress either life to the advantage of the other; but he adjusted them, and by stern and persistent resolution held them in the necessary adjustment. . . .
>
> How shall a man live sanely in presence of the small daily facts of life . . . and in presence of the vast mystery of death? . . . Shakspere's attainment of sanity and self-control was not that of a day or of a year, it was the attainment of his life. . . . His series of dramatic writings is one long study of self-control.

Walter Pater, the most sensitive of aestheticians, brings to his fifty pages of Shakespearean criticism an elegiac tone, a melancholy eye for the irony of kingship, and an extraordinary sense of the kinship of the forms of Shakespeare's plays to other art forms: picture, tapestry, children's tale, instrumental solo, ceremonial rite, and sculpture. As fully as Johnson and Arnold, he regrets Shakespeare's excesses of style and carelessness of plotting, yet he finds *Measure for Measure* to have "almost the unity of a single scene" and *Love's Labor's Lost* to play with all the variants of "the foppery of delicate language." (Pater's essays on *Measure for Measure,*

1874, *Love's Labor's Lost,* 1878, and "Shakespeare's English Kings," 1889, are collected in his *Appreciations,* 1889.)

George Bernard Shaw's Shakespearean criticism has gained in prominence since its collection by Edwin Wilson as *Shaw on Shakespeare* (1961). Much of it appeared in the *Saturday Review* near the turn of the century and is denigrating, if witty, biographical criticism that derives from a puritanical, myopic, and ahistorical reading of the plays. For Shaw, who is in some ways a latter-day Dr. Johnson, there is too little of Bunyan, too little of Ibsen, and altogether too much of the romantic commercialism that leads Shakespeare to "strain all his huge command of rhetoric and stage pathos to give a theatrical sublimity to the wretched end of [*Antony and Cleopatra*], and to persuade foolish spectators that the world was well lost by the twain." For Shaw, Henry V is "a Jingo hero"; the comedy of Beatrice and Benedick is "Much-Adoodle-do." "Thirty-six big plays in five blank verse acts," he sighs, and "not a single hero!" Of course there is more and more solid and sensitive criticism than this, especially of Shakespeare's music and imagery, but when Shaw claims that the plays offer "nothing but death made sensational, despair made stage-sublime, sex made romantic, and barrenness covered up by sentimentality," we are hearing what Tolstoy was to say again in *Shakespeare and the Drama* (1906) but without Shaw's engaging wit. Tolstoy found Shakespeare essentially cynical and romantic-commercial, writing plays, regrettably, "for the upper classes of his time and ours" and so contributing to the "direct depravation of men by presenting them false models for imitation."

If Coleridge ushers in the age of British romantic criticism, Andrew Cecil Bradley, a century later, is its last and greatest spokesman. His lectures, collected as *Shakespearean Tragedy* (1904), remain hypnotically compelling. Faithful to the texts, every line of which seems omnipresent to him as he examines the tragedies individually and collectively, sensitive both to his and to Shakespeare's multiple and idiosyncratic audiences, Bradley sets himself to determine the substance of the tragedies, their essential structures, and then to review each play analytically as life, theater, and poem, attending above all to the inner depths of the heroes around whom the others revolve. The lecture on substance, focusing on the tragic trait, the tragic impression, and the tragic triumph, seems mechanical now, curiously anachronistic in its nineteenth-century, secular perspective and sentimentally optimistic. The lecture on construction, with its richly detailed presentations of the problems and solutions of the exposition, of the rhythmic conflict of the plays' central portions, of the crisis, and of the "fourth-act problem," remains the foundation of most modern analyses of the plays' structure.

It is his analysis of the characters for which Bradley is best remembered. His conception thereof, as Kenneth Muir remarks, is "still an orthodoxy to be questioned" ("Changing Interpretations of Shakespeare," *The Age of Shakespeare,* vol. 2 of *The Pelican Guide to English Literature,* Boris Ford, ed., 1955), not because it was he who first saw that Hamlet is melancholy or Othello romantic but, rather, because with such minute fidelity to the details of both text and human experience, and with such catholic sensibility, Bradley brings them and the worlds they inhabit alive to us. One can no more synopsize such presentations than one can compress to the ten words of the ancient telegram the opening sentence of *Paradise Lost.*

Modern Criticism

Reaction: Conventions of Theater and Thought. Against Bradley and the whole tradition of analyzing characters as if they were real stand Robert Bridges, Levin Schücking, Elmer Edgar Stoll, and their critical progeny. Bridges finds the characters psychologically inconsistent, the consequence of Shakespeare's giving the audience the surprise they wanted. The surprise itself derived from Shakespeare's method, which was, in short, to take plots from old stories wherein actions followed from characters and to reverse the pattern by introducing heroes superior to their actions. Shakespeare's art was thus "to create a kind of contrast between the two"—hence Hamlet's madness, Othello's jealousy, Angelo's moral tergiversations ("On the Influence of the Audience," *The Works of William Shakespeare,* Stratford Town Edition, X, 1907).

Schücking, in *Die Charakterprobleme bei Shakespeare* (1919), grants the inconsistency and improbability of the characters but seeks to exonerate Shakespeare by appealing to a history-of-the-theater perspective. Shakespeare's art form, he declares, is a mixture of the most highly developed elements (Shakespeare's special contribution) with quite primitive elements (those of Elizabethan the-

atrical convention). The primitive elements—all such matters condemned by the neoclassical critics, such as severed heads, stage battles, ad-libbing clowns, the mixture of genres, the neglect of the unities—were what the audience expected and what Shakespeare provided. So too, by a convention now largely limited to melodrama, he provided them direct self-explanation. Not only do villains declare their own villainy, but they also acknowledge virtues in their victims that they might not be expected to perceive—as when Iago speaks of Othello's nobility and Cassio's "daily beauty"—and heroes without immodesty declare their own merits—Julius Caesar, for example, or Brutus. And because the state of the art in Shakespeare's day included multiple authorship and the commercial habit of giving audiences what they wanted, Shakespeare's characters are inconsistent. They speak out of character, as when the coarse Mercutio pays dainty tribute to Queen Mab; they act out of time or place, as when Hamlet discusses the contemporary wars of the London theater; and they act out of character, as when Cleopatra changes from fickleness to marble-hard constancy.

During more than fifty years Stoll exuberantly propounded a comparable no-nonsense interpretation of Shakespeare in such works as *Shakespeare Studies, Historical and Comparative in Method* (1927), *Art and Artifice in Shakespeare* (1933), and *Shakespeare Studies* (rev. ed., 1960). His strength, that of the historian and the theatergoer, was used ebulliently against those who would make Shylock pathetic, Falstaff noble, or Hamlet especially subtle. To understand Shylock, he argues, we must understand the views of Shakespeare's day and the practices of Shakespeare's theater with regard to misers, moneylenders, and Jews; and he explores these topics extensively. To understand *Othello* we must recognize the narrative and theatrical conventions of slander accepted, innocence calumniated, identity mistaken, soliloquy true. "Not psychological consistency but dramatic effectiveness is Shakespeare's aim, and like every other dramatist he will sell, if not his own soul, at least a character's, for a contrast." More effectively than Schücking and Bridges, because so much more extensively grounded in history and stage tradition and so enthusiastic in his demolition of his critical enemies, Stoll, if reductive in his assessment of the plays, helps set them back in their own times and theater.

Many of the contemporaries and successors of

Bridges, Schücking, and Stoll have likewise focused on conventional or nonrealistic dimensions of the plays. W. W. Lawrence in *Shakespeare's Problem Comedies* (1931) affirms that the improbable bed-trick was an archaic convention quite acceptable as "real" to an Elizabethan audience. In *The Fool* (1935) Enid Welsford traces from classical to modern times the role that provides so much resonance in *Henry IV, Twelfth Night,* and *King Lear.* Samuel L. Bethell's *Shakespeare and the Popular Dramatic Tradition* (1944) explores how Shakespeare's plays fluctuate in their address to different levels of audience awareness. Alfred Harbage analyzes the composition of the audience (*Shakespeare's Audience,* 1941), finding therein one secret of the playwright's universality. In *As They Liked It* (1947) he suggests how, by the moral valence of characters, ideas, and images, Shakespeare engages his audience on a journey that is immensely pleasurable, as are carousel rides and the like, because it takes us nowhere, only back to where we started, our moral certainties comfortably reinforced. In *Shakespeare and the Rival Traditions* (1952) Harbage examines the dramatic fare provided by the public and the coterie theaters of Shakespeare's day and determines that Shakespeare and the other dramatists for the public theaters affirmed an optimistic vision: a divine plan for the universe, the dignity of man, chastity, fidelity, and what G. B. Harrison has called "the major decencies of life."

Theodore Spencer's *Shakespeare and the Nature of Man* (1942) and E. M. W. Tillyard's *The Elizabethan World Picture* (1943) both build on Arthur O. Lovejoy's *The Great Chain of Being* (1936) to define a scheme of value and perception presumably possessed by Shakespeare's audience and incorporated in the plays. Ulysses' great speech on order provides one commonplace; Menenius' analogy of the human body and the body politic, another; Hamlet's dual vision of man, yet another. As the last instance makes clear, the positive world view had its negative, or mirror, side, induced in Shakespeare's day by the revolutionary perspectives of Copernicus, Montaigne, and Machiavelli. "New philosophy," as Donne wrote, "calls all in doubt."

To recognize one final instance of concern with generic convention, Leo Salingar's *Shakespeare and the Traditions of Comedy* (1974) identifies four comedic lines that converge in Shakespeare: (1) "popular romance drama, secular and religious" from the Middle Ages; (2) classical comedy inviting "the audience to enjoy an exhibition of some form of deceit"; (3) festive matter deriving from Italian comedy, "an explosion of high spirits licensed and ratified by custom" and (4) the plots of *novelle,* especially those, as in *Merchant, Much Ado,* and *All's Well,* dealing with "broken nuptials and a crisis involving the law." These traditions meet in Shakespeare, whose "great innovation was to treat comedy lyrically as an emotional and imaginative experience, an inward metamorphosis."

Bradley focuses on the psychological realism of Shakespeare's characters and on the realistic causality of his tragic plots; Stoll and others dwell on those historic conventions of theater and thought that remove characters and plot from reality. The living theater itself provides yet another focus; for director and actors, settings, props, lighting, and sound mediate the text to live audiences. Attention may be paid to Harley Granville-Barker, whose directing and criticism are the sources of what Ralph Berry (1979) has called the new mainstream of Shakespeare studies: Shakespeare in performance. Granville-Barker's *Prefaces* (published individually from 1923 on and collectively in 1946–1947) animatedly approach ten plays—*Love's Labor's Lost, Cymbeline,* and the major tragedies (except for *Macbeth*)—as they may be thought to have evolved half-extemporaneously, like the pulpit orations of a virtuoso preacher, in Shakespeare's workshops, the Globe or Blackfriars. For Granville-Barker they constitute a fluid fusion of characters in action on the stage under the mediation of a Shakespeare sensitive to variations of stillness and movement, the solitary and the crowded, the roughness and smoothness of verse and prose—the whole cornucopia, in short, from which this long history pours: "the play's acting in a theater."

Biography. In *The Man Shakespeare and His Tragic Life-Story* (1909), Frank Harris, Shaw's managing editor at the *Saturday Review,* joined with his theatrical reviewer in seeing through the plays to the author, but his explanations were different. For Shaw, Shakespeare wrote to please; for Harris, he wrote "to show himself to us." So Shakespeare "painted himself twenty times from youth to age at full length" and so revealed himself as "gentle, and witty; gay, and sweet-mannered, very studious, too, and fair of mind; but at the same time he was weak in body and irresolute, hasty and wordy, and took habitually the easiest way out of difficulties; he was ill-endowed in the virile virtues and virile vices . . . a parasite by nature." His "master-quality" was "his overpowering sensuality." And the leading woman in the plays, the dark lady, says Harris, "was his complement in every failing; her strength matched his weakness; her resolution his hesitation; her boldness his timidity." Harris' Shakespeare may evoke little conviction these days, but it is a Shakespeare out of the library, down from the clouds, and, like Dowden's—if with a more feverish pulse—alive.

Wyndham Lewis in *The Lion and the Fox* (1927) considers the plays from two perspectives: (1) the roles of the hero (the lion) and the Machiavellian villain who destroys him (the fox); (2) the role and character of the dramatist who, in killing off the heroes, serves as executioner in the ritual slaying celebrated in James George Frazer's *The Golden Bough.* We shall return to the first perspective. The mask of this executioner, says Lewis, "was incessantly convulsed with the most painful unprofessional emotions," for he, like Harris' Shakespeare, is essentially feminine, passive, emotionally responsive—in love, if with anybody in *Antony and Cleopatra,* "with Antony." Essentially, Shakespeare is nihilistic, which is why he writes tragedies, the drama of failure. The great characters, *"Antony and Cleopatra, Othello, Lear, Timon,* and the rest, are all splendid masterpieces, all reproducing the same music of extinction and unbounded suffering." The great outpourings of frustration, anger, and despair are Shakespeare's voice speaking through his characters' lips. Lewis' Shakespeare appears not to have written the comedies or romances. His tragedies seem to have achieved no fifth-act epiphanies, however fractional. They seem to lack Cordelia and Desdemona and, to put it simply, the substance and subject of Sonnet 116.

In the first of his many Shakespearean volumes, *Myth and Miracle* (1929), George Wilson Knight, like Dowden, argues that the plays reveal Shakespeare's spiritual life, that they culminate triumphantly in those romances Lytton Strachey found to be evidence of exhausted boredom, and that *"The Tempest* is at the same time a record of Shakespeare's spiritual progress and a statement of the vision to which that progress had brought him." That vision is not the muted melancholy of Prospero's "We are such stuff / As dreams are made on, and our little life / Is rounded with a sleep." It is instead the reverent gratitude of Gonzalo's "Look down, you gods, / And on this couple drop a blessèd crown! / For it is you that have chalked forth the way / Which brought us hither."

Caroline Spurgeon's *Shakespeare's Imagery, and What It Tells Us* (1935) speaks to us about the man and about his plays. What the images tell us in her somewhat misguided analysis (for she regards figures but not the thought they incorporate) is of a Shakespeare antipodally different from that of Harris or Lewis (there is no entry for *sex* in her index) but recognizable still. Shakespeare has an eye sensitive to change and contrast in color, in dawn and sunset, in the human face with its myriad expressions. His ear is finely tuned, hostile to discord, susceptible to sweet airs, discriminating in its response to the human voice. His sense of smell is acute, especially with respect to the foul odors of "unwashed humanity and decaying corpses." He knows gardening well, dislikes hunting, likes watching animals, the hunted, the hunters. Spurgeon examines what the images tell us of Shakespeare's thoughts on love, hate, fear, evil, goodness, time, and death, summing up the inner man in five words: "sensitiveness, balance, courage, humor, and wholesomeness." Shakespeare is "Christ-like; that is, gentle, kindly, honest, brave and true, with deep understanding and quick sympathy for all living things."

That part of John Middleton Murry's *Shakespeare* (1936) offering biographical hypothesis rather than literary interpretation assumes that through Shakespeare, from first to last, nature spoke, giving us no hint of Shakespeare's personality and very little to guess about his life. What there is, Murry proposes—relying partly on the Sonnets, partly on images that ring true to his personal experience, partly on a perceived evolution in the explicit treating of theater, actors, and audience, and partly on a perceived genealogy of characterization, especially of the male heroes—records one plunge into social humiliation from which Shakespeare "emerged with the conviction that his destiny lay in the theater," and a second plunge, which led Shakespeare to make "a new and more creative contact with the people." The Bastard in *King John,* who evolved one way into Hotspur, another into Falstaff, who can make fun of an audience as he can ridicule himself, stands and speaks for the true England. The Bastard and his line constitute embodiments of "the Shakespearean Man," a kind of self that strives to find complete embodiment in a play and so achieve extinction. This attained, Shakespeare will be able to bring his nature and art, his freedom and restraint, into a union never before completely achieved. This happens, says Murry, in *Hamlet.* Thereafter the Shakespearean Man appears no more in the plays, and in them creativity glows evenly—sometimes failing, sometimes succeeding, but never in the imbalance evident before.

In *Shakespeare's Imagination* (1946; rev. 1963) Edward A. Armstrong enters into the study of Shakespeare's images in a way far different from Spurgeon's but significantly related to that undertaken by Walter Whiter in *A Specimen of a Commentary on Shakspeare* (1794). Influenced by the doctrine of the association of ideas, and having observed certain "unnatural" clusterings of images in Shakespeare (as of candying and of fawning dogs), Whiter began the exploration of the poet's imagination; but the venture stopped with him and was not undertaken again until Spurgeon in her way, and Armstrong in his own, resumed the effort. Armstrong follows Whiter in focusing on linked images or image clusters; but whereas Whiter had dealt only with those that seemed "unnatural" or idiosyncratic, Armstrong studies natural and unnatural together and thereby develops certain understandings about their author's imagination. He sees Shakespeare as possessing a retentive memory and vigorous powers of association, the latter operating according to five principles: (1) mood; (2) the master or controlling imagery of life/death beneath which all other images are categorically subsumed; (3) natural linkage (as cart with horse); (4) unnatural linkage, as by some accidental joining of impressions in the poet's mind; and (5) contrast. From these cooperating principles derive the affective unities of the plays. Armstrong conceives Shakespeare's imaginative processes as "independent of ethical relevance" and as in no very precise way indicative of their author's personality. Yet as for Harris and Murry, and pursuing Coleridge's idea that Shakespeare created his characters from within, Armstrong finds that "in himself Shakespeare found the nucleus of Hamlet. Hamlet is cluster-thinking come to life."

In *Hamlet and Oedipus* (1949), the final form of an essay originally entitled "The Oedipus-Complex as an Explanation of Hamlet's Mystery: A Study in Motive" (*American Journal of Psychology,* 1910), Ernest Jones pushes beyond Hamlet's motives to those of Shakespeare himself. "It was a living person who imagined the figure of Hamlet with his behavior, his reflections, and his emotions. The whole came from somewhere within Shakespeare's mind." Jones notes, in the probable year in which *Hamlet* was written (1601), the deaths of Shakespeare's father and of the earl of Essex, "an obvious father-substitute"; and he sees the Sonnets as recording "some overwhelming passion that ended in a betrayal in such circumstances that murderous impulses toward the faithless couple were stirred but could not be admitted to consciousness." These elements combined, Jones thinks, to produce the oedipal eruption starkly evident in *Hamlet* and already adumbrated in *Julius Caesar.* There "Caesar represents the father," and Brutus, Cassius, and Antony represent the rebellion, the remorse, and the natural piety of the oedipal son. That such an analysis opens Shakespeare more than any other male to our view may be doubted, but it unquestionably opens the way to further psychoanalytic examination of the plays.

Style. Examinations of Shakespeare's style, as M. C. Bradbrook observes in *Shakespeare Survey* (1954), focused in the first centuries on its ease and barbarisms. Nineteenth-century critics increasingly perceived how imagery participated in the plays' organic unity; Bradley recognized that animal imagery pervaded *Lear* and that images of blood and night created the special atmosphere of *Macbeth.* In the twentieth century, stylistic interest has had two principal foci, the most extreme of which may be subsumed under the heading of "poetic drama." In reaction to the Bradleys, Stolls, and Granville-Barkers, such critics as G. Wilson Knight and Lionel Charles Knights see the plays as governed by the spatial (as distinct from narrative) principles that operate in a lyric. So Knight in *The Wheel of Fire* (1930) repudiates conventional analysis for exposing only one surface facet of a play; "but a true philosophic and imaginative interpretation will aim at cutting below the surface to reveal that burning core of mental or spiritual reality from which each play derives its nature and meaning." Well before W. K. Wimsatt, Jr., and M. C. Beardsley wrote of "The Intentional Fallacy" (*Sewanee Review,* 1946), Knight rejected out of hand the notion that "a work of art should be criticized according to the artist's 'intentions.'" Similarly, he rejected analysis deriving from source study, since true sources are the "forms of things unknown," which "the poet's pen / Turns . . . to shapes." Knight also rejected the common category of character, "since it is so constantly entwined with a false and unduly ethical criticism" and with irrelevant concern with motives.

After such repudiation, what forgiveness? Examinations of the plays that earn such praise as Hardin Craig's "I know of no Shakespeare commentary of greater eloquence and insight than his.

So great and so inspiring is his running commentary that the reader is annoyed when the author leaves off temporarily to make unimportant remarks about images and symbols. Indeed, there is a frequent contradiction between an almost perfect commentary and a most imperfect theory" (review of *The Imperial Theme*, in *Shakespeare Quarterly*, 1952). That is true. The theory often interferes with Knight's elucidation; and his language, in which he attempts to preserve absolute truth to his own imaginative reaction to the plays, veers at times toward the bombastically obscure. But the gains are enormous. Although one may hesitate at seeing Hamlet as "the ambassador of death walking amid life" or discovering in the music of *Othello* "the dominant quality" of "separation," one may find *Timon* clarified as a parabolic reincarnation of *Othello* and *Macbeth* illuminated by apprehending it as nightmare.

In *A Short History of Shakespearean Criticism*, (1968) I wrote that, seeing the plays in Knight's way,

> we lose interest, momentarily, in those old Bradleyan concerns of character and plot structure. Instead, we seek and with growing sensitivity react to the newer concerns of image and symbol and archetypal pattern. We pulse to life-themes and death-themes. We juxtapose characters and incidents. We listen for the roaring of storms, the restorative notes of sweet harmonies. For a moment, or longer, we read Shakespeare afresh and derive from that experience the power to find new meanings in the plays individually, which is the immediate goal of "interpretation," and new meanings in the plays collectively, which is its ultimate goal.

Even more strikingly than Knight, L. C. Knights's famous *How Many Children Had Lady Macbeth?* (1933) insists that "a Shakespearean play is a dramatic poem." "We start with so many lines of verse on a printed page which we read as we should read any other poem. We have to elucidate the meaning ... and to unravel the ambiguities; we have to estimate the kind and quality of the imagery and determine the precise degree of evocation of particular figures." The consequence is a reading of a play such as *Macbeth* not totally at odds with that of earlier critics but more intricately textured, more richly holistic, more emphatically visionary.

The second, or secondary, focus of stylistic criticism has been concerned less with reacting against the limitations of various critical approaches than with intensifying recognition of one supremely important dimension of Shakespeare's art, its imagery. In the following paragraphs this criticism will be our concern.

Caroline Spurgeon (*op. cit.*) reports that in every play are "certain groups of images which, as it were, stand out ... and immediately attract attention." These groups of images, which Spurgeon variously calls "floating," "leading," "dominating," "running," "iterative," and "recurrent," and which invite that "interpretative" response called for by Knight, derive in *Romeo and Juliet* from "light, every form and manifestation of it: the sun, moon, stars, fire, lightning, the flash of gunpowder." Shakespeare saw the story, "in its swift and tragic beauty, as an almost blinding flash of light, suddenly ignited, and as swiftly quenched." In *Hamlet* the dominating image is of an ulcer or tumor; in *Troilus and Cressida* it is of food; in *Othello*, "of animals in action, preying upon one another, mischievous, lascivious, cruel or suffering"; in *Lear*, "of a human body in anguished movement, tugged, wrenched, beaten, pierced, stung, scourged, dislocated, flayed, gashed, scalded, tortured, and finally broken on the wrack."

Wolfgang Clemen's *The Development of Shakespeare's Imagery* (1951; originally published as *Shakespeares Bilder, ihre Entwicklung und ihre Funktionen im dramatischen Werk*, 1936) may be considered a biographical study, but its concern is with the evolution of a talent rather than the profile or history of a mind. Clemen's antecedents include Dowden and, more especially, Coleridge. He achieves his aim, which is to trace one line in the growth of Shakespeare's art, most satisfactorily in examining the earlier plays. In these the speech is often bombastic and undifferentiated; the language "adds and accumulates," seeking "to replace clarity and definiteness by multiplicity." So it is in *Titus Andronicus*. In *Love's Labor's Lost* a slight organic gain appears because the "taffeta phrases" belong to the world of the play. *Richard III* shows maturation: the images "become briefer," the images introduced by "like" and "as" largely disappear, and "the metaphorical element gradually pervades the language." By *Richard II* the imagery in many scenes enhances and deepens "the symbolic meaning of what occurs on the stage," and "imagery becomes the characteristic manner of expression of the chief character." In Shakespeare's middle period, the images rise associatively, "in the very act of composition; one word engenders another."

And in the tragedies, the images become "an inherent part of the dramatic structure," polyphonically enlarging and multiplying its meanings to include the natural and supernatural, creating the organic unity so often praised since the lectures of Schlegel and Coleridge.

So powerful has been the influence of Knight, Knights, Spurgeon, Clemen, and the New Criticism generally, that exploration of the plays' imagery has dominated criticism for half a century. In William Empson's *Seven Types of Ambiguity* (1930), *Some Versions of Pastoral* (1935), and *The Structure of Complex Words* (1951), "multiple meanings are sought through syntactical ambiguities, puns and paradoxes: the implications of key words ('fool' in *Lear*, 'honest' in *Othello*) are explored with the ruthless ingenuity of a mathematician in search of every possible variation" (Bradbrook, *Shakespeare Survey*, 1954). Robert Heilman's *Magic in the Web: Action and Language in Othello* (1956), like his earlier *This Great Stage: Image and Structure in King Lear* (1948), explores the intricate interweaving of metaphor with its attendant ramification and elucidation of meaning. The same may be said of Cleanth Brooks's "The Naked Babe and the Cloak of Manliness" (*The Well Wrought Urn*, 1947), Maynard Mack's "The World of Hamlet" (*Yale Review*, 1952), Maurice Charney's *Shakespeare's Roman Plays: The Function of Imagery in the Drama* (1961), and one wonders how many thousands of doctoral dissertations. Two works merit special mention, those of Partridge and Mahood.

Shakespeare's Bawdy (1947) by Eric Partridge belongs with the various Shakespeare lexicons but deserves, perhaps, special note in that, like the work of Mahood and Spurgeon, it opens our eyes (and occasionally our doubts) to meanings that our Victorian forebears did not—or chose not to—see. A glossary running from "Abhorson" to "youth" ("often used by Shakespeare to mean 'youth with its sexual curiosity and amorous ardor'") follows an essay dealing with nonsexual, homosexual, and sexual bawdry in the works and concluding that the making of love and the making of poetry were for Shakespeare kindred forms of release and creativity.

According to Molly M. Mahood's *Shakespeare's Wordplay* (1957), puns are kin to metaphors, to image clusters, and are among the conscious and unconscious means by which Shakespeare develops his semantic harmonies. "Shakespeare quibbles as a poet, as a dramatist, and as a dramatic poet," both early and late in his career, says Mahood. She gives close attention to *Romeo and Juliet*, *Richard II*, the Sonnets, *Hamlet*, *Macbeth*, and *The Winter's Tale* and in a rich concluding chapter has many interesting things to say: "that the average number of puns in a play by Shakespeare is seventy-eight," that "in twenty-three out of thirty-seven plays more than half the total instances of wordplay occur in the first two acts," that "Shakespeare distinguishes the clowns from the courtiers by one group's linguistic abuses and the punning virtuosity of the other," or that Iago puns and Edmund does not. Mahood's final discussion deals with Shakespeare's "changing views of language through the sequence of his plays." From an earlier conflict "between linguistic faith and linguistic scepticism," Shakespeare came at last to a conflict between "self-doubts and his faith in his own achievement; between mistrust of poetry as a mere world of words and the vindication of poetry as the only creative mode of language."

Histories. In "Shakespeare's History Plays: 1900–1951" (*Shakespeare Survey*, 1953), Harold Jenkins identifies three periods in the evolution of criticism of the histories. The first, of which Schlegel is representative, comprised "the ten histories as one great work of which *King John* was the prologue and *Henry VIII* the epilogue," the whole constituting an epic having England itself as "the true protagonist" and expressing the national spirit. The second phase, extending well into the present century, focused on the question of genre, as in Felix Schelling's *The English Chronicle Play* (1902), and on the question of the political significance of the plays. The genre was apprehended as loose, discursive, epically comprehensive rather than dramatically concentrated. The political ideas, in such works as C. F. Tucker Brooke's *Tudor Drama* (1911), were seen to focus on statecraft, kingly responsibility, and the need for national unity. During this period Shakespeare's authorship of the *Henry VI* plays had come in doubt, and there were important questions about the text of *Henry V*. In the third phase, as Jenkins puts it,

when scholarship had once demonstrated that the historical material reached Shakespeare already shaped into a large cyclic unity, embracing cause and effect, connecting political crime with retributive civil war, it was easier for literary criticism to detect in the sequence of the plays themselves a unity more organic than was inherent in the old idea of a national epic.

And although this unity was latent in the material, the feeling grew that its realization in the plays was to be attributed to a single capacious imagination.

Further, once Shakespeare's authorship of *Henry VI* was accepted, "in these early plays, formerly dismissed as prentice patchwork, there came to be recognized, however fumbling in execution, a dramatic undertaking on the grand scale. . . . the history sequence now appeared as the major achievement of the first half of Shakespeare's career."

Few books have been devoted to the histories. Tillyard's *Shakespeare's History Plays* (1944) and Lily Bess Campbell's *Shakespeare's "Histories": Mirrors of Elizabethan Policy* (1947) agree in the historical perspectives just detailed and attributed to Hall. Upon this historical base and upon those concepts of order and degree, responsibility, and obedience earlier set forth in *The Elizabethan World Picture,* Tillyard builds close aesthetic and psychological examinations of the individual plays. He sees in *Richard II,* for example, conscious emphasis on ceremony as a means of fitting the play into its medieval time frame; he sees in Hal's "ironic detachment . . . the characteristic and most attractive side of his deliberate way of acting"; and he sees in Hal, in contrast to the provincial Hotspur, "the *cortegiano,* the fully developed man." Campbell, arguing that "histories" were designed to reflect as in a mirror instances of God's law and justice, sees the plays as instructing Elizabeth and her people in the duties of rule and obedience.

Robert Ornstein's *A Kingdom for a Stage* (1972) denies the view, held by Schelling and Irving Ribner (*The English History Play in the Age of Shakespeare,* 1957), that before Shakespeare there existed a significant dramatic-historic genre. If Shakespeare "did not originate the form of the History Play when he wrote the *Henry VI* plays, he created its vogue and shaped its tradition." Ornstein rejects the idea that the plays derive their shape and larger significance from Hall, for although the first tetralogy is based primarily on Hall, the second is based on Holinshed; whatever sources Shakespeare used, "his interpretation of the past was his own." The critic's task, says Ornstein, "is to fathom Shakespeare's unique insight and intuition, not to square his plays with a hypothetical norm of Elizabethan attitudes," which is bound to be little more than a "consensus of truisms and pieties." Ornstein's fathoming produces many fine conclusions, perhaps the most important among them that Shakespeare

places as great a value on the sanctity of personal relations in the History Plays as in the tragedies, because he intuits that order depends, not on concepts of hierarchy and degree, but on the fabric of personal and social relationships which is woven by ties of marriage, kinship, and friendship, by communal interests, and ideals of loyalty and trust.

In *Patterns of Decay: Shakespeare's Early Histories* (1975), Edward Berry discovers a significant pattern. Each play in the first tetralogy reveals "a dominant theme, expressed not only in language but in character and action, which both unifies the play and defines a single stage in the process of social and political disintegration depicted by the series as a whole." The theme of *Henry VI, Part 1,* is chivalry, embodied in Talbot, and ceremony; that of *Henry VI, Part 2,* is justice or law; that of *Henry VI, Part 3,* family; and that of *Richard III,* the self alone. In each play the focus narrows, with the decay becoming more striking until at Bosworth Field retribution completes the pattern and regeneration begins.

Comedies. In his valuable review article (*Shakespeare Survey,* 1955), John Russell Brown observes that much of the early-twentieth-century criticism of the comedies has been confined to expressions of praise and enjoyment. Ashley Thorndike (*English Comedy,* 1929) advised basking "in the sunshine" of the romances. Much criticism until the 1950s focused on the characters. One still relishes J. B. Priestley's admirable portraits of Jaques and Touchstone, Falstaff ("compared with him, we are all slaves"), Bottom ("a trades-unionist among butterflies"), and Sir Toby and Sir Andrew (*The English Comic Characters,* 1925). John Palmer (*Comic Characters of Shakespeare,* 1946) and Thomas Parrott (*Shakespearean Comedy,* 1949) had good things to say of the characters but little of the genre wherein they appeared. H. B. Charlton (*Shakespearian Comedy,* 1938) saw the plays as elucidating "the moral art of securing happiness"; and Subodh Sen Gupta (*Shakespearian Comedy,* 1950) saw them as analyzing characters profoundly, placing them "in certain situations in which they learn the deeper secrets of their own hearts."

Brown observes:

This stress on characters has had some important [and unhappy] consequences: *The Comedy of Errors, The Shrew,* and *The Merry Wives* are neglected as mere farces; . . . Shylock . . . is made the centre of *The Merchant;* Hero and Claudio are thought to be of little interest . . . ; the masque of Hymen is passed over as an unauthoritative accretion; Malvolio is sometimes allowed to play for tragedy; and the endings of *The Two Gentlemen, Much Ado* and *Twelfth Night* are called precipitous and unsatisfying.

With Northrop Frye, Nevill Coghill, and Cesar Lombardi Barber this changes.

Frye's perception is progressively set forth in "The Argument of Comedy" (*English Institute Essays,* 1948), *Anatomy of Criticism* (1957), and *A Natural Perspective* (1965). Shakespeare's comedies and romances, he argues, are nonillusionist and unrealistic. They tell stories that are self-contained conventions deriving ultimately from nature myths that present the movement from winter to spring. In them Shakespeare reveals no values except for dramatic structure, which proceeds from a harsh, anticomic society, law, or mood through a "period of confusion" and of "temporarily lost identity" to a discovery of identity (most often in marriage or betrothal, for the essential thrust of comedy is erotic) and a festive ending in which "a new society is crystallized." This structure parallels the central myth of Christianity: "Man loses a peaceable kingdom, staggers through the long nightmare of tyranny and injustice which is human history, and eventually regains his original vision" not out of his own merit but through God's grace, a point that "recurs all through Shakespearean comedy, where 'grace' is a centrally important thematic word."

The great objection to Frye is his neglect of close and sustained application of his mythic thesis to individual cases. As C. L. Barber remarks in a review (*Shakespeare Quarterly,* 1971) Frye "is not proving a theory in the ordinary sense, but pursuing a vision. . . . His neglect of individual works is part of a commitment to something else: 'it is only the individual and discrete literary experience that melts "into thin air"; what does not vanish is the total vision which contains that experience.' " (The quotation within the quotation is from Frye's response to his critics, *Northrop Frye in Modern Criticism,* Murray Krieger, ed., 1966.) The great value of Frye is that he places the romances within that large vision, the complex of myths by which man attempts to find the meaning of his life.

Coghill ("The Basis of Shakespearian Comedy," *English Association Essays and Studies,* 1950) sees Shakespeare's comedies as inheriting and expressing the vision most gloriously set forth in Dante's *Divine Comedy.* "The medieval formula for Comedy leads to the Beatific Vision." Shakespeare's comedy is "built up on a love-story, often indeed on a group of love-stories; lovers are united, faults are pardoned, enmities are reconciled." For Coghill, "it is proof how strongly" Shakespeare "held to a view of life as harmony that he later learnt how to stretch Comedy to contain sorrow and evil, and yet to show them capable of resolution in love and joy."

Barber (*Shakespeare's Festive Comedy,* 1959) similarly sets forth an anthropological perspective, although the analogies he sees between the plays and more primitive rituals seem, at first sight, less tenuous than Frye's. The plays put their characters "in the position of festive celebrants: if they do not seek holiday it happens to them." "Much of the poetry and wit, however it may be occasioned by events, works in the economy of the whole play to promote the effect of a merry occasion where Nature reigns." The characters, like festive celebrants everywhere, release energies customarily devoted to inhibition and, in the release, achieve clarification. And at the play's end, as at the end of holidays, everyday nature returns, characters and audience are brought back refreshed to the everyday world. Each of the plays Barber examines focuses on a particular kind of folly that is "released along with love—witty masquerade in *Love's Labor's Lost,* delusive fantasy in *A Midsummer Night's Dream,* romance in *As You Like It,* and, in *The Merchant of Venice,* prodigality balanced against usury." Barber's theory places more emphasis on mood then does Frye's and accounts for the interruptions to the plot provided by clowning, dance, and song. It may as well seem less to acknowledge the radical seriousness of the plays, their largeness of vision; and its definition of the comic genre is less inclusive than Frye's. It does not include the problem comedies or the romances.

Robert Grams Hunter's *Shakespeare and the Comedy of Forgiveness* (1965) follows Coghill in finding the root of Shakespeare's comedy in the medieval miracle play. The forgiveness in Shakespeare comes from human rather than divine sources, he asserts, from those who have suffered the consequence of the viciousness or folly of such as Claudio, Bertram, Angelo, and Leontes.

In *The Evolution of Shakespeare's Comedies* (1970), Larry S. Champion stresses Shakespeare's "development as a comic playwright . . . in the direction of complexity or depth of characterization." As Shakespeare's "conception of character expanded, so also did his problem of maintaining the proper perspective for the spectator." The goal at first was to develop in the audience a detachment that, as Shakespeare's subtlety of characterization grew and the audience found itself more involved, had to be importantly modified so that engagement and disengagement blended. Shakespeare progresses from comedies of situation in which the protagonist is essentially a puppet (*The Comedy of Errors, The Taming of the Shrew*), through comedies of identity in which the protagonist gains in self-knowledge (*The Merchant of Venice, As You Like It),* to the problem comedies, which are seen as unsuccessful but mediating steps to the final romances, in which the protagonist achieves new values.

Against such books as Champion's, and William J. Martz's *Shakespeare's Universe of Comedy* (1971), Wayne A. Rebhorn, to whom this discussion of the comedies owes much, protests (1979). Many works since Frye, ignoring him completely or acknowledging him only obliquely, have done either one of two things:

> approached the comedies à la Bergson through audience distance and the mockery of social deviants, or approached them through their themes and especially through their characters. . . . they tend to fall back on chronology as the chief organizing device for their studies. Thus they speak repeatedly about the *development* of the comedies, about Shakespeare's maturation as an artist, and about increasingly sophisticated portrayals of character or investigations of a theme like love.

"Their escape from Frye," he adds, "amounts to a large step backwards into the nineteenth century."

Shakespeare's Comedy of Love by Alexander Leggatt (1974) escapes some of Rebhorn's scorn, for although Leggatt rejects a generic or archetypal pattern for the plays, he recognizes this much of a scheme: "throughout Shakespeare's comedies, love seems to thrive on irrationality and confusion, and emerges from it strengthened, renewed and satisfied." Green or golden worlds are set against harsh or brazen worlds, and in the early and late, if not the problem, comedies, wish is fulfilled. Leggatt particularly stresses the shifts of style and idiom in the individual plays, the natural discourse of Benedick and Beatrice, for example, as pitted against the conventionalized talk and conduct of Claudio and Hero; but he perceives that Claudio's mourning, for all its conventionality, can bespeak just such natural feeling as many a mourner experiences at a formal funeral.

Tragedies. Under the earlier discussion of reactions to Bradley and of style enough has been said about major lines of early-twentieth-century criticism of the tragedies to let us acknowledge without further comment here the work of the Stollians (to name the tribe for its principal exponent) and the work of Knight, Knights, and their immediate New Critical successors. And there have been post-Bradleyans. One thinks especially of John Innes M. Stewart, whose *Character and Motive in Shakespeare* (1949) responds to charges of inconsistency in characterization by suggesting that poetic drama conveys truth by means other than those of psychological realism, and that conventionalized characters may refer, if only in a fossilized way, to genuine human dispositions. Here we may return to Wyndham Lewis, whose biographical theory has already been examined. Lewis finds the "master-subject" of Shakespeare's plays in the "struggle between chivalry, 'Celtism,' Christian mysticism, on the one hand, and the 'scientific spirit' of the Renaissance mind and of the modern world on the other." The lions of his Machiavellian title, the simpletons or fools, are the heroes, who speak for the former or past values in the grand style; the foxes or knaves are the Bolingbrokes and Claudiuses, the Iagos and Edmunds, who speak the language of the man of the world—"knowing" and cynical—and destroy the heroes. Lewis' view pays little regard to the achievement by the lions, if only momentarily, of a wisdom not hitherto theirs; nor does it regard the constellation of decent and loving creatures—the Horatios and Desdemonas, the Kents and Cordelias—who attend upon or sacrifice themselves for the heroes. Like the commentaries of the Stollians, Lewis' has the merit of inviting toward the plays a perspective distinctly un-Bradleyan and, despite its limitations, illuminating.

In *Shakespeare's Tragic Frontier* (1950), Willard Farnham attributes to Shakespeare three tragic worlds: early, middle, and last. The first, "without settled form," runs from *Richard III* to *Richard II;* the second, from *Julius Caesar* through *Lear,* has admirable heroes whose tragic flaws, because their hearts are incorruptible, "do not reach into the centers of their characters." The last tragic world, comprising *Timon of Athens, Macbeth, Antony and Cleopatra,* and *Coriolanus,* presents heroes "deeply flawed," all of whom "have a power, such as the heroes of the middle tragic world do not have," says Farnham, "to draw from us reactions that vary widely between profound antipathy and profound sympathy." *Timon* becomes Shakespeare's first venture into the tragic mystery of the deeply flawed yet noble character; *Antony and Cleopatra* is the play wherein it becomes "the all-absorbing tragic mystery." Farnham's analyses are sharp and, especially as he deals with the two final Roman plays, compelling. One need not agree with him *contra* T. S. Eliot, however, that *"Coriolanus* is a magnificent failure in which Shakespeare seems to have brought his tragic inspiration to an end by taking tragedy into an area of paradox beyond the effective reach of merely human pity."

Like G. Wilson Knight, Arthur Sewell in *Character and Society in Shakespeare* (1951) finds the unity of each play in the author's vision, "discovering itself in character and in conflict between characters, as though vision itself was unfolded in the play, and as though this unfolding was achieved through the embodiment in characters of various addresses to life, all presided over by one supreme and comprehensive address, which was Shakespeare's." The characters have "two different but related activities," action and speech, the one eventuating in plot, the other in style. Sewell finds the vision in the comedies and histories essentially static; but in the tragedies, confronting the metaphysical universe, "the hero undergoes . . . [a] new and uncovenanted experience" that transforms him, his creator, and the audience. Writing, in the modern rhetorical cliché, is discovery, and so, in the most profound sense, Sewell finds it in the great Shakespearean tragedies wherein "the generation of images, the fusion in language of imaginative energies into living personality, is a concrete representation, a mimesis, of a human soul in the very process of striving for identity, . . . seeking to fashion Chaos into Order." All try to find order—the disillusioned Prince of Denmark in the unweeded garden that his world has suddenly become, Othello where chaos has come again, Lear at the ultimate tribunal, Macbeth plummeting into the eternal abyss. The social, political, and philosophical disorder developing in Shakespeare's world prompted him "to create supreme drama out of the question, How shall man find the intersection between that which is in time and that which is out of time? Or, to put the matter simply, and I do not think too simply, What shall we do to be saved?"

Few efforts to fuse Bradleyan perspectives with Stollian have been more effective than Bernard Spivack's in *Shakespeare and the Allegory of Evil* (1958). Spivack examines four villains—Aaron, Richard III, Don John, and, at extraordinary length, Iago—to discover in them two conventions: the character

as live, as referrable to the motives and passions we as humans know, and the character as Vice still evolving from its inception in the medieval psychomachia. The conjunction of these conventions appears in Iago's motives, which are ambiguous; in his emotions, which he declares to be of one sort but which are, in expression, of another; and in his goals, which are simultaneously retaliatory and nonretaliatory. The motives "sound like parenthetical remarks, postscripts, marginalia—like a clutter of opportunisms for an action that was inevitable before they were ever thought of." Examined closely, the emotions reduce to jocularity, and the essential goal is the advancement of the banners of hell and night. Like Harbage, Spivack sees moral sentiment as governing Shakespeare's dramaturgy. Like Stoll he sees the plays as governed by convention. And like Bradley, with the comprehensive precision of a scholar-critic-lawyer-psychologist, he examines character.

Harold S. Wilson's *On the Design of Shakespearian Tragedy* (1957) places ten plays into three groups. The first group—*Romeo and Juliet, Hamlet, Othello,* and *Macbeth*—belongs, according to his scheme, to the "Order of Faith," the first two showing Providence working toward harmony, the second two, Providence punishing sins. The second group—*Julius Caesar, Coriolanus, Troilus,* and *Timon*—belongs to the "Order of Nature," the first pair presenting characters whose nobility withstands the trial they face; the second, characters who fail such tests. Wilson labels the first pair of plays in each quartet "thesis," the second pair "antithesis." The final two plays in his grouping—*King Lear* and *Antony and Cleopatra*—constitute the synthesis, the predominant value being human love, recognizably but not explicitly related to Christian love. If the taxonomy appears a shade too neat, and manifestly anachronistic, it nevertheless sharpens our perceptions of the values that the plays celebrate and the ways in which characters and plot dynamically embody them.

Maynard Mack's "The Jacobean Shakespeare: Some Observations on the Construction of the Tragedies" (*Jacobean Theatre,* Stratford-upon-Avon Studies 1, 1960) has been much and justly anthologized. Building on Bradley's lecture on the construction of the tragedies, Mack seeks a more inward understanding. The first part of his discussion deals with the paired voices in the tragedies, that of the overstating hero, in whose speech "there is always a residue of hyperbole," and that of his foil, whose "vocabulary [is] of a different intensity, a different rhetorical and moral wave length, to set it off." The second part deals with structure, "the cycle of change" through which the tragic hero moves: the opening phase in which the hero is enabled "to sound the peculiar timbre of his tragic music"; the second, in which "the hero tends to become his own antithesis" (the brutal Hamlet, the Iagolike Othello); and the third phase, which "represents a recovery of sorts; in some cases, perhaps, even a species of synthesis."

In *The Story of the Night: Studies in Shakespeare's Major Tragedies* (1961) John Holloway, like Knight before him, rejects the language and assumptions of conventional criticism. A Shakespearean play, he asserts, "is not a statement or insight or special kind of informativeness—not these things essentially, though it may be all of them incidentally—but is a momentous and energizing experience." And like Wyndham Lewis, Holloway perceives this experience anthropologically. Each tragedy ultimately reveals the archetypal pattern, the ritual sacrifice of the scapegoat hero; each engages the audience in this ritual, thereby enlarging its feeling for community, and, through the enacted suffering of the hero, imaginatively awakens it to the price it pays to belong to the community. The chapters on the individual plays are anything but reductive, although they do lead toward this radical pattern. That on *Lear,* which focuses on the play as doomsday ruination in the process of realization, compares Lear's experience to Job's. Each protagonist undergoes a unique

> protraction of torment, and the note is surely one of refusal to hide that from oneself, refusal to allow the terrible potentialities of life which the action has revealed to be concealed once more behind the veil of orthodoxy and the order of Nature. If there is such an order, it is an order which can accommodate seemingly limitless chaos and evil. The play is a confrontation of that, a refusal to avert one's gaze from that.

Frank Kermode calls this chapter, "like the play, incomparable" (*New Statesman,* 29 Dec. 1961).

"Although in each tragedy we find a major character who is confronted by a critical situation," says Matthew Proser in *The Heroic Image in Five Shakespearean Tragedies* (1965), "the action the hero takes is as much determined by his own conception of himself, his 'heroic image,' as by exterior circumstances." Each hero tries to live up to his self-image,

and each fails except, perhaps, in death, which, if it is sufficiently heroic, "converts the living man into an image of himself." Brutus, who misconstrues his private fears as public reasons and sees himself as Rome's savior, deserves Antony's magnificent tribute only, perhaps, when dead. Macbeth's heroic image of manliness ("I dare do all that may become a man; / Who dares do more is none") finds in the crown its symbol and, in murder (to which he finally surrenders himself), the means of achieving and maintaining it. Othello, Coriolanus, and Antony are warrior heroes, the first seen primarily in private, the second in public, and the third in both arenas. Each is intensely self-aware, perhaps never more than in the instant of making the choice that means death. Each finds a language to define his image, a language that others—Iago, for example, or Cleopatra—manipulate or reinforce.

Robert Hunter West's *Shakespeare and the Outer Mystery* (1968) attempts "to inquire reasonably what Shakespeare's tragedies do convey about ultimates in their worlds." The inner mystery is that of the human heart; the outer "is the cosmic mystery, the mystery of transcendence, of ultimate origin . . . the beyond and above; outer as outside and enclosing ordinary experience; outer as existing before and after this natural life; outer as a superior and controlling reality in which man's creation and destiny lie." West is writing in reply to such contemporizers of Shakespeare as Jan Kott (*Shakespeare, Our Contemporary,* 1964) on the one hand, and such Christianizers as Roy Battenhouse ("Shakespearean Tragedy: A Christian Interpretation," in Nathan A. Scott, ed., *The Tragic Vision and the Christian Faith,* 1957) on the other. What West has to say of the ghost in *Hamlet,* the witches in *Macbeth,* the nature of Iago's iniquity, the question of Othello's damnation or Lear's "ripeness," though developed in shrewd detail in the various chapters, is simply that "none of the tragedies seems to have a given and indisputable scheme of outerness, . . . all maintain a vast reserve, a mysteriousness that should stop the critic from more than hesitant suggestions about how they may be read, or confine him to a modest statement of personal views." Again, "the chief feature of Shakespeare's tragic outerness is an awesome mystery in which man participates. The grandeur of the mystery negates the assertion of outer blankness from which the disciples of absurdity derive their moral despair of morals, and man's participation negates the assertion of his alienness in the universe."

Paying tribute to Bradley, Baldwin, and Mack, Ruth Nevo's *Tragic Form in Shakespeare* (1972) identifies in nine of the tragedies a consistent five-act structure, to the segments of which she affixes the labels of "predicament, psychomachia, peripeteia, perspectives of irony and pathos, and catastrophe." Through these acts the hero progresses, his "development proceed[ing] through the phases of challenge, temptation or dilemma, disintegration, and despair to the final recognition in which all that was hidden is revealed, and self and destiny fully and finally confronted." Nevo's book is less a deductive demonstration of this analysis than a series of thoughtful running commentaries informed by it.

In *Shakespeare's Tragic Perspective* (1976) Larry Champion has two purposes. One is "to trace [the] development of Shakespeare's vision," a development indicated by the chapter titles: "The Search for a Perspective" *(Titus, Richard III, Richard II, Romeo and Juliet),* "The Private Dimensions of Tragedy" *(Julius Caesar, Hamlet, Othello),* "The Cosmic Dimensions of Tragedy" *(Lear, Macbeth),* and "The Social Dimensions of Tragedy" *(Timon, Coriolanus, Antony and Cleopatra).* The other purpose is "to examine the developing sophistication of Shakespeare's dramatic technique," his use of such devices as choral characters, subplots, portents, omens, soliloquies, and asides to manipulate the audience's response to the evil within the plays. Champion's analysis invites initially a strong emphasis on the individual's culpability (except in *Romeo and Juliet*) and, in the final tragedies, a diversified awareness of guilt in the society as well as the individual. "The causes of tragedy, in Shakespeare's final perspective, exist not in isolation but as a combination of destructive human forces from within and without."

"The arc of tragic action," says Susan Snyder in *The Comic Matrix of Shakespeare's Tragedies* (1979), "incorporates death's inevitability, against which develops that special dimension of the protagonist we call heroic." Comedy, by contrast, offers an " 'evitability' principle: it gets around death, either by ignoring it completely or by presenting it as nonfinal, illusory." Snyder's hypothesis is that Shakespeare, having "thoroughly explored and mastered the comic mode" earlier in his career, used its conventions "as point[s] of reference in developing tragic forms." The comic conventions that the "knowledgeable theatergoer of the 1590s" would expect and that Shakespeare had helped de-

velop include the love story that never does run smooth (though it ends happily), the significant intervention of chance or fortune, manipulative characters, earthy clowns, humor characters, disguise, confusion, "linguistic foolery," the overturning of rigid social traditions, and the like. The world embodying these conventions "is not real, yet it responds to real human needs in its refusal of restraint and finitude"; and though it holds off chaos only by its "arbitrary natural law," it "might be seen . . . as a possible starting point, or a running accompaniment, or even a constituent element, of Shakespeare's tragic vision."

The three items in that series point to chapters that illuminate *Romeo and Juliet* and *Othello, Hamlet,* and *King Lear.* "Mercutio is the clown of romantic comedy . . . the best of game-players, endlessly inventive" whose sudden death "Shakespeare makes the birth of tragedy." Both Friar Laurence and the Nurse are creatures from the comic world, but their efforts to manipulate and accommodate fail in a world where the evitable has been transformed into the inevitable, where time loses its flexibility and fortune (not character) determines the outcome. In *King Lear,* to leap to the final chapter, "Between the Divine and the Absurd," comic and tragic worlds combine in the grotesque. Snyder has good things to say about Edmund and Edgar as self-humbling ironists, the latter as Poor Tom enormously inventive (like Mercutio), about the earthy Fool, about "an incongruity verging on the comic between the king's towering emotions and the petty incidents that cause them." Most important, she makes us see both plot and character as moving through vicissitude and chaos to the happy ending that the old *Chronicle History of King Leir* and Nahum Tate's adaptation of *King Lear* provide and that Shakespeare does not.

Snyder's exploration of the comic matrix in this play leads to this conclusion:

> Shakespeare . . . is not rewriting the *Purgatorio* or anticipating *Endgame;* he is setting one vision against the other, and in their uneasy coexistence lies the play's peculiar tragic force. Dante and Beckett at their respective poles offer not tragedy but two kinds of comedy. . . . Each kind in its way diminishes man somewhat. He is either a figure in a preestablished scheme, following the way laid out for him by a higher intelligence, or he is an aimless atom in a universe of aimless atoms. Where the two comic visions are held in balance, with neither dominating, individual choice and perseverance have special significance. The uni-

verse of tragedy, and preeminently of *Lear,* intimates pattern but fails to complete it; some pieces of the jigsaw are forever missing, and some of those on hand will never fit. Man is heroic in these circumstances when, like Lear, he has the capacity to create a larger self even out of the destructive element—to make his own meaning.

Romances. In "Shakespeare's Romances: 1900–1957" (1958) Philip Edwards subgroups his subjects according to their varying foci, among which are the author himself, the mythic or allegorical significances of the plays as revealed by anthropology or comparative religion, Christian interpretation, and the genre of romance. Of the biographical meanings enough has been said, though one might add Louis MacNeice's happy poem, "Autolycus" (*Collected Poems,* 1949), which begins, "In his last phase when hardly bothering / To be a dramatist, the Master turned away / From his taut plots and complex characters / To tapestried romances, . . ."

John Churton Collins provides an early allegorical reading of *The Tempest* ("Poetry and Symbolism: A Study of *The Tempest,*" 1908). As Edwards summarizes:

> The island . . . may be considered as the world, with Prospero as the controlling divinity. The characters are various aspects of humanity. The plot tells how those subjects who have sinned against and wronged a Power are at last brought before the Power. The wrong done is answered with forgiveness, "sealed and ratified by the marriage of the child of the wronged one with the child of the wronger."

Knight (*Myth and Miracle,* 1929; *The Shakespearian Tempest,* 1932) finds in the breakdown of medieval religious ritual the possibility of new, dramatic formulations of abiding verities that Shakespeare, as critic-priest (not, as Lewis would have him, as poet-executioner), mediates to his audience. "The progress from spiritual pain and despairing thought through stoic acceptance to a serene and mystic joy is a universal rhythm of the spirit of man. . . . The Final Plays of Shakespeare must be read as myths of immortality. . . . Tragedy is never the last word." Like MacNeice, Derek Traversi (*Shakespeare: The Last Phase,* 1954) sees Shakespeare abandoning realism but setting forth a movement from breakdown in personal and political relations to reconciliation.

Edwards reacts against such interpretation:

The reduction of the complexity of Shakespeare to a striving towards a balanced view of life seems to me typical of the pallidness of all interpretations of the last plays which insist that they are symbolic utterances. . . . Sentimental religiosity . . . ; platitudinous affirmations of belief in fertility and re-creation; an insistence on the importance of maturity and balance: these are the deposits of Shakespeare's last plays once the solvent of parabolic interpretation has been applied, but these are not what the reader or the audience observes in Pericles' reunion with Marina, the Whitsun pastorals, Leontes' denial of the oracle or the wooing of Ferdinand and Miranda.

To Edwards' listing of allegorists may be added Douglas L. Peterson (*Time, Tide, and Tempest,* 1973), who sees Shakespeare as both engaging his viewers in the worlds of the plays and, by stressing their artifice, holding them at a distance. By scenes that are "speaking pictures" or emblems Shakespeare conveys truths about the benign powers ruling our universe—"Look down, you gods. . . ."

Although in *Shakespeare's Last Plays* (1938) Tillyard sees the romances as Christian in perspective, and although only *The Winter's Tale* perfectly fits his ideal pattern of a prosperous king committing evil, suffering therefor, then overcoming the evil within himself and entering with his society "by an act of forgiveness or repentance . . . into a fairer prosperity than had first existed," Tillyard does not reduce "the complexity of Shakespeare" to pallid interpretation.

Samuel L. Bethell's Christian interpretation *The Winter's Tale: A Study* (1947) stresses its emancipation from realism as the means of imaging a higher reality; the restoration of Hermione is "a carefully prepared symbol of spiritual and actual resurrection, in which alone true reconciliation may be attained."

In his remarkable *The Heart's Forest: A Study of Shakespeare's Pastoral Plays* (1972), David P. Young first defines "pastoral," then examines from generic, metadramatic, and audience-manipulation perspectives a quartet of plays that at first seem oddly dissimilar: *As You Like It, King Lear, The Winter's Tale,* and *The Tempest.* Elizabethan pastoral drama as it came to Shakespeare "was not a courtly and elegant genre based on Italian models, but a rough-hewn and ramshackle affair, dressed in the hand-me-down literary respectability it could claim through its ancestry in Sidney and Spenser." Its basic pattern was of "exile, pastoral sojourn, and return." In Young's analysis, "the vicissitudes of

Fortune as obstacles to the achievement of [the sought-after social and psychological] harmonies are stressed, with the result that the action swings curiously between intellectual discussion and spectacular event." Moreover, "almost anything is possible in this heightened, imaginary world." The pastoral joins with lyric poetry in its concern "to relate human experience to the great rhythms of the natural world," and it makes of nature "a glass that, rightly held, gave access" to the imagination. Inevitably, pastoral offers antitheses: "urban versus rural, court versus country, . . . the active life versus the contemplative," worldliness and innocence, nurture and nature, art and nature. And pastoral is, of course, hugely paradoxical. "It affects to prefer nature to art, but is itself highly artificial and turns out to have art as one of its major subjects. It confounds the exterior and the interior, transforming landscape to mood and back again. Like the imagination from which it proceeds, it is elusive, unstable, protean."

We may consider one example of Young's analyses. He begins his study of *The Winter's Tale* with its division into two halves, the first primarily tragic, the second primarily comic, the two joined by Time, as Chorus, who exists in a double mode: linear (as in tragedy) and cyclic (as in comedy). Young devotes one section to the art-nature opposition that runs through the play. The style swings from what Mack has called the "emblematic," which detaches the audience, to the "psychological," which engages it. Leontes is simultaneously the conventionalized figure of stage tyrant and the humanly realized victim of mental aberration. Perdita is the living likeness of Hermione; and Hermione is "a boy actor impersonating a woman who is impersonating a statue of herself, and this woman-statue-actor provides the climax of a fiction that might well be 'hooted at / Like an old tale.' " To Time, already mentioned, Young devotes his final section. "Time's speech," says Young, "offers the reader or spectator a unique perspective, one which partakes of the artist's attitude toward his materials (a peculiar mixture of engagement and detachment) and of a strong sense of relativity." For Young, "Time's overview refers us once more to the uniqueness that arises from the very structure of *The Winter's Tale:* its striking rehandling, through juxtaposed genres, of the pattern of extrusion and restoration, the dual worlds so characteristic of pastoral romance. The roots of the story are the same ones that gave rise to *As You Like It* and

King Lear; yet it is at least as different from them as they are from each other."

In *Shakespearean Romance* (1972) Howard Felperin defines romance as "a success story in which difficulties of any number of kinds are overcome, and a tall story in which they are overcome against impossible odds or by miraculous means." Following Coghill and sounding like Frye, whom he attacks, Felperin sees comedy and romance as issuing in "a renewed and raised society," moving from a "lower or fallen order of nature . . . into a higher order." The archetypal romance is the Christian epic. Whereas Shakespeare's earlier comedies place few genuine obstacles to ultimate happiness, the late plays stress pain and suffering for which the happy outcome never completely compensates. "It is through this technique of shadowing or qualifying or problematizing the triumphs it presents that the best romance manages to pass itself off as an image of the real."

Barbara A. Mowat (*The Dramaturgy of Shakespeare's Romances,* 1976) analyzes the techniques of these plays. She shows the back-and-forth shifts from tragic involvement and comic detachment (as does Douglas Peterson), the tragic parts comic in their hyperbole, the comic involving real pain. She points to the oscillation between illusionistic realism and highly artificial presentation. And she pays special attention to the plotting, noting the absence of the crisis in the middle and the heavy use of narrative to provide continuity. Like the plays of Aristophanes before and of Brecht after, Shakespeare's romances, as Rebhorn (1979) summarizes this point, "aim at breaking up normal patterns of expectation, and as a result, force the audience, placed at a distance from the play-world, to make the drama it has seen into a coherent, meaningful statement"—for many a critic a difficult, uncertain task.

New Emphases. As the twentieth century closes, can one see new directions in Shakespearean criticism? Perhaps there are only new emphases. The criticism of character, so strong in the nineteenth century, continues still, if informed now by such disciplines as psychoanalysis. Ernest Jones's work has already been noted. Behind it lie comments by Freud himself, ably reviewed by Kenneth Muir. In 1966 Norman N. Holland published *Psychoanalysis and Shakespeare,* a compendium of psychoanalytic criticism, the perusal of which led Maurice Charney to "four basic reasons why the psychoanalytic approach to Shakespeare has proved thus far to be so fruitless and so misdirected" (*Shakespeare Quarterly,* 1968): (1) The psychoanalytic critics are more interested in psychoanalysis than in Shakespeare; (2) their preoccupation "creates a confusion between art and life"; (3) the biographical fallacy, like the allegorical fallacy, substitutes psychoanalytic for literary and theatrical symbolism; and (4) the criticism makes an unwarranted claim to scientific validity. Emphatic as such objections may be, reinforced by such analytic aberrations as that the sonnet form is oedipal, that Lear inclines to "wet himself" or that "the skulls in *Hamlet* [are] symbolic testicles," psychoanalytic criticism proceeds apace.

In David Willbern's "Bibliography of Psychoanalytic and Psychological Writings on Shakespeare: 1964–1978" in *Representing Shakespeare: New Psychoanalytic Essays,* edited by Murray M. Schwartz and Coppélia Kahn (1980), are 461 entries. "Hermia's Dream," the first essay in this stunning collection, is by Holland himself, and in it he traces three stages of psychoanalytic criticism:

> At first we treated the unconscious processes in literary characters as though they were fact, not fiction, happening "out there," . . . . Then we set the character into an ego process embodied in the play as a whole. We began to acknowledge that we were included in that process, too, as we lent ourselves to the play. Now we have begun to make explicit the self-discovery that was only implicit and silent in those two earlier methods.
>
> . . . Just as self and object constitute each other in human development, so in the literary transaction the reader constitutes text so that text may constitute its reader. In this mutuality, Hermia's dream is not simply a dream dreamed for us. Rather, we dream her dream for ourselves, and as we know ourselves so we know the dream, until its local habitation is here and its name is us.

Holland works through psychoanalytic criticism back to the self. Madelon Gohlke, another essayist in *Representing Shakespeare,* works outward toward the possibility of a feminist psychohistory. Gohlke's concern is with metaphorical reverberations in character, plot, theme, and cultural fiction; and her analyses carry her from *Romeo and Juliet,* wherein, "read metaphorically, the plot validates the perception expressed variously in the play that love kills," through *Hamlet* and *Othello,* wherein the heroes perceive themselves as rendered powerless by the conduct of Ophelia and Desdemona, through the tragic stories of Lear and Macbeth, who find themselves rendered powerless by nurturing or maternal figures, to *Antony and Cleopatra.* Gohlke's discussion of this last play begins:

> Interwoven into the patriarchal structure of Shakespeare's tragedies is an equally powerful matriarchal vision. They are even, I would argue, aspects of one another, both proceeding from the masculine consciousness of feminine betrayal. Both inspire a violence of response on the part of the hero against individual women, but more importantly, against the hero's perception of himself as womanish, in which he ultimately hurts himself. The concurrence of these themes is particularly evident in *Antony and Cleopatra,* a play that both recalls the ritual marriage conclusion of the comedies as it deepens the sexual dilemma of the tragic hero.

From close analyses of the sexual metaphors at the center of the tragedies, Gohlke proceeds to the idea that beneath the theme of male dominance in the plays (and in the culture) lies the sense that "it is women who are regarded as powerful and men who strive to avoid an awareness of their vulnerability in relation to women." The conclusion to which she points is the need for redefining our norms of male and female natures, for pursuing the psychoanalytic goal of dislocating the unconscious and thus freshly affirming our reality.

Gohlke provides a vantage point for reviewing another of the growing critical approaches to Shakespeare, that of the feminists. Of female critics and commentators on Shakespeare there have been many across the ages: Margaret Cavendish, Duchess of Newcastle, in the seventeenth century; Elizabeth Montagu and Charlotte Lennox in the eighteenth; Anna Brownell Jameson and Mary Cowden Clarke in the nineteenth; and in the twentieth, a host among whom one may name with honor Agnes M. Mackenzie, Virginia Woolf, Caroline Spurgeon, Muriel Bradbrook, Margaret Webster, Sister Miriam Joseph, Molly Mahood. Feminist criticism, however, is not necessarily by women or about them. It is, say Carolyn Lenz, Gayle Greene, and Carol Neely, the editors of *The Woman's Part: Feminist Criticism of Shakespeare* (1980), "more a matter of perspective. . . . Feminists assume that women are equal to men but that their roles . . . have been restricted, stereotyped, and minimized; their aim is to free women from oppressive constraints: 'the struggle for women is to be human in a world which declares them only female.' "

The quotation within that quotation is from

Juliet Dusinberre's *Shakespeare and the Nature of Women* (1975), a remarkable and occasionally militant fusion of cultural and literary criticism. Dusinberre's thesis is that "Shakespeare and his contemporaries could rely on their audience's alertness to controversy about women. They shared with it an awareness of changing attitudes heightened by Puritan propaganda," especially as this focused on the sanctity of marriage. Dusinberre's work calls on or comments upon all of Shakespeare's plays. Perhaps her final sentences justly epitomize her perspective:

Shakespeare saw men and women as equal in a world which declared them unequal. He did not divide human nature into the masculine and feminine, but observed in the individual woman or man an infinite variety of union between opposing impulses. To talk about Shakespeare's women is to talk about his men, because he refused to separate their worlds physically, intellectually, or spiritually. Where in every other field understanding of Shakespeare's art grows, reactions to his women continually recycle, because critics are still immersed in preconceptions which Shakespeare discarded about the nature of women.

The bibliography of *The Woman's Part*, which lists works "appropriate to the concerns of those interested in the position of women, in relations between men and women, and in love, sexuality, courtship, marriage, and the family in Shakespeare," comprises 332 items, most of them published since 1960 and attesting by their number to the force of this critical movement.

"As We Like It: How a Girl Can Be Smart and Still Popular," an essay by Clara Claiborne Park reprinted in that volume, delightfully tells us "about the extent—and the limits—of acceptable feminine activity" in Shakespeare's world, "which in this as in other things remains . . . disconcertingly like our own." Shakespeare makes Beatrice brilliant but not uncomfortably so and able to tame herself so that the men in the audience need not attempt the task. Coppélia Kahn's "Coming of Age in Verona," to take a final instance, follows Harold Goddard (*The Meaning of Shakespeare*, 1951), seeing *Romeo and Juliet* as "constantly critical of the feud as the medium through which criteria of patriarchally oriented masculinity are voiced" and "as constantly sensitive to the association of those criteria with more humane principles of loyalty to family and friends, courage, and personal dignity." Kahn's criticism is sensitive, Freudian (when Romeo offers to cut his name from his body he is,

symbolically, castrating himself), and enlightening. Let her final remarks about hero and heroine serve as evidence:

They have come of age by a means different from the rites of passage—phallic violence and adolescent motherhood—typical for youth in Verona. Romeo's death in the tomb of the Capulets rather than in that of his own fathers reverses the traditional passage of the female over to the male house in marriage and betokens his refusal to follow the code of his fathers. And it is Juliet, not Romeo, who boldly uses his dagger, against herself.

Metadramatic criticism, which seems to be enjoying a bull market, follows Marshall McLuhan's line that the medium is the message and offers its audience most as it invites close attention to the uses of language in the plays. Among its chief exponents are Sigurd Burckhardt (*Shakespearean Meanings*, 1968), James L. Calderwood (*Shakespearean Metadrama*, 1971, and *Metadrama in Shakespeare's Henriad*, 1979), Lawrence Danson (*Tragic Alphabet: Shakespeare's Drama of Language*, 1974), and Richard Fly (*Shakespeare's Mediated World*, 1976). The bond plot of *The Merchant of Venice* is ultimately "Shakespeare's bondage to his source," suggests Burckhardt, and the business with the ring may ultimately reflect the "circularity" of the story's "own composition." *A Midsummer Night's Dream* is about imagination, says Calderwood (and many before him), and the sexuality in the play metaphorically represents "the wedding of imaginations in the theater." Perhaps more usefully, Calderwood sees Richard II's use of language as symbolic, Bolingbroke's as mere convenience. "In the deposition scene Richard, the name without a meaning, confronts Bolingbroke, the meaning without a name." Danson finds the heroes engaged in a "search for adequate expressive modes," although it may seem to some that their success in their search is a main reason we go to the Shakespearean theater. Fly presents Shakespeare in *King Lear* as, like his hero, pushing language to the breaking point. Few would disagree.

BIBLIOGRAPHY

Invaluable for the historian of Shakespearean criticism are "The Year's Contributions to Shakespearian Study," published annually in *Shakespeare Survey,* and the reviews published in every issue of *Shakespeare Quarterly.*

Robert W. Babcock, *The Genesis of Shakespeare Idolatry 1766–1799* (1931). M. C. Bradbrook, "Fifty Years of the Criticism of Shakespeare's Style: A Retrospect," in *Shakespeare Survey,* 7 (1954). John Russell Brown, "The Interpretation of Shakespeare's Comedies: 1900–1953," *ibid.,* 8 (1955). J. A. Bryant, Jr., "Shakespeare: The Lean Years," in *Sewanee Review,* 86 (1978). Arthur M. Eastman, *A Short History of Shakespearean Criticism* (1968). Philip Edwards, "Shakespeare's Romances: 1900–1957," in *Shakespeare Survey,* 11 (1958). T. S. Eliot, "Shakespearian Criticism: From Dryden to Coleridge," in H. Granville-Barker and G. B. Harrison, eds., *A Companion to Shakespeare Studies* (1934). F. David Hoeniger, "Shakespeare's Romances Since 1958: A Retrospect," in *Shakespeare Survey,* 29 (1976). John Holloway, "Criticism—20th Century," in Oscar J. Campbell, ed., *The Reader's Encyclopedia of Shakespeare* (1966). J. Isaacs, "Shakespearian Criticism: From Coleridge to the Present Day," in Granville-Barker and Harrison, eds., *op. cit.*

Seymour Kleinberg, "Criticism—17th Century," "Criticism—18th Century," and "Criticism—19th Century," in Campbell, ed., *op. cit.* M. Jamieson, "The Problem Plays, 1920–1970: A Retrospect," in *Shakespeare Survey,* 25 (1972). Kenneth Muir, "Fifty Years of Shakespearian Criticism: 1900–1950," *ibid.,* 4 (1951); "Some Freudian Interpretations of Shakespeare," in *Proceedings of the Leeds Philosophical and Literary Society,* 7, pt. 1 (1952); and "Shakespeare's Imagery—Then and Now," in *Shakespeare Survey,* 18 (1965). Patrick Murray, *The Shakespearian Scene: Some Twentieth-Century Perspectives* (1969). D. J. Palmer, "Some Recent Studies in Shakespeare," in *Critical Quarterly,* 18 (1976). Norman Rabkin, "Shakespeare at the End of the Seventies," in *Sewanee Review,* 88 (1980). Augustus Ralli, *A History of Shakespearean Criticism,* 2 vols. (1932). Wayne A. Rebhorn, "After Frye: A Review-Article on the Interpretation of Shakespearean Comedy and Romance," in *Texas Studies in Literature and Language,* 21 (1979).

M. A. Shaaber, "Shakespeare Criticism: Dryden to Bradley," in Kenneth Muir and S. Schoenbaum, eds., *A New Companion to Shakespeare Studies* (1971). David Nichol Smith, *Shakespeare in the Eighteenth Century* (1928). S. Viswanathan, *The Shakespeare Play as Poem: A Critical Tradition in Perspective* (1980). Herbert Weisinger, "The Study of Shakespearian Tragedy Since Bradley," in *Shakespeare Quarterly,* 6 (1955). Stanley Wells, "Shakespeare Criticism Since Bradley," in Muir and Schoenbaum, eds., *op. cit.*

Shakespeare and the Painter and Illustrator

W. MOELWYN MERCHANT

"I have had a most rare vision." Bottom's confusion of dreaming and waking, his mixture of biblical theology (quoting the Epistles of St. Paul and St. John, if with some confounding of the senses) with the activity of the more sinister world within the play—all this corresponds to the two poles of the comedy, the joyful reconciliation of the alienated lovers and the dark exploration of a supernatural world shot through with aggression and malice. Puck does well in the end to reveal his allegiance to "the triple Hecate," while "following darkness like a dream."

All these facets of the play demanded the flexible virtuosity—verbal, visual, and musical—of Shakespeare's stage setting within its early Baroque theater. In uniting the "stigmata . . . of a play for some courtly marriage" (in Harley Granville-Barker's phrase) with exploration of a supernatural world within which Hecate broods as darkly as in *Hamlet, Lear,* or *Macbeth,* Shakespeare here and throughout his work mobilized not only his own incomparable wordplay but also the wittiest conceits in sight and sound of which his theater was capable.

It will be my aim here to trace from this rich and complex beginning the history of Shakespearean interpretation as it is extended through paintings, engravings, and book illustrations, from the Peacham drawing of *Titus Andronicas* (1595) to our own day, and in the fruitful interplay with theater setting. For it is precisely this interplay that justifies the term *visual criticism* and makes of it (with music

as its rich associate) such a powerful instrument, indispensable as a corrective to our predominantly verbal exploration of the plays.

It is impossible here to do more than highlight a handful of examples from the many thousands of major and minor works that, for three centuries, have illuminated Shakespeare's text. And these works must carry the burden of representing very various genres; easel painting, book illustration, and theater design represent disciplines, artistic criteria, and constraints very far removed from each other; yet all three are frequently practiced by the same artist, subjecting himself creatively to their varied demands.

We may profitably begin with the first illustrated complete edition of Shakespeare, published by Jacob Tonson in 1709, edited by Nicholas Rowe, and illustrated by such modest artists as Elisha Kirkall and Michiel Van der Gucht. Tonson has an honorable place in the production of four editions, with *Paradise Lost* in 1695, Dryden's translation of *Virgil* in 1697, and Ovid's *Metamorphoses* (in English) in 1717. The illustrations to the less ambitious *Shakespeare* fulfill a variety of functions and are both illuminating concerning stage practice in the early eighteenth century and critically interesting in bringing forward certain clear aesthetic standards. For Tonson and Rowe appear to have agreed (judging by the dedication to the duke of Somerset) that "Dramatick Poetry" in general and Shakespeare in particular needed protection from manifold assaults: "She has been persecuted by

Fanaticism, forsaken by her Friends, and oppress'd even by Musick, her Sister and confederate Art." This summary of nearly a half-century of "oppression"—from the Puritans, the closure of the theaters in 1642, and from the distortions of "Shakespeare made Fitt" in the operatized versions of the Restoration—accounts for Tonson's attempt to produce an edition both carefully edited and illustrated. The convoluted history of one of these engravings, the frontispiece to *Coriolanus,* must stand for all the rest.

This frontispiece treats the scene in the fifth act when Coriolanus is confronted by Volumnia and Virgilia. The classical conflict has reached its climax, pitting the pride of a rebellious conqueror against his dual piety to his city and to his family. Kirkall (if he was the engraver) made a remarkable decision, to adapt to a vertical composition a distinguished work by Nicolas Poussin, rendering the same scene from Plutarch. This would appear to be wholly removed from the theater both in its origin and in its adaptation, yet its subsequent history and influence are remarkable. Francis Hayman's drawing for Thomas Hanmer's much finer, six-volume edition (1744–1746) adopts precisely the same composition; and after many transmutations, in theater costume and in smaller editions, it reappears in full stature in Kemble's production in 1807. Thomas Rowlandson and Augustus Charles Pugin's *The Microcosm of London* (1808) has a plate, showing the interior of the Drury Lane Theatre, that reveals in every detail a return to Poussin's painting. For over a century, then, a classical French artist's interpretation of Plutarch became the basis for both book illustration and theater presentation of this scene from Shakespeare.

Meanwhile, William Hogarth had given us two notable works, his drawing of Falstaff examining his troops (ca. 1728; Royal Library, Windsor Castle) and, some twelve to fourteen years later, the elaborate painting, *Garrick as Richard the Third—Starting from Sleep* (Walker Art Gallery, Liverpool). They show two contrasting techniques of interpretation. The drawing is swift and impressionistic, the "troops" minimally sketched in: Shallow a vacuous face, Silence a mere embodied gesture, Shadow literally a "half-faced fellow" in profile. Falstaff is rotund, decadent in his lounging arrogance, his seedy finery suggesting his darker character in *Henry IV, Part 2,* a courtier ripe for repudiation. This is the very essence of the theatrical. The portrait of Garrick in his finest role gives us the substance of Richard's tragedy frozen in a single gesture within the authentic eighteenth-century theater setting. When to this recollection of Garrick are added the lesser but still important *Garrick as Hamlet* by Benjamin West and as Romeo by Benjamin Wilson, with the two related studies of *Garrick and Mrs. Pritchard in Macbeth* by Johann Joseph Zoffany and by Henry Fuseli, we have recreated for us, in setting, authentic gesture, and atmosphere, the actor who dominated the middle decades of the eighteenth century.

A further painting remains from that period to complete its story of "visual criticism," the unique *King Lear in the Storm,* painted in 1767 by the young Scottish artist John Runciman (National Gallery, Edinburgh). The composition is majestic, the group of characters (including the Fool, not seen on the eighteenth-century stage) isolated by the intersection of the vertical line through the "novel," the sharp diagonal of the inundating wave crest, and the horizontal of the skyline on which a ship founders. The characters, identifiable both as Shakespearean and as being in the "antique manner" (from prototypes by Van Dyck and Rembrandt), are isolated on a rock near which drowned bodies float. No such scene appears in the play; after all, "For many miles about/There's scarce a bush." What Runciman, with unique insight, has painted is the imagery, which in turn renders the tragic raving of the King. Lear is "contending with the fretful elements"; we believe that the wind will indeed "blow the earth into the sea"; here are "cataracts" and "hurricanoes"; while Edgar, a crazy leadsman, calls a sounding to the deranged helmsman of the ship of state: "Fathom, and half, fathom and half! Poor Tom." Here the two natural terrors (which reappear in *The Winter's Tale*) of the feral and the flood are joined and contrasted:

> Thou'dst shun a bear;
> But if thy flight lay toward the roaring sea,
> Thou'dst meet the bear i'th' mouth.

(III. iv. 9–11)

Runciman's is a picture of rare power and rarer in its own day for its eschewing of the theater in order to center upon the text.

The British engraver and publisher John Boydell merits separate treatment from the generality of his age; for though there was a lamentable absence of unity in method and style, his project, announced in 1786, was ambitious: to set up a Shakespeare

57. Drawing for the frontispiece of *Coriolanus,* by Francis Hayman (1744).

58. *Garrick as Richard the Third,* by William Hogarth (ca. 1746).

Gallery that would do honor to Shakespeare, while assisting in the establishment of an English school of historical painting. To commission 170 paintings by some thirty-five artists was no mean undertaking, and they were a distinguished if heterogeneous gathering: Joshua Reynolds, Fuseli, James Northcote, William Hamilton, Robert Smirke, Francis Wheatley, and John Opie led the ranks, and scarcely a major artist (except William Blake) was absent from the venture. Some of the paintings had real distinction: Reynolds' *Death of Beaufort* (echoing the composition of Poussin's *Death of Germanicus*), Benjamin West's *Ophelia,* and James Barry's *Lear and Cordelia* establish the classical mode, reflecting the aims of the Royal Academy and Reynolds' discourses delivered there; while the wit of Smirke's *Sly in Bed* and the theatricality of Wheatley's *Baptista's House* and of Northcote's *Entry of Bolingbroke* raise stage echoes to the grand

manner. George Romney, however, seems on all counts to dominate the gallery, though he contributed only three works: the small fancy of *The Infant Shakespeare* and the two very substantial pictures, *Prospero and Miranda* and *Cassandra Raving* (there is a small sketch for the central figure at the Folger Library). But a series of notebooks—now in the Fitzwilliam Museum, Cambridge, and at the Folger Library—together provide an even more impressive approach to Shakespeare's text. The five notebooks at the Folger are dominated by *King Lear* (his awakening and the death of Cordelia), *The Tempest* (studies for the large Boydell painting), and *Macbeth* (notably a series of *Banquo's Ghost,* cinematic in its progressive sense of vivid movement). Here, with the swift insight characteristic of many preliminary drawings, is a rare grasp of character and a sense of theater without staginess.

The major figure absent from Boydell's gallery,

59. *King Lear in the Storm,* by John Runciman (1767).

William Blake, showed his own massive and varied insights. By comparison with his studies in Milton and in Biblical subjects, his handling of Shakespeare is more spare (fewer than thirty works, all reproduced and commented upon in my article, "Blake's Shakespeare," in *Apollo,* April 1964). Some are small exercises in historical portraiture, most notably the seven early character heads (Boston Museum of Fine Arts), among which are three moving studies of Lear. More significant and consonant with Blake's private mythology are *Jocund Day or the Dance of Albion*, verbally related to *Romeo and Juliet* (a line engraving in the Rosenwald Collection, National Gallery, Washington, D.C.) and a drawing, *Fiery Pegasus* (in the British Library Print Room in the extra-illustrated Second Folio). This is a more complex study, contrasting the spontaneity and creative wit of Hal, who develops into the regenerate King Henry, with the barren reason (the *Waste of Locke and Newton*). Still more impor-

tant are the two color-prints in the Tate Gallery, *Hecate* and *Pity.* The former vividly explores the "triple Hecate" who animates Puck and broods over *Macbeth,* the curse of Lear, and the potion in Hamlet's play-within-the-play. Blake's triple figure is surrounded by witches' familiars, recollecting *Macbeth.* That play is critically alluded to in *Pity,* for the imagery in Macbeth's speech of the "new-born babe/Striding the blast" is analyzed line by line and yet held in tension within a tight composition. Finally—and most splendidly—Blake produced a series of drawings and prints of the scene in *Henry VIII* of Queen Katherine's dream, the most notable of which (Fitzwilliam Museum and almost identical with a drawing in the Rosenwald Collection) shows a double spiral of angels bearing garlands above the recumbent queen. This series indicates vividly what we might have inherited had Blake commented visually as fully on Shakespeare as he did on Dante.

Blake's contemporaries produced important but

761

60. (Left) A sketch for *Cassandra Raving,* by George Romney. 61. (Below) A sketch from the series of *Banquo's Ghost,* by George Romney.

62. *The Vision of Queen Katherine,* by William Blake (1807).

isolated works. None was as prolific as Eugène Delacroix in France, who merits extended consideration not possible here. Fuseli characteristically drew the nightmare fantasy of Lady Macbeth's sleepwalking (Carrick-Moore notebook, British Library) and a series of drawings for Rivington's edition of the plays in 1805 (some of which were engraved by Blake). Two studies of Macbeth and the Witches surpass the sensibility of most other artists of their day: Francis Towne's drawing, in cool line and wash, endows the encounter with mystery and credibility; and John Martin's mezzotint, a more frenetic version, places the supernatural meeting in a landscape that did him notable service in his mezzotints for *Paradise Lost.* A third major work in this period is John Constable's *Jacques and the Wounded Stag,* the painting mezzotinted by David Lucas. Constable records that at Coleorton, the home of Sir George Beaumont, "On Saturday evening it was *As You Like It,* and I never heard the 'Seven ages' so admirably read before"—an experience that doubtless led to this study in the pastoral mode.

At this point in the history of Shakespeare illustration there is something of a revolution in theater practice that greatly affects the artist both in easel

63. Illustration of costume for *Richard III,* by J. R. Planché.

painting and in design for the stage. History painting, a central concern of the academicians, had required accurate settings and detail in period dress and accoutrements. Two artists, William Capon and James Robinson Planché, developed this demand with pedantic passion in stage setting. Capon was scenic director at the Drury Lane under the Kembles, and we are able from the descriptions in James Boaden's *Life of Kemble* and surviving drawings in the Memorial Library, Stratford-upon-Avon, to envisage his settings for Kemble's *Henry VIII.* The drawings indicate the aptness of Boaden's assertion that Capon's architectural settings were "from partial remains, and authentic sources of information —put together with the greatest diligence and accuracy."

Planché greatly advanced the "historical" implications of Capon's work, and the critical development can be dated with accuracy: his designs for the opening, at the Drury Lane on 19 January 1824, of Kemble's production of *King John.* His aim was declared on the playbill: ". . . Shakespeare's Tragedy of King John with an attention to Costume never equalled on the English Stage. Every character will appear in the precise HABIT OF THE PERIOD, the whole of the Dresses and Decorations being executed from undisputed Authorities, such as Monumental Effigies, Seals, Illumined Mss &c. . . ." The costume for another production, *Richard III* (Forrest Collection, Birmingham Public Library), illustrates Planché's manner. It was to dominate illustrations and theater sets for nearly a century—prolifically (but with variable success and critical acclaim) in the designs commissioned by Charles Kean, and with brilliance and scholarly discrimination in the work of Edward W. Godwin.

The visual transition from the age of Charles Kemble and Edmund Kean to that of Charles Kean is revealed quite tellingly by a verbal quirk. In the work undertaken for William Macready and Samuel Phelps we hear less of scenery than of painting. More significant, two kinds of artist intermingle their talents: the professional scene-painting families, notably the Telbins and the Grieves, who span the whole of the nineteenth century; and the painters, in particular Clarkson Stanfield and W. R. Beverley, whose work could be admired equally at the Royal Academy and the public theater. Stanfield's diorama for Macready's *Henry V* at Covent Garden in June 1839 drew from *The Times* the tribute: "We scarcely know whether most to admire the care, taste, and research displayed in the design, or the beauty of the execution.''

Charles Kean's productions at the Princess's Theatre carried the tradition to excess. So minute was the research undertaken (as we see in the play-bills and souvenirs) and so prolific the scenes designed (mainly by Grieves, Lloyds, Telbin, and Dayes) that it is difficult to isolate one work for critical examination. The 1853 *Macbeth* probably serves best. Kean's long and scholarly introduction to the published acting version (a reprint of the first fold of the playbill) cites, among others, Diodorus Siculus, Strabo, Pliny, Du Cange, and Dr. John Smith, D.D., who translated a life of St. Columba in 1798. The principal setting, by Robert James Gordon (a drawing in the Victoria and Albert Museum), indicates the success with which Kean had attained his aim of depicting the costume and daily living of a "Highlander of the eleventh century."

This conscientious pedantry was sometimes attacked by the dramatic criticism of the day, but, more potently, it was undermined by the paintings of the Pre-Raphaelites. Ford Madox Brown comments on his *Lear and Cordelia* (Tate Gallery) that accuracy in costume and setting would have been attainable in his painting, "but I have rather chosen to be in harmony with the mental characteristics of Shakespeare's work."

A sane equipoise is reached in the work of the finest artist in the theater in the second half of the century. Godwin's articles on the architecture and costume of Shakespeare's plays in *The Architect* in 1874–1875 were reprinted by his son, Gordon Craig, in *The Mask* (1908–1912). Craig quotes Godwin tellingly in his criticism of the paintings in the Academy in 1865: "The accessories in pictures, whether on canvas or on the stage, should be altogether wrong or wholly right." His comment on this statement illuminates both his own mature practice and Godwin's: "This suggestion that they may be altogether 'wrong,' that is to say incorrect,

64. Set design by Robert James Gordon for Kean's 1853 production of *Macbeth*.

65. *Lear and Cordelia,* by Ford Madox Brown (1849–1854).

is very illuminating. . . . Either the producer was to represent that purely imaginative realm of the poetic drama removed from all realities, furnished and peopled with purely imaginative forms, or to give a reflection of reality as clear as the reflection of Narcissus in the pool." Godwin prepared a detailed brief for *The Merchant of Venice,* acute in its sense of architectural history and wholly assimilable to the contemporary theater. Squire Bancroft performed the play in April 1875, and it would seem, from critical descriptions, that he came very near to realizing Godwin's intentions. In the absence of any illustrative material we rely on the *Times* report (19 April) for an indication of the visual revolution that Godwin had initiated: "It is scarcely possible to convey in writing an approximation of the manner in which, in conformity with this distribution [of scenes], a picture of old Venice is presented. No attempt is made to emulate the gorgeous revivals of Mr. Charles Kean, but the

most thorough feeling for finish and propriety prevails throughout."

The way was clear for the clarity and sober theatricality that the succeeding generations brought about, the generation of Harley Granville-Barker, William Poel, and Gordon Craig. Visually there was an abundance of theater material; but the new idea, of setting the stage with suggestive simplicity to allow the verbal complexities and the intricacies of dramatic construction to come through, is most potently demonstrated in the Cranach Press edition of *Hamlet* (1930) prepared for Count Harry Kessler, who said of Craig's influence: "It must have been about 1900 [in fact 1903] when the first stage scenes that he created for his mother, Ellen Terry, astounded London by their almost fanatical simplification and their turning away from realism. While the Meiningen Company and, in England, Beerbohm Tree were making the stage into a branch of the Arts and Crafts Museum, piling up

66. Woodcut from Act III, scene 3 of *Hamlet,* by Gordon Craig (1930).

67. Set design for *Measure for Measure,* by John Piper.

accurate historical detail, people found that Craig had used for Ibsen's *The Vikings* only curtain as background and only such properties as were indispensable to the action.'' The woodcut from the Cranach *Hamlet,* "Now might I do it pat," accurately depicts Craig's spareness.

The last half-century has seen only sporadic attempts to unify the vision of the painter, the musician, and the director in presenting the words of Shakespeare in their greatest import. Distinguished artists have invaded the theater to good effect for single productions: James Pryde designing *Othello* in 1930, Michael Ayrton and John Minton setting *Macbeth* for John Gielgud in 1942, Leslie Harry designing both the Robert Helpmann ballet and the Old Vic *Hamlet* in 1944. The production that united all the arts to give us one of the greatest Lears of our age was that directed by George Devine at Stratford-upon-Avon in 1953; Michael Redgrave played Lear, John Gardner wrote brilliantly economical music, and Robert Colquhoun designed costumes and a set, both sculpturesque and pictorial, that reinforced every nuance of the dramatic movement between barbaric splendor and

dereliction. This simple production would suffice to show that the artist need no longer be a decorator of scenes.

John Piper's settings for Benjamin Britten's *A Midsummer Night's Dream* (itself a brilliant critical commentary in music on Shakespeare's play), established new standards for the artist commissioned to design Shakespeare for the stage. The original drawings for Britten's *Dream* have not survived but the quality of Piper's insight into Shakespeare may be judged by this drawing for an unrealized setting of *Measure for Measure.* Sadly, our major companies have lacked the courage—or the stature—to venture upon a collaboration with artists of great eminence. Their work, such as that by Eric Ravilious for the Golden Cockerel Press *Twelfth Night* (1932) and Thomas P. Robinson for the Players' Shakespeare *Midsummer Night's Dream* (1941), has appeared almost wholly in illustrated editions, posing little threat to "directors' theater." An outstanding work of this kind was the series of murals for Morley College by Edward Bawden. And there is room for the swift artist's impression in the theater, as a drawing by Eric Griffiths (Art Director of

68. Opening tableau of Stratford-upon-Avon's 1983 production of *Comedy of Errors,* by Eric Griffiths.

69. Preliminary ink drawing by Josef Herman, for the "Shakespeare in Art" exhibition (1964).

Sculpture for Royal Doulton) shows in deftly re-creating the opening tableau of Stratford-upon-Avon's 1983 *Comedy of Errors.*

We must close with a large-scale work by Josef Herman, which concluded and crowned the exhibition "Shakespeare in Art," mounted by the Arts Council of Great Britain for the Shakespeare quatercentenary in 1964. It was the only specially commissioned work in an exhibition that spanned the full three centuries of "visual Shakespeare." Herman himself describes the emerging image:

Eventually the human bundle lay passively midst rocks and stones on bare earth, a heath on which nothing could grow. . . . In the distance, far from the human bundle, on the horizon, I painted the Fool sitting on a low heap of pebbles, playing a flute, totally unconcerned with Lear's fate. . . .

There exists no such scene in Shakespeare's *King Lear.* But everything in the second act suggests the gradual intensification of Lear's loneliness and grief which culminates in the wretchedness of madness. Except for the moment of dying, human isolation cannot go further.

("The Painter and Literature," in English Association, *Essays and Studies,* 1977)

The finished painting is now in a private collection, but this preliminary ink drawing declares more vividly than anything since Runciman's *Lear* the critical penetration, the formal and emotional illumination, that the artist can bring to the words of Shakespeare. It is astonishing that this powerful tool of visual criticism still lies comparatively neglected, while analytical verbosity goes untrammeled.

Shakespeare in Music

ELLEN T. HARRIS

Composers have long been inspired by the beauty of Shakespeare's lyrics, by the strength of his drama, and by the richness of his characters. Shakespearean song settings abound, operas proliferate, and instrumental music continues to be composed. Two recent catalogs (both 1964) of Shakespearean music list, for example, 124 settings of "It was a lover and his lass," fourteen operas based on *Hamlet,* twenty-four operas based on *Romeo and Juliet,* and thirty-six instrumental works based on *The Tempest.* To cover a subject of such magnitude with analytic and historical thoroughness in the present essay would be impossible. A closer look at the catalogs, however, reveals that many of the Shakespearean compositions warrant less than full scrutiny, for much musical mediocrity lurks in these lists. Although a thorough study of every score might well reveal some music unjustly obscure, in this essay no effort has been made to be comprehensive. I have tried instead to present the basic historical outlines of the vast repertoire of Shakespearean music and to illuminate that history with a look at musical practices in a few selected compositions. For clarity, the study is divided into three parts, each representing a different musical medium and a different aspect of the Shakespearean influence: songs based on original texts, operas based on adaptations of the plays, and orchestral music influenced by the characters and conflicts of the dramas.

Shakespeare and Song

There are three sources of lyrics for Shakespearean songs: the songs from the plays, other verses from the plays, and the Sonnets. The words that composers have most often been drawn to set are the song lyrics. These texts were meant for musical settings, and by and large they are constructed according to the principles for sung text summarized by John Dryden in the preface to his libretto for the opera *Albion and Albanius* (1685). The lyrics are short; they use rhymes (sometimes double); they contain short verses (sometimes of different lengths); they use frequent stops; they often contain a refrain; and they emphasize open vowel sounds rather than "clogg'd consonants." The songs from *The Tempest,* for example, fit this description well. Ariel's song of freedom follows all of the stipulations:

> Where the bee sucks, there suck I;
> In a cowslip's bell I lie;
> There I couch when owls do cry.
> On the bat's back I do fly
> After summer merrily.
Merrily, merrily shall I live now
Under the blossom that hangs on the bough.

(V. 1)

Note especially the lack of consonants at the ends of lines. In the song of Juno and Ceres (IV. i), Shakespeare additionally employs double rhyme:

plenty/empty, growing/bowing, and farthest/harvest. Ariel's two magical songs (I. ii)—"Come unto these yellow sands" and "Full fathom five"—also follow the pattern described by Dryden. The former especially contains irregular verse lengths; both songs have refrains. In fact, all of the most popular song texts follow the criteria later set down by Dryden; and these songs, not surprisingly, come predominantly from the comedies.

The Sonnets have never been as popular for song texts. Only Richard Simpson (d. 1876) set them all; his compositions, however, remain largely unpublished. Mario Castelnuovo-Tedesco set thirty-two (Op. 125, 1944–1945), all of which remain unpublished, and Dmitri Kabalevsky set ten (1953–1954); but Igor Stravinsky's setting of "Music to hear, why hear'st thou music sadly" (1953) is the only sonnet setting generally known. The reason for the relative paucity of musical settings of the Sonnets, as for the popularity of the lyrics from the plays, lies in their construction. They have long verses of even length (decasyllabic); the verses are often constructed with enjambment; and most importantly, the language is elevated. The fixed form combined with a consummate use of language creates a poem finished in itself with no need of music for completion. In this, the Sonnets and lyrics are diametrically opposed. Compare, for example, the following verses.

Blow, blow, thou winter wind,
Thou art not so unkind
As man's ingratitude:
Thy tooth is not so keen,
Because thou art not seen,
Although thy breath be rude.
Heigh-ho, sing heigh-ho, unto the green holly.
Most friendship is faining, most loving mere folly:
Then heigh-ho, the holly.
This life is most jolly.

(*As You Like It*, II. vii)

Then let not winter's ragged hand deface
In thee thy summer ere thou be distilled.
Make sweet some vial; treasure thou some place
With beauty's treasure ere it be self-killed.

(*Sonnet 6*, 1–4)

The first, one of the most popular song texts, contains simple images in short, uneven verses that can be molded without damage into different musical lengths and shapes. The second, which remains unset except by Simpson, contains difficult imagery in long sweeping lines that resist conformity to regular musical structures or metrical patterns.

Composers have occasionally chosen texts from outside the repertoire of the lyrics and Sonnets. For example, the first few verses of "I know a bank" from *A Midsummer Night's Dream* (II. i), with their vibrant depiction of a flower-covered shore, have been popular. Similarly, the lines from *The Merchant of Venice* beginning "How sweet the moonlight" (V. i) have frequently been set; music is directly invoked in these lines: "Here we will sit and let the sounds of music / Creep in our ears." In other cases, passages have become well known as song texts because of the popularity of a single setting. For example, Ralph Vaughan Williams set Prospero's magnificent speech from *The Tempest,* "The cloud-capp'd tow'rs" (IV. i), and Joseph Haydn set Violet's lines beginning with "She never told her love" from *Twelfth Night* (II. iv). All four of these excerpts are, like the Sonnets, in decasyllabic verse and also, like the Sonnets, are used rarely as song texts.

The greater popularity of the lyrics as song texts is due only in part to the technical reasons of construction and content. Practical reasons exist as well. The song lyrics are set more frequently in part because of their use in stage productions. In fact, Shakespearean songs can be divided musically into two distinct groups, depending on whether the settings were intended as part of a theatrical performance.

Perhaps the best known of the Shakespearean songs written for the theater are those that Thomas Augustine Arne composed for performances at Drury Lane and Covent Garden between 1740 and 1760. Excluding those songs written for Shakespearean productions but with texts by another author, nine Shakespearean song settings by Arne survive from six plays (representing, however, only five productions, for the two songs from *Love's Labor's Lost* were inserted into *As You Like It* to be sung by Celia). All were written for either Kitty Clive or Thomas Lowe, neither of whom had a trained voice. In *A General History of Music,* Charles Burney wrote of Clive that "her singing, which was intolerable when she meant it to be fine, in ballad farces and songs of humour, was, like her comic acting, every thing it should be." Burney described Lowe as having "the finest tenor voice I ever heard in my life" but noted that "for want of diligence and cultivation, . . . [he] could never be trusted with any thing better than a ballad, which he constantly learned by ear.'' Composing for such singer-actors places limitations on the vocal style and compass and denies the composer a free hand to express the text musically. Rather, the music accompanies the lyrics and, ideally, heightens them.

Arne's songs, if not exhilarating or profound, are at least charming. They frequently include both echo and question-and-answer between the voice and the accompaniment. Sometimes Arne combines this technique with bird calls, as in "When daisies pied" (cuckoo) and "When icicles hang" (owl). Arne also uses word painting. For example, in "Under the greenwood tree" he sets the word "turn" to a musical turn and emphasizes "rough weather" with the harsh interval of the tritone, and in "Where the bee sucks" he allows an extended vocal melisma on the verb "fly". In some songs, Arne adds musical interest to his simple accompaniments by means of counterpoint, and in such instances the accompaniment picks up the word painting. In "Under the greenwood tree," the bird mentioned in the text is alluded to in the recorder part; and in "Tell me where is fancy bred," the "fancy" seems to appear in the pervasive triplets of the violin, while the voice remains generally within the notated simple meter. In the latter case Arne may have been making a musical pun, for fantasias, or fancies, often highlighted just such rhythmic and metric ambiguity. Burney wrote of Arne that "he introduced a light, airy, original, and pleasing melody . . . [that] forms an aera in English Music; it was so easy, natural and agreeable to the whole kingdom, that it had an effect on national taste . . . [and] was the standard of all perfection at our theatres and public gardens."

More than a century later, the same striving for vocal simplicity appears in the only Shakespearean songs written by Johannes Brahms: the five songs of Ophelia (translated into German by Ludwig Tieck and August Wilhelm Schlegel) composed in 1873 for Olga Precheisen to sing at a production of *Hamlet* in Prague. The accompaniments follow and support the voice by doubling it at pitch. The rhythms are even and regular; the melodies move within a small compass. As a result the songs often sound like folk melodies or hymn tunes. Although newly composed by Brahms, the music seems commonplace, and the listener assumes that Ophelia is remembering snatches of this or that. Her confusion and utter desolation are shown by her singing these pseudofamiliar melodies in an inappropriate context. Ophelia has lost touch with reality, and

Brahms's songs express this clearly on the stage. But it is the situation, not the music, that is dramatic; and perhaps for this reason Brahms later derided his songs as "make work."

Generally speaking, lyrical songs, such as those set by Arne, survive better out of the theater than dramatic songs, such as those set by Brahms, which are too closely tied to their function within the play. Many composers, however, have been drawn to the lyrical and dramatic aspects of Shakespeare's words without the impetus of a stage production. In these songs the music takes on greater importance. For example, Richard Strauss's six *Ophelien Lieder* (1919) were never intended for a theatrical production; and as concert pieces they stand outside any dramatic context that might infuse them with meaning. Thus, in the tradition of "mad songs," the music, not the text, tells the story, carries the meaning, and relays the singer's confusion and instability. Whereas Brahms's Ophelia songs make their effect by using commonplace music in an inappropriate dramatic situation, Strauss's songs use commonplace words with agitated and dissonant music. This difference is immediately clear in the openings of the first songs. Strauss creates rhythmic agitation in the accompaniment through the constant syncopation of the chords, and he increases the tension by adding a chromatic melody in anticipation of the voice and then insistently hammering out the dissonant interval of the tritone. He maintains this accompaniment after the entry of the voice, whose melody is broken up into little fragments. Brahms, on the other hand, uses no independent accompaniment, and his melody comprises four parallel phrases that are hymnlike and without rests.

Franz Schubert composed songs to three Shakespearean texts, two of which have become justly popular: "Horch, horch, die Lerch" ("Hark, hark, the lark" from *Cymbeline*) and "Was ist Sylvia?" ("Who is Sylvia?" from *The Two Gentlemen of Verona*). Although lyrical, like Arne's songs, both were written outside the theatrical tradition. They make their effect not by striking dramatic means but rather through their tuneful, strophic simplicity. The long vocal phrases, however, require the singer's support and strength, especially for the upper tones. Thus, despite their simplicity, these songs are not for the amateur or singing actor. The uncomplicated form and harmony, the tunefulness, and the regularity of the rhythm reflect the innocence of the texts, which would be suffocated by untoward sophistication. However, by freeing the voice from the accompaniment (unlike most of the theatrical songs) and by molding the lyrics into long phrases, Schubert allows his melody to soar.

Songs written to texts other than lyrics from the plays follow the tradition of the concert songs. Haydn's setting (1795) of "She never told her love," from *Twelfth Night,* may be the first example of a song taken from the spoken text of a play. It draws heavily on the conventions of classical opera, including a long introduction full of textural and dynamic contrast. The abbreviated text (Haydn omits a line and a half from the middle) is stretched out by repetition and by piano interludes, and the music reacts violently to the content of each line or half-line, thereby creating a song of great dramatic contrasts. It was this kind of approach to texts other than songs that led to the many Shakespearean operatic settings of the nineteenth century.

Following this explosion of Shakespearean opera, twentieth-century composers have retreated somewhat from the strikingly dramatic approach to song composition apparent in Haydn and Strauss. The songs of this century tend more toward the lyrical, often through a folk idiom like that employed by Virgil Thomson in his Shakespeare songs. Stravinsky's setting (1953) of Shakespeare's Sonnet 8, "Music to hear," although certainly not a folk song, also emphasizes the lyrical mode. The composer has chosen a text with a strong musical metaphor: both people and notes are better when wedded in concord than when single. The text could easily resonate with additional meanings to a twentieth-century composer, however. Lines such as "Music to hear, why hear'st thou music sadly?" or "If the true concord of well-tunèd sounds, / By unions married, do offend thine ear, / They do but sweetly chide thee" could speak directly to the modern composer, who is often in conflict with his audience. Furthermore, the rigidity of the verse structure and the esoteric language remove Shakespeare's Sonnets, like much contemporary music, from the popular domain. Stravinsky was probably drawn to this poem, therefore, by the relation of its content, language, and structure to modern music and its acceptance. He sets the text by devising a four-note motivic cell based on a fixed intervallic pattern. This set can be varied by beginning on different pitches and by inversion—either by melody or by interval. Stravinsky underscores the sonnet form by repeating at pitch his original group of three sets at the beginning of the first two quatrains

and final couplet; but even more importantly, the seemingly rigid compositional technique mirrors the poetic structure, which depends on fixed verse lengths and fixed rhyme patterns that often conflict with freer sentence structure and phrase rhythm. In the hands of lesser artists, sonnet form and serial composition can become dry and mechanical, but Shakespeare and Stravinsky both excel in overcoming the potential limitations of structure. Stravinsky's song is light and lyrical; its message may well be its apparent effortlessness.

In a way, Stravinsky's interest in structure brings full circle the concern for structural appropriateness so apparent in the seventeenth century. At first, only the lyrics from the plays were considered suitable for musical setting—and then usually in a theatrical production. But by the late nineteenth century, composers began to treat the sonnets, too, as appropriate song texts despite the seventeenth-century "rules." (Although Henry Lawes set an anonymous variant of Sonnet 116 before 1659 [beginning, in Lawes's setting, "Self-blinding error seazeth all"], these poems were not used frequently as song texts until about 1875.) In the meantime, composers also began to treat the spoken portion of Shakespeare's plays as suitable for musical setting. With a few forgotten exceptions, this trend can be said to have begun with Haydn.

As composers began to reach toward other portions of Shakespeare's works, stepping outside the theatrical tradition to the concert stage, it was only natural that Shakespearean opera should develop. In these works the word itself loses its primacy; what remains of Shakespeare is the dramatic situation and conflict.

Operatic Treatments

Operatic composers are not drawn to Shakespeare's plays by the beauty of the language or the structure of the verse. What is primary is the emphasis on strong passions, characters, and conflict. For this reason, the comedies that contain most of the favorite song texts have rarely been set as operas. *As You Like It,* for example, can boast of only two operatic adaptations: Veracini's *Rosalinda* (1744) and Florence Wickham's *Rosalind* (1938). Of the plays popular for their song lyrics, the two fairy plays, *A Midsummer Night's Dream* and *The Tempest,* have been used most frequently—fourteen and thirty-one times, respectively—but the settings fall predominantly outside the nineteenth century. In seventeenth- and eighteenth-century England these two plays were operatic favorites because the fairy element lent a touch of verisimilitude to the continual singing. *Macbeth*, too, was put in this category on account of the witches. In the twentieth century the fairy plays seem to have found favor again because they lend themselves to utterly fantastical treatment. On the other hand, nineteenth-century composers seeking passion and character development in their librettos found it in *Romeo and Juliet* (eight settings), *The Merry Wives of Windsor* (four), *Macbeth* (five), and *Othello* (two).

Operatic treatment of Shakespeare began during the Restoration with the literary adaptations written by Sir William Davenant *(Macbeth)* and John Dryden *(The Tempest)*. In these works, called "dramatic operas" or "semi-operas," the torso of a play was used to sustain a succession of musical interludes combining chorus, solo song, and dance. Often the texts for the musical sections did not derive from the original play but were newly written for the adaptation. For example, the music written by Henry Purcell for *The Fairy-Queen* (1692), which is based on *A Midsummer Night's Dream*, occurs in discrete sections placed at the ends of the five acts. These are meant to serve as entertainments for Titania and are sung by her fairies. The main characters—the young lovers, Theseus, Hippolyta, Titania, and Oberon—do not sing, and Purcell never sets any of Shakespeare's own words.

In the middle of the eighteenth century, three all-sung Shakespearean operas were performed in London: Veracini's *Rosalind* (1744), mentioned above, and two operas by John Christopher Smith, *The Fairies* (*A Midsummer Night's Dream*, 1755) and *The Tempest* (1756). All were heavily altered. In the late eighteenth century, however, the number of Shakespearean operas on the Continent exploded concurrently with the rise of realistic comic opera. In the era of *The Barber of Seville* and *The Marriage of Figaro*, it is no surprise to find *The Merry Wives of Windsor* suddenly an extremely popular libretto. At the same time, multiple settings of *Romeo and Juliet* heralded the romantic era. None of the late-eighteenth-century operatic versions of these two plays, however, is as important as the adaptations that followed in the nineteenth century: for example, Charles Gounod's *Roméo et Juliette* (1867), Otto Nicolai's *Die lustigen Weiber von Windsor* (1849), and Verdi's *Falstaff* (1893). Shakespearean operas have continued to be writ-

ten in the twentieth century. In addition, particularly fine adaptations have been created for the Broadway stage: Richard Rodgers' *The Boys from Syracuse* (*The Comedy of Errors*, 1938), Cole Porter's *Kiss Me Kate* (*The Taming of the Shrew*, 1948), and Leonard Bernstein's *West Side Story* (*Romeo and Juliet*, 1957).

All operatic adaptations follow similar principles in revising the original texts. Since words, because of the sustenance of sound and musical repetition, take much longer to sing than to speak, a play must be cut. This is done in a number of ways. First, subsidiary plots and characters are reduced or eliminated, allowing attention to be focused on the main story. Second, scenes based on punning or wordplay are omitted, as they lose most of their effectiveness when set to music. Third, long philosophical texts are also eliminated; lacking passion or drama, they are deemed inappropriate to musical setting. Fourth, the societal background is usually eliminated; the passion displayed is thus intended to be independent of both time and place. Finally, where it is not already the main focus, the love interest is increased.

Gounod's *Roméo et Juliette* serves as an example. The four opening scenes depicting the quarrel between the Montagues and Capulets are cut, thereby eliminating much punning and wordplay, as well as long speeches by Capulet and the Nurse. It also leaves out the social context of the feud in which the action unfolds. In this regard it is also striking that the opera ends with Juliet's death, thus eliminating the discovery of the bodies and the reconciliation of the parents. Indeed, Montague is omitted entirely, as is the Nurse, whose comic and bawdy role adds such earthiness to the play. Friar Laurence's role is also much reduced; in particular, his beautiful speech beginning "The grey-eyed morn smiles on the frowning night" (II. iii. 1) is cut. These alterations change the story from one about families to one about passion. That we are left with only the title characters—and little else—illustrates the greatly reduced importance of Shakespeare's own words in operatic adaptations. No play that develops an intricate character motivation through the subtlety of language can serve without adaptation as an opera libretto.

Still, with all that is cut, there remains in great Shakespearean operas a strong scaffold for musical setting. It is an error to compare librettos with the Shakespearean plays on which they are based and dismiss the adaptations as having little or no literary value. Without their scores these librettos are incomplete. The music adds the most important dramatic content to the finished opera, often serving to replace much of the lost text, for music can convey quickly and effectively what it might take pages of words to accomplish. Arrigo Boito, a composer who was also the librettist for three Shakespearean adaptations—Franco Faccio's *Amleto* (1865) and Verdi's *Otello* (1887) and *Falstaff*—understood this well. During the composition of *Otello,* he wrote to Verdi:

> An opera is not a play; our art lives by elements unknown to spoken tragedy. An atmosphere that has been destroyed can be created all over again. Eight bars are enough to restore a sentiment to life; a rhythm can re-establish a character; music is the most omnipotent of all the arts; it has a logic all its own—both freer and more rapid than the logic of spoken thought, and much more eloquent.
>
> (Quoted in Julian Budden, *The Operas of Verdi,* III, 303)

Music can be used, as in Nicolai's *Die lustigen Weiber von Windsor,* to underscore characterization. In Shakespeare's play one finds many deliberate pairings and cross-pairings of characters by resemblance or contrast. Mistress Ford and Mistress Page are paired by their receipt of identical letters from Falstaff. Slender and Dr. Caius are the two unsuitable suitors. Dr. Caius and Sir Hugh Evans are verbal antagonists with risible accents; both are duped by the Host. The Host and Mistress Quickly both deal in deception, and Falstaff, when he accepts Ford-Brook's offer, is also paired with Quickly, who will do any errand if she is well paid. Nym and Pistol are paired in wanting revenge on Falstaff; Shallow also wants revenge on Falstaff, and Falstaff in his wooing pairs himself unintentionally with the two foolish lovers. Ford and Caius are insanely jealous; Slender and Shallow are both dim-witted.

In Nicolai's libretto, by Salomon Hermann Mosenthal, much is omitted. The elimination of ten characters (Shallow, Sir Hugh Evans, Pistol, Nym, the Host, and Mistress Quickly among them) serves also to reduce the subplots and the social context. Falstaff is no longer seen as a person against whom many have grudges, and the fight between Evans and Caius (in a scene containing much punning and wordplay) is deleted. (In the libretto, the names of the characters from Shakespeare's play are not all retained; to facilitate a comparison of the works, the Shakespearean names are used here.)

The opera begins with the wives reading their letters together, for the only plots remaining are Falstaff's attempted love affairs and the wooing of Anne Page. Indeed, the love interest between Anne and Fenton is greatly expanded; in the opera, Act II contains an extended love scene between the young couple that is surreptitiously watched by Caius and Slender. This is all newly written material.

The libretto, which follows all of the conventions of adaptation listed above, is thus much less rich than Shakespeare's text. But Nicolai's music sustains the idea of pairings so evident and important in the play. The composer oversaw much of the writing of the libretto and described in a letter to Mosenthal the characters as he envisioned them:

> Mrs. Ford: a young, pretty, merry woman, 20 years old . . . Mrs. Page: a well-preserved woman of 35, lively but less so than her friend, Mrs. Ford . . . Anne Page, her daughter, 17, much in love, beautiful, sentimental, but not too much so . . . Mr. Ford, 40, violent, very jealous and energetic (The most important male part in the opera) . . . Fenton, 25, heart and head in the right place, really loves Anne . . . Mr. Page, 50, fat, very miserly, phlegmatic. Falstaff . . . Falstaff.

These descriptions illustrate changes. In particular, it is surprising to find Mrs. Ford and Mrs. Page separated by fifteen years and Mrs. Ford and Anne Page only three years apart. But this restructuring enables Nicolai to create flexible pairings that differ from, but are stylistically similar to, Shakespeare's original. He uses two means: vocal range and duet pairings.

Mrs. Ford and Anne are shown to be young and similar in age by being sopranos. Deep love is portrayed by the use of coloratura: Anne's one aria, "Wohl denn! Gefasst is der Entschluss—O selige Träume," shows her taking flight musically and emotionally. Mrs. Ford well remembers these feelings, for she herself is still young. When she ponders how to respond to Falstaff, therefore, she immediately picks up the mode of flowery coloratura. In her aria "Verführer! Warum stellt ihr so," she parodies the singing style that Anne will later use; the setting in this aria of the words "I love you" is marked to be sung "with caricature."

Slender, Caius, Fenton, and Falstaff are all wooers. Nicolai pairs Slender and Fenton vocally by making them tenors; Caius and Falstaff are basses. Slender and Fenton are lovesick and lack self-assurance. As in the musical relationship between Mrs. Ford and Anne, Slender's repeated and mooning outbursts of "O süsse Anna!" caricature the deeper, truer and extended lyricism of Fenton's aria, "Horch, die Lerche singt im Haine."

Caius and Falstaff, on the other hand, both exude self-confidence and woo with bravado. In his first entrance, Caius sings repeated sixteenth notes on a single tone as he threatens to kill Slender; he is referred to as a rooster. Falstaff's entrance is preceded by a fanfare; he is another rooster who enters preening. Military motives recur regularly in both wooers' music.

Nicolai makes other pairings clear in his duets. Love duets are traditionally composed so that the voices begin apart and gradually move together to a unison, a musical consummation. Nicolai uses this technique to show who is united with whom musically. Mrs. Ford and Mrs. Page in their opening duet take turns reading their identical letters, but they sing the signature—John Falstaff—in unison, and much of the rest of the duet in parallel thirds.

The opera offers other examples of this technique. In Act II, Ford comes to Falstaff disguised as Brook. They sing in alternation and then agree upon a plan that has each of them deceiving the other. At the words "I look ahead with great anticipation; we both shall reach our goal today and find our consolation" they come together in unison—two deceitful men who belittle women's morality. Anne and Fenton, the only couple who are united in the course of the play, are united musically as well. At the words "Long ago my heart decided (and you're mine for evermore)" they arrive at a unison. Anne's successful scheming leads to her marriage to Fenton. Promoted to the role of a "Merry Wife," she joins the other two wives in the epilogue.

This technique is not used where it would be inappropriate. Although Mr. and Mrs. Ford sing a duet, they are not united in thought, and their opposition is maintained musically throughout. Similarly Mr. Page and Fenton remain opposed musically throughout their one duet. Like the best Shakespearean operas, *Die lustigen Weiber von Windsor* sensitively relates in music an integral part of the original—in this case by carefully maintaining Shakespeare's concept of paired characters.

Another important aspect of musical settings, and one that can be found equally in Gounod's *Roméo et Juliette* and Benjamin Britten's *A Midsummer Night's Dream* (1960), is the use of closure. Because themes, harmonies, and rhythms can be restated exactly, it is possible to enclose an aria, scene, or act in repetition and have it represent an extended or frozen moment. This glorification (and seemingly endless expansion) of single moments is typical of opera. In the example most ripe for parody, the hero challenges his adversary to a duel and pauses for an elaborate aria about his emotions before making the first thrust. In opera, verisimilitude is as much stretched by the distortion of time as by the singing itself; and musical, as opposed to real, time exists especially within the closed forms of music.

This kind of closure often has a striking impact on the opera's dramatic shape. In Shakespeare's *Romeo and Juliet* the lovers are carefully placed within a social context; although their love blooms and grows outside societal restraints, it also serves as the means for social reconciliation. In Gounod's opera, the social context is lacking, but the lovers are still carefully separated from the other characters by the use of musical closure. Their first three love scenes are closed, and the last, in the tomb, is infused with musical reminiscences of the third love scene, their wedding night.

Act I, encompassing the ball, is naturally closed by the recurrent strain of the dance music. This theme accompanies the opening chorus, "L'heure s'envole," and continues in the background during the following conversation. After Capulet has introduced his daughter and sung the welcoming song "Allons! jeunes gens!" the dance music swells again into the foreground.

When Roméo and his friends enter, the dance theme is again suppressed. Mercutio sings of Queen Mab, and events now follow one another with great speed. Juliette sings her aria, "Je veux vivre dans le rêve"; Juliette and Roméo meet and sing a duet, "Ange adorable"; and Roméo's identity is revealed. When the fighting breaks out, Capulet and his guests try to restore the good humor by singing a reprise of "Allons! jeunes gens!" The act ends with the dance theme once again flooding in.

How long does all this action take? Nothing close to the time it takes to sing, unless one wants to argue that Capulet has requested his orchestra to play one tune all evening. Thus, musical time governs this first act in a series of frozen moments. The opening chorus, Capulet's song, and Mercutio's song are all closed harmonically and melodically in the form ABA. Each is merely an interruption of normal time. Juliette's song, too, is written in ABA form with a coda for vocal display. When Roméo and Juliette meet, time stands still, and Gounod makes this particularly apparent when Juliette realizes Roméo's identity. Standing dazed amid the tumult, she sings a series of repeated notes over a single repeated chord. The action around her must freeze; it and the agitated music resume immediately after she finishes. The reprise of "Allons! jeunes gens!" and the dance music then close the act.

Just as this act is musically closed, so, too, are the two impassioned love scenes. The balcony scene (Act II) and the wedding-night scene (Act IV, scene 1) both begin with clearly stated orchestral themes that close the scenes as well; like the dance tune, they are never sung. At the end of Act II, after Juliette's exit, Roméo sings repeated notes while the act tune wells up; at the end of Act IV, scene 1, after Roméo's exit, Juliette sings against the orchestral tune.

That Gounod places the lovers in their own world by this musical means is all the more apparent by contrast to the open-ended nature of the other scenes. The wedding at Friar Laurence's cell, the street fight leading to the deaths of Mercutio and Tybalt, and the scene between Capulet and his daughter leading to Friar Laurence's plan all push forward musically and dramatically to a climax. None is closed by musical means.

The final act ends with the deaths of Roméo and Juliette; the tomb scene is expanded, however, by David Garrick's textual additions in which the lovers have a scene together before Roméo dies. Because of the dramatic nature of the action, the scene is not closed, but Gounod re-creates the lovers' world by reprising music from their wedding night. Roméo's impassioned song to the apparently dead Juliette "O ma femme!" is sung to the Act IV, scene 1, theme. Just before Roméo takes the poison, this theme, now agitated rhythmically, recurs in the orchestra. After revealing to Juliette that he has taken poison, Roméo becomes delirious and reprises his song from Act IV, scene 1, insisting that he hears the nightingale, not the lark. And after Juliette stabs herself, the lovers' final embrace is accompanied by the orchestral interlude that had accompanied their final embrace on their wedding night. Thus, Gounod has achieved a kind of closure in Act V by using musical motives familiar from another

scene. But now the end is different. Instead of separating, and having the moment die, the lovers, singing in unison, find death and eternal union in each other's arms. Whereas in Shakespeare the lovers transcend society, in Gounod they transcend time.

In Britten's *A Midsummer Night's Dream* these techniques of closure are used to depict the timelessness of fairyland and sleep. The time span in Shakespeare's play is itself problematic, and various commentators have assessed it in various ways. Britten's response to the play best coincides with the interpretation of George Lyman Kittredge: "No audience would note [any temporal] discrepancy, for the night in the enchanted forest is long enough to bewilder the imagination. What, indeed, is time in our dreams, especially on a magic midsummer eve?"

Although Britten's adaptation is closer to its original than perhaps any other Shakespearean opera, he, too, eliminates the controlling social framework by beginning not, as Shakespeare does, with Theseus and Hippolyta in Athens but with the fairies in the enchanted wood (II. i of Shakespeare). The lovers are thus first encountered in the wood, but some of their lines from the first act are transferred into this environment. The rustics' first meeting also occurs, somewhat inexplicably, in the wood; the lines from Shakespeare's first act are simply inserted into this new context. Although interrupted with insertions from Act I, Shakespeare's second act (Britten's first) proceeds in order, except that Titania's bewitching is placed at the very end.

These changes permit all of the characters except Theseus and Hippolyta to be introduced in the wood and enable Britten's first act to begin and end with a scene for the fairies. The atmosphere is depicted by a mysterious and unnatural-sounding theme played at first on the lowest strings with *portamento* slides from chord to chord. This theme begins the act, recurs after each group of characters is introduced, and closes the act. All is enchanted within this wood. The "fairy theme" encloses not only the characters but the act as well and lends it timelessness.

The second act represents the enchanted sleep of Titania, Bottom, and the four lovers. It is similarly closed, but its theme is used less pervasively. Only the last act, representing the human world, is directional and open-ended. During this act, all awake restored—first Titania, then the lovers, and finally Bottom. At this point Theseus and Hippolyta appear for the first time. Athens replaces the forest, humans untouched by enchantment appear, and the turn to reality is complete. The royal couple sing their opening lines from Shakespeare's play; and after the lovers enter from the wood, the opera continues with the dialogue in Shakespeare's play spoken when the lovers are discovered in the wood; it then proceeds with the rustics' play, and so on to the end.

By means of judicious cutting (Egeus and Philostrate are omitted completely, for example) and transposition of text, Britten's opera presents three separate worlds progressing gradually from illusion to actuality: from fairy enchantment to restorative sleep, to joyful reality. Only the first two are timeless and musically closed.

Perhaps no composer has ever succeeded in using music to illustrate dramatic change or conflict as well as Giuseppe Verdi. Verdi set three Shakespearean operas: *Macbeth* (1847), *Otello,* and *Falstaff (The Merry Wives of Windsor).* The last two were set to librettos by Boito; the first had a libretto originally coauthored by Francesco Maria Piave and Andrea Maffei that was substantially revised by Piave for the Parisian performances in 1865. The first two of Verdi's Shakespearean operas illustrate many of this composer's techniques.

In his libretto for *Otello,* Boito omits the opening act in Venice and closes with Othello's death, cutting out Lodovico's final speech with its reference to Venice. (The English spellings of names will be used throughout this discussion.) Thus, the societal frame is, as usual, eliminated. This also precludes our knowing the characters before their arrival on Cyprus. In Shakespeare's first act, for example, the audience hears negative reports of Othello from his enemies, sees him placing trust in an avowed foe, and witnesses the Moor's self-assurance and pride in the scene before the senate. Without this introduction, Othello becomes a less complex character. In the opera, Iago can no longer precipitate an action that is logical and natural, given the weaknesses of the other characters; rather, he becomes the sole cause of all the destruction. It is noteworthy that Boito described Othello and Desdemona in purely positive terms; he wrote not that Othello is destroyed by his own jealousy, but that he is "the supreme victim of the tragedy and of Iago."

In Shakespeare's play, then, Othello is much spoken about before he enters, and when he appears, he is on stage throughout the scene, speaking first with Iago and afterward with Brabantio. There follows the scene before the senate. In the second act, when Othello arrives safely on Cyprus, he has three speeches, exits, and reenters to signal the start of festivities. In the opera, on the other hand, the action begins with the storm raging and with Othello's ship foundering off the coast of Cyprus. We learn nothing of Othello. After his entrance, he sings three lines and then exits. His text is not only brief but uninformative:

Rejoice! The mussulman's pride is buried in the sea;
The glory is ours and heaven's!
First our arms, and then the storm defeated him.

In a spoken drama this would undoubtedly be insufficient as an introduction of character. In *Otello,* however, it becomes through the music an absolute depiction of Othello's character.

Just as Boito omitted the first act of the play, Verdi eschews the formal introduction or overture to the opera and—like Boito with the storm—begins musically in *medias res* with no sense of boundary, beginning, or shape. The opening music has no tonal stability, rhythmic coherence, or melodic continuation. Only when Othello enters does the turbulent music settle into a single tonality, bringing closure for the first time. Othello is thus depicted as hugely powerful, for it is he who brings cadence and coherence to the music. His style changes perceptibly, however, when he comes under Iago's spell.

In Act II, when Othello is first affected by Iago's scheming insinuations, he is angered and upset. He says goodbye to a "tranquil mind," "to fame," and "to glory" in music that is still firmly in one key, its rhythms martial; but more and more throughout the brief aria the chromaticism that Verdi uses to characterize Iago emerges in the accompaniment. By the end of the act, Othello as we have known him is indeed lost. In his duet with Iago it is hard at first to make out Othello's part, for so much of it is in monotone. Only when Iago enters do we understand, for it is he who has the melody—who literally is calling the tune. Othello's accompaniment is ultimately fitted to Iago's melody, illustrating clearly that he has lost control over the music and thus over himself and the situation.

By the third act Othello cannot regain his composure even while alone. Just as in the first act his presence was felt musically even after his exit (by the sustenance of his key), Iago's presence is now musically apparent even in his absence. In "Dio! mi potevi scagliar!" (the speech beginning with IV. ii. 48 of Shakespeare), Othello cannot muster a tune but is reduced again to a monotone; he is accompanied, moreover, by Iago's chromatically descending lines, and, worst of all, he maintains no tonal stability.

The changes in Othello's character as depicted musically lead directly to the crisis of the last act. Boito omits the scenes in which Othello questions Emilia about Desdemona's conduct, Desdemona complains of Othello's behavior to Emilia and Iago, and Desdemona and Emilia talk about marriage before Desdemona goes to bed. They would have been overly long and tedious in musical settings, as well as unnecessary, for the use of economical musical gestures has been more than adequate to depict both Desdemona's constancy and Othello's change of character.

In the play, Desdemona retires at the end of Act IV, and Act V begins with the scene in which Roderigo sets upon Cassio and is killed. Only then is a return made to Desdemona's bedchamber for Othello's entrance and his speech beginning "It is the cause, it is the cause, my soul." In the opera Desdemona retires at the beginning of the last act: she says her prayers—as added by Boito—and goes to bed. Immediately Othello enters. There has been no act break, no intermediary scene. In real time Desdemona could not possibly have fallen asleep. But in the opera Othello does not speak. His previous solos have illustrated his degradation, and this musical style would be wholly inappropriate to the text of his soliloquy. Thus, he remains mute. Verdi has the orchestra alone depict his thoughts, taking the drama up without any assistance from the sung word. This orchestral interlude also accounts for the elapsed time that would allow Desdemona to fall asleep. Here Verdi uses musical closure, not like Gounod to expand time, but to contract it; and the interlude takes less time than the various actions would take in reality.

In the play, Othello muses both on the necessity of killing Desdemona and on the method. He draws an analogy between putting out the light and quenching Desdemona's life spark. Drawn to her sleeping form, he kisses her. The relationship of this speech to Verdi's interlude can readily be noted in the specific stage directions in the score: "Othello appears at the threshold . . . he comes forward . . . he lays a scimitar on the table . . . he stands before the candle undecided whether to ex-

tinguish it or not . . . he looks at Desdemona . . . he extinguishes the candle . . . he goes to the bed," and so on. But more important, when Othello leans over to kiss Desdemona, Verdi recalls the music that accompanied the culmination of the love duet of the first act (added by Boito and fashioned out of text from Shakespeare's Act I), where the lovers also kiss. The repetition of this motive signifies not only their kiss, but also their great love, evoking the time when Othello was a different person.

This so-called kiss motive returns once more at the very end of the opera after Othello has stabbed himself. Before he dies, he leans over to kiss Desdemona. Although his last word—*bacio* (kiss)—is given in the libretto, Othello is not given a note for the last syllable, and its omission in the score is Verdi's final stroke of characterization. Othello's inability to complete the obvious cadence, to complete a gesture that had served to characterize him definitively upon his entrance, reveals that not even in death, not even for a moment, can he return to his former glory.

The use of repetitive musical motives and wordless musical speeches also plays an important part in Verdi's *Macbeth*. The overture is of critical importance, and Verdi wrote of it to Piave: "Once it is done I'll leave you all the time you want, because I've got the general character and the color of the opera into my head just as if the libretto were already written."

What can this mean? The overture opens with a short, eerie introduction. Knowing the opera to be *Macbeth,* one might guess that this section represents the witches; and indeed, this music recurs in the Act III scene with the witches. In the overture, then, as in the drama, the witches precipitate the action. The main part of this movement thereafter consists of an opposition of two themes—one violent and loud, the other poignant and lyrical. As they play off one another, the listener is regularly led to expect cadences or closure, but that expectation is always thwarted by deflection, silence, or an onrush of new material. Even the final cadence of the overture continues longer than one might anticipate.

Many commentators, after associating the opening theme with the witches, connect the two main themes with Macbeth and Lady Macbeth. In fact, the beautiful and expressive second theme does recur at the beginning of Lady Macbeth's sleepwalking scene. Nevertheless, this interpretation seems lacking. The operatic Lady Macbeth could not possibly be represented by such a touching theme, for she is truly monstrous. Unlike her literary counterpart, she not only urges the death of Duncan, but also joins with Macbeth in deciding to murder Banquo. She and Macbeth agree to the deaths of Macduff's wife and children, shouting, "Revenge, revenge, revenge, hour of death and of revenge." By the time of the sleepwalking scene, however, Lady Macbeth herself has been destroyed by guilt and is more pitiable than frightening. Surely, then, the theme from the overture used here cannot represent her character, because this is the one scene most unrepresentative of her. Rather, the overture's themes must represent the two emotional states—rage and pity—that suffuse the play and struggle within Macbeth's character. Duncan is killed; his death causes rage and pity. The Macbeths rage against their enemies, but ultimately we must pity the desolation of their lives and their destruction. Rage and pity, two opposing states, form the basis of the play. Macbeth himself realizes this early on, before Duncan's death, in a speech omitted from the opera.

> Besides, this Duncan
> Hath borne his faculties so meek, hath been
> So clear in his great office, that his virtues
> Will plead like angels, trumpet-tongued, against
> The deep damnation of his taking-off;
> And pity, like a naked new-born babe
> Striding the blast, or heaven's cherubin horsed
> Upon the sightless couriers of the air,
> Shall blow the horrid deed in every eye
> That tears shall drown the wind.
>
> (I. vii. 16–25)

The overture contrasts the "trumpet-tongued" outcry, the call for revenge, with the tearful pity. It is as apt a musical representation of this speech as one could ask for.

Such wordless instrumental movements as appear in Verdi's operas—and also, for example, in Hector Berlioz's dramatic symphony *Roméo et Juliette* (1839)—coincided with the emergence of independent programmatic musical movements, called symphonic or tone poems, which attempted to represent extramusical images or ideas in purely musical terms. Many of these works were based on Shakespearean plays. In them, composers dispensed entirely with the text, allowing music alone to tell the story. Most often, this was done by as-sociating a particular theme with each character of the drama.

Orchestral Treatments

Nineteenth-century symphonic music tends to create dramatic effects through the use of strong conflict, usually followed by a resolution of some kind. The sonata principle, which underlies the majority of nineteenth-century orchestral works, relies on this concept: two contrasting themes in opposing key areas are presented (exposition); developed through expansion, fragmentation, juxtaposition, and other means (development); and then restated in the home key (recapitulation). The dramatic character of this form seems to have made composers consider it a perfect vehicle for representing a stage drama: the compositional structure follows dramatic form nicely (statement, crisis, denouement), but it also gives the composition an absolute form apart from any programmatic meaning. Thus, it is possible to hear such works as satisfactory, if not excellent, compositions without ever recognizing the programmatic intent. Indeed, there can never be a one-to-one relationship between a musical theme and a literary character. Without reference to the title—and some imagination—one cannot know that the opening theme of Berlioz's *King Lear* Overture (1831) represents Lear or that the opening of Tchaikovsky's *Romeo and Juliet* Fantasy Overture (1869; revised 1880) represents Friar Laurence. However, when both the plays and the composer's purposes are known, it is possible to guess characters and dramatic situations with ease. The best of these programmatic compositions not only follow the play's story line but also conform to traditional sonata form. The prepared listener can thus be simultaneously delighted by the composer's success at both levels.

Felix Mendelssohn's Overture to *A Midsummer Night's Dream* (1826) is the locus classicus of the genre. It begins with four sustained chords in a cadential progression played by wind instruments. The pattern of closure makes an odd opening; Mendelssohn begins with an end. The restatement of these chords at the end of the overture, however, clarifies their meaning. They are the gateway in and out of fairyland; their cadential structure thus marks a boundary between two worlds. This effect is heightened by having the chords follow a harmonic progression typical of sacred music, which connotation, along with the soft dynamic, adds something of the supernatural, something *misterioso,* to the passage. Like Britten in his later opera, Mendelssohn carefully closes off the fairy world from everyday life.

The fast, staccato, and sprightly first theme, played by the violins, introduces the fairies. Its forward motion is twice interrupted by single chords played by the winds, reminiscent of the opening chords. One has the sense of an intrusion through the gateway by humankind, and, in confirmation of this, the first theme group ends with the regal theme for full orchestra that can later be associated with Theseus and Hippolyta, whose actions precipitate the ensuing disturbance in the wood. (Their wedding is the cause of Titania and Oberon's presence near Athens and the rustics' decision to produce a play; moreover, Theseus' edict leads to the lovers' decisions to enter the wood.)

After a long transition, the second theme group represents the various mortals as they appear: first the lovers, then the rustics with a theme including an ass's bray, and finally Theseus and Hippolyta combined with the calls of their hunting horns. Needless to say, this compresses the action of the play into a very reduced time frame. The development section thus plays on the urgency of action by pitting the fairy theme against the horn calls, seemingly depicting Puck's speech beginning "My fairy lord, this must be done with haste, / For night's swift dragons cut the clouds full fast, / And yonder shines Aurora's harbinger" (III. ii. 378–380).

At the end of the development a downward scale passage is played four times. It is unrelated to any previous material, but the return of the lovers' theme immediately after this section connects it to them. (I assume it represents the fairy magic descending on each lover in turn, but see Roger Fiske's slightly different interpretation in Hartnoll.)

The recapitulation begins with a repetition of the gateway chords. We must now be at the reawakening—first of Titania, and then, after a much shortened transition, of the lovers, and finally of Bottom. Only then is the listener transferred to Theseus' palace; the royal couple's theme is thus delayed until the end of the recapitulation. In the coda the fairies return; and just before the end, the theme of Theseus and Hippolyta returns as if from a great distance. The overture closes with the gateway chords.

The major themes in this overture all represent specific characters, and the drama of the music resides in the clarity of their conflicting natures. Not all Shakespearean plays, to be sure, contrast kings and clowns, fairies and mortals, but in *A Midsummer Night's Dream,* Mendelssohn is able to depict the action by manipulating his themes in traditional ways. For example, Theseus and Hippolyta do not appear in the development, during which the fairy magic is worked; but their hunting horns represent the impending dawn. In the recapitulation their theme is delayed until each of the characters affected by fairy magic awakens. It is rare to find an absolute musical form so successfully wedded to a specific dramatic program.

Other Shakespearean overtures tend to be more general in their approach. Berlioz's *King Lear* Overture contrasts a raging theme marked "disperato" with one that is lyrical. Only by means of an extended introduction can we infer the meaning behind them. The work begins with a violent passage played in unison by the lowest strings. After a brief interjection by the horns, this theme is repeated quietly by the upper strings, followed by more extensive interjections from the other winds. When the lowest strings resume their monologue, the first part is echoed in the upper strings and, after an outburst from the winds, the second part is repeated in the bass. Then, very tentatively, a beautiful theme emerges in the oboe; expanded by all the woodwinds, it is finally confirmed richly by the brass instruments. A wild outburst from the entire string section, repeating the opening theme, ends the introduction.

There can be no question that this section of music represents the Council scene. Lear speaks (lower strings), demanding. Goneril and Regan mirror his thoughts by responding as he expects, and their music (upper strings) mirrors his. Throughout these passages there are quiet comments for solo horn, and perhaps it is not too farfetched to notice that *corno* (horn) and *Cordelia* are both abbreviated *Cor.,* but when Cordelia's turn to respond comes, she is at first represented by the oboe. Her theme is beautiful and lyrical; and its many rests make it seem hesitant. It becomes full only when repeated first by all the winds, and then by the horns. These three statements represent Cordelia's growing responses to her father: her first words (I. i. 87 and 89), her first speech (91–93), and her final explanation (95–104). The denunciation of her by Lear, Goneril, and Regan, all of whom are represented by strings, ends the introduction. (Again, see Fiske for a variant interpretation.)

The sonata form that follows then portrays the ensuing events. The first theme, *disperato,* represents Lear's distress, perhaps even the storm on the heath. The second theme group represents compassion and comprises two themes: the first (for solo oboe) depicts Cordelia; the second (for solo bassoon) possibly depicts the Earl of Kent. The use of solo winds for characters representing truth and compassion follows naturally from the introduction, where the wind instruments clearly contradict Lear's strings.

The development combines the *disperato* theme with Kent's; Cordelia's theme does not appear. In the recapitulation the *disperato* theme returns. Before Cordelia's theme is reintroduced, however, Lear's theme from the introduction is heard and gradually fragmented, representing his madness. Only then do the Cordelia and Kent themes recur, depicting the reunion of father, daughter, and Kent in the French camp. In the coda, drums are heard and the battle ensues. Lear's theme returns in the basses in altered rhythmical values, as the old man appears carrying Cordelia's body. The overture ends with music similar to the *disperato* theme.

Berlioz's overture differs from Mendelssohn's. Its primary theme represents a feeling or action rather than a person, and it is contrasted with a lyrical, "compassionate" theme group. Indeed, it is more like Verdi's overture to *Macbeth* than it is to Mendelssohn's *A Midsummer Night's Dream.* The compassion of Cordelia and Kent, for example, can only be tentatively identified, by the range and placement of these themes within the sonata form. The introduction, however, is quite specific in its depiction of Lear, and the recurrence of this theme helps clarify the dramatic action throughout the overture. Like Mendelssohn but unlike Verdi, Berlioz uses the sonata form and molds it to his purposes. It is a virtuosic achievement to have captured so much of the richness of *King Lear* while maintaining an independent musical structure.

Peter Ilyich Tchaikovsky's *Romeo and Juliet* Fantasy Overture (1869; rev. 1880) is, of the three overtures discussed here, the least programmatically specific. The long hymnlike introduction is meant to represent Friar Laurence, as we know from Tchaikovsky's correspondence; the same arpeggiated harp chords return toward the end of the overture. It is unclear why Tchaikovsky chose to frame his composition with this character, but the churchlike music lends a mysterious and sacrificial background to the violent passions of the drama.

The *sonata allegro* begins with a vigorous and energetic theme, after which the string and woodwind sections alternate measures as if in argument, and then irregularly spaced, crashing chords in the winds and percussion resound against rushing sixteenth notes in the strings. Surely this is the street fighting of Act I, scene 1. The second theme group, contrasting directly with this, represents the young lovers. The familiar "love theme" expresses Romeo's longing, and a second theme that tends to vacillate between two notes must represent Juliet's hesitation, although it has never, to my knowledge, been identified as such. After their initial statements, Romeo's and Juliet's themes are united, the entire section presumably representing the balcony scene.

The development contrasts the fighting theme with Friar Laurence, perhaps in an attempt to show evil and good in contention. The fighting quickly overpowers the ineffectual friar, and the ensuing violent music must represent the deaths of Mercutio and Tybalt.

The fighting music recurs briefly in the recapitulation. The second theme group then begins with Juliet's theme, indicating her worry and apprehension for Romeo's safety and her fear that she will not see him before his exile. But Romeo enters triumphantly, and the two themes are immediately combined. This sequence of themes is easily heard as the wedding-night scene. After this point, however, the music loses direct reference to the story.

An ominous, insistent motive in the violins appears against the love theme. Shortly thereafter, the love theme is fragmented and reduced to its opening motive, which is repeated without completion. This leads to a repetition of the fighting theme. Perhaps Tchaikovsky meant this to represent Romeo's banishment and Juliet's struggle with her family. The coda begins with a repeated figure in the timpani. Romeo's theme is heard quietly in the bassoon, and Juliet's returns in the winds—thematic appearances that may represent the lovers' deaths. The harp theme of Friar Laurence then takes over, but the overture ends with four measures of *fortissimo* chords that are reminiscent of the fighting theme. Like Shakespeare (and unlike Gounod), Tchaikovsky concludes with references to the families.

Composers, regardless of their medium, often respond similarly to Shakespeare's plays. For example, the overtures of Mendelssohn and Tchaikovsky are both closed by musical repetition, just as the operas by Britten and Gounod based on *A Midsummer Night's Dream* and *Romeo and Juliet* use musical closure to set off the fairy world and the lovers' world, respectively. In the operas and overtures, however, musical characterization differs. The overtures typically identify characters with a single theme that can be varied, combined with other themes, or fragmented. Because in operas the actors appear on the stage and sing, thematic identification is unnecessary. In Verdi's *Otello,* for example, the changes in Othello's character are illustrated not by variations on a single theme but by changes in musical style.

Ballet, like opera, has characters on stage; but the action is mimed, and the characters are usually represented musically, as in the overtures, by thematic identification. Sergei Prokofiev's *Romeo and Juliet* (1935–1936) offers one example. As opposed to the symphonic overtures, which last about fifteen minutes and omit subplots and characters, Prokofiev's three-act ballet is virtually all-inclusive. Its fifty-two scenes divide the play into a series of individual actions or characters, such as (in the first act): Romeo (scene 2), The street wakens (scene 3), The fight (scene 6), and The young Juliet (scene 10). Specific thematic tags are given, for example, to Romeo, Juliet, Mercutio, Tybalt, and the Nurse; only Romeo's and Juliet's themes, however, change as the action unfolds. At least in this aspect of the score, Prokofiev seems to have been influenced by Tchaikovsky, and, generally speaking, this ballet undoubtedly derives from the tradition of the programmatic Shakespearean overture.

Unlike the overtures examined above, however, Prokofiev's ballet adheres to no fixed repetitive form. It follows the play closely, with no character or action omitted, and takes its dramatic shape from Shakespeare's play alone. Nevertheless, the musical depiction of the drama resides in the thematic representation of characters and their interactions (as in the overtures), and the overall musical shape is determined by the continual repetitions of these themes. The result is not as dramatically satisfying as in the overtures, for the compositional process precludes a crisis and resolution (as in sonata form) and is merely additive. It is no surprise, then, that

Prokofiev combined selected movements into three highly popular orchestral suites; without the stage action, the ballet is not successful as a dramatic entity, but the individual movements contain superb music.

From the setting of Shakespeare's words in songs, to the operatic reworkings of the dramas, to the wordless orchestral representations of the characters and themes, musical transformations of Shakespeare abound. In some cases composers have been drawn to the melody and rhythm of the verse itself; in other cases composers have been inspired by the dramatic conflict and passion of the plays. In all the most successful adaptations, the music is not mere accompaniment to Shakespeare, but analysis and interpretation; and listening to a good musical setting of Shakespeare enables us to learn something about the original.

BIBLIOGRAPHY

Catalogs. Alan Boustead, *Music to Shakespeare* (1964). Phyllis Hartnoll, ed., *Shakespeare in Music* (1964), esp. Part 2.

Bibliographies. A Shakespeare Bibliography: The Catalogue of the Birmingham Shakespeare Library, 7 vols. (rev. ed., 1971). Frederick W. Sternfeld and Eric Walter White, "Shakespeare," in *The New Grove Dictionary of Music,* XVII (1980).

Studies. Roy E. Aycock, "Shakespeare, Boito, and Verdi," in *Musical Quarterly,* 58 (1972). Julian Budden, *The Operas of Verdi,* 3 vols. (1973–1980). Doug Coe, "The Original Production Book for *Otello:* An Introduction," in *19th Century Music,* 2 (1978–1979). Edward T. Cone, "The Old Man's Toys: Verdi's Last Operas," in *Perspectives USA,* 6 (1954), on *Otello* and *Falstaff,* and "The Stature of *Falstaff:* Technique and Content in Verdi's Last Opera," in *Center,* 1 (1954). Roger Covell, "Seventeenth-Century Music for *The Tempest,*" in *Studies in Music* (Australia), 2 (1968).

Winton Dean, "Shakespeare in the Opera House," in *Shakespeare Survey,* 18 (1965), and "Verdi's *Otello:* A Shakespearean Masterpiece," *ibid.,* 21 (1968). Francesco Degrada, "Lettura del *Macbeth* di Verdi," in *Studi musicali,* 6 (1977). John R. Elliott, Jr., "The Shakespeare Berlioz Saw," in *Music and Letters,* 57 (1976). Peter Evans, "Britten's New Opera: A Preview," in *Tempo,* 53–54 (1960), and *The Music of Benjamin Britten* (1979).

James A. Hepokoski, "Verdi, Giuseppina Pasqua, and the Composition of *Falstaff,*" in *19th Century Music,* 3 (1979–1980), and *Giuseppe Verdi: Falstaff* (1983). Joseph Kerman, "*Otello:* Traditional Opera and the Image of

Shakespeare," in *Opera as Drama* (1956). David R. B. Kimball, "The Young Verdi and Shakespeare," in *Proceedings of the Royal Musical Association,* 101 (1974–1975), on *Macbeth.* David Lawton, "On the 'Bacio' Theme in *Otello,*" in *19th Century Music,* 1 (1977–1978). R. W. S. Mendl, "Berlioz and Shakespeare," in *Chesterian,* 29 (1955). David Rosen and Andrew Porter, eds., *Verdi's Macbeth: A Sourcebook* (1984).

Daniel Sabbeth, "Dramatic and Musical Organization in *Falstaff,*" in *Atti del III Congresso internazionale di studi verdiani* (1974). Roger Savage, "The Shakespeare-Purcell *Fairy Queen:* A Defence and Recommendation," in *Early Music,* 1 (1973). Gary Schmidgall, *Literature as Opera* (1977), ch. 6. Herbert M. Schueller, *"Othello* Transformed: Verdi's Interpretation of Shakespeare," in Wayne State University, Dept. of English, *Studies in Honor of John Wilcox* (1958). Eric Walter White, *Benjamin Britten* (2nd ed., 1983).

In my work on Shakespearean opera, I have benefited greatly from the insights of David Bevington, with whom I co-teach a course entitled "Shakespeare at the Opera."

Major Shakespearean Institutions: Libraries, Museums, Organizations

RALPH BERRY

Shakespeare is hard to categorize. One learns this truth early, discovering that comedy and tragedy have a wide overlap to which the First Folio classification does no justice. The works of Shakespeare constantly reveal transformations from one category to another, blurred edges, definitions that escape from themselves into proposals for new mutations. And this problem of definition is extended into the institutions that form my subject. Often it is not possible to make a clear distinction between Shakespearean and non-Shakespearean institutions. That is because the study of Shakespeare is part of a larger whole and in practice has at least two dimensions. Shakespeare is, in the first instance, a Renaissance poet and dramatist, to be studied in a library or collection devoted to the Renaissance. He is also a man of the theater, who demands to be studied via the record of stage performance. The libraries that I describe here will emphasize at least one of these dimensions. But that dimension, rather than Shakespeare, may well be the formal reason for the library's existence.

For the purposes of my brief, I have preferred to concentrate on a fairly narrow interpretation of the term *Shakespearean*—that is, I deal for the most part with institutions solely or very considerably devoted to Shakespeare. For example, the Library of Congress has a vast accumulation of Shakespearean material, as must all great libraries that encompass the humanities. But the Shakespearean scholar who visits Washington, D.C., is likely not to work in the Library of Congress at all. He will go to the Folger

Shakespeare Library, across the street, where there is an incomparable concentration of Renaissance and Shakespearean works, together with many theatrical records. Hence, the Folger Shakespeare Library falls within my field, and the Library of Congress, outside. The determination of relevance is often, but not always, made easy by the presence of "Shakespeare" in a title. The Huntington Library, with its vast Renaissance and Shakespearean holdings, demands inclusion. So does the Garrick Club Library, a collection known to all theater historians and rich in specifically Shakespearean materials. But then, almost by definition a major theater collection will have a high proportion of Shakespeareana. Shakespeare is ubiquitous, and this article describes only the most obvious places where one can study him in detail.

Libraries are in any case appraised somewhat differently today, compared to a generation ago. Then, *Shakespeare Survey* ran in its early numbers a series of articles devoted to the major Shakespearean collections. These articles are essential reading for what they tell us about not only the libraries but also the times in which they were written. Shakespeare, it is clear, is presented as a literary figure. His most important bequest is the First Folio and the single-text quartos; libraries are therefore to be judged primarily on the numbers of folio and quarto holdings. It is illuminating to read L. W. Hanson on the Bodleian Library, as well as his patient rebuttal of Joseph Quincy Adams' account of the league tables. (Do two copies of the

Fifth Quarto of *Richard III*, one in poor condition, rate as the equal to a Bad Quarto of *Romeo and Juliet?*) Nothing, of course, can shake the primacy of the four great collections of early Shakespeare editions: the British Library, the Bodleian, the Folger, and the Huntington. But nowadays one would wish to shade the picture, making more, for example, of Birmingham's collection of Shakespearean music and stressing the all-around balance of the Folger. Simply, one has reservations about a game played with the same (largely unchanged) counters as in the past. The revolutionary feature of today's scene is the place found for Shakespeare in performance. It is true that theater collections often grow rapidly and without a sense of direction, lacking the identity of the older institutions, but they constitute a force that reflects, even as it shapes, a changing perception of Shakespeare.

Within Shakespearean institutions in general, one finds great diversity, not to say quirkiness. It is as though such institutions partake of the generic variousness of their genius. They come into being for a host of personal, local, and national reasons. The Germans founded *Shakespeare Jahrbuch* as a conscious act of homage to the man whom they perceived as their national poet; the English founded the Shakespeare Birthplace Trust for no other cause than that a house came onto the market, and an American was bidding for it; the Folger Shakespeare Library is in essence the personal creation of a great collector, Henry Clay Folger; the Stratford Shakespeare Festival in Ontario, Canada, is the work of a single enthusiast, Tom Patterson. We are left with the facts that *Shakespeare Jahrbuch*, now well into its second century, is by far the oldest Shakespeare journal; that there is no Shakespearean institution of great antiquity in England (barring the buildings themselves); that the largest collection of folios and quartos is in Washington, D.C.; and that the most important Shakespearean festival outside Stratford-upon-Avon is in a small town in Ontario. Anyone can found a Shakespearean institution, and no one knows what it will grow into.

It follows that an account of Shakespearean institutions should be alert to these quirks of context. This prescription is not best served by setting up a category, such as "library," and pursuing it across the nations. Shakespeare is a world playwright—*the* world playwright—but in a sense the title is quite unreal, for he exists through perceptions formed by nation-states. And however inviting it is to celebrate the international variousness of Shakespeare—the two Indian journals devoted to *Hamlet,* the Centre d'Études et de Recherches Élizabéthaines at Paul Valéry University, and *Shakespeare Studies (Japan),* to name but a few—it seems best to concentrate on those institutions that have put down deep roots over time in a few countries. Hence, my plan of organization is based on national context, and I have chosen to develop the subject through Great Britain, the United States and Canada, and the German-speaking peoples.

Britain: Stratford-upon-Avon

Geography is the key to the English Shakespearean institutions. If one sets aside the holdings of early Shakespearean editions in Oxford and Cambridge, the major Shakespearean institutions are based on (or related to) Stratford-upon-Avon and London. This situation mirrors one fact of Shakespeare's life, his shuttling between Stratford and London; and this must have set up in him a certain creative tension between his birthplace and workplace. Such a tension is replicated in the Shakespearean institutions. On the one hand, there is Stratford-upon-Avon, heir to, and guardian of, the Shakespeare tradition; behind Stratford lies Birmingham, with its great Shakespeare Library and the Shakespeare Institute at the University of Birmingham. On the other hand, there is London, with its theaters, libraries, and metropolitan allure. Each center has a claim to Shakespeare, and the facts of his life are ambivalent, for though he retired to Stratford, he is known to have bought property in London—a pied-à-terre, surely—in the later years of his life. This ambivalence is illustrated, above all, in the Royal Shakespeare Company (RSC). The RSC has two homes, in Stratford-upon-Avon and London. It is the perfect symbol of the English Shakespeare.

Stratford-upon-Avon, a market town in the center of England, whose position in the world owes everything to its association with Shakespeare, is the home (or at least one home) of three major Shakespearean institutions: the Shakespeare Birthplace Trust, the Shakespeare Institute, and the RSC and its Royal Shakespeare Theatre. Twenty miles to the north is Birmingham, with its own Shakespeare Library.

Shakespeare Birthplace Trust. The trust came into existence in 1847, purely as a reaction to Phineas T. Barnum's plan to buy Shakespeare's "birthplace" and transport it to the United States. Appalled at this prospect, the English bestirred themselves: the trust was formed, committees set up, money found, and the birthplace purchased for £3,000. The trust thus found itself responsible for the preservation and maintenance of the birthplace, with income derived from subscriptions and admission fees. From this modest beginning, the trust has expanded notably. It has acquired other Shakespeare properties: Anne Hathaway's Cottage, the Nash House (New Place), Mary Arden's House, and Hall's Croft, as well as other less famous properties that act as a buffer against unwanted development. The trust has also bought the land at Welcombe that Shakespeare originally owned. Purely as a property holding, the trust is formidable, requiring a staff at most recent count of 182, of whom fourteen are gardeners.

That is one major role of the trust, guardian of the Shakespearean matériel. Another is promoter of the general advancement of Shakespearean knowledge and appreciation, to which end it engages in educational and cultural work. Much of this is based on the research facilities provided by the extensive library. The Shakespeare Birthplace Trust Library, housed in the Shakespeare Centre, has a rich collection of Shakespeareana that includes copies of the first four folios, much local archival material, and a number of early acting editions and prompt copies. Theater history is a great strength of the Shakespeare Centre Library, for it contains the archives of the RSC. These include press cuttings from 1874, when the movement for the Shakespeare Memorial started, playbills from the theater's opening in 1879 on, and promptbooks for all performances from 1922, with a few gaps. The RSC now routinely deposits its promptbooks and other production records with the Shakespeare Centre Library, to which a regular file of press reviews (for Stratford and London performances) is attached. The library is not only a major theater history collection but also a clearinghouse for inquiries dealing with Shakespearean subject matter. Dr. Levi Fox, O.M., director of the Shakespeare Birthplace Trust, is also secretary to the International Shakespeare Association.

Shakespeare Institute. The institute, a part of University of Birmingham, was established in 1951 in Mason Croft (Marie Corelli's old house in Church Street, still the Stratford home of the institute) by Allardyce Nicoll, with the object of promoting international collaboration in Shakespearean scholarship and teaching. The growth of the institute's research and teaching activities led in 1963 to the setting up, by Terence Spencer, of the library and postgraduate center in the university grounds at Edgbaston, Birmingham. With this dual location the institute fulfills a variety of functions. It offers courses leading to advanced degrees and special courses for the general public and university students from all over the world. The focus is on Shakespeare, but the institute's work extends to Shakespeare's contemporaries, seventeenth-century literature, later English drama, and the contemporary theater. At Stratford, courses are related to the productions of the RSC. All this is reflected in the library, whose stock of books, periodicals, and microfilms now approaches 100,000 and whose strengths lie in Renaissance literature, English drama, and the contemporary stage. To the world of Shakespearean scholarship, the institute is known best as a convener of conferences, above all the biennial International Shakespeare Conference. In 1981 the International Shakespeare Association Congress—conveniently, if not quite correctly, known as the World Shakespeare Congress—was held in Stratford, an event that the institute took a large part in organizing.

The institute has also become a center of publication. Within the last generation, publications edited at the institute and involving contributions from its academic staff have included *Shakespeare Survey; Stratford-upon-Avon Studies; Modern Language Review; Yearbook of English Studies;* the New Penguin Shakespeare and the Penguin Shakespeare Library; and the Cornmarket Series of Reprints of Acting Editions and Adaptations of Shakespeare Plays. The institute continues to work with *Shakespeare Survey,* which publishes a selection of the papers delivered at its biennial conferences. The New Cambridge Shakespeare and most of the New Arden Shakespeare volumes were edited by those connected in some way with the institute, whether as officers, fellows, students, or occasional lecturers. In sum, the Shakespeare Institute is a stronghold of Shakespeare publishing in England and has no institutional competitor.

Birmingham Shakespeare Library. The Shakespeare Library, a part of the City of Birmingham Public Library, is the largest Shakespeare library in the country. Its scope was signaled in 1861 by George Dawson, president of the local Shakespeare club, who wrote: "I want to see founded in Birmingham a Shakespeare Library which should contain (as far as practicable) every edition and every translation of Shakespeare; all the commentators, good, bad, and indifferent; in short, every book connected with the life and works of our great poet. I would add portraits of Shakespeare, and all the pictures, etc., illustrative of his work." Opened in 1868, burned down in 1879, and reborn immediately after, the library owes its strength to a century of consistent policy: buying every new book on the subject as it was published, and the older books as they came upon the market. The results are now formidable. The early Shakespearean publications are represented by two copies of each of the four folios and a number of quartos. The library's main strengths lie in the eighteenth century, for which period it possesses many acting versions, and the nineteenth century, for which it has over 800 editions of the works. The foreign language section includes editions in ninety languages, ranging from Abkhasian to Zulu.

For stage history, the archive contains prompts, criticism, programs, publicity, and pictures: these document many hundreds of opera productions, films, radio and television programs, ballets, and marionette shows. There are 2,000 pieces of Shakespearean music in the library. Illustrated material covers all periods from 1709 to the present and is represented most richly in the seventy-six folio volumes of the H. R. Forrest Collection.

The catalog to the Shakespeare Library, published in dictionary form, has since 1971 been computerized. Work continues on classifying the older material, while the library's zeal to remain up to date remains undiminished. It subscribes, on an international basis, to newspaper clippings, which are classified and mounted in volumes. A systematic attempt is made to obtain some record of every English and foreign Shakespearean production, as it occurs.

To sum up, one has first to recognize a Stratford-Birmingham axis and then to register the great triangle of archives. Birmingham's Shakespeare Library, the Library of the Shakespeare Institute in Edgbaston, and the Shakespeare Centre Library in Stratford constitute the central resource for scholars in England. It is agreed by the librarians of all three institutions that there is a common need for greater cooperation. It is conceivable, for example, that in the future a measure of coordination in purchasing policies will be enforced by the sheer pressure of costs. However, the emphases and needs of each archive vary considerably, and these libraries

will no doubt continue their diversity of character and development.

Royal Shakespeare Company. Not until the late nineteenth century did the idea take hold that Stratford should be the scene of regular festival performances of Shakespeare plays. The festival dates from 1879; the Shakespeare Memorial Theatre received its royal charter in 1925; and the present theater was opened in 1932. At first it was assumed that it was possible to bring together a company at Stratford for a limited season, but no more. By the 1950s that assumption was no longer acceptable; a framework had to be found for an acting corps with a permanent base. The appointment in 1960 of Peter Hall as artistic director provided the impetus for change, starting with the theater's name. "Memorial" was felt to be too Victorian in its associations, and from 1961 on, plays were staged at the Royal Shakespeare Theatre, home of the RSC. At the same time, a London base was found at the Aldwych Theatre, and three-year contracts were introduced, thereby giving actors and other personnel a degree of security never before known to them. The way was thus made clear for an exceptionally large company, based simultaneously in Stratford and London, providing a repertory of Shakespearean and modern plays for virtually the entire year.

Britain: London and the Universities

Theaters. The RSC provides our transition to London. Its present base there is the Barbican, opened in 1982, with two auditoriums corresponding neatly to Stratford's. The Barbican's main stage is the London counterpart of the Royal Shakespeare Theatre at Stratford-upon-Avon, and The Pit (at the Barbican) is the equivalent of Stratford's The Other Place, a small experimental theater seating some 100 to 150 in conditions of extreme austerity. This correspondence is central to the RSC's existence. Typically, several Shakespearean productions are introduced each season at Stratford-upon-Avon (never in London) and then, during the following season, transferred to London. The Barbican thus presents productions that have been run in, improved, perhaps somewhat recast—in any case drawn from the most successful of Stratford's previous season. It is a two-stroke cycle system, and the RSC directorate plans in terms of two-season units, London upon Stratford. This is not of course a rigid pattern; theater is not like that. David Edgar's adaptation of Dickens' *Nicholas Nickleby,* for example, was so great a hit in London and New York that it is said to have destroyed the company's logistics for a year. But the system does offer a principle of planning.

Shakespeare is the house dramatist of the RSC, but he is not its sole writer. It is central to the RSC's thinking that its repertory should contain modern playwrights, that Shakespearean theater should not be hermetically sealed off from the rest of the dramatic tradition. The main theater at Stratford-upon-Avon is almost exclusively devoted to Shakespeare's plays. Pilgrims to Stratford expect to see Shakespeare at the main theater. But The Other Place has recently offered Ibsen and Bulgakov, as well as several of Shakespeare's contemporaries, such as Ford, Dekker, and Fletcher, and the Barbican is open to all contemporary influences. The RSC executes a balancing act between regular presentation of Shakespeare and a roving commission in contemporary and world drama. As one of the two great state theaters (its funding from the Arts Council is extensive but notoriously inadequate) the RSC is the arbiter of Shakespeare on today's stage.

The National Theatre, it should be added, is not a Shakespearean institution. Although it opened with Peter O'Toole's Hamlet and then staged Olivier's Othello, the most famous Shakespearean performance of the 1960s, the National Theater has never accepted any major responsibility for staging Shakespeare. It sees this as the affair of the RSC. Consequently, the National Theatre mounts on the average one Shakespeare production in a year. In this its policy resembles that of most English repertory companies.

London has as yet no neo-Elizabethan theater in which Shakespeare could be staged in authentic surroundings; but it will have. The International Shakespeare Globe Centre is dedicated to this end and has made impressive progress. The major purpose of the Shakespeare Globe Centre, as its brochure *This Wooden O* tells us, is

to rebuild Shakespeare's Globe Theatre on the South Bank of the River Thames as an international working monument to the world's greatest playwright. The new Globe will be built close to the original site on Bankside and as faithfully as possible to its sixteenth-century original. It will provide a unique facility for the experimental production of the plays of Shake-

speare and his contemporaries, and stand at the center of an important complex of complementary facilities, to include a full-scale replica of Inigo Jones' Theatre (1617) and a new museum and research centre of the Shakespearean stage.

The complex, in short, will be "an international resource centre for people everywhere." The Bankside site has been chosen, and the redevelopment there has been authorized by the government, other authorities having given their blessing. A wide-ranging list of patrons, advisers, and supportive societies has been announced, headed by the most distinguished of patronage. In 1984, legal difficulties with Southwark Council delayed the beginning of construction work on the site. Nevertheless, it is clear that this project, which has owed a great deal to the tireless advocacy of Sam Wanamaker, is moving steadily toward fruition.

British Library. There is no institution in London called "The Shakespeare Library," or anything like it, at which one could work in a concentrated and extensive way on Shakespearean topics. No doubt matters will be different when the Bankside Globe is completed. At present one has to pursue Shakespeare in libraries by no means exclusively geared to him, the most famous of which is the British Library (previously known as the British Museum, and no doubt still better known that way). The foundation of the British Library's holdings in Shakespeare is David Garrick's library of "old English plays." The second notable addition was the library of George III, and later came J. O. Halliwell-Phillipps' collection. In 1910 the library was able to complete the "set" of First Quartos. The Department of Printed Books, English Antiquarian Section, contains the listings under Shakespeare in the General Catalogue, but has no other access to Shakespeareana. Small pockets of Shakespeare came in with collections like the Ashley Library or the Huth quartos, but they do not form large separate parts of the overall holdings. The Department of Manuscripts is likewise without a division devoted to Shakespeare. The most comprehensive statement of the department's holdings is to be found in the relevant section of the *Index of English Literary Manuscripts, Volume One, 1450–1625* (Peter Beal, ed., 1980) and in Samuel Schoenbaum's *William Shakespeare: Records and Images.*

Theatre Museum, Victoria and Albert Museum. The Theatre Museum is a striking emblem of the disarray in which theater history finds itself. It was established as recently as 1974 and has been housed, inadequately, in a small portion of the Victoria and Albert Museum. Various new sites were canvassed, and Covent Garden was eventually fixed upon. The move there was threatened, first, by an adverse official report that was overthrown by a massive combined effort on the part of the theater world, and second, by a cutback in government spending (1983) that caused a delay in the official commitment to the project. Happily, these planning problems have been overcome. Building conversion work at Covent Garden started early in 1984, with completion scheduled in two years. A further six months is required by the authorities to set up and open the museum, in 1986. The Theatre Museum will be completely closed for the last year of this period.

The outcome will be a Theatre Museum situated in the old flower market near Covent Garden, lying at the heart of London's theater district, within easy walk of forty theaters. The main area will contain three exhibition galleries; also on the premises will be the bulk of the Theatre Museum's basic research collections, which contain only material associated with performance. Associated facilities—including a theater for performances, seminars, and conferences—are also planned. The museum will be for the general public as well as for the researcher; and for the latter, the resources will match the magnitude of the project. The existing house catalogs will in time be replaced by a centralized computer catalog based on the Tandem system developed by West German theater museums. In addition to being a place for serious study, the Theatre Museum should provide an information switchboard where questions can be answered or referred to other collections. And when the Theatre Museum has been linked up with the Tandem computer system it will eventually be possible to link directly with theater institutions on the same system around the globe.

For the Shakespearean, the Theatre Museum has certain special collections of unique interest. Foremost is the Gabrielle Enthoven Collection, which includes over a million playbills, programs, newspaper clippings, autograph letters, manuscripts, illustrations, music, and texts relating to the London stage from the early eighteenth century, as well as to regional theater in the United Kingdom from the early 1970s. The Harry R. Beard Collection of English and European theatrical portraits, prints, and drawings includes many Shakespearean sub-

jects and performers from the eighteenth and nineteenth centuries. The promptbook collection contains William Poel's prompts. For photographs, there is the Guy Little Collection, covering the Victorian era, and the Houston Rogers Collection of twentieth-century photographs. Scene designs and scenic models for the twentieth century are also represented extensively, and the Paintings Collection includes many performers in Shakespearean roles from the eighteenth century on. There are of course many scrapbooks, account books, and personal files. At the Theatre Museum one will be able to study Shakespeare onstage in theatrical context and on a scale not yet possible anywhere else.

Garrick Club Library. The Library of the Garrick Club, established in 1831 to serve the needs of its members, is an exceptional theater collection. Generally strong on eighteenth- and nineteenth-century material, the library houses 10,000 playbills and programs from Drury Lane from 1716 on, together with fifty promptbooks, 3,000 play texts, and 500 volumes on the theater arts. The club also owns a large collection of theatrical paintings, which depict the history of the British theater from the eighteenth century. Admission is limited to scholars, by appointment only.

Raymond Mander and Joe Mitchenson Theatre Collection. This private collection of theatrical memorabilia, started in 1949, is now an immense storehouse. The collection includes material on all aspects of theater: playbills, costumes, theatrical china, properties, and books dating back to 1664, the whole being quite eclectic in character. It is widely used as a source of illustration and information, by publishers and others in the mass media. After filling to overflowing the small Victorian house in which it has been lodged, the collection is now in transition to much larger premises. Beckenham Place, Lewisham, a Georgian mansion dating back to 1780, has been offered to the museum; a capital grant for work on refurbishing the mansion has been approved by the Greater London Council. The museum, now a registered charity, has launched an appeal for funds and is due to open to the public in the spring of 1985.

British Institute of Recorded Sound. The institute has made sound recordings of many productions staged by the National Theatre Company at the Old Vic and the South Bank, and the RSC at the Aldwych and the Barbican. These recordings date back to the early 1960s.

National Film Archive. This archive covers features, documentaries, and newsreels shown in Great Britain, irrespective of their country of origin, from 1895. The collection does not contain film of stage productions, but it does include many notable theatrical figures in film productions, such as Forbes-Robertson in *Hamlet* (1913). The Shakespearean section goes back to 1909, with *Brutus* (an Italian version of *Julius Caesar*) and J. Stuart Blackton's Vitagraph production of *A Midsummer Night's Dream.*

Universities. At Oxford, the Bodleian Library contains Edmond Malone's collection of folios and quartos. (Matters are now better ordered than when the librarian disposed of the Bodleian's First Folio, it having been superseded by the superior Third Folio.) At Cambridge, the Library of Trinity College has Edward Capell's collection. And Edinburgh has its superb collection of dramatic material bearing upon Shakespeare, to be found at the National Library of Scotland and Edinburgh University Library.

What emerges from this survey is that Britain is now rediscovering its theatrical past. Some extremely important theater collections, with a strong Shakespearean component, are now in a period of rapid growth and institutional stabilization. I have no doubt that within a few years, the theatrical records of the past will be studied in exemplary circumstances at Covent Garden, the Bankside, and the Mander and Mitchenson Collection in Lewisham. But these are projections. To my knowledge, the only major theater collection in England to be fully cataloged is in Bristol. The University of Bristol Theatre Collection contains, among a good deal of memorabilia, three major archives: the Beerbohm Tree Collection; the Richard Southern Collection; and the Old Vic archive. The last accession reflects a conscious intent on the part of the National Theatre, the natural heir to the Old Vic records, not to expand into the museum-archive area. This outlook is common to theaters, I think. It is as though theater people feel that the vital essence of their work must be separated from the preservation of records. Theater history is a constant grapple with haphazard record-keeping, and only now are archives moving into a period of consolidation. They illustrate the general tenor of Shakespearean institutions in Britain, an impression of rather haphazard birth and development, identity but not clarity of definition.

Shakespeare Survey. The journal has had as its subtitle, from its founding in 1948, *An Annual Survey of Shakespearian Study and Production,* properly symbolizing the confluence of two great streams. It also points to the editor's problem. How is "Shakespearian production" to be surveyed? Its sheer range and bulk call for brutal discriminations. In practice, *Shakespeare Survey* confines itself to well-considered coverage of Stratford and London. This is manifestly less than just to the excellent repertory companies in, for example, Birmingham and Bristol; but the scale of the problem defies any less hardy solution.

The mainstay of *Shakespeare Survey* is its scholarly and academic content. Each volume has a stated theme ("Shakespeare in the Twentieth Century" is that of issue 36), normally the same in alternate years as that of the biennial International Shakespeare Conference. Volumes, which are illustrated, also contain articles on other topics and regularly include surveys of the previous year's work in Shakespearean criticism; Shakespeare's life, times, and stage; Shakespeare editions and textual studies; and a review of productions. Each volume is indexed and ten-year indexes are also provided. *Shakespeare Survey* has an international circulation, and a normal print-run of some five thousand copies. Editorial continuity has been marked: the first eighteen volumes were edited by Allardyce Nicoll, the next fifteen by Kenneth Muir, and succeeding volumes by Stanley Wells. *Shakespeare Survey* is the touchstone of the English Shakespeare tradition.

The United States and Canada

The distinctive features of Shakespearean institutions in the United States are the resources of the major libraries and the range of theater festivals. The East Coast has the Folger Shakespeare Library, and the West Coast has the Huntington Library; theater festivals with Shakespeare at the masthead are everywhere. The map suggests an emblem of the American scene, the strongholds of scholarship flanking the lights of the theaters. These institutions have great and diverse strengths.

Folger Shakespeare Library. The Folger, in Washington, D.C., is an independent research institution, devoted to advanced study in the Renaissance. Simply, it is the finest Shakespeare library in the world. Everything in it stems from the character and intentions of its founders, Henry Clay Folger and Emily Jordan Folger. From the lecture by

Ralph Waldo Emerson at Amherst College, which Henry Folger attended, through the copy of the Fourth Folio on which Folger bid for "with fear and trepidation" at a New York auction in 1889, securing it for $107.50, to the choice of Washington as the site of the great collection and the opening of the Folger Shakespeare Library in 1932—all unfolds in a sequence astonishing in its impression of ordered design: it is a completed life-statement. The Folgers intended a monument more enduring than brass, and they succeeded.

To glance at a résumé of the library's holdings is to sustain this sense of astonishment. The bare statistics are stunning: 79 copies of the First Folio; more than 100 copies of the Second, Third, and Fourth folios; 208 quartos; 1,700 promptbooks; 16,000 books printed in English before 1641; 30,000 continental titles for the years 1500–1700; 50,000 prints; 250,000 American and British playbills. The extent of the Folger holdings defies characterization; the researcher has first to orient himself very carefully. But it would be wrong to convey an impression of haphazard riches. Everything has developed according to design, even if the collectors' plan is necessarily opportunist in its moments. Nothing, I think, better conveys the flavor of the collection's early days than Joseph Quincy Adams' account (in the Folger facsimile) of the pursuit of the first edition of *Titus Andronicus,* which turned up among the possessions that a Swedish post office clerk had inherited from his father, and news of the find was reported in early 1905:

Mr. Folger was thus enabled to read of the discovery in an eight-line dispatch to *The New York Times* of January 11. In great excitement he cabled to his London agent, Henry Sotheran and Company, to send a representative post-haste to Sweden to negotiate for the purchase of the treasure, and then waited, he tells us, in growing apprehension. Five days later came over the wires the laconic message: "Representative now in Sweden"; the following day came a second message: "Bought. Cable immediately two thousand pounds direct to account of Petrus Johannes Krafft, Ricksbanken, Malmö, Sweden"; and a short time later the prize was in his hands.

That is still the only copy known to exist. It is a far cry from those heroic days to the ordered accessions policy of later years (1,770 titles acquired in 1981–1982).

Today's Folger Shakespeare Library reflects its founders' wishes, in itself and in its address to the world. Within a classical exterior is a Tudor interior; within that are steel vaults controlled for humidity and temperature, to guarantee the absolute security of the library's treasures. The harmonization of styles conduces to the library's ambience, at once restful, stimulating, and subtly re-creative. The Exhibition Gallery is an exhibition in itself, yet the core of the library is the Reading Room, intended to evoke the style of the great hall of an Elizabethan college or house. At hand is an Elizabethan stage, home to the Folger Theatre Group; and there is a resident music ensemble, the Folger Consort. Academic programs burgeon: the library is home, for example, to the Folger Institute of Renaissance and Eighteenth-Century Studies, now cosponsored by more than twenty major universities. The institute is engaged in a sustained collaboration with the Newberry Library Center for Renaissance Studies (Chicago); the two centers cooperate on summer institutes, seminars, and other academic programs. O. B. Hardison, Jr., director of the Folger Shakespeare Library from 1969 to 1984, has stressed the need to link the library with the Washington community, and a well-developed docents program makes use of many volunteers. The Folger is a most remarkable example of what a library can achieve as a scholarly resource and in its relations with the world.

Huntington Library. When Kenneth Muir and Michael J. B. Allen were preparing their facsimile edition of the quartos, *Shakespeare's Plays in Quarto* (1981), in only three instances did they need to look outside the Henry E. Huntington Library (San Marino, California) for their copy. The first edition of *Titus Andronicus* exists only at the Folger, and *The Contention (Henry VI, Parts 2 and 3)* and *The True Tragedie (Henry VI, Part 3)* were reproduced from copies at the Bodleian Library. All the other quartos—nineteen of them—were reproduced from first editions held by the Huntington Library. Only the British Library can match the double of the Bad and Good Quartos of *Hamlet. Shakespeare's Plays in Quarto* is a considered emblem of the power of the Huntington.

Henry E. Huntington came late to the serious business of collecting, though he had acquired books for many years before his retirement around 1910. In a series of forceful coups, he bought up whole collections at a time. A hundred of these purchases were described in the first issue of the *Huntington Library Bulletin* (May 1931): the four great collections were those of Elihu D. Church, Frederic R. Halsey, the Bridgewater House Library, and John Philip Kemble and the duke of Devonshire. The Huntington Library has been called "a collection of collections or a library of libraries"; but its subsequent development has been more measured since the coups of the early years. It is in fact part of a complex comprising a library, an art gallery, and botanical gardens, the whole occupying 208 acres. All this was part of the Huntington estate, which was established as a trust (1919) and bequeathed to the public on the death of its owner. The great strength of the Huntington is its Renaissance holdings: there are 13,000 book titles printed before 1641, which include a unique copy of Kyd's *The Spanish Tragedy* (1599) and the only complete copy of Marlowe's *Tamburlaine* (1590). Later eras have not been neglected, and the library contains a major nineteenth-century acquisition in the Turner Shakespeare, a forty-four-volume extra-illustrated set of original drawings and prints. The ambience of the Huntington has been greatly appreciated by generations of scholars; its statement of interests emerges from the title of its publication, founded in 1937: *The Huntington Library Quarterly: Studies in English and American History and Literature.*

Theater Collections. Theater collections are hard to describe usefully in this context, since there will be a Shakespearean presence in almost all of them, but special mention must be made of the Billy Rose Theatre Collection of the New York Public Library, located at Lincoln Center for the Performing Arts. This collection has a great deal of material on Shakespearean productions on stage, in films, and on radio and television. Holdings take the form of programs from the early eighteenth century through the twentieth century; photographs; typescripts and promptbooks; posters; clippings, including reviews; and correspondence and business papers having to do with those productions. Since 1970, the establishment of Theatre on Film and Tape (TOFT) permits the filming or videotaping of live performances for the record, and the TOFT collection includes productions of Shakespeare. Overall, the emphasis is on American and other English-language productions, with the greatest strengths lying in the nonbook materials cited above. The Billy Rose Theatre Collection is a primary archive for research into Shakespeare on the American stage.

Other archives of quality are to be found at Columbia University, Harvard University, and Yale University. Columbia University in New York has the Brander Matthews Collection, with over sixty editions of the complete works of Shakespeare. Important manuscript collections are the Randolph Somerville Papers and the Roger Wheeler Theatrical Memorabilia Collection: the major strength is in Shakespeare on the American stage in the nineteenth and twentieth centuries. Harvard University has, besides its general collection in the Houghton Library, the Harvard Theatre Collection. No list of its holdings is publicly available, but this is a major and growing collection. Yale University's holdings are exceptionally strong: the Elizabethan Club, in addition to the four folios, possesses a choice set of early quartos. These include an uncut *Midsummer Night's Dream* (1600), *Venus and Adonis* (1594), and *Hamlet* (1604). There is extensive support material in the Sterling Memorial Library (the university's main library) as well as in the Beinecke Rare Book and Manuscript Library (both constituents of Yale University Library). The Beinecke contains many seventeenth-century editions of fifteen plays of Shakespeare (including the 1608 quarto of *King Lear*) and many eighteenth-century editions. Finally, the Yale Center for British Art addresses itself to dimensions beyond the purely literary. It is, for example, most interested in illustrations of Shakespeare. In 1981 the center staged a major exhibition, *Shakespeare in Art,* which aptly expresses its vista on Shakespeare.

American Shakespeare Festivals. "To say that Shakespeare is America's leading playwright hardly does the situation justice." That was Edwin Wilson's appraisal (*Wall Street Journal,* 18 July 1980) of the network of Shakespeare festivals proliferating in North America, and time has underscored that judgment. The tally is kept by *Shakespeare Newsletter,* which listed (April and May 1981) a total of forty-one Shakespeare festivals within the continental United States. Some of these were fairly small events and appear not to have been repeated. The same journal published a consolidated list of twenty-five festivals for 1982 (April–May 1982), and by 1983 the number had risen to thirty-one. I give them as listed in *Shakespeare Newsletter* (Summer 1983):

Alabama Shakespeare Festival, Anniston,
Alabama
American Players Theatre, Spring Green,
Wisconsin
Baltimore Shakespeare Theatre, Baltimore,
Maryland
Berkeley Shakespeare Festival, Berkeley,
California
Champlain Shakespeare Festival, Royall Tyler
Theatre, University of Vermont,
Burlington, Vermont
New York Shakespeare Festival, New York,
New York
Oregon Shakespeare Festival, Ashland,
Oregon
Pleasure Faire of the Renaissance, Sterling,
New York
Riverside Shakespeare Company, New York,
New York
Shakespeare and Company, Lenox,
Massachusetts
Shakespeare-by-the-Sea Festival, Virginia
Beach, Virginia
Shakespeare in Central Park, C. Douglas
Ramey Amphitheatre, Louisville,
Kentucky
Shakespeare in Delaware Park, State
University of New York, Buffalo, New
York
Shakespeare in the Park, Fort Worth, Texas
Shakespeare/Santa Cruz Festival, Performing
Arts Building, University of California,
Santa Cruz, California
Shakespeare Society of America, Globe
Playhouse, Los Angeles, California
Utah Shakespearean Festival, Cedar City, Utah
Cockpit in Court, Essex Community College,
Baltimore, Maryland
Colorado Shakespeare Festival, University of
Colorado, Boulder, Colorado
Shakespeare Festival of Dallas, Dallas, Texas
Great Lakes Shakespeare Festival, Cleveland,
Ohio
Garden Grove Shakespeare Festival, Garden
Grove, California
Houston Shakespeare Festival, Miller Theatre,
Houston, Texas
Illinois Shakespeare Festival, Illinois State
University, Normal, Illinois
Theater at Monmouth, Monmouth, Maine
New Jersey Shakespeare Festival, Drew
University, Madison, New Jersey

North Carolina Shakespeare Festival, High
Point, North Carolina
Oak Park Festival Theatre, Oak Park, Illinois
Old Globe Festival Theatre, San Diego,
California
Virginia Shakespeare Festival, College of
William and Mary, Williamsburg, Virginia
Wisconsin Shakespeare Festival, Platteville,
Wisconsin

That is a notable list, the more so since it omits the American Shakespeare Theater at Stratford, Connecticut. This festival has had periodic difficulties but retains the promise of its title and location: it has the genetic code of greatness. Even if one assumes that some of the festivals listed here are destined for no long life, many will certainly take hold—have in fact done so—and more will be initiated. Of the thirty-one, one only is a newcomer (Baltimore): all the others have a past, sometimes an extensive one. In 1983, for example, Colorado held its twenty-sixth annual season; the Old Globe, San Diego, its thirty-fourth; Oregon, its forty-eighth. Many more are effectively permanent institutions, with loyal cadres of returning spectators and stable funding. The contrast with England is interesting, for Shakespeare festivals are not widespread there. (The RSC, together with St. George's Theatre in Tufnell Park and the Regents Park Open-Air Theatre, accounts for most of the regular Shakespeare seasons.) Habitually, a Shakespeare play is included in most companies' repertory seasons in England; the American tendency is to build a season around Shakespeare. The list testifies to the enormous appetite of the American public for Shakespearean theater.

And the most intriguing of festivals is still to come. For some years now, Wayne State University in Detroit has been committed to a major project, the reconstruction of the Globe Playhouse. This building, known as the Third Globe, is now well into its planning stage. A neo-Elizabethan stage project is not unique, but this one has an exceptional combination of institutional support (from Wayne State University and the Detroit authorities) and expert advice from an international advisory committee. The dimensions of Shakespeare's Globe have passed beyond definitive calculation, but Detroit's reconstruction is based on a formidable reassessment of the evidence. The project vies with the Bankside Globe as one of the most ambitious re-creations of Shakespeare's stage in our time. It will have to wait for several years, however, before fruition. The project has been handed over to private developers (Schervish, Merz, and Vogel) who are actively seeking funding. Shane Park is already open, and the target date for the opening of the theater itself is 1988. The Detroit Globe will no doubt take its place as an authentic focus of Shakespearean theater.

Stratford Festival, Canada. Stratford, Ontario, is now the foremost Shakespearean festival in North America. Born in a tent in 1953, with Alec Guinness playing Richard III, it has expanded enormously. The Stratford Festival has three permanent theaters, of which the Festival Stage is the most important. An Elizabethan adaptation created by Tyrone Guthrie and Tanya Moiseiwitsch, the stage thrusts into the audience, which surrounds it on three sides. The festival offers a program of classical and modern plays, always with a large proportion of Shakespeare, and musical productions. Including school previews, the 1983 season ran to twenty-three weeks, playing to a total audience of half a million.

"Festival," though a traditional component of the title, no longer carries the implication of impermanence. Though the Stratford Festival has pulled back from its longest season (twenty-seven weeks in 1980), it remains broadly true that it plays for half the year and is in rehearsal for half the remaining period. One day, perhaps, the festival may achieve the relationship with Toronto that the RSC has with London. It remains a major institution, with a sizable administration, an archive with full records of all its productions, an acting corps of over 100, and fourteen to sixteen productions to mount each season. With few exceptions, usually guest artists of eminence, the theater personnel are Canadian. Such an operation requires and receives government funding, and the festival is supported by the Canada Council and the Province of Ontario. It nevertheless generates most of its income from box-office receipts and private contributions. In effect, if not name, the Stratford Festival is the National Theatre of Canada.

American Journals. The growing strength of the Shakespearean stage is fully registered in the major American journal of Shakespeare, *Shakespeare Quarterly.* Born in 1950, two years after *Shakespeare Survey,* it bears the impress of two editors: the late James G. McManaway and John F. Andrews. *Shakespeare Quarterly* has always been a journal of high scholarship. Its interests are shared with comparable journals, but the areas of its special emphasis are most interesting. More than any other journal, *Shakespeare Quarterly* has responded to what J. L. Styan termed "the Shakespeare Revolution," the realization that stage and study are coequal partners in Shakespeare. And as a quarterly (whose bibliography, indeed, is now a supplement, a fifth issue) it has been able to respond to the stage in ways not feasible for annual publications. Hence, in the later 1970s, *Shakespeare Quarterly* embarked on the gigantic enterprise of recording much of Shakespeare in contemporary performance. The contrast with the past is instructive. Twenty years ago, *Shakespeare Quarterly* might publish reviews of half-a-dozen festivals—the English, Canadian, and American Stratfords and Shakespeare in the Rockies, in New York, and in Oregon. In the early 1980s, the summer issues of *Shakespeare Quarterly* ran to as many as forty theater reviews. These covered virtually all American festivals and much in the outside world, such as Shakespeare in Finland, Israel, and West Germany. The stream overflowed into other issues, and today the policy is of general dispersal: that is, one reads theater reviews in *Shakespeare Quarterly* on the same basis as book reviews; they occur in every issue in roughly equal numbers. It is a striking and cogent means of registering the temper of the times.

Shakespeare Quarterly, then, can be seen to have borne out the introductory statement of its present editor: "Shakespeare is not easily circumscribed, and it can be argued, I think, that a journal devoted to study and appreciation of his work should not be easily circumscribed either." In its blend of authoritative scholarship and sensitivity to the outside world, *Shakespeare Quarterly*—edited from the Folger Shakespeare Library, with a print order of over 4,500—is central to American Shakespeare.

Mention should also be made of *Shakespeare Studies* (University of New Mexico, Albuquerque), an annual publication dating from 1965. *Shakespeare Newsletter* (Evanston, Illinois) now appears four times a year and has, since 1950, been much valued by Shakespeareans as a source of news, reviews, announcements of forthcoming events, jokes, abstracts, and the miscellanea and properties of the Shakespearean world.

Shakespeare Association of America. The SAA focuses the interests of American and Canadian Shakespeareans. Founded in 1923, the association took on new life following the World Shakespeare Congress in Vancouver, in August 1971. There a call went out to form national organizations in all the English-speaking countries and to set up an international organization. J. Leeds Barroll went back to the University of South Carolina and began to form an American group. With some funding from his institution and advice from a national committee of interested scholars, he was able to incorporate the association in 1972. Mary Hyde then agreed to vacate the name of the old SAA so that the new group could use it, thus continuing a long-standing tradition of similar aims.

The first annual meeting was held in Washington, D.C., in 1973 and was attended by more than 200. Before long the International Shakespeare Association (ISA) had been formed, and in 1976 the SAA hosted the first World Congress sponsored by that international group in Washington, D.C. The second congress, also a joint meeting with the SAA, was held in Stratford-upon-Avon in August 1981.

Membership in the SAA is open to anyone with a serious scholarly interest in Shakespeare's life, times, and theater; most members are college and university professors. Membership fluctuates between 500 and 700. Attendance at the annual meeting ranges between 175 and 400, though larger numbers attended the ISA congresses in 1976 (1,000) and 1981 (650). The meetings feature papers, symposia, and seminars on a wide variety of subjects. A high percentage of research prepared for these meetings finds its way into books and journals. A distinguished scholar is honored each year by being asked to deliver the annual lecture. Additionally, the SAA has fostered a growing dialogue between scholars and theater professionals, with contributions from the RSC and from most of the major Shakespeare companies in North America.

German-Speaking Peoples

Of all peoples other than the English-speaking, the German have the longest and closest associations with Shakespeare. That *unser* [our] *Shakespeare* still holds good is plain, as one looks at Germany. The German theaters, as recorded in *Shakespeare Quarterly*, regularly revive Shakespeare in productions of great distinction. The Bodmer Foundation of Zurich has easily the finest continental collection of early editions. The Shakespeare Library of the University of Munich, founded in 1964, is a well-developed center of Shakespearean resources. A major function is to collect all material relevant to the historical and present-day reception of Shakespeare in the German-speaking countries (Shakespeare translations from the eighteenth century to the present, unpublished stage versions and adaptations, reviews of Shakespeare productions). It is well equipped as an information center for the editors of the *Englisch-deutsche Studienausgabe der Werke Shakespeares;* it keeps in touch with the various theaters in the Federal Republic of Germany; and it organizes seminars for schoolteachers. Munich is the center of Shakespeare studies in West Germany.

All this is a crystallization of the Deutsche Shakespeare-Gesellschaft (German Shakespeare Association), which first met for Shakespeare's tercentenary in 1864 and commenced publication of *Shakespeare Jahrbuch* the following year. This remarkable journal is of an antiquity not matched in England and America. And it has an even greater claim on our attention, for the way in which it has responded to the facts of twentieth-century politics. In 1963 the German Shakespeare Association was split up into two independent societies, both carrying on the original tradition. What is still called the Deutsche Shakespeare-Gesellschaft (at Weimar) is now confined to the German Democratic Republic, while the Deutsche Shakespeare-Gesellschaft West (at Bochum) covers the Federal Republic of Germany, Switzerland, and Austria. Since 1964, each of these societies has published its own *Jahrbuch*. (The West German *Shakespeare Jahrbuch* is still known, confusingly, by the acronym *SJH*, though its place of publication was changed in 1982 from *H*eidelberg to *B*ochum.)

As one contemplates the rows of *Shakespeare Jahrbuch* side by side on the same shelf—the Shakespeare of Weimar and the shakespeare of Bochum, the blue binding of the East and the red binding of the West—one cannot but marvel at the serene adaptability of the author. It is, as it seems, still possible to find in the secular church of Shakespeare a unity and accord not available elsewhere. The affair is in fact less paradoxical than it looks. The essence of Shakespeare defies classification. We must expect to find something irregular and unpredictable in the institutions that acknowledge him as their inspiration.

BIBLIOGRAPHY

H. M. Adams, "The Shakespeare Collection in the Library of Trinity College, Cambridge," in *Shakespeare*

Survey, 5 (1952). David Addenbrooke, *The Royal Shakespeare Company: The Peter Hall Years* (1974). Henrietta C. Bartlett, *A Census of Shakespeare's Plays in Quarto 1594–1709,* rev. ed. (1939). Sally Beauman, *The Royal Shakespeare Company: A History of Ten Decades* (1982). Georges A. Bonnard, "Shakespeare in the Bibliotheca Bodmeriana," in *Shakespeare Survey,* 9 (1956).

Godfrey Davies, "The Huntington Library," *ibid.,* 6 (1953). Levi Fox, *In Honour of Shakespeare,* enl. ed. (1982), and *The Shakespeare Centre, Stratford-upon-Avon* (1982). F. C. Francis, "The Shakespeare Collection in the British Museum," in *Shakespeare Survey,* 3 (1950). L. W. Hanson, "The Shakespeare Collection in the Bodleian Library, Oxford," *ibid.,* 4 (1951).

Mary C. Henderson, "With the Compliments of the Raymond Mander and Joe Mitchenson Theatre Collection," in *Performing Arts Resources,* 2, Ted Perry, ed. (1976). C. Walter Hodges, S. Schoenbaum, and Leonard Leone, eds., *The Third Globe: Symposium for the Reconstruction of the Globe Playhouse* (1979). Mary C. Hyde, "The Shakespeare Association of America to the Folger Shakespeare Library on Its Fortieth Anniversary, 23 April 1972," in *Shakespeare Quarterly,* 23 (1972), 219–229.

Betty Ann Kane, *The Widening Circle: The Story of the Folger Shakespeare Library and Its Collections* (1976). Nati M. Krivasky and Laetitia Yeandle, "Theatrical Holdings of the Folger Shakespeare," in *Performing Arts Resources,* 1, Ted Perry, ed. (1975). Marion Linton, "National Library of Scotland and Edinburgh University Library Copies of Plays in Greg's *Bibliography of the English Printed Drama,*" in *Studies in Bibliography,* 15 (1962). George Rowell, "The University of Bristol Theatre Collection," in *Performing Arts Resources,* 4, Mary C. Henderson, ed. (1978). S. Schoenbaum, *Shakespeare: The Globe and the World* (1979) and *William Shakespeare: Records and Images* (1981).

The Shakespeare Institute: University of Birmingham (n.d.). *The Shakespeare Library: Birmingham Public Libraries* (n.d.). *Stratford Festival Story 1983* (official publication, updated annually, with the title date adjusted). *This Wooden O* (1982), brochure of the International Shakespeare Globe Centre. Louis B. Wright, *The Folger Library: Two Decades of Growth. An Informal Account* (1968).

Shakespeare and the Modern Writer

ANTHONY BURGESS

The year 1916 was, at least in Shakespeare's own country, too distracted for multicentennial celebrations. But 1964 saw something like a blaze. The twenty-third of April was a Thursday, a publication day, and there was a publisher's cocktail party on the Monday to wet the head of my novel *Nothing Like the Sun,* which is about Shakespeare. The same evening had been chosen for the opening of a new television channel, BBC-2, and, as television critic of *The Listener,* I had an obligation to stay at home and watch. But the publication party had priority. Fortunately Battersea power station broke down, and the inauguration of BBC-2 had to be postponed until the following evening. Thus, I was able to see *Kiss Me, Kate,* one of the exemplifications of the "new" approach to Shakespeare—unstuffy, irreverent, but laterally authentic, since the Bard might be regarded as being closer to Cole Porter and Broadway razzmatazz than to the scholars who were picking him raw.

BBC-2, which at the beginning of its career was permitted to confine its appeal to a minority audience, was able in that quatercentenary spring to present a fair spectrum of contemporary approaches to Shakespeare. There was a program on his life and personality, written by Ivor Brown but drawing also on Leslie Hotson's *The First Night of "Twelfth Night."* Duke Ellington's *Such Sweet Thunder* was performed. There were presentations of Laurence Olivier's films of *Henry V, Hamlet,* and *Richard III.* There was even an hour-long Shakespeare anthology in Elizabethan pronunciation,

demonstrating that rigorous linguistic research could also furnish entertainment. Though 1916 had seen a film version of *The Merchant of Venice,* with Matheson Lang in the lead, the otherwise muffled celebration of that bad year had hinted that World War I and Shakespeare had little to say to each other. Was that to be true of the whole disenchanted era? Nineteen sixty-four was quite sure that Shakespeare belonged to the modern world.

Shakespeare certainly did not seem to have much to say to the fighting poets of World War I. Here were depths of misery and boredom, a long, muddy stalemate variegated by slaughter on a scale previously unimaginable, the death of patriotism, a cynicism that found no echo in readings of *Troilus and Cressida*—a play apparently unknown to young officers who had come straight from public-school literature courses. Rupert Brooke, dead in 1916, had written sonnets in 1914 with a St. Crispin's Day flavor, but the task of poets like Robert Graves and Siegfried Sassoon was to express the inexpressible through a bland medium suitable for weekend joy in cottage gardens. Wilfred Owen saw the futility of Georgian rhyme but could not write blank verse. He used slant rhyme instead and occasionally, perhaps without knowing it, evoked the rhythms of Dante. The impossibility of yoking the inherited literary tradition to a new and, as it turned out, unique experience was best exemplified in David Jones's *In Parenthesis* (1937), where characters from *Henry V* sit very strangely in the Flanders mud. The significant literature of the twentieth century did not emerge from its most terrible nightmare. If Shakespeare had anything to say to writers, they had first to be cut off from the fighting experience: they had to be Americans like Pound and Eliot, or they had to sit out the war in a neutral zone, as did James Joyce. The continuity of literature in English, which must always mean learning something from Shakespeare, had to be sustained outside the battle.

In *Language and Silence* (1967) George Steiner affirms, in inappropriately grandiloquent prose, the inefficacy not only of literature but of language itself to express the horrors of the Nazi holocaust. "After Auschwitz, only silence." In other words, we have to accept the limitations of Shakespeare. No such limitations were recognized by the romantics, while the Age of Reason perceived that its own limitations were a virtue that Shakespeare barbarously transgressed. It is perhaps only since the armistice of 1918 that Shakespeare has been recognized as a journeyman writer of genius subject to the errors and ineptitudes enforced by rapidity of execution or produced by sheer insouciant carelessness. "Others abide our question; thou art free," said Matthew Arnold. Shakespeare had been a mountain, a god. By 1964 he was acceptable as a human being. There was less reverence but far more understanding; there was also more affection. It was possible to think of Shakespeare as Will. Milton has never been known as Jack.

There had been a time when the private life and personality of Shakespeare had been as little relevant to his work as those of Homer (who might, anyway, be a congeries of anonymous bards) had been to his. When disreputable biographical facts were known, they were frequently brushed aside. That Shakespeare's first child was born six months after his marriage was excused by reference to nonexistent customs of affiancement: "No moral delinquency may be imputed to him," wrote E. K. Chambers. The nineteenth century was much concerned with Shakespeare as a proto-Tennyson, a model of probity. Indecencies in his work were edited out or glossed falsely. In the "Scylla and Charybdis" episode of *Ulysses,* John Eglinton objects to Stephen Dedalus' prying into the life of a great man. "The poet's drinking, the poet's debts. We have *King Lear,* and it is immortal." But Joyce, in a long chapter, claims a right previously claimed by two other Irishmen to consider Shakespeare as a man and to use the plays as material for speculation on his life and character. Oscar Wilde had already done this and made a fanciful identification of Mr. W. H.; while Bernard Shaw had, in *The Dark Lady of the Sonnets,* put a comic Shakespeare on the stage. Frank Harris was the pioneer in fanciful Shakespeare biography, but Will as a figure of fun was an emanation of Shaw's vaunted superiority to him as a playwright. Yet it was seen, in all the fictional travesties of Shakespeare the man that followed Shaw's, that no ingenuity (save perhaps that of Edward Bond in his play *Bingo*) could render him unsympathetic. What twentieth-century writers have found in the fancied personality of Shakespeare are the preoccupations that afflict or bless any writer, great or small—concern about money, marriage, children, extramarital love, deadlines, social position, even disease.

Shaw's Shakespeare is an actor of poor memory and limited imagination, who snaps up good things that he hears, his poetic ear not as good as it should be, something of a lecher, a skilled wheedler of favors, a snob vastly concerned with his own social position. Such a portrait could not have been sustained beyond the limits of a one-act play whose true theme, anyway, is Britain's need for a national theater. The first full-length fiction about him seems to be John Brophy's *Gentleman of Stratford* (1939), a novel of "popular" intention in which there is no stink from Fleet Ditch, no pederasty, no hangman's hands, nor indeed anything to upset the average subscriber to a popular book club. The Bard is a little weary, very genteel, a sufferer from a marriage threatening to become too philoprogenitive, and the guilt of adultery—as well as a hopeless schwarmerei for an aristocratic woman he calls my dear Lady Disdain. Presumably each age gets the Shakespeare it requires, whether in personality or art, but a comic or even farcical Shakespeare is safer than a romantic one. Thus, the entertainment called *No Bed for Bacon,* published in 1941 by Caryl Brahms and S. J. Simon, presented a Shakespeare whom the reader was not expected to take seriously and hence, safe from an expected posture of reverence, surprisingly found almost plausible. This Shakespeare, who spends much of the book trying out new spellings of his name, is regarded as an expert on orthography. He is always dreaming of a "shining" play called *Love's Labor's Found,* in which he never gets further than some such opening as "The Garden of Eden. Enter a Snake." When he proposes dalliance with a young girl and she demurs, he grins and says, "It's all right if it's Shakespeare." Such a diversion links hands with

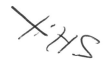

Shaw's playlet. Shakespeare's plays are so great that we can afford to see their creator as a figure of farce, one who, in the British manner, is forbidden to be exalted by the unbidden additions of genius. The greatness is, in other words, an irrelevance to be laughed off.

My own novel of 1964, *Nothing Like the Sun,* sums up in its title the diminishing approach: if the brightness of Shakespeare's mistress' eyes must not be exaggerated, neither must his own stature as a moral being. Borrowing from Thomas Mann's *Doctor Faustus,* I speculate about the possibility of Shakespeare's catching syphilis from the Dark Lady or the earl of Southampton or both, and the relationship between the spirochete and the genius of tragedy. I cannot justify such an approach on any grounds other than the prevalence of the French pox in Elizabethan England and Shakespeare's own very accurate summary—in *Timon of Athens*—of its symptoms, which he could have recognized in himself. Yet the aristocrat of the diseases, as it has been called, seemed to me to be a very useful symbol of the breakdown in civic order that Shakespeare certainly observed in the later days of Elizabeth's reign and brooded on in the dark comedies as well as the great tragedies. No novelist need ask his readers, especially his scholarly ones if any, to take his depositions as biographical fact; but he has the duty of at least contriving a credible language, ambience, and psychology—the duty, in short, of being scholarly while trying to entertain. The task of preparing such a novel as *Nothing Like the Sun* involves more scholarship than the average reader need be aware of—a kind of soaking in of atmosphere and language and the imposition of various limitations, for the Elizabethans did not know what we know: they were, for instance, pre-Freudian and pre-Marxist, as well as pre-Newtonian.

My fictionalization of Shakespeare very nearly, in 1968, reached the cinema screen. This was the age of the four-hour, "hard-ticket" film; it was also the age of permissiveness, well able to present a syphilitic Shakespeare grappling with the Dark Lady and others (even the earl) in frontal nudity. Such a film, unmade because of the final timidity of Warner Brothers, could have contributed something to scholarship. Olivier, in the opening and closing sequences of *Henry V,* put the Globe playhouse on the screen; my own film was to make much of the carting over the Thames of the demolished timbers of the Shoreditch Theatre and the erection, under Peter Street, of the new structure on the Bankside.

It also proposed presenting the Essex rebellion and the preludial performance of *Richard II* that signaled its commencement. The quashing of the rebellion and the execution of Essex had to be related directly—following the needs of the plot rather than of history—to Shakespeare's own situation in a year in which he mostly wrote nothing but, in the autumn, brought out *Hamlet,* and it was through brooding on plot that a significance could be imposed on an event known by scholars but never interpreted by them. Essex was executed on Ash Wednesday; the Shrovetide revels proceeded as usual before, and the Lord Chamberlain's Men performed at court on the eve of Essex's death. What play was presented? Only pedantic negativism would deny that it was *Richard II,* that the queen watched it, and that she gave orders for the players to witness the execution on Tower Hill to remind them of the dangers of allowing trivial entertainment to become mixed up in politics. This sequence was suggested by my producer, William Conrad, an actor who is no scholar: he required that the Lord Chamberlain's Men should so perform, and the record of a performance obeyed him, though it did not give the name of the play. The rest seemed to follow logically. An artist's instincts are always, especially when they are set to work on Shakespeare, of immense value.

It is in Joyce's *Ulysses* that the most magisterial fictional examination of the relationship between Shakespeare's life and work is to be found. Stephen Dedalus, in the National Library in Dublin, puts forward drunkenly a thesis that nobody is forced to accept and that nobody does. (Drunkenness is a useful device for hedging imaginative bets: the narrator of *Nothing Like the Sun* gets progressively drunker on Chinese rice spirit.) Stephen will not have it that Shakespeare's plays are, like Beethoven's music, divorced from the private preoccupations of the artist. It is, for instance, impossible for a playwright to ignore the private significance of his characters' names. In *Richard III* a Richard courts an Anne; Shakespeare's wife was an Anne and one of his brothers, a Richard. Anne and Richard remain in Stratford while the husband and brother lives high in scortatory London. Adultery follows wooing; Anne is "hot in the blood." The incestuous aspects of the affair are given fuller treatment in *Hamlet.* Richard becomes Claudius, whose name means "limper," Gertrude is Anne, Shakespeare himself plays the dispossessed Ghost, seeing in Hamlet the lineaments of his own dead son Hamnet as he might have been had he lived. All this is, of course, unsound as scholarship; but fictional insights, as well as psychoanalytical ones like the oedipal theory of Ernest Jones (which influenced Olivier in his film *Hamlet*), must perhaps be drawn on when critics like T. S. Eliot find a disparity between the content of a play and the emotional force that inspissates it.

Certainly, the "problem" of *Hamlet* is partially resolved when one ceases to see the play as an aesthetic structure and considers that it may, in its less active phases, be an outlet for personal obsessions. There is more of Warwickshire in Denmark than plausibility should permit—the queen's floral cadenza, a conflation of the accidentally drowned Ophelia and the suicidally drowned Kate Hamlett of Shakespeare's youth, with its consequent wrangle about lack of burial rights in consecrated ground and "crowner's quest law." And Hamlet seems to be summarizing the earlier career of his creator for Horatio when he philosophizes about the skulls of a lawyer, a nobleman, and a clown called Yorick who is probably the Richard Tarleton of the Queen's Men, Shakespeare's first acting troupe.

It is to be noted that the biographical approach —wholly justifiable in fiction, especially when it is *Ulysses*—seeped into scholarship in a manner that might be considered wholly alien to the rationale of the scholar. G. B. Harrison's *Shakespeare at Work* reads like a novel, as does Hotson's *The First Night of "Twelfth Night,"* though the thesis of the latter seems sometimes to go further than the most extravagant novelist might permit. Moreover, to view the plays in the light of the circumstances in which they were written is often to substitute human excuses for objective appraisal when the playwright is not at his best. *King John,* for instance, becomes interesting not as a play but as a record of the psychological turmoil that the author was undergoing while writing it—the moving passages about the death of a son and the danger of a new Spanish invasion transposed to a medieval England become implausibly Protestant.

It would be wrong to consider Joyce's concern with Shakespeare the man as a mere interlude in the plot of *Ulysses,* for that novel is as much myth as realistic fiction, and Shakespeare is being drawn upon as a contributor to myth. The relationship between Shakespeare, his adulterous wife, and his short-lived son is forced into presiding over the situation of Leopold Bloom, who has also lost a son and whose wife is unfaithful. Moreover, Shakespeare becomes the ghost of Hamlet's father, and his relationship to Hamlet is of a mystical order that finds a parallel in Bloom's adoption of Stephen Dedalus as a son-surrogate. Stephen wears a "Hamlet hat" and is in mourning. He is Japheth in search of a father, as well as Telemachus waiting for Odysseus to come; he is dispossessed of his kingdom, whether this be the Martello Tower, for which he pays the rent, or the bigger realm of literature, which he cannot enter without the sponsorship of a mystical father. Theologically father and son are of the same substance, and Hamlet is both prince and king. When, in the phantasmagorical brothel scene, Bloom and Stephen look simultaneously into a mirror, they see Shakespeare as a joint reflection—a comic cuckold who has lost even the gift of language, a caricature of total dispossession. Shakespeare presides over *Ulysses* more solidly than does Homer, not only in the sense that his language dominates the interior monologues of Stephen, as idle speculations about *Hamlet* flit through the musings of Bloom, but as the creator of myth who is himself a myth. Penelope is a weaver, but Bottom is one also, and Bloom can enter the ghastly fairyland of nighttown (where a true midsummer night's dream is enacted) only by wearing an ass's head. A bottom of good sense, to use Dr. Johnson's term, meets the overly rarefied young Hamlet. But this Hamlet is also a dead Hamnet (Bloom's son Rudy) come back to life, and this turns Bloom into a kind of Shakespeare.

Adaline Glasheen is inclined to believe that the hero of *Finnegans Wake* is also Shakespeare (or Shapesphere) disguised as H. C. Earwicker. His wife is named Ann and he has three children, two of whom are twins—the exact Shakespeare constellation. He may be regarded as the summation of all Shakespeare's male characters, from Lackbreath to Fallstuff; but this is as much as to say that, being universal sinning man, as well as universal creating man, he has to find his historical analogue in Shakespeare, who, next to God, has created most and—necessarily, according to Joyce's implied thesis—sinned most. The sins of creative man have to be sexual: to erect one must have erections, and libido (Shakespeare's "Will") is the force behind art as well as sex. One must not pursue this too far, but it is in order to see Shakespeare as one of the primary fertilizing forces behind Joyce.

Ulysses appeared in 1922, and that year saw the publication of T. S. Eliot's *The Waste Land,* which, independently of Joyce, drew on Shakespeare to create a kind of synthetic mythology. The postwar age is dry of belief and awaits the revivifying rain: death by water is preferable to death through drought, and Ophelia and the father of Ferdinand in *The Tempest* ("Those are pearls that were his eyes") join Phlebas the Phoenician and King Ludwig II of Bavaria as watery sacrificial victims who may assist our regeneration. Shakespeare has become a great giver of symbols, and it is the culture that begot him that stands in critical juxtaposition to our own. When the sterile opulence of Belladonna, Lady of the Rocks, has to be invoked, this is done through an ironic reminiscence of Cleopatra—"The Chair she sat in, like a burnished throne,/ Glowed on the marble." When a more literal sterility is presented—Lil of the bad teeth refusing to have children—Ophelia's final words before her drowning are heard. Shakespeare provides a literary shorthand, and one of the conditions for understanding Eliot is an assumption that Shakespeare, like the Bible, has been absorbed into our culture and become virtually proverbial. "On the Rialto once"—"Lights, lights": the phrases in *Burbank with a Baedeker: Bleistein with a Cigar* are intended to spark not merely reminiscences of entire plays *(Othello* and *Hamlet)* but images of entire cultures that have been betrayed.

It is not, of course, quite as simple as that. The ambiguity of Eliot, especially in *The Waste Land,* is a device of contrapuntal complexity that ensures the artistic validity of the work and prevents it from becoming tendentious. Elizabethan England had dirty ears that could hear "jug jug" in a nightingale's song, and Elizabeth and Leicester on the Thames joke about the possibility of marriage—a marriage that would be sterile. "That Shakespeherian Rag," which is so elegant, so intelligent, traduces Shakespeare, but Shakespeare has the stuff of self-betrayal in him. There is, to Eliot, no useful moral content in Shakespeare, as there is in an Upanishad, but there is at least a live tradition that it is the duty of twentieth-century literature to recover. The strength of Shakespeare lies in many things, none of which have much to do with the rigorous Thomism of Dante, whom, as a Christian, Eliot reveres in a manner that transcends purely literary judgments. The major Shakespearean strength lies in his achievement of a verse medium capable of a multitude of tonalities, some of which are pertinent to the needs of a twentieth-century poet.

In discussing the formation of his own verse technique, Eliot spoke of the influence of Jules Laforgue, evident enough in the rhymed works, such as *The Love Song of J. Alfred Prufrock,* and of the post-Shakespearean dramatists—Middleton and Webster more than Beaumont and Fletcher. Eliot, with a kind of humility, refused to be influenced directly by Shakespeare but accepted his influence at a remove. This seemed to be a means of testing the validity of the blank-verse medium itself as used not only by Shakespeare but also by his predecessors and contemporaries. To submit to Shakespeare directly, as to Joyce, is to risk becoming an imitator of what cannot easily be imitated. When, in *Murder in the Cathedral,* Eliot makes his Third Priest say

Go venture shipwreck on the sullen coasts
Where blackamoors make captive Christian men,

he is very nearly going back as far as *Gorboduc,* but he is justified because the verse of *Gorboduc* is behind Shakespeare. His most sustained effort in free verse that is not far from blank verse is *Gerontion,* where the tone is of a highly intelligent playwright who, having learned from Shakespeare in the year 1615 or thereabouts, has gone to sleep and awakened in the twentieth century. He has bypassed classicism and romanticism and is fitting an early-seventeenth-century technique to twentieth-century pessimism.

The romantic poets were willing to learn from Shakespeare's blank verse, but they failed to understand its closeness to speech rhythms. To approach Shakespeare was to count syllables and to use tropes and inversions that, though obsolete, gained a certain glamour through association. Lacking both stage experience and an important theatrical tradition, they produced a rhetoric that was neither lyrical nor dramatic. Though neither Eliot nor Pound began with theatrical ambitions, both had an innate dramatic sense (hamstrung for a time in Pound because of his devotion to Browning), recognizing that all verse that is not song is essentially dramatic, in that it gains its vitality from heightened speech and that the imagined voice that utters it is, to a certain extent, that of an invented character. Yeats, though he wrote verse for the theater, was inhibited by a lyrical approach that accepted what Shakespeare learned to overcome—the line, and not the verse-paragraph, as the unit of utterance. His finest blank verse is more primitive than Shakespeare's:

The blood-dimmed tide is loosed, and everywhere
The ceremony of innocence is drowned;
The best lack all conviction, while the worst
Are full of passionate intensity.

(The Second Coming)

This is wonderful but not as wonderful as Ulysses' lamenting in *Troilus and Cressida* the breakdown of order. More cunningly than Yeats, Eliot saw that the modernity of Shakespeare lay in a desire to obscure the five regular beats of the blank verse line and even, in the interests of approximating to speech, to truncate it on occasion.

Dr. Johnson had berated Shakespeare for his "quibbles"—the fatal Cleopatra for which his world was well lost—but extravagant wordplay, conceits, deliberate complexities, too "metaphysical" for the Age of Reason, were to Eliot's taste and also to William Empson's, as exemplified not merely in his poetry but also in a revolutionary handbook called *Seven Types of Ambiguity* (1930). The mature Shakespeare, it was disclosed, rarely made plain statements. Sometimes he created complexities straight out of the unconscious, as in the famous "Ariachne" of *Troilus and Cressida,* where "Ariadne" and "Arachne," both concerned with lines and labyrinths, are instinctively fused. The task of editors had previously been to disentangle what they saw as confusion and declare for one name or the other, but the portmanteau nature of the coinage was now to be seen as very modern and a justification of Joyce's contrapuntal technique in *Finnegans Wake.* It proved necessary also to view Shakespeare's wordplay in terms of his pronunciation. In *Henry IV* reasons are as plentiful as blackberries because the digraph *ea* has an "Irish" pronunciation. The unrounded *o* in "solid" makes Hamlet's flesh sallied and sullied. Where Shakespeare's puns had been deplored they were now seen as justifiable devices of irony. If *Macbeth* could play with "gild" and "guilt," Eliot's Phlebas and Mr. Eugenides could meet in a pocketful of currants and a current under sea. If Wordsworthean simplicity was no longer acceptable and a whole line could be filled up with "polyphiloprogenitive," this was because Shakespeare liked long words.

The revival of the verse play in the 1930s had little directly to do with the influence of Shakespeare. Nineteenth-century poetic drama had tried to learn from Shakespeare but reproduced only the least important aspects of his rhetorical surface.

With Stephen Phillips there was altogether deplorable pseudo-Shakespeareanism, as well as a blank verse that did its utmost to point a gap between live speech and stage diction. Perhaps the most shameful of all attempts to make acceptable verse drama was Clemence Dane's *Will Shakespeare* (1921), which, having as theme an improbable love rivalry between Shakespeare and Marlowe, had to be resolutely Elizabethan and in blank verse too. When, in 1935, Eliot produced his *Murder in the Cathedral,* he tried to obliterate the possibility of comparison with Shakespeare by using free verse for his chorus and a mixture of verse forms for his dialogue, rhymed, half-rhymed, unrhymed, which should carry more of the flavor of the medieval guild plays than that of a more sophisticated theater. In the plays with a modern setting that followed—*The Family Reunion, The Cocktail Party, The Confidential Clerk*—the aim was to avoid the rhetorical altogether and produce a mode of stage speech indistinguishable from Monsieur Jourdain's prose but cunningly marked by a soft regular tetrametric beat that could justify a sudden heightening into poetry. It is notable that in *The Cocktail Party* the only poetry occurs in a long quotation from Shelley's *Prometheus Unbound.* Any undue heightening of speech would have sounded, so Eliot must have felt, like an approach to Shakespeare and thus embarrassed both poet and audience.

In other words, Shakespeare was no longer suitable as a theatrical influence. The verse plays of Auden and Isherwood were closer to Brecht than to anything in the English tradition, though in Auden's *The Ascent of F6* both Michael Ransom and his mother are made to speak a blank verse close to Wordsworth at his most pedestrian:

Give me the crystal—let me look again
And prove my former vision a poor fake.

Christopher Fry, who because of cricketing associations was often linked unjustly with Eliot, was believed for a time to have imported into stage comedy an Elizabethan gusto. It was possible for a character to describe the moon as "a circumambulating aphrodisiac" and please middle-class playgoers with an impression that they were being uplifted as well as diverted. But Fry has not lasted, except as a film scenarist and translator of Anouilh and Rostand, and the whole brief prospect of a permanent revival of verse in the theater has proved to be a chimera. The modern stage has yielded finally to prose.

In *Finnegans Wake* the dead god-giant is sacramentally consumed, and his uneaten or regurgitated limbs and organs lie scattered on the wide champaign of the book. Shakespeare is in much the position of a god who, being also man, and a man apparently indifferent to the fate of his work, can be broken and consumed more casually. We have seen in the theater versions of Shakespeare that deny not only the setting and dress of the original plays but also their presumed meaning. (I have witnessed on French television a production of *Hamlet* in which the Ghost is a woman. This goes further than Leopold Bloom's speculation that the Prince himself might be a woman and hence have good reason for spurning Ophelia.) Charles Marowitz's *Hamlet* was not intended to be Shakespeare, though it rifles *Hamlet* for some of its lines. Edward Bond's *Lear* makes of Shakespeare's plot and characters an exercise in twentieth-century violence that seems to scorn Shakespeare's historical innocence. In nondramatic literature it seems possible for writers to filch from Shakespeare what they wish, ignoring the presumed total artistic intention of a poet too big—and also too dead—to complain. If Eliot has made of Elizabethan (properly Jacobean) verse a medium suitable for the sensibility of the age between two wars, it is presumably possible for a modern writer to take over Shakespeare's characters and make them new.

The separation of Shakespeare's characters from his plays began early, but chiefly with the French romantics. When the British Shakespeare company that contained Harriet Smithson appeared in Paris in the 1820s, there was great excitement at the content but disappointment with the form. Shakespeare, it was assumed, would have been a novelist if the novel had properly existed in his time; he was forced to work in an unsympathetic and barbarous medium from which he must now be rescued. It was the musician Hector Berlioz who set out to present an idealized *Romeo and Juliet* in which even the words of the original were subdued; for them was substituted the universal language of sound, so that Romeo became a clarinet and Juliet an oboe, Mercutio's Queen Mab speech was transferred to the orchestra, and what few words were retained were to be mumbled by the chorus. Tchaikovsky got all the main elements in his *Romeo and Juliet* fantasy-overture—Friar Laurence chorale, Capulet-Montague dissension, love theme—and a number

of later composers, including Strauss *(Macbeth)* and Elgar *(Falstaff)*, accepted the assumption (quite apart from operas) that parts of Shakespeare were greater, or at least more useful, than the whole. This was a musical parallel to the tendency of scholars like A. C. Bradley and the authoress of *The Girlhood of Shakespeare's Heroines* to separate characters from their aesthetic context and to accord them an almost historical reality.

Though Elgar's symphonic study *Falstaff* does not properly come into my survey, its aesthetic finds a parallel in all literary attempts to separate the fat knight from his total context. Verdi's opera follows *The Merry Wives of Windsor* and, through reminiscences of the *Henry IV* plays and exaltation of the music to *nobilmente* levels, makes a lesser Falstaff into a greater one. But it is dangerous to separate the Falstaff of the historical plays from the history to which he is a foil. Elgar has his Prince Hal themes, but his concentration on the Falstaff episodes of the two *Henry IV* plays makes great music out of a falsification of Shakespeare. Sooner or later, perhaps under the influence of Elgar, Falstaff had to appear as the hero of a novel, and in 1976, Robert Nye produced a lengthy piece of fantastic fiction that sought to make the fat knight into a kind of Rabelaisian hero, with more uncleanliness than Shakespeare would have countenanced. Thus, there is a whole chapter dedicated to "Sir John Fastolf's prick," complete with a sub-Rabelaisian catalog of nicknames for the organ. There is a certain amount of willful, and unworthy, anachronism, as when Falstaff or Fastolf claims to have recognized the rogues at Gadshill and says, near-quoting Bing Crosby, "Buckram becomes you; it goes with your eyes." This whole *Falstaff*, part Shakespeare, part garbled history, mostly invention, is amusing enough, but it leaves out of account the cunning with which the original Falstaff is fitted as a foil into a serious and even tragic historical chronicle. Evidently, as one sees also in Orson Welles's film *Chimes at Midnight* and the number of British pubs called the Falstaff Arms, Falstaff (the meat, as L. C. Knights says, that most readers regard as the only edible material of the *Henry IV* sandwiches) has become a folk spirit of demotic hedonism, an English Silenus into whom is rolled, for more than good measure, the sub-Falstaff Sir Toby Belch. He represents that side of the English character, wholly demotic, that is also summed up in Donald McGill's seaside picture postcards and the drunken spirit of northern wakes weeks. His knighthood is forgotten, as is also his wit. Elgar does not ignore either, and he superadds a nostalgia for boyhood innocence and a love of the English countryside. Or at least, music having no true verbal referents, this is what he appears to do.

Falstaff has been separated from his context in his own name. Hamlet has been dragged out of Denmark in a number of guises. The melancholy young man, dispossessed, learned, highly articulate, not at home in the world of action, is, as we have seen, easily transmuted into Stephen Dedalus. Such a character, needing the solidity of an understanding father, in whom emotion, according to Eliot, is in excess of any possible excitatory cause, has been almost a cliché in the twentieth-century novel. He is Denis in Aldous Huxley's *Crome Yellow* and Gumbril in *Antic Hay,* as well as Paul Pennyfeather and William Boot in, respectively, Evelyn Waugh's *Decline and Fall* and *Scoop.* Waugh's trilogy *Sword of Honour* presents a kind of negative hero, Guy Crouchback, who finds something morally rotten in the whole world— World War II is a symptom of this, not a cause— but, caught up in a machine controlled by powers greater than himself, takes up arms with no prospect of quelling a sea of troubles. Behind Crouchback stands Ford Madox Ford's hero Christopher Tietjens, dispossessed of his lands and honor, the stoic good soldier who observes the decay of morality and is himself attacked by forces that have power but no responsibility. All these essentially nontragic characters survive by virtue of their stoicism. According to Eliot, Hamlet's stoicism, like that of the Duchess of Malfi (whose "I am Duchess of Malfi still" echoes Seneca's "Medea superest"), is merely a desperate assertion of identity in the face of destruction. This is because the Prince is the hero of a tragedy. The contemporary Hamlet is stoic in the face of battering that is too exaggerated to be other than comic.

On the whole, Shakespeare has given little to the modern novelist, and this is surprising. For a legitimate fictional exercise would be the relegation of the Shakespearean soliloquy, and even much dialogue, to the unspoken stream of consciousness— following, of course, the *Ulysses* technique—and the provision of something like plain, colloquial speech for the spoken exchanges. Yet neither *Hamlet* nor *Macbeth* has been turned into a novel. Such a transformation would be the contemporary equivalent of the Lambs' *Tales from Shakespeare* and perhaps, for readers scared of Shakespeare, more useful. It is Shakespeare's fellow playwrights who have felt more disposed to paraphrase or tamper— from Shaw with his new ending for *Cymbeline* to Tom Stoppard with his *Rosencrantz and Guildenstern Are Dead.* But as so much tampering is allowed to stage directors, failed playwrights nearly all, such genuinely creative fiddling would seem to be supererogatory.

What Shakespeare can give to the modern writer, and sometimes does give, is a sense of the importance of his craft and of the resources of the English language. Add to this an endless pragmatic wisdom and a humanistic tolerance, and we have what British citizens like to think is their main contribution to civilization. But language comes first as last, and it is in the complexity of the later plays, some of the Sonnets, and *The Phoenix and Turtle* that we best learn the actual and potential resources of English.

As the most valuable product of a Western civilization seen, in our own century, as in grave danger from the totalitarian forces within and without, Shakespeare remains more a symbol than an influence in a certain kind of writer. Aldous Huxley's *Brave New World* presents a scientific totalitarianism in which strong emotions are recognized as a danger to social stability and in which literature has been tamed to a branch of "social engineering." The savage who enters this stable, hedonistic, yet infantile society comes with a tattered volume of Shakespeare that symbolizes a braver if older world: Shakespeare is immune from censorship because he has become unintelligible. George Orwell visualized a time in which Shakespeare would be read no more but saw in him what he saw in Charles Dickens—an ebullience and love of the processes of life that totalitarianism, like Ben Jonson, would wish to sufflaminate. Winston Smith, the doomed hero of *Nineteen Eighty-four,* wakes one morning with the name Shakespeare on his lips. He does not understand what the name means, but the unconscious, as yet unsubmissive to the metaphysics of Ingsoc, certainly does. In the real 1984, Shakespeare remains for the modern writer, as for modern literate man in general, a standard for judgment of morality as well as of art. And, more than in the past, he is seen also as a fellow human being and a fellow artist.

Shakespeare and the Modern Playwright

PETER USTINOV

When we consider the influence of Shakespeare on the modern playwright, it cannot mean merely the choice of plots, since Shakespeare borrowed them from other sources and from history itself. The lessons he teaches are not merely narrative or indeed those of architecture but, rather, the all-important ones of texture. Shakespeare was an actor—whether great or even good is of no consequence. Whether he would have won one of the ephemeral prizes awarded for the gratification of the few and the sorrow of many in this time of instant communication is neither here nor there. What is certain is that he had to have been at least a most interesting actor to have written works as divergent in aim as *King Lear* and *The Comedy of Errors.* He knew in the most subtle detail the possibilities of the actor's craft and elevated them to the level of great art.

Paradoxically, he lived at a time when the sophistication of audiences had not yet come to demand such refinements as directors and stage designers, so that far more had to be relegated to the realm of imagination. In this domain Shakespeare had no peer. When there are battles, we are shown isolated pockets of conflict, redolent of the prevailing chaos. A solitary king craves the solace of a horse; mortal enemies meet by chance, owing to an evident breakdown in their chains of command. What emerges from the paucity of the physical means at Shakespeare's disposal is an extraordinary insight into the grotesque inefficiency inherent in the very nature of human conflict: the rodomontade and

pageantry that precede it, the arbitrary shift of fortunes that accompanies it, the utter desolation and disruption that follow in its wake.

The suggestive powers of the actor bore a far greater burden then than they do today, for time and space had to be peopled and decorated by the power of the word and gesture. The traditional Chinese theater has always relied as heavily on the performer's resources as did the theater of Shakespeare. A boatman rowing across an unseen river finds the way of suggesting not only water but also wind and current by the movements of his body. This is total acting, and the public understands every mimetic allusion and responds by an effort of reciprocal imagination.

Naturally enough, technical advances of three centuries have served to diminish the demands on the public imagination and to relegate the actors to the roles of mere instruments in an ever-growing orchestra. The upper and lower stage of the Elizabethan playhouse, which were certainly inherited from the medieval mystery play, and their need to dramatize celestial as well as mundane—and even, at times, infernal—activities, yielded in the seventeenth century to the proscenium stage that we know today. On the picture-frame stage, usually decorated with a predilection for elegance and equilibrium, perspective became all-important, distant temples in man-made parklands serving as a background to almost every dramatic manifestation that was not specifically comic in character. Shakespeare was performed under what must have been extraordinarily ponderous conditions, with hooped and garlanded skirts abounding, to say nothing of headdresses heaped high with feathers. Gesture became as formal as the physical limitations imposed by the costumes demanded. Tragedy evolved into a rite performed to meticulously prescribed rules, rather than an expedition into the depths of the human spirit.

After the disturbing uncertainties of the Cromwellian revolution, this new order inevitably settled into a kind of genteel somnolence, once the roystering hedonism and cynicism of Restoration comedy had burned itself out and the happy ending became a social necessity.

The sharper edges of Shakespeare were honed away, and King Lear was allowed, in Nahum Tate's adaptation (1681), to survive his risky adventures on the heath in order to bestow his blessing, with rediscovered benignity, on the nuptials of Cordelia and Edgar. Thomas Bowdler's *Family Shakespeare* (1807) erased the saltier passages of the ancient texts. That Shakespeare's genius survived these incursions on its integrity is a mark of its unique power. The next hurdle was the seductive art of theatrical machinery. The playbills of the early nineteenth century reveal the enormous change of emphasis that the purely mechanical aspect of the theater had undergone, a change so great that the spectator was no longer enticed by the performers or the play but, rather, by the stage engineer's legerdemain, made manifest in such events as Vesuvius in full eruption, a brigantine sinking in a storm at sea, or the walls of Jericho tumbling down. As in the films of Cecil B. DeMille, the fury and majesty of nature silenced the human spirit. After all, what is there to talk about while crossing the Red Sea under a canopy of frozen breakers? And why speculate about being or not being in an accurately reproduced tempest, under scudding clouds and the sting of rain? Shakespeare needs calm for reflection and a launching pad of silence in order to ascend into his particular orbit. Introspection was out of style, to permit the theatrical designers to regale the public with exceptionally brilliant reproductions of natural disasters and other acts of God.

Only with the intellectualization of the theater and the introduction of the so-called fourth wall was the expansiveness of the epic finally forced into retreat, to be eliminated entirely by rising costs and the advent of films. With the newfound intimacy and the quieter tones of Chekhov and of Ibsen—to mention only two heralds of the rediscovery of human relations—the focus returned to the individual. Shakespeare, no more fitted to this atmosphere than he had been to the era of the engineer, was, on the whole, treated with perhaps excessive reverence, as befits a "classic," a definition that somehow suggests an inherent remoteness. The declamation of his verse was emphasized in dramatic academies, sometimes at the expense of content. With one or two notable exceptions, costumes and sets were still painfully accurate realizations of what it was deemed Shakespeare's intentions would have been, had he been able to envisage the evolution of dramatic art. It was a theater without surprises, as reverent as a ritual, and often duller than Shakespeare has any right to be.

The footnotes of the many editions for students shed a harsh light on the scholarship and, too often, on the pedantry of those who have loved the author unwisely and too well. Only recently has Shakespeare been liberated from the various constraints to which he has been subjected over the centuries. This is not to say that there were not extraordinary performances of his works, even during fallow times, which served to keep the torch aflame. Edmund Kean must have been an exceptional actor by any standards—a revolutionary temperament, tawny and bibulous, the victim of every passing temptation, wayward, disreputable, and probably intensely modern, collapsing on the stage during a performance as befitted his highly developed sense of occasion. Sometimes the words of detractors lend credence to the praise of admirers, and the critic of the ominously entitled London *Theatrical Inquisitor* wrote scathingly, "Either Mr. Kean is energetic, or he is nothing." This critic must have been a partisan of the Kembles, the noble tragedian and his sister, Mrs. Siddons, of the stately gesture and the measured phrase.

The history of the arts is replete with examples of purveyors of widely divergent styles, powerful enough to animate passionate followers and thereby to create public conflict. The battleground of this particular war was invariably Shakespeare, who, despite the Bowdlers and Tates, retained his universality and greatness to the extent that at all times his plays were yardsticks of achievement, the Everest on every ambitious actor's horizon.

What this genius has offered to actors is clearer perhaps than his well wrapped and discreet gifts to authors. When rehearsing Shakespeare, the actor is often compelled to use one of the many useful scholarly editions, in which the footnotes at times occupy more space on the page than the text itself. Naturally the actor tends to pore over these bits of erudition, which are the residue of centuries of scholarship, as pointers toward his own interpretation. Frequently the notes are valuable, but at times they betray a pedantry that is the antithesis of the freedom required by any interpreter: the trees obscure the wood. As rehearsals progress, there is naturally less and less reference to the footnotes; after the first night they are forgotten altogether. However, it is a curious and salutary experience to look at them again after three or four weeks. One then has the odd impression of being at sea with the benevolent Bard as one's only companion, traveling ever further from the shore, with the footnotes, like seaside bungalows, solid and insensitive, receding gradually into the mist.

Why this impression? Perhaps because many are privileged to read Shakespeare as one would read any author. Some have it as a vocation to study the works in depth. A few have the ineffable joy of actually interpreting him and sharing his solitude. It is the latter, the actors, who approach him most closely and who are able, in moments of dramatic grace, to extract a few of his secrets from him. The authors watch from afar, from the shoreline. And how often have they been deceived, despite their appreciation—perhaps because of their appreciation?

Catherine the Great, a woman of notorious sensibility, both physical and mental, who corresponded as an equal with Voltaire, wrote a series of historical dramas "en imitation de Shakespeare." As a German and a newcomer to the grim vagaries of Russian history, she studied Shakespeare with myopic energy, bestowing on posterity some of the most inadequate imitations ever written. Her tragedies are mercifully short but require enormous casts, whose members address each other with a full regard for protocol before killing each other off for specious reasons without for a moment engaging the spectator's emotions. Had she not described her contribution as being in imitation of Shakespeare, these works would have passed unnoticed into the great limbo of literature, but her betrayal of the source of her inspiration renders her total inability to understand the nature of her model's genius a phenomenon of abiding interest.

Even the dramatists who followed Shakespeare, the Drydens, the Sothernes, and others, tended to smother single thoughts or actions under mountains of rhetoric, as though quantity were the hallmark of quality, and volume a guarantee of substance. This procedure may have satisfied the ambitious playwright, but it induced monotony and immobility in the actor, who could only express more and more of the same, instead of being able to dart from thought to thought with the alacrity of a dragonfly.

And here we come to perhaps the most outstanding and inimitable of Shakespeare's attributes, his astonishing capacity for fully engaging in the details of human behavior while being Olympian at the same time. Julius Caesar could be interpreted in Fascist Italy as confirmation of the need for dictatorship or, by Orson Welles, as a denunciation of its evils, with no alteration of the text but merely a change of emphasis.

Henry V, in the hands of the youthful Laurence Olivier, became a symbol of patriotism and courage in wartorn Britain; but some time later, in the hands of an even more youthful schoolboy, the king was played in a Youth Theatre Performance as an uncertain and devious monarch who spent his time tiptoeing around his encampment in order to overhear what simple soldiers were saying about him. When Olivier cried, "Once more unto the breach, dear friends, once more," it became a clarion call, an inspiration. When the schoolboy cried the phrase, it was merely well-phrased propaganda contrived to incite already weary men to further sacrifice in an uncertain and selfish cause.

And so, with the generous elbow room allowed by the author, unrestricted by the meticulous instructions of more recent dramatists, it is possible to play Macbeth as an uncouth, ferocious monarch or as a weakling under the thumb of an unscrupulous wife. And Lear can be played as a creature of intrinsic majesty or as a petulant, self-indulgent dotard, always without betraying the author's intentions. But today's authors and audiences are too intellectually developed and too politically aware to allow their characters such latitude.

Shakespeare and Bach, two titans of human achievement, have something in common in their modesty and in the functional austerity of their attitude toward their work. Shakespeare's prompt copies are certainly not devoid of error or misprint. Bach did leave a few instructions on his manuscripts, but they were almost invariably for his own use, since he foresaw no posterity for himself but only a thorough concentration of his talents at a given time and place.

Nowadays, attitudes have changed. In Bach's day composers were merely musicians who wrote music as part of their more immediate chores, such as conducting choirs and orchestras and teaching. At the celebrated Mermaid Tavern there was the same kind of blurred image, the same kind of wonderful negligence and pragmatism. Poets contributed to each other's works, and scenes were sketched on tables wet with overflowing ale. There was as yet no possessiveness about work in progress, and everyone borrowed shamelessly from one another; there were no literary guilds or protective associations for writers. The finder kept, but the thief stole. Thoughts, rhymes, scenes, motivations were common property. Only genius was inviolate, and it took time to manifest itself, with Bach as with Shakespeare.

This inevitability is entirely foreign to contemporary dramatists, who are on the whole notoriously devoid of self-reliance because of the precipitate advance of progress, the huge increase in the size of populations, and the ever-increasing hours of leisure to fill. In 1942 Henry A. Wallace proudly declared the coming century to be that of the common man. It is turning out to be largely the century of the middleman, as clever folk invent jobs for themselves as go-betweens, agents, managers, lawyers, and consultants. The Elizabethan hull plowed through pristine seas; the contemporary hull cuts through a polluted ocean, gathering barnacles as it makes heavy weather of what were once a calm sea and auspicious gales.

This and the advance in awareness of the theatergoing public have forced the playwright to come to grips with intellectual considerations that merely colored the instinct of great poets of the past. The most penetrating works of art that could be described as Freudian were invariably written well before Freud, by authors as diverse as Shakespeare, Dostoevsky, and Melville. Such men were so well versed in the appearances of existence that they delved with extraordinary perception into the depths of human motivation, extracting, refining, and distilling their works of art with a freedom that now eludes us. Just as it is impossible to disinvent nuclear weapons, so it is impossible to rediscover that original simplicity which gave the canvas its limitless dimension. We simply know too much. We know the moon is dust. And we know the world is small.

It is useless to complain about what is nothing but evolution. We live at a specific period in history and must find our own way, knowing that headlong advances in technique will only render the task of future generations even more difficult. Haydn wrote more than 100 symphonies, Mozart 626 compositions in a life span of thirty-five years, Schubert eight symphonies and nearly 1,000 other compositions in only thirty-one years. Artistic problems in those times were dictated by the size and capability of musical ensembles and by patrons addicted to circumscribed concepts of beauty, in their architecture and furniture, as in their dress and comportment.

Since then, there has been the romantic movement, its gradual disintegration into atonality, the dodecaphonic system, and now the opulent musical chaos of our times, with every possibility except perhaps that of shocking or surprising. The same is true in the theatrical arts. How much further can one go in sheer austerity than Samuel Beckett? How much further in spectacle than the average American musical, even when shirts are lost on them?

The question then arises, To what extent can Shakespeare influence a contemporary playwright? Had there been critics in his day other than the public barometer, he would no doubt have been castigated for certain inconsistencies and told to prune before opening night—not after. The erosion of time has hardened all of Shakespeare's vagaries into a mold as recognizable as the presidents' heads on Mount Rushmore. We no longer know what is great, what is merely fine, and what is less than fine. We no longer even ask if one head resembles the original more than the others. Shakespeare is Shakespeare, whether he is Bacon or indeed, as Mark Twain so perspicaciously alleged, someone else of the same name. His influence on us is his huge, cool shadow over the history of the theater, now as much as ever before.

We could, if it were possible, take heed of the continuous changes of texture, the amazing changes of direction in the middle of phrases, the arresting succinctness after moments of expansiveness, the extraordinary space accorded to those instruments of his orchestra, the actors, a latitude that gives the executant his head and enables him to extract the best of his talents.

But all of us, as was Shakespeare, are of our times. Our canvas is smaller than his because we know more and are therefore raddled with inhibitions. We are induced to have a point of view, to take a position. We are encouraged by the critical faculty to do what has never been done before while conforming to rules imposed by fashion.

Plays are written and rewritten, tried out and altered on the road under the pressure of producers, committees, and experts—either accredited or self-appointed—on what the public wants. Two hundred years ago playwrights wrote and wrote again; we write, rewrite, and rewrite again. And there is absolutely no guarantee that the results are better than they would have been in the past. To maintain such a presumption would be tantamount to believing that the telephone has improved the quality of conversation.

Had "To be, or not to be" been written today, the author would be upbraided both for an odious pretentiousness and for posing a question as obvious as it is infantile. To make such a speech palatable, three and a half centuries are needed, together with the knowledge that the author is safely on the celestial stock exchange—with some slight fluctuation in his value as fashions change, but amazingly stable, considering that he was once as mortal as we are.

Each author may see in Shakespeare what he will, as may each member of the public; but to speak of influence is dangerous. The contemporary author is far too close to the prejudices and practices of his own times to admit of any influence other than a private wonder at the diabolical cleverness of the technician, awe for the skill of the journeyman actor who knew how to write for the instruments of his choosing. As for Shakespeare's genius, one can only marvel at it. Genius cannot touch those of mere talent. And if there are a few writers of genius around today, it is too soon for us to realize it, and they have no need to be influenced in any case. They might even resent the supposition that such an absurdity is desirable. Did not George Bernard Shaw endlessly carp and cavil at Shakespeare? And was it not Tolstoy himself who said that Shakespeare was the antithesis of an artist, that his sense of character was rudimentary? Genius is an unreliable critic of genius. That is what ordinary folk are for.

Shakespeare and the Modern Director

JONATHAN MILLER

One of the questions I'm often asked is which Shakespearean play interests me the most. I find that difficult to answer because my experience has been that the play I'm working on at a given time is the one that most thoroughly engages my attention. For me, and I suspect for most directors, it is work on a play that makes it interesting. It seems to expand into a universe of its own, so that at that time no other play seems to matter. This doesn't mean, of course, that work on one play excludes consideration of all other plays, because one of the things I've always felt is that when you're doing one of Shakespeare's plays it's advisable, if not inevitable, that you use the other plays as prefaces and checkpoints, as reminders of and guides to Shakespeare's characteristic preoccupations.

On the whole I don't subscribe to the view that each play should be wrenched out of context or used for something that is relevant to our own time. I'm against the idea of using Shakespeare for relevant purposes. I'm not opposed to modernizing the presentation, because once a way of presenting Shakespeare becomes "canonical" it becomes fossilized. But I think that it is silly to suppose that all artifacts from the past, Shakespeare's plays included, are of interest only insofar as they can be used as vehicles or devices for expressing or conveying something that is of current interest.

There are two extremes, both ludicrous, which

This article is based on an interview between Jonathan Miller and the editor.

should be avoided at all cost. One is the notion that one should use the plays to say something about an urgent political issue or social concern. That, to my mind, is fatuous—a consequence, as T.S. Eliot would have said, of overvaluing our own time. The other extreme is to assume that there is, in fact, a readily identifiable author's intention that can be excavated intact from Shakespeare's own time. I realize that there are intentionists in this business who claim that a controlling authorial design is what has to be identified before you can really satisfactorily do any work, either critical or productive, on a play. This extreme is not as ludicrous as the first alternative, but it has certain absurdities built into it because, as one well knows, authors may not be fully aware of what they intend. They may be in a position to exclude certain things that they certainly don't intend, I suppose—but since Shakespeare is dead, he is not in a position to do even that. No, I think that the most an intelligent reading can do to recapture an author's intention is to identify a cluster of probabilities and work with those.

But this prompts another question. Is it possible to realize all these identifiable Shakespearean probabilities in settings and in contexts that are different from the ones in which he would have seen his own plays staged? There is a widespread and, to my mind, curious belief that the best way to present Shakespeare in order to realize his intentions is in the format, in the costumes, or in the settings that he would have used. You can, of course, construct an argument in support of the view that using Elizabethan staging conventions is the best way to re-create the conditions of the original rehearsals at which Shakespeare was present and therefore in a position to say what he did not want, even if we grant that he was not in a position to say everything that he did want. Perhaps. But I think that even if we were capable of reinstating the prototype, it would be of no interest at all for modern audiences. They wouldn't understand the gestures; they wouldn't understand the rhetorical mode. And even those familiar with all the codes of that dramatic style would probably find that it doesn't work the same way now. So the modern director has the job of trying to realize something approximating Shakespeare's original intentions with idioms and modes of dramatic presentation that may be completely at odds with the ones that Shakespeare was familiar with.

Short of going back and attempting to re-create the staging conventions of the 1590s and early 1600s—which, as I say, is fraught with difficulty—what you have to do, if you're interested in recapturing some of the sensibility of the playwright as it was manifested visually and aurally on the stage in Shakespeare's own time, is to look for other resources from which it may be possible to retrieve energies consonant with the past. Thus, although it may not be altogether precise to look for Shakespearean parallels in the Italian painting of the Renaissance, attempting to do so is one of the ways in which you can try to recover something of the feel of the Elizabethan and Jacobean theater. There's a sumptuousness and exoticism in *Antony and Cleopatra,* for example, with the extraordinary baroque richness of its language, that seems to me to be remarkably compatible with the atmosphere in the paintings of Paolo Veronese. And in any event, whatever else it does, using Veronese as the visual basis for a television setting of the play (as with my BBC production of *Antony and Cleopatra*) enables you to escape the simple-minded literalism of reproducing archaeologically orthodox images of the historical period represented in Plutarch's narratives and, by derivation, in Shakespeare's tragedies. It keeps you aware that when a character mentions an object or a place from classical antiquity, it doesn't necessarily mean that what the character (or the playwright who created him) has in mind is what we would recognize as an archaeologically accurate image today.

Unlike ours, the sixteenth-century view of the past was extremely odd and syncretic. It drew from a diversity of sources, most of them fragmentary and few if any of them properly distinguished from the others, to create an image of classical Greece and Rome that is to ours as a crude sixteenth-century map of the world by Claudius Ptolemaeus is to a twentieth-century atlas based on the kinds of surveys now made possible by satellite reconnaissance photography and computer technology. We have the capacity to reinstate the past with a great deal of fidelity to detail because our archaeology is much more sophisticated than Shakespeare's. But paradoxically—and precisely because of this disparity between our technology and Shakespeare's—the better our archaeology becomes, the more anachronistic an application of it becomes as a means of re-creating the visual images of Shakespeare's theater. Shakespeare himself had no access to our archaeologically restored images of the ancient past. He was simply writing verse and drama for the Renaissance English theater, drawing much of his material from narratives of classical antiquity. So if we were to place Shakespeare's verse and drama in front of the actual Roman and Alexandrian settings to which he nominally referred, we would find ourselves confronted by a jarring incongruity. A more recent parallel may be found in Verdi's opera *Rigoletto,* where the composer seems to be referring to sixteenth-century Mantua but actually gives us the oompa-oompa of a nineteenth-century town band as the curtain goes up. The dissonance between these two historical frames of reference is more apparent to us today than it would have been to audiences in Verdi's time. The nineteenth-century character of Verdi's music would not have been noticeable as such to a nineteenth-century audience, but it is immediately obvious to a twentieth-century audience. By the same token, the sixteenth-century character of Shakespeare's spoken text is audible as such to us in a way in which it couldn't have been audible to Shakespeare's audience. As a general rule, the discrepancy between a given text and its earlier "historical" setting becomes more pronounced the more distant the audience gets from the time at which the author wrote.

But does it follow that a modern director's task is to strive for as little discrepancy, as little dissonance, as possible? Not necessarily. I think that as long as you are explicit and deliberate about the dissonance, you are free to exploit it for whatever artistic purposes you consider legitimate. The awful thing is when you simple-mindedly happen upon dissonance because you haven't thought it out. It's all very well to have dissonance in the Brechtian sense, because then you are deliberately creating an effect that is calculated to move the audience in a certain preconceived way. But if you happen upon a dissonance merely because you literal-mindedly reproduce the setting to which Shakespeare nominally refers, you are faced with a dissonance that is unlikely to work to your advantage. It is simply dissonance *de facto,* by default. If you deliberately undertake a dissonance for the purpose of creating a sense of dramatic distance, a sense of staging the thing as an object to be looked at, that can be artistically exciting. You have to be aware of the ontological status of every single act that you commit on stage. If you are not, then you run the risk of making a fool of yourself.

I hate to have to resort to the fashionable terms of semiotics, but what I'm saying is that when you produce a play, what you present on stage is a cluster of signs, and the status of those signs has to be very clearly understood by the person who is making them. Otherwise the object is giving off not your signals but impressions that are incorrectly interpreted as your signals. Anything that is giving off impressions, giving off sensory evidence, may be taken by the audience as contributing to a sign system. If it is not intended as such, then it may produce a very confusing effect on the audience. Ideally, what you do with a production is control every impression that comes off the stage so that it brings about one effect by contrast with something else. It's the same as the way in which language is structured. Language is a system of morphemes, the purpose of any one of which in a particular instance is to be seen or heard in contrast with all of the other morphemes that might have occupied a given position in a statement but do not.

But, of course, just as an author will sometimes generate unanticipated effects, so will a director. There may be certain things that he can clearly indicate and articulate as being his intentions, but he is usually surprised to find, by hindsight if not at the time, that things that quite clearly by their coherence would have to be labeled as intentions are not necessarily the intentions with which he started—or at least intentions of which he was fully aware at the time he was designing his production. Some things come about by accident, but they can become incorporated into the director's intentional system by his deciding to keep them. What starts out as an incidental feature becomes a deliberate one once you decide to keep it rather than exclude it. An accident that is kept in by accident is obviously a mistake; but an accident that is kept in by design becomes an intention.

I strongly prefer to work in an atmosphere that encourages spontaneity. Because anyone who supposes that he has such control over the future that every single one of the contingencies of the real world are manageable in advance is deluding himself. What you do is to begin with a broad design, a series of things that you feel to be preferable, and then you start working on the physical, concrete material, which is the setting and the people who are playing the parts. And because you do not in fact have control over the future, you are constantly being surprised by it. Every now and then something comes up which is quite clearly valuable and interesting. So what you do is keep it. I like that: keep it. That's part and parcel of the job of being a director. There are, as we all know, obsessive directors who feel that their conscious creativity is in some way jeopardized if they include things that are contributed by someone or something other than their own private imagination. But that, I think, is a completely unrealistic view of the function of the imagination. First of all, you are constantly being surprised by your imagination, which contains things that you don't know. And secondly, the world is always coming up with things that you don't know, because it is actually much more complicated than you could ever know. Which is what makes it interesting. And which is why, to me, directing is interesting.

Until fairly recently, of course, directors were relatively unimportant. During much of the nineteenth century, for example, producing plays was much more simple-minded than it is now. Directors in the modern sense weren't really needed. Shakespeare's plays were sentimentalized and turned out in a succession of easily identified virtues and vices, so that going to the theater was rather like looking at row after row of Shakespeare Toby Jugs. Because audiences were comfortable with these stereotypes, each Toby Jug cloned to look exactly the same as the ones that people had long been used to seeing, theater producers had little incentive to offer up anything new. To be sure, there were a few gifted people in the early years of the twentieth century —Harley Granville-Barker and Tyrone Guthrie, for example—who shook things up a bit. But the modern era of the director really began, I think, in the 1950s, when the theater began attracting directors and actors who had studied English at Oxford and Cambridge and who had been taught to subject the plays to close literary analysis. All of a sudden it became possible to see something more than Toby Jugs in Shakespeare's plays: it was permissible to get away from the didactic, oversimplified stereotypes of the past and bring some subtlety to the process of interpreting the script.

Predictably, this disturbed a lot of people, including academic critics like Helen Gardner, and many of them still look back on the 1950s as the time when Shakespearean production began to deteriorate. They yearn for the good old days when you went to the theater for the actors and never even heard the names of the directors. They deplore the threat to Toby-Jug Shakespeare that they see in directors like Peter Hall, Peter Brook, and John Barton—not to mention Jonathan Miller—and they clamor for an end to directors' Shakespeare. And, of course, many of them write for the popular press and do their best to make life miserable for people who try to give them something other than the stereotyped images of Shakespeare that they bring with them to the theater or the television screen. I find it debilitating to worry about offending these kinds of audiences and critics. So, like most other modern directors, I strive to please a constituency of intelligent and curious people who are not afraid to see things made over new again. Although I think that, in the sense I've already described, Shakespeare meant what he meant, I also think that there are different ways of discovering what he meant. So I direct for the kind of audience that Hamlet identified as the "judicious." Not necessarily the scholars who can pick up esoteric references to Renaissance iconography. No, I'm referring to ordinary people whose intuitions are disciplined and informed and open to new experiences. If you're a director, it's from their souls that you recognize what you are doing and how well you are doing it, because their souls are well furnished and responsive to what you give them in the theater.

In some ways, I suppose, I don't really think of audiences as such—I think of people in the audience, one by one. I know that there will always be some who will be querulous, who will complain about not getting what they liked before, or who will object that I have departed from some canonical version of the play that they have just seen. But there will also be those people who are so delighted that it is as if they have just seen the play for the first time, people who instantly understand what I'm getting at; and not necessarily, as I say, because they're deeply informed. Often it's merely that they have good antennae and they've received something that you've been trying to transmit through the production. These are the people I aim for.

But the only way I can reach them is through the actors with whom I work. On the whole, I prefer to have actors who are unexpected—what the professional people think of as dangerous—actors from whom I never quite know what I'm going to get next. Unpredictable but not corny, not hams, not mandarin, certainly not sentimental. People who are prepared to be hard and peculiar and often quite disturbing. Above all, I look for actors who can always be funny, even in the most serious plays—perhaps particularly in the most serious plays—actors who can suddenly startle me and everyone else on the set with something absolutely absurd. Because I think it's a terrible mistake to be too solemn with Shakespeare. There are certain critics of my work who are so frivolous that they can only be grave. I'd much prefer to be in the company of people who are sufficiently serious to know that they can also be frivolous. So I look for a sense of playfulness in the actors and designers I surround myself with, and I occasionally enjoy planting a little joke in a production—like the picture of Cranach's Eve that I pinned up on the pole in Ajax's tent in the BBC *Troilus and Cressida,* for example, or the easel I put in the background of the Greek council scene with preliminary specifications for the Trojan Horse. But getting back to the actors, it's nice if they do some reading and thinking of their own about the play we're working on, but it's by no means necessary because I can supply that. And they, in turn, will supply something that I can't. What I ask them to bring with them into the rehearsal room is the totality of their experience. Some of it may have to do with reading, some with what they've seen in the street, or with very accurately recalled images of friends or relatives. What I look for, mostly, is accurate and unsentimental recall, both of reading and of immediate experience.

I've normally sketched out at least a theoretical construct of the production before I assemble the actors. I've already met with the designer and the costumer and developed an overall "look" for the production. So with me there is a creative relationship with the actors that precedes any actual encounter simply by virtue of my having chosen one group of actors rather than another for the various parts. I've already developed a rough idea of who it is that might have meant these lines or those, and that idea has informed my selection of this actor rather than that actor. But even though I will have already preempted a certain amount of the decision-making that goes into a production, I tend to be much more intuitive and haphazard and spontaneous in my rehearsals with my actors than my explicit commitment to theory might lead you to expect.

My rehearsals, I think, are felt by the profession to be rather easygoing, and I try not to drum actors into interpretations that they find alien. I never begin with a read-through because it's a humiliating ordeal; some actors are very good sight readers, others are not, and I see no reason to make anyone feel uncomfortable on the first day of rehearsal. So what I do is spend the first morning explaining roughly what my ideas for the play are. I show the actors the set and costumes, and then we sit around, drink coffee, and chat. I find that I'm less talkative in the early stages now than I once was. My first day on the set used to be rather like a university tutorial. Now I feel more comfortable just getting people on their feet and letting the scenes develop as we fudge our way toward what seems to be a coherent expression of the play. The actors will contribute things I didn't expect, and as the production grows the combination of ideas that I had at the beginning becomes more and more complicated. Unforeseen contingencies enrich the mixture of ingredients, and gradually the finished product begins to emerge. I don't block it. I don't force it. I simply try to let it take the final shape that seems most natural under the conditions and in the context in which my actors and I find ourselves working.

I've been asked whether I find Shakespeare's plays archaic, and if so whether I attempt to enter them by means of Renaissance iconography, say, or Renaissance psychology. I find that kind of question intriguing, but in fact I've seldom found it possible to bring much historical knowledge into a production in such a way as to make it intelligible to a modern audience. I may find it illuminating to read a book like Erwin Panofsky's *Studies in Iconology,* or even to go back to such Renaissance sources as Cesare Ripa's *Iconographia* or Timothy Bright's *Treatise of Melancholy.* It may help me to get a feel for Shakespeare's staging of certain scenes if I understand something about the way Shakespeare's audience read emblem books. And it may be valuable for my approach to some of Shakespeare's characters to have a general notion of the way a playwright like Ben Jonson caricatured people by his systematic application of humor psychology. But I can't honestly say that I do historical reading in order to understand the plays more fully. It's just that I read that stuff all the time anyway. In a way, I suppose, I put the cart before the horse. To me, Shakespeare's works offer good practical experiments in that they allow me to play with the ideas I get from my historical reading. So when I say that I don't do historical reading in order to understand the plays, what I really mean is that I do the plays in order to get a clearer view of what the history means.

In some of my television productions for the BBC, I tried to relate the work of modern historians such as Lawrence Stone to the relationships between the sexes in *The Taming of the Shrew,* or to the emergence of a contractual society from one rigidly structured in terms of status as illustrated by Shakespeare's portrayals of villains such as Iago and Edmund. But the closest I've come to using the visual sign systems embedded in Renaissance iconography is in my use of, say, Wylie Sypher's *Four Stages of Renaissance Style* to help identify stylistic parallels, such as those relating a mannerist painter like Tintoretto to a mannerist play like *Hamlet.* I like Sypher's notion—which, of course, he derived from Heinrich Wölfflin—that there may be some kind of elective affinity between the pictures of a period and the plays of a period. The notion of the sister arts is important, something I take note of, and it's one of the means by which I've tried to achieve artistic coherence in my television productions for the BBC.

But as much as I strive for coherence in a production, I am also intent on allowing the text's latent ambiguities to emerge. Once I've decided what will be fundamental, I will emphasize that. But I also want to give the audience an experience of the complexities that accompany that primary emphasis. It's like plucking a string. A fundamental is what you are most conscious of hearing; but in order to get an interesting timbre, you encourage overtones related to that fundamental so as to enrich it and make it somewhat ambiguous. William Empson talks about this sort of thing in *The Structure of Complex Words.* By definition, complex words have many connotations. You develop one as the key, and then you try to control the others in such a way as to achieve harmonics as one connotation plays off against all the others.

Sometimes in directing you can do this by transposing a play from the time in which Shakespeare set the action to another historical period that will set off slightly different resonances. The trick is to choose a historical setting whose resonances will help to reinforce the dominant tonality of the original text. When I first directed *The Merchant of Venice,* for example, I set it in the 1880s in order to get the effect of idle young men of that period as they lounged around places like Trieste. I was struck by certain similarities between the Bassanio-Antonio relationship and the relationship of Oscar Wilde and Lord Alfred Douglas. Wilde was a rather tigerish young masher who enjoyed parasitizing his patron while giving him little or nothing in return; Douglas, for his part, must have agonized with jealous love. I recognized when I decided to build on this kind of parallel that I would have to sacrifice certain aspects of the original text, but I felt that the gains were worth the price. It was a deliberately playful way of dealing with Shakespeare; it wasn't in any respect frivolous or arbitrary, however, nor was it in any way an attempt to make Shakespeare "relevant." Rather, it was part of an effort to bring out some of the resonances latent in the original play by setting off one idea against several levels of allusion. There were allusions to Verdi, for example, and I used the music in the production to suggest parallels between the treatment of Rigoletto and the mocking and rejection of Shylock. The effect of the production as a whole was to illustrate the potency of that wonderful line in *All's Well That Ends Well* where we are told, "The web of our life is of a mingled yarn, good and ill together" (IV. iii. 66–67).

Nothing is ever simple in Shakespeare. His plays continually remind us that our vices and our virtues are all mixed up in a ball with one another. We do the right things for the wrong reasons, and the wrong things for the right reasons. The virtuous are often vindictive, and the vengeful are often virtuous and affectionate. Although it was Jack Gold rather than I who directed the BBC television version of *The Merchant of Venice,* I worked with him as producer for that rendition of the play, and I thoroughly approved of the searing moment at the conclusion of the trial scene when Shylock's "conversion" to Christianity was sealed by the plac-

ing of a crucifix around his neck. Here what was ostensibly an act of mercy came across as something that also had a strong element of malice in it. Shakespeare was too complicated a human being to wish Shylock to be a mere pantomime villain: witness the "Hath not a Jew eyes" speech (III. i.). And Shakespeare was too much aware of the "mingled yarn" principle in human life to present the Christians in the play as exponents of pure compassion and unquestionable virtue.

The more I've thought about *The Merchant of Venice,* the more I've found myself meditating on its many plays on words connoting affinity—words like *kind, kindness, kin, kindred, gentle, gentile.* These words all have to do with being kind to people of your own kind, gentle to people of your own "gentility." One of my favorite speeches in the play is "Hie thee, gentle Jew. / The Hebrew will turn Christian; he grows kind" (I. iii. 173–174). Since *kin* and *gen* derive from the same root, meaning *generation,* Shakespeare reminds us here and elsewhere that kinship and gentleness are related to one another. We are obliged to be kind to those to whom we are in some way kin. But what the play illustrates, in fact, is that there are people of the same race who are utterly unlike one another, and even people of the same family (Shylock and his daughter Jessica, for example) who share few if any character traits. On the other hand, there are people of different races or family groupings who are very similar to one another. At the end of the trial scene in *The Merchant of Venice,* Shylock is dogged off the stage by a character whose name, ironically, is Gratiano. Though Gratiano is nominally a Christian, he is in some ways the most vengeful character in the play; his spitefulness is the very antithesis of the spirit of grace implied by his name. As a consequence of Gratiano's scornful interjections as the moneylender's defeat becomes unavoidable, Shylock's forced conversion, which Christians in Shakespeare's original audience were evidently expected to respond to as a bestowal of unmerited mercy, is difficult to distinguish from the "justice" that Shylock had been insisting upon prior to his discomfiture by "the learned judge."

In Gratiano we hear the first faint rumblings of the virulent anti-Semitism that was to produce such unutterable horrors in our own century. In saying this, however, I am by no means suggesting that *The Merchant of Venice* is anti-Semitic in a modern sense. I see the play as susceptible of having our more recent kinds of anti-Semitism poured into it (as sometimes happens when it is performed today before audiences prone to racial bigotry); but in fact the "anti-Semitism" of *The Merchant of Venice* is the theological anti-Semitism of the Middle Ages. It is the view of human history that is depicted on the front of Strasbourg Cathedral, for example, where there are two effigies, one blindfolded and representing the Old Law and the Synagogue, and one with eyes raised to heaven and representing the New Law and the Ecclesia, the congregation of the redeemed. In *The Merchant of Venice,* Shylock's sin, such as it is, can be removed by baptism because it is the sin of Judaism, the outgrowth of a spiritual blindness rather than a genetic defect; if the Jew's fault stems from his failure to acknowledge Jesus as the Messiah, he can be forgiven that fault by consenting to become a Christian. The proper expression of this kind of "anti-Semitism," in other words, is to bring the Jew to the font—against his will, if necessary—in Christian compassion.

This may not be very palatable to a twentieth-century society that places a high premium on tolerance and cultural pluralism, but it is nevertheless a far cry from the very different kind of secular anti-Semitism that Nazi Germany based upon a racial theory. According to that theory, you would only exacerbate the problem by bringing the Jew to the baptismal font. For if the Jew's fault was defined as genetic, the only way to eradicate it was by extinguishing its carrier. Once racial anti-Semitism supplanted theological anti-Semitism, it was no longer thinkable to address the spiritual fault in the Jew by showing him the light; the only imaginable solution was to bring him to the gas chamber instead. Because of what happened under Hitler, it is difficult for a modern audience, and particularly a Jewish one, to sit through a performance of *The Merchant of Venice.* But I would not favor removing the play from the repertory, in part because it is an interesting piece of archaeological literature that helps us understand something of what the Renaissance inherited from the Middle Ages, in part because as such it gives us a valuable perspective on today's anti-Semitism, and in part because, like all of Shakespeare's plays, it reminds us that human beings are so complex, so confusing a mixture of good and bad elements, that "final solutions" are never going to work as ways of bringing about improvements in society.

What I've been referring to as the "mingled yarn" principle has also guided my approach to the directing of other Shakespeare plays. Thus I find it impossible to view Iago in Coleridge's terms as a pure embodiment of evil, a manifestation of "motiveless malignity." So when I selected Bob Hoskins to play the part in the BBC television production of *Othello,* I set out to portray Iago as a credible social type: a dwarf petty officer whose Cockney accent immediately set him off as a man of lower-class origins and thus of limited opportunities for military advancement. As I directed the play, it was clear that Iago's envy of upper-class twits was what motivated him to punish the Moor: Othello would come to see that it was bad judgment to hold Cassio's "bookish theoric" in higher regard than the experience of a pragmatic soldier like Iago. I wanted to depict Iago as a profoundly diseased person, afflicted by both class prejudice and racial prejudice; I did not want the audience to come away thinking of him as a morality-play devil who takes pleasure in villainy simply because he is by definition evil.

If Iago is a character with some grounds for a grudge, however, if he has a personality that makes him something more complicated than a simple embodiment of evil, I would insist by the same token that many of Shakespeare's more attractive characters are something other than the paragons of virtue they are often considered to be. Take Brutus, for example. I find him spinsterishly Victorian and lacking in generosity. In the quarrel scene with Cassius, he seems somehow to take pleasure in the collapse of his fellow conspirator, so intent is he on maintaining his own dignity as "the noblest Roman of them all." And Hamlet. I've directed *Hamlet* three times, and I've come increasingly to find a pinched mean-mindedness in the Prince. Hamlet is not a magnanimous person: he finds fault where there is none, and he brings about a great deal of unnecessary grief and suffering. I've grown more and more impatient with his infantilism—his refusal to believe that his uncle can have any positive qualities (notwithstanding the play's clear indications that Claudius is in many ways an effective ruler and an affectionate husband to Gertrude), his obsession with his mother's "lechery" (and his inability to see that she might be attracted to Claudius in a perfectly normal way), his monstrous behavior toward Ophelia (which drives this delicate girl to schizophrenia and death), his cruelty toward Polonius (both before and after the moment of rashness when Hamlet stabs the "foolish, prating" old counselor through the arras), and finally his cavalier dismissal of Rosencrantz and Guildenstern. In my last production of the play, at London's Donmar Warehouse in 1982, I had Horatio withdraw somewhat as Hamlet boasted of his plot to have his former schoolmates "put to sudden death, not shriving time allowed" (V. ii. 46–47). And at the very end of the play, as Claudius reached out for Gertrude in death, the Hamlet in this production angrily rushed to pull their hands apart. It wasn't that I was trying to deny Hamlet any sympathy from the audience. It was rather that I was interested in developing aspects of his personality that hadn't emerged in previous productions. And, of course, I found in doing so that I was also compelled to take a fresh look at the other characters, most of whom (Claudius, Gertrude, Polonius, for example) came off more attractively than they had in my previous interpretations of the play.

Over the years I've learned that you must be careful never to take what one character says about another as being what Shakespeare necessarily meant us to think about that other character. Shakespeare's characters are frequently unreliable in what they say about others; and just as frequently they are unreliable as guidelines about themselves. Quite often, in fact, the most revealing indications they provide occur in the remarks that spill out by accident—when you know that they are not intending to convey something but when they nevertheless do so incidentally and inadvertently. It's in the slips of the tongue that someone really tells you what they're like. So as you read the text, if you're a director, you treat it in much the same way that a psychoanalyst treats the discourse of his patient. You try to overhear statements that lie beneath the surface of what is actually being said. Like Polonius, you try by indirections to find directions out. And in doing so you recognize that Shakespeare was writing for an audience that was capable of picking up a great deal of information from the subtlest of hints.

I sometimes wonder what kind of Shakespeare we'll be producing fifty years from now. Life is changing so fast now, and we are getting more and more remote from many of the works of the past that we think of as classics. The Bible is totally unknown to many people today. I was watching people at the Art Institute in Chicago recently, and it suddenly occurred to me that many of them were confronting pictures about subjects that they knew nothing about. As I watched them looking at medieval and Renaissance religious triptychs, it seemed to me that they were desperately trying to make them generate some kind of beauty that didn't depend on the pictures' subject matter. It was as if they believed that beauty was a substance that could be held in a container, rather like some kind of aerosol spray, and that you could get at it if you only applied the right kind of scrutiny to the container. But, of course, medieval and Renaissance pictures do have the quality of being about something, and their beauty is involved in and partly constituted by what they are about. And if you don't know what they are about, then you are not actually in a position to understand or appreciate them at all.

The farther we get from the assumptions and beliefs of a Christian Europe, the harder it will be to be moved by its art. This is certainly true of the paintings that were familiar to Shakespeare and his contemporaries. And it is no less true for the dramatic works of Shakespeare himself. The job of the modern director is to do what he can to keep renewing Shakespeare, to persevere in the effort to maintain Shakespeare's plays in the repertory as long as there are audiences capable of understanding and responding to him. But if our society fails to do its part to perpetuate the idea of a classic and to sustain the kinds of cultural literacy upon which the apprehension of a classic depends, there isn't much the director can do to keep Shakespeare alive by himself.

Tradition, Style, and the Shakespearean Actor Today

SIR JOHN GIELGUD

Tradition, according to the dictionary, is "the handing down of customs, opinion, or doctrines from ancestors to posterity, from the past to the present, by oral communication; an opinion, custom, or doctrine thus handed down; principles or accumulated experiences of earlier generations handed on to others."

It is often said that the English stage has none of the great tradition of acting that has given dignity and substance to the theaters of France, Germany, and Russia in their finest days. Today the National Theatre and the Royal Shakespeare Company at the Barbican are hoping to create a similar tradition in England, a permanent company for acting classic plays with style.

Style (I read again in my dictionary) is "the general formal characteristics of any fine art." A broad generalization, surely, and not a particularly illuminating definition. What exactly is style in acting and stage production? Does it mean the correct wearing of costume, appropriate deportment, and the nice conduct of a clouded cane? Does it mean correct interpretation of the text without extravagance or eccentricity, an elegant sense of period, and beautiful (but unselfconscious) speaking, by a balanced and versatile company of actors, used to working together, flexible instruments under the hand of an inspired director? Such were the theaters of Konstantin Stanislavsky in Russia, of Jacques Copeau and, afterward, the Compagnie des Quinze in France, and, during certain years of his supremacy, of Max Reinhardt in Germany.

An individual actor can have style. A production can achieve a general style. A company can be said to play with style. And this word *style* can apply equally to a modern play or to a costume piece, to comedy and tragedy alike.

It is a doubtful question whether tradition and style can be studied and learned in a dramatic school or acquired by watching fine actors, still less by reading accounts of the performances of the great players of the past. Every year students flock to England from many parts of the world (and especially from the United States) to learn the way to act Shakespeare and to interpret his texts. It would be interesting to know what conclusions they carry away with them. For the glamor and the past traditions of the theater merge so imperceptibly into the theater of today that it is hard to know which influence is the stronger. Both actors and audiences know the familiar plays of Shakespeare far too well and the unfamiliar ones far too little. It is a sad disappointment to find the recent production of *Alls Well That Ends Well,* after being acknowledged as a superb and original production of the Royal Shakespeare Company both by the British public and by the London and New York critics, failing on Broadway owing to swiftly decreasing audiences.

Some actors and directors try to escape altogether from the web of tradition, especially in the best-known Shakespearean plays and parts. Too often in the last fifty years they have achieved sensational modern innovations and freakish quirks of originality at the expense of the plays themselves.

The actors who are asked to play Shakespeare dressed in clothes of some other period—Macbeth in Byronic costume, Rosalind as a Watteau lady—have a double task, for they have to play in the manner of a much later period as regards deportment and behavior while interpreting characters conceived in the Renaissance. Shakespeare has already tended to confuse the issue with his anachronisms, but too much ingenuity in decorating his plays will only add to the confusion. Harley Granville-Barker has suggested that some of the Roman plays should be staged with Renaissance-classical costumes, in the manner of Veronese and Tintoretto, and this legitimate experiment has been tried with varying success—most happily in the obvious case of *Antony and Cleopatra,* to which it is particularly suited.

But style in acting does not consist solely of the external elegances. Sergei Diaghilev introduced painters into the theater, and a designer of fine taste can help the pictorial side of a production by insisting upon correct detail, not only in scenery, costume, and properties, but also with wigs and makeup (though he cannot teach the actor how to wear them). But this is only the beginning. Each actor has his own qualities and methods of approach, and it is the subtle task of the director to study his players before trying to weld them into a particular unity of manner, pace, grouping, and variety of attack. He is apt to be influenced considerably by his designer, and by the limitations as well as the outstanding qualities of his leading players. (He should, of course, influence and collaborate with the designer in planning the production, and together they will have considered the physical limitations of the theater in which the play is to be given, as well as those of each player in the cast.)

In the process of invention and interpretation many strange complications may ensue. A designer of genius, as Claude Lovat Fraser was, may invent an original version of the period he is to convey. In his famous designs for *The Beggar's Opera* (1920), Fraser stripped the costumes of all trimmings and superfluous detail (preserving the line and using plain but brilliant colors) and simplified his backgrounds to the barest suggestion. Sir Nigel Playfair, the director, invented a presentational style for the actors and singers that also simplified and stylized the eighteenth-century atmosphere, and, in complete harmony with his designer, a new and delightful effect was achieved. This was a rare example in the theater of a marriage of true minds, but subsequent developments of the same kind and treatment (even by Playfair himself) seemed comparatively inferior, imitative, and sometimes quite indifferent.

True originality comes from within—an instinctive feeling on the part of some person connected with a production who is strong enough to control and influence everybody concerned. But if this originality, however brilliant, runs counter to the intrinsic quality of the author and his text, the result will not be a happy one.

It is seldom customary nowadays for the author to read his new play to the company at the first rehearsal, though this was often done in the past by men like Sir Arthur Wing Pinero, himself a masterly director, and by George Bernard Shaw, who always read with a rare vivacity and sense of character. Sir Henry Irving, too, always read a play to his company, whether by Shakespeare or anyone else. But readings are apt to be unsatisfactory occasions, since the interest of each actor in his own part is apt to make him inattentive to everybody else's. Also, if the director attempts to give too many theoretical hints of what he hopes to achieve at such an early stage, he may only succeed in confusing his actors before they get down to work. He will have some main essentials worked out for himself through his preliminary talks with the designer and with the author, in the case of a contemporary play, but he will often find it best to wait to elaborate his views until he has seen, from the first few rehearsals, how the cast he has to work with fits into the imaginary pattern he has in mind. As regards a classical play, however, several readings will be found needful (though not necessarily at the first rehearsal) for elucidating meanings, discussing rhythm and phrasing, and offering a broad suggestion of character-drawing, interplay, and the manner in which the director hopes to proceed.

Most actors like to set their movements and business at an early stage, and they find it very exasperating when the director changes his mind continually on these matters up to the very last minute—as, I regret to say, I have so often done myself when I have directed Shakespeare. Some extremely skilled directors (Granville-Barker, Michel St. Denis, Theodore Komisarjevsky) who had their plans worked out in great detail in advance could bring an almost perfect scheme, prepared in every detail, to the early rehearsals, and the movement of the play could then be rehearsed and set in the first weeks, leaving two weeks or more for the development of detail, pace, character, and the finishing touches. This is certainly the ideal method of production—but few directors are sufficiently clear-headed, or certain enough of the abilities of their company, to achieve it. There is also a danger that, if the director provides too much set detail, the actors will become lazy and cease to contribute their share in the creative work they have to do. They begin to move to order like puppets. It is important that they should feel they are bringing something of their own to add to the effect that the director is trying to contrive. Naturally, he must remain the guiding influence, since he sees them as a first audience, from the front, and he must be the final judge of their efforts, for they may easily, amongst themselves, create a somewhat different result from what he had imagined, and he must remain alive to the possibility of exciting developments throughout the rehearsals that he never envisaged from his own conception in his preparations. A modern author, too, must be prepared to be similarly influenced in the matter of cuts and rewriting.

The actor, then, should be receptive but not dumbly submissive, obedient but not slavishly imitative, and the director, if he is also an actor, must not try to force his own personality upon the members of his cast who seem to him lacking in personalities of their own. It is better for him to indicate subtleties of mood and character than to go up onto the stage and illustrate what he requires by showing off his own superior technical skill or caricaturing faults—a cruel discouragement to self-conscious or inexperienced actors. Only if he finds a player negligent and deliberately uncooperative is he justified in making an example of him before his fellows.

Since the 1950s, the supremacy of the director has lessened the tradition of the importance of the so-called star, and the public is far better informed as to the director's contribution, through newspapers and television interviews, than ever before—though actors and actresses, of course, in my own early years, were familiar with directors' names and reputations. Granville-Barker unhappily was no longer working in the 1920s, but Dion Boucicault was still a skilled director (especially of Sir James M. Barrie's plays) as was Basil Dean (a feared and respected martinet). Sir Charles Hawtry and Sir Gerald du Maurier, both better known to the public as actors, were acknowledged masters of direction, too, helping many aspiring authors and players to success.

I myself began to direct plays in 1932 and found it fascinating to work with a number of established players, whose willing obedience to my untutored efforts surprised and delighted me; and for many years before and during World War II, I directed twenty or thirty plays with increasing enthusiasm. I never found difficulty in blending the talents I was fortunate enough to find among older players with the less experienced skills of my own generation, so many of whom were destined to achieve subsequent supremacy in their art. I learned much of my increasing efficiency as a director from Komisarjevsky, St. Denis, and Playfair, with all of whom I had worked as an actor, and from whom I had gained some sense of grouping, pace, decor, music, and lighting. But I never felt that I had sufficient originality to put a greatly individual stamp on my productions—especially when I was lucky enough, in 1950, to work for the first time under Peter Brook, who, still a very young man, made a brilliant success at Stratford-upon-Avon with his *Measure for Measure,* in which I played the part of Angelo. His later successes, in which I was also fortunate enough to participate, were *The Winter's Tale* in London in 1951, and a Stratford *Tempest* a few years later. Since then, Brook's productions of *Titus Andronicus* and *A Midsummer Night's Dream,* among many others, were perhaps two of his most acknowledged triumphs.

Meanwhile, Sir Peter Hall, John Barton, Trevor Nunn, Terry Hands, and Jonathan Miller have all contributed an important succession of achievements, aided by a brilliant number of talented players such as Judi Dench, Ian McKellen, Albert Finney, and Alan Howard, as well as established stars of an older school, such as Dame Peggy Ashcroft and Paul Scofield—all of whom have readily adapted themselves to innovations of every kind, especially to the problem of becoming accustomed to open stages and uncut texts. They have demonstrated exemplary discipline in teamwork and a resolute determination to avoid the old-fashioned dangers of ranting.

What are the most important qualities in an actor? Imagination, sensibility, and power. Relaxation, repose, and the art of listening. To speak well and to move gracefully are elementary feats that can be mastered with hard work and practice, though some great actors, Irving in particular, seem to have succeeded without them. At first the young actor is bound to be greatly influenced by the acting he admires, and a love of tradition combined with a natural respect for experience may lead him to admire the less subtle excellences of the actors he watches at work. His own taste may not be good. But as he grows older, he will be increasingly influenced by the pictures he sees, the books he reads, the music he hears, rather than by the acting of other players. He will come to trust more to his own instinct and to his increasing knowledge of character and emotion, as well as to his experience of acting in many different kinds of plays. A fine actor of modern parts who plays for the first time in a costume play may sometimes bring a far truer sense of style to his performance than an actor who is steeped in tradition and can boast of a long career in Shakespeare.

As he grows in experience and power, the actor discovers more and more how the make-believe side of acting has to be strangely combined with a naked admission of self-revelation. At first he enjoys pretending, living in another character. But he has at the same time to imagine himself, say, into the character of Macbeth, a warrior capable of committing a murder for the sake of ambition, and also to discover his own personal reactions to the speeches and situations with individual truth and sympathy. However well he may simulate the externals of the part—the age, deportment, and physical aspects of his impersonation—he can only execute the promptings of his imagination within the limits of his own technical instrument and range of personality. And it is here that Shakespeare provides so wonderfully for the actor. In his great characters there is such a wide sweep of creation, such subtle variety of temperament, that a dozen actors may choose a dozen ways of playing them, and—if only they succeed within their own personal expression to the full—the result will be a fine performance. Lord Laurence Olivier, especially in his performances of *Titus Andronicus, Macbeth,* and his controversial but strikingly powerful and original *Othello,* is an outstanding example of this.

The director has his most subtle task in conducting the rehearsals so that the actors may feel confident that he is stretching them to the extreme limit of their potentialities, yet not demanding the impossible. Only with this object in view is he justified in any liberties he may take in adjusting the balance of a scene, for the total effect of the play will be greatly influenced by the qualities of the leading performers, and they need all the assistance possible to enable them to dominate the action, though only when it is justifiably required by the text.

Some directors believe in preliminary discussions and many days of readings. Others work without trying to explain their views to the actors. Others, again, look to the leading players to set the pace and style. They try to teach, parrot-fashion, the actors of the smaller parts or seek to cover their deficiencies with a mass of movement, comic invention, and pretty groupings. But how seldom is the intrinsic atmosphere of a period achieved (especially when the play is written in prose or verse of complicated pattern and full of archaic references and jokes), and how often is a false effect superimposed as a result.

I have said that relaxation is all-important in acting. For myself, I have always found it the most difficult quality to attain. Relaxation is best learned, perhaps, in acting the plays of Anton Chekhov. I believe any actor who has appeared in one of his plays will agree with me. There is a lack of urgency, an inner truth of domestic substance in his characters, that comforts the actor. Though the Chekhov men and women are frustrated, unhappy, nervous, yearning, they are very natural. It is curious that it seems easier for our actors to interpret the humors and tragedies of these Russians than to give convincing performances of the simple English rustics of Shakespeare, Richard Sheridan, and Oliver Goldsmith. It may be that the mixture of comedy and tragedy in the Chekhov plays makes the burden easier to sustain. The mood is continually flexible and changing, and the director may exercise his talents to the full in controlling these varieties of mood and atmosphere, leaving the actors to concentrate on details of characterization. Besides, the parts are very evenly divided, no single character dominates the action, and the period style is comparatively unimportant and not so very far from our own day.

It is very difficult to sustain the tragic plane in a tragedy like *Macbeth* or *Othello,* where the principal characters are of such heroic size and there is little comic relief. But it is equally difficult to sustain the changing moods of Shakespeare's comedies, with their alternating scenes of verse and prose, romance and knockabout, or the brilliant heartlessness of William Congreve and Oscar Wilde, without wearying the audience, especially today, when the restlessness of modern life and the familiar hectic rattle and whisper of the microphone makes it harder for an audience to concentrate attentively during a long performance in the theater. Pace, in classical playing, is essential, but it is equally important for the actors to play closely with one another, picking up cues, welding scenes together in contrasts of varying speeds and intensities, than for the producer to achieve a general effect of violent hurry and restless vivacity. Unless the leisure of an earlier generation is achieved upon the stage, the brilliant talk seems wearisome and over-elaborate, the characters jerky puppets, grimacing and posing in a wealth of improbable affectation.

Tradition can only be handed down, a delightful but ephemeral mixture of legend, history, and hearsay. But style evolves afresh in the finest players and directors of each succeeding generation, and influences, in its own particular era, the quality of acting and production. The theater needs both, thrives on both, for both are the result of discipline, of endless experiment, trial and error, of individual brilliance and devotion. And genius may always be relied on to appear suddenly from nowhere, breaking all rules and confounding all theory by sheer magnetism and originality.

William Poel and Harley Granville-Barker worked continually to clear away the melodramatic gestures, slow delivery, and old-fashioned declamatory manner of the Victorian and Edwardian theaters. Thanks to their influence, Shakespeare's plays began to be acted, for the first time, in the right order of scenes and with a minimum of cuts. Business was allowed only if it seemed to arise naturally from the text and was not spun out or elaborated into effective tableaux or used as a means for working up applause. All this was greatly to the good. But the director, however forceful in personality, has to withdraw once the curtain goes up. The actors have the final word. Then, after six weeks of consecutive performances, the pace has dragged, new business has been introduced. Even the most conscientious players tend to flag when the audience is unresponsive, and they begin to find their parts monotonous and devoid of spontaneity. Rehearsal is the only remedy, and English actors do not relish rehearsing a play in which they are already acting eight times a week. So it is obviously an advantage from the actors' point of view to be playing several plays in a changing repertoire. But such a program confuses the public, costs a fortune in scenery changes and lighting rehearsals,

and risks the dangers of miscasting, since the same actors must somehow be fitted to several parts at once.

We have never till now achieved a permanent classical company in England, though in the period 1937–1938 and again in 1944 and 1953 I myself ventured on three repertory seasons using a group of the same actors with some success. Granville-Barker achieved one or two brilliant beginnings and foundered with World War I. Nigel Playfair and J. B. Fagan benefited by his example and (to a limited extent) created theaters of integrity and style. They used a nucleus of actors and actresses whose early training, under the actor-manager stars (Sir Herbert Beerbohm-Tree, Sir Frank Benson, Sir George Alexander), had developed their talents to a point where they were admirably fitted to become members of a company in which the policy was bent toward interpreting good plays without sacrificing their balance.

English character actors are surely as fine as any in the world; and, as the body of every repertory company, they are essential. They are versatile and loyal. But, curiously enough, they seem to do their best work under an autocrat—whether he be actor, director, or a combination of both. For it is the leader of a company who creates his own tradition of style and ensemble playing. But soon the more brilliant among the younger members of such a company begin to find themselves cramped. They break away from the nursery and, as they become increasingly successful, begin a new tradition of their own. So it happened with Mrs.—afterward Dame—Madge Kendall, Dame Ellen Terry, Irving, Sir Johnston Forbes-Robertson, Beerbohm-Tree, Alexander, Granville-Barker, and in our own day with Dame Sybil Thorndike, Dame Edith Evans, Sir Ralph Richardson, Olivier, Sir Alec Guinness, Sir Michael Redgrave, and myself.

The struggle is always the same: between the actor's personal magnetism, the public's preference for outstanding personalities, and the author's dependence on actors to interpret the leading roles that they write. It is evident that the star must always exist. But is he to sacrifice his choice of parts and the development of his personal career to the establishment of a theater of which he is the head? If so, he must stand down in certain productions, and either play a small part, or direct, or not appear at all. In that case he must have in his company one or two actors at least of equal talent and drawing-power as himself—a very difficult achievement, since star actors are always greatly in demand. In addition, he must guarantee his company long-term engagements—but not so long that they will become exhausted and dissatisfied. Also, his actors must agree not to accept film and radio work, since they will be required to rehearse continually. And sufficiently attractive parts must be provided for each player—at least one good part in a season, say, of four plays.

Experimental plays must be alternated with some of the well-known classics (which are most certain to attract the public), and modern authors must accept a ready-made cast (which may imperil the chances of their work, since in a repertory company a certain amount of less-than-perfect casting is inevitable) as well as a limited run. It is essential that a classical company should sometimes work on an original script, even though a Shakespearean team is seldom well suited to act a modern play, in which the women's parts are so often predominant and in which there are seldom enough parts to accommodate the whole company. If actors are laid off for a certain play (which may be an admirable respite for them), they must be paid or they will go elsewhere. Economically, as well as artistically, the prospect is a bleak one; and it seems to me remarkable that, with the interruption of the two wars, the advent of films, radio, and television, and the enormous rise in expenses in every department of the theater—all these crises following one another in rapid succession—the experiments in classic repertory and semipermanent companies made in England during the last sixty years have succeeded as well as they have.

Patrons such as Lord Howard de Walden, Lord Lathom, Sir Barry Jackson, and Anmer Hall cheerfully risked and lost fortunes in the English theater, but distinguished work was still achieved through their enthusiasm and altruism. Lilian Baylis used to boast that the Old Vic was really the National Theatre and there is no doubt that her extraordinary career succeeded, despite endless struggles with inadequate means, in proving an inspiration. After her death her example bore fruit in shaming the endless prevarications and postponements of the government into the long-promised creation of the National Theatre and the Barbican. But even in her lifetime she had accomplished the remarkable feat of rebuilding (and establishing after several difficult years) the Sadler's Wells Theatre. She also enabled Dame Ninette de Valois to triumph in the founding of her ballet company, while she continued to provide opera in English at cheap prices for her ever-enthusiastic audiences, even though her knowledge of the arts was utterly naive (style and tradition meant nothing to her). But Miss Baylis combined shrewdness and unfaltering determination with her faith in God and her conviction that with his help she would accomplish the work he had given her to do. She must be remembered as something of a saint, with all the doubts, fears, eccentricities, and frequent disagreableness that must ever be associated with sainthood.

The Old Vic and Stratford were, until the creation of the two subsidized theaters, the only two houses for many years to pursue an uninterrupted policy of presenting Shakespeare. Both underwent periods of unequal criticism and popularity. At the Vic, Robert Atkins, Harcourt Williams, Michael Benthall, and Tyrone Guthrie were important influences, while at Stratford, Walter Bridges-Adams, Barry Jackson, Anthony Quayle, Glen Byam Shaw, and Peter Hall contributed a number of memorable seasons and productions. The much-criticized Arts Council did a great deal of work—invaluable especially during and soon after World War II—in helping and encouraging experimental and classical ventures throughout the country. Both at the Vic and at Stratford the star actors who appeared over the years—Sybil Thorndike, Edith Evans, Laurence Olivier, Paul Scofield, Peggy Ashcroft, Maurice Evans, Charles Laughton, Godfrey Tearle, Paul Robeson, Ralph Richardson, Alec Guinness, Ruth Gordon, Michael Redgrave, and myself, as well as many others, all distinguished players—were content to appear, shorn of West End salaries and star billing, to the great and valuable development of their talents. And, at both these theaters, from 1920 to 1970, the work reflected their devotion to their craft and to the interpretation of Shakespeare and the classics.

The repertory system, with the establishment of the two subsidized theaters, has now at last been achieved, and the public, which for so many years was supposed to be unable to support a series of productions given on alternate nights, now appear to take the scheme for granted, and take the trouble to make certain that they are booking seats for the production that they wish to see. This is an enormous step forward and was considered quite out of the question as recently as the early 1960s. But it is sadly ironic that this state of things should have been achieved only in a time of inflation, when production costs, industrial disputes, salaries, and cutbacks have endangered the entire theatrical profession and forced the staggering increase in transport and the price of theater seats.

It is sad that when at long last a really fine production has materialized, it cannot be kept in the repertoire of a theater, to be revived at intervals over several years and shown in the United States and the great capitals of Europe, too. But that is the glory of the theater as well as its fallibility. Talented players develop quickly and cannot be kept in a subordinate position for long. The best ensemble will deteriorate after a hundred performances of the same play. Actors cannot work together happily for too many years at a time. Directors become stale. Style changes. Stars become too old to wish to continue playing the great parts in which they made their reputation a few years ago. (This was not always so, and surely it is a sign of grace.)

The repertory theater and the classical theater must always be nurseries. They will attract talented young people who wish to learn their business. A few of the best stars and character actors will always be glad to work in them—but only for a limited period, for the work is intensely concentrated and demanding, and the rewards financially inferior. In addition there are the purely material considerations to deter an actor who is no longer young—continuous rehearsals and learning of new parts, sharing of dressing-rooms, unfeatured billing, and the binding terms of a long contract.

Practical men of vision are rare in the theater. It is seldom that one man can combine the talents of impresario, financial manager, director, and actor. He may have a smattering of all these qualifications, but if so he is best fitted to work in a theater building that belongs to him and to devise his own policy for running it. He will certainly not work so well under a committee or board of governors. But if he makes wrong decisions or becomes tired or ill after a concentrated period of hard work, he will collapse as Irving did. It was obviously a bitter disappointment to Olivier that, after so many years of brilliant work and endless managerial troubles, he was not after all well enough to remain director of the National Theatre when at last it opened.

Under present-day conditions there is little possibility that an actor can back his own ventures, so that he is bound to be financially responsible to a patron or a syndicate, or else he must work, under someone else's management, in whatever theater that management is able to provide for him and, to some degree, under supervision. The conditions cannot be ideal, however one looks at them. The demand is always far greater than the supply as far as talent is concerned—and the temperament of theater people is notoriously incalculable. Actors are inclined to be loyal in adversity and difficult when things are going well.

But there is a great new public for the theater since World War II. The little clique of middle-class theater-lovers of the Victorian and Edwardian days has disappeared. Regular and critical playgoers, but conventionally minded, following the favorite authors and actors of their day, they were, on the whole, fearful of experiment and suspicious of innovation. They loved Shakespeare chiefly as a stamping ground for stars and spectacle and reveled in the melodramas that the cinema has usurped today. Books are more widely read; films, radio, and television have increased the public demand for entertainment; and an appetite for literature, acting, spectacle, and the spoken word has spread to millions of potential playgoers who would never have dreamed of entering a live theater fifty years ago. Plays are read, listened to, and discussed as well as seen. There is a much wider interest in the production of intelligent work. Criticism is more general, if often less well-informed and expert. And though one may venture to resent pipes and open shirts in the stalls of a theater, they represent a far more widely representative audience than the snobbish, socially-divided house of former days.

For myself, I am in two minds as to some of the most drastic practical changes that have come to the theater in these last years. I cannot like the open stage or theater in the round, both of which demand a completely different method of projection from actors trained to appear on a proscenium stage. In an otherwise brilliant production of *The Duchess of Malfi* that I saw recently at the Roundhouse the continuous turning and changing of positions made it impossible for me to watch the facial play of the cast and forced me to miss hearing a large proportion of the intricate text—though this fact, I must admit, did not seem to trouble the audience or the majority of the critics.

Lighting has become far more brilliantly and imaginatively used, and experts in this department now have highly respected and invaluable posts in all the best theaters, as well as being successfully provided with booths at the backs of auditoriums so that they can direct their work satisfactorily.

Scenic design has veered in a number of directions, both realistic and abstract, and the curtain has been largely abolished (destroying anticipation, complicating the ends of scenes, and necessitating laborious curtain calls). For several years steeply raked floors became the fashion—very effective from the stalls, less popular with the actors, whose balance was apt to be seriously threatened by them. Overhead lighting is now almost always in view, but this does not seem to trouble audiences (many of them used to open ceiling lights in their own homes), though personally I cannot help resenting their somewhat freakish intrusion on the pictorial effect of a scene.

The subsidized theaters have enabled directors to rehearse far longer than the three or four weeks customary in London for so many years. This is undoubtedly a great advantage, though I cannot say that I believe long discussions, exercises, and improvisations are always necessary. I myself rehearsed with Peter Brook for ten agonizing weeks on the *Oedipus* of Seneca in 1968, and the result, though controversially received, was undoubtedly for me a rigorous and intimidating experience.

Peter Hall rehearsed his production of the *Oresteia* for almost a year, almost rivaling the historic precedents of Stanislavsky and Felsenstein. But the stage director must possess almost the equivalent staying power of a film director to keep the trust of a company for so long. And quite a different discipline must then be demanded of the actors as well as the already taxing task of acting eight times a week before an audience. It is for a younger generation than mine to learn how to stay the course. The labors of applying their skills to the new media in which they do additional work— broadcasting, films, and television, as well as the persistent interviews and other forms of promotion and publicity on television and radio talk shows— make their lives increasingly exhausting and deprive them of any sort of private life.

Audiences are still traditionally minded. They still applaud (as a rule) and hiss (a good deal less frequently than of old). They still stand in queues, arrive late, drop tea trays, and demand speeches and autographs from their favorites.

Behind the curtain, too, tradition remains, as much an inevitable part of the theater magic as the plush curtain, the jumbled property room, the narrow, bleak passages and staircases where the actors pass, now in costume, now in their street clothes, and the dressing rooms with their pinned-up yellowing telegrams, strangely assorted mascots, and reminders scribbled in greasepaint across the mirrors. An age-old tradition, even in a young company playing in a theater that has been newly built (though how much happier most actors feel when playing in an old one—the Haymarket or the Theatre Royal in Bath or Bristol). But Tradition is not a God to be worshiped in the theater, for that encourages sentimentality and looking backward. We may best use it as a warning as well as an example, a danger as well as an ideal.

To play with style—the style that expresses the actor's individual personality, serves his author intelligently, and is flexible enough to give and take for the benefit of his fellow actors, either in classical or in modern plays—this is a worthy and constructive aspiration for a talented young actor to pursue. He may achieve it, perhaps, when he comes to his maturity, in a different, yet equally brilliant, way from his predecessors. But the theater muddles on. I believe it will muddle forward and muddle through.

The Cultural Phenomenon of Shakespeare

JOSEPH G. PRICE

Sometime around the turn of the seventeenth century, William Shakespeare sat down at his worktable to continue writing a play of revenge that he would call simply *The Tragical History of Hamlet, Prince of Denmark.* The title would attract audiences familiar with an earlier, popular melodrama on the same subject. Although he had worked his way into the third act, Shakespeare felt uneasy about his protagonist. Hamlet had taken on a complexity that an actor, even the great Richard Burbage, perhaps could not clarify for the spectators. Indeed, Shakespeare had created a problem for himself. When in Act I he had written into Hamlet's reply to Gertrude's question the line "But I have that within which passeth show," he contradicted the theater itself. "Show" is what the stage is about; the theater can hardly allow a character to pass—that is, bypass—"show."

How then to externalize "that within" the protagonist? The only solution was a soliloquy. The complexity also needed to be simplified. Hamlet had seen a ghost, discovered his mother to be adulterous and incestuous, knew his uncle to be a murderer and usurper, and had vowed himself to be an avenger. An outrageous situation and an introspective character must be brought together within the understanding of the audience. Groundlings and noblemen alike must be moved. What did Hamlet share with the rest of mankind? "To be, or not to be—that is the question." The evils of the world force the question, Which is preferable, existence or nonexistence? Does one attack these evils or endure them passively? Why choose life over death? As he expanded the speech over some thirty lines of poetry, Shakespeare coined a phrase, "ay, there's the rub"; wrote of human fears "when we have shuffled off this mortal coil"; described death as "the undiscovered country"; and generalized that "conscience does make cowards of us all." The words took on an enduring life of their own.

In the eighteenth century, Samuel Johnson sketched out a very early psychological analysis of the speech already famous by then: "Of this celebrated soliloquy, which bursting from a man distracted with contrariety of desires, and overwhelmed with the magnitude of his own purposes, is connected rather in the speaker's mind·than on his tongue, I shall endeavor to discover the train, and to show how one sentiment produces another." In the nineteenth century, Samuel Taylor Coleridge declared, "This speech is of absolutely universal interest"; and so it was, for German philosophers adopted it as an explanation for the paralysis in German politics—"Deutschland ist Hamlet." In the twentieth century, existentialists found in it a sounding board for the modern debate over essence and existence.

The soliloquy has long since become a part of the popular imagination. "To be, or not to be" is so pervasive throughout our culture that its author need never be identified. The phrase has been used as title for two films; it frequently headlines advertisements; its parodies appear in comic strips. Why should the world put such stock in that phrase?

Why should it define so many important issues? Why do the words spring to the lips of those who have never read a line of *Hamlet*? What beyond its mere simplicity leads to its universal application?

For Shakespeare as he outlined his third act, the more practical problem was the increasing complexity of his protagonist. The playwright was satisfied with what he had written for the first two acts. In the play's first scene, he had wanted to establish the reality of the Ghost and still convey popular superstitions. To a minor character, Marcellus, soon to disappear altogether from the play, he gave the speech:

It faded on the crowing of the cock.
Some say that ever 'gainst that season comes
Wherein our Saviour's birth is celebrated,
This bird of dawning singeth all night long,
And then, they say, no spirit dare stir abroad,
The nights are wholesome, then no planets strike,
No fairy takes, nor witch hath power to charm.
So hallowed and so gracious is that time.

(I. i. 157–164)

Shakespeare would never know that these line, out of their context, would appear on countless Christmas cards in the 1980s. In the second scene, contrast between Hamlet and Laertes was established early. Although the king gave Laertes permission to return to the university at Paris, he denied Hamlet's request to return to Wittenberg. (Shakespeare could not anticipate André Gide's witty observation that Hamlet's whole problem was that he had gone to a German university.) As Shakespeare wrote Hamlet's first soliloquy, did he foresee that the line "Frailty, thy name is woman" would be immortalized by controversy?

In the third scene, Shakespeare fashioned a father's advice to his departing son as Laertes set sail for France. Perhaps he drew on commonplaces of his own time, but when Shakespeare turned the phrase "Neither a borrower nor a lender be," the world listened and has quoted it ever since. Polonius went on to preach, "To thine own self be true." On 31 May 1984, Anthony Lewis, without mentioning Shakespeare, so entitled his article on Israel for the *New York Times*. More frivolously, an advertisement for Omaha steaks appeared in the *New Yorker* with the banner "To thine own self . . . be good!"

In the last two scenes of the first act, Shakespeare had worked quickly over Hamlet's first confronta-

tion with his father's ghost. He scattered phrases that would fall upon fertile ground and grow into the language of English-speaking peoples everywhere: "to the manner born," "a custom more honored in the breach than the observance," "nature's livery," "at a pin's fee," "something is rotten in the state of Denmark," "leave her to heaven," "one may smile, and smile, and be a villain." Near the end of the first act, he composed the simple, poignant couplet "There are more things in heaven and earth, Horatio, / Than are dreamt of in your philosophy."

There were more things in store for Shakespeare, both heavenly and earthly, than his own philosophy could possibly have imagined. Seven years after Shakespeare's death, Ben Jonson, his rival and friend, enshrined him in the verses introductory to the First Folio:

But stay, I see thee in the *Hemisphere*
    Advanc'd, and made a Constellation there!
Shine forth, thou Starre of *Poets*.

Sixty-two years after Shakespeare's death, John Dryden in the preface to *All for Love* "profess'd to imitate the Divine *Shakespeare*." Three centuries later, John Bartlett in his *Familiar Quotations* listed seventy-seven pages of quotations from Shakespeare, thirty-one from the Bible.

In Act II, Shakespeare had created two minor characters with the amusing names Rosencrantz and Guildenstern. How unlikely that they would be inflated into the title characters of Tom Stoppard's play *Rosencrantz and Guildenstern Are Dead* (1966). To divert them from their spying mission on behalf of the king, Shakespeare's Hamlet says:

What a piece of work is a man, how noble in reason, how infinite in faculties; in form and moving how express and admirable, in action how like an angel, in apprehension how like a god: the beauty of the world, the paragon of animals! And yet to me what is this quintessence of dust?

(II. ii. 300–305).

The lines have prompted generations of readers to meditate on the dichotomy in human nature. Out of the dialogue with these insignificant characters comes a perspective of life that gleams through Shakespeare's plays. We can imagine the surprise of audiences when they heard these lines sung in the 1960s rock musical *Hair*.

Shakespeare concluded Act II with the lines "The play's the thing / Wherein I'll catch the conscience of the king." During the American presidential campaign of 1984, the *New York Times* printed a caricature of the Democratic candidate, Walter Mondale, accompanying it with an article captioned with those lines. There was no need to identify the source or clarify the allusion. During the same campaign, Secretary of State George Shultz spread alarm when he insisted, "But we cannot allow ourselves to become the Hamlet of nations, worrying endlessly over whether and how to respond." The world understood his meaning; the mental state conveyed in the second soliloquy had become the prototype of inaction, of bewildered delay.

Now Shakespeare returned to the "To be, or not to be" soliloquy. He cut off Hamlet's reverie with the entrance of Ophelia. The lovers had not spoken to each other since Polonius ordered his daughter to repel Hamlet's letters and deny him "access" to her. The angry Hamlet cries out, "Get thee to a nunnery," and the rebuke would echo in the ears of many rejected maidens.

When Shakespeare finished the nunnery dialogue and the play-within-the-play, these scenes must have seemed to him straightforward in their theatricality. No doubt he discussed with his fellow actors whether Hamlet was aware that Claudius and Polonius were overhearing his tirade against Ophelia and, if so, when the actor should convey this to the audience. In all likelihood, Shakespeare himself would stage-manage the play-within-the-play. Claudius would reveal his guilt when he heard his own crime reenacted, but should he also watch the dumb show that foreshadows the murder in pantomime? Were the ghost of Shakespeare now to prowl the stacks of any large modern library, it would grow even paler counting the pages of scholarly argument and critical commentary debating these two scenes. Gasping at the record of contrivances by means of which actors and directors coped with problems of the stage business, the specter would catch a glimmer of what has become the Shakespeare industry.

For his own world, the Globe playhouse, Shakespeare introduced a band of itinerant actors into *Hamlet* to play "The Mouse-trap" or "The Murder of Gonzago" and let Hamlet instruct them:

Speak the speech, I pray you, as I pronounced it to you, trippingly on the tongue. But if you mouth it, as many of our players do, I had as lief the town crier spoke my lines. Nor do not saw the air too much with your hand, thus, but use all gently, for in the very torrent, tempest, and (as I might say) whirlwind of your passion, you must acquire and beget a temperance that may give it smoothness.

(III. ii. 1–8)

For just one year (1982) the index to the "World Bibliography for Shakespeare" published by *Shakespeare Quarterly* lists by name four thousand actors and actresses who had either been mentioned in reviews of performances or were alluded to in articles of criticism. Probably all of them, at one time or another, were taught to follow Hamlet's advice. Over the centuries, most performers, professional and amateur, have been told to speak the speech trippingly on the tongue.

The actor may be expected to know Shakespeare, but would the sportsman? Toward the end of Act III, scene ii, Hamlet mocks Polonius about the shape of a cloud. In an article on fishing in *Sports Illustrated* (13 September 1982), an inventor explains why he has called his new fly "Hamlet's Cloud": "Most fish are like Polonius. They see what they want to see, and this fly can be anything." In the same issue, Earl Weaver, then manager of the Baltimore Orioles, is quoted as arguing with one of his players: "You're wrong. As Polonius said to his son Laertes before he left for Paris. . . ."

Shakespeare has been called a cult hero, but such a designation only dwarfs his immensity. His influence spreads far beyond a cult of worshiping fans; he is present in every aspect of modern life. These allusions from *Hamlet* only hint at the popularity of expressions from his other plays, enough to fill volumes from the last thirty years of our popular culture alone. Manufacturers, advertisers, authors, publishers, and entertainers assume instant recognition of Shakespeare's name, characters, and expressive language. A television commercial, with no further identification, represents the face of Shakespeare in an appeal for funds for higher education. Alfred Dunhill markets Shakespeare vintage cigars; Falstaff beer is a tavern staple; a disc jockey plays a jazz piece labeled "Ode to a Shylock." The lyrics of a 1950s popular song include, "Someone once said, 'All the world's a stage.'" A local newspaper complains of a federal health report that describes the five periods of human life: where, by the way, did we mislay the other two of the seven ages of man? Woody Allen stars in a film, *A Midsummer Night's Sex Comedy*. A television character murmurs disappointedly to his friend, "Et tu, Brute." A florist advertises "A rose by any other name." A *New York Times* editorial, "Every Inch a King," explains the conduct of the owner of a professional baseball team in terms of King Lear. A Hollywood hit, *Flashdance*, itself a cult film, stages a scene in a sleazy Pittsburgh bar, where the voice of the pop singer, Donna Summer, blares, "He's my boy, he's my Romeo." And scores of popular novels are published with titles such as *Nothing Like the Sun, The Grave-maker's House, Something Wicked This Way Comes, Cry Havoc!*, and *Caliban's Filibuster*.

Rather than cult hero, Shakespeare may better be described as the cultural phenomenon of the post-Renaissance world, which now extends beyond Western boundaries to comprise every culture. His internationalism might have been predicted as early as 1607, when *Hamlet* was performed aboard a British vessel at anchor off the Atlantic coast of Africa.

One understands the phenomenon in Great Britain and the United States. Since the beginning of the twentieth century, students in elementary and secondary schools, colleges, and universities have studied Shakespeare. Small children act out "Bottom and the Fairies." Creeping "like snail unwillingly" to Shakespeare, students suffer through the silly questions appended to the school texts of *Julius Caesar* yet thrill to the cries of "The will, the will! We will hear Caesar's will." Impatiently they skip over lines in *Romeo and Juliet* that were fashioned out of sixteenth-century rhetorical conventions, yet make the story their own when Juliet whispers:

> O, I have bought the mansion of a love,
> But not possessed it; and though I am sold,
> Not yet enjoyed.
>
> (III. ii. 26–29)

As in every age, contemporary adaptations, like *West Side Story*, make more forceful the modernity of Shakespeare. The fear with which students approach "the greatest writer in the history of the world" dissipates before the killing of Julius Caesar, the tormented conscience of Macbeth, the revelry of Falstaff, the topicality of Othello, the magnetism of Richard III, the wit of Rosalind, the magic of Cleopatra, and the poetry of plays and sonnets. "Shall I compare thee to a summer's day?" and "When, in disgrace with Fortune and men's

eyes," seep into the memory, to be recalled at curious moments years later.

The sophisticated student would come to recognize so much of his culture as Shakespeare's sphere: fiction such as William Faulkner's *The Sound and the Fury*, music such as Mendelssohn's *A Midsummer Night's Dream* and Duke Ellington's *Cymbeline*, opera such as Verdi's *Otello*, painting such as J. M. W. Turner's *Juliet and Her Nurse*, ballet such as Prokofiev's *Romeo and Juliet*, theater such as Tom Stoppard's *Rosencrantz and Guildenstern Are Dead*, and musical comedy such as Cole Porter's *Kiss Me, Kate*.

If there is a cult for Shakespeare, no doubt its principal members are his fellow artists; the evidence is well documented in other essays of this volume. The effect of Shakespeare on the arts has been described in many books; for example, Martin Scofield's *The Ghosts of Hamlet: The Play and Modern Writers* (1980) analyzes the influence of a single play. To this evidence, I would add only a curious, little-known, privately printed work, *Book Titles from Shakespeare* (1901). It is a confirmation of the popular writer's indebtedness to Shakespeare. The book is not the work of a scholar and carries a charming disclaimer:

> The act or scene in which these quotations occur is not given, as those unfamiliar with the text will enjoy the search and, failing to at once find the lines, are sure to hit upon some others well worth the reading. Nor does this list claim completeness—indeed it may be, while this is printing, a half score of others are in process of incubation!

Nevertheless, the author lists authors and titles for 132 books published principally in the preceding twenty years whose titles spring from Shakespeare. His disclaimer is prophetic. In a second edition in 1911, the books have increased to 400. Today, of course, the computer would turn up thousands.

The book carries an endnote: "This list of Book Titles from SHAKSPERE was collected by Volney Streamer and privately printed for him and Louis Francis Eggers and their friends, at The Calumet Press in New York in the year MCMI." Volney Streamer and his friends constitute another cult of Shakespeare, amateurs who take more than a casual or scholastic interest in the Bard. Shakespeare becomes their hobby, sometimes their avocation. Bardolatry had its roots in Victorian England and was nurtured by public lectures, popular readings, and prettily printed "beauties" of the poet, anthologies of favorite passages. Since then, the practice has only grown. The Shakespeare Society of Philadelphia, an impressive group, is the oldest continuing organization devoted to the dramatist. The society was founded in 1852 by a group of lawyers, and its membership today still is limited to twenty-five men drawn from the highest levels of Philadelphia's corporate executives, judges, doctors, and other professional people. For years the society met twice a month at a private club in black tie for dinner, followed by a reading of a Shakespearean play for which each member, seated along a rectangular table, read assigned lines. Although less formal today, the group continues biweekly meetings presided over by a scholar "dean" who answers questions and moderates disputes of interpretation.

Many have served this rigorous dedication to Shakespeare for decades. The zeal with which the founding members read the plays led to a monumental research project still in progress by scholars under the auspices of the Modern Language Association of America. Horace Howard Furness, a lawyer and charter member, apparently became annoyed by the discrepancies, inaccuracies, and omissions of the various editions in use around the table. He wondered why all the information and editorial commentaries for a play could not be contained in a single volume. He began work on a variorum edition that would list all the variant readings and explications, from the earliest editors at the beginning of the eighteenth century to his own day. Furness moved from the ranks of amateur to professional with the publication of his first New Variorum Edition, *Romeo and Juliet,* in 1871.

In 1980 the Old Cambridge Shakespeare Association of Massachusetts celebrated its centennial. This society numbers about sixty members, including many couples, meets monthly at the home of a member, and reads a play with roles previously assigned to individuals. Among its most famous members was John Bartlett, beloved for his *Familiar Quotations* but even more industrious in his attempt to record alphabetically every word in the Shakespearean canon in its every appearance. *The Harvard Concordance* (1973), compiled by Marvin Spevack through computers, has now accomplished this task, but Bartlett in 1894 managed to list two-thirds of the words in a volume of almost two thousand pages. For the association's anniversary, the mayor of Cambridge proclaimed Shakespeare Day.

There are dozens of such societies and, no doubt, hundreds of such proclamations—all testaments to love of the words of Shakespeare.

The poetry in itself, however, cannot explain such devotion. In an address before the International Shakespeare Association entitled "Is It True What They Say About Shakespeare?" Tom Stoppard synthesized claims of earlier critics:

It should be already clear from what I have said that yes, it is true what they say about Shakespeare. In him we find two separate forms of genius which are rare indeed when encountered separately but almost unprecedented when found together in the same writer. To observe human nature with a clear eye, and to understand human behaviour with an unclouded mind, is rare; to express these things in verbal cadences which simultaneously manage to suggest compression and expansiveness, defies analysis.

I have mentioned Hamlet both as archetype and as client for psychoanalysis. Long before Freud, however, Shakespeare had been praised for his consummate psychological skill. In one of the earliest assessments of his plays, in 1664, Margaret Cavendish, duchess of Newcastle, wrote in a letter:

Shakespeare did not want Wit, to Express to the Life all Sorts of Persons, of what Quality, Profession, Degree, Breeding, or Birth soever; nor did he want Wit to express the Divers and Different Humours, or Natures, or Several Passions in Mankind; and so Well he hath Express'd in his Playes all Sorts of Persons, as one would think he hath been transformed into every one of those Persons he hath Described; and as sometimes one would think he was really himself the Clown or Jester he feigns, so one would think, he was also the King, and Privy Counsellor; also as one would think he were really the Coward he Feigns, so one would think he were the most Valiant, and Experienced Souldier; Who would not think he had been such a man as his Sir John Falstaff? and who would not think he had been Harry the Fifth? & certainly Julius Caesar, Augustus Caesar, and Antonius, did never Really Act their parts Better, if so Well, as he hath Described them, and I believe that Antonius and Brutus did not Speak Better to the People, than he hath Feign'd them.

The understanding and representation of human nature are the transcendent elements in Shakespeare's art to which each succeeding century and every country have paid tribute. When he predicted that Shakespeare was "not of an age, but for all time," Ben Jonson may have understood that his friend had unraveled mysteries of the soul for all generations. We are still compelled to analyze the psyches of the deformed Richard III, the arrogant Caesar, the Machiavellian Iago, the alien Othello, the disillusioned Troilus, the self-indulgent Antony.

The characters confront primal questions. Hamlet touches the rawest nerve of human existence— "Should I live? Should I die? Should I act? *Can* I act?"—or the essential question of human conduct and, perhaps, of all philosophy: What motivates, or dictates, our actions? Are we free, are we governed from outside ourselves, are we controlled by our environment? Macbeth is tormented by the three possibilities. Is it his own nature? "I have no spur / To prick the sides of my intent, but only / Vaulting ambition." Other Shakespearean characters agree. Cassius insists, "The fault, dear Brutus, is not in our stars / But in ourselves." In *King Lear* the bastard son of Gloucester exclaims, "This is the excellent foppery of the world, that when we are sick in fortune, often the surfeits of our own behavior, we make guilty of our disasters the sun, the moon, and stars; as if we were villains on necessity." Macbeth, however, is less certain and debates the meaning of the witches: "This supernatural soliciting / Cannot be ill, cannot be good." The blind Gloucester in *Lear* sees the futility of all human decisions: "As flies to wanton boys are we to th' gods; / They kill us for their sport."

Hamlet resigns himself to divine intervention: "There is special providence in the fall of a sparrow. If it be now, 'tis not to come; if it be not to come, it will be now; if it be not now, yet it will come. The readiness is all." Like all of Shakespeare's protagonists, Macbeth is pressured by external forces, in his case, his wife. When he first decides not to kill the king, Lady Macbeth scorns his retreat:

> From this time
> Such I account thy love. Art thou afeard
> To be the same in thine own act and valor
> As thou art in desire?
>
> . . . .
>
> When you durst do it, then you were a man.

Coriolanus is begged by his mother, wife, and son not to sack his native city, Rome:

> You have said you will not grant us any thing;
> For we have nothing else to ask but that
> Which you deny already; yet we will ask.

In comedy, Beatrice demands of her newly confessed love, Benedict, that he kill his best friend. He cries, "Ha! not for the wide world!" A moment later, he has yielded: "Enough, I am engaged. I will challenge him." Here are the ambivalent resolutions to the question of free will; each response is given full justification throughout the plays; in *Macbeth,* each is weighted equally against the others.

We are drawn into the particular character who represents our own philosophy, our own psychology. Shakespeare, however, as Cavendish writes, is drawn into all of his characters. George Bernard Shaw praised him for holding a mirror up to nature, but whose face is reflected there—Shaw's, yours, mine?

To praise the reality of the characters, to label Shakespeare a master psychologist, falls short of explaining the mythic stature that our culture has bestowed upon him. Many writers, especially among modern novelists, may be praised as analysts of human nature. But something extraordinary happens with the Shakespearean character. The historical Caesar and Antony "did never Really Act their parts Better, if so Well, as he hath Described them," nor did Brutus and Antony speak as well to the Roman mob as did Shakespeare's characters. Shakespeare moves beyond the reality to create the ideal; he is not recording history but infusing it with a mythology of his own. Because his characters are "feigned" to act better and speak more fluently than their historical counterparts, they become archetypes: Shakespeare's Cleopatra, not the Egyptian queen, today symbolizes woman's "infinite variety." His full cast of characters constitutes a mythic race as formidable as the gods and goddesses of primitive legends.

From the beginning, Shakespeare's fame has been wafted on whispers of the divine, a hint of mystery and myth, a disposition toward worship. In 1599, John Weever published the sonnet "Ad Gulielmum Shakespeare":

> Honie-tong'd *Shakespeare* when I saw thine issue
> I swore *Apollo* got them and none other,
> Their rosie-tainted features cloth'd in tissue,
> Some heaven born goddesse said to be their mother.

Elizabethan poetry abounds in such extravagances, yet Jonson's remarks personalize the mythologizing and give credence to the reverence, "for I lov'd the man, and doe honour his memory (on this side Idolatry) as much as any." Sixteen years after Shakespeare's death, Milton wrote of his "hallow'd Reliques"; Dryden, as noted earlier, of the "Divine" Shakespeare; Thomas Otway, of his "thoughts that were immortal as his mind." Alexander Pope and Samuel Johnson led the eighteenth-century praise, echoing "divine" and "immortal." The genesis, growth, and persistence of Shakespearean idolatry has been traced by scholars in great detail; random examples will suffice here. Ralph Waldo Emerson predicted that if creatures from outer space ever landed on our planet, they would know it as Shakespeare, not Earth. The most famous self-acclaimed agnostic of nineteenth-century America, Robert Green Ingersoll, declared that the Bible could be destroyed, for the works of Shakespeare alone would provide the world with moral guidance and "raise the intellectual standards of Mankind." Comparisons of the plays with the Bible had by that time become common, and Shakespeare was elevated to the greatest of moral teachers. John Quincy Adams remarked that "no man can understand him who did not study him pre-eminently as a teacher of morals."

A most intense endorsement came from Andrew Carnegie, who aspired to build a library in Stratford-upon-Avon adjacent to the house in which Shakespeare reputedly was born: "The birthplace of Shakespeare is to me the most sacred spot in the world, more sacred than the Holy Sepulchre itself. Shakespeare taught me more than all other books put together. I have dreamed of that birthplace all my life." Henry Clay Folger, another millionaire and chairman of the board of Standard Oil, built a remarkable cathedral to the man from Stratford, the Folger Shakespeare Library (1931), which now houses the world's rarest and largest collection of materials on Shakespeare.

Although those who deny Shakespeare's authorship of the plays blame their failure to convince on a conspiracy to protect the selfish interests of academics and of the Shakespeare industry, the fact is that Shakespeare has been protected by enthusiasts of all classes and climates, for they love the man on either side of idolatry. In a more profane vein, Edwin Arlington Robinson has captured what perhaps we all feel:

Tell me, now,
If ever there was anything let loose
On earth by gods or devils heretofore
Like this mad, careful, proud, indifferent Shakespeare!

Charlton Ogburn's *The Mysterious William Shakespeare: The Myth and the Reality* (1984) is only the latest attempt among many to demonstrate that the canon was written by someone other than Shakespeare. Debunking is always a component of mythology. In "Shakespeare as Culture Hero" (1966), Alfred Harbage brilliantly describes the mythmaking process and the psychology of the debunkers. His application to Shakespeare of the first mythmaking step forecasts the later stages:

But let us look at the Shakespearean case in its general outlines. Shakespeare, as even the Baconians concede, was a living man, whose birth, marriage, death, whereabouts, possessions, and acting career are mentioned in contemporary documents. But these ordinary facts seemed increasingly inadequate as the extraordinary nature of his accomplishments became manifest, and they began to be pieced out with myth. Lord Raglan [in *The Hero*] estimates that the process of mythmaking begins about fifty years after the subject's death, when his mark remains, but his person is fading from memory. About fifty years after Shakespeare's death, there was no written biography available, but his mark was visible indeed: his works were about to go into their third edition, playhouse managers were competing for rights to perform his plays, and three successive poets-royal—Johnson, Davenant, and Dryden—had hailed him as a nonpareil. A story now became current that he was driven from Stratford by Sir Thomas Lucy for poaching his deer. Scholars point out that Lucy possessed no deer park and the story seems unlikely; but it is otherwise identifiable as myth, combining as it does two traditional motifs usually associated with culture heroes—that of his turbulent behavior in youth and that of the persecutor who hounds him into exile. In other words the process of transformation has begun.

After tracing the parallels between the development of the Shakespearean myth and classical legends, Harbage employs the Freudian explanation of hero worship in terms of the child's substitution of the hero for the father, whose dimensions shrink in proportion to the child's growth. He then analyzes the personalities of the debunkers, whose numbers include Mark Twain and Freud himself. We need not pursue Harbage's analysis of the abnormality that Ernest Jones found in his master when Jones wrote, "I am suggesting that something in Freud's mentality led him to take a special interest in people not being what they seemed to be." From our own experiences, we need only realize that every hero has his detractors, that even legendary heroes have their debunkers. We should not be angry, Harbage points out: "It is not the least of Shakespeare's distinctions that he has been singled out to become the one culture hero of modern times, the single addition to ancient pantheons."

The contrast between the "ordinary facts" of his life and the "extraordinary nature of his accomplishments" is at the heart of Shakespeare's mystique. The Shakespearean myth works in two ways. Because we want to know more, we invent more. No one has felt the longing more deeply than Henry James, who, in his introduction to *The Tempest,* wrote:

> So it is then; and it puts into a nutshell the eternal mystery, the most insoluble that ever was, the complete rupture, for our understanding, between the Poet and the Man. There are moments, I admit, in this age of sound and fury, of connections, in every sense, too maddeningly multiplied, when we are willing to let it pass as a mystery, the most soothing, cooling, consoling too perhaps, that ever was. But there are others when, speaking for myself, its power to torment us intellectually seems scarcely to be borne.

To satisfy himself with his own artistry, James conjures up an image of Shakespeare writing his last play; the dramatist becomes "a diving musician who, alone in his room, preludes or improvises at close of day. He sits at the harpsichord, by the open window, in the summer dusk; his hands wander over the keys." The image is an invention, and with integrity James confesses, "One can speak, in these matters, but from the impression determined by one's own inevitably standpoint." From the plays, all of us form impressions of Shakespeare and concoct images of the playwright as a Prince Hal whose rowdy youth preceded his greatness, a Richard II who speaks in exquisite verse, a Hamlet who broods over the meaning of life, an Othello or Lear who explodes in passion, an Antony betrayed by the "dark lady," a Prospero whose "revels now are ended"—or as not a bourgeois Stratford landowner at all but an earl, Edward de Vere; a lord chancellor, Francis Bacon; or a scoundrel, Christopher Marlowe. Like a chameleon, Shakespeare changes color to blend with our own landscapes.

The more objective determinant in the myth is the universal acclaim of his greatness. Here, too, James may lead the way, "for it is never to be forgotten that we are here in presence of the human character the most magnificently endowed, in all time, with the sense of the life of man, and with the apparatus for recording it." Shakespeare's contemporaries were far more prolific. In 1609, a few years before Shakespeare's retirement, Lope de Vega, the great Spanish dramatist, boasted that he had written over four hundred plays. Shakespeare by then had written about thirty-five and would write only two or three more. But through those works he had recorded the life of man and woman, from the adolescence of Romeo and Juliet through the mature passion of Antony and Cleopatra to the senility of King Lear and the regeneration of Prospero, where Shakespeare became, in James's words, "irresistibly aware, in the depth of his genius, that nothing like it had ever been known, or probably would ever be again known, on earth."

BIBLIOGRAPHY

Robert W. Babcock, *The Genesis of Shakespeare Idolatry, 1766–1799* (1964). Ivor Brown and George Fearon, *Amazing Monument: A Short History of the Shakespeare Industry* (1939). Margaret Cavendish, "Letter CXXIII," *CCXI Sociable Letters* (1664). Ruby Cohn, *Modern Shakespeare Offshoots* (1976). Gwynne Blakemore Evans, ed., *Shakespeare: Aspects of Influence* (1976). Israel Gollancz, ed., *A Book of Homage to Shakespeare* (1916). Frank E. Halliday, *The Cult of Shakespeare* (1957). Mrs. Septimus Harwood, *Shakespeare Cult in Germany from the Sixteenth Century to the Present Time* (1907). Edward Hubler, "Three Shakespearean Myths: Mutability, Plenitude, and Reputation," in *English Institute Essays, 1948* (1949).

Clement M. Ingleby, *Shakespeare's Centurie of Prayse* (1874). Oswald LeWinter, *Shakespeare in Europe* (1963). William Dodge Lewis, *Shakespeare Said It* (1961). Louis Marder, *His Exits and His Entrances: The Story of Shakespeare's Reputation* (1963). Samuel Schoenbaum, *Shakespeare's Lives* (1970). Herbert M. Schueller, ed., *The Persistence of Shakespeare Idolatry* (1964). David Nichol Smith, *Shakespeare in the Eighteenth Century* (1928). Tom Stoppard, "Is It True What They Say About Shakespeare?" International Shakespeare Association Occasional Paper no. 2 (1982). Franz J. Thimm, *Shakespeariana from 1564 to 1864* (1865). Nancy Webb and Jean Francis Webb, *Will Shakespeare and His America* (1964). Alfred Van Rensselaer Westfall, *American Shakespearean Criticism, 1607–1865* (1939).

Shakespeare and the Humanities

JACQUES BARZUN

"Shakespeare Without End." Such was the title of an essay that Goethe wrote, in two parts, in 1813 and 1816. It was not a long essay—the two fragments are short, but they are meaty. Their intention was to "place" Shakespeare in the world of art and thought, as well as acknowledge again the powerful influence he had had on Goethe as poet, playwright, and thinker. It was just then, in the early 1800s, that Europe as a whole was entering upon what has been called Bardolatry—idolizing Shakespeare above all other authors since ancient times. The title of Goethe's essay clearly implies that Shakespeare's thirty-seven plays form an inexhaustible source of knowledge and wisdom, poetry and artistry, which mankind can draw on forever.

If we followed Goethe's lead, to discuss Shakespeare and the humanities would mean pointing out how and where in our western culture the plays (and poems) had contributed knowledge, wisdom, and art since their writing at the turn of the sixteenth century—say 1590 to 1610. Then one could add some estimate of Shakespeare's cultural potency today. But the question of his influence is much more complicated than the fact of his reputation would suggest. Today, there is no need to promote the bard; he is a fixture and an industry: dealing with Shakespeare keeps several occupations going, and the people thus employed show the advantages of the division of labor; each group handles a part of the business in a different way. The scholars, the actors, the critics, the biographers, the schoolteachers, the publishers, and the vague assemblage called the general public or—more flatteringly—the "general educated reader" play diverse roles in relation to the man and his work and hold different views about him.

That is what we should expect in an age of specialization: it has dispersed the united bardolaters of Goethe's time, and in so doing it has brought some thoughtful students to regard Shakespeare as a strange—indeed a unique—case, for reasons that have little to do with his great genius and powerful works. And those reasons prove to be instructive about the humanities as we find them now and in earlier times.

Perhaps the word *humanities* as used here needs a short definition, or rather, delimitation. For the present purpose, the humanities comprise the several arts and all the studies that center on man as a conscious creature—religion, philosophy, law, history and its offshoots, the various *ologies*. Physical science is also one of the humanities when it is considered historically as a sequence of intellectual achievements. Shakespeare, needless to say, did not directly contribute to any of these branches of thought and learning, except the one art of literature. But, as readers of this volume can tell by simply looking at the table of contents, he has been read—scanned, studied, scrutinized, examined, investigated, put on the rack—with a view to assessing both his knowledge of all this learning and the influence of his works upon it during the last three hundred and fifty years.

The humanist's first question is therefore: why

this unusual digging "without end" in the Shakespeare quarry? The answer belongs to the broadest of the humanities, cultural history. And it suggests at once a question of literary criticism: why should this special treatment have been accorded to *him?* To say that he was the very greatest poet and playwright who ever lived will not do, for it is a bardolatrous answer, no longer congenial to the modern temper, as we shall see. But to understand even what these questions and answers mean, we must first know how the crystallization of superlative praise around Shakespeare's name occurred and what it actually stands for.

Shakespeare's situation at any time since his living days has been so peculiar and variable that to become aware of it is in itself a lesson in the nature of the humanities. It takes us straight into the evolution of criticism; the shifts of taste and assumptions from age to age; the development of schools and universities; the changing forms of social imitation and snobbery; the history of painting, music, and ballet; the techniques and conditions of staging, lighting, and acting; and the economics of the enterprise by which Shakespeare's works are studied, discussed, and published. Such a task exceeds the limits of an essay, as well as of any one writer's detailed knowledge. Only a sketch of the terrain can be given. But it should be enough to make clear what a reader of Shakespeare can find in him that throws light on the place and the bearing of the humanities.

The Crusade

The widespread acceptance of Shakespeare's greatness was slow in coming. It took roughly two centuries, counting from his death in 1616; and as we might infer from Goethe's essay, it was finally achieved by the poets, painters, musicians, and essayists of the Romanticist period, from 1790 to 1830. We shall shortly notice how the crusade was conducted and by whom. The point here is that it was the work of professionals—artists making a great to-do over another artist long dead.

This summary does not mean that until the 1800s Shakespeare had been totally neglected—far from it. But he was not "the supreme genius" of the western world. In his own day he was popular enough to earn a fair living at writing plays; his good points were appreciated by his fellow craftsmen in the usual way; that is, with a mixture of

reservations and some envy. There is nothing odd in the fact that he should have been extravagantly praised and savagely attacked, that he should be noted by one fellow-writer solely for his "copious industry," or that a little past the midpoint of his career, a younger poet should parody him along with the melodramatist Heywood: their "stuff" had begun to sound old-fashioned. Again, the fullest tribute, by Ben Jonson, sternly criticized aspects of Shakespeare's art, as is normal between contemporaries who are also rivals.

All this proves once more that genius does not go unrecognized. Even the most eccentric and solitary of writers, Blake, was known to a few in his lifetime as a fine wild poet. But several dozen testimonials by good judges do not insure renown, let alone general or even national fame. These depend on a multitude of factors and chances. The world of letters in Shakespeare's time differed from ours in many ways affecting this matter of repute. There were no newspapers and magazines to review plays. There was no effectual copyright, so theatrical companies had an interest in keeping plays from being published. Shakespeare himself seems to have felt no ambition to extend his reputation through publishing his plays. During his life, poor texts of some of them came out in print, without stage directions, locales, or lists of characters. After his death, thanks to the devotion of two close friends and associates, a first folio edition of all but one of the plays was published, but again the text was often faulty and hardly two copies were alike. Still, Shakespeare had readers, perhaps persons other than the playgoers who gave him his livelihood. This theatergoing public, then as now, was mixed and wayward in its judgments. Ben Jonson called them "illiterate fools," an "uncapable multitude." Their breath, according to Webster, another playwright, would poison and kill the most perfect play. Despite the lack of reviewers, authors then felt sufficiently misunderstood to utter their customary curses.

But even though readers took up Shakespeare and he continued to be played, during the century after his death, many more references have been found to Ben Jonson as the great English dramatist: "Renowned Jonson, the glory of the land," wrote Martin Parker in 1641. Jonson was more regular—i.e., artistic—more learned, and at the same time less difficult, more straightforward in action, more lucid in speech.

The year after Parker's verse appeared, the closing of all theatres for the eighteen years of Revolution and Civil War (1642–1660) interrupted the native dramatic tradition; and what is more, the Restoration of the Stuarts brought with it a taste for things from France. Charles II and his court, and the town aping the court, were impatient with the old plays; manners and language and ways of judging good and bad in literature had changed.

This cultural shift helps to explain both the preference for Jonson, who had exploited the classical Latin models, and the hostile judgments of Shakespeare uttered by a lively mind of the new time, Samuel Pepys, Secretary of the Navy and diarist. For example, in 1662 Pepys went to *Romeo and Juliet,* "a play of itself the worst that I ever heard." A year later, after seeing *Midsummer Night's Dream,* he vows never to go again to "the most insipid, ridiculous play that I ever saw in my life." But the dancing was good and there were some handsome women. As for *Twelfth Night* early in 1663, it was well acted, "though it be but a silly play."

Pepys in fact thought it was a new work; he never mentions Shakespeare's name. The common practice was not so much to follow an author's work—that is a modern fashion—as to "go to the play," whatever one or another theater might offer. This authorlessness was quite appropriate, since the productions were arrangements, improvements to suit the current taste. The *Romeo and Juliet,* for instance, included a new character, the wife of Count Paris. A little earlier, William Davenant had taken *Measure for Measure,* cut it, sandwiched in Beatrice and Benedick from *Much Ado About Nothing,* and called it *The Law Against Lovers.* Pepys records that it was well done and that he particularly enjoyed "the little girl's singing and dancing."

In these conditions it is obvious that no surge of public opinion would single out Shakespeare as conspicuously great. The question did not arise, either for the public or for the theatre managers who, between 1660 and 1710, produced some twenty-five heavily mutilated versions of Shakespearean works. This is to say that the interest in them was practical—entertainment on the public's side, profits on the producers'. Indeed it was this utility that caused Shakespeare to be "improved" on the simple plan later expounded by John Dennis, a famous critic: "I have alter'd everything which I disliked."

It was the professionals once more—the poets—who in reading Shakespeare and sometimes in improving him for stage production were caught by his verbal and dramatic virtuosity. Milton, Dryden,

Pope all wrote eulogies, with harsh reservations. Pope compiled a volume of Shakespeare's "beauties"—not his heroines, but his fine passages. Dryden did over *Antony and Cleopatra,* altered *Troilus and Cressida,* and had a hand in other manglings, yet sincerely admired his great victim.

For, being professionals, all these poets and critics had strong objections to a good deal in Shakespeare. His "sweetness" and "power" were evident, but his lack of form, lack of taste, lack of human judgment, love of lowlife, love of exaggeration, love of puns and irrelevant jokes were noted and condemned. In a word, the enlightened opinion was: Shakespeare is a rough, untutored genius, enormously gifted but incapable of "art." Certainly, the plays cut and patched into musicals, or *King Lear* with dancing bears at intervals between the acts, demonstrate what little connection "art" had with his name and fame. The neo-classical ideal of literature was the tyrant on the throne, and bears went well with old Shakespeare's "barbarism."

Across the English Channel, the dramatist whose works were the admiration of all Europe—Voltaire—had gained some acquaintance with the plays in England in the 1720s and, while also borrowing from them, had ratified the English verdict: Shakespeare was a savage with not an ounce of taste or judgment.

But by the last third of the eighteenth century the tide began to turn. Dr. Johnson directed the full force of his strong mind on the plays and produced an edition with a long Preface. Here at last was a critic in the honorific sense of the word. He knew at first hand what he spoke of and he spoke after mature reflection and comparison. His own ideal in language and drama was not Shakespeare's and could not stretch to encompass it. But his experience of the world was wider and his emotional depth greater than those of his predecessors, so that he could accept as true and fine what others had rejected as wild and barbarous. Still, this acceptance went to Shakespeare's power and insight rather than to his art. Johnson declared that one could not find in Shakespeare six lines without a fault and that the comedies were finer works than the tragedies; he also thought the plays as a whole "the worse for being acted," particularly *Macbeth.*

About the same time, in Germany, the poet and playwright Gotthold Ephraim Lessing, then writing drama criticism in Hamburg, was beginning a campaign against the tragedies of Voltaire. He found them shallow, contrived, incapable of teaching anybody anything new about human life and the human heart. Lessing's standard of comparison was Shakespeare. To Voltaire's *Zaïre,* in which love and jealousy spin the plot, he opposed *Othello,* which he called a "complete textbook" on those passions.

His bringing up Shakespeare again and again must have annoyed readers who did not know a word of the plays, for Lessing asks rhetorically: "Must it always be Shakespeare?" And he answers Yes. He recommends reading the translation by Wieland (another poet), conceding that it has faults, but it will do for a good while—until we Germans have all learned our Shakespeare. By that time—1767—it was but three years till Goethe, a youth of 21, discovered Shakespeare for himself and was soon to declare him one of the two greatest influences in his artistic life.

What was happening at the hands of these men of slightly different generations was the undermining of the neo-classical style that had ruled European culture for a hundred and twenty-five years. In Lessing and Goethe among others, we see the stirrings of a new conception of life and art called Romanticism. The name is unsatisfactory in its irrelevant suggestion of "romance," but it is the historical name and there is no changing it now. One of the features of the new outlook was its liking for nature, not trimmed or tamed, but primitive and wild. One sees at once how Shakespeare's characteristic manner fits this preference. Listen to Maurice Morgann, a Welsh friend of Dr. Johnson's and the man who could claim to be the first of the idolators: in an *Essay on the Dramatic Character of Sir John Falstaff,* published in 1777, he says that in spite of others' neglect or censure, "there are those who firmly believe that this wild, this uncultivated Barbarian [Shakespeare] has not yet obtained one half of his fame." He admits the "spots" and "impurities" that mar the works, but he predicts that "when the very name of Voltaire, and even the memory of the language in which he has written shall be no more, the Apalachian mountains, the banks of the Ohio, and the plains of Sciota [Illinois] shall resound with the accents of this Barbarian."

Such remarks and others of the same kind by English and German writers of the time indicate that Shakespeare was being touted, not only for himself but also as a champion in the struggle to overthrow the tyranny of the French in manners, language, and artistic standards. Shakespeare was the perfect instrument with which to cast off a double yoke. English national pride could now begin

to say: *our* great poet, and soon the Germans would say *unser* Shakespeare, because his native tongue, his freedom from rules, his deep and violent feelings, his wildness—in short—suddenly seemed very close to ancestral Germanic traditions. For some years, in fact, the urge to renew cultural links with the national past had been widely felt in Europe—except in France. The old popular ballads and heroes and the old medieval architecture (despised as "Gothick") were being studied and prized anew. Shakespeare's structures were Gothic too—asymmetrical, wayward, and perverse, and his characters' actions and feelings followed the same irregular patterns now revalued.

So went the first phase of Shakespeare's rehabilitation. It said in effect: we like him the way he is, crude and full of faults. In the next phase, another wave of professionals—men such as Coleridge, Hazlitt, Carlyle, De Quincey, the mature Goethe, and after them the youngest French writers and artists (notably Stendhal, Victor Hugo, and Berlioz), proposed the startling idea that far from being a wild untutored barbarian Shakespeare was an artist of consummate intelligence and judgment. In 1818 Coleridge had stated the case: "Let me now proceed to destroy . . . the popular notion that he was a great dramatist by mere instinct, that he grew immortal in his own despite, and sank below men of second- or third-rate power when he attempted aught besides the drama." No one, he went on, should talk of Shakespeare "as a sort of beautiful *lusus naturae* [freak of nature], a delightful monster—wild, indeed, and without taste or judgement, but like the inspired idiots so much venerated in the East. . . . I have said, and I say it again, that great as was the genius of Shakespeare, his judgment was at least equal to it." Coleridge's conclusion, supported by a close analysis of the works and echoed by the other enthusiasts, dictated what the world's attitude should henceforth be: "The Englishman who without reverence, a proud and affectionate reverence, can utter the name of William Shakespeare, stands disqualified for the office of critic."

Ten years later, in the long preface to a "Shakespearean" play on Cromwell with eighty-two characters and large mobs, Victor Hugo ranks Shakespeare with Homer and the poets of the Bible; he is the "sovereign" maker of the modern age in poetry, his faults taken in stride as the rugosities of the "giant oak" which he is. De Quincey likewise uses the simile of Shakespeare as a force of nature, "to be studied with entire submission of our facilities."

By the next generation this creed became established fact and was extended over the wide world. In "The Hero as Poet" (1841), Carlyle writes: "Of this Shakespeare of ours, perhaps the opinion one sometimes hears a little idolatrously expressed is, in fact, the right one; I think the best judgment not of this country only, but of Europe at large, is slowly pointing to the conclusion, that Shakespeare is the chief of all Poets hitherto."

The Other Arts Respond

There was an underside, a countercurrent to this extraordinary transformation from untutored genius and accidental maker of poetry to the office of Chief Poet, Wisest of Men, and Most Judicious Artist; and I shall return to it. But first we must look at some of the effects of the proclaimed preeminence on the rest of Europe. It did not express itself in a great burst of popular enjoyment such as greeted the novels of Walter Scott or the poetry of Byron. It remained what I have called for want of a better word "professional," instigated (not to say engineered) from the top, by and among artists.

The first results of the Anglo-German part of the crusade were naturally translations and performances. Wieland's unsatisfactory one, mentioned by Lessing, was replaced by those of August Schlegel, Dorothea Tieck, and Count Baudissin in the years 1796–1810. In France, Letourneur was similarly followed by others, of whom Emile Deschamps and Alfred de Vigny proved the most acceptable. At first, the influential performances were rarely the native efforts to put on these translated plays; they were rather the productions by visiting English troupes. In Paris, in 1822, for example, such a company was hissed off the stage, partly for political reasons—the English defeat of Napoleon in 1815 and the occupation of the city by foreign armies was too recent in the memory and Shakespeare was called "Wellington's aide-de-camp"—a sign of the force nationalism exerts on artistic opinion. But in 1824-5 a "Catherine and Petruchio" (*Taming of the Shrew*) was put on without outcry, and by 1827 the whole Parisian world of art and intellect went wild over a new group of English players in *Romeo and Juliet, Hamlet,* and *Othello,* with John Kemble and the beautiful Irish actress Harriet Smithson in the leading roles.

Young Hector Berlioz, the composer who later married her, now began, like other enthusiasts of his age, to learn English so as to read Shakespeare in the original. For the majority in the audiences that applauded these English players did not understand one word of the text. They were struck by the action alone—its freedom and naturalness compared with French tragedy. They relished the exhibition of violence and horror on the stage (instead of its recital at second hand), as well as the ease with which the imagination, prepared by a synopsis, could move from one scene to another distant in time or space—a radical change from the neoclassic unities that required one spot and one day for all tragic depictions.

These changes of method in representing reality were of enormous importance to all the arts thereafter. The three greatest artists ever influenced by Shakespeare were Goethe, Pushkin, and Berlioz, and in all three it is clear that it was the English dramatist's form, coupled with his lifelikeness—what has since been called "realism"—that liberated their thought and practice. Goethe's *Faust* is written in discontinuous, far-flung scenes, sordid or lofty, whose unity and coherence lie in the developing theme, not in passages contrived to link one with the next. The very subject could not have been handled at all under neo-classic restrictions. Pushkin, having first been captivated by Byron, purged himself of the Childe Harold mood and adopted Shakespeare as the richer spirit and in 1825 composed *Boris Godunov,* a true history play on the English model and, much later, the inspiration of Mussorgsky for the opera with the same title and corresponding form. Berlioz, working with the joint examples of Goethe and Shakespeare before him, fashioned his twelve musical dramas on the same plan. His treatment of the Dido and Aeneas story from Virgil in *Les Troyens,* though it is a "classical" theme, follows the Shakespearean pattern, as did his *Romeo and Juliet* symphony twenty years earlier. And his very last work, the comic opera *Beatrice and Benedict,* is similarly adapted from *Much Ado about Nothing.*

Between the two visits of Shakespeare actors to Paris in 1822 and 1827, another Frenchman had supplied in a pair of pamphlets that became famous an esthetic theory detailing what the new art should be. Henri Beyle, who wrote under the name of Stendhal, had become acquainted in Italy with young artists who preached *romanticismo* against the still prevailing neoclassic doctrines, and as an aspiring playwright he shared their views. To make the contrast clear in France, Stendhal called his two essays (soon joined in one volume) *Racine et Shakespeare.* The solemn spectacle, the "noble" language, the pace of Racine's tragedies were familiar to Stendhal's readers. Shakespeare had to be described, and the conclusion made plain that to write a neo-classical tragedy was "to write so as to please our grandfathers," whereas to write like Shakespeare was to please the living generation. Shakespeare, he affirmed after detailing his artistry and explaining away his bombast, was "the hero of the Romanticist poetics." The curious word *hero* in this context was shorthand for what the Romanticists took a great artist to be—a genius, a seer, a lofty spirit to be revered. What was heroic about the genius was his struggle against the surrounding mediocrity (remember Ben Jonson) and their prolonged incomprehension. Neglect was always due to the artist's uniqueness: his contemporaries resisted his strange new vision of life. But his power to convey his perceptions added to man's self knowledge and was in time recognized as a priceless gift to humanity.

Independently, in Russia and virtually in the same year as that of Stendhal's second pamphlet (1823), Pushkin was writing to a critic friend that all he heard about Romanticism was wrong; the true Romanticism was in Shakespeare. What he had in mind was the artful combination of the comic and tragic, of bliss and horror, of the commonplace and the startling—a comprehensive realism. It did not seem odd, apparently, that the new model for young artists should be a writer not living or recent, but one whose works had been "written to please" their great-great-great grandfathers. As it turned out, the Shakespearean example had to be modified a good deal to produce plays acceptable to the audiences of the 1830s and 1840s in France, Italy, Spain, and Germany. The French model, entrenched for almost two hundred years and supported (as was commonly thought) by the precepts of Aristotle and the example of the Greek and Roman classics, died hard.

In France, Victor Hugo was able to make the language of his poetic dramas almost as free as Shakespeare's and he accustomed the public once and for all to changes of scene at will. The little list of places we find printed in our programs—Scene 1: A wooded hill near Ase's farm; Scene 2: A clearing in the forest; and so on—became familiar, as if they had always been in use. But the true Shake-

spearean freedom and movement were never fully recaptured. This is a fact to be reckoned with when we try to assess Shakespeare's art as distinguished from the clichés about Shakespeare's art. The further history of his plays abroad reinforces the point and their first use there shows how cultural assimilation proceeds.

But before crossing to the continent one must interpose some marginal effects in England of Shakespeare's elevation to stardom. One was the attempt to forge manuscripts of "lost" plays by him. Another was the rediscovery of his contemporaries in drama, including Marlowe. "The Elizabethans" meant nothing until nearly the middle of the nineteenth century. Charles Lamb effected this resurrection with a volume of specimens from their works, previously regarded as crude and childish. Lamb and his sister also started the profitable genre of *Tales from Shakespeare:* by now we have reached *Shakespeare for Today, Shakespeare's Plays in Digest,* and even *Macbeth* in cartoons, variously intended for hesitant producers, speed readers, and students shaky before examinations.

What is suggestive on the European scene is that the plays, well before their acceptance as such, were sources of ideas for librettists and composers of ballets and operas. Mozart's unlucky contemporary Salieri composed a *Falstaff* opera in 1798, and before and after him there came into being some half dozen *Romeo and Juliet* operas, all but one dreadfully mangled, lacking Mercutio and the Nurse and adding various new characters. In two of the pieces Romeo is sung by a woman, so she and Juliet can warble in thirds. An early ballet based on *Macbeth* consisted mainly of bringing on the ghosts of Duncan and Banquo to disturb Macbeth at his ill-timed dinner. *Coriolanus, Othello,* and *Hamlet* followed, as it were on tiptoe, this successful translation of tragedy into pirouette and pantomime. Operas by Rossini and others also used Shakespearean plots and characters, and Mozart's librettist Da Ponte drew on the comedies for good situations. One might say that the very materials Shakespeare had borrowed from others were being torn from his works for re-use by still others.

In Italy, faithful productions of his plays were slow in coming. His Italian settings should have exerted some appeal; but one after another, the tragedies that were tried out achieved at best a succès d'estime, that is, something appreciated rather than enjoyed. Nor was this result always obtained. In 1843 a leading Italian actor put on

Othello in Milan with the greatest care, hoping that the public's familiarity with the ballet and with Rossini's *Otello* would soften resistance to the tragedy. But the audience, after whispering and murmuring early in the play, broke out into an uproar of shouts and hissing so that the curtain had to be brought down before the end. They had come to see a tragedy in the manner of their own Alfieri and they were given scenes of common life as in the comedies of Goldoni. Not until the 1860s did the public become more tolerant and enable Ernesto Rossi to win some battles with his *Macbeth* and *King Lear.*

An account of Shakespeare's fortunes in the Hispanic world would be to the same effect. One obstacle there was the national cult of Lope de Vega and Calderón, whose plays, congenial to start with, were sufficiently numerous and varied and "Gothic" to satisfy the desire for a true portrayal of life.

In Russia, thanks to Pushkin, the situation was different, and not just because of his *Boris Godunov.* Pushkin had planned to write a series of miniature plays in the manner of Barry Cornwall's *Dramatic Scenes,* themselves a by-product of England's revaluation of the Shakespearean form. Pushkin wrote four such plays and through them inspired a follower named Alexander Ostrovsky. It has been said on good authority that he and Shakespeare are the two playwrights whose popularity in Russia has never waned. Ostrovsky adopted the Shakespearean form of brief successive scenes and was not afraid to use the Shakespearean monologue, his subjects from common life corresponding to the "vignettes" that Shakespeare inserts in his plays to link high affairs of state or contrast the fancies of love with the rude comedy of workaday doings. In the one work of his that is well known outside Russia, *The Snow Maiden* (made into an opera by Rimsky Korsakov), Ostrovsky was visibly inspired by *Midsummer Night's Dream.*

But perhaps the Russian readers' knowledge was not as accurate as has been reported. In 1865 Nikolai Leskov wrote a novella called *Lady Macbeth of Mtsensk,* whose title is associated nowadays with the opera that Shostakovich composed on the tale in 1934. In both works the title refers to a nickname given to the heroine by her neighbors, but she is hardly Shakespeare's character; she is only a brutal, sexually obsessed woman of coarse mind and habits. Thus do names and attributes as they spread denature original creations. More recently still, when Pasternak was suspect to the authorities for

his early stories, he was allowed to publish his translations of Shakespeare. So we may at least conclude that Russia has been with Germany the European exception in taking Shakespeare into its continuing repertory for the stage.

In the other arts, it was in the 1820s and '30s that Shakespeare fertilized the imagination of the young creators. Composers found in him songs to set, plots to turn into operas or ballets, and even more important, ideal themes on which to compose instrumental music. For it was then that the orchestra, following Beethoven's lead, was expanding its means and modes of expression independently of words and voices—dramatic music without a libretto. In this new genre, Berlioz, who had already written an overture to Scott's *Waverly,* went on to compose a *Tempest* fantasia, a *King Lear* overture, a *Death March for the last Scene of Hamlet,* and the dramatic symphony *Romeo and Juliet.* Mendelssohn wrote a suite for *Midsummer Night's Dream;* Tchaikovsky a *Romeo and Juliet* fantasy and music for *Hamlet,* which play also inspired Liszt's tone poem. Several famous operas have drawn on the plays, notably Verdi's *Macbeth, Falstaff,* and *Otello;* and, in our day, Barkworth's *Romeo and Juliet,* Malipiero's *Julius Caesar,* Getty's *Tempest,* Britten's *Midsummer Night's Dream,* and Samuel Barber's *Antony and Cleopatra.* The output of "music to Shakespeare" is huge and the studies entitled "Shakespeare and Music" correspondingly numerous—aptly so, because there is every reason to infer from his words that the poet himself was a passionate lover of music.

The painters, too, were caught in the stream of Shakespearean adulation during the heyday of Romanticism. In England, the young Bonington—soon to die—produced several scenes from Shakespeare in watercolor and what is perhaps the loveliest painting based on any of the plays, Slender and Anne Page, from *The Merry Wives.* The older Turner, whose self-education was largely based on classic mythology and history, paid his homage with half a dozen canvases on subjects from *The Merchant of Venice* and *Romeo and Juliet.* The Italian scene in each was no doubt Turner's chief interest, for he was seldom at ease with human figures, especially in groups.

In France, meanwhile, Delacroix had drawn a series of *Hamlet* lithographs that are to be counted among his early masterpieces. He also painted *Macbeth With the Witches,* a subject that Corot later also treated with great power. And everywhere, but especially in England, the editions and translations of the plays kept engravers busy providing illustrations. For it was the custom then as now to illustrate books, and the commonest practical means was by engraving. None of the sets thus produced showed outstanding merit except those by the Swiss-English painter Fuseli, who also did a Milton series. As it happens, two of Fuseli's Shakespeare illustrations were engraved by William Blake who, though often citing Shakespeare as one of the great artist-seers of the world, made only a few sketches illustrative of Shakespeare. The one design in Blake's characteristic manner is "A spirit vaulting from a cloud to turn and wind a fiery Pegasus." The lines, somewhat altered, are from *Henry IV, Part 1* (IV. i.), and as one might expect, this watercolor fresco turns the image into an allegory showing the Horse of Intellect leaping from the cliffs of Memory and Reasoning, a barren waste representing "the world of Locke and Newton."

The truth is that Shakespeare's plays, though full of memorable scenes, do not lend themselves to visual reinterpretation. Their force comes from the web of associations with the events that precede and follow, and especially with character. They thus differ from the incidents of classical mythology, which are violent climaxes whose antecedents or agents need not be known in detail. Shakespeare's scenes resemble rather those of the Christian scriptures, but these have the advantages of having their context known at a glance, as Shakespeare's plots and poetry can scarcely hope to be, for reasons that will appear.

Happy Novelists, Unhappy Playwrights

It may surprise if among the arts affected by the early Shakespeare worship I include the art of the novel. To begin with, the short-lived German theory of the novel, evidently inspired by Shakespeare and formulated by Friedrich Schlegel, declared that the modern novel should be all-inclusive: prose narrative, lyrics, dramatic dialogue, and digressions of all kinds—literary, scientific, and supernatural. And many such works, including Goethe's *Wilhelm Meister,* were written on this plan. But a far greater influence came from the prominence in Shakespeare of what we now know as characterization. The common reader tends to assume that this ele-

ment has always been part of literature, but it is not so. Until the Elizabethans and for a good while after, the persons in a story or drama spoke and acted in keeping with their station in life and their purpose in the situation. They portrayed a kind of average expectable human behavior, heightened only by the suspense or terror of the predicament they were in. One might say they were recognizable through and through; they did not lead the beholder on into unknown depths which the author had, first, observed then striven to reproduce so as to present a unique individual. Certainly the ancient Greek tragedians did not so treat their characters, however ably they designed their types. And in early modern times the prose narrative, like the French neo-classic theatre or English Restoration comedy, continued to fashion types.

Those narratives should properly be called *tales,* to distinguish them from what we understand by a novel. It is with the onset of Romanticism (after a few remarkable anticipations) that the individual becomes the great object of literature. And it is through the individual who invites our interest and sympathy as a unique person that the modern reader comes to see "society" as another kind of being, most often hostile and cruel to the "hero" on whom our attention is centered. Society, in other words, replaces the ancient Necessity—the gods or the mythic curse prophesied before the action begins. But since society is made up of human beings whose habits and institutions seem capable of reform (as the gods are not), the novel becomes the medium not only of character depiction but also of social criticism.

The "revelation" of Shakespeare in the nineteenth century gave impetus to these literary and moral intentions. In the two novelists who established the novel as a distinct genre, Scott and Balzac, Shakespeare's influence is manifest. Scott knew the plays intimately—he even wrote pastiche quotations in their style to head his chapters—and in the great scenes of his Scottish series, he is (and was called) a prose Shakespeare. His linking of high and low life, his picturesque dialogue, his rendering of the irrational in thought and action—all highly original when they broke upon Europe between 1814 and 1830—owe their inspiration to the great plays. And in his medieval series one detects the manner and movement of the Shakespeare chronicles. Thus the subgenre "historical novel," invented by Scott, extends the Shakespearean conception into prose literature and, as the modern historian Trevelyan has said: it taught Europe history.

As for Balzac, he was first influenced by Scott and then directly by Shakespeare: the tragic story of Père Goriot and his two daughters is adapted from *King Lear.* Still more significant is Balzac's conception of character as at once individual, recognizably planted in contemporary reality and, by virtue of ideas, a carrier and emblem of a view of life.

The main device for characterization and its anchoring in social reality is the particular, the telling detail, often irrelevant-seeming. Thus when Hamlet's father's ghost is first reported, Bernardo interrupts his eerie recital and says: "The bell then beating one—." It has an electrifying effect, no one can quite say why. Again, when Lear weeps over the dead body of his daughter Cordelia, he breaks off his outburst of grief to ask: "Pray you undo this button. Thank you, sir." It is "touches" like these, of which Shakespeare is full, that create the semblance of a person possessed of autonomous life within a world felt as actual. The modern novel (at least down to the 1920s) similarly relies on the accumulation of details; it is a mass of such particulars.

They constitute in fact the artistic basis of Romanticist art. In attacking the old French tragedy, Stendhal had an easy time showing—among other denials of the particular—the absurdity of clinging to a single locale, an indefinite, featureless spot, "where the conspirators come to complain of the tyrant, and then the tyrant comes to complain of the conspirators." A little earlier, Blake had jotted down the aphorism: "To Generalize is to be an Idiot. To Particularize is the Alone Distinction of Merit."

After this brief glance at the arts and theories that made use of Shakespeare's example, it remains to look at playwriting itself. A word has already been said about Victor Hugo's reform of French ideas and habits of stagecraft. He wrote successful plays in verse for a dozen years and with him the French poetic drama came to an end. In England, where one might have expected a rebirth of that genre, it did not come to pass. To begin with, the Shakespearean model was too overwhelming to do anything but crush all new works under the burden of comparison. Byron wisely limited himself to "closet drama," that is, poems in dialogue, like Goethe's *Faust.* After Byron, three other great poets, Tennyson, Browning, and Swinburne, tried their hand at large-scale poetic and historical drama

and all failed. Browning's other poems showed that he possessed the dramatic instinct, but neither he nor the other two could fashion a blank verse adapted to their needs. The language had changed, Elizabethan freedom of feeling and expression had shrunk, the world of machine industry discouraged lyric flights in mundane situations. Even if it had been possible to disregard these handicaps, self-consciousness would have lost the battle, in the same way that nineteenth-century veneration for the Gothic cathedrals stifled originality. Only the utilitarian buildings of that time, those making no pretensions to "art," now seem to us genuine architecture.

Yet by the end of the century in England it seemed so incredible that no modern had been able to follow in Shakespeare's footsteps that every young poet who emerged was incited to make the attempt. In 1900, the actor-manager Alexander commissioned the rising star Stephen Phillips to write for him a poetic drama. The resulting *Paolo and Francesca* was produced to great acclaim; but Phillips sensed the futility of going on and tried to pattern his next works on the ancient Greek model —in vain: his blank verse, his notions of scene and character were hopelessly tied to Shakespearean ways, so that his industrious output is little better than a parody of the compelling idol. Consider another instance. When in 1937 Shaw rewrote the fifth act of *Cymbeline* for a special occasion, one could see how well Shakespeare's blank verse could be imitated by a prose master of words; not indeed the verse in its highest flights, but in its compression and narrative speed. Such cases illustrate the humanistic generality that in art, a technique or manner has value only when it is fresh from the mind of the creators. Afterwards any competent workman can reproduce it, but the magic is gone.

The Man Everybody Knows

The sweep of the Shakespeare cult over the artistic elites of Europe solidified the assumption that their great master was known and held at the same valuation in every corner of the globe and by all classes of society. Goethe had launched the idea that there was such a thing as "world literature" and it seemed obvious that Shakespeare must head the list of the moderns in that category. We saw this unprecedented confidence expressed by Carlyle; a generation later it inspired the dedicatory words of

Charles and Mary Cowden Clarke's *Shakespeare Key,* a thick volume that classified under a couple of hundred headings lines from Shakespeare indicative of his attitudes, handling of words, and profound observations. The dedication read: "To the True Shakespearean All Over the World . . . in Token of Cordial Fraternity." We may take it that by that date—1879—Shakespeare had definitively "arrived."

Everybody within the reach of western civilization recognized his name, and many could cite one or two of his plays. Literary conversation was punctuated "without end" by a refrain of "Take Shakespeare . . . ," as if he embodied all the problems and solutions of esthetics. When a name was needed to point up an argument his rose automatically to the lips. Thus when Dimitri Pisarev, late in the century, attacked Pushkin as a writer for the idle rich, he argued: "a pair of boots is more useful than a Shakespeare play." Down to our time, when advertisers want to suggest the highest reach of excellence in a product, they invoke Shakespeare as a standard, using a new conventional effigy of his features and dress. His only rival in that department of culture is the Mona Lisa.

After 1870, the rapid spread of the creed was due to the systems of free and compulsory public schools established in western countries about that time. No child escaped the truant officer or a Shakespeare play. A usual choice, and an appropriate one for democracies, was *Julius Caesar.* It was hard reading and might leave few traces beyond "lend me your ears" plus the sense of duty done once and forever; but thanks to the teacher's rapt admiration and the introduction to the annotated text, the requirement made "Williamshakespeare" a four-syllable household word.

In private schools, especially girls' schools, the graduation play was inevitably Shakespeare and probably *As You Like It.* In colleges and universities, the usual Literary Society followed suit with an annual play production—*Julius Caesar* again, or possibly *King John.* This ritual was sustained by the family's owning of a complete Shakespeare, in double columns, cheaply bound and printed, and pressingly sold from door to door even in remote farming districts.

In bourgeois families, before the advent of film and television, a Shakespeare reading, with parts assigned to old and young, was considered good entertainment. And for this purpose the edition in ten volumes prepared in the early 1800s by Dr.

Thomas Bowdler was a godsend. He is made fun of now, because he cut out the bawdy passages, but he should be regarded as a dedicated Shakespearean who advanced the cause immeasurably by enabling "a" Shakespeare to circulate among a population that was prudish or fastidious—depending on one's point of view—and would not have exposed women and children to the raw product of Shakespeare's muse.

One must add that it is to Bowdler's credit that he actually read Shakespeare and knew when the bard's dirty mind was at work. Many of the English were make-believe readers, as appeared in the incident that Mrs. Trollope, mother of novelists, reports in her book on America. She had come to Cincinnati in 1836 to make her fortune by running a dry-goods store, and in a conversation with one of the worthies of the town the subject of literature came up. He disappointed her with his provincial views, so she asked the inevitable question: "And Shakespeare, sir?" "Shakespeare, madam, is obscene, and we are advanced enough to have found it out." The man from Cincinnati had evidently read him, as possibly Mrs. Trollope had not; or if she had, it was in a bardolatrous haze that veiled the off-color jokes. Those two in Cincinnati admirably typify the ordinary state of things Shakespearean in the century of his promotion to "chief of poets hitherto."

If one looked only at the fact that Shakespeare turns up in all the places and activities so far enumerated, one might suppose that he plays in our culture the role that Homer played in the Greek. But though the appearance is there, the reality is not. With us, schoolchildren are not deliberately and thoroughly made familiar with the whole Shakespeare canon—they have a brush with it, if so much. Especially today, when "the language arts" courses offer only the works easiest to read among the most recent fiction, and when the memorizing of poetry is thought to stunt mental growth, Shakespeare is to the young but a proper name of uncertain spelling. Adults do acquire and repeat a number of Shakespeare's phrases, some inaccurately (gild the lily; a poor thing but mine own), others with a false meaning (more honored in the breach; a touch of nature makes the whole world kin). One that they do not get wrong is: "To be, or not to be"; but many of the commonest two hundred or so listed in books of quotations are either avoided as "dreadful clichés" or not recognized as being Shakespeare's at all. Thus his minted wisdom and arresting situations do not serve us, like Homer's in ancient times, as "a directory for human life."

Besides, a civilization based on paper and print like ours is not receptive to communal traditions in the Greek manner. Even so, may it not be said that within the indifferent mass of young and old there is a wide public, over and above the professional group of artists and writers, that "loves Shakespeare" and follows him, gratefully to the playhouse and thoughtfully in the study? Judging by the frequent use of phrases from Shakespeare as the titles of novels (especially crime fiction), such people do exist. But the truth is that since the days of Garrick, who popularized the big roles in the mid-eighteenth century, the wide public's interest in Shakespeare has been through the personality of great actors, men and women who could draw a crowd to see them in any "vehicle"—the very word tells the story. Shakespeare's posthumous life is the sequence, first, of his editors and adapters, and then of his dedicated actors, from Garrick, Kean, Kemble, Mrs. Siddons, Ira Frederick Aldridge (the first black Othello, 1826), Macready, Irving, Forbes-Robertson, Benson, Barrymore, and Beerbohm-Tree, down to Margaret Webster, Sybil Thorndike, Donald Wolfit, Maurice Evans, Ralph Richardson, and Laurence Olivier in our own times. The talk of the town that moves the crowd has been the paired names: Salvini's Hamlet, Irving's Shylock, Webster's Ophelia, and so on "without end."

That it is the histrionic power, rather than the poetic, which weighs with the audiences is illustrated by the remarkable career of Salvini, just mentioned. He was a great Italian actor of the 1860s, who had the good fortune to convert with his *Hamlet* a leading critic named Bianchi and thus helped to acclimate Shakespeare in Italy. Browning, the poet, who lived there at the time, approved Salvini's interpretation and so did the British ambassador. Thus encouraged, Salvini took his troupe and repertoire of five Shakespeare plays to Paris and London. He was received with divided coolness and warmth in Paris. Sarcey, the leading drama critic, wrote that Shakespeare "irritated him." Zola, annoyed at first by having to hear a play in a foreign tongue, finally joined in the enthusiasm of the Shakespearean wing of the audience. In London, Salvini was widely acclaimed. The only thing to be inferred from these events is that Shakespeare's lines apparently do not matter much. The poetry, translated into Italian, and then delivered to Parisians and Londoners in that language,

surely gets lost along the way. The drama is in pantomime. Well, but does not that demonstrate Shakespeare's wonderful power of dramatic construction? It might if experience did not show that no actor or producer leaves the constructions untouched. Take away the verse and the craftsmanship and what is left? The stories, of course, and these we know are not Shakespeare's inventions, but borrowings from earlier historians and novelists.

The dependence of Shakespeare's fame on great actors has other consequences. Great actors want large parts. The plays of Shakespeare that do not contain such parts—*Troilus and Cressida, Cymbeline, Winter's Tale*—are very rarely put on. Out of the thirty-seven, not more than twelve are such as to exalt star performers, and all too often the great acting offered to the public is confined to the star part. Nor is this all. As was indicated a moment ago, the first thing the Shakespearean actors and directors do as they go to work is to cut lines, invert and omit scenes, and generally remake the play. Garrick rewrote the ending of *Romeo and Juliet* "to make it more tragic." We have the testimony of Bernard Shaw, perhaps the most qualified and devoted of Shakespeare students, that until the early 1900s the plays were never given on the English stage complete or as written. Shakespeare's normal relation to the theater is neatly summed up in Shaw's remark that "Augustin Daly thought no price too extravagant for an addition to his Shakespeare relics; but in arranging Shakespeare's plays for the stage he proceeded on the assumption that Shakespeare was a botcher and he an artist." *King Lear*, when put on by Irving, was so thoroughly "adapted" that spectators who did not know the plot were unable to figure out what happens to Gloucester and why. The idea of fidelity to the text was unheard of. When Forbes-Robertson exceptionally restored the part of Fortinbras in *Hamlet* and some good lines by Polonius, the public got a somewhat clearer notion of the work. Granville Barker gave and acted in several plays "as written" but that proved a treat mainly for connoisseurs at little theaters. And when Benson presented all of *Hamlet*—some 4,000 lines—in two sittings, the idea was found eccentric and uncalled for. Maurice Evans was more successful a generation later, but I may add to the record that having missed that production, I have been able to see, in a long life of Shakespeare-hunting, only one uncut *Hamlet,* an amateur production at Princeton University.

It may be said that it is a tradition of the theater everywhere to cut and tamper and that Shakespeare doubtless manhandled his own plays. That is true, but in modern times the practice applies to works in the making: they are tested on the stage with the help of actors and directors; but, again in modern times, respect for the admired classics has prevailed. One cannot always be dead sure that Molière, Sheridan, Congreve, Ibsen, Wilde, Pirandello, Strindberg, O'Neill, or Shaw will be presented as written, but it is almost always so. The words are all there and the scenes in their proper order; the creative instinct of the theatrical profession confines itself to interpretation, stage business, and details of scenery.

Not so with Shakespeare. For one thing, he is always too long for modern taste. For another, some of his lines are unsayable or dull, or suspected of being meaningless. For a third, some of the short scenes he was fond of seem purposeless, and since the last commuter train leaves at 11:10, "out with those scenes!" In *King Lear,* for instance, the unwinding of the plot from Act IV, scene vii onwards is usually so cut and hurried that unless one knows the play from reading it, one cannot follow from seeing it.

Trifling details like these evince a fear that the audience will grow restless and bored. And for the same reason it is felt desirable to spice up the action by novel tricks. Margaret Webster put a red stocking on one arm to show that Ophelia was out of her mind. Lear's fool came on with a whited face and a putty nose. Mrs. Patrick Campbell was persuaded that she should play Lady Macbeth "as if seen through a sheet of glass." Such alluring details, when advertised, help to stir up public interest. Thus we have had *Hamlet* in modern dress, *Midsummer Night's Dream* with Oberon's world permanently peopled by acrobats, *Much Ado* changed so as to take place on a ship at sea, *The Taming of the Shrew* turned into a musical, and *Lear* much rewritten by Ingmar Bergman. From Russia has come an Ophelia of peasant type shown roaring drunk, so that when her Hamlet was shown raving mad and dying in convulsions, it seemed fortunate for all concerned. Meantime, A. L. Rowse, a scholar formerly at Oxford, has "translated" all the obsolete phrases in the plays and recast the lines he thought hard to understand.

Many of these productions and alterations, it is only fair to add, meet with warm approval from audiences and critics. Shakespeare is once again found entertaining and theatrically impressive. These many efforts certainly argue a kind of devotion to the original author, but cannot be called respect for his art. To sum up, for four centuries Shakespeare's work has been like the article which a young writer carefully composed and published and submitted to a magazine; it was promptly accepted by the editor, who wrote back enthusiastically: "lovely material to cut from!" This conclusion compels us to face a paradox. If Shakespeare lives on the stage thanks to the cult of personality —and not his own personality, but the magnetic power of his interpreters—does the fact not conflict with the claims advanced for his genius as a dramatist?

Except for odd efforts—the determination of an English amateur group to put on all the plays (in 1966) or the non-stop "dramatic reading" of the plays *and* poems taking some forty hours (in 1975) —only one-third of Shakespeare's plays reach the stage; and they are subjected there to mutilations that leave the text never twice the same. Adding tricks and "ideas" is relied on to help the author overcome an expected resistance. Where, one asks again, is Shakespeare's "supreme art"? The public cannot have it both ways, pretending, first, that it cherishes Shakespeare for his mastery and then allowing him to be pulled about and presented "improved" and incomplete. If one turns to a towering figure in another art, equally demanding on the interpretative side, and considers Beethoven, the contrast is striking. Nobody would tolerate a "Shakespearean" treatment of the symphonies, the *Missa Solemnis,* or *Fidelio.*

This thought raises the question, in what sense Shakespeare is "universally popular." At various times and places Shakespeare has been offered as free entertainment in public parks. The attendance is usually large, which suggests popular liking— provided presence is matched by attentiveness. During the second world war an abortive attempt was made in England to "make Shakespeare popular" by free productions for the troops on furlough. James Agate, the drama critic and diarist, who was a great Shakespearean, refused to back the plan. "Shakespeare," he said, "is already popular with me." All of which would seem to imply the disconcerting conclusion that Shakespeare remains an intellectual sort of pleasure. When he is taken in his own shape and his own words, the playwright in the top position lives on mainly through books.

Play-Acting, in Two Senses

Before going on to examine the reasons that have been advanced by what we may call the "reading party" among Shakespeare admirers—those who think Shakespeare is best unacted, or even unactable—we should stop a moment to form an impression as to the number of competent admirers, those familiar enough with the plays to be annoyed at cuts and alterations and at the county-fair conditions of the open-air productions.

At the height of the idolatry, the late eighteen-twenties, Hazlitt, who knew the plays as few have done and whose critical writings contain unsurpassed commentaries on Shakespeare as poet, dramatist, and thinker, writes regretfully that in cultural competition with France, the English always bring forward Newton and Locke. "Shakespeare, we are shy of bringing forward. . . . There, Racine is a religion; with us, Shakespeare forms a sect, and, if the truth were to be spoken, not a very numerous one. . . . Even well-informed people among us hardly know the difference between Otway and Shakespeare." (Hazlitt means: appreciate the qualitative difference).

A generation later, in Paris, Berlioz expressed astonishment at the number of his friends, educated and even "artistic" people, who knew little or nothing of Shakespeare: "Not to know *Hamlet* by middle age is like having lived all one's days in a coal mine," he told them; and he began to give readings of the chief plays to private gatherings of these ignorant Parisians, taking all the parts himself and commenting as needed. It is likely, though, that before their initiation at Berlioz's hands, those same people would have counted themselves (and been counted) as upholders of Shakespeare's world-wide fame. This kind of cultural pretense is usually perfunctory, but sometimes hypocritical, as in the incident Northcote relates of Dr. Parr, the noted English scholar: "I remember at the time of the Ireland controversy [over the Shakespeare forgeries] a man like Dr. Parr going down on his knees and kissing the pretended manuscript! It was not that he cared about Shakespeare; he merely worshipped a name."

An important by-product of discovering that Shakespeare has been more celebrated than *well known* in the strict meaning of those words is the light it throws on the place of the humanities in society. Few students have given thought to the makings of fame; systematic studies have not gone beyond retracing the ups and downs of some reputations, one at a time; so that, like the general public, the critics and scholars make assumptions that are demonstrably false. They believe concerning the indefinite list of great names that everybody holds them in much the same esteem, and they attribute that esteem to natural causes—truth will out; the clear merits of the artist, slowly perceived perhaps, will finally be "recognized," the way one recognizes as one's own a piece of property long mislaid or stolen. According to this view, there is a consensus about artists and it is not local or temporary but universal and permanent.

The facts reviewed in the present essay should be enough to cast doubt on this conventional attitude. And to them must be added other elements and influences which, being elusive and unprovable, are conveniently left out of history and criticism—the element of chance (meetings, personal connections); the influence of vested interests, individual or collective; and everpresent, the force of fatigue with the old and desire for the new. All these are potent and their action is not that of intrinsic merits in works of art or rational judgments on the part of seasoned critics.

We may now return to the opinion, expressed by critics who did know their Shakespeare thoroughly, that the plays are "the worse for being acted." The phrase, it will be remembered, is Dr. Johnson's, but he gave no reasons for his dictum. It was Charles Lamb who went into the question in a famous essay on the tragedies and put the case for the "readers only":

> It may seem a paradox, but I cannot help being of opinion that the plays of Shakespeare are less calculated for performance on a stage than those of almost any other dramatist whatever. Their distinguishing excellence is a reason that they should be so. There is so much in them which comes not under the province of acting, with which eye, and tone, and gesture have nothing to do. The glory of the scenic art is to personate passion and the turns of passion; and the more coarse and palpable the passion is, the more hold upon the eyes and ears of the spectators the performer obviously possesses. . . . But . . . in Shakespeare . . . the form of *speaking,* whether it be in soliloquy or dialogue, is only a medium, and often a highly artificial one, for putting the reader or spectator into possession of that knowledge of the inner structure and workings of mind in a character which he could otherwise never have arrived at . . . by any gift short of intuition.

Lamb then makes the point that even the best acting does no more than exhibit a sort of standardized passion. The players know how to express anger, joy, disbelief, fear, contempt, but not *this* anger, *this* fear, *this* joy, because gesture, face, and voice are physically limited and thus limit the spectator's imagination. As a result, "the sort of pleasure Shakespeare's plays give in the acting seems to me not at all to differ from that which the audience receives from those of other writers; and, they being in themselves essentially so different from all others, I must conclude that there is something in the nature of acting which levels all distinctions."
Then follow some examples:

> I have never seen a player [in *Hamlet*] who did not exaggerate and strain to the utmost these ambiguous features—these temporary deformities in the character.... All the Hamlets that I have ever seen rant and rave at [Ophelia] as if she had committed some great crime, and the audience are highly pleased, because the words of the part are satirical and they are enforced by the strongest expression of satirical indignation of which the face and voice are capable.
> ... So to see *Lear* acted, to see an old man tottering about the stage with a walking-stick, turned out of doors by his daughters in a rainy night, has nothing in it but what is painful and disgusting. We want to take him into shelter and relieve him. That is all the feeling which the acting of *Lear* ever produced in me. But the Lear of Shakespeare cannot be acted.... On the stage we see nothing but corporal infirmities and weakness, the impotence of rage; while we read it, we see not Lear, but we are Lear—we are in his mind, we are sustained by a grandeur which baffles the malice of daughters and storms.

Lamb's point is Johnson's unfolded: Shakespeare's plays are made into something else by acting and that something else is worse, because it reduces Shakespeare's characters and conception of life to the kind we get from other able playwrights. His uniqueness is gone. "I am not arguing," Lamb adds, "that *Hamlet* should not be acted, but how much Hamlet is made another by being acted." He shows further and in detail how the public has acquired from the great actors an impression of Richard III's character which is virtually the opposite of Shakespeare's. Nor are these the judgments of a man who dislikes or has a prejudice against the theater: "Never let me be so ungrateful as to forget the very high degree of satisfaction which I received some years back from seeing for the first

time a tragedy of Shakespeare performed.... It seemed to realise conceptions which had hitherto assumed no distinct shape. But dearly do we pay all our life after for this juvenile pleasure, this sense of distinctness."

Independent opinion to the same effect, though less detailed, is found scattered through the literature of criticism. One more may be quoted in confirmation of Lamb's central thesis: Goethe, fond of the stage as a writer, a director, and even an actor, has this to say: "Shakespeare's works are not for the physical vision.... Shakespeare speaks always to our inner sense. Through this, the picture-world of imagination becomes animated and a complete effect results of which we can give no reckoning. ... If we study the works enough, we find that they contain much more of spiritual truth than of spectacular action." We are reminded here of the painters' rare attempts to render Shakespeare's scenes on canvas.

On this question of To act or not to act, it should be remembered that in the span between Shakespeare and our day, the stage has varied enormously. I am not thinking merely of the familiar ascribing of Shakespeare's peculiarities to the Elizabethan theater. It does account for the descriptions of place and time uttered in the plays to orient the spectators or stimulate their visual sense. But when the theater came permanently indoors and offered the spectators the picture-window scheme, with painted scenery, artificial lighting, women actresses, and dis-illusioning intermissions, there began a conflict between imagination and physical make-believe. The "materializing" that Lamb mentions in another part of his essay was first attempted with crudely painted scenery and flickering oil lights that cast odd shadows and soon filled the hall with stench and smoke; all this was bound to work hardship on poetry and passion, indeed to disfigure the works that were most passionate and poetical.

But the trend toward "realism" was irresistible, and beginning in the 1830s it became a main concern of producers and actors, as well as inventors of stage machinery. Whereas formerly the public "went to the play" for the new plot and the great acting, now it was drawn in also by the "effects." The introduction of gas-lighting made scene painting, costuming, and other visual elements ever more "exact"; and with gas in the 1860s came elaborate machines for setting up and changing scenes, creating thunder and lightning, making the moon cross the heavens, showing mist and snow and rain, running streams, boats pitching and rolling, and cannon firing and recoiling. Stages grew larger, audiences bigger. By the time of Henry Irving in the eighteen nineties, the verbal Shakespeare with his fiery moments and quieter nuances was competing with the spectacular Shakespeare designed by actor-managers. That is what made Shaw so fiercely critical of Irving, for whom the text was but something to wrap around his personality and his apparatus.

Still, Irving and his leading lady, Ellen Terry, did carry on the tradition of acting as the art of voice and movement. After them, in our century, came a further turn in the march of artistic truth, under the names of Naturalism and Symbolism. The "great acting" of the older school was felt to be melodramatic ranting, asides were foolish, soliloquies stopped the action, and Shakespeare's iambic pentameter, with its eloquence and its rhyming tags at the end of scenes, destroyed belief. The poetry must therefore be spoken as much as possible like prose—the lines broken up into their constituent phrases. Actors accordingly devoted less time to training their voices and their bodies and more to reshaping their minds and souls to follow the patterns supposedly lying deep beneath the words of their parts. Psychology was no longer the playwright's monopoly. Since the imaginative, poetic effects were no longer verbal, they must come from subtle lighting in varied colors (thanks to electricity and gelatins), and from symbolic scenery made up of non-representative pillars and stairways or stylized forms of human shelter. Shaw broke through these doctrines by saying that he would not give sixpence for a play that could not be acted in a set of drapes, thus, like a good Shakespearean, throwing back the bard on his own original resources.

Yet when it came to actual productions, the outlay and the risk led producers to compromise. Though by the 1920s the day of the great actor-manager was past, the realistic setting lingered. At Shakespeare's birthplace, for instance, the opening words of *The Tempest,* which beautifully describe the terror of the storm at sea, were regularly drowned out by the howling wind machine.

A better kind of Shakespearean lifelikeness, one might have thought, would be achievable on film when movies became talkies in the thirties. But the attempts to transfer the bard to the screen have been few. Perhaps the best was Olivier's *Henry V,* in which the actor's love of shouting and the enactment of the battle made a good show. But the same

actor's *Hamlet* movie was a travesty. The audience was at the outset directed to believe that here was "the tragedy of a man who could not make up his mind," and it was played on that assumption, coupled with the Freudian one that Hamlet was in love with his mother: the chamber scene was a near rape. Yet the inconsistency between the two causes assigned for the tragedy was never cleared up. Meanwhile, the visual side, which in a film is a main point of interest as well as a great opportunity, was unsatisfactory from start to finish.

The latest mode of staging, television, has so far done no better. Olivier in his old age has played *King Lear,* with evident sincerity of purpose; he poured all his physical strength into the exacting part. But the production showed the great limitations of the medium: its reduction of the human figure to pygmy size and its distortion of the human voice. Whenever more than three characters were seen together, they looked indistinct and far away. To obviate this difficulty, most of the play was shown in close-ups, often one face at a time, or two faces and upper bodies clinging and talking nose-to-cheek without reason. Not surprisingly, the tragedy breaks up into a series of purely individual affairs—the play is gone: *Lear* without space is a contradiction; opponents heard seriatim generate no conflict; and faces scanned so close and so long freeze the emotion they express.

To overcome this defect, perhaps, blood and violence were lingered over and added to. Gloucester's mutilation was made sickening in fact as well as in thought, the duel between Edmund and Edgar was needlessly prolonged, and Lear in his physical distress was shown disemboweling a small creature and eating a piece of it raw. Lamb would have said of the entire staging: "I told you so."

The Underside

The various ways in which Shakespeare's art and craft, poetry and dramatic skill are implicitly denied by the actors and by the opinions we have been surveying bring us back to what I have called the underside of Shakespeare's glorification, the current running counter to the ultimately victorious movement that enthroned the Bard. That stream of heresy has continued flowing to the present day; the resistance to Shakespeare on the part of sober critics, great writers, and others among the articulate and cultivated is not imaginary or sporadic, though often it is half-repressed or embarrassed in its utterance. And it has followed without a break the open expression of dislike, derision, or apology that characterized the age of Pepys, Dryden, and Pope. For convenience one may date the underground movement from the anecdote reported by Fanny Burney, the young novelist whose successful *Evelina* made her famous overnight. She was at court talking with George III in the 1780s and he used the privilege of a king to speak out his private notion of Shakespeare's works: "What! Is there not sad stuff? What? What? But one dare not say so!"

Napoleon Bonaparte, who started out in life as a man of letters, had the same opinion: "It's impossible to finish reading any of his plays; they are pitiful." It might seem as if heads shaped for wearing crowns were thick ones of philistine mould. But it is not possible to ascribe philistinism to the long series of skeptics and dissenters from the cult. William Gifford, the editor of the *Quarterly Review*, kept muttering about Shakespeare's "gorgons and hydras" and hoped out loud that "God would forgive Shakespeare for the plays he has written." Matthew Arnold had strong reservations offsetting his praise and kept urging them against the conventional view. Samuel Butler, a genuine and astute reader of Shakespeare, who advanced a persuasive reconstruction of the story in the sonnets, confessed he could not stomach several of the best known plays. William Ernest Henley declared that "Shakespeare often writes so ill that you hesitate to believe he could ever write supremely well." James Russell Lowell's last word was: "If we take up a play thinking it is his, it is astonishing how many things we excuse, and how many we slur over, and so on, for various reasons not very satisfactory, I think, if strictly examined." George Moore wrote a play caricaturing "the world's greatest playwright" and pointed out all the absurdities in *Macbeth:* "I cannot endure a play with thirty-two curtains." Arnold Bennett was inclined to concur: *Troilus and Cressida* was "great stuff" but "it takes the fellow three acts to come to the real point of the plot." And Logan Pearsall Smith put the best light on the English resisters' discomfort when he suggested the Shakespeare paradox: "Of all great artists, the most completely devoid of all artistic conscience."

On the continent of Europe also, the grumblers and dissenters would make an impressive list, with Tolstoy at their head. (Dostoevsky was unhappy but less violent). *Hamlet,* Tolstoy thought, was "crude, immoral, senseless." *Macbeth* was "a farcical play, written by a clever actor with a good memory, who had read many books." And in his "Essay on Shakespeare," written at the turn of the century, he concludes that the world has been suffering from an extraordinary delusion: Shakespeare's greatness ranks with the worst superstitions of history. From Tolstoy's letters it appears that he received messages of agreement from Germany, France, and elsewhere.

The new century Tolstoy was ushering in with his diatribe had further reasons (as we shall see in a moment) for distrusting the tenets of the faith in Shakespeare. But one must first understand what the majority of the doubting critics had in mind when they questioned his art and hence his supremacy. What they were judging was what had bothered Dr. Johnson: the "faults"—"not six lines" without one. Whatever these may be in detail, play by play, there are three ways of "taking" them. Lowell's words just quoted confess to one way, which is that of the devotees—they excuse the faults, slur over them, because they are Shakespeare's: the King can do no wrong. The second way follows the logic indicated by the nineteenth-century critic, Richard Holt Hutton: "If I am not competent to affirm without a doubt that it was an execrable and most undramatic conceit in Shakespeare to make Laertes dry his tears over his drowned sister with the wretched effort at jocularity, 'she has enough of water', I do not suppose I am competent to understand the tragic character of Ophelia's fate."

The third way is to concede the faults—not excuse or slur over them—but maintain that they are so far outweighed by the merits as to be negligible. That was the way of the original idolater, Morgann, and it has been the way of the most thorough and comprehensive readers of Shakespeare from Hazlitt to Shaw. Says Hazlitt: "If he had been only half of what he was, he would perhaps have appeared greater." The pivotal word here is *appeared.* Hazlitt goes on: "The natural ease and indifference of his temper made him sometimes less scrupulous than he might have been." (This was Ben Jonson's complaint: Shakespeare should have "blotted"—struck out—"a thousand lines.") "His very facility of production would make him set less value on his own excellence and not care to distinguish nicely between what he did well or ill." The implication is: we should distinguish between the good and the bad, but be sure to set a high value on the excellent;

to encourage which, Hazlitt concludes with a piece of irony: "He was fonder of puns than became so great a man."

Victor Hugo has often been quoted on Shakespeare and his faults: "I admire it all like a brute." The remark is from the long, rambling introduction to his son's translation of the plays into French, and it comes after acknowledging contemporary objections, still outspoken in France in 1864. What Hugo is preaching and giving an example of resembles Kent's love and admiration of King Lear, knowing the worst of him but feeling "Nevertheless!" Another sentence from that same Introduction should be quoted as often: "Shakespeare is the most difficult problem that esthetics has to settle." Esthetics not being a science but a rationalizing of an apparent consensus at a given time and place, it will not solve the problem; yet discussing it may teach us truths about the humanities.

The salient fact about Shakespeare's faults is their relativity—what Blake meant by "blemishes which are beauties." For example, the "age of reason" could not easily swallow the undignified, barbaric spectacle in *The Winter's Tale:* "exit pursued by a bear." The age of surrealism finds it an attractive, symbolic idea, and the searching scholarship of the modern age underwrites it confidently, like a lawyer fingering a precedent: "Bears appear in other plays of Shakespeare's time; tame bears were not unknown, and bears were easy for an actor to impersonate."

There is, further, the relativity of mode. Faults that strike us in reading may disappear under acting (or be removed in the acting version). Conversely, what looks like digression or excess on the stage may afford pleasure in reading, when the pace is set by our thought, not by the continuous motion of voluble human beings. The public, of course, does not tell what it feels, except by its behavior toward the box office. No repertory theatre offers Shakespeare the year round except in England; and there, in the form of a National Theatre, it took over half a century of agitation since the 1890s to get it established. At the three Stratfords (England, Canada, and the United States), the season is short and linked with the tourist interest and the financing ever precarious. It is conventionally said that Shakespeare is the playwright most often performed, though in some years he is outstripped by Gilbert and Sullivan; but as we noticed earlier, it is rather Shakespeare's raw material that is put on, with alterations by wiser hands. Of the fifteen pro-

ductions reported on by the *New York Times* during the unusually rich season (1983–84), only one was textually unchanged, the rest being not merely cut but more or less transformed.

In any case, a qualified reader's or spectator's judgment is the resultant of innumerable forces, from temperament and training to intellectual maturity or artistic purpose. Thus Goethe, early promoter of Shakespeare though he was, found "the two comics" in *Romeo and Juliet,* Mercutio and the Nurse, "unbearable," and he cut them out of the version he made for his own theater at Weimar. Berlioz, on the contrary, was amazed that none of the composers of operas based on the play kept Mercutio or the Nurse, whose presence would in his view justify music happily contrasting with the lyric and the tragic portions. Going further, John Jay Chapman, who wrote a superb little book called *A Glance Toward Shakespeare,* thinks a passage in the Nurse's part "a stroke of dramatic genius, unforeseen and startling in its power," for he sees in it the trigger that sets off Juliet on her course of action.

In any work of art the faults impugned by criticism are necessarily particulars—*this* line, *that* character trait, *these* actions in sequence, *those* reasons given for the denouement. But in the discussion of artistic principles it is the writer's habit and tendency that are praised or attacked. It is not only Shakespeare's puns that betray his "lack of artistic conscience"; there is his ever-ready exuberance, his lack of judgment, his exaggerated comparisons, his lack of a well-balanced mind. Walter Bagehot, an earnest defender, thought it best to admit the charge: "He is deficient in . . . the *definite proportion* of faculties and qualities suited to the exact work in hand."

That summary foreshadows what happened to Shakespeare's supremacy at the turn of the nineteenth century and has gone on since. A new generation of artists was trying then to throw off the heavy load of masterpieces produced in the previous era; in other words, to repudiate Romanticism and its offshoots down to the 1880s. The young were tired of grandeur, antithesis, realistic detail, lyric effusion, serio-comic contrasts, heaven-storming, and loose though massive construction. It was boring to be overwhelmed. Logically, getting rid of Romanticist works and techniques meant a depreciation of Shakespeare. The very notion of the heroic genius had to be ridiculed and another artistic model set in its place, that of the superior craftsman who lavishes patience and care on every detail of his work, determined to create a perfect form. Form, not feeling or message, was now the true aim of art.

In keeping with this passionate preference, the work of the so-called Metaphysical Poets, who came after Shakespeare in the early seventeenth century, was revalued. Their poems were taken as guides to coherence in symbol and idea, sustained imagery and spare diction. These criteria are what led the American poet and "New Critic" John Crowe Ransom to dismiss the famous "Tomorrow and tomorrow" speech in *Macbeth:* its imagery "doesn't work out." It may be dramatically effective—the critic doesn't know or care about that; it isn't poetry in the true sense. In the same spirit, T. S. Eliot concluded about *Hamlet* that "so far from being Shakespeare's masterpiece, the play is most certainly an artistic failure."

As usual, even critics who share the same advanced views disagree among themselves. André Gide, brought up to read English and admire Shakespeare, and later moved to translate and explain him to French skeptics, was repeatedly taken aback by the works themselves: *The Tempest* had bored friends who had seen it; Gide rereads the play and records in his diary: "A strange drama, which leaves one more unsatisfied than any other by Shakespeare." As for *Richard II:* "One of the least perfect, least constructed of Shakespeare's dramas." Of *Henry V:* "One of Shakespeare's least good plays; mediocre and even very bad in spots. . . ." The repetitive phrasing should be noted: "one of the least perfect, one of the more unsatisfactory"—these numerals imply several other plays in each inferior kind. Then comes *King Lear:* "Do I dare write what I think? I am almost on the point of considering this play execrable, of all Shakespeare's tragedies the least good—and by far."

The new standards for twentieth-century art were plainly intended to reinstate the classical virtues of strict form, "objectivity," and visible logic. In an article of the period between world wars, G. K. Chesterton, not wanting to give up Shakespeare yet responding to cultural change, is compelled to say: "In a much deeper sense, Shakespeare was classical, because he was civilised. . . . He was not a barbarian . . . he was not even a German." By civilised, Chesterton means belonging to the Latin tradition. To writers striving for "Latin" merits, Shakespeare's headlong rush and lordly indifference to art in the sense of fine polish must be a source of both wonder and irritation. It left little free mind to enjoy what he had chosen to do—or rather, what he had done, seemingly without pausing to choose. And among theater reviewers, no less than among theorists and high-flying critics, the same unease is voiced in the staged presence of the bard. One proposes to "divide the faults" between the great actor and the playwright; another explains the rare performing of *The Tempest* by its inherent difficulty—it is closer to a piece of music than to a drama; a third thinks the transformation of *The Taming of the Shrew* into a good show is one of the modern miracles of the theatre; yet another, after seeing *All's Well,* complains of "the author's slow exposition, crabby poetry, and infelicities of structure and characterization"; and a last one calls *Lear* "one of the most muddled and preposterous melodramas ever conceived by the human mind. . . . There isn't a character in it, not omitting the virtuous Cordelia, who arouses in me any permanent emotion more exalted than hilarity."

With such words the wheel has certainly come full circle. Lamb and Coleridge wrote intellectualized rhapsodies to rescue *Lear* from its detractors; André Gide and Wolcott Gibbs find in the play only execrable and hilarious melodrama. Perhaps the harshness of expression in such verdicts springs from resentment against the unique measure of glory still supposed to be paid to Shakespeare. There is in modern criticism (as in modern biography) a strong urge to pull down. True, the critics do not want to send back Shakespeare among the neglected; they want him demoted into the common herd of geniuses, where he could be denigrated without sacrilege or the suspicion of eccentricity.

What the critics forget is that bardolatry at the outset was not arbitrary or pointless; it was an essential force in establishing the modern doctrine of Art with a capital A as the highest spiritual activity of man. When religious orthodoxy declined in the nineteenth century, art took its place, a secular religion. Its great works were a species of revelation, and the artist-prophet had to be accepted with all his obscurities of statement. Shakespeare happened to be the earliest and largest-looming of a succession that has certainly not ended with Rimbaud, Joyce, or the masters of the Absurd. All are treated according to the assumption applied by the religious to the Bible: given these scriptures, let us make them consistent and full of meaning.

Establishment and Industry

The kind of labor just referred to as unavoidable for bringing order into "revelations" can only be done by people with an interest either in the contents of the particular tidings or in getting them accepted, or both. Such people must also have a love of texts and a passion for research. They must be, or become, scholars. The scholarship about Shakespeare and his works took its rise in an obvious necessity: the plays existed in poor, inconsistent printings and the facts or traditions about his life were few and uncertain. To satisfy the world's curiosity about him and supply readable texts, researchers in ever-increasing numbers have gone to work on the records of his period and have collected every discoverable contemporary copy of the plays and poems. In addition, Shakespeare's growing fame inspired forgeries (recall Dr. Parr kissing such a script) that had to be exposed, and the Elizabethan ways of collaboration called for assigning or questioning authorship in doubtful parts of the canon.

Besides, the man or woman of today who wants to read Shakespeare needs something more than a clean text. There must be notes to give the meaning of obsolete words, to explain the frequent puzzles that Shakespeare's use of language occasioned, and to describe customs and practices incidental to the action of the play. Add an introduction about the Globe Theatre and Renaissance England, and you find that in a good modern edition *Hamlet* takes up 255 pages and the commentary, exclusive of footnotes, 320. An easier play, *Othello,* manages with 120 of comment to 198 of text and footnotes. Such figures indicate that since the first Folio of 1623, with its brief and touching preface by two of Shakespeare's friends, editors and researchers have found a good deal to say. A demanding reader would make one more request—that Shakespeare's plays be printed like those of other dramatists, with the name of the character centered above each speech. Only one modern edition takes the space to provide this visual and intellectual comfort. Instead, the name of the character, usually abbreviated, is printed in italics, and stuck to the be-

ginning of each verse. Hard reading and absurd alternations are the result: *Ant. Por. Shy.; Ham. Ger. Pol.; Sic. Mess. Sic.* Why must Shakespeare differ from others in all things?

At first the editing of the texts was undertaken by independent scholars, who worked at their leisure or (like Dr. Johnson) were backed or commissioned by publishers. But after the middle of the nineteenth century, a great change took place in this kind of enterprise. The universities reformed their curriculum to include, as an alternative to "classical studies," "modern studies." Instead of reading only the ancient Greek and Roman writers, the moderns, native and foreign, could be chosen for study in the same exacting ways. Shakespeare and his peers passed from being "works of diversion" (in the Yale University library catalogue of 1750) to being raw material for examination (in both senses of the word). In most European countries, the shift in curriculum was powered by cultural nationalism. In England, for example, it was decided that the nation's original language and literature were Anglo-Saxon. So Shakespeare entered the university as the pièce de resistance near the historical midpoint of the degree-bearing course. The spirit of science was at work, too: every subject must be studied not by the light of simple reason and tradition, but by methods ever more refined and numerous. To do Shakespeare justice, academic lecturers began the painstaking research "without end" that has erected the huge pyramid known as the Shakespeare "literature."

Nowadays, it is taken for granted that every college and university in English-speaking lands (and in a great many elsewhere) will offer a course in Shakespeare, which almost always means a scholar who specializes in the subject and is expected to publish papers on it. But he or she is far from being a standardized creature. There are species and subspecies of "Shakespeare people," as well as fashions in what type of work is thought most important. There have been those who counted—short lines, or words and phrases denoting themes (sleep, death, water, etc.)—so as to draw conclusions about either Shakespeare's obsessions or the structural elements in a play. Others have discovered myths behind the stories, as well as symbols, not visible on the surface, in remarks or actions by the characters; and a few—notably Freud's biographer Ernest Jones—have interpreted these psychoanalytically. Still others have sought sources and parallels in other plays and literatures. Scholars with an historical bent have raked through the relics of Shakespeare's age and thrown light on the common behavior and beliefs that we should bear in mind when reading or seeing the plays. Recently, minute scrutiny has extended to the typesetting of the first editions of the works. It has been thought possible to distinguish typesetter A. from B., plus assistants (or printer's devils), whose habits and mistakes, when compared, are taken as helpful in making emendations. Scholars can now argue in the *Times Literary Supplement* whether or not it was the proofreader of *Lear* who would fold the sheets after correcting them.

Nor is this all. Another set of textual analysts, mostly outside the academy, have found mysterious hints and sometimes full ciphers in the blank verse, and with their aid have identified as the real author "behind" Shakespeare one or another of his contemporaries. The first doubts about authorship go back to the 1780s, but the initiator of a world-wide and continuing movement was an American woman, Delia Bacon, who found the true author of Shakespeare's works to be Francis Bacon, the jurist and philosopher of science. (But the so-called Baconian Theory is named after her, not him.) Other investigators have preferred earls—Oxford, Rutland, Derby; or established writers—Marlowe, Burton, Defoe: in all seventeen candidates for the post. Upwards of 4,000 books and articles contain the arguments and ciphers.

The postulate in these "demonstrations" is that a mere actor, brought up as a middle-class boy in Stratford, could not have acquired knowledge and brilliance enough to write the works published under his name. The reasoning in favor of these dark horses is not borne out either by evidence or by comparison with the cases of geniuses in other times and other arts. A powerful mind can learn enormous amounts in spite of any early surroundings. What is not to be explained is the use to which the genius puts the learning, small or great. And it does not appear that any but one of the pretenders to Shakespeare's mantle could lay claim to a universal mind. That one was Bacon, whose mind we know through his acknowledged works, a wise but four-square soul not likely to have written the lyrics, the bawdy, or the rodomontade lavished upon the plays. As for the so-called evidence of the ciphers, it has been demolished once and for all by William and Elizabeth Friedman, expert cryptologists, who show in *The Shakespearean Ciphers Exam-*

ined that the decoding techniques of all the main users of the proof-by-cypher are invalid. One could extract any message one wanted by their means. Yet as one sober scholar has remarked, the Baconian and other hypotheses, by enlisting another contingent of diggers, contributed valuable information from the historical record.

One might add that the so-called serious scholarship can give cause for skepticism and impatience too. Interminable controversies—for example, that between de Perott and Thomas about Spanish sources for the plays—sound like trifling; indeed, the insubstantiality of the idea of "source" or "influence" is plain in much of the research. A scholar's summary of one paper suggests how close to parody the source-hunting literature often is: "It is possible that a play on the subject of Romeo and Juliet originated in the South Netherlands. Since, if there was such a play, it has been lost, the possibility of its having influenced Shakespeare can be no more than a hypothesis."

All this scanning and burrowing and surmising, which shows no sign of abating, suggests that what may be called the Shakespeare establishment has been unaffected by the shift in literary opinion away from Romanticism and bardolatry. The high schools and colleges may have felt it and diminished Shakespeare accordingly, but not the graduate school departments, where in addition to specialist scholars there are academic critics. The latter take the text and its apparatus from the former and go on to discuss Shakespeare's form, morals, art, philosophy, language, and imagery. It is taken for granted that the works do possess these features and that their author had artistic, moral, and those other purposes in writing as he did. The late Alfred Harbage wrote several persuasive and enlightening books in that vein. But academic critics also fall into worshipful tautologies that ratify the principle not only of Shakespeare's perfection but that of a perfectly conscious and highbrow Shakespeare: "In this final scene, plot finally assumes its full status as the crown of an intricate development of poetic resources. Technique becomes the free and adequate instrument of experience, and the development of imagery which we have traced . . . is given an adequate external consummation, seen as logically complete." Tell that to the manipulative stage director and the disaffected literary critic, and the two will raise their voices in a duet of derision.

It would, to be sure, leave the academics unmoved. One reason is that the world of scholarship all over the earth is solid—courses, degrees, meetings, promotions, chairs, journals, libraries form an impressive organization. And its products—books, texts, "materials"—constitute another vested interest, the publishers', which until the end of the last century involved the engraving trade. Up to that time but to a lesser extent now, the schoolteachers could also claim a stake in the bard—preparing innumerable texts with an introduction and notes addressed to the youthful and presumably reluctant understanding. The combination of groups resembles an industry with a church on top.

Secondary Motives

This state of affairs certainly makes Shakespeare unique *now,* whether or not he was so in the beginning. And his case, being conspicuous, brings out a number of points about the humanities as they exist in the lives of men and women, rather than as we think of them from speeches and college-catalogue assertions of their importance.

Most obvious is the fact that people usually need a reinforcement of their cultural concerns, a secondary interest or motive, which acts like a flywheel to keep their admiration steady. These secondary interests are not to be despised; they make for the continuous transmission of culture as a whole which, if left to the pure reader or simple enjoyer, would be a much feebler stream—indeed it would be divided into many rivulets, periodically subject to drying up.

One such secondary interest is the passion for collecting—books, memorabilia, "association items." We saw how Augustin Daly, who thought nothing of carving up Shakespeare, also thought nothing of paying a high price for some relic associated with the Bard. And some people, as Shaw pointed out, develop a delight in a famous author "as they might have delighted in a particular breed of pigeons if they had never learnt to read." Such antiquarian zeal brings together individuals of a like taste and leads to research and lectures, clubs and societies and their exhibitions and newsletters. In an age when history is a habit of mind, these institutions grow up around many of the world's great figures in art and letters. Everybody knows of the Janeites, not an East Indian sect, but the admirers of Jane Austen. Another such group among the latest devotes itself to the pursuit of James Joyce over the streets of Dublin and Zurich, camera in

hand and text in the memory. It is said that there exist today over three-hundred "single-author societies" in the English-speaking world.

One may reasonably infer that for many persons —perhaps for most—an interest in literature or some other art tends to be exclusive; it is difficult to be catholic, easier to concentrate on the one artist whose work or personality is most congenial —the word should be taken in its original meaning: "of the same breed." There is a kind of convenience too in promoting one alone. The reliance on the star for attracting the public is based on this propensity. Besides, vesting all one's emotions in a single figure satisfies them all at once. If the apostle is free of snobbery, then it is pride in knowing, discovering, explaining, defending, *owning* the sole great master—indeed, there may even be the pride of feeling humble before him, mingled with the joy of using him in the public competition for glory.

An attachment of this kind also denotes the wish not to be superficial in the liking but to know "all about" Shakespeare, Dickens, "Jane," or Joyce; it is a vicarious life whose achievement, in turn, fulfills the desire to add to knowledge, to be a scholar too, in a modest way. The authors, such as Shakespeare, whose lives or works present the greatest number of puzzles and uncertainties are found to have the most fervent followers. In France, for example, none are more indefatigable than the *beylistes,* as the devotees of Stendhal call themselves. In the English-speaking world, Shakespeare outtops the rest in "problems." As Matthew Arnold said in a different context: "Others abide our question;" Shakespeare remains elusive, his secrets protected by history.

Earlier we noted the influence of another secondary interest—cultural nationalism—in first making Shakespeare's reputation and then keeping it high. "Our Shakespeare," say the English—or some of them—and persuade themselves not only that they collectively had a hand in giving him birth, but also that he is representative, a regular Englishman, though on the heroic scale. But when on another occasion the same English people tell us of their "stubborn national dislike of putting things too strongly," one can only laugh at the nationalist trick of having things both ways; for if anyone ever "put things too strongly" it was Shakespeare. It is his extravagant speeches that have made him attractive to great actors and unattractive to modern poets and critics. Yet how could a poet make his mark as a perpetual understater?

Other kinds of nationalism—racial, political—can also play a role in culture, but more fitfully. For example, what enabled the Germans to say *unser* Shakespeare was the belief in a Teutonic or Nordic race, whose tastes in literature were assumed to be uniform from the Danube to the Irish Sea. But the growth of Goethe- and Wagner-worship in Imperial Germany tended to let Shakespeare drift back to his own country. In France, a little before and during the second world war, adroit political use was made of Shakespeare, despite the Parisians' ordinary lukewarmness toward him. In the midst of the troubles of 1934, when a dictatorship was threatening, a production of *Coriolanus* aroused intense feeling and may have helped to rally democratic opinion. For no mere partisan playwright was making the point—it was Shakespeare. Later, during the German occupation of the country, the official theatres put on *Richard III* and *Julius Caesar* to great applause. These plays were ideal for attacking tyranny without incurring reprisals from the Gestapo—who could object to the great Nordic poet's regaling the French with high thoughts?

It would be a mistake to infer from this complex state of affairs that the admiration for Shakespeare and the enjoyment of his works were all derivative or unreal, a kind of collective pretense, as Tolstoy thought. There are true-blue Shakespeareans, as there are Dickensians and Berliozians, Wagnerites and Ibsenites. Who and where are they? Let us go back a moment: if we survey Shakespeare's following during the last century and a half, we find it made up somewhat as follows: first, his actors and producers; then that part of the public which merely recognizes his name; next in order: the amiable or hypocritical ready-believers in his greatness; the theatergoers and reviewers who enjoy the plays; the contingent of academics—a large and solemn body, itself subdivided among several kinds of teachers, scholars, and editors; and last, the many whose business or profession it is to publish and promote not Shakespeare's works alone, but also the huge number of commentators. If we subtract from all these the cynical and the bored, the rest together form a loose but tenacious world following united by scriptures much pondered and articles of faith seldom examined. Shakespeare is Shakespeare and his establishment need not justify itself. One asks again, in the census just taken, where are the thoroughbred Shakespeareans and how may we know them?

One answer springs to mind: they must be peo-ple not moved by these secondary interests but only by love of literature and simple enjoyment. There are such people; they know the works and feel their power and have studied enough to sift the criticisms leveled at their preferred artist. They need no further motive to go on reading him or seeing him acted. But they are not the only "firsthand" Shakespeareans. There is no reason why someone moved by a secondary concern should not also be a genuine lover. Among the actors and scholars many must have experienced that heartfelt attachment. It is only a presumption that a person engaged in counting short lines and weak endings or indexing themes ("Sleep that knits up the raveled sleave of care"—see: "Knitting") will tend to be less of a Shakespeare devotee and more of an entrepreneur in the establishment. Nor is it blamable: we do not expect the surgeon at his work to be full of affection and admiration for his patient, yet we know he is performing what all hope is a useful task.

Wherever found, on the stage or in the study or out camping, the true Shakespeareans are readily known. They read the plays over and over again; their admiration does not mean keeping at a respectful distance; it means, on the contrary, a frequent commerce with an overwhelming, often puzzling, and sometimes irritating intellect. The stout Shakespeareans venture beyond the standard dozen plays and find the rest as rich in crystallized emotion and perception as the well-known. These readers' minds become populated with Shakespeare's figures and thoughts; quotations flow from them at the touch of a resemblance or contrast in real life. It was this propensity that led one of the tribe to make a delightful little book called *Essays of Shakespeare* and which consists of short "articles" —each five hundred words or so—made up of lines from the plays joined into consecutive thought upon a topic: Truth, Time, Love, Nature, Music, Honor, and fifty others, including Drinking: For and Drinking: Against. Scholars would say the work is not scholarship, true; but its composition argues an enviable familiarity with the text. Again, some would decry the juggling with fragments, but after all the garbling for the stage, it seems a little late to make that a punishable offense.

Shakespeareans of this quality naturally divide into the modest and the great. The great have left us their opinions, which have themselves become objects of discussion, as these pages have shown. Lessing, Goethe, Coleridge, Monti, E. T. A. Hoffmann, Hazlitt, Lamb, Keats, Berlioz, Victor Hugo,

De Quincey, Pushkin were the first missionaries who spread their conviction among the indifferent and the infidels. Later came G. M. Hopkins, Emerson, Abraham Lincoln, Walter Bagehot, Samuel Butler, Frank Harris, Oscar Wilde, Yeats, Bernard Shaw, C. E. Montague, Granville Barker, Christopher Morley, James Agate, as well as notables of the theater whose words—they not being writers—come to us at second hand.

The clan of the modest are the private persons who neither act nor write, but are content to reflect and enjoy. I have known but two such, a retired architect and a taxi driver. On my first meeting with the former, someone expressed surprise at his being retired, to which he replied: "I am older than you think. To tell the truth, I am like Jane Nightwork, 'I cannot choose but be old.'" He said the words from *Henry IV, Part 2* not as if quoting but as if embroidering a thought that had often occurred to him—as indeed it had. As for the taxi driver, whose acquaintance I made by introducing myself into his cab, he had formed a Shakespeare club in his New York neighborhood, to hold readings and discussions altogether for pleasure. At one of these I learned that with his unassuming friends he had worked out to his satisfaction the locale of *The Tempest:* it was not Bermuda, as scholars believed, but one of the Elizabeth Islands, off Cape Cod. "Actually," he said, "it's Cutty Hunk."

It is in these situations, as in the Victorian family readings of Shakespeare (or the drawing-room playing of Chopin), that culture—the humanities—may truly be said to live. Books on the shelf and their elaborate preparation are indispensable; but they are only instruments, dead until used and used right. No modern reader or spectator of the plays can do without the scholarly aids or the wisdom of the great Shakespeareans of the past. But at some point, Shakespeare's mind itself, alone, must touch some other mind. And this must be with Shakespeare's own purpose to the fore, rather than that of the receiving mind—not to elucidate a point, prove a thesis, discover a new typesetter, or discourse on "Comedy as Sadness Overcome in *Twelfth Night.*"

The Modest Shakespearean

This last observation may warrant concluding this essay with a few remarks drawn from one reader's cultivation of Shakespeare over the years. Not that

any account can or should serve as a model. Everybody reads for and as himself, and it is a mirage of the academic to imagine a correct view of Shakespeare's plays. Any view must of course be defensible and any may be shown incorrect by reference to details; but when one recalls the diversity of opinion among the great critics on all subjects whatsoever, there can be no hope of the orthodoxy that one Shakespeare scholar demanded in the name of "reading score" accurately. His very metaphor spoke against him, since no amount of markings in a score will keep a piece of music from sounding widely different under various, quite faithful interpretations. It is of the nature of the humanities—it is their humanity—that makes them many things to many men.

This truth provides a good entrance into Shakespeare's work, so long and so regularly praised for the depiction of characters. The playwright, it is said, knew human beings through and through, and in every speech delivers a lesson in psychology. His people are lifelike and we know at once the kind to which they belong. But reading the plays does not bear out this confused claim. Psychology studies common traits, types of people, not individuals. And Shakespeare's characters do not stand for any type *or* individual. They are not like any people we know. No one has ever seen anybody who resembled Falstaff, Othello, Cleopatra, Hamlet, Lear, or Lady Macbeth. True, one can classify each of them under a *part* of his or her make-up—bragging, jealousy, erotic passion, and so on; but as beings they are not only more complex, but also larger and less comprehensible than any human creature. No doubt Emerson had this impression when he said that "Shakespeare's creations indicate no anxiety to be understood," inside the play or outside. Think of the 250-year debate about Hamlet; the factual inconsistencies in Lady Macbeth; the unfathomable motives of Iago; the absurd behavior of Lear and Othello; the deliberate vileness of the future Henry V; and the attitude that made James Agate (a great Shakespearean) say: "Mention in the whole of dramatic literature a greater gumph than Cordelia."

It is no rebuttal to point out that there are gumphs and fools and villains in real life. In life they are not interesting; we pity or despise them. In Shakespeare they all possess extraordinary intelligence; they see into themselves in a manner never equalled on earth; and they make remarks about the world like writers of philosophical maxims. Finally, they all talk like Shakespeare, with—among other traits—his bent toward exaggeration. It is in fact his exaggerative force ("Forty thousand brothers . . ." "Had all his hairs been lives . . ." "the multitudinous seas incarnadine . . .") that makes Shakespeare aggrandize his characters; he adds to their native core other, enormous possibilities of life. Shaw thought that Shakespeare's hyperbolic words were due to his conceiving and feeling more vividly than ordinary men. A similar overgrowth of the shaping power gave us his characters.

The exceptions occur only among the lowliest of his lowlife people. They, no doubt, are "copied straight from life"—the ones who chitchat as we may suppose Elizabethan porters and potboys did; they are so true to life we often fail to catch their meaning, the slang and joshing of the time having died. But above this level, that is, from shepherds and court fools to kings and queens, the figures are endowed not so much with life as with power over our own perceiving and conceiving faculties, making us find real what Shakespeare has fashioned by his lightning association of ideas. Take the shepherd who is about to discover Perdita in the desert in *The Winter's Tale:* "I would there were no age between ten and three-and-twenty or that youth would sleep out the rest; for there is nothing in the between but getting wenches with child, wronging the ancientry [older people], stealing, fighting." This lecturette is not needed for plot or character. There is really no likelihood in this Bohemian shepherd-sociologist, but we treasure his words as if he had conducted a "study."

What then are we to say of Shakespeare as the supreme creator of character, whose influence on novel-writing, noted earlier, derives from this very power? I think an appropriate statement would be that he created in character form huge extensions of human experience, imaginable states of being, within which we recognize with terror or delight acts and motives and nameless sensations just because they have been magnified. Surely, if Jane Austen and Flaubert draw with the finest pen characters who fit without effort into our world, then Shakespeare does something else: he makes the stuff out of which such characters could be made. The only other writers who work in Shakespeare's vein are Scott and Balzac, and their decline in popularity since the grand surprise of their first appearance may be due to this making of giant beings, which the later, perfected novel has taught us to suspect or dislike. Moreover, as novelists they

lacked the aid of poetry in transporting us out of the realm where the human scale prevails.

Some great Shakespeareans, notably Shaw and William James, have been bothered by Shakespeare's unwillingness to make his figures, ready as they are to comment on life, demonstrate by their behavior what the meaning of life is. This complaint no doubt leads to the twentieth-century revival of interest in Dante and explains, for example, Santayana's omission of Shakespeare in his discussion of great poets or Charles G. Osgood's neglect of him in his books about the humanities and in *Poetry as a Means of Grace.* The bard has no philosophy, though some think he inclines to pessimism. Now if, as Lamb pointed out, we no longer go to the theater like Shakespeare's contemporaries and first descendants, "to escape from the pressure of reality, but rather to confirm our experience of it," it is easy to understand why modern critics and poets and actors feel the want of a point of view in Shakespeare. His men and women do not lead us along a course of action that can be summed up— it makes no moral (or immoral) point such as we have come to expect from every novel and prose drama. The result is that although Shakespeare does "confirm our experience of reality," he extends it so far that, again unlike our modern writers, he never leaves us oppressed by further proofs of life's painful constraints.

Yet the impulse to moralize (in this sense) is so strong that even great Shakespeareans have repeatedly tried to show what one or another of the plays "comes down to." This has been particularly true of *Hamlet* as perhaps the most galvanizing of all the plays. A long tradition has it that Hamlet is the man who cannot make up his mind and who comes to grief as a result. But in that tradition are also doubts, and a scholar has found it necessary to write a 300-page book entitled *What Happens in "Hamlet,"* quite as if the play couldn't tell us on its own. To the extent that Hamlet himself is discussable as an ordinary character, he is clearly a man of thought *and* action; he proves it in the way he evades the plot to exile and despatch him. Indeed, his delaying is due in part to his knowing what action is: he is caught in a political situation as well as in a family predicament. The King and his party miss no chance to dispose of him one way or another. After their first try fails, they follow it up with spying and finally with the poisoned cup and poisoned sword. Denmark *is* rotten.

But modern readers have lost the Elizabethans' familiarity with royal politics, at the same time as they seem to forget their own refined sensibilities; they want Hamlet to take the earliest opportunity to stab Claudius, not seeing that they would be the first to ask embarrassing questions: Was Hamlet sure the ghost's message was genuine? How can an educated and thoughtful prince act like that brainless, impulsive Laertes? It is politics again that makes Hamlet distrust and dismiss Ophelia and kill Polonius, rightly suspecting betrayal and possibly murder from behind the arras. Everything ends disastrously, as is bound to happen in situations balanced on a knife edge; for (to repeat) there are two parties struggling over the sovereignty, not just Hamlet mismanaging his private revenge in a passive setting. The young Yeats, future dramatist, saw this clearly: "I wished to be able to play with hostile minds as Hamlet played, to look in the lion's face, as it were, with unquivering eyelash." And later he disagreed with the actors' mooning Hamlet, because in spite of reflectiveness, Shakespeare "thrust between his fingers agile rapier and dagger."

What has misled interpretation further is the bad biographer's habit of using a man's confidences as facts for an indictment. Hamlet's soliloquies, which take us well beyond characterization, express the momentary doubt or self-reproach of a conscious mind. We should require these hesitations as signs of decency if they were absent; and when we compare and judge fairly, we see that it is Macbeth, not Hamlet, who is the great vacillator, lost without his wife. The last word said, by Fortinbras, praises Hamlet as one likely to have done well "had he been put on." It shows what those who saw things close to thought about a prince obviously unlike our traditional "melancholy Dane."

Shakespeareans who cling to the do-nothing Hamlet might get a shock of surprise from a remarkable book by the well-known playwright William Gibson entitled *Shakespeare's Game.* Using his intimate knowledge of the theater and much reading besides, Mr. Gibson reviews the great plays and argues that what we read is probably *Hamlet* with scenes nonsensically transposed. His rearrangement is persuasive and brings out the activist Hamlet who pursues his end without stalling. And while we shake our heads with a "Yes, but" at this bold suggestion, Mr. Gibson clinches his case: the scheme is not his own: it is the layout of a 1603

printing of the play, corrupt in text, but lucid in organization; the printer's tout misremembered the verse, but not how the action went. The date and the facts remind us that Shakespeare's plays are now and forever approximations, reconstructions by editors from the versions of his time, in which dozens of lines omitted from one source are found in another that lacks dozens of the first. We need Shakespeare's ghost to sort them out and tell us his final wishes.

It is not psychology, then, that we learn from Shakespeare, though his superhuman creatures perpetually tempt us to psychologize and seldom deny us the pleasure of carving from them life-size persons according to our experience. Nor do we learn a philosophy—not even pessimism; for with all his furious hatred of life in *Lear* and elsewhere, he faces evils with the kind of courage marked by gaiety, not resignation. The plays contain a superabundance of life (compare Chekhov or Samuel Beckett), and that is why reading Shakespeare we acquire a sense of how things go in the world, the historian's sense of its *miscellaneous* character. It is rational and non-rational; there is a fatal logic of events and also a perpetual intrusion of the irrelevant and the absurd. Like the historian (and not just in the history plays), Shakespeare shows the diversity of truths and their dependence on perspective. Life has a meaning but not *one* meaning.

This rare undogmatic love of the Many rather than the One seems in Shakespeare always at full strength, not limited in any direction. The normal, the grandiose, the vulgar, the silly, the unheard-of, the inexplicable, the sensible, the flighty, the ghostly are equally on tap and may gush forth at any moment, leaving us startled and pleased and forever unable to say why. For example, in *Macbeth* there suddenly turns up for conversation with the two murderers a third one, who has no role to play but this bit of talk. The man is unnecessary; the effect is marvelous. Often in Shakespeare we are moved in this way, as much by what he thinks of doing as by how he does it.

He had, of course, a great advantage over modern playwrights in being free to present the moods and acts of the mighty. With us, "real" characters are abundant, ever more subtly drawn, more odd, and yet still believable. The difficulty is to keep up the assumption that what they do or think will matter, that their griefs and deaths have weight. Shakespeare's dukes, soldiers and princesses matter because they are responsible for multitudes—partisans, armies, nations. They have private desires as well, lead double lives, so that their vagaries and successes or failures cause *events*. Death of a salesman? Very sad, but there are ten million salesmen left after he goes, and one can feel neither "the deep damnation of his taking off" nor that "the soldiers' music and the rites of war speak loudly for him."

Quoting as I have just done immediately brings to mind the fact that Shakespeare's language is extraordinary, in the literal sense. He is the only writer who has had a complete grammar composed about him, or rather, out of him. It is not only that he followed the custom of his age in using high-flown rhetoric, nor that English then allowed freedoms in diction and syntax that later usage abolished; it is also that the same power of unlimited association of ideas led Shakespeare to put together words in clusters whose facets reflect multiple meanings, like light, in every direction. To take a simple example, Edgar in *Lear* is about to open a letter not meant for him, a prosaic enough business in any play; but he says:

> Let us see.
> Leave, gentle wax; and, manners, blame us not.
> To know our enemies' minds, we rip their hearts;
> Their papers, is more lawful.

And after he has learned of Goneril's treachery, he exclaims:

> O indistinguish'd space of woman's will!

The first three lines are another instance of superfluity; they add strangeness to ordinary actions—sealing a letter with wax, "gentle" because it was soft when applied. Then the breach of manners in reading somebody else's mail is personified into a critic, but the thought jumps to the fact that it is less blamable to tear open a letter than to kill our enemies, as is readily done in Edgar's world, in order to find out (and stop) what they intend. Goneril's letter is shocking, but Edgar's first cry is not of anger or indignation. It marvels at what a determined woman can do: her will knows no bounds, it fills space, where no distinguishing marks of limitation can be imagined.

It is all very well to point out that poetry is just this art of arranging words to make them mean more than they say. All poets forge compact, evoca-

tive, unexampled phrasings that transfix a sensation or an idea and are thereby memorable. But Shakespeare condenses meaning and feeling into tighter cores and does it repeatedly, under no pressure from plot or "psychology" and with unprecedented success. One has only to compare him with twentieth-century poets who have deliberately distorted grammar and vocabulary to achieve the same compression: one scans their work in vain for Shakespeare's naturalness and felicity. James Joyce's radical method of punning and hybridizing words has the same purpose of giving simultaneous impressions; but being a method it requires laborious decoding, and aside from purely atmospheric passages, it feels forced instead of spontaneous.

Shakespeare can fail, too, when his leap of thought is miscalculated or when he succumbs to one of his obsessive associations—for instance his automatic linking of tears with water or washing. These are a kind of punning on ideas, and they annoy not by playing on similars but by being obvious or repetitive. Misjudgment spoils a line also when the image is not merely out of scale with reality but much too much out of scale, as in Prospero's request to Miranda whose gaze he wants to direct toward her future love: "The fringed curtains of thine eye advance." These curtains are her eyelids and the fringes are the lashes, from which it follows that "advance" stands for "raise"—as bad a term as the whole image is clumsy. It makes one visualize a beautiful girl with thick straight lids on retractable rods.

Such faults of conception and language cannot be excused in either of the usual ways: "he did it to please the groundlings;" or: "reflect further and the fault will turn out to be a fine stroke as well as an error of judgment on your part." These explanations take care of many of the passages that have diversely angered successive generations; those might be called Shakespeare's revolving faults, and a reader must not trip over them through an unwillingness to reflect. But the tired puns and the indecencies that were at no time clever are still there, like the bad images. Among these I would class the second and third lines of Ariel's famous song: "Full fathom five thy father lies," which raise a hideous picture of the drowned man; pearls and coral become ghastly deposits when thought of as replacing human features.

The Shakespearean's attitude toward such faults need not be blindness; it should be magnanimity. That was Morgann's recommendation two hundred years ago and it is still good. All great works of the human spirit are studded with faults, and the greater the work the worse do the faults appear. So much is readily conceded by all but the classical perfectionists, who hedge against possible lapses by refusing to tackle vast subjects and heterogeneous materials. But here again, Shakespeare goes beyond others, surpasses the faultiness of the faulty. He does what must cast doubt on his being competent at all, as Henley said, the choice being either to throw him overboard or to take him as he is. Those who go on reading him show that they accept the faults. Magnanimity may be difficult, but it is a simple thing: not letting the faults subtract anything from the merits—which is also a precept of wide application in the humanities.

One more benefit rewards the Shakespearean, besides living ideally with outsize characters, relishing an incomparable language, and pondering through a plot and commentary the miscellany of life. All these combine to develop in the reader the double vision that was Shakespeare's own. The dramatist is necessarily inside the world, observant of its most trivial details, feeling what his creatures feel each in turn; but the poet is outside, living a richer life than any and recording that fuller life. He can do this because the split into two is only a figure of speech; the undivided Shakespeare has lived all his people's lives plus his own. The realm where they are at one is named Imagination, not the word that means decorative fancies, but that which means divining the unknown and bringing it within the common reality.

No one can deny that Shakespeare's imaginings have added to our Real. They were the cause of the Romanticists' becoming Shakespeare worshippers. He had accomplished without theory the kind of work they were hoping to do more consciously. The fusion of the seen and the unseen, expressed in sensory forms dramatic as life, was that complete art that Goethe and Pushkin and Berlioz and the rest wanted to recapture. In retrospect, Shakespeare stands out as primarily an artist's artist—for artists of a certain kind. Fortunately, he can also be, for anyone who takes the pains to orient himself rightly, a transcendent master; and for such followers he is at the same time master of the revels, where the only aim is enjoyment.

BIBLIOGRAPHY

James Agate, *The Later Ego*, Jacques Barzun, ed. (1951). Walter Bagehot, "Shakespeare—The Man," in *Literary Studies*, 1, (1879). Gerald E. Bentley, *Shakespeare: a Biographical Handbook* (1961). Hector Berlioz, *The Memoirs of Hector Berlioz*, David Cairns, ed. and trans. (1969). Samuel Butler, *Shakespeare's Sonnets Reconsidered* (1899; repr. 1927). John Jay Chapman, *A Glance Toward Shakespeare* (1922). Marchette Chute, *Shakespeare of London* (1949). Samuel Taylor Coleridge, *Lectures on Shakespeare, Etc.* (1930). Paul S. Conklin, *A History of Hamlet Criticism, 1601–1821* (1947). Thomas De Quincey, "On the Knocking at the Gate in *Macbeth*," in *De Quincey's Literary Criticism*, H. Darbishire, ed. (1909).

William and Elizabeth Friedman, *The Shakespearean Ciphers Examined* (1957). William Gibson, *Shakespeare's Game* (1978). Johann Wolfgang von Goethe, "Shakespeare Ad Infinitum," in *The Permanent Goethe*, Thomas Mann, ed. (1948). Selma Guttman, *The Foreign Sources of Shakespeare's Works* (1947). Alfred Harbage, *As They Liked It* (1947). William Hazlitt, "Sir Walter Scott, Racine, and Shakespear," in *The Plain Speaker*, vol. 7 of *The Collected Works*, A. R. Waller and Arnold Glover, eds. (1903) and "Travelling Abroad," "Our National Theatres," and "Covent Garden Theatre," in *New Writings*, P. P. Howe, ed. (1925). Charles Lamb, "On the Tragedies of Shakespeare," in *The Works of Charles Lamb* (1926).

William A. Neilson and Ashley H. Thorndike, *The Facts About Shakespeare* (1913; repr. 1959). G. B. Shaw, "Better Than Shakespear?" in *Three Plays for Puritans* (1900); "Foreward" to *Cymbeline Refinished*, in *Geneva, Cymbeline Refinished, and Good King Charles* (1946); "Preface" to *The Dark Lady of the Sonnets*, in *Misalliance, Dark Lady of the Sonnets, and Fanny's First Play* (1914); and "Mr Frank Harris's Shakespear," in *Pen Portraits and Reviews* (1932). David Nichol Smith, ed., *Shakespeare Criticism: a Selection*, (1916; repr. 1942). Hazelton Spencer, *Shakespeare Improved* (1927). A. C. Swinburne, *The Age of Shakespeare* (1908). George Coffin Taylor, *Essays of Shakespeare* (1947). Oscar Wilde, "The Portrait of Mr. W. H.," in *The Novels and Fairy Tales* (1915). John Dover Wilson, *What Happens in Hamlet* (1935).

Shakespeare and the Modern Critic

JOHN SIMON

Shakespeare is the measure of many things, among them the critic. Just as actors and directors must cut their teeth on Shakespeare, so the dramatic critic must sharpen his discrimination on him. That is to say, there is no way of being a serious theater critic without having evolved a set of criteria based on what one thinks can or cannot be done to Shakespeare. This is particularly true today, when "director's theater" is having its anarchic heyday and when every stage director who wishes to be a playwright—or who wants to make a name for himself by rewriting a few masterpieces —must improve on Shakespeare by distorting him into whatever shape the director sees fit to sensationalize him into. It would seem that no sooner had hack dramatists like Nahum Tate stopped disfiguring Shakespeare than the actor-managers and star actors fell to it. And when *they* were finally brought to their senses—or, failing those, their knees—up rose the directors to do him in.

It is fortunate that critics and professors do not matter much to men and women of the theater, and that some of the weirder notions about Shakespeare as promulgated by the press and academe have left relatively little mark on Shakespearean productions. There have, no doubt, been mountings suggested by the ideas of scholars and critics, but, in my opinion, only the Jan Kott–Peter Brook axis has produced anything like notable damage to Shakespeare in the English-speaking world. Directors such as Laurence Olivier, Peter Hall, and Trevor Nunn have avowed their debt to F. R. Leavis, but

it seems to have done no harm to their work. It remains to be seen whether such a potentially deleterious figure as A. L. Rowse, with his modernizations of Shakespeare's texts, will gain a foothold in the theater.

This is where the critic can be of use. Even if he does not influence what is actually done—and why should he?—he can and ought to have some useful advice about what must not be done. The prime function of the modern drama critic in the Shakespearean arena is to protect Shakespeare against those who want to make director's theater—or, to call it by its rightful name, mincemeat—out of him. A strong stand against unwarranted experimentation is greatly needed, as is encouragement of directorial insights that illuminate rather than obscure. There are such ideas, but they are hard to come by and are not likely to be splashy—indeed they bring no sensational publicity to the director who provides them or the critic who promotes them.

The governing principle in my reviews of Shakespearean productions has been the now highly unpopular one that, by and large, Shakespeare should not be tailored to the audience but that the audience should accommodate itself to Shakespeare. Theatergoers ought to be courted not by making Shakespeare in various (usually objectionable) ways more appealing to them, but by allowing them to appreciate him in his excellence, which needs very little, if any, tampering with. It is not that a slight cut here or there cannot be countenanced or that the transposition of a scene, or even a small addition in the spirit of the work, is unconscionable. Thus in *Henry V,* IV, vii, Henry declares "I was not angry . . . Until this instant." Earlier in the scene, Fluellen protested, "Kill the poys and the luggage?" But already in IV, v, the Boy deplored leaving only boys to guard the luggage: "The French might have a good prey of us." And in between, in IV, vi, Henry orders that "every soldier kill his prisoners." Clearly, something is missing or out of sequence here, and the best way to explain how the humane Henry has become merciless is to insert a bit of pantomime at the end of IV, v, in which the Boy is slaughtered. (On this subject, see note 73 in Sally Beauman, ed., *The Royal Shakespeare Company's Centenary Production of "Henry V"* [1976].) But major liberties—and a good many minor ones—should not be taken, especially if their avowed purpose is to make the play more "comprehensible" or "accessible" to contemporary audiences. That kind of education is the job of the schools, newspaper and magazine articles, and program notes. It behooves us to modernize or simplify Shakespeare as much as it does to dilute a vintage wine in order to make it palatable for children or to convert the outside staircase of a majestic Renaissance palazzo into an inclined platform for the benefit of paraplegics, generous as such aims may be.

Yet critics everywhere hail this or that hotshot director for having staged a Shakespearean play with the kind of "present-day relevance" that would make students, Broadway audiences, television addicts, and other alleged illiterates become interested in Shakespeare. If Ben Jonson could content himself with few company but fit, Shakespeare, a fortiori, can do without those who require Rowse and his kind to reduce him to their level or an Andrei Serban or Peter Sellars (the wunderkind, not the comedian) to reduce him to their visual level. The democratic—or populist—notion that the masses *must* have Shakespeare can only harm Shakespeare and not satisfy the hunger of those who have been bred on television and circused on rock concerts.

In his lecture "Shakespeare and the Grand Style," George Saintsbury said something of paramount importance about Shakespeare: "It seems as if he had deliberately determined that no special mould, no *recipe* of mixture and arrangement, should be capable of being pointed out as his secret, or even as one of his secrets, of attaining gran-

deur." If this is so, and I believe that it is, one may want to stress one or another aspect of a Shakespearean play, but not so much as to sacrifice the rest entirely. One should rigorously attempt to offer as faithfully as is humanly possible (humanity is so easily abrogated in favor of gimmickry) all that one can of what is there. And what is there first of all is the language: Shakespeare's poetry aflame even in the prose passages. But that poetry, alas, is often the first to suffer in contemporary productions. Yet even more fundamental than what directors do with Shakespeare's language is the question of what language the actors speak. If they speak American English, they cannot, in my considered opinion, do justice to Shakespeare's musical peaks.

Faster than you can say Helge Kökeritz, people will point out that Shakespeare's English was different from, say, John Gielgud's or Laurence Olivier's and more like today's Virginia Tidewater speech. But that is not the point. Geoffrey Tillotson once remarked ironically about a production of Shakespeare at Harvard, where he was guest lecturer in 1948, a production in which the young actors made concerted efforts to sound British: "How touching of them to have gone out of their way to study up on Shakespeare's pronunciation." One man's Oxford is another one's Ozark.

No matter how Shakespeare or Burbage or any Elizabethan pronounced those words, the English language has developed a great musicality, a range of pitch and cadence—indeed, a melody—that the American language, a much flatter and unmelodious thing, lacks. And there is no appealing to the past in these matters. It is of small import that Beethoven composed for the fortepiano or that a horn of Mozart's era produced a much more modest sound than today's horns. We have to use the best instruments we have evolved to do justice to the music; in harps, for example, regardless of the "state of the art," geniuses, we may safely assume, always heard the heavenly variety in their minds. To put it another way, we do not stage a Shakespearean play today as it was supposedly done at the Globe; or, if we do, it has only curiosity value. Bluntly stated, Shakespeare deserves the best linguistic instruments we have; and the best speech melody, the best music, is to be had in high British speech—even if British actors, as often as not, try to get away from it or cannot manage it any more. American actors trying to reproduce British English run the risk of sounding ridiculous. Still, if, unlike those Harvardians, they can carry it off, by all means let them. If not, let them resort to the best kind of American stage English they can produce—some sort of compromise, or Midatlantic, accent. But let the audience realize that it is getting a second-best bed.

A somewhat similar, though more ticklish, problem in Shakespearean productions in the United States is the casting of black actors. There is no difficulty if the performer can, visually and aurally, pass for white; but I firmly believe, and have put this belief in writing, that one cannot cast a black as, say, Mark Antony or Prince Hal. History, even in a work of fiction, has certain prior claims. And, even beyond history, plausibility has its unalienable rights: to see a black Benedick or Beatrice does not work because it contradicts too many aspects of the internal logic of the play as well as of the social conditions of the period and place. I think, however, that the world of fantasy escapes such strictures and that, for instance, the fairies in *A Midsummer Night's Dream* can be played by blacks, provided they are all of them black. What, however, could have been more wrongheaded than David Jones's production (1981), in which one of the four Athenian lovers—and that precisely Lysander—was black. This had to set up the wrong associations in an audience: Egeus simply did not want his daughter to marry a black.

This is a matter of the black actor's not looking right; as often, though, it is a matter of his not sounding right. The argument presented for that type of casting is that in the interest of democracy and fair employment and social justice, we must be color-blind and tone-deaf. The answer is that in art there is no such thing as democracy: you hire someone because he is the best person for the job. And consistency, homogeneity, and seamlessness are part of a good production. There is no way in which either our sense of history or our sense of logic can accept a black Cordelia alongside a white Regan and Goneril. No matter how unnaturalistic a Shakespearean play may be, it needs its foothold in reality from which it can transport us to realms of poetry, symbolism, and eschatology. Credibility of the humblest sort is flouted at the peril of depriving the imagination of a firm launching pad. Start with manifest inconsistencies, and disbelief becomes unwilling to let itself be suspended.

But such considerations are politically odious in this society, and in vain do I look for critics who will address this issue. Perhaps they do not see it that way; perhaps they or their editors or publishers are cowards. Certainly I have been accused by entire organizations (such as the Actors Equity Association), as well as by individuals, of racism for holding such views. And though some of my colleagues have agreed with me privately, I have yet to see or hear them make this agreement public. My position does not mean that I am against black actors, only that I am even more for Shakespeare and opposed to whatever perverts his meaning and lessens his impact.

For related reasons I could not accept Peter Brook's much lauded and influential production (1970) of *Dream* for the Royal Shakespeare Company. It was of no consolation that Brook did not tamper with the text (as he did in his *Lear*); meddling with the looks of the play can be equally damaging. Turn the forest outside Athens into a gym, hospital room, lunatic asylum—or whatever the gleaming white box inside which Brook staged his circusy nightmare was supposed to represent—and the wrong reverberations are started. At the very least, you make the audience admire the cleverness with which you have transposed the forest, the dexterity with which you juggle your transposition, and thus deflect the attention from the essentials to something irrelevant. When Giorgio Strehler did *The Tempest* at the Piccolo Teatro di Milano—another Kott-inspired production—he unveiled, at the end, his theatrical mechanism—seemed, in fact, to dismantle the entire orchestra pit and part of the stage. But this matched Prospero's breaking his staff and was an ingenious addition consonant with the meaning of the play: the director, like the playwright, was abjuring his magic. Meaning was perhaps not deepened, merely broadened, but it certainly was not altered.

"There is a filiation without the heart," John Donne admonishes in his Third Prebend Sermon. It is up to the contemporary critic to recognize and evaluate to what extent a production of Shakespeare pays him more than lip service. It is therefore encouraging to read the following in the 6 June 1978 entry of *Peter Hall's Diaries:* "I am now militantly classic, which is not popular at the moment when everybody expects to see Shakespeare directed from one single interpretative viewpoint. I don't believe in that any more, so there can be accusations of ordinariness or blankness." Yet the way around ordinariness and blankness is suggested by Hall himself in an earlier entry (26 September 1977): "The main problem we moderns have with Shakespeare [is] rhetoric." Now, I think that by rhetoric Sir Peter means poetic diction or, more simply, the problem that modern actors have with speaking verse and modern audiences with listening to it. I cannot be entirely sure, but I would like to believe that any good poetry, Shakespeare's or another's, will receive sufficient hearing if properly delivered. (Once again, I am no more concerned with the tone-deaf than with the color-blind.) But how are we to get actors—American ones in particular—to speak poetry well?

The first requirement is for the schools, even at the lowest level, to teach good poetry, to make students memorize it, and to elicit from them at least the rudiments of the art of declamation. (Shakespeare's songs, by the way, would go over nicely even with young pupils.) The second requirement is for actors, having learned something in school, to develop this skill further and to be able, as their European counterparts are, to give an occasional poetry recital and hold their audience spellbound. In this way rhetoric ceases to be anathema. The trick in the delivery of dramatic poetry is the balancing of two modes: the musical mode, which comprises metrics and various aspects of sonority; and the intellectual-psychological mode, which comprises the conveying of meaning and the evocation of the feelings accompanying that meaning. Unfortunately, what passes in the United States for truthful, Stanislavskian acting is in fact Lee Strasberg's bastardization of it (itself a stylization, albeit a grubby one), so that in the postwar years the American stage was swamped with a "method" that had mostly madness in it and one that is still surviving directly or indirectly to the detriment of other acting styles, notably the poetic, unnaturalistic, stylized one. In method acting, getting at some sort of psychoanalytical truth is all, and scansion has never been thought of, much less heard. But never mind metrics, the mere notion of several consecutive words spoken trippingly on the tongue is highly suspect: emotional truth comes not in flowing cadences, only in fractured prose.

Under such conditions, Shakespeare cannot thrive. And, indeed, poetic drama was never undertaken by the Actors Studio; accordingly, teachers, actors, and students joined in ignoring verse. The upshot is that actors who can speak Shakespeare are, in America, even harder to find than directors who can stage him honestly and selflessly. But the delivery of Shakespearean verse—or, for that matter, prose—suffers from yet another malady: the need to deliver famous lines "originally":

differently at all cost, even if it kills the meaning. Thus odd emphases are inflicted onto unlikely words; pauses are introduced where they are uncalled for and withheld where they are needed; and tempo, volume, and even minimal audibility are fiddled with in nonsensical ways. Well, not entirely nonsensical; the aim is always to make the actor appear interesting—and interesting he may well be, but not good.

The contemporary critic must defend Shakespeare assiduously against such abuse, because the nobler the monument, the greater the urge of fools to deface it: if there were no guards at the Louvre, it is on the Venus de Milo that imbeciles would clamber to scrawl their names. Similarly, it is off Shakespeare, by scratching their signatures all over his work, that boneheads and charlatans figure they can thrive best—and often do. And not only actors and directors but also textual editors—especially when directors set themselves up in that capacity—must be guarded against. I am thinking not even of wholesale philistinism à la Rowse here but of that odd bit of seemingly harmless updating, as when a director decides that nothing is lost by modernizing *Hamlet*'s "And each particular hair to stand an end / Like quills upon the fretful porpentine" (I. v. 19–20) into "fretful porcupine." The rationale would be that the meter is not interfered with, the cadence barely, and the meaning made clearer to contemporary audiences. But no: the assonance in "*end*," "fr*et*ful," and "porp*enti*ne" is part of the Shakespearean music, and the internal alliteration in "*f*ret*f*ul" and "*porp*entine" conveys a bristling set of parallelly perpendicular quills or hairs that the *p-c* sequence in "porcupine" undercuts. Besides, it is nice to be reminded of old terms or of older forms of current words. "Shakespeare works through the living word," observed Goethe, and, true enough, many a word is still living or partly living because of Shakespeare. Such linguistic conservationism should not be sabotaged.

All this is not to be understood as an attempt to hamstring either the actor or the director. There is such dizzying richness in Shakespeare—such a wealth of legitimate meanings within individual verses, speeches, scenes, and characters, not to mention entire plays—that there is room for individual interpretation without having to overstep the boundaries of what is stated or implied, without having to reach for what demonstrably could not have been intended even unconsciously. Only lack of imagination and sensitivity—as well as excess

870

ego—would impel a lesser mortal (and who, up against Shakespeare, is not lesser?) to substitute his feeble fancies for the supreme dramatist's mighty inventions.

The trouble, to be sure, is that we tend not to have the actors and actresses to embody the easeful masculinity and generous femininity of Shakespeare's heroes and heroines. (It is irrelevant that the playwright had to content himself grudgingly with fat Burbages and boy Cleopatras.) Thus an *Othello* directed by Peter Coe at Stratford, Connecticut (1981), and later seen at the Kennedy Center and on Broadway, used up three Desdemonas without finding a satisfactory one; and the Circle in the Square *Macbeth* (1982), directed by and starring Nicol Williamson, went through three actresses (in forty performances) without hitting upon a suitable Lady Macbeth. (The backstage phone was answered with "Queen for a Day.") Today's unisex young men and women, living in an age of militant feminism and complementary male overcompensation or abjection, are psychologically and physiologically unfit for Shakespearean lovers, quite aside from insufficient or incorrect training.

What devolves on the critic in such an age? The need to develop his standards through voracious seeing, reading, and rereading of Shakespeare, as well as intensive study of historical and critical works. This means the perfecting of one's critical taste not only in Shakespearean matters but also in theater in general, for, to a much greater extent than the uninitiated might think, the two overlap. And it means not falling for notions such as this one from Jonathan Miller, one of Shakespeare's most determined misdirectors: "The bottom line in Shakespearian production is anything goes. If I smear tar over Picasso's 'Guernica,' I've destroyed a masterpiece. If I muck up Shakespeare, I, not he, look like an ass. The text remains, and Shakespeare will survive." That is the Bottom line indeed, and spoken like an ass. For one ass begets others, and if they are not gelded, they will be numerous enough to overwhelm and ravish even a clear-eyed Titania.

The question today is, Who will declare mucked-up Shakespeare a scandal? Not the untutored audiences, who don't know any better; not the media, ravenous for a new work of genius every hour on the hour; not the foundations, itching to swamp the boondocks with classics; and not the critics, vying with one another to be the first to hail the latest reinterpretation and transmogrification of a masterpiece. And that is how the isle gets peopled with Calibans.

BIBLIOGRAPHY

Sally Beauman, ed., *The Royal Shakespeare Company's Centenary Production of "Henry V"* (1976). Peter Hall, *Peter Hall's Diaries: The Story of a Dramatic Battle,* John Goodwin, ed. (1983). Helge Kökeritz, *Shakespeare's Pronunciation* (1953). Jan Kott, *Shakespeare, Our Contemporary,* Bołesław Taborski, trans. (1964). F. R. Leavis, *The Common Pursuit* (1964). George Saintsbury, "Shakespeare and the Grand Style," in *Essays and Studies by Members of the English Association,* 1 (1910). Nahum Tate, *The History of King Lear . . . Reviv'd with Alterations* (1681).

Teaching Shakespeare: Tradition and the Future

HOMER SWANDER

For anyone professionally interested in Shakespeare, the sixty middle years of this century—from about 1920 into the decade of the eighties—have been a fascinating time to be alive; and the next half-century or so promises to be so fascinating that one wants to defy the actuarial charts in order to be part of it. Every great artist contributes, mysteriously, to the mysteriously expanding universe of the human spirit. Teachers and scholars at their best serve both the mystery and the expansion. Those who teach and study Shakespeare work, alongside actors and directors, in the very heart of the mystery, where they are possessed of a strange charge: to increase what we know so as to heighten our sense of excitement and awe before what we know we can never know. In our time, Shakespeareans of all kinds, in both the theater and the academy, have responded to that charge with a degree of resourcefulness, nobility, and commitment that has brought us ever closer to the historical Shakespeare—the Elizabethan playwright as his contemporaries might have perceived him—and, equally, has revealed to us the expanding nature of his art as no Elizabethan could have known it. As a result, we stand on the brink of even greater discoveries that will lead us into ever deeper responses to the always expanding theatrical world that Shakespeare left us.

Ideally, therefore, to speak about teaching and studying Shakespeare today we should bring together, and build upon, the contributions of a truly dazzling array of thinkers: traditional literary schol-ars, literary critics of the no-longer-new New Criticism, estheticians and semioticians, historians and biographers, editors and bibliographers, theoreticians and practitioners of the theater, scholars and critics of the ''stage-centered'' school, structuralists and deconstructionists, and day-to-day classroom teachers from both English and drama departments. In the Shakespearean theater, classroom, and study, we live in a time of unparalleled exploration, variety, challenge, and conflict. To teach, to study, or to act Shakespeare in the closing decades of the twentieth century is to participate in a constantly and rapidly changing adventure, and we owe our opportunities to an old and still-evolving community of seekers for whom what is known today is never enough for tomorrow.

What perhaps most distinguishes ours from previous times is in part a gift from science. We are the first generation ever to have ''Shakespeare''—whatever that comes to mean under conditions of such variety—available to us in five fundamentally different media: theater, print, film, television, and recorded sound. And we benefit from many other firsts; they vary in kind and significance but all contribute to new depths and complexities of Shakespearean experience. We are the first to have a trustworthy edition of the First Folio so easily and inexpensively available that we can all have it in our studies. We are the first, ever, to have in our studies accurate copies of virtually all the known documents relating to Shakespeare's life and work. We are the first to profit from the kind of intense exploration of Shakespeare's text that became (and could only have become) possible through the birth of a theater company with the unique resources, stability, policies, and dedication of the Royal Shakespeare Company (RSC). We are, astonishingly, the first generation since Shakespeare's own to know that the First Tetralogy is entirely his work. And these are but typical examples. One could make a very long list.

Equally important, of course, in defining our uniqueness is the whole twentieth-century world in which we work, seeking in our own time, and therefore inevitably in own way, to understand more deeply and more legitimately the work of a man whose birthdate, already four hundred years behind us, we are fleeing at the rate of sixty minutes an hour. As we flee, we are at every turn invited to look through new sets of spectacles in order to see more fully the works that, for our solace, we carry with us.

Thus, of great significance to teachers and students in our century has been the work of those critics and theoreticians who have asked to what degree and in what ways the discoveries of Freud, Jung, Marx, Einstein, Darwin, and Wittgenstein, for example, help us to see more deeply into Shakespeare than, say, Dryden, Samuel Johnson, Coleridge, and Lamb ever did. But a valuable counterquestion persistently arises: Does Freud illuminate Shakespeare or does Shakespeare illuminate Freud? That is, what is the true relationship between the great varieties of investigations—artistic, scientific, psychoanalytic, philosophic—into the human condition? How do we properly use new knowledge to illuminate old but profound works of art?

The problems of literary criticism, and therefore of reading and teaching Shakespeare as literature, are attacked even more directly by those whose work falls under such labels as structuralism, deconstruction, semiology, postmodernism, and reader response: Ferdinand de Saussure, Claude Lévi-Strauss, Roland Barthes, Jacques Derrida, Stanley Fish, the Prague schools, and the Yale Group. Their often philosophic investigations into the nature of language, of signs, and of communicable meaning constitute one of the newest challenges to traditional literary thought. Their challenge is particularly unsettling because it seems often to suggest—and even aggressively to assert—that coherent, shareable literary meaning is impossible. To the degree that Shakespearean criticism embraces

such a possibility, severe pedagogical problems clearly arise: In the absence of a shareable meaning for *Hamlet,* what does one share in the classroom? The underlying question is even more searching: If modern thought "deconstructs" Shakespeare, do the plays fundamentally change? That is, do we come to understand the plays more deeply, or will we (once again) only be changing them to fit new and rapidly shifting ideas of the nature of man? The least one can say is that whether we like it or not, whether we admit it or not, Shakespeareans in and out of the classroom are today challenged by—and in fact are increasingly involved in—the problem of the meaning of meaning.

If we try to express the problem in simpler and more specific questions, we are likely to find ourselves asking, as only one example, something like the following: As women come to perceive both themselves and men differently, and alter their place with respect to men in the social structure, do they understand "Shakespeare's Portia" or "Shakespeare's Kate" more truly, or do they now see Portia and Kate through a new distorting glass created by their fidelity to their own new image of human possibilities? If Shakespeare "means" one thing for the Victorians (who had their own images of humanity) and another for us, one thing in modern America and another in modern Saudi Arabia, one thing for Professor Jones (a traditional male chauvinist) and another for Professor Smith (a dedicated feminist), one thing for the Elizabethans or for Shakespeare himself (whatever that may have been) and another for Sir John Gielgud, how are scholars and teachers to define their subject matter, properly explore the play, and choose legitimate strategies for the classroom?

A challenge of another kind asserts itself increasingly with each passing year: the sharp challenge or heavy burden created by the almost daily increase of knowledge that seems relevant, and is often claimed as essential, to a satisfying comprehension of Shakespeare. New books and articles rapidly join the thousands that already exist on every conceivable aspect of the Middle Ages and the Renaissance, enriching our understanding of the literary, theatrical, social, political, theological, philosophical, scientific, and economic contexts in which Shakespeare worked and of the myriad, centuries-long developments that created those contexts. Faced with an expansion of knowledge that seems like one long, constantly exciting explosion, even the most energetic Shakespearean must at some point pause to wonder about the nature of the relationship between such knowledge and a student's enjoyment of the works that are basically part of a popular art form. How much about the theology of grace must one know to understand (and thus "properly" enjoy) *Romeo and Juliet*? About the theology of conscience to follow Hamlet's analysis of himself? About Elizabethan marriage laws and customs to respond authentically to Isabella, Mariana, and the Duke in *Measure for Measure*? About Castiglione's Neoplatonism to detect the Prince of Morocco's flaw and thus to sympathize with Portia's response to him in *The Merchant of Venice*? About the Renaissance belief in a close relationship between astronomy and music to respond fully to music and dance in *The Merchant of Venice, A Midsummer Night's Dream,* or *The Tempest*? I find myself in each of these cases wanting, out of my own kind of enjoyment, to say, "A very great deal." But whatever one answers, the consequences for our scholarship and teaching are endless. How can we open new worlds to our students without creating a witness in the classroom to the belief that only those with a Ph.D. and time for continuing research can truly appreciate Shakespeare?

We should pause here to notice that the exuberant spirit with which I began this essay has already given way to notes of concern. And, indeed, as one surveys the current pedagogical scene, it is often difficult to maintain one's high spirits. On the basis of the available evidence, it is possible to argue that the teaching of Shakespeare is, for the most part, a distressing failure. We all know that just beneath his constantly refurbished reputation as our greatest cultural icon lies his equally persistent reputation as the Champion of Boredom. In the schools and universities, his name often seems synonymous with such a state, and it is useful to remind ourselves that this greatest playwright of all time has in fact bored more people than any other human being in history. Only through the misguided efforts of actors and teachers, to be sure; but that is exactly the point. If university teachers were doctors of medicine instead of philosophy, someone would surely observe that our patients are dropping dead as they leave our offices, and he might wonder if anything short of a deliberate conspiracy could kill so many. Serving as grim witness to a vast pedagogical failure are those millions who have passed through our classrooms and are, in Shakespearean terms, the walking dead: in them there is not the faintest desire ever to read or to see *King Lear* again. Kenneth Muir, one of our most distinguished scholars, is not alone in suggesting that the best way to encourage a fresh and lively interest in Shakespeare's work would be to ban the teaching of his plays. It is certainly arguable that the most effective move we teachers can make is simply to get out of the way, on the grounds that we do more harm than good.

The least that must be said is that the teaching of Shakespeare remains an experiment; the spectacular successes of many individual teachers in no way alter the fact that no system of universal education has yet proved that to require the study of Shakespeare in the schools and universities achieves the presumably desired effect of turning more people toward than away from the plays. The experiment is essentially of the twentieth century. Toward the end of the nineteenth, as the English-speaking nations moved more fully into systems of universal education, it became clear that classics in English must replace the classics in Greek and Latin that had served well enough in more aristocratic times. And Shakespeare, securely defined and canonized by nineteenth-century critics as the greatest literary genius in our language, was the obvious choice to replace, without loss of quality, even the greatest of the Greeks.

As a result, ours is the first century in which nearly everyone who speaks English is required to study Shakespeare and consequently the first in which nearly all Shakespearean scholarship and criticism comes from scholars and critics who are in the first instance professional teachers—and, more than that, teachers of literature. "We are now," Richard L. Levin observed with respect to Shakespeare, "so used to the near-monopolization of literary criticism by professors of literature that we may sometimes forget that it is a relatively recent phenomenon, yet it will inevitably affect the nature of this criticism" *(New Readings vs. Old Plays)*. Levin goes on to point out that it will also affect the nature of what happens in the Shakespearean classroom. This intimate, circular relationship between teaching Shakespeare and meeting the academic requirements for literary research and publication is, for better or worse, one of the major direct consequences of grafting a basically democratic idea of education upon the basically elitist conception of a learned community devoted primarily to research.

That Shakespeare journeys through the twentieth century in the company of more critics and teachers than actors is neatly symbolized, at the exact start, by the professional life and influence of A.C. Bradley. His own education was in classical literature, yet he was a professor of English, the first at Oxford University. His book *Shakespearean Tragedy* (1904), dedicated to his students and based on his lectures to them, was essentially a nineteenth-century work that became, through the schools and universities of the twentieth century, the most influential book ever written about Shakespeare. Through at least the first third of this century, most Shakespearean classrooms felt, directly or indirectly, its presence. And I cannot imagine anyone disagreeing with the frequently expressed view that Bradley's work contains in perfect synthesis the forces that have moved us into one of the least questioned orthodoxies of our time: that Shakespeare's plays are central to a literary education and are, moreover, essential to the schooling of any educated person.

Possessed of an easy, unforced confidence that Shakespeare's meaning in each play not only is accessible but also can be demonstrated to the shared satisfaction of all reasonable readers, Bradley's work has in fact satisfied a wider range of readers, from scholars to undergraduates, than has any other Shakespearean work ever available to teachers. That fact alone has made his book and his method—even when much diluted for the young—unusually useful in the academy. For three decades the very existence of Bradley's book helped both to create and to verify a comforting sense of coherence around a body of knowable, and therefore teachable, plays. What he wrote about each play was at last not as important as a quality implicit in the basic nature of his approach. He was not so much announcing a "new" Shakespeare—a new interpretation that would astonish the world and prove everyone else quite wrong—as, indeed, doing almost the opposite. In a most reassuring way, his manner and method seemed to be suggesting, beyond any specific conclusions, that the plays "meant" what most educated people who read them carefully had always supposed they meant. Although his work is gently Hegelian and is introduced by chapters on tragedy and construction, what remains most persistently in the minds of his readers is his exploration of Shakespeare's characters, whom, through descriptions and analysis, he brings vividly "to life" in his pages. Understandably enough, teachers sought to do the same in classroom lectures or discussions and to draw students toward essays on such matters as "The Char-

acter of Portia" or, more specifically, on "Portia's Relationship with Her Father." Even eighty years after its publication, one need not travel far to discover classrooms in which the influence of *Shakespearean Tragedy* is still alive.

During the years in which a Bradleyan criticism dominated Shakespearean pedagogy, Shakespearean scholarship was almost entirely historical and philological. Because the scholars were themselves teachers with their own classrooms, were thus the teachers of teachers, and were also the authors of an increasing number of articles and books aimed primarily at a growing academic audience, their discoveries—about Elizabethan social mores, about Shakespeare's literary sources, about the medieval and Renaissance theater, or about printing-house practices that affected the texts—provided the kind of background information that readily supported a way of lecturing about the plays that soon became commonplace. Although major scholars like Levin Schücking and Elmer Stoll did raise objections to Bradley's work, in actual day-to-day classroom practice the historical-philological scholarship, transformed into lectures and reading assignments, comfortably accompanied the prevailing Bradleyan critical approach. Thus, neither the criticism nor the scholarship most influential in the classroom forced the teacher to depart from the received view in which plays were seen as fundamentally like other forms of narrative fiction. That they were "dramatic" in structure, employed verse, had been written for a nonrealistic stage, and were limited to dialogue as a narrative strategy did not, for most teachers, imply any need for pedagogical practices essentially different from those that were employed in teaching the eighteenth-century novel.

In the 1930s, Shakespeare became quite suddenly a poet instead of a novelist, a transformation that offered what appeared to be the first fundamental challenge to the classroom procedures based on Bradleyan criticism and historical scholarship. Until 1930 important disagreements about the plays normally occurred only as a consequence of some accretion of historical or literary knowledge, usually external to the plays themselves. But with the publication in that year of G. Wilson Knight's *The Wheel of Fire,* the Shakespearean world encountered for the first time ever a major disagreement—one with implications for all criticism and scholarship, for every teacher, and for the theater as well—based on a radically new perception of the internal nature of Shakespeare's plays. The New Critics, led by F. R. Leavis and L. C. Knights and following at once upon Knight, earned their capital letters by calling, for the first time in the history of Shakespearean criticism and pedagogy, for a complete break with the past. They were new indeed. A Shakespeare play, said Leavis in 1937, was not "a psychological novel written in dramatic form and draped in poetry"—not, that is, a novel to be read and taught like any other novel but, said Knights in 1933, "so many lines of verse on a printed page which are read as we should read any other poem." A poem, that is, that we should teach like any other poem. Knights insisted in his famous essay *How Many Children Had Lady Macbeth?* that the total response to a Shakespeare play can be obtained only "by an exact and sensitive study of the quality of the verse, of the rhythm and imagery, of the controlled associations of the words and their emotional and intellectual force, in short by an exact and sensitive study of Shakespeare's handling of language." As the critics of no previous age had ever undertaken such a study, it became clear that the desired total response was one that the world was only upon the brink of discovering. And the discovery rested upon nothing more—but nothing less—than an "exact and sensitive" reading of the text itself: "read with attention, the plays themselves will tell us how they should be read." With a radicalism never before asserted and to the dismay of historically oriented critics and teachers, the text standing gloriously by itself was granted a state of very high privilege. Shakespearean classrooms were about to undergo a fundamental change.

Bradley's work, based on a perceived continuity of literary tradition, had been reassuring, cohesive in its force; the new work was either infuriating or exhilarating. During the 1930s and 1940s and even into the 1950s, the Shakespearean academy was divided as never before, with the revolutionaries doing their best, as good revolutionaries must, to render a middle position untenable. Since teachers in the classroom are for the most part extraordinarily conservative, they tend to follow the dominant trends of scholarship and criticism that had been absorbed by the time they completed their own university studies, thus requiring a generation at least for even the most persuasive revolution to replace the old guard. However, at some point in the 1950s, with the New Critics becoming senior citizens, the excitement and the gunfire dis-

appeared. If the revolution had joined—or even become—the establishment, where did that leave the average Shakespearean teacher?

The most significant academic impact of the New Criticism was to legitimize interpretation—a bold and often bald statement of meaning based entirely on textual evidence—as both a publishing and a pedagogical strategy and to encourage a shift away from character and background studies toward interpretation based upon the "new critical" perception of imagery patterns. As classroom necessities had encouraged dilutions of Bradley's method, often resulting in crude sketches of character abstracted from the complex web of the play, and a highly developed historical scholarship had just as often led to oversimplified background lectures as a substitute for facing the play, now the New Criticism—which had dealt harshly with both—led, under similar pedagogical pressures, to an analogous abstraction of imagery patterns. Of all the many poetic elements to be analyzed and interpreted in that "exact and sensitive" study demanded by Knights, imagery patterns proved to be the most attractive: they were there for anyone to see (how could previous generations have missed them?), yet they yielded real pleasures of discovery and seemed, most seductively, to lead to the richest caves of meaning.

Thus, by the 1960s three great schools or methodologies of criticism—Bradleyan, historical, and New—were available for any teacher of Shakespeare as literature. Practitioners of each school, in their desire to illuminate Shakespeare's work for colleagues or students, had made contributions complex and sophisticated enough to challenge the finest minds. And each school was also offering its own colorful, attractive, easy-to-use classroom package: Studies in Character, Background, or Imagery. Each school also, of course, tried to place its own major interest in the context of its own idea of dramatic structure, and each promised to enrich us and our students with the truth of Shakespeare's real themes and ultimate meanings.

It is true that the "new" was in: Bradley was old-fashioned, and historical scholarship was after all for specialists, but any teacher of English literature could "interpret" a play. And any university teacher, forced to publish or perish, could, like Bradley, turn a classroom interpretation into an article or a book. With unprecedented regularity, college and university classrooms fed the journals and the presses. Classrooms provided the testing grounds, the journals and the presses were hungry for "new interpretations" of every Shakespeare play, and the flood of interpretative articles and books made its greatest and most direct impact back in the classrooms. By the 1950s this intricate relationship between the published and the pedagogical criticism of Shakespeare was simply taken for granted; by 1970, furthermore—as demonstrated, for example, in *Modern Shakespearean Criticism,* a collection of essays by twenty-four writers published specifically for classroom use—it was possible to believe in an achieved unity of critical perception that could fairly be called modern. Modernity, in this view, accepts the rejection of Bradley and shows only incidental interest in criticism based directly on historical investigation. The editor of the collection, Alvin B. Kernan, finds his critics "in remarkable agreement about the fundamental tenets of Shakespearean criticism, about the ways in which the plays are to be approached and understood" and therefore taught. Explaining for his audience of teachers and students what the *modern* of his title means, he says, "What these critics share is a belief that Shakespeare's plays are most usefully and properly approached, not as realistic imitations of human nature and affairs, but as symbolic structures, elaborately intertwined and interworking parts that combine to create, not a photographic representation of the world, but an image of reality as it is perceived by the imagination." Kernan's is of course but one of the many ways taken to describe, in a context meant to be directly suggestive for teachers and students, the "insight" that was "first fully projected and used to illuminate the nature of poetic drama and Shakespeare's plays" in 1930 but that by 1970 had become the orthodoxy by which to guide "modern" teachers of Shakespeare.

We may be allowed to doubt that the agreement was ever as great as Kernan suggests; and it is certain that even as he perceived it, it was about to disappear. The freedom to interpret, as inadvertently encouraged by the New Criticism, was already under fire from the left and the right. Knight, Knights, and Leavis had never intended to suggest that everyone, not even every critic or every teacher, was capable of the "exact and sensitive" readings that the new age required. But by the 1970s what seemed clear to many observers was that even the most exact and sensitive critics or teachers—whoever they were, and everyone had

his own list—were unable to agree on the interpretation of any single play. On the left, the apparent chaos fed in obvious ways the suspicion and the belief that literary meaning, in any traditional sense, is mere illusion. On the right, however, the same chaos led in the opposite direction: to the belief that modern literary—and therefore Shakespearean—criticism is little more than a variety of irresponsible madness, the dismaying, even if unintentional, betrayal of a tradition that recognizes in literature the existence of real meaning that can be discovered, described, retained, and widely shared: *taught,* that is. Looking at exactly the same period of history as that represented by Kernan's collection (1930–1970), Levin finds "one of the most striking features" of the period to be a "remarkable proliferation of reinterpretations or 'new readings' " that are "radically" opposed to the "traditional views" of the plays "held, . . . by *virtually all spectators and readers down to the present time* [italics added]." And he leaves no doubt about what he believes to be the basis for this traditional consensus that always exists beneath the apparent chaos and to which, in his view, critics and teachers must return: "The universally and profoundly moving experience of the characters, regarded not as symbols or representatives of some abstract truism, but as unique personalities sharing and calling out to our common humanity." This is to turn Kernan's statement quoted above precisely inside out. We are—some of us, anyway—back in the land of Bradley.

Thus, it is once more respectable to assume in one's teaching that the plays "mean what generations of spectators and readers have taken them to mean." One is obliged, of course, to try to discover what that consensus is with respect to each play and then to trust it over one's own "new" reading, which, in the view of the neo-Bradleyites, will be no more than an idiosyncratic and thus valueless revelation. In a classroom judged from such a position, the response to a play by a majority of the readers (who happen to be students) may suddenly weigh more than the learned but "new" response of the teacher. "It is not pleasant" for Levin "to contemplate what goes on in some of those classrooms, where the critic-as-pedagogue is in absolute control, and his interpretations are not subject to even the minimal accountability that publication provides." Levin is concerned that the idiosyncratic ingenuities of the teacher will function as a substitute for real knowledge and that what students will learn is that their own interpretations "are always wrong, because the work never means what it seems to mean." They will also learn, he believes, that a play is "something to be 'studied' rather than experienced," that it "cannot be merely enjoyable or moving," and that "the meaning of the play is not found in our direct experience of it but in an elaborate intellectual operation quite separate from that experience."

Levin's concerns are widely shared, and his analysis of the problems widely accepted. But to teacher-critics who, though concerned, do not want simply to jettison the last fifty years (or to accompany the deconstructive armies into the night), Levin's "Modest Proposals" for improvement seem, in Norman Rabkin's phrase *(Shakespeare and the Problem of Meaning),* mere "banal suggestions" that offer no hope whatever for our current crisis of confidence. As advice for teachers in a time of crisis, the proposals do boil down rather quickly to a single strategy by which to protect oneself against the idiosyncratic impulse and thus to remain inside the tradition: one must simply believe and remember that "meaning is to be sought in our actual dramatic experience," in "the actual experience of the play," in the "immediate impression derived by ordinary people," in the "concrete facts of character and action," in the "literal representation of particular human actions." Such overlapping and never-defined phrases, such slippery words as *immediate, ordinary,* and *literal,* do indeed possess little force in today's highly demanding pedagogical world. Though to sound his useful warning Levin repeatedly invokes tradition, he provides, even as his term *modest* implies, little or no energy for its enrichment.

In *Shakespeare and the Problem of Meaning,* Rabkin provides precisely that energy. His book, though not so intended, is the closest thing we have, in the developing critical and pedagogical tradition of the center, to a modern primer for teachers of Shakespeare as literature. Published in 1981, it is a book of and about the 1970s, bringing us close enough for our purposes to today. It explicitly avoids—or even quarrels with—the extremes that Rabkin sees as characterizing the beginning and the end of the 1970s: early on, "the ubiquitous critical tendency to explicate meanings" and, only ten years later, the growing tendency to deny "the very notion that literature . . . can be said to have meaning." In large part agreeing with Levin about idiosyncratic interpretations, Rabkin nevertheless places himself in a tradition that includes and develops the work of the

New Critics; and he believes "as not only the New Critics but the establishment they replaced did that one [can] speak for a community that look[s] out on the same world," that it is possible for critics and teachers to create "descriptions of literary works that come close to being definitive" (he even withholds the qualification "for our time"), that "literary works mean, and that there are ways in which we can talk about"—*and therefore teach*—"their meanings."

When he praises the critics of *The Merchant of Venice* for integrating "the techniques developed in the last half-century for literary study"—"They hear verbal nuances and know how to talk about them; they know the significance of motifs and echoes, of dramaturgic and metrical effect, of structure and symbol, character and genre"—he is speaking of techniques that would in his view distinguish the Shakespearean pedagogy of any good teacher of literature and would be essential to the Shakespearean education of any good student of literature. But he also argues that even the best criticism (and, by implication, pedagogy or education) resulting from such techniques "leaves us with the sense that it has somehow failed to come to grips with or has even in some way denied the existence of essential qualities of the play."

On the one hand, the revolutionary techniques that began to surface in 1930 have served us well and must be seen as genuine progress in our attempt to appreciate Shakespeare fully: "Even at their worst they speak for the conflicts, tensions, implications, and significant fields of force that contribute to our sense that a play is an autonomous, coherent, and meaningful whole." On the other hand, the specific formulations that result are always "narrower than the play," reveal "some conflict" between what the critic "identifies on reflection and his actual experience of the play," deny to "Shakespeare's intention or the play's virtue what the comedy actually *does* to us," are in fact so "inadequate" that they "serve very poorly . . . what is communicated by the plays they describe." That is, they are "reductive" (this is perhaps his key critical term).

Rabkin's most significant contribution to our teaching is his identification of this apparent contradiction—such virtues and such apparently contradictory sins in the same body of criticism—as merely one way to describe the nature of Shakespearean drama. In each play, he insists, resides a meaning that can be—even demands to be—recognized and explicated; but, he also insists, even the fullest possible meaning is not the complete experience of the play. In the very nature of the plays as great art there is a force that literally drives us to seek, define, and share intellectually their "central mystery," but it is in the nature of that mystery to remain so: "The essence of our *experience* [italics added] is our haunting sense of what doesn't fit the thesis we are tempted at every moment to derive."

The consequences for the teacher-critic are clear enough, and Rabkin spells them out in a set of required virtues that are—and this is crucial—in addition to, not in conflict with, the virtues listed above as associated with the revolution of 1930:

> He must find terms in which the oppositions and conflicts and problems within a play can be stated while recognizing the reductiveness of those terms. He must fight the temptation to proclaim what it boils down to; he must fight against the urge to closure which, as a gifted audience, he feels with particular intensity. He must learn to point to the centers of energy and turbulence in a play without regarding them as coded elements of a thematic formula. And while rejecting narrow conclusions drawn by other critics, he must be able to learn from the perceptions that have led to those conclusions.

Writing of his own excitement in sensing "that we are making communal progress in our understanding of Shakespeare," Rabkin defines, as he sees it, the challenge to criticism; and in an age in which the major activity in Shakespearean classrooms is one or another form of literary criticism, the challenge clearly applies to pedagogy as well. We need, he believes,

> to embark on a self-conscious reconsideration of the phenomena that our technology has enabled us to explore, to consider the play as a dynamic interaction between artist and audience, to learn to talk about the process of our involvement rather than our considered view after the aesthetic event. We need to find concepts other than meaning to account for the end of a play, the sense of unverbalizable coherence, lucidity, and unity that makes us know we have been through a single, significant, and shared experience.

To call Rabkin's book a primer for teachers of Shakespeare as literature is not to say that he discusses pedagogical theory or classroom strategies, and it is certainly not to imply that the book is elementary in any pejorative sense. Quite the contrary. Any teacher of Shakespeare who wishes to experience the literary tradition of the center working at its best, and who wishes to keep that tradition thoughtfully alive in his or her own classes, should turn to this book first. For the contribution it can make to our teaching in the present moment is clear, strong, and direct; and it is a contribution that deliberately conserves the valuable past as it optimistically points toward an even richer future. Teachers who follow the suggestive standards and challenges—the implications of both theory and practice—to be found in Rabkin's work will not need pedagogical details spelled out but will, instead, be led to create their own specific strategies out of their own teaching and Shakespearean experience, in Rabkin's sense of the word.

All of the individuals or schools of thought that we have thus far briefly examined or glanced at—Bradley, the historical-philological scholars, the New Critics, the Freudians, the Marxists, the feminists, the structuralists, the postmodernists, Levin and the neo-Bradleyites, and Rabkin—in spite of whatever revolutions, radical adjustments, or bitter disagreements they have had, are, in a sense that we must now examine and try to define, fundamentally united. They are all teachers, critics, and scholars of literature and of Shakespeare as literature. The discipline upon which they rely—the basic point of view toward words on a page, the initiating attitudes and assumptions, the modes of investigation, the strategies in the classroom, the defining goals and critical or scholarly methods—derives its sanction entirely from literature, from the nature of the literary experience, and from the possibilities or challenge of literature as an object of study. It has no roots whatever in the art, craft, or discipline of theater. It derives no sanction, needs no nourishment, achieves no identity from the theatrical experience, from the possibilities and challenges of theater as an object of study. When Shakespeare was canonized for educational purposes, replacing the Greeks and Romans in curricula, he came as a literary saint, and the theology of the established church was, and remains, literary. No one said that Bradley, for example, was unqualified for the priesthood merely because he knew substantially nothing about theater, and the credentials demanded of those who would teach or write about Shakespeare in the English departments of the 1980s still exclude theatrical validation of any kind. Received opinion continues to place a Shakespearean scholar most properly in the library, not in a theater.

There has of course always been a minority voice, and especially since about the middle of the century it has been possible to detect a growing nervousness, a dissatisfaction even, arising out of the uneasy perception that there may be something lacking in an exclusively literary response to a body of work that was designed exclusively for the theater. The positive signs of this dissatisfaction are various. Among recent political signs, we find the International Shakespeare Association in 1981 holding its world congress—with the theme of "Shakespeare: Man of the Theatre"—in Stratford-upon-Avon not primarily because it is the writer's birthplace but because it is the working home of the Royal Shakespeare Company. The Shakespeare Association of America in 1983 convened its annual meeting in the small, out-of-the-way town of Ashland, Oregon, entirely because it is the home of the Oregon Shakespearean Festival. The existence and influence of these theater companies and the constantly growing number of theaters devoted partly or entirely to Shakespeare have furthermore allowed teachers who enjoy theater to introduce their students to Shakespeare in performance. Teachers themselves have been able to see more Shakespeare on the stage as well as in the library, and the impact on scholarship has been growing. Actors have, in significant numbers, been invited into classrooms to share their way of looking at, and working with, Shakespeare. There has been nothing especially controversial about any of this activity. It has without much difficulty taken its place in the system, and teachers and scholars of the so-called stage-centered school can now, in a way that was not possible even in 1970, win both approval and promotion.

In fact, there appears to exist fairly widespread agreement that the most significant development in Shakespearean scholarship and teaching since the 1960s has been in the area of the so-called theatrical dimension: this dimension has, in one fashion or another, invaded many classrooms, been the subject of numerous books and articles, and stimulated a considerable amount of discussion at scholarly meetings. There remains, however, much disagreement about its nature, its proper place in the established configuration of Shakespearean studies, its long-term staying power, and the relative value of classroom practices associated with it. In some quarters, many of them powerful and prestigious, there continues to be outright opposition. To give but one example, when Maynard Mack, one of our most justly influential scholars and a teacher of great reputation, presented in 1979 the first occasional paper of the International Shakespeare Association, he dismissed the "school of performance" as only a passing "vogue," only a "more or less cloudy prism that, if properly angled, may refract some shadow" of the Shakespearean truth. Mack's title, "Rescuing Shakespeare," exactly describes his purpose, which derives its importance from what he sees as the tendency of such "vogues" (the New Criticism and the "School of Psychoanalysis" are also included) to "eschew history" and thus seriously to subvert the proper "academic study of Shakespeare."

John L. Styan, however, sees not a fad but a revolution, not a subversion but a new integration of knowledge that for the first time ever will truly bring the theater and the academy together in a common endeavor. For scholars, critics, or teachers "to stop short at the text is now," Styan believes—and his book, The Shakespeare Revolution, was published two years before the occasion of Mack's paper—"a kind of surrender, for the text will not tell us much until it speaks in its own medium." And the future, as he sees it, is bright: "Actor and scholar will teach each other not what Shakespeare 'means,' but what his possibilities are beyond logic. Nor will these be exhausted. The scholar will modify the actor's illumination, the actor will modify the scholar's, a process of infinite adjustment. Shakespeare remains uncharted territory waiting to be explored and articulated." If Styan is right, a new discipline is developing that will transform our Shakespearean world: its scholarship, criticism, teaching, and even theatrical performance.

More than any other person, Styan has been, for the academy, the leader and chronicler of the Shakespeare revolution. His unique importance lies in the fact that, like Bradley, Leavis, Rabkin, and Mack, he is nominally—institutionally—a teacher and scholar of English literature but that the very titles of his books (a series that started appearing in the 1960s) tell a new and different story: The Challenge of the Theatre; Chekhov in Performance; Drama, Stage and Audience; The Elements of Drama; Modern Drama in Theory and Practice; and Shakespeare's Stagecraft. For those teachers and students who wish to recognize and accept Shakespeare's work for what Shakespeare would presumably have thought it to be—drama or theater, not literature—Styan's books are alone in being what one might reasonably call indispensable.

The first fourteen pages of *Drama, Stage and Audience* (1975) combine theory with descriptions of drama and the study of drama, for the best such discussion available anywhere. The following definitions or descriptions are basic to it:

Discipline: "Drama has its own discipline, one which is not an extension of that of literature. . . . At its centre is the theatre experience, which is capable of analysis, recreation and judgment of its methods and purposes like those of any other art."

Medium: In drama, "medium calls for as much consideration as . . . content: we must know the theatre at least as well as we know the play."

Script: "The signs on the printed page are signals for something to happen in the theatre . . . a coded pattern of signals to the actor."

Performance: "The theatre is the testing ground for the validity of words and images . . . performance is a further coded pattern of signals to the spectator."

Study: "The study of the drama is the study of how the stage compels its audience to be involved in its actual processes. . . . Any study of a play is impossible without an initial decoding of all signals."

The literary mode of study is to take words on the page not only as primary evidence but also as legitimate, sufficient, and comprehensible in themselves, the first and final object of study, leading to nothing but the reader's experiences. The temptation to employ this mode in studying and teaching Shakespeare derives from an understandable desire to deal with what is relatively stable. The text, demonstrably and sufficiently challenging as literature, lies before us on the desk and can be placed, literally, in the hands of our students. But to succumb to the temptation is, Styan believes, to deprive the words of their true function in the process that identifies drama, the process that legitimizes the words as drama.

However important the script, it "is not the play"; and the play—not just the script—is what Shakespeare created, writing the script, in fact, only to create the play. What Styan calls the "irreducible theatre event" requires "three elements": script, actors, audience. And thus the vexed problem of meaning in Shakespeare—the challenge usefully confronted by both Levin and Rabkin in literary terms—will not, in Styan's view, yield to methods of scrutiny and interpretation derived from litera-

ture (however frequent, polite, or enthusiastic may be the references to audiences or theatergoing):

It is beyond dispute that dramatic meaning cannot lie in words alone, but in voices and the tone of voices, in the pace of the speaking and the silences between; and not alone in this, but also in the gesture and expression of the actor, the physical distinctions between him and others, the statuary of tragedy and the curlicues of comedy, stylistic suggestion beyond reckoning. There are so many variables simultaneously working to create meaning on the stage that it is impertinent to identify it in terms other than its own. The experience is the meaning.

And the experience here suggested differs fundamentally from the literary experiences offered in the work of Bradley, Leavis, Levin, or even Rabkin.

I do not mean to suggest that the ground from which Styan argues has only recently come into view. The discovery that Shakespeare was not a novelist or a poet but a wright, that he wrote scripts and made plays, is one of those odd discoveries of the obvious that the human race has until now seemed as determined to ignore as to make—over and over again, for example, in our own century. What could be more clear or, in terms of our still-prevailing literary tradition, more radical than to say that Shakespeare's "dramatic quality . . . can hardly be grasped by mere reading," that "unacted action comes rather near to being a contradiction in terms," and that "to stagecraft, to action, which is what stagecraft embodies, everything else in [Shakespeare] is subordinated" (Styan, 1977). Yet, symbolically enough, the speaker was Bradley's successor at Oxford as professor of poetry, John W. Mackail; and, confusingly enough, the year was that crucial one for Shakespearean studies, 1930, when anyone stirring revolutionary fires was listening to quite another music.

Six years later, when already the only Shakespearean news that seemed to carry a reshaping or revitalizing force was coming from the camp of the New Critics, John Dover Wilson made no news at all when he declared: "It is one of the most important literary discoveries of our age that Shakespeare wrote, not to be read, but to be acted, that his plays are not books but, as it were, libretti for stage-performances. It is amazing that so obvious a fact should so late have come to recognition." From this obvious fact he drew two conclusions that, had any significant number of Shakespeareans paid heed, would have turned us definitively toward the

Shakespeare of the theater nearly half a century ago:

For scholars, editors and critics: "We students of Shakespeare must try out his effects in action upon a stage, if we are to understand them," for no Shakespearean knowledge is "safe" that is "divorced from theatrical experience."

For students and the general public: "Never believe what the scholars and professors tell you about a Shakespeare play until you have seen it on the stage for yourself."

For teachers, Wilson's conclusions would seem to have made inescapable a pedagogy composed of playgoing and playmaking; yet all but a small minority of teachers did in fact escape, remaining snug and warm inside the literary stockade. Although Wilson was one of the most influential scholars of his time, his failure in this matter could hardly have been more complete. The world was not yet ready to believe his most simple truth: that only those who know the theater intimately and deeply can know the works of the theater and therefore of Shakespeare, intimately and deeply. Nearly a quarter of a century later, Sir Tyrone Guthrie, lamenting the historical development that in European culture had divorced "theatrical performance and the literary study of drama," accurately observed that not only Shakespeare but all other major dramatists are, "in schools and universities," seen primarily as "men of letters" instead of "men of the theatre," their works "still studied as literature."

Perhaps the divorce lamented by Guthrie need not have happened, and yet the basic confusion seems always to have been with us. In Shakespeare's own time, the playwright John Marston, in his introduction to *The Malcontent,* thought a script that had been "enforcively published to be read" was an "unhandsome shape" and that the words could give true pleasure only when presented in the theater "with the soul of lively action"; but John Heminge and Henry Condell, the editors of the First Folio, presented the plays "To the great Variety of Readers" with every indication that these two lifelong actors, two of Shakespeare's closest friends and collaborators, thought a full understanding of his scripts available merely from the page, though you might need a "Friend," a "guide," some professor of literature, perhaps, to assist you:

It is not our province, who only gather his works, and give them you, to praise him. It is yours that reade him. And there we hope, to your divers capacities, you will finde enough, both to draw, and hold you: for his wit can no more lie hid, then it could be lost. Reade him, therefore; and againe, and againe: And if then you doe not like him, surely you are in some manifest danger, not to understand him. And so we leave you to other of his Friends, whom if you need, can bee your guides: if you neede them not, you can leade your selves, and others. And such Readers we wish him.

A pedagogy based on Marston would certainly lead to playgoing, possibly to classroom visits from the actors, to long discussions about scripted versus literary words, and even perhaps to doing scenes in class. A pedagogy based on Heminge and Condell would lead, with Bradley, Leavis, or Rabkin as our guides, mainly to literary analysis and criticism. Theatrical experience—though seen as pleasant, sometimes useful, and occasionally even to be personally treasured—would not be considered essential.

It must surely seem strange to any outsider that a profession as solid, venerable, and knowledgeable as that large group of scholars, critics, and teachers gathered around Shakespeare has arrived in 1985 radically divided about the most basic professional matter of all, quite unable to agree among themselves even on what it is they are studying and teaching. What can surprise no one is the resulting confusion. If as scholars we cannot define a common object of study, as teachers we will clearly not possess a common subject matter. A set of words called *Hamlet*—yes. But what is *Hamlet*? A play? A drama? A theater event? A literary work? A text? A script? A complete work of art? Only part of a process? Each term presents the same set of words under a label that quarrels with one or more of the other labels, and what you get in class depends entirely on the teacher that fate gives you.

The fact is that we do not share even a basic professional vocabulary of sufficient stability and precision to enable us to understand one another in the work that we must do together. For most Shakespeareans, what appears on the page is a drama, and to teach *Hamlet* from a book is to teach the art of drama. What, then, to do in the face of the following perfectly traditional definitions?

Bernard Beckerman: "Drama occurs when one or more human beings isolated in time and space present themselves in imagined acts to another or others" (*Dynamics of Drama*).

Emrys Jones: "The peculiarity of drama is its embodiment in actual human beings: the actors who provide the dramatist with his indispensable medium. Their activities are the language through which he must project his imitation of reality" (*Scenic Form in Shakespeare*).

Susanne K. Langer: "Drama is not made of words as a piece of literature is, . . . [nor is it] literature embellished with concurrent appeals to the sense of sight . . . but is poetry in the mode of action" (*Feeling and Form*).

What has proved impossible over the years is to create a discipline, in the study not only of Shakespeare but of other dramatists as well, based on such definitions and at the same time compelling enough to convince a majority of Shakespeareans. Few teachers or scholars openly quarrel with the definitions. It is apparently easier to ignore them or, through some trick of the mind, to exempt Shakespeare from them. It is also easier to accept the obvious—that Shakespeare was a working dramatist—but avoid the consequences in the details of one's own working life. Certainly, very few members of the profession follow such basic and unexceptionable definitions to the consequences for teaching and scholarship that the definitions obviously imply, consequences that land us with both feet in the theater and consequences toward which Styan, Beckerman, Jones, Langer, Alan Dessen, John Russell Brown, Glynne Wickham, Richard Southern, and others have, each in his or her own way, been vigorously pointing.

We have no direct helpful testimony of any kind from Shakespeare himself. Everything that we know about him, however, suggests that what mattered to him most was not the script or the reader but the production and the audience: "poetry in the mode of action." So much does this seem to be the case that it is reasonable to suppose that he would have agreed with the modern playwright Athol Fugard: "I have always regarded the completed text as being only a half-way stage to my ultimate objective—the living performance and its particular definition of space and silence" (Introduction to *Statements: Three Plays*). If, furthermore, we press into Shakespeare with such orthodox definitions of drama as those by Beckerman, Jones, and Langer fixed firmly in our minds, we inevitably find ourselves studying Shakespeare's language as something that differs essentially from the language of literature,

> a theatrical language where the word is never dissociated from the place where it is spoken or from the concrete language of the stage, where the word is never conceived outside the framework of the accompanying gesture, the movement, place, the physical stance and the bodily posture . . . where the word in its relationship to the gesture, the phrase to the movement, the language to the body, the writing to the direction, are all thought out and explored to their extreme limits.

That this is a description of Samuel Beckett's work by Pierre Chabert (*Gambit,* no. 28), an actor who has worked closely with him, in no way decreases its importance for our understanding of Shakespeare. Even more than Fugard and Beckett—as much as anyone who comes to mind—Shakespeare worked in the theater, lived in the theater, thought and composed theatrically. It is hard to imagine that he would have been happy with a response to his work that allowed the words to be isolated from "the concrete language of the stage." And it is thus hard to believe that we are not obliged, in studying and teaching Shakespeare, to avoid such a response. The obligation that in our time increasingly forces itself upon us is to search the word in each of Shakespeare's scripts for the "gesture, the movement, place, the physical stance and the bodily posture" that is an integral part of the conception, to think out and explore "to their extreme limits" the "word in its relationship to the gesture, the phrase to the movement, the language to the body, the writing to the direction." Is there not, that is, a scholarly and pedagogical discipline that would embrace Fugard, Beckett, and Shakespeare but be inappropriate for Spenser, Wordsworth, and Faulkner—inappropriate, in fact, for Shakespeare's sonnets and Beckett's novels?

The contribution of the theater itself toward such a discipline, a New Discipline that might, in its logic and rigor, bring a majority of teachers and scholars to accept the full consequences of perceiving Shakespeare's plays as drama, has, in the unique presence of the RSC, been absolutely central. For the first time in history we have had since 1961 the theatrical equivalent of a modern research center that is constantly testing its conclusions in the marketplace. No other theater since Shakespeare's own has had as profound an impact upon the way the world thinks of his plays. The RSC and the modern technology that allows actors and audiences to travel have taken many academics, with an educative frequency, out of their studies and into a theater where they have been able to experience productions that combine fidelity, challenge, and popular appeal with a degree of complexity that is indisputably more authentic—by which I do not mean historically imitative—than any other large body of Shakespearean work since Shakespeare's death. For the first time in the history of Shakespearean scholarship, criticism, and pedagogy, the academy has been granted an extended series—a living library—of performances capable of suggesting, and often of demonstrating, that Shakespeare did in fact write not for readers but for actors and audiences, that his language and his dramatic structures are more precise, full, profound, and available in the theater than in the study.

What is deliciously ironic about all of this is that without the academy—and I mean the academy in one of its most aggressively literary, antitheatrical rages—the RSC would never have done the work that has been so influential. The work that has defined the company at its best is that in which it deliberately absorbed, and then in theatrical terms validated, the New Critical revolution of the 1930s, most specifically, however, as it manifested itself not in a book or series of articles but in the classroom of F. R. Leavis in the 1950s, from which Peter Hall and later Trevor Nunn emerged to lead the RSC. Hall, in his *Diaries,* says: "All the textual seriousness at the basis of Trevor's work and of mine comes from Leavis, and there is a vast band of us. Comical to think that Leavis hated theatre and never went to it. He has had more influence on the contemporary theatre than any other critic." At the heart of that influence was a force that helped to drive Shakespeare's text to the center of Shakespearean production as never before, the text suddenly free to make its own demands with greater urgency: less cutting, longer rehearsals, a barer stage, thinking actors, a more intellectual probing of theme and structure, a new attention, in speaking the verse, to form, rhythm, meter, and lineation.

The RSC was from the first a directors' theater—directors who shared a commitment to language and ideas as well as to theater. They tended to arrive at the first rehearsal with a reading derived from the study—readings as analytical as any by Leavis, as thematically visionary as any by Knight,

or as idiosyncratically "new" as any condemned by Levin—but then, in greater or lesser degree, they subjected that reading, as no critic or scholar need do, to the intense collective scrutiny of an increasingly articulate company and to an analysis through voice and body that can occur only on the floor of a rehearsal room populated by actors who have been given a new sense of themselves as members of a thinking, developing, permanently valued ensemble. The vocal and physical contributions to be expected from the theater were, that is, an integral part of the new textual work. For example, there arose an interest in finding a new discipline for the voice based on a more precise awareness of the nature of Shakespeare's verse. At a time when, in American theatrical circles, the most-repeated cliché about English acting had to do with what was perceived as an empty, extravagant singing of the verse, Hall and, especially, John Barton (to whom Hall entrusted most of the teaching in the company) had analyzed that problem, had recognized the equally serious dangers of the naturalistic speaking that was an attractive but mindless response to singing, and had done more (partly under the influence of another Cambridge professor, George Rylands) to follow the verse itself into a concrete, specific way of speaking based on "shape, form, and colour" than has any other theater to this day.

Thus, inside the RSC a new kind of scholar appeared—directors and actors who would have been surprised and uncomfortable (and still are) to find themselves so labeled but who were nevertheless developing a new scholarly discipline, one truer to the nature of Shakespeare's words than any that has ever reigned in the academy. Accepting as fully and rigorously as any New Critic the demands of the text, they were learning, out of a necessity that most critics and scholars feel no pressure to face, the nature of a Shakespearean script: words, yes—like literature in that—but words wholly unlike literature in their primary function, words in search of voices, bodies, a space, in search finally of a form that resolves itself only and precariously in the active presence of an audience. A director or an actor whose work is conditioned by such a discipline explores, as does a scholar, an unknown or mysterious territory with tools appropriate to the task, and returns to report on what he has found; but he does so collectively by presenting a play instead of individually by writing a book.

The RSC came only slowly to the knowledge that

the discipline it had developed had given birth to new offstage possibilities, perhaps even to a new offstage responsibility. By 1978, however, Trevor Nunn was stating the case with clarity and force: "Our textual studies and the methods we employ to unlock texts could certainly be more successfully shared. We don't do anything like enough work in schools and colleges; we probably do too much of our analysis behind close doors. . . . The RSC has a responsibility to influence the way Shakespeare is taught" (*The RSC 1978,* 4). To feel the need for such influence, and publicly to define one's own responsibilities in such terms, is more than a casual offer of assistance and may in fact suggest, very politely, a belief that the traditional academic grasp of the shared subject matter is at best inadequate and at worst illegitimate. In any case, Nunn gave his full support to a project based at the University of California at Santa Barbara called Actors in Residence (AIR) that is guided by precisely such a belief and exists primarily to create a new kind of collaboration, in teaching and research, between RSC actors and directors and American scholars and teachers. Over a hundred actors and directors from the RSC are members of AIR, and thousands of faculty members and students throughout the United States have worked with them in a program that places actors in residence on American campuses and students in residence at the RSC. The line from Cambridge through the RSC to "literature" classes in American universities is clear and straight, a fact that would surely have astonished Leavis.

Through the textually oriented theatrical energies of the RSC, what could have ended as only one more brilliant literary distraction—Shakespeare as poet instead of Shakespeare as novelist—became what its own self-proclaimed revolutionary force cried out for: a radical transformation of our awareness of Shakespearean possibilities in the area that in his own professional life Shakespeare himself claimed. As a literary procedure applied to Shakespeare, the New and neo–New Criticism has perhaps earned the ridicule that Richard Levin aims at it, though he fails to perceive the source of its weakness. But as an intensely analytical procedure that owes its discoveries to a full submission to the processes, discipline, and nature of theater, it has—without losing any of its force or brilliance—found a home in the Shakespearean tradition that matters most: the one in which infinitely complex arrangements and qualities of words accept the challenge

of highly trained voices and bodies, of varying but carefully considered spaces, of intelligently informed and perceptive audiences, and (not quite paradoxically) of the hazards that accompany a popular art form.

The point that matters is that the intricate union of language and theater created with unique success by the RSC is its greatest accomplishment thus far and—true to its origins at Cambridge—is the one that most clearly reveals the rich area of identical interest that fundamentally unites academic and theatrical Shakespeareans. Whether our activity of the moment is scholarship, pedagogy, criticism, or production, there is—as John Styan has argued so forcefully—only one legitimate discipline, necessarily of the theater, in which each activity plays its proper role. The theater of Shakespearean drama and the academy of Shakespearean drama need one another. Theater, as Hall and Nunn saw, needs to be sustained by the constant, intense investigation of language (in all its elements: diction, syntax, imagery, prosody, prose rhythms, punctuation, and so on) characteristic of the New Critics. And equally, commitment to such an investigation of Shakespeare's language, more traditionally located in the academy, needs to be sustained by the constant, intense awareness and exploration of the physical possibilities of theater. Put this way, there may still remain the appearance of two tasks proceeding side by side. It is therefore necessary to emphasize that only if we understand the radically unitary nature of the work will we have learned the most important lesson available from the RSC experience, and only if we allow ourselves, in the academy and in the theater, to be guided by that understanding will we be able deliberately, instead of haphazardly, to continue the progress that the RSC has demonstrated to be possible.

It has not been the purpose of this essay to propose or review specific strategies for teaching or studying Shakespeare. The most effective strategies, in any case, arise from the daily experience of individual teachers who are as alert to their own and their students' possibilities as they are to the nature and content of Shakespeare's scripts. But the essay would be incomplete, I think, without some brief reference to the pedagogical consequences that appear to attend a genuine acceptance of Styan's theory and definitions, Dover Wilson's claims and observations, the quoted definitions of drama, the implications of the work of Fugard and Beckett, or the textual work of the RSC, for the pedagogical challenge that defines our time is precisely there: Will the actual daily classroom procedures in schools, colleges, and universities be grounded in and receive their sanction from the nature of literature or from the nature of drama? If one chooses to teach or study Shakespeare as drama instead of as literature—and a scholarly regard for the needs of our historical moment would lead to such revealing classifications—what are the initial consequences in and around the classroom?

The first and governing consequence is a new definition of our collective venture: to educate audiences for Shakespearean theaters instead of readers for Shakespearean texts. In actual fact, our students will learn, more swiftly and deeply than ever before, how to read a Shakespearean script; and student actors who wander into our courses will leave enriched, much better prepared to create Shakespearean stages. But the central task that requires our attention and defines our professional activity is audience development, in the broadest and deepest sense.

It is easy enough to point to the major areas of activity toward which the logic of the New Discipline (if for convenience I may continue to call it that) appears to lead any interested teacher: playgoing; using film, television, and video cassettes (though with great care for the differences among the media); bringing professional theater people into class; doing scenes in class with the students as performers (what Styan calls the "direct method"); practicing the kind of reading demanded by scripts but not by literature; and probing (through demonstration, discussion, and assignments) the theoretical and specific differences between drama and literature. What is needed is fifty years of exploration and experiment in class, nourished by fifty years of investigation and dialogue by scholars committed to the discipline.

What is already clear—a negative but salutary consequence of thinking clearly—is that the discipline moves us forever out of that illusory halfway house called the "theater of the mind." The theater we must work with and in is the one in which space and silence are measured by feet and minutes, where Shakespeare's words propel real bodies into real space and real voices into real silence so as to participate in the intricate process that Hamlet describes: "Suit the action to the word, the word to the action." As it is the only process for which the scripted words were designed, we must find ways of helping our students to discover what such words are like, how they differ from words not so designed, how they function in the process as signals to actors, and how such signals are transformed into signs for an audience. And we must also find ways of helping the students to perceive and respond to such signs in the living theater; to become increasingly aware of, and sophisticated about, the unlimited multiplicity of theatrical signs; and to grow in their ability to contribute as audience to the unfolding revelation and form toward which the script and the actors have hoped the collective experience would move. These are the two areas of learning that the New Shakespearean Discipline embraces: the nature of scripted signals and the nature of performed signs. The future is going to tell us much about them—and thus much about Shakespeare's art—that, strangely and excitingly enough, we do not yet know.

BIBLIOGRAPHY

John Barton, *Playing Shakespeare* (1984). Peter Brook, *The Empty Space* (1968). Alan C. Dessen, *Elizabethan Drama and the Viewer's Eye* (1977) and *Elizabethan Stage Conventions and Modern Interpreters* (1984). *Peter Hall's Diaries: The Story of a Dramatic Battle* (1983). Alvin B. Kernan, *Modern Shakespearean Criticism* (1970). G. Wilson Knight, *The Wheel of Fire* (1957).

Richard Levin, *New Readings vs. Old Plays* (1979). Norman Rabkin, *Shakespeare and the Problem of Meaning* (1981). J. L. Styan, *Shakespeare's Stagecraft* (1967); *Drama, Stage and Audience* (1975); and *The Shakespeare Revolution* (1977). Stanley Wells, *Literature and Drama* (1970).

Contemporary Issues in Shakespearean Interpretation

MAURICE CHARNEY

Each age re-creates Shakespeare in its own image, thereby renewing his works with a tremendous vitality. It should therefore not be surprising to learn that there are whole books devoted solely to listing books and articles on a single play and that there is scarcely a play of Shakespeare that does not have a book devoted to it. Since criticism goes out of date so quickly, such a ferment of ideas and opinions about Shakespeare is all to the good. Each national culture and ethnic group has its own special ideas and vested interests in Shakespeare, as the annual international bibliography in *Shakespeare Quarterly* abundantly witnesses. Each country even seems to have its favorite Shakespeare play.

A good deal that has been written on Shakespeare is out of date and needs to be rewritten, reconceived, and renewed in relation to modern tastes, interests, and sensibilities. I have arbitrarily limited the scope of this article to the years since 1960, with special emphasis on the period since 1970. I have not attempted the impossible task of presenting a brief and compendious survey of all Shakespeare criticism in this period, but I have concentrated on trends, movements, and special concerns. I have divided the subject rather arbitrarily into eight areas: theater, film, feminism, psychoanalysis, Marxism, iconography, metadrama, and Shakespeare's relation to the drama of his time. My purpose in choosing these areas is to set out some of the newer ways of thinking about Shakespeare.

Theater

The most basic transformation in our approach to Shakespeare since 1960 is that his plays are no longer considered primarily as long poems but rather as theatrical works intended to be performed —indeed works, like musical compositions, that can only be fully realized in performance. As Bernard Beckerman has phrased the matter, "There is evidence all around us that an important change has occurred in Shakespeare studies. Far from being supplemental and peripheral as in the past, analysis of Shakespeare through performance is now conceded to be a proper and perhaps central way of approaching Shakespeare" ("Explorations"). We are now in a period of stage-centered readings of Shakespeare.

Important work is being done on understanding and reconstructing the playhouses and other playing spaces in which Shakespeare was first presented. Theatrical historians like Richard Hosley have increasingly turned to the professional study of architecture in order to solve technical problems. The inner stage, miraculously invented for Shakespeare by Germanic scholarship, has more or less disappeared, and there is a general feeling that historical concepts must be workable as theater. This has resulted in a notable decline in the use of the balcony or upper stage and the windows on the side or the "top" mentioned in *The Tempest*. In general, antiquarianism has ceded to effectiveness, and we tend to think of Elizabethan theaters as much more festive and popular places than we used to. There is also a link between Elizabethan stages and those on the Continent, as George R. Kernodle has demonstrated from art works of the period.

For our purposes, the emphasis falls on dramaturgy rather than the architectural features of stage and theater design—in other words, how a play is put together, its technique, its relation to an audience, its conventions of representation. Dramaturgy is, of course, dependent on the physical theater and the conditions of performance. We must take into account the fact that Shakespeare's plays were generally presented in daylight, in the afternoon, in a theater that did not use changeable scenery or have the benefit of electric lighting. But this does not exclude intensely realistic effects, such as a liberal use of stage blood in scenes of violence. It is quite probable that actors, although more eloquent and formal than they are now, were not at all trying to imitate orators, as Bertram Joseph has claimed. In contemporary accounts, Richard Burbage, the leading actor of Shakespeare's company, was praised for his lifelikeness and his ability to arouse strong emotions.

Modern critics such as Bernard Beckerman, John Russell Brown, and John L. Styan have been interested in re-creating the feeling of an Elizabethan performance—its fluidity, its extensive use of contrast, its wide range of emotional and declamatory effects. All three of these critics have a practical association with theater, so that their studies of Shakespeare are strongly oriented toward performance. We must acknowledge that we are all primarily readers of Shakespeare on the printed page, yet there is a way of reading, highly developed by Brown, that takes account of our experience of performance as it might occur in the theater of the mind. We must learn to read Shakespeare in a way that is meaningful theatrically, just as a musician reads a score with some feeling for what it might sound like.

Beckerman's *Shakespeare at the Globe, 1599–1609* is a crucial book for the development of the theatrical point of view of Shakespeare. On the basis of fifteen Shakespeare and fourteen non-Shakespeare plays that were presented at the Globe between 1599 and 1609, Beckerman sets out general characteristics of staging, dramaturgy, and acting, as they affected the Chamberlain's (King's) Men, in which Shakespeare was the leading playwright, a principal "sharer" (or owner), and an actor. His chapter on dramaturgy has been especially influential because Beckerman tries to establish premises for a study of Shakespearean dramatic form.

In Beckerman's pages on scene structure, it becomes clear that the scene is the basic structural unit in Shakespeare and the Elizabethan drama. We should discard entirely our modern notion of acts, most of which were supplied by later editors. The sequence of scenes is quite different from that of a modern play, with much more attention to a rich, episodic development than to the forward movement of narrative. Multiple actions, as in *King Lear,* often alternate and interweave the scenes of one plot with those of another. As Beckerman puts it, "Within the framework of an Elizabethan scene, perhaps the most marked characteristic is the placement of emphasis not on the growth of action but on the character's response to crisis." Thus, the dramatic theme is realized through the effects it produces. Other books that concentrate on the architectonic power of the scene are Emrys Jones's *Scenic Form in Shakespeare* and Mark Rose's *Shakespearean Design.* Rose develops the idea of pictorial and emblematic scenes arranged in triptychs, a structural image from the fine arts.

The most persistent and most prolific of the stage-centered critics of Shakespeare has been John Russell Brown, who has shown himself to be both extremely radical in insisting that we immerse ourselves totally in the performed play and extremely practical in his step-by-step guide through various plays of Shakespeare. It is hard to imagine a more seductive proselytizer. Some of the chapter titles in his *Discovering Shakespeare* are a good index to Brown's approach: "Shakespeare Dead and Alive," "Parts for Actors," "Motivation and Subtext," "Shows for Audiences," "Stage Action," "Context," and "Engagement." The same rubrics could also serve for a study of Ibsen or Pinter.

Brown's point of view is most lucidly stated in the essay "The Theatrical Element of Shakespeare Criticism." With a dulcet and decorous tone, Brown asks us to make a giant leap in our commitment to Shakespeare in the theater. It is not enough merely to pay lip service to performance, both contemporary and historical. The responsible critic of Shakespeare must take the inevitable step of "becoming involved directly, at firsthand, with the process of a play in rehearsal and performance." Brown does not try to minimize the difficulties this method might encounter, but he is committed to pursuing a theatrical approach to Shakespeare wherever it might lead: "The true choice is not between a verbal reading and a theatrical one, but whether or not to allow Shakespeare's words to awaken—to create, as it were, on their own account; in the theater, which is its element, his text is the originator and energizer of all that we see and hear."

John L. Styan has also written and lectured extensively—and wittily—on how we are to interpret drama and especially Shakespeare, and even more especially, difficult and ambiguous examples of dark comedy. His book *Shakespeare's Stagecraft* gathers together everything we need to know about the theater to be wiser and more insightful readers of Shakespeare. Styan is always reminding us of the whole stage situation—for example, the mere presence of the silent Ophelia while Hamlet delivers his "To be, or not to be" soliloquy is a comment on that speech, or the menacing but wordless Aufidius, who is an observer of Coriolanus' yielding to his mother, defines the nature of that capitulation. "Gestic poetry" is one of Styan's apt phrases for the way in which action is projected into language: "Shakespeare's identification with his character worked so strongly within him that physical gesture forced itself upon the lines, moving the actor to reproduce its muscular activity," as in Hamlet's miming of his rage: "Who calls me villain?" (II. ii. 557). This is a kind of histrionic onomatopoeia, which insists that the verbal and nonverbal aspects of drama cannot be separated.

There has been a shift of emphasis in our period from director's Shakespeare to actor's Shakespeare. In other words, we no longer depend so heavily on the director's bright idea to carry a production but rather on the actors, individually and in ensemble, being able to realize the inherent powers of Shakespeare's text. No one has written more eloquently on this subject than Michael Goldman in *Shakespeare and the Energies of Drama* and *The Actor's Freedom*. Goldman succinctly states his concern in "Acting Values and Shakespearean Meaning: Some Suggestions": "The medium of drama, as I understand it, is not words or the stage, or even actors; it is acting, and I am trying to learn to read Shakespeare's plays as compositions in the medium of acting." Goldman's studies of Shakespeare are not so much directed to actors as to readers who are valiantly trying to come to grips with Shakespeare through an understanding of his characters as dramatic roles.

The chapter on *King Lear* in *Shakespeare and the Energies of Drama* is so moving because Goldman calls upon us to endure with the old King the painfulness and terror of his part. It is as painful to us as it is to him because it arouses in us pity and fear, the workings of which lead to what Aristotle in the *Poetics* called catharsis, a purgation of emotion. By the end of *King Lear,* "we should have been made to see and feel a succession of competing shocks, tortures, and degradations whose rhythm we recognize as bound up with our own abiding misery, which we make every effort to ignore or to convert into something less troublesome: our experience of the nothing that comes of not being all." In positing such a close compact between audience (or reader) and actor (or text), Goldman is making tremendous demands on us to participate in the experience of the play.

One practical spin-off of the theatrical approach to Shakespeare is the attempt to understand various nonverbal aspects of his plays, what we may call his presentational imagery. This is a departure from the exclusive concern with language in imagery studies in the tradition of Caroline Spurgeon. One good example of this nonverbal interest is Frances A. Shirley's *Shakespeare's Use of Off-Stage Sounds.* My essay "*Hamlet* Without Words" experimented with the idea of *Hamlet* as a nonverbal structure, or at least attempted to interpret the play without referring to the spoken language. Using a more modern linguistic approach, Brownell Salomon offers an engaging account of "Visual and Aural Signs in the Performed English Renaissance Play."

One problem remains: Whatever our good intentions and whatever our stated commitment to theatrical values, we must still deal with Shakespeare primarily through the medium of reading. The critics we have been discussing all require us to be extraordinary readers, with insights that cannot possibly come from the printed page alone. There is no way to resolve this paradox, but at least we are no longer required to think of Shakespeare's plays as extended poems and to approach them as we would a difficult poem by John Donne.

We must tackle the problem of "Shakespeare's unpoetic poetry," as in my short essay of that name. Eloquence on the stage is essentially different from the eloquence of metaphysical poetry; Cordelia's ineloquent "And so I am! I am!" and Lear's "Pray you undo this button" are intensely moving in their dramatic context. The question is most cunningly discussed by Inga-Stina Ewbank in "'More Pregnantly Than Words': Some Uses and Limitations of

Visual Symbolism" and by Dieter Mehl in "Visual and Rhetorical Imagery and Shakespeare's Plays." Alan C. Dessen has many shrewd and telling points to add to this topic in *Elizabethan Drama and the Viewer's Eye.*

We can bring this discussion of the theatrical aspect of Shakespeare to a conclusion by considering Jean E. Howard's *Shakespeare's Art of Orchestration.* We look in vain here for studies of sources, intellectual traditions, the background of ideas, or even character studies, an account of imagery or dominant symbols, or language and style as something separable from theatrical expression. These older topics have disappeared. Instead, we have various aspects of Shakespearean orchestration, which is a nice musical analogue of dramaturgy. Without feeling the need for defensive argumentation, Howard assumes many of the radical theatrical ideas that Shakespeare critics have so passionately debated for more than a decade.

The purpose of the book is stated with unequivocal boldness: "In this book I want to look at some of the ways in which Shakespeare works his theatrical magic. Specifically, I will examine his orchestration, through the playscript, of the aural, visual, and kinetic dimensions of stage production—in other words, his control of the sensory dimensions of the implied performance." The use of the word *playscript* rather than *play* is a sign of a new way of thinking about Shakespeare. It is not that Howard has points to make that are essentially different from Beckerman, Brown, Styan, or Goldman, but rather that she so coolly and confidently assumes that the reader is familiar with her methodology and will more or less agree with her values. The final chapter on *Twelfth Night* is simple, straightforward, and eminently practical, but it demands from its readers a degree of theatrical sophistication that would have been unthinkable in 1960.

Film

The study of Shakespeare as performed on film and on videotape is also part of a renewed interest in performance. Cinema and television have been used extensively in teaching Shakespeare, especially in areas where there is little or no access to theater. The preferred method is to show two or more film or television versions of a single play, which can then be discussed in relation to each other as well as to the printed text. Film and televi-

sion reach out to a large new audience that would not otherwise be exposed to "live" Shakespeare. There is a *Shakespeare on Film Newsletter* filled with reviews of productions and general information, and there are many relevant reviews in the *Literature/Film Quarterly.*

Jack J. Jorgens' *Shakespeare on Film* is the basic book in this area, and what makes it so admirable is the largeness of the author's vision. He is not narrowly technical or professional about the film medium; he thinks of it as continuous with the needs and concerns of theatrical expression. Jorgens' opening chapter, "Realizing Shakespeare on Film," sets out some of the critical questions that arise when we move from one medium to another. Should the film version of a Shakespeare play be theatrical and try to transcribe and re-create the theatrical experience? Should the Shakespeare film take advantage of the camera's unique ability to photograph the real world and emphasize settings, as Renato Castellani did in his version of *Romeo and Juliet?* Or should the film work in a completely filmic medium, translating and recasting the play into effective aural and visual images, as Orson Welles and the Russian director Grigori Kozintsev do? It is obvious where Jorgens' sympathies lie, and he is not alone in his high praise for Welles's *Chimes at Midnight* and *Othello* and Kozintsev's *Hamlet* and *King Lear.*

It is not surprising that academic purists never like Shakespearean films—or most stage productions—since they are not reconciled to the idea that the text of the play is not immutably fixed and established on the printed page. One axiom of Shakespearean filmmaking seems to be that the closer the film is to the text the duller it is, which may explain why it is so difficult to make excellent movies out of classic and much-loved novels. Film is not primarily a verbal medium, yet the problem of making a Shakespeare film lies not so much in the language itself as in translating that language and all it implies into the film medium. The most effective Shakespeare films make free and imaginative use of the text.

Kozintsev delivered some eloquent remarks on this subject to the World Shakespeare Congress of 1971. He rejects the shallow attractions of realism: "If I were offered the opportunity of shooting *Hamlet* at Elsinore itself, I wouldn't take it. Historical and geographical authenticity are not the authenticity of poetry. They are often contradictory. What one sees in the mind cannot easily be translated into visual terms." This in part answers the facile cinematic demand that everything in the play be converted into a visual equivalent—most literally, that what is spoken about in the poetry should be pictured on the screen. Kozintsev is careful not to fall between the stools of theater and cinema. If film is indeed a visual art, then the problem in a Shakespeare film is how to shift the stress from the aural to the visual. The answer is not simple: "The poetic texture has itself to be transformed into a visual poetry, into the dynamic organisation of film imagery." One never feels in Kozintsev's *Hamlet* or *King Lear* the indifference or actual contempt for Shakespeare's poetry that is so strongly evident in Franco Zeffirelli's *Romeo and Juliet.*

One of the most searching discussions of realism versus poetry in film is John Fuegi's essay "Explorations in No Man's Land: Shakespeare's Poetry as Theatrical Film." The no-man's-land of the title is that shadowy area between literature and cinematography. Fuegi decisively rejects realism as an end in itself, and he stresses the importance of sound as well as sight. The author is optimistic about achieving poetic effects in Shakespeare films because the text is not a barrier, as has usually been thought, but a great stimulus to the filmmaker's imagination.

On the subject of the sound track, Charles Hurtgen objects to grand-opera techniques in scoring a film, because they tend to make the spoken words sound like recitative (as in Olivier's "To be, or not to be" soliloquy). His essay "The Operatic Character of Background Music in Film Adaptations of Shakespeare" is a plea for a better balance between words and music in Shakespeare films. Directors should try to overcome their obvious embarrassment with Shakespeare's poetry and not try to drown it out with grandiose music.

Another approach to this question is the imaginative use of nonmusical sounds that relate symbolically to the words being spoken, as in the movies of Orson Welles. Samuel Crowl praises Welles's creativity in *Chimes at Midnight* for improving the balance of the Henry IV plays and for redressing the overemphasis on Prince Hal in most stage productions ("The Long Goodbye: Welles and Falstaff"). The next logical step is to ask if we should rewrite Shakespeare to conform with the movie. The question is absurd because we are speaking of interpretation and performance rather than the establishing of a definitive text. Later interpreters of the *Henry IV* plays, both in the theater and on film, will undoubtedly want to do them differently. As

spectators of performance we are asked to affirm our willing suspension of disbelief so that the moviemaker or director can present his own authentically imagined and integrated version of the play we read.

Two practical books in this area, with detailed filmographies, are Robert Hamilton Ball's *Shakespeare on Silent Film* and Roger Manvell's *Shakespeare and the Film.* There is a good collection of essays by Charles W. Eckert, *Focus on Shakespearean Films.*

The issues we have been discussing are more or less summed up in Sidney Homan and Neil Feineman's "The Filmed Shakespeare: From Verbal to Visual." The authors present five general theories on the possibility of translating Shakespeare's plays to a primarily visual medium such as the cinema: (1) It is impossible to translate any play into a movie while retaining the aesthetic integrity of both media. (2) Shakespeare can be translated to the screen, but the resulting product can at best only be inspired by the play. (3) Shakespeare can be translated to the cinema, not just adapted, but everything verbal must find a filmic or visual equivalent. (4) In the cinema, words and images are not inimical, and a proper combination of the two allows for fidelity to Shakespeare's intentions. (5) One should just film the play, perhaps taking some advantage of the camera's ability to provide close-ups and other cinematic tricks to heighten tension. The gamut of possibilities raises questions that cannot be definitively answered at this stage in the development of the Shakespearean film.

The related issue of Shakespeare on television cannot be considered in the same terms as Shakespeare on film, since videotaping is essentially a different art from filmmaking. The BBC-TV series of the early 1980s, which includes all of Shakespeare, has generally seemed disappointing to critics, who thought that too many of the productions were rather static (especially the early ones) or so far from the play as to be almost in competition with it (as in Jonathan Miller's oddly deflationary and debunking interpretations).

Is there a distinctively televisionary style analogous to the filmic style that Jorgens favors? Actors have always complained about the tightness of the television setting and the lack of mobility in videotaping, even with three or more cameras. This is similar to viewers' objections to the constricted quality of plays made for television. The excessive use of close-ups as a way of rendering Shakespeare's soliloquies made *Henry VIII* and some of the earlier plays seem like a progression of talking heads. Studio productions tend to seem stagy and artificial and to lose that quality of vivid realism associated with on-location shooting, but for reasons of economy and ease, the BBC had to make most of the series in a studio. Thus, *Twelfth Night* was neatly and domestically confined, whereas *As You Like It,* videotaped out-of-doors at Glamis Castle in Scotland, had a certain pastoral excitement that we tend to associate with festive comedy. *As You Like It* was more filmic than *Twelfth Night,* which may not seem like such a good thing to television purists. Some of these generic issues are raised in my review "Shakespearean Anglophilia: The BBC-TV Series and American Audiences." The directors of the BBC series are so steeped in theater techniques that they are diffident about bringing Shakespeare to life on the home screen.

Feminism

The feminist approach to Shakespeare developed with enormous rapidity, especially after 1970. Was Shakespeare a feminist? The question has been debated with great zeal on both sides, and Shakespeare has been accused of a sexist and patriarchal bias that he would have found difficult to understand. Unlike most of his fellow dramatists, Shakespeare creates bright, witty, resourceful, and intelligent heroines—something unusual for his period. Except for Juliet, these lovely and forceful heroines occur chiefly in the comedies, whereas in the tragedies there are a great many tigerish and antimaternal women (like Lady Macbeth and Volumnia) or whorish vamps (like Cressida and Cleopatra in some interpretations). There is also a good deal of disillusioned sex nausea in the tragedies, especially in such characters as Hamlet, Troilus, and King Lear. Feminist critics have been especially disturbed by Lear's mad diatribe against women:

But to the girdle do the gods inherit,
Beneath is all the fiend's.
There's hell, there's darkness, there is the sulphurous
pit, burning, scalding, stench, consumption.

(IV. vi. 125–128)

Linda Fitz has very cleverly nailed male critics of *Antony and Cleopatra* for their alarmingly chauvinist views of the play ("Egyptian Queens and Male Reviewers"). Male critics feel personally threatened by Cleopatra and all she represents of aggressive and destructive sexuality. Cleopatra is converted from a tragic heroine in a play with historical roots to an archetype of woman—incomprehensible, torridly sexual, and ultimately living only for pleasure and self-fulfillment. The political issues of the play are more or less forgotten in relation to Cleopatra. Fitz has latched onto a splendid topic, male fear of women, but it is not clear whether the critics are only stand-ins for Shakespeare himself, who must have had all the same anxieties as his Antony.

The first book of feminist criticism of Shakespeare was Juliet Dusinberre's *Shakespeare and the Nature of Women,* which has proved to be the most influential. The book deals with both Shakespeare and Elizabethan drama, but its real interest is in the intellectual currents of the time. Reviewers have taken the author to task for her overly optimistic view of both humanism and Puritanism as movements that tended to value women highly and to support feminist ideas in this period. She is too much interested in the role models supplied to dramatists by vigorous women in public life such as Queen Elizabeth and Moll Frith, the Roaring Girl. Is the drama from 1590 to 1625 really "feminist in sympathy," and are Shakespeare's women "not an isolated phenomenon in their emancipation, their self-sufficiency, and their evasion of stereotypes"? Dusinberre is thinking chiefly of the women in the comedies. Despite a certain overzealous commitment, Dusinberre has affected most later feminist criticism by the seriousness and boldness of her approach. She attracts attention, for example, to the significant topic of the boy actors who played all women's parts and of women characters disguised as men, by which means they could speak their minds freely. This is not really androgyny, as some feminist critics have claimed, but a kind of cross-gender license like that of the Fool.

One of the most subtle critiques of Dusinberre is Martha Andresen-Thom's "Thinking About Women and Their Prosperous Art: A Reply to Juliet Dusinberre's *Shakespeare and the Nature of Women."* The author salubriously reminds us that Shakespeare is a writer of romance, who uses standard themes, stereotypes, and literary commonplaces in relation to women. There is no reason to think that, by privileging feminist criticism, we can immediately separate women from all other romance materials. Her account of the myth of the Silent Woman is especially fascinating. Surely Desdemona is so wonderfully loquacious and insistently sexual in the earlier parts of *Othello* that one wonders why she becomes the Silent Woman, so patiently anticipating her ritual slaughter? Why doesn't she protest vociferously, as she might have done in Act I? Andresen-Thom rightly insists that Shakespeare's most direct sources for his women were fictional and literary rather than drawn from social fact, as Dusinberre suggests. Without ignoring the ferment of ideas in Shakespeare's time and the wealth of models he could have drawn from public life, domestic life, or life in Stratford, a critic could hardly call his plays documentary.

The best way to sample feminist criticism of Shakespeare is in the excellent anthology *The Woman's Part,* put together by Carolyn Ruth Swift Lenz, Gayle Greene, and Carol Thomas Neely. The editors' introduction sums up both feminist values and the basic assumptions of a feminist approach to Shakespeare. They quote a sentence from Dusinberre that has become a rallying cry for feminist critics: "The struggle for women is to be human in a world which declares them only female." There are four primary objectives of the feminist criticism of Shakespeare: (1) to "liberate Shakespeare's women from the stereotypes to which they have too often been confined"; (2) to "examine women's relations to each other"; (3) to "analyze the nature and effects of patriarchal structures"; and (4) to "explore the influence of genre on the portrayal of women." There is a sense of freshness in this volume, as if the critics were reading Shakespeare for the first time.

The essay by Clara Claiborne Park, "As We Like It: How a Girl Can Be Smart and Still Popular," considers the heroines of Shakespeare's comedies. Park plays with the paradox of the brilliant, energetic, witty, beautiful, and desirable heroines of Shakespeare's comedies—Rosalind in *As You Like It,* Viola in *Twelfth Night,* Portia in *The Merchant of Venice,* and Beatrice in *Much Ado About Nothing.* (We could add Juliet and Desdemona to this list for at least the early part of their plays.) Why is it paradoxical? Because "if the bright young girl is to be made acceptable—to audiences, to readers, perhaps even to her creator—ways must be found to reduce the impact of her self-confidence, to make sure that equality is kept nominal."

From Park's perspective, Shakespeare's come-

dies are not so feminist as they might seem because there is a self-regulating system at work. Shakespeare's high-spirited comic heroine is a woman who will tame herself:

> She offers both men and women that most precious of assurances—that they can have it both ways. To women, a girl like Beatrice affirms their bright potentialities, but also the warm safety of their conviction that these should never be displayed in any way that could threaten men. The men in the audience—like the men in the play—can enjoy her company, free from both the threat of insubordination and the necessity of putting her in her place.

This is a wonderfully practical argument that more or less undercuts all of Dusinberre's extravagant claims.

Park's position is reinforced by male disguise, which allows the heroine to extend her role in exciting ways not possible for a decorous woman. She can jest broadly and even woo for herself without fear of recrimination. Rosalind in disguise as "Ganymede" (which is also an Elizabethan slang term for an effeminate man) takes charge of her love affair and makes Orlando seem terribly passive. Male disguise offers a kind of license to seize the prerogatives otherwise denied to properly brought up women. "With male dress we feel secure. In its absence, feminine assertiveness is viewed with hostility. . . . Male dress transforms what otherwise could be experienced as aggression into simple high spirits."

Madness, either involuntary or assumed, functions as another form of disguise by which otherwise decent women can assert themselves, indulge in a free associational lyric excess, talk dirty, and sing snatches of bawdy songs, as Ophelia does in *Hamlet.* Like the putting on of male attire, madness represents the assumption of a new role with its own special speech. (This subject is explored in "The Language of Madwomen in Shakespeare and His Fellow Dramatists," by Maurice Charney and Hanna Charney.)

The Woman's Part is so rich and various a collection that it is difficult to focus on just a few characteristic essays. On the negative side is the character analysis offered by Rebecca Smith in "A Heart Cleft in Twain: The Dilemma of Shakespeare's Gertrude," which is very shaky. Smith objects violently to the sexist criticism of Gertrude as a sensual, deceitful woman, and she supports her position by the portrait of the queen as she actually is in the play: "a soft, obedient, dependent, unimaginative woman who is caught miserably at the center of a desperate struggle between two 'mighty opposites.'" But how can Smith, operating on sound feminist principles, presume to bowdlerize the play of Hamlet's, and to some extent of Claudius', view of Gertrude? That is what the play is about, and whether or not we believe literally in Hamlet's inflamed and febrile imaginings, there can be no soft Gertrude apart from the way the other characters see her. This reduces feminist criticism to a rescue operation for Shakespeare's fallen women.

Linda Bamber takes heterodox positions in *Comic Women, Tragic Men.* She is dissatisfied with just about all feminist critics, with the possible (or impossible) exception of Leslie Fiedler, because she thinks they make the soppy assumption that Shakespeare must be a feminist. She is particularly concerned with the powerful misogyny of Shakespeare's tragedies, which suggests that he was preoccupied with the dark side of female sexuality. How are we to explain such "nightmare female figures" as Goneril, Regan, Lady Macbeth, and Volumnia? "For these characters are not just women who happen to be evil; their evil is inseparable from their failures as women." We have come a long way from the relatively easy optimism of Dusinberre's *Shakespeare and the Nature of Women,* whose cheerfulness and good tidings were no longer viable a mere decade later.

We should also note Irene G. Dash's theatrical study, *Wooing, Wedding, and Power: Women in Shakespeare's Plays,* which is grounded in theatrical history and has wonderful illustrations. The feminist argument emerges clearly from the evidence of promptbooks prepared by directors. The cuts, the alterations, the notes on performance all indicate the sexist bias of most Shakespearean productions, which should not surprise anyone who believes that the theater is a mirror of its times. Garrick, for example, rewrote *The Taming of the Shrew* as *Catherine and Petruchio,* and it dominated the stage from 1756 to 1886. Through elaborate cutting, his Kate is no longer an intelligent, witty, vigorous, rational young woman who has more or less been abandoned by her father in favor of her younger sister. At the very end, Garrick's Kate proclaims, without irony, "I see 'tis vain to struggle with my Bonds."

Psychoanalysis

The psychoanalytic approach to Shakespeare is closely intertwined with the new feminist criticism, because feminist critics want to lay bare the psychosexual underpinnings of received attitudes. Thus, Coppélia Kahn's *Man's Estate: Masculine Identity in Shakespeare* is both feminist and psychoanalytic in its assumptions. It is typical of the newer psychoanalytic criticism in the sense that it is not exclusively dependent on Freud. The names of Erik Erikson, Margaret Mahler, Edith Jacobson, and D. W. Winnicott appear frequently, and there is an attempt to extend psychoanalysis beyond the individual to the family and to society. Part of Kahn's book is devoted to the boyhood of Shakespeare's heroes; another significant part concerns itself with the larger context of the growing-up process.

The chapter on *Coriolanus* and *Macbeth* pairs the milking babe and the bloody man as countersymbols of an unsatisfied dependency on feminine influences. It is as if the hero is compelled to be violent and bloody in order to prove himself manly enough to be accepted by his exigently heroic mother-wife. Lady Macbeth is constantly harping on an ideal of manliness that has almost more effect on her than it does on her husband, as she rejects the milkiness of the maternal role and becomes the unsexed Amazonian warrior. Volumnia in *Coriolanus* is a later development of the Lady Macbeth role, more uncompromising because more firmly steeped in the Greco-Roman heroic tradition. Kahn sees "a paradox of sexual confusion" at the heart of *Macbeth* and *Coriolanus.* "Their virile warrior-heroes, supreme in valor, are at the same time unfinished men—boys, in a sense, who fight or murder because they have been convinced by women that only through violence will they achieve manhood." The women themselves are "half men." One could argue that Kahn is introducing a sentimental critique of manliness that is quite foreign to Shakespeare's own classical ideals, as Reuben Brower so forcefully argues in *Hero and Saint: Shakespeare and the Graeco-Roman Heroic Tradition* (1971).

The most important study of the psychoanalytic approach to Shakespeare is Norman N. Holland's long, detailed, and impressive *Psychoanalysis and Shakespeare.* My first reaction to the massive contribution of psychoanalytic critics to Shakespeare is to be repelled by the barbarousness of the language, the callous disregard of literary and theatrical values, and the zaniness of some of the symbolic thinking. There is an unhealthy interest in Shakespeare the man, playing various fictionalized roles as boy, husband, son, father, brother, and friend, as if the life of the author could be reconstructed from the fantasy materials of his works. But some of the psychoanalytic critics are highly imaginative, and the use of an entirely different symbol system frees criticism from its inherent prejudices. Ernst Kris, for example, comes to Shakespeare through the study of art history, and his *Psychoanalytic Explorations in Art* is stimulating and complex.

Nonpsychoanalytic readers will approach Holland's book as a compendium of insights, some preposterous and others exhilarating. Thus, to choose a few points at random, it is fascinating to follow up Alexander Grinstein's parallels between the play-within-the-play in *Hamlet* and the dream within a dream, or to pursue Franz Alexander's oedipal argument about Prince Hal, Falstaff, and the Henry IV plays. "We like Falstaff," Alexander concludes, "because he represents the child that remains forever in us and whom we prize, the 'narcissistic nucleus of human individuality.' "

Many of the papers Holland speaks about are included in M. D. Faber's large anthology *The Design Within: Psychoanalytic Approaches to Shakespeare*, which very well represents the older psychoanalytic criticism of Shakespeare. For one thing, it is overwhelmingly Freudian and orthodox, so that most of the critics create the illusion that they are only expanding on suggestions in Freud and writing the papers that Freud might have written himself, had he so wished.

It is interesting to see Robert J. Stoller, one of the leading authorities on sexual identity, both physiological and psychological, commenting on Coriolanus and his problems. Volumnia is the classic "phallic mother":

> For such a mother, a son is the literal embodiment of her phallus which from infancy she had wished to attain by one means or another. Subjected to such relentless pressures, her son may either surrender and become virtually emasculated, or he may be able partially to salvage his virility by acting out his mother's fantasy as her surrogate until his repressed (feminine) identification with her—and his guilt about his repressed hatred of her—lead him to contrive his destruction.

If we can get past the rebarbative psychoanalytic jargon, this is an excellent account of the psychodynamics of the play and one that has influenced many later critics. It is evident why *Coriolanus*, next to *Hamlet*, has attracted the most psychoanalytic interest. Both plays are painfully enmeshed in oedipal conflicts, as is also *The Merchant of Venice* (Shylock vs. Jessica), another favorite of psychoanalytic critics.

A more up-to-date anthology than Faber's is *Representing Shakespeare: New Psychoanalytic Essays,* edited by Murray M. Schwartz and Coppélia Kahn. This is strikingly more literate than Faber's collection, there is much less interest in constructing a hypothetical biography of Shakespeare from the evidence of his works, and the range of reference is much wider—R. D. Laing, Erikson, Winnicott, and Mahler compete for attention with Freud. Psychoanalysis in this volume is more closely allied with the study of literature, the other arts, and philosophy, and the one-to-one allegorizing that used to be practiced in the name of psychoanalytic criticism has fortunately disappeared. We are no longer oppressed with images of Hamlet losing control of his sphincter or Lear wetting himself on the heath.

One laudable tendency of this volume is the use of psychoanalysis to explore difficulties in Shakespeare—resistances, blockages, and ambiguities—rather than to restate the obvious in technical, scientist terms. Leonard Tennenhouse formulates the principle with admirable lucidity in his study of *The Merchant of Venice:* "A psychoanalytic description of literature seeks the subject's own vantage point in discovering the configuration of what is avowed, repressed, and defended. Psychoanalytic criticism thus has as its provenance the disturbing or seemingly incoherent features of a text." The two locales of the play, Venice and Belmont, are an aspect of Shakespeare's dramatic style "in which emotionally different areas of action are marked off by means of geographical boundaries." But in *The Merchant of Venice*, as in *Antony and Cleopatra*, the two locales stand for sexual identifications. Venice seems "masculine, competitive, and commercial," whereas Belmont seems "maternal, bountiful, and generous." Despite this firm symbolism, something seems to have gone wrong with the ending of the play, and we are left with an uncomfortable and disturbing resolution. A dark cloud hangs over Belmont in the fifth act.

Meredith Skura also uses psychoanalytic methods to engage difficult plays or to untangle problems in interpretation, and her literary sophistication is by no means sacrificed to psychoanalytic simplifications (which may be disguised by jargonistic display). Her essay on *Cymbeline* is offered as an experiment "to see how a psychoanalytic bias can be of use in coming to terms with difficult works ... which do not readily fit into expected patterns." The psychoanalytic categories are posited to explain "puzzling details." Skura argues her case against a general background of romance assumptions, especially the paradox of the family so evident in kinship studies: "The family is so important that characters cannot even imagine themselves without one, yet every family must bring on its own destruction." Thus, the story of Posthumus learning how to be a proper son is a shaping influence on the story of his learning how to be a proper husband: "There is no way for him to find himself as husband until he finds himself as son, as part of the family he was torn from long ago." Skura's discourse is sinuous and subtle.

The most impressive essay in the volume is Janet Adelman's " 'Anger's My Meat': Feeding, Dependency, and Aggression in *Coriolanus.*" Some of these themes have already been touched on by Kahn and Stoller, especially the relation of the nonnurturant mother to her ferocious son. In the reversal of values at the heart of the play, "blood is more beautiful than milk, the wound than the breast, warfare than peaceful feeding." The act of eating is debased as a form of physiological dependence, and the tragic issue in the play is Coriolanus' almost hysterical claim to stand alone "as if a man were author of himself / And knew no other kin" (V. iii. 36–37). This inhuman goal is unattainable, and the hero is destroyed by his capitulation to his mother in sparing Rome. Adelman shows us how we can combine imagery study, old-fashioned scholarship, and a sensitivity to dramatic language with psychoanalytic concepts to illuminate a difficult play.

In this light, Skura's *The Literary Use of the Psychoanalytic Process* reads like a devil's advocate's statement of everything that could possibly go wrong with the psychoanalytic approach to literature. This wise book is not exclusively concerned with Shakespeare, although there is a substantial discussion of *Measure for Measure.* The play is particularly amenable to psychoanalytic comment just because it is difficult and problematic. Psychoanalysis can bring to the discussion "its distrust of literal reference; its lack of tact and its openness to coun-

terintuitive meanings; and its self-consciousness about the process of interpretation." Are the problems in the play sexual or economic? Either way, they center on exchange, "either a holding back—whether represented by Angelo's cold righteousness, Isabella's religion, the neurotic distrust of sexuality that has been hinted at in both characters, or even simple modesty like Mariana's—or else the opposite, a sexual exchange that occurs only in a dehumanized way." What is so rewarding about this commentary is that it makes no attempt to simplify complex issues. The best rationale for psychoanalytic criticism is that it is uniquely suited to explain Shakespeare's paradoxes and ambiguities.

A final sample of the possibilities of psychoanalytic explanations is Barbara Freedman's study of *The Comedy of Errors:* "Errors in Comedy: A Psychoanalytic Theory of Farce." This essay offers a lively theory of an entire genre whose dreamlike quality is produced by an attempt to block aggression. Freedman defines farce as "a dramatic genre deriving laughter chiefly from the denial of the cause (through absurdity) and the effect (through surrealism) of aggressive action upon an object." It is the intent of farce to seem meaningless and nonsensical in order to divert attention from its underlying aggressive impulses. "The secret of the strange enjoyment of farce may be that although we enjoy fulfilling forbidden wishes, we enjoy punishing them just as much, if not more, particularly when we can do so in a plot which is apparently devoid of logic, meaning, and harm." Freedman then goes on to a highly subtle analysis of what has generally been thought of as one of Shakespeare's simplest plays.

Marxism

The Marxist approach to Shakespeare is difficult to define, since Karl Marx made only scattered remarks on Shakespeare, and his social, economic, and political insights do not have a direct relation to literature. Nonetheless, Marxist critics have more or less common assumptions about the nature of society as it is depicted in Shakespeare's works, and they come to the plays with both a high level of sociological generalization and their customary set of critical terms.

One of our best Marxist critics, Paul N. Siegel, proposes a series of questions a Marxist might ask about Shakespeare and his historical and intellectual milieu. In relation to E. M. W. Tillyard's non-Marxist synthesis, *The Elizabethan World Picture,* for example, a Marxist would want to know "what were the material and ideological forces that brought about the modification of the medieval 'world picture' . . . and how the Elizabethan world picture is a rationalization of the social position of the Elizabethan ruling class and an expression of its outlook." Or about Falstaff: "How does the social psychology of the Elizabethan class of which he is a member affect his depiction? What are the material roots of this social psychology?" Or about the exciting intellectual movements of the 1590s and early 1600s: "How did the developments in the economy, political events, and shifts in thought and feeling interact upon each other to produce 'the Shakespearean moment'?"

These questions echo the strong link between history and literature—or more properly, society and literature—posited by Marxist critics, who seek out a kind of historical determinism in their study of Shakespeare. No author is sui generis, and in order to understand Shakespeare one must study Elizabethan and Jacobean society and the ideological context in which his work was written and presented. Siegel raises these important issues in a special number of *The Shakespeare Newsletter* devoted to Marxist interpretations.

Siegel's book *Shakespearean Tragedy and the Elizabethan Compromise,* first published in 1957, was reissued in 1983 with the subtitle *A Marxist Study.* The author explains in his new introduction that most readers of the earlier edition did not perceive the Marxist orientation. This is either a tribute to Siegel's lack of dogmatism or the vagueness of the book's debt to a specifically Marxist criticism. Siegel's Christian humanism, for example, could hardly be construed as a Marxist topic. The new introduction tries to make the Marxism of the book much more explicit: "I argued that the analysis of Shakespeare's ideological position helps us to perceive the better the aesthetic patterns of his plays and that the perception of these patterns provides us with an experience that both has significance for us today and is affected by our own life's experience." Siegel attempts to refute the anti-Marxist thesis of Ann Jennalie Cook's *Privileged Playgoers of Shakespeare's London, 1576–1642,* which claims that Shakespeare's audience was not at all popular and plebeian. It is crucial for the Marxist view of Shakespeare that the audiences of the Elizabethan public playhouses be composed of artisans, small shopkeepers, and their apprentices, as Alfred Harbage claims in *Shakespeare's Audience.*

Siegel's essay "Marx, Engels, and the Historical Criticism of Shakespeare" is also a valuable introduction to our subject. He presents in some detail Marx's comments on Shakespeare (and, to a lesser extent, those of Engels), chiefly on *The Merchant of Venice* and *Timon of Athens.* These plays, and especially *Timon,* helped Marx define an acquisitive and capitalist view of life: "a world of atomized, mutually hostile individuals" in which there is "no other nexus between man and man than naked self-interest." *The Economic and Philosophical Manuscripts* of 1844 contain Marx's commentary on Timon's two apostrophes to his newly found gold: "Shakespeare portrays the essence of money excellently. . . . If money is the bond that binds me to human life, that binds society to me and me to nature and men, is not money the bond of all bonds? . . . It is the universal whore, the pander between men and peoples." Marx's trenchant remarks echo the language of both Shylock and Timon.

Kenneth Muir discusses Marx's use of *Timon* in a fascinating essay, *"Timon of Athens* and the Cash-Nexus." The reading of *Timon* came early enough in Marx's career to be influential on his thinking. Muir playfully suggests that Shakespeare was one of the spiritual godfathers of *The Communist Manifesto:* "Marx would doubtless have become a Communist even if he had never read *Timon of Athens,* but his reading of that play helped him to crystallize his ideas." We recall that *Timon of Athens* also exercised a peculiar fascination on Vladimir Nabokov in *Pale Fire* (1962).

Robert Weimann is undoubtedly the most sophisticated, subtle, and abstract of the Marxist critics of Shakespeare. His *Shakespeare and the Popular Tradition in the Theater* has been translated, condensed, and brought up to date by Robert Schwartz from a work first published in German in 1967. Unfortunately, although the translation uses English words, it is not fully rendered in spoken English. Despite his enormous learning, Weimann's thesis is extremely simple: that we have neglected the popular theatrical tradition that lies behind Shakespeare and have preferred instead literary and classical models even when they are not relevant. This is also the point of view argued by David Bevington, Alan Dessen, and Glynne Wickham.

Like Siegel, Weimann is aware that the assumption of a popular audience and a tradition of popular, native plays is indispensable for the Marxist link between theater and society:

> It is only when Elizabethan society, theater, and language are seen as interrelated that the structure of Shakespeare's dramatic art emerges as fully functional—that is, as part of a larger, and not only literary, whole. To understand verbal artistry as an element in the total function of the Shakespearean stage, dramatic speech must be considered both as a process between actors and audiences and as a vision of society, as an integral part of the history of the nation that Shakespeare's theater both reflected and helped to create.

That "vision of society" represents Marxist criticism at its most eloquent, and Weimann, of course, rejects the theories of a coterie drama that Harbage posits in *Shakespeare and the Rival Traditions.* In Weimann's approach the subliterary culture assumes an almost excessive importance for Shakespeare, and folk plays, moralities, and interludes are featured in place of more learned and classically derived sources.

In "Shakespeare's Wordplay: Popular Origins and Theatrical Functions," this attitude extends to Weimann's attack on the rhetorical approach. Critics like T. W. Baldwin and Sister Miriam Joseph ignore Shakespeare's vital connection with a medieval tradition of punning and wordplay, especially as this is linked with the questioning of authority in festive comedy. Wordplay is a subversive medium that undermines the public, officially sanctioned language. It also conveys "the actor's sense of his social identity." Weimann is here very close to the theories of comedy and society in Mikhail Bakhtin's *Rabelais and His World.*

In Weimann's eloquent essay "The Soul of the Age," *historical,* as in the "historical approach" to Shakespeare, functions as a code word for the Marxist approach, and sometimes the word *humanist* is used in the same way. It is historical in the sense that Shakespeare is seen in his historical and ideological context. In order to understand the plays properly, "we can (and we must) reconstruct the economic conditions, the social status, the moral assumptions, and the literary tastes of the typical representatives of Shakespeare's audience." While this kind of cultural perception of Shakespeare in his own time is valuable in itself, it would be equally valuable to understand Shakespeare in relation to Elizabethan literature, classical models, and the history and conventions of the theater. It is the old, insoluble argument of the indebtedness of literature to life and to other literature.

Actually, most of the critics in Arnold Kettle's Marxist anthology *Shakespeare in a Changing World* are much more inclined to discuss Shakespeare in critical and theatrical terms than in historical terms (in Weimann's sense). The Marxist orientation is not obvious in many of the essays. The most overtly Marxist contribution, at least in phraseology, is Raymond Southall's *"Troilus and Cressida* and the Spirit of Capitalism." In Southall's formulation the world of chivalry and romance in the play is set against "the powers of personal and social corruption inherent in the appetitive spirit of capitalism." To make Pandarus a representative of emergent capitalism in a period that saw the weakening of feudal relations is to distort the fictive status of the play for the sake of ideological values. "The undermining of the old feudal relations and the emergence of a potent bourgeois ethic" may be "pertinent to any truly sociological consideration of Elizabethan literature," but I have my doubts whether it helps us understand *Troilus and Cressida.*

One of the best Marxist essays of the 1970s is Paul Delany's *"King Lear* and the Decline of Feudalism." Delany makes good use of European Marxist theory (György Lukács, Lucienn Goldmann) to develop a thesis similar to Southall's but more relevant to the play. Like Pandarus, Edmund typifies the "new bourgeois ethic of irreverent, individualist acquisitiveness," and the play demonstrates a dialectical conflict between the old order of the feudal aristocracy, of which Lear is the chief representative, and the new order of the emergent bourgeois state, represented by Goneril, Regan, Cornwall, and Edmund. One of the gratifying points of Delany's essay is the tacit acknowledgment that even Marxist critics, with a full load of ideological baggage, must still work close to the texts they are writing about.

Anne Paolucci is by no means a committed Marxist critic—probably just the opposite—yet her essay "Marx, Money, and Shakespeare: The Hegelian Core in Marxist Shakespeare-Criticism" is extremely informative. It is interesting how much Marx borrows from Hegel, especially in his *Timon*-related philosophy of money; Marx had written and published an introductory critique to Hegel's *Philosophy of Right* in 1843. Paolucci is scandalized by the fatuousness of some Soviet Marxist criticism of Shakespeare, as in the dismissive judgment of Anatoli Lunacharski: "Shakespeare's tragic outlook on the world was consequential upon his being the dramatic expression of the feudal aristocracy, which in Elizabeth's day had lost their former dominant position." For Paolucci, this makes a mockery of the complexity of Marxist-Hegelian thinking.

Iconography

The iconographic approach to Shakespeare flourished after 1960, stimulated by the high value placed on the union of the arts and tempted by the difficulties inherent in any interdisciplinary subject. The main inspiration for literary critics has been the work of Erwin Panofsky, especially *Studies in Iconology* (1939), although other critics associated with the Warburg and Courtauld Institutes and the journal they publish have also been influential (for example, Fritz Saxl, Rudolf Wittkower, and Julius Held). Critics of Shakespeare have invoked the visual and pictorial traditions of the emblem books (both English and continental), of the arts of design (especially needlework), and of the great storehouse of symbols in paintings, sculpture, and the graphic arts. Engraved frontispieces and title pages of books, for example, have been a rich source of visual imagery.

The best place to begin this discussion is with William S. Heckscher's magisterial essay "Shakespeare in His Relationship to the Visual Arts: A Study in Paradox." With wide learning and copious illustrations, this article touches on most of the important aspects of iconography. In his introductory topics, for example, Hecksher has a note about Falstaff's pillow as a dramatic emblem. To Dürer, in the engraving *The Doctor's Dream,* as to Shakespeare, "the pillow spelled out the vice of *Acedia* with a capital letter. The systems of the deadly sins had taught that Sloth-*Acedia* prepares the ground for the vice of *Luxuria*." A large part of Heckscher's essay is devoted to explicating the figure of Patience, as she appears in two passages in Shakespeare *(Twelfth Night* and *Pericles).* These texts are perfectly explicit in themselves, yet the wide network of classical allusion and visual archetype provides a richness of background that is not immediately predictable from Shakespeare alone. The iconographical approach supplies a depth of perspective to the allusions in the text.

This expansive effect is abundantly evident in John M. Steadman's splendid "Falstaff as Actaeon: A Dramatic Emblem." It enriches our understanding of *The Merry Wives of Windsor* to learn how closely Falstaff as Herne the Hunter is modeled on Actaeon, who was torn to pieces by his own dogs —an emblem of the self-destructive quality of lust. Shakespeare had already used the Actaeon myth in *Twelfth Night* for the mooning Duke Orsino, whose "desires, like fell and cruel hounds, / E'er since pursue me" (I. i. 23–24). Obviously we do not need Steadman's learned study to reveal to us that the aging Falstaff is lustful and will be appropriately chastised in all of his adventures. But Steadman's own adventures in Renaissance iconography and mythography enlighten our understanding of Shakespeare's artistry in *The Merry Wives.* It is surprising how close Shakespeare is to the received pictorial traditions for Actaeon. The fine arts do not play a large role directly in Shakespeare's work— although Giulio Romano is remembered as the sculptor of Hermione's statue in *The Winter's Tale* —but Shakespeare seems to have shared with many artists of his time the same heritage of pictorial representation.

Steadman's valuable "Iconography and Renaissance Drama: Ethical and Mythological Themes" argues for a humanistic tradition on which Renaissance poets and painters drew, with the same ethical and mythological values. It is no surprise, therefore, that they should convey subject matter or meaning in similar ways. Yet there is great danger in making facile links between visual and verbal icons; the symbolic tradition is "not only complex but often ambiguous and equivocal." Only rarely can contemporary emblems and iconologies provide us with demonstrable sources for Renaissance drama. It is rather a question of analogues and parallels. Steadman recognizes that the problems of ascertaining iconographical sources are much greater in the drama than in poetry. The poet tends to be much more explicit in his communication with the reader than the playwright with his audience.

In "Trends and Problems in the Study of Emblematic Literature," Peter M. Daly learnedly corroborates Steadman's conclusion that it is difficult, and perhaps not very valuable, to hunt for specific sources, especially in the study of Shakespeare. Since the emblematic literature is so extensive, reaching beyond emblem books as such, it is not rewarding to try to pin down what is essentially a common symbolism.

In an interesting pair of articles, Dieter Mehl demonstrates what can be done with "Emblems in

English Renaissance Drama'' but also warns us against the misuse of ''Emblematic Theatre.'' In the first essay, Mehl states that emblematic elements have three main functions in English Renaissance drama: (1) They can be directly borrowed or quoted, but in their dramatic context they tend to lose their static and pictorial character and are hardly recognizable as emblems. (2) They can be inserted as ''allegorical scenes or tableaux providing a pictorial commentary on the action of the play, thus creating that mutually illuminating combination of word and picture which is central to the emblematic method.'' (3) They could enter more organically into the plays as emblematic images in the course of a scene, presentational images that combine verbal and pictorial expression. Mehl comes to the emblem literature through the study of drama rather than through art history, so that he is admirably cautious in using emblems to enrich the verbal context. In ''Emblematic Theatre,'' he is rather aghast at the indiscriminate and fashionable application of emblems to the study of Renaissance drama. Many of the visual effects claimed for Shakespeare are, paradoxically, read into the plays and projected into performance by a too-zealous subtlety.

Hamlet has lent itself especially well to iconographic study. Roland Mushat Frye has written an informative account, ''Ladies, Gentlemen, and Skulls: *Hamlet* and the Iconographic Traditions.'' Beginning with Hamlet's contemplation of the skull of Yorick in the graveyard, Frye leads us through the traditions behind that visual commonplace, especially the high points of the memento mori imagery. As in many iconographic studies, there are no surprises that might impinge on our understanding of the play; the visual analogues are rather directed to deepening our awareness of a familiar theme. In another direction, they should also clarify the staging of this crucial image, for the staging itself is another visual analogue for the written text.

Bridget Gellert Lyons' essay ''The Iconography of Ophelia'' is unusual among studies of this sort for the light it casts on the interpretation of Ophelia. She is, for Hamlet and for the audience alike, ''a problem in iconography,'' and her part is conceived in almost excessively emblematic terms. When her father sets her up to be reading as she encounters Hamlet, she immediately evokes the familiar image of the Virgin reading at the moment of the Annunciation. Everything about Ophelia is

double and ambiguous. Her mad flower-dispensing scene calls up the image of Flora, who is both a pastoral nature goddess and an urban courtesan. The overt sexuality of this scene makes it easy to associate the offering of flowers with deflowering. Perdita, too, offers flowers in the sheep-shearing scene of *The Winter's Tale,* but she controls the symbolism in a way that is not available to the mad Ophelia. There is definitely a gap between the pastoral world and the contaminated world of Claudius' Denmark. This study is a model of how iconographical learning can be combined with subtle literary criticism.

Lawrence J. Ross is undoubtedly the most learned, the most surprising, and the most prolific commentator on Shakespeare's iconography. Ross comes to the study of visual materials with a background in Shakespeare and Elizabethan drama and a deep commitment to Christian symbolism. His range of allusion is astonishing, and he presents his case with polemical fervor.

An early essay, ''The Meaning of Strawberries in Shakespeare,'' is typical of the method. Beginning with three allusions to strawberries—in *Othello* (the ''spotted'' handkerchief), *Henry V* (the strawberry beneath the nettle), and *Richard III* (Richard's request for strawberries)—Ross expands his theme and all of the contradictory meanings that strawberries might bear. Like most symbols, they can be either negative (hypocrisy, the snake in the grass) or positive (perfection of spirit as in representations of the Virgin with strawberries), so that the immediate context is crucial in interpretation. Desdemona's spotted handkerchief carries the double connotation very effectively. Ross begins and ends with allusions to Shakespeare, but the purpose of his soaring edifice is hardly to explicate these passages. It is clearly there for its own sake: to establish a grandiose iconographic perspective that lies behind even the simplest and most innocent of allusions.

This is eminently true of Ross's bravura piece ''Shakespeare's 'Dull Clown' and Symbolic Music.'' The humble passage in *Othello* of the musicians offering their services stimulates a magnificent discourse on music theory and on esoteric doctrines of the relations of love and music, with abundant visual correlates. The dull clown of *Othello* is safely stowed away until the very end of the paper, where he makes a brief and insignificant reappearance.

The method has much wider scope for expression in the long essay ''Wingless Victory: Michelangelo, Shakespeare, and the 'Old Man.' " Ross has a field day with *vetus Adam* (the fallen Adam) versus the New Man of Christianity. Falstaff is clearly the unregenerate Adam of the Old Testament, but what he has essentially to do with Michelangelo's statue *Victory* remains puzzling, despite Ross's attempt in the end to pull everything together. It may well be true that Michelangelo and Shakespeare's Henry IV plays share the same humanistic traditions, but why bring them to impinge on each other? It is not that Ross does not have plausible explanations for these seemingly farfetched juxtapositions both in this essay and in "Art and the Study of Early English Drama." The question really boils down to this: At what level of generalization do we wish to be instructed or entertained?

Finally, in John Doebler's learned book *Shakespeare's Speaking Pictures: Studies in Iconic Imagery* the word *iconic* is used for visual and aural symbolism on stage, *iconographic* being reserved for symbolism in the graphic and plastic arts. Doebler, in studying the presentational imagery of six Shakespeare plays, moves freely between stage imagery and its correlates in the visual arts. His most curious chapter is on the mousetrap symbolism in *Hamlet*. *The Murder of Gonzago* is also called *The Mousetrap*, by which Hamlet will trap the conscience of the King. Doebler reminds us, with many visual examples, that in Augustinian thinking God incarnated himself in Christ as a way of baiting the trap for the devil. Doebler asks us to believe that "by Shakespeare's day, mice, traps, and probably even St. Augustine's mousetrap set by God for the devil, had a host of conventional symbolic associations for ordinary Englishmen." The complexity of the web of allusions, both theological and aesthetic, poses a practical problem for iconographic and iconic studies. Who, except the critic himself, could possibly master and evoke all of this humanistic and pictorial material?

Metadrama

Lionel Abel's little book *Metatheatre: A New View of Dramatic Form* lies behind the study of Shakespeare's metadrama. Abel delights in paradoxical overstatement, and all metatheater tends to the ideal form of Pirandello's *Six Characters in Search of an Author*. Metatheater proposes a self-conscious and reflexive Shakespearean drama in which the idea of tragedy as we know it is more or less an-

nihilated. Abel postulates that Shakespeare, finding the *Hamlet* story almost impossible to convert into a tragedy, "turned toward various play-within-a-play devices." It is not tragic to kill one's uncle, but, Abel asks with mock portentousness, "Would *Hamlet* have been a tragedy if the Ghost had told Hamlet to kill his mother, along with Claudius?" Abel's joking, taunting, teasing tone—in which everything is open and all that was once so difficult is now so simple—establishes a characteristic style for metatheatrical and metadramatic criticism.

To Abel, "Hamlet is an objective expression of Shakespeare's inability to make of his play a tragedy." Hamlet's problem is that "he has a playwright's consciousness." He is the "first stage figure with an acute awareness of what it means to be staged. How be dramatized when one has the imagination to be a dramatist?" Abel's speculations on the author-character relationship are part of that doublenss of vision we now take for granted. Metatheater and metaplays are "theatre pieces about life seen as already theatricalized."

Abel makes certain Pirandellesque assumptions about the relations of theater and life. If the characters on stage are real and autonomous, then the audience must be theatricalized. If all the world's a stage, then the clear lines between stage and world disappear. Luckily, none of the metatheatrical critics mean any of these postulates literally. There is a built-in playfulness about the method, a permanent hypothecation of literature and life, that is covered under the general rubric "self-consciousness." In other words, Shakespeare is always conscious of himself writing a play, and his characters are conscious of themselves as characters in a play. Whatever suspension of disbelief is demanded is only local and temporary. The play reflexively turns on itself and explores the difficulties both of writing this particular play and of writing plays in general.

James L. Calderwood is our most important critic of "Shakespearean metadrama," which phrase serves as the title of his first book in a series that includes *Metadrama in Shakespeare's Henriad: "Richard II" to "Henry V"* and *To Be and Not to Be: Negation and Metadrama in "Hamlet."* An introductory chapter in *Shakespearean Metadrama* defines the subject. Borrowing from Abel's definition of metatheater as a dramatic genre that goes beyond drama, "becoming a kind of anti-form in which the boundaries between the play as a work of self-contained art and life are dissolved," Calderwood develops an approach more suitable to Shakespeare than to Abel's favorite dramatists, Pirandello, Brecht, Genet, and Beckett.

Shakespeare's plays are not only about the various thematic issues that have been claimed for them. They are also about Shakespeare's plays in the sense that "dramatic art itself—its materials, its media of language and theater, its generic forms and conventions, its relationship to truth and the social order—is a dominant Shakespearean theme, perhaps his most abiding subject." This is part of the larger aesthetic assumption that "each poem contains its own poetics" and is essentially self-interpreting. Shakespeare uses many dramatists within the plays, characters such as Aaron, Oberon, Iago, and Prospero, "whose successes and failures in governing men and events reflect Shakespeare's in governing them." Shakespeare's king-killers, Brutus, Hamlet, and Macbeth, ponder and select an appropriate style in which to kill the king. They "may indicate obliquely how Shakespeare, whose imagination is stained with the blood of many kings," goes about "marshaling the weapons of tragic art in the cause of death." Calderwood's style sets for other metadramatic critics a high standard of punning, epigrammatic, gnomic, vatic, and paradoxical understatement.

The lively and witty essay on *Titus Andronicus* in *Shakespearean Metadrama* is typical of Calderwood's approach. He refuses to accept the play at its face value or conventional estimation. T. S. Eliot's fulminations against *Titus* as "one of the stupidest and most uninspired plays ever written, a play in which it is incredible that Shakespeare had any hand at all," serve as a goad to Calderwood to defend it and explain it. His metadramatic interpretation is strangely Victorian in its defense of Shakespeare against his rude and barbarous audiences. *Titus Andronicus* "presents us with a rape of language, with the mutilation that the poet's 'tongue' suffers when forced to submit to the rude demands of the theater. The major image of this barbarizing of language by the theater is of course the rape and mutilation of Lavinia by the Goth brothers." No historical evidence is cited to support the "barbarizing of language by the theater"; that would spoil the imaginative fun. Metadramatic explanations tend to be pure and ahistorical. They imitate the figments of the imagination they set out to explore.

The *Hamlet* book is more subtle and eloquent, and in many ways less overtly metadramatic, than Calderwood's previous work. It is really a poetic meditation on the play. The author is disturbed by the onomastic poverty of *Hamlet*. Both Hamlet and Fortinbras lack a distinct identity of their own but are merged in the names of their fathers, and Claudius is never mentioned by name at all, although a mysterious Claudio transmits Hamlet's letter from the pirates. This book establishes *Hamlet* as Shakespeare's primary metadramatic text. Calderwood is brilliant—brilliantly inventive and fertile—on the style of Hamlet's soliloquies, which is interruptive, disjunctive, spasmodic, and reflexive. "By means of these interruptions Hamlet, as though to transcend the solitude of soliloquy, generates within his own utterance a responsive audience. Interior monologue becomes interior dialogue." Hamlet seems to be an outside observer of his own mental processes, so that he can add to the text of his soliloquies "a metatext devoted to self-critical comment and query." Thus, Hamlet is able to create the impression that "we are being presented not with the conclusions of thought but with thought itself." In his interpretation, Calderwood, in some literal sense, needs to re-create the play, as if he, rather than Shakespeare, were writing it.

All the metadramatic critics of Shakespeare owe a powerful debt to the strange and extraordinarily original book of Sigurd Burckhardt, *Shakespearean Meanings,* published posthumously in 1968. Burckhardt is here perversely committed to the old-fashioned notion that Shakespeare always knew exactly what he was doing, but in the essay on *Julius Caesar,* "How Not to Murder Caesar," Shakespeare's intentionality is given an odd twist. The anachronism of striking clocks in ancient Rome, a schoolboy boner if there ever was one, is put in deliberately by Shakespeare to remind us how anachronistic Brutus' assassination style is. As plotters in the dramatic sense, Cassius brings Brutus in as coauthor "to give the production the kind of prestige and styling that will make it a hit with the audience, the Roman populace." But Brutus, unfortunately, wants to put on a tragedy of classical, almost Aristotelian purity. Brutus is not guilty of treachery or bad politics but of anachronism. "The clock, striking as soon as he irrevocably committed himself to the Old Style, signifies to us—though not to him—that time is now reckoned in a new, Caesarean style." There are wonderful essays in this book on the quality of nothing in *King Lear* and all the intricacies of the bond in *The Merchant of Venice.*

Kirby Farrell acknowledges a large debt to Burckhardt in *Shakespeare's Creation: The Language of Magic and Play.* His theme is often literally the implications of play (in Johan Huizinga's sense) and magic in Shakespeare, but we are usually dealing with these themes at two or three removes from the allusions in the text. Farrell postulates a histrionic Hamlet, whose identity keeps shifting because his imagination is so powerful: "he fears that reality is but the caprice of 'conceit.' " Farrell reasons like a metadramatic critic in the sense that he supplies the characters with motives and metaphors that go beyond anything that can be demonstrated in the play itself. He re-creates Hamlet's role for Hamlet rather than for Shakespeare, and he assumes that Hamlet is in some sense alone in the play trying to find his way and/or trying to make up his part. Thus, Farrell interprets the Ghost as a projection of Hamlet's imagination and sees their encounter as a way to objectify the self-destructive process in Hamlet, "for the apparition undermines him, imposing an insupportably negative task, exciting an inhuman idealism in him." Father and son are mythologized as impossibly angelic or demonic—in other words, in terms of annihilation. "It fixes both father and son in the posture of martyrdom *whether or not* their revenge is carried out." It is obvious that Farrell's argument is based more on his own play than on Shakespeare's.

Lawrence Danson's *Tragic Alphabet: Shakespeare's Drama of Language* is metadramatic in its emphasis on language almost to the exclusion of plot, character, and the movement of the action. This is a subtle and self-conscious book, and the author introduces another dimension of reflexivity in his comments on his own critical reasoning. In the chapter on *Coriolanus,* the centrality of metonymy and synecdoche is effectively argued. Unlike metaphor, these are "figures of fragmentation and usurpation—or parts representing the whole and of the whole absorbing its parts." *Coriolanus,* too, is a world of "fragments," and Danson makes much of Menenius' fable of the belly and the members, which is metonymic rather than metaphoric in character. This rhetorical distinction offers an ingenious key to the play.

Many of the issues and conclusions of the metadramatic approach to Shakespeare are summed up in Sidney Homan's plain and practical book *When the Theater Turns to Itself: The Aesthetic Metaphor in Shakespeare.* It is a relief to find metadramatic criticism that is not in itself arcane, ironic, and hubristically re-creative. By using the phrase "aesthetic metaphor," Homan indicates that he wants to go

beyond theatrical references in the text to "metaphors based on all the components of the theater," both the subtext and the overtext. In the chapter on *Hamlet,* for example, he takes up the following topics: Hamlet's fascination with the theater; the play's own sensitivity to the theater; "the possibility that Hamlet suspects he is in a play"; theater as a metaphor for the corruption and duplicity of the Claudius faction; the enervating effect of Hamlet's theatrical consciousness; and the tremendous split between Hamlet's theatricality and reality, "between the demands of the stage and the inexorable demands of life." Another summing-up of metadramatic criticism is Michael Shapiro's review article "Role-Playing, Reflexivity, and Metadrama in Recent Shakespearean Criticism," which deals with other critics than those discussed here.

Shakespeare's Relation to the Drama of His Time

Shakespeare's relation to the drama of his time has, since 1960, taken a quite different turn from the source studies and verbal parallels that prevailed in a previous era. Verbal resemblances, in the form of borrowings or influences, seem much less important than similarities in construction, character relations, and dramatic technique. This is part of the new value placed on Shakespeare as a man of the theater.

There has also been a fortunate ebb in the flood of Shakespeare idolatry, which assumes that anything Shakespeare wrote is automatically and by definition superior to anything written by any of his contemporaries. This attitude may be sampled in its fullest fatuousness in David L. Frost's *The School of Shakespeare: The Influence of Shakespeare on English Drama, 1600–1642:* "All the dramatists with whom this study is concerned are minor, if our standard is to be anything but parochial or chauvinist; and we must guard against the vice of the specialist, who hails as a masterpiece anything that noses above the swamp." The derogatory image makes it clear that Frost will devote his efforts to putting down the upstart dramatists who dare to compete with Shakespeare. Actually, according to G. E. Bentley in *Shakespeare and Jonson,* Ben Jonson's reputation was much grander in his own time than Shakespeare's. Later in the century, many worthy commentators thought Shakespeare much inferior to Francis Beaumont and John Fletcher.

The subject of Shakespeare's reputation compared to other Elizabethan and Jacobean playwrights' is wittily pursued by T. J. B. Spencer in "Shakespeare *v.* The Rest: The Old Controversy." Although John Dryden thought Shakespeare deficient in female characterization in comparison with Fletcher (Shakespeare "writ better betwixt man and man; Fletcher betwixt man and woman"), by the nineteenth century Samuel Taylor Coleridge made the great discovery that "Shakespeare's women characters were remarkable in that you felt like marrying them." Spencer also takes historical account of the slow and halting progress in the study and publication of the "Old Dramatists," whose main failing was in not being Shakespeare.

It is generally more rewarding to study Shakespeare's use of the drama of his time than to approach the subject through Shakespeare's influence on his fellow dramatists and those who came immediately afterward. The latter is more obvious and has been the subject of much fuller research. In my essay "Shakespeare—and the Others," I try to emphasize Shakespeare's indebtedness to "the others": "The truth becomes more and more evident that Shakespeare is always working from models. He seems always to be trying out a kind of play that others had done before him."

But it is also vital, as a way of countering bardolatry, to insist that there is a large segment of Elizabethan and Jacobean drama that develops apart from Shakespeare. For example, Shakespeare did very little with the comedy of London life that we find so vigorously expressed in Jonson, Thomas Middleton, Thomas Dekker, and Thomas Heywood. Only *The Merry Wives of Windsor* even approaches this kind of "realistic" comedy. Shakespeare was not a writer of court masques, as Jonson, Middleton, and many of his contemporaries were, although some splendid masques and antimasques appear in his late romances. Also, Shakespeare never created the brilliantly lustful and sophisticated women that we find in Beaumont and Fletcher, Middleton, Cyril Tourneur, and others. Cressida and Cleopatra are more or less innocents compared to Middleton's Livia in *Women Beware Women* and Beaumont and Fletcher's Evadne in *The Maid's Tragedy.* Cloe's line in Fletcher's *The Faithful Shepherdess* is strikingly un-Shakespearean: "It is Impossible to Ravish mee, / I am soe willing."

Shakespeare and Christopher Marlowe offer the most intriguing possibilities in their literary and theatrical relationship. They were both born in 1564, within a few months of each other, and when Marlowe died in 1593 at the age of twenty-nine, his accomplishments were much more considerable than Shakespeare's at the same age. There was no Shakespearean "mighty line" to match Marlowe's grand and soaring theatrical energy. Nicholas Brooke has written with admirable complexity about "Marlowe as Provocative Agent in Shakespeare's Early Plays." Brooke is one of the few critics who take seriously Marlowe's influence on Shakespeare even though one cannot cite an avalanche of parallel passages. Rather, "there are a number of eruptions in Shakespeare's work of passages which are unmistakably Marlovian in tone and attitude, to a degree which would almost justify a disintegrator in identifying them as Marlowe's work." The influence flows both ways, and *Edward II,* Marlowe's last play, definitely profits from the Shakespearean style of character creation in the early history plays.

Everything seems to point to the fact that Shakespeare was dazzled by his brilliant and powerful contemporary. Aside from the Marlovian eruptions that Brooke speaks about, Shakespeare never tried to imitate Marlowe directly. Even though *The Merchant of Venice* is clearly based on Marlowe's *The Jew of Malta,* it is strikingly different from the earlier play. It is as if Shakespeare were determined to avoid the kinds of effects that Marlowe could do so well, and his Shylock is strangely inarticulate compared to the grandly rhetorical Barabas, who is another Marlovian overreacher in style and theme. The puzzling relations of these two plays are explored in my essay "Jessica's Turquoise Ring and Abigail's Poisoned Porridge: Shakespeare and Marlowe as Rivals and Imitators." This essay considers the implications of the anxiety of influence so provocatively set out in Brooke's account. We still have no fully satisfactory explanation of Brooke's conclusion: "Marlowe seems to have been for Shakespeare not only a great poet, as his tributes imply, but the inescapable imaginative creator of something initially alien which he could only assimilate with difficulty, through a process of imitative re-creation merging into critical parody." This is the direction in which the study of Shakespeare and Marlowe needs to move.

Shakespeare's relations with Jonson are similarly puzzling and complex. The two men are as far apart temperamentally as Shakespeare and Marlowe, and Jonson mingled high praise for his fellow dramatist with little carping examples to show that Shakespeare "wanted art." In other words, Shakespeare did not have the classical learning or high sense of formal perfection of his self-educated contemporary. It is with Jonson that there begins the myth of Shakespeare as a poet of nature, one who flowed so freely that he never needed to revise a line. Nancy S. Leonard cleverly undermines the old distinction that Shakespeare's comedies are romantic and Jonson's satiric in "Shakespeare and Jonson Again: The Comic Forms." Actually, the two forms of comedy are "essentially and inextricably involved with each other, even dependent on each other." What is surprising about this discussion is not that Shakespeare makes wide use of satiric comedy but how deeply Jonson is committed to the assumptions of romantic comedy. This would explain the function of such anomalous innocents as Bonario and Celia in *Volpone.*

Robert Ornstein, in "Shakespearian and Jonsonian Comedy," confirms Jonson's suppressed penchant for the sweetness and amiability of romance: "Contemptuous as he was of romantic fabling, Jonson had, moreover, an instinct for romantic variety and multiplicity which, though severely disciplined in *Volpone* and *The Alchemist,* burst forth in the noisy carnivals of *Epicene* and *Bartholomew Fair.*" Ornstein's essay is an eloquent meditation on the two playwrights. Would it were longer!

Harry Levin presents a masterful comparison of Shakespeare and Jonson in "Two Magian Comedies: *The Tempest* and *The Alchemist.*" These two plays were presented in 1610 and 1611 by the King's Men, Shakespeare's company, and it is likely that Richard Burbage played both Prospero and Subtle. Levin sees the two playwrights as polar opposites, one concerned with illusion and the other with delusion. "Jonson's dramatic method is to tell us the respective methods of his dramatis personae. He is nothing if not analytic, where for Shakespeare we must use such Coleridgean adjectives as *organic* and *esemplastic.* Where Shakespeare fuses things together, Jonson sorts them out; he breaks them down, where Shakespeare builds them up." As in Edward Bond's fictional re-creation of Shakespeare and Jonson in the play *Bingo* (1974), Levin projects Jonson as always being astonished how Shakespeare could get away with it.

The relation of Shakespeare to John Lyly offers a much neater topic than his relation to Marlowe or Jonson. Lyly's brilliantly artificial comedies of courtly love undoubtedly influenced Shakespeare's early comedies, yet Shakespeare is radically different from Lyly. The Lylian formulas are affectionately burlesqued in *Love's Labor's Lost.* Marco Mincoff sets out the main lines of the subject in his substantial essay "Shakespeare and Lyly." Love is the main business of Lyly's courtiers, but it is rather what we would call flirtation or the witty love-game. There is something charmingly frothy and frivolous in Lyly that tends to disappear in Shakespeare as the witty lovers are humanized, psychologized, and satirized.

Peter Berek gives a good account of this "realistic" transformation of Lyly in "Artifice and Realism in Lyly, Nashe, and *Love's Labor's Lost.*" Although Lyly was Shakespeare's best teacher in the art of structuring comedy, Shakespeare breaks the Lylian mode in *Love's Labor's Lost,* which demands our emotional engagement whereas Lyly does not. In Shakespeare, "the person, not the idea, matters most."

Richard S. Ide's *Possessed with Greatness: The Heroic Tragedies of Chapman and Shakespeare* offers a model for how the parallel argument might be conducted of Shakespeare's relation to a fellow dramatist. The subject at first seems highly unpromising, since Shakespeare and George Chapman have so little in common, yet Ide manages to demonstrate in some detail that Shakespeare is reacting to Chapman's model of heroic tragedy. This is especially true of *Coriolanus* and its connection with Chapman's two-part play *The Conspiracy and Tragedy of Charles Duke of Byron* (1608). Ide considers Shakespeare's play a response "not only to the *Byron* plays but to Chapman's theory of titanic heroism as well." The argument is intertextual, since *Coriolanus* was fashioned on the model of Byron (and probably of Bussy D'Ambois, too) and cannot be fully conceived outside the context of Chapman. "It is as if Shakespeare set out to create a superior version of Chapman's hero so that he might criticize not only Bussy and Byron, but the defective epic ideals on which Chapman's conception of heroism is based." Whether or not Ide's strong claims are literally true, he does suggest a mode of relationship between Shakespeare and his fellow dramatists that could profitably be explored further.

So much as been written about the relations of Shakespeare and Webster that the topic is almost exhausted. Webster is certainly the most popular of all the Elizabethan-Jacobean dramatists, yet his reputation rests almost entirely on two plays, *The*

White Devil and *The Duchess of Malfi*. In terms of solid theatrical accomplishment, "he is the most spectacular under-achiever among Elizabethan dramatists." This is a judgment from my essay "Webster vs. Middleton."

I object strongly to the fact that Webster has become the yardstick for what is "Shakespearean" in Elizabethan and Jacobean drama, as if a lyrical and metaphysical intensity in the verse is the only criterion of Shakespearean values. On the contrary, it seems to me that the satirical and highly polished eloquence of Webster has little to do with the typically unpoetic poetry of Shakespeare's tragedies. In this sense, Shakespeare is much closer to the understated and contextual poetry of Middleton, especially in *The Changeling*. We need to revise our thinking about what is most Shakespearean about Shakespeare and pay closer attention to the qualities of his theatrical art.

Conclusion

Our heroic survey of Shakespeare criticism in the past twenty-five years has now come to an abrupt end. By limiting the topic to only eight areas—theater, film, feminism, psychoanalysis, Marxism, iconography, metadrama, and Shakespeare's relation to the drama of his time—we have left out a great deal that is important in recent thinking about Shakespeare. One notable line of inquiry, mostly of the past five years, has been the "new historicism," which considers Shakespeare in his own culture from a historical, anthropological, and political point of view. This kind of thinking is well analyzed by Jonathan Goldberg in "The Politics of Renaissance Literature: A Review Essay." In his own book, *James I and the Politics of Literature* (1983), Goldberg articulates the relationship between society and literature, especially as it concerns James I and his projection of a Roman style. Shakespeare's *Julius Caesar* and *Coriolanus* demonstrate the paradoxical connection between the "staging of power and the powers of the stage." The Roman plays reflect the realities of public life, "the continuities of history, the recreation of Rome as England's imperial ideal."

Goldberg acknowledges a strong debt to the work of Stephen Orgel, especially on Renaissance masques and courtly entertainments. Orgel's short book, *The Illusion of Power*, is subtitled *Political*

Theater in the English Renaissance, and he consistently emphasizes the two-way relationship between events on stage and the staging of the king in the audience. The masques embody and validate a certain concept of monarchy, a political ideology. These ideas are well summed up in Orgel's essay, "The Royal Theatre and the Role of King" in *Patronage in the Renaissance*. On one side are "the kinds of roles and imagined worlds Renaissance monarchs caused to be created for themselves," and on the other are "the kinds of theatres they required in which to perform those roles." Orgel finds an intimate link between monarchy and theater.

In the general area of theater and society, we should also notice the more speculative studies by Greenblatt, Montrose, and Dollimore, as well as many essays appearing in the journal *Representations*, which began publication at Berkeley in 1982. Stephen Greenblatt's *Renaissance Self-Fashioning* has been particularly influential. *Othello*, for example, is considered under the rubric of "The Improvisation of Power," and Iago becomes the archetypal Greenblattian hero, constructing a narrative into which he inscribes and inserts those around him. In his commitment to role-playing and the histrionic, Iago is a typical Renaissance man.

Among the new breed of Shakespeare critics, Louis Adrian Montrose makes the most significant use of anthropology as a way of looking at a text in its cultural milieu. In " 'The Place of a Brother' in *As You Like It*: Social Process and Comic Form," Montrose considers the implications of primogeniture for the play, which he sees as illustrating the "dialectic between Elizabethan dramatic form and social process." In his study of *A Midsummer Night's Dream*, " 'Shaping Fantasies': Figurations of Gender and Power in Elizabethan Culture," Montrose insists that the fantasies that shape the play are also fantasies to which it gives shape. Montrose examines the social anthropology of theater and acting in yet another essay, "The Purpose of Playing: Reflections on a Shakespearean Anthropology."

Finally, Jonathan Dollimore offers a highly idiosyncratic and original view of Shakespeare and the drama of his time in *Radical Tragedy: Religion, Ideology and Power in the Drama of Shakespeare and His Contemporaries*. Political radicalism is brought to bear on the interpretation of a number of plays, among them *King Lear* and *Coriolanus*. Dollimore comes up with some surprising conclusions about the mob in *Coriolanus*, who he thinks is represented with complexity and sympathy. In doing so, Dollimore reminds us that the class war of the play is what made it so appealing to Brecht.

In all of the topics we have considered there has been an unstated assumption that Shakespeare is writing for the theater and that performance is closely connected with interpretation. I notice with interest that even the newer textual studies are insisting on the essential relation of the printed text with the performed play and that the notion of an ideal dramatic text, fixed forever and immutable, is disappearing.

We must conclude from our survey that Shakespeare seems more and more to be a figure connected with popular theater and with popular culture rather than an erudite and esoteric figure who wrote for a small coterie of those capable of understanding him. There is a new emphasis on a free Shakespeare that is available to all. It is remarkable how many miscellaneous students are crowding in to study Shakespeare in universities. If "Bird Lives," as the popular graffito for Charlie Parker, the alto saxophone player, claims, then so does Shakespeare. "Shakespeare Lives" has taken its place beside "Bird Lives" and "Kilroy Was Here" as a legendary assertion of immortality. Shakespeare's mythic status helps to validate our elaborate account of trends in Shakespearean criticism. If indeed "Shakespeare Lives," then in the future we may be sure that an entirely new account will have to be rendered.

BIBLIOGRAPHY

Theater. Bernard Beckerman, *Shakespeare at the Globe, 1599–1609* (1962) and "Explorations in Shakespeare's Drama," in *Shakespeare Quarterly,* 29 (1978). John Russell Brown, *Shakespeare's Plays in Performance* (1966); "The Theatrical Element of Shakespeare Criticism," in Rabkin; *Shakespeare's Dramatic Style* (1971); *Free Shakespeare* (1974); and *Discovering Shakespeare* (1981). Maurice Charney, *"Hamlet* Without Words," in *Journal of English Literary History,* 32 (1965) and "Shakespeare's Unpoetic Poetry," in *Studies in English Literature,* 13 (1973). Alan C. Dessen, *Elizabethan Drama and the Viewer's Eye* (1977). Inga-Stina Ewbank, " 'More Pregnantly Than Words': Some Uses and Limitations of Visual Symbolism," in *Shakespeare Survey,* 24 (1971). Michael Goldman, *Shakespeare and the Energies of Drama* (1972); *The Actor's Freedom* (1975); and "Acting Values and Shakespearean Meaning: Some Suggestions," in *Mo-*

saic, 10 (1976–1977). Jean E. Howard, *Shakespeare's Art of Orchestration,* 1984. Emrys Jones, *Scenic Form in Shakespeare* (1971). Bertram Joseph, *Elizabethan Acting* (1951; 2nd ed., 1964). George R. Kernodle, *From Art to Theatre: Form and Convention in the Renaissance* (1944). Dieter Mehl, "Visual and Rhetorical Imagery and Shakespeare's Plays," in *Essays and Studies,* n.s. 25 (1972). Norman Rabkin, ed., *Reinterpretations of Elizabethan Drama* (1969). Mark Rose, *Shakespearean Design* (1972). Brownell Salomon, "Visual and Aural Signs in the Performed English Renaissance Play," in *Renaissance Drama,* n.s. 5 (1972). Frances A. Shirley, *Shakespeare's Use of Off-Stage Sounds* (1963). John L. Styan, *Shakespeare's Stagecraft* (1967).

Film. Robert Hamilton Ball, *Shakespeare on Silent Film* (1968). Maurice Charney, "Shakespearean Anglophilia: The BBC-TV Series and American Audiences," in *Shakespeare Quarterly,* 31 (1980). Samuel Crowl, "The Long Goodbye: Welles and Falstaff," in *Shakespeare Quarterly,* 31 (1980). Charles W. Eckert, *Focus on Shakespearean Films* (1972). John Fuegi, "Explorations in No Man's Land: Shakespeare's Poetry as Theatrical Film," in *Shakespeare Quarterly,* 23 (1972). Sidney Homan and Neil Feineman, "The Filmed Shakespeare: From Verbal to Visual," in Sidney Homan, ed., *Shakespeare's More Than Words Can Witness* (1980). Charles Hurtgen, "The Operatic Character of Background Music in Film Adaptations of Shakespeare," in *Shakespeare Quarterly,* 20 (1969). Jack J. Jorgens, *Shakespeare on Film* (1977). Grigori Kozintsev, *"Hamlet* and *King Lear:* Stage and Film," in Clifford Leech and J. M. R. Margeson, eds., *Shakespeare 1971* (1972). Roger Manvell, *Shakespeare and the Film* (1971).

Feminism. Martha Andresen-Thom, "Thinking About Women and Their Prosperous Art: A Reply to Juliet Dusinberre's *Shakespeare and the Nature of Women,* " in *Shakespeare Studies,* 11 (1978). Linda Bamber, *Comic Women, Tragic Men: A Study of Gender and Genre in Shakespeare* (1982). Maurice Charney and Hanna Charney, "The Language of Madwomen in Shakespeare and His Fellow Dramatists," in *Signs,* 3 (1977). Irene G. Dash, *Wooing, Wedding, and Power: Women in Shakespeare's Plays* (1981). Juliet Dusinberre, *Shakespeare and the Nature of Women* (1975). L. T. Fitz, "Egyptian Queens and Male Reviewers: Sexist Attitudes in *Antony and Cleopatra* Criticism," in *Shakespeare Quarterly,* 28 (1977). Carolyn Ruth Swift Lenz, Gayle Greene, and Carol Thomas Neely, eds., *The Woman's Part* (1980). Clara Claiborne Park, "As We Like It: How a Girl Can Be Smart and Still Popular," *ibid.* Rebecca Smith, "A Heart Cleft in Twain: The Dilemma of Shakespeare's Gertrude," *ibid.*

Psychoanalysis. Janet Adelman, " 'Anger's My Meat': Feeding, Dependency, and Aggression in *Coriolanus,* " in Schwartz and Kahn. M. D. Faber, *The Design Within: Psychoanalytic Approaches to Shakespeare* (1970). Barbara Freedman, "Errors in Comedy: A Psychoanalytic Theory of Farce," in *Shakespearean Comedy,* Maurice Charney, ed., *New York Literary Forum,* 5–6 (1980). Norman N. Holland, *Psychoanalysis and Shakespeare* (1966). Coppélia Kahn, *Man's Estate: Masculine Identity in Shakespeare* (1981). Murray M. Schwartz and Coppélia Kahn, eds., *Representing Shakespeare: New Psychoanalytic Essays* (1980). Ernst Kris, *Psychoanalytic Explorations in Art* (1952). Meredith Skura, "Interpreting Posthumus' Dream from Above and Below: Families, Psychoanalysts, and Literary Critics," in Schwartz and Kahn, and *The Literary Use of the Psychoanalytic Process* (1981). Robert J. Stoller, "Shakespearean Tragedy: *Coriolanus,"* in Faber. Leonard Tennenhouse, "The Counterfeit Order of *The Merchant of Venice,"* in Schwartz and Kahn.

Marxism. Mikhail Bakhtin, *Rabelais and His World,* Helene Iswolsky, trans. (1981). Ann Jennalie Cook, *The Privileged Playgoers of Shakespeare's London, 1576–1642* (1981). Paul Delany, *"King Lear* and the Decline of Feudalism," in *PMLA,* 92 (1977). Alfred Harbage, *Shakespeare's Audience* (1941) and *Shakespeare and the Rival Traditions* (1952). Arnold Kettle, ed., *Shakespeare in a Changing World* (1964). Kenneth Muir, *"Timon of Athens* and the Cash-Nexus," in *The Singularity of Shakespeare and Other Essays* (1977). Anne Paolucci, "Marx, Money, and Shakespeare: The Hegelian Core in Marxist Shakespeare-Criticism," in *Mosaic,* 10 (1976–1977). Paul N. Siegel, *Shakespearean Tragedy and the Elizabethan Compromise: A Marxist Study* (1957; rev. ed., 1983); as special ed., Marxist number of *The Shakespeare Newsletter,* 24 (1974); and "Marx, Engels, and the Historical Criticism of Shakespeare," in *Shakespeare Jahrbuch* (Weimar), 113 (1977). Raymond Southall, *"Troilus and Cressida* and the Spirit of Capitalism," in Kettle. Robert Weimann, "The Soul of the Age: Towards a Historical Approach to Shakespeare," in Kettle; "Shakespeare's Wordplay: Popular Origins and Theatrical Functions," in Clifford Leech and J. M. R. Margeson, eds., *Shakespeare 1971* (1972); and *Shakespeare and the Popular Tradition in the Theater,* Robert Schwartz, ed. and trans. (1978).

Iconography. Peter M. Daly, "Trends and Problems in the Study of Emblematic Literature," in *Mosaic,* 5 (1972). John Doebler, *Shakespeare's Speaking Pictures: Studies in Iconic Imagery* (1974). Roland Mushat Frye, "Ladies, Gentlemen, and Skulls: *Hamlet* and the Iconographic Traditions," in *Shakespeare Quarterly,* 30 (1979). William S. Heckscher, "Shakespeare in His Relationship to the Visual Arts: A Study in Paradox," in *Research Opportunities in Renaissance Drama,* 13–14 (1970–1971). Bridget Gellert Lyons, "The Iconography of Ophelia," in *Journal of English Literary History,* 44 (1977). Dieter Mehl, "Emblems in English Renaissance Drama," in *Renaissance Drama,* n.s. 2 (1969) and "Emblematic Theatre," in *Anglia,* 95 (1977). Lawrence J. Ross, "The Meaning of Strawberries in Shakespeare," in *Studies in the Renaissance,* 7 (1960); "Art and the Study of Early En-

glish Drama," in *Research Opportunities in Renaissance Drama,* 6 (1963); "Shakespeare's 'Dull Clown' and Symbolic Music," in *Shakespeare Quarterly,* 17 (1966); and "Wingless Victory: Michelangelo, Shakespeare, and the 'Old Man,' " in *Literary Monographs,* 2 (1969). John M. Steadman, "Falstaff as Actaeon: A Dramatic Emblem," in *Shakespeare Quarterly,* 14 (1963) and "Iconography and Renaissance Drama: Ethical and Mythological Themes," in *Research Opportunities in Renaissance Drama,* 13–14 (1970–1971).

Metadrama. Lionel Abel, *Metatheatre: A New View of Dramatic Form* (1963). Sigurd Burckhardt, *Shakespearean Meanings* (1968). James L. Calderwood, *Shakespearean Metadrama* (1971); *Metadrama in Shakespeare's Henriad: "Richard II" to "Henry V"* (1979); and *To Be and Not to Be: Negation and Metadrama in "Hamlet"* (1983). Lawrence Danson, *Tragic Alphabet: Shakespeare's Drama of Language* (1974). Kirby Farrell, *Shakespeare's Creation: The Language of Magic and Play* (1976). Sidney Homan, *When the Theater Turns to Itself: The Aesthetic Metaphor in Shakespeare* (1981). Michael Shapiro, "Role-Playing, Reflexivity, and Metadrama in Recent Shakespearean Criticism," in *Renaissance Drama,* n.s. 12 (1981).

Shakespeare and the Drama of His Time. G. E. Bentley, *Shakespeare and Jonson: Their Reputations in the Seventeenth Century Compared* (1945). Peter Berek, "Artifice and Realism in Lyly, Nashe, and *Love's Labor's Lost,"* in *Studies in English Literature,* 23 (1983). Nicholas Brooke, "Marlow as Provocative Agent in Shakespeare's Early Plays," in *Shakespeare Survey,* 14 (1961). Maurice Charney, "Webster vs. Middleton, or the Shakespearean Yardstick in Jacobean Tragedy," in Standish Henning et al., eds., *English Renaissance Drama* (1976); "Jessica's Turquoise Ring and Abigail's Poisoned Porridge: Shakespeare and Marlowe as Rivals and Imitators," in *Renaissance Drama,* n.s. 10 (1979); and "Shakespeare—and the Others," in *Shakespeare Quarterly,* 30 (1979). David L. Frost, *The School of Shakespeare: The Influence of Shakespeare on English Drama, 1600–1642* (1968). Richard S. Ide, *Possessed with Greatness: The Heroic Tragedies of Chapman and Shakespeare* (1980). Nancy S. Leonard, "Shakespeare and Jonson Again: The Comic Forms," in *Renaissance Drama,* n.s. 10 (1979). Harry Levin, "Two Magian Comedies: *The Tempest* and *The Alchemist,"* in *Shakespeare Survey,* 22 (1969). Marco Mincoff, "Shakespeare and Lyly," in *Shakespeare Survey,* 14 (1961). Robert Ornstein, "Shakespearian and Jonsonian Comedy," in *Shakespeare Survey,* 22 (1969). T. J. B. Spencer, "Shakespeare *v.* The Rest: The Old Controversy," in *Shakespeare Survey,* 14 (1961).

Conclusion. Jonathan Dollimore, *Radical Tragedy: Religion, Ideology and Power in the Drama of Shakespeare and His Contemporaries* (1984). Jonathan Goldberg, "The Politics of Renaissance Literature: A Review Essay," in *ELH* (1982) and *James I and the Politics of Literature: Jonson, Shakespeare, Donne, and Their Contemporaries* (1983). Stephen Greenblatt, *Renaissance Self-Fashioning: From More to Shakespeare* (1980). Louis Adrian Montrose, "The Purpose of Playing: Reflections on a Shakespearean Anthropology," in *Helios,* n.s. 7 (1980); " 'The Place of a Brother' in *As You Like It*: Social Process and Comic Form," in *Shakespeare Quarterly* (1981); and " 'Shaping Fantasies': Figurations of Gender and Power in Elizabethan Culture," in *Representations* (1983). Stephen Orgel, *The Illusion of Power: Political Theater in the English Renaissance* (1975) and "The Royal Theatre and the Role of King," in Guy Fitch Lytle and Stephen Orgel, eds., *Patronage in the Renaissance* (1981).

LIST OF CONTRIBUTORS

List of Contributors

JOHN F. ANDREWS
National Endowment for the Humanities, Washington, D.C.
Ethical and Theological Questions in Shakespeare's Dramatic Works

J. H. BAKER
St. Catharine's College, Cambridge
Law and Legal Institutions

J. LEEDS BARROLL
University of Maryland
Thinking About Shakespeare's Thought

JACQUES BARZUN
Charles Scribner's Sons, New York
Shakespeare and the Humanities

BERNARD BECKERMAN
Columbia University
Shakespeare's Dramatic Methods

GERALD EADES BENTLEY
Huntington Library, San Marino (Calif.)
Shakespeare's Reputation—Then Till Now

RALPH BERRY
University of Ottawa
Major Shakespearean Institutions

DAVID BEVINGTON
University of Chicago
Shakespeare's Professional Career: Poet and Playwright

M. C. BRADBROOK
Shakespeare and His Contemporaries

J. PHILIP BROCKBANK
University of Birmingham
Shakespearean Scholarship: From Rowe to the Present

JOHN RUSSELL BROWN
National Theatre, London
Shakespeare's Tragicomedies and Romances

ANTHONY BURGESS
Shakespeare and the Modern Writer

MAURICE CHARNEY
Rutgers University
Contemporary Issues in Shakespearean Interpretation

D. C. COLEMAN
Pembroke College, Cambridge
Economic Life in Shakespeare's England

PATRICK COLLINSON
University of Sheffield
The Church: Religion and Its Manifestations

ANN JENNALIE COOK
Vanderbilt University
Shakespeare and His Audiences

ARTHUR M. EASTMAN
Virginia Polytechnic Institute and State University
Shakespearean Criticism

G. R. ELTON
Clare College, Cambridge
The State: Government and Politics Under Elizabeth and James

GEORGE P. GARRETT
University of Michigan
Daily Life in City, Town, and Country

LIST OF CONTRIBUTORS

SIR JOHN GIELGUD
Tradition, Style, and the Shakespearean Actor Today

ANTHONY GRAFTON
Princeton University
Education and Apprenticeship

MARGRETA DE GRAZIA
University of Pennsylvania
The Sonnets

ANDREW GURR
University of Reading
Theaters and the Dramatic Profession

JOHN RIGBY HALE
University College London
Shakespeare and Warfare

ELLEN T. HARRIS
University of Chicago
Shakespeare in Music

S. K. HENINGER, JR.
University of North Carolina
The Literate Culture of Shakespeare's Audience

JOHN DIXON HUNT
University of East Anglia, Norwich (Eng.)
The Visual Arts in Shakespeare's Work

JACK J. JORGENS
American University
Shakespeare on Film and Television

ARTHUR KIRSCH
University of Virginia
Shakespeare's Tragedies

F. J. LEVY
University of Washington
Patronage of the Arts

JOHN L. LIEVSAY
Shakespeare and Foreigners

MICHAEL MACDONALD
University of Wisconsin
Science, Magic, and Folklore

W. MOELWYN MERCHANT
Shakespeare and the Painter and Illustrator

JONATHAN MILLER
Shakespeare and the Modern Director

ANNE PAOLUCCI
St. John's University (N.Y.)
Shakespeare as a World Figure

MARGARET PELLING
Wellcome Unit for the History of Medicine, Oxford
Medicine and Sanitation

J. G. A. POCOCK
Johns Hopkins University
The Sense of History in Renaissance England

JOSEPH G. PRICE
Pennsylvania State University
The Cultural Phenomenon of Shakespeare

ROGER PRINGLE
Shakespeare Birthplace Trust, Stratford-upon-Avon
Sports and Recreations

DAVID B. QUINN
University of Liverpool
Travel by Sea and Land

PETER SACCIO
Dartmouth College
Shakespeare's Treatment of English History

S. SCHOENBAUM
University of Maryland
The Life: A Survey

CHARLES H. SHATTUCK
University of Illinois
Shakespeare in the Theater: The United States and Canada

J. L. SIMMONS
Tulane University
Shakespeare's Treatment of Roman History

JOHN SIMON
Shakespeare and the Modern Critic

MEREDITH SKURA
Rice University
Shakespeare's Psychology

ARTHUR J. SLAVIN
University of Louisville
Printing and Publishing in the Tudor Age

HALLET SMITH
Huntington Library, San Marino (Calif.)
The Poems

LACEY BALDWIN SMITH
Northwestern University
"Style Is the Man": Manners, Dress, and Decorum

MARVIN SPEVACK
Westfälische Wilhelms-Universität, Münster
Shakespeare's Language

F. W. STERNFELD
University of Oxford
Music in Shakespeare's Work

LIST OF CONTRIBUTORS

HOMER SWANDER
University of California, Santa Barbara
Teaching Shakespeare: Tradition and the Future

WYLIE SYPHER
Simmons College
Painting and Other Fine Arts

JOAN THIRSK
Indian Institute, Oxford
Forest, Field, and Garden

PETER USTINOV
Shakespeare and the Modern Playwright

BRIAN VICKERS
Swiss Federal Institute of Technology, Zurich
Shakespeare's Use of Prose

STANLEY WELLS
Balliol College, Oxford
Shakespeare on the English Stage

GEORGE WALTON WILLIAMS
Duke University
The Publishing and Editing of Shakespeare's Plays

C. R. WILSON
University of Reading
Music in Shakespeare's Work

GEORGE T. WRIGHT
University of Minnesota
Shakespeare's Poetic Techniques

DAVID YOUNG
Oberlin College
Shakespeare as a Writer of Comedy

LIST OF ILLUSTRATIONS

List of Illustrations

7 *(p. 126).* An engraving, possibly by Renold Elstrack, of Queen Elizabeth opening a new Parliament in the White Chamber in 1586. Reproduced from Robert Glover, *Nobilitas Politica vel Civilis* (1608), a book on the major dignitaries and nobles of England. *Rare Books and Manuscripts Division, The New York Public Library; Astor, Lenox, and Tilden Foundations.*

8 *(p. 130).* An engraving by Vasari's pupil J. Stradanus, showing the interior of a sixteenth-century printing shop. This is the fourth in a series of twenty engravings from the drawings of Flemish artist Jan van der Straet, illustrating the new technology and crafts of the day. They were widely reprinted after 1580 by Galleus at Antwerp under the title *Nova Reperta. Reproduced by courtesy of the Trustees of the British Museum, Ill. 5–174.*

9 *(p. 131).* An engraving of a large paper mill in operation. Reproduced from Vittorio Zonca, *Nova Teatro di Machine et Edificii* (1607), a book on the subject of early mechanical engineering. *Rare Books and Manuscripts Division, The New York Public Library; Astor, Lenox, and Tilden Foundations.*

10 *(p. 133)* and 11 *(p. 133). The Printer* (l.) and *The Illuminator* (r.), reproduced from a facsimile of Jost Amman's *A True Description of All Trades* (1568), a collection of 114 woodcuts illustrating all manner of trades and professions of the sixteenth century. Each woodcut is accompanied by doggerel verse composed by the popular Nuremberg poet Hans Sachs. The verses provide much less information than the woodcuts by Amman (1539–1591), which have contributed to the importance of the book as a historical document on the social and industrial life of the period by illustrating, in exacting detail, the work of a variety of craftsmen. *Print Collection, The New York Public Library; Astor, Lenox, and Tilden Foundations.*

12 *(p. 134).* Printing in England was performed in small offices, such as the one illustrated in this woodcut, for more than three centuries. The wooden hand press was about six feet high. *By permission of the British Library, Harleian Ms. 5906b, no. 134.*

13 *(p. 134). Death Among the Printers* from *Danse Macabre,* printed by Mathias Huss at Lyons (1499). The pressman is arrested by Death at the moment of pulling the press; his colleague, meanwhile, is beating the ink balls to replenish them for the next application; the compositor, with his case of type, composing stick, and two-page form on the bench beside him, is setting from copy propped up before him; and in the adjoining bookshop the shopman is halted in the act of displaying a volume of his wares. *By permission of the British Library, IB.41735, leaf b1 recto.*

14 *(p. 137).* Illuminated frontispiece from a hand-copied version of *Dicts of the Philosophers* (1477), which was presented by Anthony Earl Rivers to Edward IV in the Royal Palace of Westminster at Christmas 1477. The full-length figures (from l. to r.) are the scribe Haywarde; Rivers in full plate armor with a surcoat bearing his arms and the Sun of York; Richard, Duke of Gloucester (the future Richard III); Chancellor Thomas Rotherham; King Edward IV; the little Edward, Prince of Wales (the future Edward V, who Richard murdered in the Tower); and Edward's Queen Elizabeth Woodville, Rivers' sister. *Dicts of the Philosophers* was the first dated book printed in England; it had been translated from the French by Rivers for his friend William Caxton (1422?–1493), England's first printer. *His Grace the Archbishop of Canterbury and the Trustees of Lambeth Palace Library, Ms. 265, fol. 1v.*

15 *(p. 138).* The only known example of a printer's advertisement published in England during the fifteenth century. Caxton had also used his Type 3 for headlines after about 1476. *The Bodleian Library, Oxford, Arch Ge 37.*

16 *(p. 139).* Richard Pynson (d. 1530) was the first printer in England to introduce Roman type, which came from Paris. He first used it to print a speech by the Bishop of Forli, Petrus Gryphus, in 1509. The speech was intended to be delivered before Henry VII, but the death of the king prevented this. *By permission of the British Library, G1203.Aij.*

17 *(p. 141).* Title page from the so-called *Bishops' Bible* (1568), printed by Richard Jugge (d. 1577). The *Bishops' Bible* displaced Thomas Cromwell's *Great Bible* (1539) and held its place until the coming of the Authorized Version of 1611. The portrait of Elizabeth is generally attributed to Franciscus Hogenberg, a craftsman in the employ of the Archbishop of Canterbury, Matthew Parker. *By permission of the Folger Shakespeare Library, STC 2099 c.1.*

18 *(p. 142).* An initial letter cut, reproduced from *The Cosmographical Glasse Containing the principles of cosmography, geography, hydrography or navigation* (1559), written by the Norwich physician William Cunningham. The book contains diagrams and maps, a portrait of the author, and a plan of Norwich, as well as a number of large woodcut pictorial initials. *Rare Books and Manuscripts Division, The New York Public Library; Astor, Lenox, and Tilden Foundations.*

19 *(p. 202). Sir Walter Raleigh* (1598) by Sir William Segar (d. 1633). Oil on panel. 43 × 33 in. Although inscribed with the date 1598, the general appearance of Raleigh in this portrait more likely reflects a later period in his life, possible shortly after his release in 1616 from the Tower of London, where he had been confined on a charge of treason against James I. The sash or ribbon-garter tied around his left arm is not an article of female attire; such a sash in such a position may indicate a commander in the field. Early in life, Raleigh was noted for the magnificence of his clothes, even at a court where external appearances carried much weight, and at a period when the extravagance of fashion at the French, Spanish, and Austrian courts made dress a matter of international competition. Fine clothes were not a mere foible of vanity to Raleigh, but part of a deliberate program in

his career. A map of Cadiz can be seen in the top left corner. *National Gallery of Ireland, Dublin.*

20 (p. 207). Illustration by Iris Brooke, reproduced from J. E. Morpurgo, *Life Under the Tudors* (1950). *Courtesy Falcon Educational Books.*

21 (p. 207). Basic Medieval look, ca. 1380, showing a style that appeared during the fourteenth century, the fashion for "tippets"—bands of material, usually white, some three or four inches wide and worn above the elbow, falling in a long streamer almost to the hem of the gown. The "fitchets"—pocket-like slits in the garment—were worn by both men and women and became a feature of the "surcote" during the closing years of the thirteenth century, their use being as a means of access to the belt worn on the "kirtle" or "gipon," where purse and knife were kept. Reproduced from *A History of English Costume* (1937), written and illustrated by Iris Brooke. *Courtesy Methuen Publishers.*

22 (p. 208). *Henry VIII* (ca. 1560–1570), by Hans Eworth (1540–1573). Oil on panel. 85½ × 48½ in. The portrait is derived from Hans Holbein's wall painting designed for the Privy Chamber in Whitehall Palace, showing the king at approximately forty-nine years of age. *Devonshire Collection, Chatsworth. Reproduced by permission of the Chatsworth Settlement Trustees. Photograph: Courtauld Institute of Art.*

23 (p. 209). Illustration by Iris Brooke, reproduced from J. E. Morpurgo, *Life Under the Tudors* (1950). *Courtesy Falcon Educational Books.*

24 (p. 210). *Robert Devereux, Second Earl of Essex* (ca. 1596), by Marcus Gheeraedts the Younger (1530?–1590?). Oil on canvas. 84 × 50 in. Without a doubt, this is the original ad vivum portrait of Devereux (1567–1601), a favorite of Queen Elizabeth, painted shortly after his return from the Cadiz expedition, to which there is an allusion in the background, with a view of a town (presumably Cadiz) in flames in the distance. *By kind permission of the Marquess of Tavistock and the Trustees of the Bedford Estates.*

25 (p. 212). *Elizabeth I* (1592), by Marcus Gheeraedts the Younger. Oil on canvas. 95 × 60 in. The queen was aged fifty-nine when this portrait was painted to commemorate her visit in 1592 to Ditchley, Oxfordshire, on which county she is standing. *National Portrait Gallery, London.*

26 (p. 213). Illustration by Cecil Everitt and Phillis Cunnington, reproduced from C. Willett Cunnington, Phillis Cunnington, and Charles Beard, *A Dictionary of English Costume 900–1900* (1960). *Courtesy Adam and Charles Black Publishers.*

27 (p. 247). *The French Ambassadors* (1533), by Hans Holbein (1497–1543). Oil and tempera on wood. 81½ × 82½ in. Dinteville (l.) was a knight of the order of St. Michael, who was five times ambassador of King Francis I in London. Selve (r.) was a great scholar and music lover, who thirteen years later represented France at the Diet of Spires. He was one of the few people occupying a high position among the French clergy who harbored sympathy for the Reformation. *Reproduced by courtesy of the Trustees, The National Gallery, London.*

28 (p. 254). *Queen Elizabeth Confounding the Three Goddesses* (1569), by Hans Eworth. The symbolism in Eworth's allegorical painting is derived from the school of Fontainebleau, which favored allegorical figures of this kind who were crowned with wreaths, holding the appropriate emblems of their office, and who were frequently naked to the waist. An elegant flattery to the queen, the composition was no doubt on a program laid down by a literary patron of the artist. It is a "Judgment of Paris" in modern dress, with Elizabeth (as Paris), who surprises the Goddesses—(l. to r.) Juno, Minerva, and Venus, each of them wearing the classical chiton—by awarding the apple, the prize for beauty, to herself. From the painting in Hampton Court Palace. *Reproduced by gracious permission of Her Majesty, The Queen.*

29 (p. 271). A woodcut illustration reproduced from *The booke of faulconrie or hauking; for the onely delight and pleasure of all noblemen and gentlemen: collected out of the best authors, aswell Italians as Frenchmen, and some English practises withall concernyng faulconrie* (1575), written by George Turberville (1540?–1610?). *By permission of the Folger Shakespeare Library, STC 24324.*

30 (p. 273). A woodcut illustration reproduced from Turberville, *The noble arte of venerie or hunting. Wherein is handled and set out the vertues, nature and properties of fiuetene (fifteen) sundry chaces, together with the order and manner how to hunt and kill every one of them* (1575). The book is an adaptation, both as regards text and engravings, from the French classic *La venerie,* by DuFouilloux, which was translated by Turberville and George Gascoigne. *By permission of the Folger Shakespeare Library, STC 24328.*

31 (p. 273). A woodcut illustration reproduced from *Minerva Brittana or A Garden of Heroical Deuises, furnished and adorned with Emblemes and Impresa's of sundry natures, New devised, moralized, and published, By Henry Peacham* (1612). *By permission of the Folger Shakespeare Library, STC 19511.*

32 (p. 274). A woodcut illustration reproduced from *The shepheardes calendar, conteyning twelve aeglogues proportionable to the twelve monethes* (1586), written by Edmund Spenser (1552?–1599). Each eclogue has a woodcut at the beginning and glossary at its end. *By permission of the Folger Shakespeare Library, STC 23091 c.1.*

33 (p. 275). *A Fete at Bermondsey* (ca. 1590), by Joris Hoefnagel (1545–1600). Oil on canvas. 31 × 29 in. This painting, once described as representing the marriage of Henry VIII and Anne Boleyn, then as *Horselydown Fair,* was later known as *A Marriage-fete at Bermondsey. Reproduced by permission of the Marquess of Salisbury, Hatfield House. Photograph: Courtauld Institute of Art.*

34 (p. 276). A woodcut illustration reproduced from *Minerva Brittana* (1612), by Henry Peacham (1576?–1643?). *By permission of the Folger Shakespeare Library, STC 19511.*

35 *(p. 277) and* 36 *(p. 277).* Two copper engravings reproduced from Peter Rollos, *Le Centre de l'amour* (1680), a collection of ninety-two engravings depicting various amusements, with preface and additional text in French. The book was previously published in Berlin around 1630 with German verse. *Spencer Collection, The New York Public Library; Astor, Lenox, and Tilden Foundations.*

37 *(p. 278).* A woodcut frontispiece reproduced from *Annalia Dubrensia* (1636), printed for editor Matthew Walbancke. The book contains poems celebrating the annual Cotswold Games, popular during Shakespeare's time. *By permission of the Folger Shakespeare Library, STC 24954.*

38 *(p. 279). Four Gentlemen of High Rank Playing Primero* (ca. 1530–1573), by John Bettes (d. 1573?). Oil on panel. 38½ × 61¾ in. Bettes was an eminent miniature painter during the reign of Queen Elizabeth. *From a private collection.*

VOLUME II

Frontispiece. A Midsummer Night's Dream (1908), by Arthur Rackham (b. 1867). Watercolor and ink on paper. 7¼ × 10½ in. In this drawing, Rackham depicts the Wedding Scene in Shakespeare's play. *From the Art Collection of the Folger Shakespeare Library, ART Box R122, no. 6.*

39 *(p. 427). Sir Henry Unton* (ca. 1596), by an unknown artist. Oil on panel. 64¼ × 29⅛ in. The painting was commissioned by Lady Unton just after her husband's death as a perpetual reminder of his achievements. The detail, showing Unton and his wife presiding over a banquet, had been described as a wedding feast; but art historians now agree that the scene does not represent a marriage celebration because the bride would not wear black. The foreground of the same detail shows a masque in progress at Wadley. The masque is a unique visual document and depicts Mercury as presenter of Diana together with a train of maiden huntresses. It is accompanied by a broken consort; the stress on music is reflective of Unton's known connections with John Dowland and John Case. *National Portrait Gallery, London.*

40 *(p. 428).* Two woodcuts illustrating the popular broadside "Poor Robin's Dream," commonly called "Poor Charity." Its tune belonged to Laurence Price's "Win at First, Lose at Last." The cuts are intentionally transposed; compare *Troilus and Cressida* (III, iii), "Time hath, my Lord, a wallet at his back, Wherein he puts alms for oblivion." Reproduced from Joseph W. Ebsworth, *The Bagford Ballads: illustrating the last years of the Stuarts* (1878), printed for the Ballad Society of London. The original collection of seventeenth-century broadside ballads was made by John Bagford (1650–1716). *General*

Research Division, The New York Public Library; Astor, Lenox, and Tilden Foundations.

41 *(p. 429). Anamorphic Head of a Woman, Usually Called Mary, Queen of Scots* (ca. 1542–1587), by an unknown artist. Oil on pleated wood panel. 330 × 248 cm. *National Galleries of Scotland, Edinburgh.*

VOLUME III

Frontispiece. The New York Shakespeare Festival in association with Joseph Papp presented *Henry V* on the outdoor stage of the Delacorte Theatre in Central Park, New York City, during the summer of 1984. The production was directed by Wilford Leach, with scenery by Bob Shaw, and costumes by Lindsay W. Davis. Kevin Kline starred in the title role, with George N. Martin (Chorus); George Guidall (Archbishop of Canterbury, King of France); Clement Fowler (Bishop of Ely, Governor of Harfleur, Sir Thomas Erpingham); Earl Hindman (Duke of Exeter); Morgan Strickland (Duke of Gloucester); David Warshofsky (Duke of Bedford); Jack Stehlin (Dauphin); Richard Backus (Constable of France); Kristine Nielsen (Queen of France, Hostess Quickly); and Mary Elizabeth Mastrantonio (Princess Katherine). *Photograph © 1984 by Martha Swope.*

42 *(p. 684) and* 43 *(p. 684). Henry V.* Great Britain 1944. Production: Two Cities Film, presented by Eagle-Lion; Technicolor, 35 mm.; running time 153 min., some versions 137 min. Produced by Laurence Olivier, with Dallas Bower; screenplay by Laurence Olivier and Alan Dent; directed by Laurence Olivier; photography by Robert Krasker; edited by Reginald Beck; art direction by Paul Sheriff; scenic art by E. Lindgaard; music by William Walton; costume design by Roger Furse. The film is dedicated to the Commandos and Airborne Troops of Great Britain, "the spirits of whose ancestors it has humbly attempted to recapture." Filmed in Enniskerry, Eire, and at Denham and Pinewood Studios, England. In 1946, a special Academy Award went to Laurence Olivier for Outstanding Achievement as Actor, Producer, and Director in bringing *Henry V* to the screen. Cast: Leslie Banks (Chorus); Felix Aylmer (Archbishop of Canterbury); Robert Helpmann (Bishop of Ely); Nicholas Hannen (Duke of Exeter); Michael Warre (Duke of Gloucester); Laurence Olivier (King Henry V); Freda Jackson (Mistress Quickly); Harcourt Williams (King Charles VI of France); Leo Genn (Constable of France); Max Adrian (Dauphin); George Robey (Sir John Falstaff); Robert Newton (Pistol); and Renee Asherson (Princess Katherine). Midway through World War II, Olivier was released from his military duties to produce, direct, and star in this film. Because the play is so patriotic, it was thought by the British government that the project would be a wonderful piece of nationalistic propaganda. Olivier had previously played King Henry

at the Old Vic, and he knew what he wanted to achieve —a movie version that would restore glory to the common man's thinking about his own country. © United Artists. *Photographs courtesy The Museum of Modern Art Film Stills Archive.*

44 *(p. 686). Hamlet.* Great Britain 1948. Production: Two Cities Film; black and white; running time 155 min. Produced and directed by Laurence Olivier; text edited by Alan Dent; photography by Desmond Dickinson; art direction by Carmen Dillon; production design by Roger Furse; music by William Walton. Filmed in Elsinore, Denmark. Winner of five Academy Awards in 1948: Best Picture, Best Actor (Olivier), Best Art Direction, Best Production Design, and Best Costumes. Cast: Eileen Herlie (Gertrude); Jean Simmons (Ophelia); Norman Wooland (Horatio); Harcourt Williams (Ghost); Basil Sydney (King Claudius); Felix Aylmer (Polonius); and Terence Morgan (Laertes). © Universal Pictures. *Photograph courtesy The Museum of Modern Art Film Stills Archive.*

45 *(p. 687)* and 46 *(p. 688). Richard III.* Great Britain 1955. Presented by S. L. O. in association with London Films; Technicolor; running time 158 min. Produced, adapted, and directed by Laurence Olivier; photography by Otto Heller; edited by Helga Cranston; art direction by Carmen Dillon; production design by Roger Furse; music by William Walton. Cast: Laurence Olivier (Richard III); John Gielgud (Clarence); Ralph Richardson (Buckingham); Claire Bloom (Lady Anne); Alec Clunes (Hastings); Cedric Hardwicke (King Edward IV); Stanley Baker (Henry Tudor); and Mary Kerridge (Queen Elizabeth). © United Artists. *Photographs courtesy The Museum of Modern Art Film Stills Archive.*

47 *(p. 689)* and 48 *(p. 689). Othello.* Morocco 1952. Production: Films Marceau; black and white; running time 91 min. Written and directed by Orson Welles; photography by Anchise Brizze, G. R. Aldo, George Fanto, Robert Fusi, and Obadan Troiani; art direction by Alexandre Trauner; music by Francesco Lavagnino and Alberto Barberis. Cast: Orson Welles (Othello); Suzanne Cloutier (Desdemona); Mícheál Macliammoir (Iago); Robert Coote (Roderigo); and Fay Compton (Emilia). Welles made the film without a production company, working as an actor in order to raise additional funds. He set the assault on Cassio in a Turkish bath because he didn't think he could find tailors in Morocco who would be capable of cutting Renaissance doublets. He moved his crew and cast from Morocco to Venice, Rome, Paris, and London, stopping the filming for several months when funds ran out, and restarting some scenes after a gap of two years. On one occasion, he even shot some scenes himself when he had no money to pay the cameraman. © United Artists. *Photographs courtesy The Museum of Modern Art Film Stills Archive.*

49 *(p. 691)* and 50 *(p. 692). Throne of Blood.* Japan 1957. Black and white; running time 105 min. Produced by Shojiro Motoki and Akira Kurosawa; screenplay by Shinobu Hashimoto, Ryuzo Kikushima, Hideo Oguni, and Akira Kurosawa; directed by Akira Kurosawa; photography by Asakazu Nakai; art direction by Yoshiro Muraki and Kohei Ezaki; music by Masaru Sato. Cast: Toshiro Mifune as Washizu (Macbeth); Isuzu Yamada as Asaji (Lady Macbeth); Takashi Shimura (Odagura); Minoru Chiaki (Miki); Akira Kubo (Yoshiteru); Takamaru Sasaki (Tsuzuki); Yoichi Tachikawa (Kunimaru); and Chieko Naniwa (Witch). © Toho Productions. *Photographs courtesy The Museum of Modern Art Film Stills Archive.*

51 *(p. 694). Chimes at Midnight,* also known as *Falstaff.* Spain 1966. Presented by Harry Saltzman; black and white, 35 mm.; running time 119 min., English version 115 min. Produced by Emiliano Piedra and Angel Escolano; executive producer, Alessandro Tasca; screenplay by Orson Welles, adapted from *Henry IV, Parts 1 and 2, Henry V, Richard III, The Merry Wives of Windsor* by Shakespeare and the *Chronicles of England* (1577) by Raphael Holinshed; directed by Orson Welles; photography by Edmond Richard; edited by Fritz Muller; art direction by José Antonio de la Guerra and Mariano Erdorza; music by Francesco Lavagnino; costume design by Orson Welles. Filmed in Barcelona, Madrid, and other locations in Spain. Cast: Orson Welles (Falstaff); Jeanne Moreau (Doll Tearsheet); Margaret Rutherford (Hostess Quickly); John Gielgud (King Henry IV); Keith Baxter (Prince Hal, King Henry V); Marina Vlady (Kate Percy); Norman Rodway (Henry Percy, called Hotspur); Alan Webb (Justice Shallow); Fernando Rey (Worcester); and Ralph Richardson (Narrator). © Internacional Films Española and Alpine Productions. *Photograph courtesy The Museum of Modern Art Film Stills Archive.*

52 *(p. 695). The Taming of the Shrew.* United States– Italy 1966. Production: Royal Films International F. A. I.; Technicolor; running time 126 min. Produced by Richard Burton, Elizabeth Taylor, and Franco Zeffirelli; screenplay by Paul Dehn, Suso Cecchi D'Amico, and Franco Zeffirelli; directed by Franco Zeffirelli; photography by Oswald Morris; edited by Peter Taylor; production design by Renzo Mongiardino and John De Cuir; music by Nino Rota. Made in Dino de Laurentiis Cinematografica Studios, Rome. Cast: Richard Burton (Petruchio); Elizabeth Taylor (Kate); Michael Hordern (Baptista); Cyril Cusack (Grumio); Michael York (Lucentio); Natasha Pyne (Bianca); Vernon Dobtcheff (Pedant); Alfred Lynch (Tranio); Alan Webb (Gremio); and Victor Spinetti (Hortensio). © Columbia Pictures. *Photograph courtesy The Museum of Modern Art Film Stills Archive.*

53 *(p. 697). Romeo and Juliet.* Great Britain–Italy 1968. A B.H.E. Film. Technicolor; running time 138 min. Produced by Anthony Havelock-Allan and John Brabourne; screenplay by Franco Brusati, Masolino D'Amico, and Franco Zeffirelli; directed by Franco Zeffirelli; photography by Pasquale de Santiis; edited by Reginald Mills; art

direction by Luciano Puccini; production design by Renzo Mongiardino; music by Nino Rota. Made with Cerona Produzione S.r.l. and Dino de Laurentiis Cinematografica S.p.A. Cast: Leonard Whiting (Romeo); Olivia Hussey (Juliet); Michael York (Tybalt); John McEnery (Mercutio); Pat Heywood (Nurse); Robert Stephens (Prince of Verona); Milo O'Shea (Friar Laurence); and Natasha Parry (Lady Capulet). © Paramount Pictures. *Photograph courtesy The Museum of Modern Art Film Stills Archive.*

54 *(p. 698). King Lear.* Great Britain 1970. Production: Royal Shakespeare Company; black and white; running time 137 min. Produced by Michael Birkett; directed by Peter Brook; photography by Henny Kristiansen; edited by Kasper Schyberg; production design by George Wakhevitch. Cast: Paul Scofield (King Lear); Irene Worth (Goneril); Jack MacGowran (Fool); Alan Webb (Duke of Gloucester); Cyril Cusack (Duke of Albany); Patrick Magee (Duke of Cornwall); Tom Fleming (Earl of Kent); Susan Engel (Regan); Annelise Gabold (Cordelia); Ian Hogg (Edmund); Barry Stanton (Oswald); and Soren Elung Jensen (Duke of Burgundy). © Filmways, Inc. *Photograph courtesy The Museum of Modern Art Film Stills Archive.*

55 *(p. 699)* and 56 *(p. 699). Korol Lir (King Lear).* Soviet Union 1970. Black and white, 35 mm.; running time 140 min. Produced, scripted, and directed by Grigori Kozintsev, from Boris Pasternak's translation of *King Lear;* photography by Jonas Gritsius; production design by Yevgeny Yenei; sets by Vsevolod Ulitko; music by Dmitri Shostakovich; costumes designed by Suliko Virsaladze. Filmed in the Soviet Union. Cast: Yuri Jarvet (King Lear); Elsa Radzinya (Goneril); Galina Volchek (Regan); Valentina Shendrikova (Cordelia); Oleg Dal (Fool); Karl Sebris (Earl of Gloucester); Leonard Merzin (Edgar); Regimantas Adomaitis (Edmund); Vladimir Emelyanov (Earl of Kent); Alexander Volkach (Duke of Cornwall); Alexei Petrenko (Oswald); Yumas Budraitis (King of France); and Donatas Banionis (Duke of Albany). *Korol Lir* was the last film of Kozintsev's long career, which began with the experimentalism of the early 1920s and ended with two adaptations of Shakespeare plays—his version of *Hamlet* is probably the better-known of the two. © Lenfilm. *Photographs courtesy The Museum of Modern Art Film Stills Archive.*

57 *(p. 759).* A drawing by Francis Hayman (1708–1766) for the frontispiece of *Coriolanus,* Hanmer's edition (1744). In the picture Hayman, who was a historical painter, depicts Act V, scene iii, of the play. The composition of the drawing is derived from the painting *Coriolanus,* by Nicolas Poussin. *By permission of the Folger Shakespeare Library, PR 2752 1744 c.2 v.5 Sh.Coll.*

58 *(p. 760). Garrick as Richard the Third* (ca. 1746), by William Hogarth (1637–1764). Oil on canvas. 75 × 98½ in. Garrick's *Richard III* was staged at Lincoln's Inn Fields in 1741. In the painting, Garrick is shown at the climax of the play, when Richard (in his tent) has awak-

ened from a nightmare on the eve of his fatal battle. Hogarth painted this picture for the distinguished art collector Mr. Duncombe, uncle of the Earl of Feversham. *Walker Art Gallery, Liverpool.*

59 *(p. 761). King Lear in the Storm* (1767), by John Runciman (1744–1768). Oil on canvas. 17 × 23¼ in. The painting depicts Lear standing on a small plateau of rock facing a stormy sky and sea. Arranged around him are Edgar as Poor Tom, Kent, the Gentleman, and the Fool rendered as a young boy cowering before the storm. In his composition, Runciman has isolated the imagery that reflects the King's mental chaos. *National Galleries of Scotland, Edinburgh.*

60 *(p. 762).* A sketch for *Cassandra Raving* (1790–1792), by George Romney (1734–1802). Pen with brown ink and wash on paper. $3^{13}/_{16} \times 6^{3}/_{16}$ in. *From the Art Collection of the Folger Shakespeare Library, ART Vol. c61, no. 9.*

61 *(p. 762).* A sketch for the Banquet Scene in *Macbeth* (1790–1792), by Romney. Pen with brown ink and wash on paper. 6⅛ × 7¾ in. Romney produced so detailed a series of drawings of the appearance of Banquo's ghost during Act III, scene iv, of *Macbeth* that it is remarkable that no large-scale history painting on this subject was ever done. *From the Art Collection of the Folger Shakespeare Library, ART Vol. c59, no. 61.*

62 *(p. 763).* The Vision of Queen Katherine (1807), by William Blake (1757–1827). Pen, gray wash, touches of color, and traces of a pencil underdrawing on paper. $15^{11}/_{16} \times 12^{5}/_{16}$ in. The drawing is recorded as Rosetti's number 86, drawn for Thomas Butts. The composition is derived from the stage directions of the Vision Scene in *Henry VIII.* In the picture, an elaborate double spiral of visionary figures springs from the ground carrying harps, cymbals, and trumpets, two of whom hover above Katherine's head bearing the garland. The design is framed within delicate Gothic arches and is strongly based on the brooding figures of Patience and Griffith, the latter possessing a dignity similar to Blake's Jehovah, a symbolic figure that links this visionary drawing with many in the Milton and Job series. *Reproduced by permission of the Syndics of the Fitzwilliam Museum, Cambridge.*

63 *(p. 764).* Costume design by J. R. Planché (1796–1880) for *Richard III.* Planché was a writer of burlesque, melodrama, pantomime, and serious libretti, in addition to being an authority on heraldry and author of *History of British Costume* (1834). His statement of principle claimed that the time for a merely generalized period effect or atmospheric suggestion was past. Planché approached Shakespeare's history plays with an eye for costuming each character in the precise "habit of the period" based on the authority of Monumental Effigies, Seals, and illuminated manuscripts. *Reproduced by permission of the Birmingham Shakespeare Library, Birmingham Central Libraries.*

64 *(p. 765).* Set design by Robert James Gordon for Edmund Kean's 1853 production of *Macbeth,* presented

at the Princess's Theatre. Watercolor on paper. 10 × 14 in. Kean employed a team of four artists—Gordon, Dayes, Cuthbert, and F. Lloyds—to design the sets for his production of *Macbeth.* The artists sometimes drew two versions of a scene, first a plain one as a set, and then one containing a significant moment of action. Gordon has depicted the appearance of Banquo's ghost during Act III, scene iv—the banquet. He is also credited on the playbill with the single setting for the second act, "Court within Macbeth's Castle at Inverness." *By courtesy of the Board of Trustees of the Victoria and Albert Museum, D-1427-1901.*

65 *(p. 766). Lear and Cordelia* (1849–1854), by Ford Madox Brown (1821–1893). Oil on canvas. 28 × 39 in., with arched top. The painting illustrates Act IV, scene vii, of *King Lear* at the moment of Cordelia's soliloquy in her tent in the French camp. The artist justified his choice of sixth-century costume in his notes in the exhibition catalog of 1865 in this way:

Having its origin in the old ballad, Shakespeare's *King Lear* is Roman-pagan-British nominally; mediaeval by external customs and habits, and again, in a marked degree, savage and remote by the moral side. With a fair excuse it might be treated in Roman-British costume, but then clashing with the mediaeval institutions and habits introduced; or as purely mediaeval. But I have rather chosen to be in harmony with the mental characteristics of Shakespeare's work and have therefore adopted the costume prevalent in Europe about the sixth century, when paganism was still rife, and deeds were at their darkest. The piece of Bayeux tapestry introduced behind King Lear is strictly an anachronism but the costume applies in this instance, and the young men gaily riding with hawk and hounds contrast pathetically with the stricken old man.

Courtesy the Tate Gallery, London.

66 *(p. 767).* A woodcut by Edward Gordon Craig (1872–1966) illustrating Act III, scene iii, of *Hamlet:* "Now might I do it pat. . . ." Craig created stage scenes for his mother, the actress Ellen Terry, that astounded London audiences by their almost fanatical simplicity and their turn away from realism. His set design opened the possibilities of presenting Shakespeare free from elaborate nineteenth-century decorations and in terms of twentieth-century theater. Reproduced from *Hamlet,* Cranach Press edition (1930), printed for Count Harry Kessler at Weimar. *Rare Books and Manuscripts Division, The New York Public Library; Astor, Lenox, and Tilden Foundations.*

67 *(p. 767).* Set design by John Piper (b. 1903) for Act V, scene i, of *Measure for Measure,* when the Duke resumes his power in a purified Vienna. The throne, a tall elaboration of the Elizabethan chair of state, is the central object in the decor. Piper's use of it as a dominant set piece stresses and enhances its significance for an audience who would be less sensitive than Shakespeare's to the overtones. This is characteristic of Piper's method of stage setting, to simplify the moods and themes of a play to a single unity, a dominant visual tone, and then to use the utmost subtlety in elaborating it. Reproduced from W. Moelwyn Merchant, *Shakespeare and the Artist* (1959). *Courtesy W. Moelwyn Merchant and the Oxford University Press.*

68 *(p. 768).* A drawing by Eric Griffiths of the opening tableau from Stratford-upon-Avon's 1983 production of *The Comedy of Errors. Courtesy W. Moelwyn Merchant.*

69 *(p. 769).* A preliminary ink drawing by Josef Herman for a painting commissioned by the Arts Council of Great Britain for the "Shakespeare in Art" exhibition, mounted in celebration of the Shakespeare Quatercentenary in 1964. The picture depicts Herman's interpretation of Act II of *King Lear. Courtesy W. Moelwyn Merchant.*

INDEX

Index